Foundations of Social Policy

Social Justice in Human Perspective

THIRD EDITION

AMANDA SMITH BARUSCH
University of Otago, New Zealand

BROOKS/COLE
CENGAGE Learning

Australia • Brazil • Japan • Korea • Mexico • Singapore • Spain • United Kingdom • United States

BROOKS/COLE
CENGAGE Learning

**Foundations of Social Policy:
Social Justice in Human Perspective,
Third Edition
Amanda Smith Barusch**

Acquisition Editor: Seth Dobrin

Assistant Editor: Meaghan Banks

Editorial Assistant: Diane Mars

Technology Project Manager: Andrew Keay

Sr. Marketing Manager: Karin Sandberg

Marketing Assistant: Ting Jian Yap

Marketing Communications Manager:
  Shemika Britt

Sr. Content Project Manager: Pat Waldo

Creative Director: Rob Hugel

Art Director: Caryl Gorska

Print Buyer: Paula Vang

Rights Acquisitions Account Manager, Text:
  Mardell Glinski Schultz

Production Service: Rebecca Logan,
  Newgen–Austin

Rights Acquisitions Account Manager,
  Image: Don Schlotman

Text Researcher: Paula F. Sutherlland

Copy Editor: Janet Tilden

Cover Designer: Cheryl Carrington

Cover Image: David Leach/Getty Images

Compositor: Newgen

For product information and technology assistance, contact us at
Cengage Learning Customer & Sales Support, 1-800-354-9706.
For permission to use material from this text or product,
submit all requests online at **cengage.com/permissions.**
Further permissions questions can be e-mailed to
permissionrequest@cengage.com.

Library of Congress Control Number: 2008922517

ISBN-13: 978-0-495-50716-1

ISBN-10: 0-495-50716-4

Brooks/Cole
10 Davis Drive
Belmont, CA 94002-3098
USA

Cengage Learning is a leading provider of customized learning solutions with office locations around the globe, including Singapore, the United Kingdom, Australia, Mexico, Brazil, and Japan. Locate your local office at **international.cengage.com/region.**

Cengage Learning products are represented in Canada by Nelson Education, Ltd.

For your course and learning solutions, visit **academic.cengage.com.**
Purchase any of our products at your local college store or at our preferred online store **www.ichapters.com.**

Printed in the United States of America
1 2 3 4 5 6 7 12 11 10 09 08

To my dad,
Gilbert Teemley Smith

Brief Contents

Contents

Preface

Social workers promote social justice....
PREAMBLE TO THE *NASW CODE OF ETHICS* (1996)

Social justice is central to the mission of social work and the focus of intense debate throughout the world. On behalf of vulnerable individuals, social work professionals contribute to these debates by providing a deeply personal and empathetic understanding of the consequences of injustice. At the same time, we struggle to understand what constitutes social justice.

Like most people, social workers (and social work students) understand justice less in the abstract and more in terms of events and conditions that affect people. This text begins with people. Major chapters start with human perspective examples that focus our analysis and critique of contemporary U.S. social policy on the people who are most affected. The content is organized around personal problems and vulnerable populations. Discussion of the history of social policy includes biographical material on leaders and advocates. Choice of contemporary policies is based on the importance of those policies for people affected by them. This broadens the lens for policy practice, preparing students not only to operate in the traditional social work "turf" but to expand their influence into important policy arenas that have not yet been the focus of social work intervention and to serve as voices for vulnerable people throughout the United States and the world.

ABOUT THE BOOK

This book is designed for use in foundation social policy courses. It has three parts. Part I offers an introduction to U.S. social policy and policy practice, Part II addresses personal problems that have been (or are becoming) accepted targets for collective action, and Part III focuses on vulnerable populations. A brief conclusion introduces global social policy concerns and organizations. Discussion topics, web-based exercises, suggested readings, and interesting websites are included at the end of each chapter.

Theoretical content is interspersed throughout. Theory related to social justice is addressed in detail in Chapter 1. The introduction to Part II offers a theoretical framework for understanding when and why some personal problems become the targets of collective action. The introduction to Part III considers discrimination and oppression from a theoretical perspective. Finally, theories of liberation are touched on in the Conclusion.

Part I includes Chapters 1 through 3. Chapter 1 discusses social justice from theoretical and philosophical perspectives, tying these viewpoints to contemporary U.S. social policy. The role of government in promoting social justice is the focus of Chapter 2, which links philosophical perspectives to contemporary politics, and then offers a brief description of the structure and function of the U.S. government and an introduction to the nation's tax system. Chapter 3 begins with a case study in advocacy and then presents several approaches to policy analysis before addressing philosophical and tactical considerations in policy practice.

Part II introduces a framework for determining when a society will develop collective responses to personal problems. Chapters in this part of the book examine problems that have been approached through collective action in the United States: Social Security (Chapter 4), poverty (Chapter 5), physical illness (Chapter 6), mental illness (Chapter 7), and disability (Chapter 8). Each chapter opens with a human perspective case. These human perspectives are based on interviews with people who are chosen to illustrate the complexity of each area of study. We explore the development of policies and services, as well as contemporary policy issues and debates. These chapters provide background material necessary for students to apply the policy analysis frameworks introduced in Chapter 3.

Part III introduces the concepts of discrimination and oppression. Each chapter explores a population that has experienced oppression in the United States: people of color (Chapter 9); gay, lesbian, bisexual, and transgendered individuals (Chapter 10); children (Chapter 11); women (Chapter 12); the elderly (Chapter 13), and working Americans (Chapter 14). The structure of these chapters mirrors that applied in Part II with the addition of major social/demographic trends affecting each population.

The book closes with a glance toward the future of our profession in an international context. Following an introduction to theories of liberation, the Conclusion returns to the philosophical perspectives presented in Chapter 1, using them to consider the implications of globalization and rising inequality for the social welfare state and the social work profession.

WHAT'S NEW IN THE THIRD EDITION

Those familiar with previous editions of this book will find some changes in this edition. I have, of course, updated demographic figures and policy discussions, as well as the web-based exercises. In addition, I continue to revise in hope of making the book more interesting and more readable. There are also some specific revisions:

- A human rights perspective has been added to Chapter 1 and integrated throughout.
- There is expanded coverage of international policy developments and social issues.
- Interspersed throughout the text are examples of successful advocacy initiatives by social workers. Students and faculty describe their experiences in the advocacy arena, reflecting on the lessons and insights they gained.
- The concept of devolution is introduced in Chapter 2.
- Working Americans have been identified as a vulnerable population, and a new chapter (Chapter 14) has been added to address labor policies.
- Finally, organization has been tightened and language streamlined throughout.

AN INVITATION

Since the first edition of this book was published, I have received phone calls, e-mails, and visits from readers offering suggestions, corrections, and compliments. These prove terrifically valuable as I update the book. Whether you are an instructor or a student, I would love to hear from you! Let me know what works and (more important, really) what doesn't work in this new edition. Please send your comments to Amanda.barusch@socwk.utah.edu, with "foundations text" in the subject line, or write me at the College of Social Work, 395 South 1500 East, University of Utah, Salt Lake City, UT 84112. I look forward to hearing from you.

ACKNOWLEDGMENTS

Each edition of this book benefited from the talents and energies of my students, colleagues, and friends at the University of Utah. To that mix is now added the staff and students at University of Otago, my home away from home in New Zealand.

The third edition of this book reflects the creative energies of several colleagues. Bob Schneider of Virginia Commonwealth University is a continuing source of inspiration for his work with Influencing State Policy, and I'm grateful that he let me refer to his website for advocacy case examples. Drawing from his experience as a leader in the United Steelworkers Union, Wayne Holland Jr., Chair of the Utah Democratic Party, gave me a fascinating introduction to the issues faced by working Americans. Sharilynn Robinson-Lynk helped bring

Chapter 10 up to speed through her insightful critique and valuable suggestions. Mary Beth Vogel helped me learn about TANF. Janet Tilden and Rebecca Logan edited the manuscript with care and good humor. Marcella Hurtado was a great help with updates and website checks.

People from various walks of life shared their experiences with me to contribute to the education of professional social workers. The stories they told me enrich each chapter. I can't name them here but will always be grateful for the time we spent together.

As always, this is all about my family, Ariana, Nathan, and Larry Barusch, each a strong advocate. Ariana continues to organize for social change, Nathan is working to understand social justice from an international perspective, and Larry strives to eliminate homelessness. They inspire my work and fill my days with joy.

Policy Analysis

Frameworks and Tools

Solidarity and justice go hand-in-hand.

Social justice is an integral part of social work practice. But what is it? This topic is the focus of Part I, which moves from broad theoretical consideration of social justice, through the role of government as a vehicle for promoting social justice, to the application of a social justice framework in policy practice. Chapter 1 reviews modern and postmodern approaches to defining this surprisingly elusive concept and then examines four philosophical conceptions of social justice. Understanding these divergent perspectives will strengthen our analytic skills, enabling us to recognize assumptions underlying arguments of others and to frame our own arguments in terms more likely to persuade. Following a brief discussion of inequality, the chapter explores the role of social work in America's pursuit of social justice and presents a brief biography of one of the profession's early policy practitioners.

Government is an important vehicle for defining and promoting social justice. Chapter 2 offers a general description of the structure and processes of the U.S. government, organized around the levels and branches of government. The tax system is introduced as an important vehicle for promoting justice. It is vital that social workers be "tax literate" in the twenty-first century, as taxes are increasingly used to advance social goals. Toward this end, Chapter 2 offers a brief introduction to the nation's tax system that considers not only the mechanics but also the philosophical assumptions that drive the system. For some readers, this chapter will be review, but for most it will provide new insights and useful reference material.

Chapter 3 turns to policy practice skills, focusing on policy analysis and advocacy strategies. We begin with a human perspective, examining an advocacy effort on behalf of free public education. Next, we present a brief definition of policy practice followed by a section on policy assessment and analysis. This section expands on the social justice themes introduced in Chapter 1, bringing them into the practice arena through policy analysis. We then explore other analytic approaches and advocacy skills. This chapter offers a general perspective on policy practice, along with specific advice from advocates throughout the country.

1

Social Justice and
Social Workers

No, no, we are not satisfied until justice flows down like water
and righteousness like a mighty stream.
MARTIN LUTHER KING JR.

This chapter focuses on the search for social justice and begins with a case study involving domestic violence. Next, we define social justice from modern and postmodern perspectives and examine four distinct philosophical conceptions of justice: oligarchy, libertarianism, liberalism, and socialism. Following a brief discussion of inequality, the chapter reviews the life and achievements of Bertha Reynolds, a leading social worker, and then explores the role of social workers in the search for social justice.

SOCIAL JUSTICE DEFINED

In August 1996, the Delegate Assembly of the National Association of Social Workers approved a new code of ethics. The preamble to this document states that "Social workers promote social justice" (NASW, 1999). Justice revolves around a simple question: is this fair? For Aristotle justice was proportionality or balance. So, as we see later in this chapter, he held that a just distribution of resources among two people is found midway between unjust distributions that favor one or the other. Others define justice as the absence of injustice, and still others promote a utopian vision of the just society.

Efforts to define social justice can be divided into two distinct approaches: "modern" and "postmodern." The modern approach is based on the notion that

A HUMAN PERSPECTIVE   Melissa Williams

In June 1996, 150 people, mostly women, met in a hotel to discuss welfare and domestic violence. The program was led by a social worker and attended by state legislators, social workers, welfare administrators, academics, advocates, and religious leaders. In the context of a national debate about welfare reform, this session was designed to raise awareness of the importance of welfare as a resource for women leaving abusive homes. One such woman was Melissa Williams. During the luncheon she and three other women told their stories.

Melissa is an attractive young woman with flowing blond hair and a gentle, reflective way of speaking. Clearly intimidated by the size of the group and the lectern in front of her, she spoke haltingly of her experiences with welfare and domestic violence.

Melissa grew up in a working-class family. Her father worked for a mining company and had little interest in children, let alone female children. Her mother was a silent woman, struggling to raise a large family on a miner's salary. Neither parent was physically abusive, but both reminded the children repeatedly that they were "worth less than nothing." For Melissa this emotional abuse intensified during puberty. Miserable in her own family, Melissa saw marriage to her boyfriend, Will, as a way out.

Will was strong, energetic, and determined. He seemed to have the world by the tail and promised the protection and appreciation that Melissa had never enjoyed. At 16, she married him. She laughed, recalling that "everyone thought we had to get married, but I wasn't even pregnant!"

Melissa did get pregnant immediately and left high school. Her husband finished high school and found a "good job"—one with health benefits. They rented an apartment and settled in. Three children were born in rapid succession. Will's job began to feel more and more like a dead end, and he took to hanging out in bars with old high school friends. He'd come home drunk and take out his anger on Melissa.

Her medical records show three visits to the emergency room with facial bruising, lacerations, and a broken arm.

Suffering from a debilitating depression, Melissa was not roused to action until Will attacked one of the children. It was just a slap, but it was enough to send Melissa back to her parents' home, where her depression worsened. Her parents encouraged Melissa to stay away from her husband, but they could not afford to support Melissa and her three children. So, one day, Melissa and her mother took the bus to the welfare office. Melissa was enrolled in the "self-sufficiency program" and awarded emergency housing assistance. Depression was identified as a barrier to employment, and her caseworker arranged for counseling and medication. She also introduced Melissa to a women's advocacy group called JEDI Women (Justice, Economic Dignity, and Independence for Women).

At the time of the conference, Melissa was living independently with her children. She had divorced her husband and did not expect to remarry. Antidepressants and a support group were critical to her ongoing success. Her children had residual health and behavioral problems from witnessing domestic violence.

Deeply moved by Melissa's experience, her audience resolved to ensure that welfare reform in their state would not eliminate a key resource for women leaving abusive relationships. A few weeks later, President Clinton signed an executive order establishing a national hotline for victims of domestic abuse. Today the state exempts victims of domestic violence from lifetime limits on public assistance.

This commitment to devote public resources to protect abused women represents a public decision about what constitutes social justice in today's society. It reveals a belief that the suffering caused by domestic violence is not a cost that women should bear alone, but a social problem that demands a collective response. As we review diverse approaches to defining social justice, consider the implications of each approach for Melissa and women like her.

justice exists as an objective, achievable end or goal. Utopian writings often take a modern approach, setting forth the characteristics of a just society. We will see other examples of the modern approach in the next section as we consider social work writings on the subject. The postmodern approach rejects the idea of an objective standard of justice, arguing that justice is socially constructed. This view focuses attention on the process involved as groups and societies define what is just.[1]

Defining Justice: A Modern Approach

Lee Ann Bell offers a clear vision of a just society as one "in which the distribution of resources is equitable and all members are physically and psychologically safe and secure. We envision a society in which individuals are both self-determining (able to develop their full capacities), and interdependent (capable of interacting democratically with others)" (Bell, 1997, p. 3). Like Bell, others, from Plato to Ayn Rand, have shared their visions of just societies. Some of these visions may strike us as utopian.

What is justice? The absence of injustice or a Golden Mean?

Plato's *Republic* offered a utopian vision in which rulers did not own private property so they could concentrate on the common good. His "best-ordered state" has a communitarian feel: "[W]hen any one of the citizens experiences any good or evil, the whole state will make his case their own" (Edman, 1956, p. 416).

Social work writings tend to define a just society as one without injustice. So, for example, in their description of "emancipatory learning," Van Soest and Garcia (2003, p. vii) suggest that "[u]ltimately, the goal is to prepare social workers and other helping professionals to transform oppressive and unjust systems into non-oppressive and just alternatives." Similarly, van Wormer (2004) defined injustice as the result of inequality and oppression, and urged social workers to devote themselves to eliminating these conditions through a commitment to restorative justice.

Thoughtful consideration of this issue is found in Gil's inspiring work, *Confronting Injustice and Oppression* (1998). A social work professor at Brandeis, Gil locates the inspiration for this work in his experiences during the 1938 German occupation of Austria, which left him committed to reversing cycles of injustice and oppression regardless of who were the victims. Gil defines justice as the opposite of injustice and oppression and directs social workers' attention to five key institutions of social life:

1. Stewardship (care of natural and human-created resources)
2. Organization of work and production
3. Exchange and distribution of goods, rights, and responsibilities
4. Governance
5. Biological reproduction, socialization, and social control

He argues that just societies treat people as equals, with equal rights and responsibilities in each of these five institutions.

Gil explicitly states two assumptions shared by all four of these social work authors: that oppression is not inevitable, and a just society is achievable. Indeed,

---

1. The terms "social justice," "social and economic justice," and "distributive justice" are often used interchangeably. In this book I use the term "social justice" to be consistent with our professional literature.

it is hard to imagine anyone who did not share this belief devoting his or her life to social work. Our moments of despair come when events challenge this cherished belief. Like Engels (*The Origin of the Family, Private Property, and the State,* 1884/1972), Gil (1998) argues that perfectly just human societies existed before technological and social change allowed for a stable economic surplus. But utopian visions need not be defended on the basis of practicality. In describing his ideal city-state, Plato rejects criticism that such a state had never existed, saying, "We were enquiring into the nature of absolute justice and the perfectly unjust, that we might have an ideal . . . would a painter be any the worse because, after having delineated with consummate art an ideal of a perfectly beautiful man, he was unable to show that any such man could ever have existed?" (p. 430). Justice is a virtue, and a just society an ideal. The modern approach articulates that ideal and energizes social workers by focusing their efforts on striving for an inspiring goal.

Defining Justice: A Postmodern Approach

The postmodern approach is not limited to contemporary scholars. In ancient Greece Aristotle wrote, "[F]ire burns both in Greece and in Persia; but *conceptions of justice shift and change*" (Barker, 1962, p. 365, italics added). More than two thousand years later, in 1863, John Stuart Mill made a similar observation:

> The entire history of social improvement has been a series of transitions by which one custom or institution after another, from being a supposed primary necessity of social existence, has passed into the rank of a universally stigmatized injustice and tyranny. So it has been with the distinctions of slaves and freemen, nobles and serfs, patricians and plebeians; and so it will be, and in part already is, with the aristocracies of color, race, and sex. (Sterba, 1980, p. 104)

The accelerated pace of change has brought this observation into focus in these "postmodern" times. For many, this era has brought a rejection of "objective" or "absolute" truth and a dawning recognition that truth is socially constructed. Thus, conceptions of justice vary from group to group and change throughout the history of societies, families, and individuals. *Absolute* justice is a misnomer. Groups of all sizes strive to achieve an acceptable state of *relative* justice. Our focus then shifts from the end (justice) to the *process* involved as people strive for justice and the *perceptions* and *roles* of individuals and groups. In this book we use the following postmodern definition of social justice:

Justice is fair allocation of the costs and rewards of group membership.[2]

---

2. While doing research for the second edition of this book, I discovered the work of David Miller, a fellow at Oxford College. Miller's definition of justice offers a similar approach: "[T]he subject-matter of justice is the manner in which benefits and burdens are distributed among men . . . whose qualities and relationships can be investigated" (1976, p. 19).

Social justice issues related to the *costs* of group membership can come up in groups of any size. They arise in families, for example, when new parents struggle to decide how to divide the responsibilities of rearing their baby. Cost issues arise in societies as well; as when members of the U.S. Congress debate tax reform proposals. Disputes about how many diapers a father should change or how much tax a corporation should pay are fundamentally debates over how to allocate the costs of group membership.

Benefits of group membership are also allocated through social justice mechanisms. Mundane decisions about who gets to use the family car reflect fundamental beliefs about what is a "just" or "fair" distribution of this benefit. In the United States, the benefits of citizenship include entitlements such as Social Security, tax deductions for home mortgage interest, and Medicaid. Distribution of these benefits is often the subject of debate.

Justice in Process

Sometimes the decisions involved in allocating these costs and rewards are informal and subtle. As background in our lives they are rarely questioned. A major contribution of critical theory and related perspectives in the social sciences has been to question allocation rules that are normally taken for granted. Other times, as is usually the case with formal social policy, decision-making processes are open and public (and laborious!).

Social justice process refers to the way a group of any size allocates the costs and benefits of membership. Good process does not guarantee a fair outcome. Yet wars have been fought and tears shed over unfair processes, which are virtually guaranteed to produce an outcome that is at least perceived as unjust. Fair process is necessary but not sufficient for achieving just outcomes. Groups and cultures differ widely in what they consider fair processes. In some contexts the decision of a single authority figure is taken as final and fair. The nature of the decision may determine what we consider a fair decision-making process, with some types of decisions left to the authority of a single executive and others subject to democratic processes. If the rules of allocation used by the group are considered fair by members of that group, then the group has achieved a measure of social justice.

In the Western democratic tradition we have general agreement about what is and is not fair in the decision-making process. Our first "Fair Process Principle" holds that members of a society should be treated as political equals. The belief in political equality is central to liberal philosophy and democratic thought. Though some people are privileged by birth and others by wealth, these privileges should not extend to the political sphere. To the extent that they do, this principle is violated.

Justice in process involves three key concepts: membership, voice, and the rule of law. "Membership" refers to the group's boundaries for distinguishing between "us" and "them." These boundaries often work to exclude what Bruce Jansson (2002) calls "out groups." People who differ from the majority of group members are vulnerable to being labeled "other" and deprived of

Fair Process Principle #1: Individuals should be treated as political equals.

membership. These subgroups are vulnerable, as their rights to the benefits of group membership may be subject to dispute. For example, a family may question its obligation to provide care to an elderly grandmother on the grounds that she is not really a member of the immediate family. A nation may question the provision of cash benefits to immigrants who are not really citizens. As we will see in later chapters, most of the history of the United States has been marked by progress toward extension of political and civil rights to those once considered "beneath" these benefits. Women's suffrage and the civil rights movement are examples of a society redefining the terms of membership.

Fair Process Principle #2: All parties affected by a decision should have a voice in the decision.

"Voice" refers to a person's ability to influence decision making within the group. At all levels of social organization, an individual's voice will be determined by the extent to which others hear and attend to that person's concerns. Americans have a strong preference for giving voice to people who are affected by decisions. Thus, our second fair process principle holds that *all parties affected by a decision should have a voice in the decision*. Violation of this principle was the stated cause of the famous Boston Tea Party. In grade school Americans are taught that wild-eyed colonists dressed up as Indians and threw bags of British tea into Boston Bay shouting, "No taxation without representation!"

Fair Process Principle #3: Formal rules should apply equally to all similarly situated parties.

The rule of law is a third important component of just process. But if a policy is legal, is it necessarily just? Does majority rule make for fair decisions? Like most of us, Aristotle answered "not necessarily." Aristotle distinguished between equity and justice, arguing that, although they are made of the same stuff, equity is more universal and more natural than justice. For him, equity is akin to natural justice, which is broader than legal justice. Legal justice establishes rules that, even if perfectly followed, can lead to inequitable results. "The same thing, then, is just and equitable, and while both are good the equitable is superior" (Bostock, 2000, p. 133).

Nonetheless, when formal rules are not universally and consistently applied, we cry "foul." In our country we expect the law to be applied equally to everyone. The notion of equal protection is embedded in the U.S. Constitution. But legislators cannot anticipate every eventuality, and individuals may disagree on what is a "similarly situated" party. This ambiguity keeps judges and lawyers occupied but does not detract from our general belief that no one is above the law.

Components of Social Justice

Miller (1976, 1999) identifies four components of social justice: desert, need, rights, and equality. The first three can be illustrated using a simple hypothetical situation adapted from Miller (1976). Suppose I hire three children to clean my windows, and I promise to pay them one dollar each for their efforts. Throughout the day I watch them work, and I observe that one child (the first child) is industriously cleaning. This child does more than her fair share of the work and does it very well. The other two dawdle along. One of them (the second child) looks ill. When I ask what's wrong, he tells me that he hasn't eaten for two days because his family has no money for food. The third child has no explanation for her sloughing but looks forward to receiving her dollar at the end of the day.

The first child represents *desert*. An outcome is considered just when each person involved gets what he or she deserves. In America we believe that someone who works hard and does a good job deserves to be rewarded.

The second child represents *need*. Just outcomes take into account each person's need. In our hypothetical example, this child clearly needed money more than the other two.

The third child represents *rights*. From a contractual perspective, a right is an outcome to which we are entitled, based on a prior agreement or contract. Apart from whether she deserves or needs the money, the third child reminds me that under our contractual agreement she has the right to receive a dollar. We will consider rights in greater detail in the next section.

My task, as the all-powerful policy maker in pursuit of justice, is to balance the deserts, needs, and rights of these three children to achieve a just distribution of the reward. This task is illustrated in Figure 1.1. Similarly, analysis of the impact of policy on social justice should consider each of these components, particularly as they relate to vulnerable populations. For example, analysis of a proposal to provide public clinics for people who do not have health insurance might consider first whether these people deserve health care; second, whether they need the care; and finally, whether their rights as citizens are violated if the care is not provided. Equality is the fourth component of justice, and a policy's impact on inequality merits careful consideration. Now let us turn to more detailed consideration of two components of social justice: rights and equality.

Human Rights. Most Americans can recite from our Declaration of Independence, "We hold these truths to be self-evident, that all men are Created equal, that they are endowed by their Creator with certain unalienable Rights, that among these are Life, Liberty and the pursuit of Happiness." When

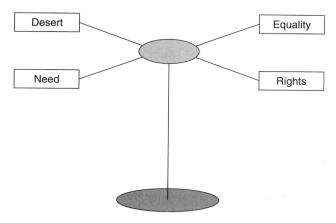

FIGURE 1.1 Balancing the components of social justice.

Thomas Jefferson penned these words, he was part of a tradition extending back to ancient civilizations and reflected in documents written as early as two thousand years before the birth of Jesus, including the Code of Hammurabi (Mesopotamia), the Cyrus cylinder (Persia) and the edicts of Ashoka (ancient India) (Robertson & Merrills, 1996). Each of these documents treats human rights as universal and inalienable. Thus, rights are possessed by all people, and they cannot be (as my grandmother would say) "begged, borrowed, or sold."

In more recent times, the horrors of the holocaust inspired members of the United Nations (UN) General Assembly to adopt the Universal Declaration of Human Rights drafted by a committee chaired by Eleanor Roosevelt in 1948. Although the declaration is not legally binding, it sets forth principles toward which many nations strive. Roosevelt characterized it as an "international magna carta of all men everywhere" (in his address to the United Nations, December 9, 1948, Paris), but other U.S. politicians have been less enthusiastic. For instance, Jeane Kirkpatrick, U.S. Ambassador to the UN during the Reagan administration, reportedly described the declaration as "a letter to Santa Claus" (http://www.humaninfo.org/aviva/ch65.htm, accessed January 9, 2008).

Nonetheless, the Declaration was promptly ratified by the U.S. in a process consistent with constitutional provisions regarding international treaties. While the President of the United States has authority to sign UN declarations, conventions, and treaties, ratification requires Senate approval. As a result, there can be a lengthy gap between the President's signature and Senate ratification. The status of U.S. ratification on other UN conventions affecting human rights (as of this writing) is listed in Table 1.1.

Civil and political rights in the United States are elaborated in the first ten amendments to the Constitution—the Bill of Rights—and in the civil rights legislation discussed in Chapters 9 and 14. Where there is a strong tradition of protection for established civil rights in the U.S., the nation does not recognize

TABLE 1.1   UN Conventions on Human Rights

Title	Year	Status in U.S.
Declaration on Human Rights	1948	Ratified by the U.S. Senate
Convention on the Prevention and Punishment of the Crime of Genocide	1951	Ratified by the U.S. Senate with the proviso that America was immune from prosecution without its consent
Convention on the Elimination of All Forms of Racial Discrimination	1969	Ratified by the U.S. Senate
Convention on the Elimination of All Forms of Discrimination Against Women	1981	Signed by the president but not ratified by the U.S. Senate
Convention Against Torture	1984	Ratified by the U.S. Senate with stipulations
Convention on the Rights of the Child	1989	Signed by the president but not ratified by the U.S. Senate

economic, social and cultural rights, or solidarity rights, some of which were identified in the Universal Declaration of Human Rights (Vasak & Alston, 1982).

Equality. We can identify three types of equality: social, political, and economic. Social equality exists to the extent that community esteem for individuals is not based on a hierarchy. This is seldom the case, because informal hierarchies govern most of our social interactions; however, the lack of social equality is seldom a matter for policy intervention. Social policies more often target political and economic inequality. As we have seen, political equality is a fundamental value in democracy, personified by the notion of "one person, one vote." To the extent that a political system deviates from this value it is considered unjust. Finally, economic equality—the equitable distribution of income and wealth—is affected by social policy. As we will see in Chapter 2, U.S. tax policy influences the degree of economic inequality in this country, as does the Social Security system outlined in Chapter 4. Of course, few Americans believe that income and wealth should be equally distributed, but most endorse the concept of equal opportunities.

Aristotle's concept of proportional rewards offers one rationale for unequal distribution of benefits. For Aristotle, justice, merit, and proportion are closely aligned. A just distribution of rewards is based on "merit" and is proportional. So an individual's rightful share is proportionate to the person's merit (Bostock, 2000, pp. 112–133). Aristotle acknowledges that not all people specify the same sort of merit, but "democrats identify it with the status of freeman, supporters of oligarchy with wealth (or with noble birth), and supporters of aristocracy with excellence" (p. 113). Contemporary definitions of merit may hinge on skill in performing tasks, dedication or sacrifice, or personal characteristics. Most of us operate across settings that define merit in different ways.

Equality might be achieved by balancing disparate claims. In the *Ethics,* Aristotle argues that in the exchange of goods justice is the intermediate point between two unjust extremes. So a just price for a good lies between two prices that would be unjust (too low a price is unjust to the producer, too high is unjust to the consumer): "[T]he virtuous man tends to take less than his share" (p. 130). In *Politics,* Aristotle suggests that a just state rewards individuals according to their contributions to the goals of the state, and the goals of a just state include a good quality of life.

As we have seen, equality is a complex aspect of social justice. Most philosophical conceptions of justice stem from or elaborate upon Aristotle's views. Aristotle saw distributive justice as the equal distribution of shares among people who are equal, and unequal distribution among people who are unequal. But the devil is in the details. Policy makers, family members, and philosophers struggle to determine the conditions and extent to which inequality should be considered just. This controversial topic will be revisited as we examine four major philosophical approaches to the definition of social justice:[3] oligarchy, libertarianism, liberalism, and socialism.

---

3. Summaries of the philosophical approaches are provided in Sterba (1980).

Oligarchy and Social Justice

Distributive Principle: From each according to his status; to each according to his status.

As we saw in the last section, Aristotle noted that "adherents of oligarchy take it [merit] to mean wealth or noble birth, ... aristocratic excellence" (Bostock, 2000, p. 113). From the perspective of an "oligarchist," individuals are born to a station in life that is divinely ordained and entails well-established benefits and responsibilities. Justice involves providing and receiving what is due. Inequality is the natural, and perhaps intended, result. The basic premise of this view often stems from a belief that God created an orderly world and humanity's challenge is not to improve upon but to understand and accept God's work.

Americans have long rejected the notion of a divinely ordained aristocracy, but we find remnants of oligarchy in the view that human nature and abilities are determined by innate factors. The idea of genetic destiny or predisposition has replaced that of divine ordination in explaining what is just or expected. Scholars who link IQ with race or ethnicity often make this argument. For example, Eysenck argued that 80 percent of IQ is genetically determined, and that social class is "determined quite strongly by IQ" (1973, p. 159). Jensen took the argument a step further, suggesting that American whites and blacks differ markedly in their IQ scores and that "something between one-half and three-fourths of the average IQ difference between American Negroes and whites is attributable to genetic factors, and the remainder to environmental factors and their interaction with the genetic differences" (1973, p. 363). Richard Herrnstein and Charles Murray achieved notoriety by making a similar argument in their 1994 book, *The Bell Curve*.

Some have gone further, arguing that in human society inequality is not only inevitable but desirable. For example, Davis and Moore (1967) offered a functionalist theory of stratification, arguing that society's most important positions require scarce talents and that higher rewards are required to recruit people with such talents into these positions. "Social inequality is thus an unconsciously evolved device by which societies insure that the most important positions are conscientiously filled by the most qualified persons" (Davis & Moore, 1967, p. 47).

Social Darwinism is closely related to this outlook. The principle of survival of the fittest, when applied to social and economic relations, implies that those who have great wealth are in some way superior to those who do not. A natural consequence of this perspective is the view that vulnerable groups such as children, people with disabilities, or welfare recipients are not capable of participating intelligently in debates that affect them. Social work policy practice can counter this tendency by bringing the voices of the vulnerable back into the dialogue.

From the perspective of oligarchy, Melissa's experiences reflect her status as a woman of working-class background who married a man of limited means. This status is fixed and brings with it certain costs and rewards. At one time in the United States, marriage carried with it the risk of physical abuse for women. That risk was simply one of the costs endured. Today our understanding of the status of wives has changed. Americans no longer expect wives to submit to physical or emotional abuse.

Libertarian Conceptions of Social Justice

Distributive Principle: From each according to his choice; to each according to his product.

Allocation of resources according to product is central to a libertarian understanding of justice. Emphasizing liberty over equality, libertarians argue that inequality is acceptable and promotes social well-being. Oliver Wendell Holmes exemplified this view when he said, "I have no respect for the passion for equality, which seems to me merely idealizing envy" (Hayek, 1960, cited in Sterba, 1980, p. 126). Hayek argues that the only form of equality that does not interfere with liberty is equality before the law. With respect to the role of government, a libertarian view would hold that there is no justification for the state to treat people differently. "Before the law . . . people should be treated alike in spite of the fact that they are different" (p. 127).

Equal treatment under the law inevitably leads to unequal distribution of resources. For libertarians, this is the price of freedom and does not require correction by the government. Libertarians typically view taxes as the coercive taking of private property. Thus, for example, Hayek argues that "economic inequality is not one of the evils which justify our resorting to discriminatory coercion or privilege as a remedy" (p. 128). This general objection to the use of government coercion to achieve equality leads libertarians to oppose taxation and policies designed to promote equal opportunity in education and job opportunity, such as affirmative action. The pursuit of equality is seen as antithetical to individual freedom and hence an inappropriate goal for government.

Robert Nozick's 1974 work, *Anarchy, State, and Utopia,* exemplifies the libertarian perspective. Nozick argues that inequality is not necessarily an indication of injustice if it results from a process that treats people fairly and equally. The fact that a free market results in disparate incomes is not cause for government intervention. Nozick disputes the notion of communal responsibility for poverty, offering an example involving 10 Robinson Crusoes on 10 separate islands. If these men have different levels of well-being, these differences result from variation in their abilities or the availability of natural resources on the islands. In Nozick's view, since none of the Crusoes is responsible for any other Crusoe's disadvantages, none would be justified in demanding that the others transfer resources to him.

In a similar vein Milton Friedman, one of President Reagan's economic advisers, argued that failure to allocate resources on the basis of productivity undermines the prosperity of society. He suggested that the appropriate ethical principle for distribution of income in a free society is "[t]o each according to what he and the instruments he owns produces" (Wood & Woods, 1990, p. 366). Under this view, wealth and high incomes come to those who are fortunate (inheritance) and who take risks (speculation). The community as a whole benefits from the presence of the wealthy, in part because they provide "independent foci of power to offset the centralization of political power" (Friedman, 1962, cited in Sterba, 1980, p. 145) and in part because they become "patrons" of experimentation, novel ideas, and the arts.

Libertarians emphasize the benefits of the free market over an economic system regulated by the government, arguing that a free-market society enjoys greater productivity among its workers and greater incentive to accumulate capital and pass it on to the next generation. A by-product of this capital accumulation is lower interest rates. Further, the free market encourages innovation and risk-taking by offering high rewards for success in uncertain ventures such as speculative investment. Finally, proponents of this view argue that the free market is preferable to government coercion in the allocation of resources because it does not interfere with individual liberty. A classic libertarian treatise is found in Ayn Rand's ode to individualism, *The Fountainhead*. Rand was a strong proponent of libertarian philosophy.

Several aspects of the libertarian view have direct implications for welfare policy. With its general opposition to taxation, a libertarian perspective on social justice would clearly oppose the use of public funds to redistribute income toward the poor. The value placed on a free-market economy would suggest that welfare, as an alternative to paid work, should be made available only as a last resort. Finally, the emphasis on personal freedom, when extended to welfare recipients, would oppose coercion as a means of social control.

A libertarian perspective would emphasize Melissa's free choice in marrying Will and having children. Libertarians would note that Will chose his job. While acknowledging the problems that resulted from these choices, the libertarian would not condone the use of tax funds to help Melissa improve her situation.

Liberal Conceptions of Social Justice

Distributive Principle: Economic liberty and political equality for all.

Central to most liberal conceptions of social justice is the attempt to combine liberty and equality, specifically economic liberty and political equality. Liberal thinkers have taken two different approaches to defining justice: the contractual and the utilitarian. The contractual tradition views the just state as one based on an unwritten contract between free and independent citizens. In contrast, the utilitarian tradition rejects the centrality of a social contract, defining justice as that which optimizes the total well-being of a society. John Rawls is widely cited for his contractual approach, while John Stuart Mill's work exemplifies the utilitarian tradition.[4]

A Contractual Approach (John Rawls). John Rawls developed what he termed "a procedural interpretation" of Immanuel Kant's theories in his classic

---

4. See Locke's *Second Treatise of Government*, Rousseau's *The Social Contract*, and Kant's *The Foundations of Metaphysics* for examples of the contractual tradition. For the utilitarian tradition, see John Stuart Mill's *Utilitarianism*.

book *A Theory of Justice*. According to Rawls, justice is a rational choice made behind a "veil of ignorance." This veil of ignorance represents a hypothetical position in which individuals ignore their personal advantage in making decisions, because "no one knows his place in society, his class position or social status; nor does he know his fortune in the distribution of natural assets and abilities, his intelligence and strength and the like" (Rawls, 1971, p. 137).

Rawls reasons that behind this veil people would rationally choose distributive rules that employ a "maximin" strategy—rules that would maximize the welfare of the least well-off. This conservative strategy, Rawls argues, would naturally be adopted if individuals were unaware of the chances that they might be among the least well-off.

For Rawls, distributive justice includes not only the fair distribution of economic goods and services but also nonmaterial "social goods," including opportunity, power, and the social bases of self-respect. He argues that a "social minimum" in all of these should be established, below which citizens of a state would not be allowed to fall. One general rule for determining the social minimum is that it be set as high as possible consistent with maintaining an efficient economic system (this condition being essential to the long-term well-being of the least advantaged).

Also central to Rawls's conception is the "just savings principle." Arguing that the veil of ignorance would deprive people of knowledge about the generation or cohort to which they belonged, Rawls suggests that "the just savings principle applies to what a society is to save as a matter of justice" (p. 288) to ensure the economic and cultural well-being of successive generations. This insures against one generation spending all of society's resources and leaving subsequent generations impoverished.

Rawls formulated two principles of justice that he believed would be derived under these circumstances:

Principle I. Special Conception of Justice

1. Each person is to have an equal right to the most extensive total system of equal basic liberties compatible with a similar system of liberties for all.
2. Social and economic inequalities are to be arranged so that they are both
    (a) to the greatest benefit of the least advantaged, consistent with the just savings principle, and
    (b) attached to offices and positions open to all under conditions of fair equality of opportunity.

Principle II. General Conception of Justice

All social goods—liberty and opportunity, income and wealth, and the bases of self-respect—are to be distributed equally unless an unequal distribution of any or all of these goods is to the advantage of the least favored.

Suggesting that Rawls is "perhaps the most instrumental [writer] in widening the scope of the concept of distributive justice," Wakefield has applied Rawls's concepts to the practice of psychotherapy by social workers (1988, p. 193). His conclusions are discussed near the end of this chapter in the section on social work and social justice.

Rawls's concept of social justice contrasts sharply with the libertarian view in its treatment of the disadvantaged. Under his general conception of justice, inequality is tolerable only when it benefits the least-advantaged members of society. For Rawls, the welfare problem would be turned on its head. Welfare mothers themselves would not be seen as "the problem." Instead, concern would focus on the presence of extreme wealth that does not contribute to the well-being of the poor.

A Utilitarian Approach (John Stuart Mill).   Mill sought to describe justice in his essay "On the Connection between Justice and Utility" (1998). He begins with the premise that humans have a natural "feeling of justice"—that we intuitively recognize and respond negatively to injustice. But that feeling of justice stems from the desire for social well-being. Mill argues that justice must be understood as that which is most "useful" to society as a whole or, to use his terms, that which generates the highest "utility"—the greatest good or well-being—for the greatest number.

Members of a subgroup of utilitarian liberals called egalitarians argue that the highest utility is achieved through equal distribution of wealth and income. This conclusion is based on a "diminishing returns" argument, which holds that the satisfaction arising from possessing a good diminishes as the good becomes less scarce. Stated more concretely, a poor person will value an additional $50 per month more highly than a rich one. So, as Dalton argues, "unequal distribution of a given amount of purchasing power among a given number of people is . . . likely to be a wasteful distribution from the point of view of economic welfare" (1925, p. 84). In other words, giving an additional $50 to the rich person produces less overall well-being than giving it to the poor one.

Central to the utilitarian argument is the principle that the happiness of each person is valued equally. For Mill, this "involves an equal claim to all the means of happiness except insofar as the inevitable conditions of human life *and the general interest in which that of every individual is included set limits to the maxim*" (Sterba, 1980, p. 103, italics added). Mill argues that unequal access to "the means of happiness" is justified only when it is in the interest of society as a whole— unlike Rawls, who argues that inequality must favor the least-advantaged members of that society.

While both contractual and utilitarian approaches would place limits on inequality in a just society, utilitarians might tolerate inequality if it produced greater good for society, regardless of its implications for the poor. Nonetheless, both perspectives place a high value on providing benefits to the disadvantaged.

In Melissa's case, both liberal approaches (contractual and utilitarian) would support intervention. From the viewpoint of a contractual liberal such as Rawls, Melissa's depression and abuse would place her below an acceptable social minimum. His philosophy would support the use of community resources to bring her above that minimum. A utilitarian liberal would emphasize Mill's concept of an intuitive feeling of justice. Within this perspective, our abhorrence of domestic violence is a clear indicator that it constitutes injustice. Further, since a utilitarian liberal perspective values the happiness of each individual equally, relief of Melissa's suffering would merit the use of community resources.

Socialist Conceptions of Social Justice

Distributive Principle: From each according to his ability; to each according to his need.

Describing his vision of a communist utopia, Marx writes, "In place of the old bourgeois society, with its classes and class antagonisms, we shall have an association, in which the free development of each is the condition for the free development of all" (Marx, 1888, cited in Sterba, 1980, p. 195). Under socialism, justice would consist of individuals contributing to the communal well-being to the extent of their ability. Free from the alienation imposed by a capitalist system, labor would become not a means but an end—an activity done for its own sake.

In its ultimate form, justice under socialism would involve distribution "to each according to his need," but this goal would be reached only after generations of workers had been raised in a cooperative society. For Marx, communist society "emerges from capitalist society" and thus is "still stamped with the birthmarks of the old society from whose womb it emerges" (p. 197). During the early phases of socialism, distributive justice would consist of returning to each individual according to that person's contribution. Several costs would first be subtracted from the "total social product," including (1) replacement of the means of production as needed; (2) costs of expansion of production; (3) a reserve or insurance fund to provide against "misadventures, disturbances through natural events, etc."; (4) costs of administration not belonging to production; (5) costs of meeting communal needs, such as schools and health services; and (6) funds for those unable to work.

The remainder, called the "diminished proceeds of labor," would be distributed to workers according to their work effort. Marx acknowledges that this would be an unequal distribution. Workers with greater strength or natural abilities contribute more work effort than those less fortunate. Also, workers who were supporting families would receive less per capita. But in Marx's view, "these defects are inevitable in the first phase of communist society. Right can never be higher than the economic structure of society and the cultural development thereby determined" (p. 198).

A Marxist perspective would hold that the current status of the poor in America is the result of the oppression of laborers by those who own the means of production. In this view, welfare is yet another means of controlling the disadvantaged while maintaining the labor pool at a subsistence level. Debates regarding the welfare system are irrelevant because this stage of societal development will inevitably yield to a higher one in which welfare will be obsolete.

Marxist analysis of Melissa's situation might see her abuse as the natural result of the oppression of laborers. Growing up in a working-class setting, Melissa was systematically taught to devalue herself, just as a capitalist society devalues laborers. Similarly, Will's violence can be seen as a response to alienating work and limited opportunities. Indeed, this violence may be seen as a harbinger of revolution. Intervention simply to alleviate the suffering would only perpetuate oppression. A Marxist viewpoint would support intervention that would teach Melissa and Will to view their situation as part of a broader socioeconomic context.

Summary of Philosophical Approaches

The distributive principles associated with each of these philosophical perspectives, as well as their implications for Melissa's situation, are summarized in Table 1.2.

The labels commonly assigned to these conceptions of social justice are best applied to ideas, not people. Each approach described here represents a pure type seldom found in human form. A "neo-Marxist" who publicly espouses the equality of humanity may dominate a household marked by rigid gender roles. A "libertarian" who values distribution of benefits on the basis of production may contribute generously to her favorite charity. Meanwhile, those of less clear-cut ideological persuasions may leapfrog from one philosophy to another as issues or personal interests dictate.

Effective policy practice requires the analytic capacity to respond to arguments stemming from these philosophical approaches. Equally important is the

T A B L E   1.2   Summary of Philosophical Approaches to Social Justice

Philosophical Perspective	Distributive Principle	Approach to Melissa
Oligarchy	"From each according to his status; to each according to his status."	Melissa's working-class status defines her opportunities and assigns her burdens. Abuse may be one of those burdens.
Libertarianism	"From each according to his choice; to each according to his product."	Melissa chose to marry Will. Will chose his job. Tax funds that are taken coercively from others should not be used to intervene in their lives.
Liberalism	"Economic liberty and political equality for all."	Intervention to bring Melissa above a social minimum is in order. Relief of her suffering will enhance community well-being.
Socialism	"From each according to his ability; to each according to his need."	Melissa's abuse is the natural result of capitalistic oppression of laborers. Intervention should educate her about the societal roots of her suffering.

ability to communicate and argue without polarizing, rejecting, or demonizing those of divergent views. Social workers who are familiar with these conceptions will be able to "speak the language" of those whose worldviews differ from theirs. So, for example, when talking with a libertarian, an advocate for public assistance might find it more effective to emphasize the loss of freedom we all experience when extremely poor people roam the streets. Utilitarian liberals might be persuaded by a presentation that articulates the suffering experienced by the disadvantaged. Contractual liberals are likely to respond to an explanation that emphasizes how deprivation reduces people to a level below certain acceptable standards (social minimums). A socialist audience may be attuned to the impacts of oppression but unsupportive of interventions that perpetuate the status quo. Finally, while it is hard to dispute a belief that the social order is divinely (or genetically) controlled, it might be possible to persuade such a person that mercy toward those who are suffering is part of the divine plan.

We rarely find a distributive principle clearly labeled as such. Instead, as we listen to arguments and examine how policies work, we can identify their philosophical underpinnings. Thus, for example, when a legislator argues that "It is not fair that our tax dollars support women just because they are mothers—welfare mothers should work for their money like the rest of us," the legislator is rejecting an oligarchic principle that says benefits should flow directly from status as a mother, and taking a libertarian perspective that says one should be paid for economic productivity. An advocate who argues, "Welfare mothers are not able to work; we should support them because they need help!" is presenting a need-based distributive principle with roots in socialist philosophy. Finally, the student who argues that "It doesn't hurt Bill Gates to pay his taxes, and public programs make a huge difference in the quality of life of the poor" is taking a utilitarian liberal perspective. In Chapter 2, which focuses on government, we will consider the ways in which these philosophical perspectives are reflected in electoral politics.

The remaining sections of this chapter turn to social work practice. We will begin by exploring social justice themes in "micro" practice. Next, we will present a brief biography of a leading social work practitioner. We will conclude the chapter by examining social justice as a defining mission for the social work profession.

SOCIAL JUSTICE: THEMES FOR "MICRO" PRACTICE

Social workers often assume that working for justice is the exclusive province of "macro" or "policy" practice. Yet social justice is a vital concern for "micro" or "clinical" practice as well. This is illustrated in the three themes examined in this section, with reference to Melissa's case: (1) social justice is personal and political,

(2) families teach social justice, and (3) injustice undermines social bonds and nation–states.

Social Justice Is Personal and Political

In response to cultural and historical pressures, many social workers "psychologize" human misery and ignore or avoid the political and economic dimensions of their clients' pain. They provide opportunities for introspection and personal change but fail to offer transformative insights rooted in understanding of broader social forces (Saleebey, 1990; Specht & Courtney, 1994). A therapist working in this vein might lead Melissa to see how her selection of a spouse was conditioned by childhood experiences, or encourage her to view her tolerance of abuse as a symptom of low self-esteem.

Yet, as Saleebey notes, "Even the most private problems of relationship and consciousness have political and social dimensions" (1990, p. 38). A social worker might empower Melissa to seek transformative change by encouraging her to participate in an advocacy group such as JEDI Women. Participation in the group could increase Melissa's awareness of the social and political forces that contributed to her abuse, and she could begin to experience herself as a capable change agent. Failure to acknowledge the social and political roots of individual misery can leave professionals as well as their clients in what Jacoby (1975) terms "the isolation that damns the individual to scrape along in a private world" (p. 44).

The diverse social, economic, and political forces that have influenced Melissa's life are elaborated throughout this text. Some are introduced below:

1.   She was born into a society that does not provide universal family planning services. Melissa's parents had a large family. Melissa, herself, bore three children she could ill afford. Nor does the United States offer direct financial support to parents. Nations such as Germany and Sweden offer limited financial support to all parents in the form of children's allowances. This is a "universal" approach to the income maintenance needs of children. The United States has adopted a "residual" approach, providing public assistance only for the most needy.
2.   Melissa's decision to leave high school during her first pregnancy may reflect a lack of support for education of pregnant teens. Programs for teenage mothers remain limited to major metropolitan areas where they serve only a small proportion of those who could benefit.
3.   Will's "good job" provided health benefits but did not offer career mobility. Lack of universal access to health care often traps workers in unrewarding jobs. The resulting tension may have contributed to Will's abuse of Melissa and the children.
4.   Recent welfare reforms provided for treatment of Melissa's depression. Although depression often goes untreated, Melissa was fortunate that her state's welfare program supported identification and treatment of barriers to employment. With antidepressant medication and counseling, Melissa can

remain in transitional employment. Her ability to support her family will depend on continuing support through her state's welfare program. Mandates at either the state or the federal level might cut off that support by imposing time limits on welfare.

5. Entering the labor market as an unskilled worker, Melissa will encounter the effects of discrimination against women. She may find employers who pay her 70 cents for work of "comparable worth" to that done by a man for a dollar. Or she may be unable to care for her children when they are ill because federal legislation exempts small companies from providing medical leave.

Clearly, social policies significantly influence the lives of Melissa and her family. Conversely, Melissa herself has affected public policy. By sharing her experiences, she helped mobilize key stakeholders to protect welfare in her state. She has also become active in a women's organization, thereby joining an emerging grassroots effort to give voice to the concerns of vulnerable women like herself. For Melissa this involvement triggered a transformation—she began to see herself not as a victim but as an agent of change.

Families Teach Social Justice

In her feminist critique of major political theories of justice, Susan Okin argued that (with the rare exception of John Stuart Mill) philosophers from Aristotle to Marx have confined their discussions to the public sphere, from which women historically have been excluded. Yet, as Okin, Rousseau, Mill, and others have

---

BOX 1.1   Charity or Justice?

President George H. W. Bush promoted the concept of "a thousand points of light," arguing that volunteerism and charity should substitute for professional assistance and entitlement. In making this suggestion, the president articulated the view that instead of demanding their right to assistance, the poor should ask for charitable support. This is compatible with a libertarian understanding of social justice, as it preserves the freedom of donors to deny aid—a liberty not enjoyed by taxpayers who are coerced into paying for entitlements. Charity also substitutes the warm glow of beneficence and personal gratitude for the cold bureaucratic exchange and the stigma associated with public assistance. Rather than demanding their rights, recipients of charity ask for help—behavior that the donors view as much more appropriate from the lower classes.

Justice, on the other hand, confers rights—rights that society is obliged to defend. Recipients of assistance emerge, not as sympathetic individuals humbly asking for relief, but as members of an interest group using the politics of protest and the tools of jurisprudence to enforce public obligations. Bertha Reynolds and others have suggested that justice confers greater dignity than charity on the recipient of assistance. For example, she noted that during the Depression, social workers were surprised to find that "[t]hey [clients] did not seem to feel the 'stigma' which social workers attached to assistance, and some, indeed, came to prefer public aid . . . to which they felt they were entitled, to private 'charity'" (Reynolds, 1963, p. 140).

observed, the moral development of children takes place in families, not in courts or legislatures. It is primarily in families that we "learn to be just" (Okin, 1989, p. 297). Politicians and developmental psychologists alike have linked the structure and operation of families to the broader structure and operation of nations.

Clearly, social justice is a significant concern within families, just as it is in the workplace and in national policy. By helping families grapple for a fair allocation of costs and benefits, social workers who promote social justice in this context may have as much impact on the nation's well-being as those who focus on legislative advocacy.

Injustice Undermines Social Bonds and Nation-States

People often disagree on what is just. Like children, adults find it difficult to transcend self-interest and consider the well-being of the group as a whole. Central to this task is long-term commitment to the group. This commitment stems first from receiving the benefits of group membership, then from recognizing them as such, and later from observing that the benefits and costs of membership are fairly allocated. On a personal level, the thrill of newfound intimacy brings two individuals into a committed couple relationship. That relationship is sustained by the partners' belief that costs and benefits are fairly allocated (i.e., that the relationship is just). Injustice is also destabilizing at a more macro level. Governments do not endure when a significant number of their citizens view them as unjust. The long history of revolution emphasizes the role of perceived injustice as a trigger. Examples include the French, American, Russian, and Chinese revolutions, the overthrow of the Marcos reign in the Philippines, and the dissolution of the Soviet regime. By promoting social justice, social workers enhance the long-term stability of groups and nations.

SOCIAL WORKERS AND SOCIAL JUSTICE

Bertha Capen Reynolds (1885–1978) was instrumental in promoting social justice both within and outside her profession. After examining Reynolds's contributions, we will discuss how social work professionals can continue to carry out her mission of building a more just society.

Bertha Capen Reynolds: A Profile

The Bertha Reynolds Society was established in 1985 to honor a singular figure in the social work profession. Bertha Capen Reynolds was one of the nation's first professionally trained social workers, with experience spanning the first half of the twentieth century. Her autobiography chronicles the personal development of an inquiring and sensitive practitioner who entered the profession determined to master the psychiatric techniques she and her peers believed were the key to unlocking human potential. After graduating from Smith College in

1918, Reynolds spent most of her career as associate director of the school's social work program. But her practice ranged from academic pursuits to serving and residing in residential facilities for the mentally ill, supervising social workers providing relief during the Depression, and serving the seamen's union during World War II.

During the Depression, Reynolds joined the "rank-and-file" social workers of her time to call for a new social order. Dissatisfied with the "passivity" she observed among caseworkers, Reynolds began to call for a professional commitment to community development. She noted that "the community is always involved in any professional relationship" (Reynolds, 1963, p. 147) and argued that "the future of social work is bound up with the coming of a sounder social order . . . the members of this profession have not only the obligation to work for justice which good citizenship applies, but the professional duty" (p. 141).

Reynolds saw in Marxism the key to establishment of a sounder social order. At a student's suggestion she read the works of Marx and Engels and was persuaded that their theory of dialectical materialism accurately reflected the inevitable progress of society. She watched the development of the Union of Soviet Socialist Republics (USSR) with interest. Unfortunately, she did not live to observe its dissolution. Her intellectual response to these events undoubtedly would have enriched and inspired the profession.

With her own brand of "brilliant common sense," Reynolds observed a parallel between the psychodynamic theory of her early training and the Marxism she discovered later in life. Both saw conflict as a necessary prerequisite to growth, and both relied on the clash of opposites (id–ego and capitalist–proletariat) to produce a synthesis that represented a higher order of development.

Reynolds never married. She cultivated and treasured her close relationships, in some cases carrying on lengthy correspondence with people she had never met. She said, "If one word is needed, then, to begin to sum up what fifty years of living have taught me, that word is *relatedness* . . . many people do not know that they stand in any particular place in society, and so they judge their viewpoint to be the only one possible for anybody. I believe it indispensable to a sound relatedness to others to know where one is to start with, for what biases and blind spots to make allowance, and to know that there exist other and quite different viewpoints" (Reynolds, 1963, pp. 314–315).

Social Work and Social Justice

Bertha Reynolds saw social justice as the hallmark of the profession and argued that social work techniques are authentic only to the extent that they serve this mission. She suggested that activities that focus exclusively on what she called the "mental hygiene" of the client should not be considered social work. For Reynolds, the proper clients for social work were the needy. She offered principles for social work practice during the Depression, saying, "They were, first of all, that social work exists to serve people in need. If it serves other classes who have other purposes it becomes too dishonest to be capable of either theoretical or practical development" (Reynolds, 1963, p. 173).

Jerome Wakefield pursued the same line of reasoning to arrive at a more elaborate conclusion. He agreed that distributive justice is the "organizing value" of the profession and that "the purpose of social work is to see to it that anyone falling below the social minimum in any of the social primary goods is brought above that level in as many respects as possible" (Wakefield, 1988, p. 205).

But, as Wakefield notes, "for better or worse, social work has become one of the mental health professions" (1988, p. 187). Noting that "[s]ocial workers probably provide more care for the severely mentally ill than any other professional group," the National Institute of Mental Health acknowledges social workers as important providers of mental health services in the United States (NIMH, 1992, p. 5; see also Task Force on Social Work Research, 1991). Further, the growth of private practice in social work is one of the most significant trends in the recent history of the profession. Between 1975 and 1985, the number of social workers in full-time private practice increased dramatically, so that in 1985, more than a third of the members of the National Association of Social Workers were engaged in private practice (Hardcastle, *Social Work Labor Force,* cited by Specht & Courtney, 1994).

Wakefield sought to integrate this trend with the overall mission of the profession by specifying the conditions under which psychotherapy promotes social justice. Relying on Rawls's conceptualization, Wakefield argues: "It is the focus on minimal distributive justice that differentiates clinical social work from traditional psychotherapy" (1988, p. 206). Social workers focus on clients who are deprived or who fall below a basic social minimum. So, for example, a professional woman whose fear of flying interferes with her advancement is not an appropriate target for social work intervention. Even with the fear of flying, she enjoys social benefits well above any social minimum.

But, as numerous authors have noted (e.g., Leighninger, 1990), the status and credibility of a profession are largely determined by the power and affluence of the people it serves. Social workers who focus on the concerns of the middle and professional classes enjoy a measure of security and stature. This is the case for social workers in private practice and those who work in employee assistance programs (EAPs).

Social workers in these settings often struggle to integrate their professional mission of service to the needy with their day-to-day activities. Social workers in EAPs must regularly confront the reality that their paychecks depend on their ability to satisfy the members of the managerial ranks. Similarly, social workers in managed care environments confront the conflict between achieving cost-containment goals and meeting the care and treatment needs of patients. The ethical practice of social work requires that the client, not the employer or health-care provider, be the focus of professional concern.

SUMMARY: SOCIAL JUSTICE CONCEPTS

We began this chapter by contrasting modern and postmodern approaches to the definition of social justice. While modern approaches are popular and offer satisfying definitions of what is and is not just, I believe a postmodern approach leads us to a more nuanced and humanizing definition of this elusive concept. We also examined four philosophical perspectives on social justice, suggesting that familiarity with these approaches can help us analyze the basic assumptions underlying most social policies. We then turned to "micro" practice, arguing that social justice is an important consideration in this arena, and identifying three themes in support of this perspective: social justice issues are personal and political, families teach social justice, and failure to correct injustice can break up families and topple governments. Finally, using Bertha Reynolds as an example, we explored the role of social work and social workers in the pursuit of social justice.

The pursuit of social justice resembles the quest for the Holy Grail. It is time consuming and hazardous, its goal is ephemeral at best, and it is an integral part of the human experience. Policy practice, with its alternating victories and setbacks, brings social workers into this quest. Effective policy practice requires a clear vision of social justice and the ability to operate within existing social, economic, and political frameworks to promote that vision. In Chapter 2 we will turn to the role of government in the search for social justice.

KEYWORDS

Economic justice	Civil rights movement	Social justice
Egalitarianism	Social Darwinism	Civil rights

THINK ABOUT IT

1. For Aristotle justice consisted of equal treatment for people who are of similar merit. How is merit defined in your classroom? In your family? In your practicum site? Which setting do you find the most personally rewarding?

2. Which of the four philosophical approaches is most congruent with your worldview? Do your classmates differ in this regard? Are some conceptions not represented among them?

3. Identify a personal conflict or negotiation that involves the allocation of costs and/or rewards of group membership. How was this conflict resolved? Did the process adhere to the "fair process principles" outlined in this chapter?

4. Select your favorite utopia. Describe one to three key allocation principles that are applied in this utopia and identify the philosophical approach they most nearly represent. Is this consistent with the political philosophy of the author?

5. Suppose that the members of a group agree that a practice (such as genital mutilation of young girls) is acceptable but an outside observer finds it abhorrent. Is the practice just? Does the outsider, a social work professional,

have the responsibility to intervene if no one who is involved objects to the practice? What about the young girls? Do they have a voice?

WEB-BASED EXERCISES

For direct links to all the sites in these exercises, log on to the Student Companion Site for this book at academic.cengage.com/social_work/barusch, and choose Chapter 1.

1. Go to the website of the Foundation for Critical Thinking at http://www .criticalthinking.org. First, explore the site and develop your own concise definition of critical thinking. Look for the "Thinker's Guide Series" on this page. Find "Critical Thinking Concepts and Tools," and scroll down on the page. You'll find a sample of the guide's contents that can be viewed at no charge using Adobe Acrobat. In that sample is a single-page graphic illustrating the "Elements of Thought." Print out the graphic and carry it to your social work classes for a week. Use it to determine how frequently these elements are used by your colleagues and instructors. Compare your findings with those of a friend or colleague.

2. Go to the United Nations website at http://www.un.org/Overview/rights .html. Review the provisions of the Universal Declaration of Human Rights. Identify which articles are and are not consistent with U.S. law. Which articles do you think pose problems for leaders in Islamic nations?

SUGGESTED RESOURCES

Bostock, D. (2000). *Aristotle's Ethics*. New York: Oxford University Press.

Finn, J. L., & Jacobson, M. (2003). *Just Practice: A Social Justice Approach to Social Work*. Peosta, IA: Eddie Bowers Publishing.

Mill, J. S. (1998). *Utilitarianism* (R. Crisk, Ed.). New York: Oxford University Press. (Original work published in 1863).

Reynolds, B. C. (1963). *An Uncharted Journey: Fifty Years of Growth in Social Work*. New York: Citadel Press.

Sterba, J. P. (1998). *Justice for Here and Now*. New York: Cambridge University Press.

2

The Government's Role

All I want is the same thing you want. To have a nation with a
government that is as good and honest and decent and
competent and compassionate and as filled with love as are the
American people.
JIMMY CARTER, 1976

In the last chapter we noted that the central mission of the social work profession is to promote social justice. This chapter will focus on the role of government in that endeavor. We begin by applying the philosophical approaches introduced in Chapter 1 to modern labels such as "liberal" or "Republican." We then describe the structure of the U.S. government along two dimensions: levels and branches. Despite its complexity, the U.S. government must be seen not as an end point for democracy but as the latest stage in a continuing process of development. Our nation's history has been marked by debate about the extent to which government should assume responsibility for social welfare. We will consider the process of privatization as it illustrates this ongoing debate about the role of government. The chapter closes with a brief overview of U.S. tax policy. It is vital that social workers understand the tax system. Taxation is an important tool of social policy, not only because it represents the cost side of the social justice equation but also because tax policy is often used to accomplish social goals.

PHILOSOPHICAL PERSPECTIVES AND CONTEMPORARY POLITICS

Some readers of this text may have snoozed through or skimmed the discussion of philosophical perspectives in Chapter 1, thinking, "This has no relevance today." Here we will demonstrate that these philosophies have direct relevance to contemporary politics in the United States. We can find remnants of oligarchy in U.S. politics, and libertarian and liberal perspectives are well represented. Socialist philosophy is seldom evident in mainstream U.S. politics, which leads some conservatives to crow that "the left is dead." Rather than debate this issue, let us consider political parties and political labels.

Political Parties

A political party is an association of like-minded individuals organized to accomplish shared goals. In most states voters are given the opportunity to declare a party preference when they register. Voter registration rolls are available to the public, and parties use them to organize their Get Out the Vote efforts. Candidates wishing to run under a party must have the official sanction of the party before they register to be on the ballot. While electoral politics in the United States operates on a two-party system, third parties have been established and at times exercise considerable influence.

The Republican Party (also known as the Grand Old Party, or GOP) emerged in opposition to the compromise of 1850 (Fugitive Slave Act). Antislavery activists allied with advocates for free distribution of western lands, protective tariffs, and a transcontinental railroad. Thus the GOP's business orientation was present at its inception. The party also has a strong foundation in libertarian philosophy. Its first presidential nominee, John C. Fremont, ran under the banner, "Free soil, free labor, free speech, free men, Fremont!" Abraham Lincoln ran for president as a Republican, as did Theodore Roosevelt, Ronald Reagan, George H. W. Bush, George W. Bush, and others.

The libertarian beliefs manifest in John C. Fremont's campaign slogan can still be found in subsequent Republican rhetoric. For example, Barry Goldwater ran for president in 1964 as a "classical conservative." He focused "on three general freedoms—economic, social, and political. . . . [T]he conservative movement is founded on the simple tenet that people have the right to live life as they please, as long as they don't hurt anyone else in the process" (Karger & Stoesz, 2002, p. 15).

This commitment to liberty evolved into a "neoconservative" opposition to government, "big" government in particular. Government is portrayed in Republican rhetoric as an obstacle to personal achievement and economic growth. This position has found eager support among business interests, which often chafe at government regulation. Thus the Republican Party generally serves as a champion for business. This role creates some interesting contradictions, as when businesses seek (and Republicans deliver) government protection from foreign competition (George W. Bush's protective steel tariffs) or government relief from unanticipated business losses (the savings and loan bailout). In these cases Republican opposition to government intervention is set aside in favor of measures that support business interests. While conservatives were generally isolationist, except when confronted with the global threat of communism, neoconservatives aspire to a global American hegemony—with roots reaching back to Theodore Roosevelt's "big stick" and William McKinley's acquisition of foreign lands.

The election of 2004 was a victory for the social conservative element of the Republican Party. Social conservatives find changing gender roles and family forms abhorrent and do not hesitate to use the government to enforce their moral code. This election signaled an end to, or at least a pause in, what Piven and Cloward have called "electoral economism" (1997)—that is, the tendency of elections to revolve around economic issues. The slogan of the 1992 Clinton campaign was "It's the economy, Stupid!" In 2004, as we will see when we consider the tax code in a later section, most Americans did not vote their pocketbooks. The 2004 Republican victory is widely attributed to the ascendance of "moral values" over economic considerations in the minds of American voters. Piven and Cloward were prescient when, in 1997, they wrote that "fundamentalism is flourishing in American politics" (p. 77).

The Democratic Party traces its roots to 1792, when the "Democratic Republican" Party was organized by Thomas Jefferson to support the Bill of Rights. It was known as "the party of the common man" when Jefferson was elected president in 1800, serving from 1801 to 1809. In the 1820s the party was transformed by Andrew Jackson. The Jacksonians eliminated the property requirement for voting (which expanded suffrage for white males), reduced government control over national banking, and instituted a "spoils system." Democrats organized immigrants under city "bosses" and under Polk achieved America's "manifest destiny" of seizing one-third of Mexico and extending the U.S. border to the Pacific Ocean.

Emphasis on equality characterizes many of the positions supported by the modern Democratic Party and is reflected in its composition. Some have described the party as "a big tent" that welcomes working-class Americans, people of color, immigrants, gays and lesbians, and other traditionally disenfranchised groups. Unlike Republicans, Democrats do not necessarily view government as a constraint on personal liberty. For example, both President Kennedy and President Johnson promised to use the power of government to eliminate social ills caused by poverty and discrimination.

In 1992, Bill Clinton ran as a "new Democrat" and embraced some positions traditionally associated with Republicans. He was an active participant in the elimination of Aid to Families with Dependent Children (AFDC), and through "reinventing government" initiatives the Clinton administration reduced the size of the federal government.

Some say the 2000 election was not decided by the major parties but by a third-party candidate—Ralph Nader. In 1996 and 2000, Nader was the presidential candidate for the Green Party, one of the best known of over 35 "third" parties in the United States that include the American Reform Party, the Libertarian Party, the Personal Choice Party, the Constitution Party, the U.S. Pacifist Party, the Socialist Workers Party, the Prohibition Party, Communist Party USA, the American Nazi Party, and others. (Please see http://www.politics1.com/parties.htm for an overview of the rich array of third parties in the United States.)

A well-known consumer advocate, Nader was the first presidential candidate for the Green Party, and his 1996 and 2000 campaigns catapulted the party into national awareness. In 2000, the Green Party was on the ballot in 44 states, and Nader secured more than 2.8 million votes. It is unclear what proportion of these votes would have gone to Democratic candidate Al Gore, but given the election's close margin some believe the presence of Nader helped secure victory for George Bush. Nader's party fell short of the 5 percent required to secure federal matching funds for its campaign, however, and Nader was not nominated by the Greens in 2004. (He ran as an independent candidate and received fewer than 400,000 votes.)

Political Labels

In the American political arena, the words "conservative" and "liberal" have assumed connotations that go far beyond their strict definitions. But let's begin with definitions. *Webster's Dictionary* defines "conservative" as "Tending or disposed to maintain existing institutions; opposed to change or innovation." "Liberal" is defined as the converse of conservative, referring to "a person who favors a political philosophy of progress and reform and the protection of civil liberties" (http://www.webster-dictionary.org/definition/conservative, accessed November 11, 2004).

While these definitions may hold true in a broad sense, the terms *conservative* and *liberal* have taken on greater meaning as they've become political bywords. For example, the conservative movement in the United States emphasizes personal liberty and argues against government involvement in the economy. Indeed, conservatives tend to favor a laissez-faire approach to the economy characterized by minimal government regulation. But the conservative movement is a coalition of groups and individuals whose agendas do not always agree. Social conservatives favor government regulation of personal and familial decisions in areas such as reproductive rights and marriage. Fiscal conservatives seek to minimize government spending and regulation. Some argue that the contradictions within the conservative movement threaten to break up the coalition that kept President George W. Bush in office (Michlethwait & Wooldridge, 2004). Fiscal conservatives were outraged by the rising deficit, though they appreciated Bush's commitment to tax cuts and a pro-business regulatory environment. Social conservatives resented his "compromise" on stem cell research but were delighted to support a constitutional amendment to define marriage as the union of one man and one woman.

The terms "liberal" and "progressive" have also taken on political connotations that go beyond their strict definitions. Historically, liberals have looked to government as a tool for social change, supporting legislation such as the New Deal, Johnson's Great Society antipoverty programs, the civil rights legislation of the 1960s, and the Clean Air Act. Oddly enough, once these legislative reforms are in place, roles become confused. Conservatives advocate for radical reform in Social Security (privatization, see Chapter 4) and liberals fight to maintain what was once a liberal reform and is now part of the country's institutional structure! Yet essential features of liberal and progressive politicians continue to be (1) their willingness to embrace (or at least accept) broad social changes, (2) their view of government as a tool for social improvement, and (3) their defense of civil liberties. So you seldom find a self-professed liberal who advocates recriminalizing abortion. But liberals are not libertarians. They value freedom and equality. By freedom they generally mean civil liberties, as opposed to property rights. So when environmental preservation steps on the toes of property owners, self-identified liberals tend to value community well-being over personal property.

In this section we have explored the philosophical underpinnings of contemporary political debates. Often these debates are fundamentally about the role of government in American society, a topic we will return to later when we examine the privatization of government functions. But first, a basic understanding of the structure and operation of government is in order. (Those who have recently completed a civics course may choose to skim these sections.)

LEVELS OF GOVERNMENT

Governance in the United States is shared among three levels of government: federal, state, and local. At the federal level, Congress is vested by the Constitution with the power to tax, provide for the common defense and general welfare, borrow money, regulate interstate commerce, manage immigration and naturalization, regulate bankruptcies, coin money, set standards for weights and measures, establish post offices, issue patents and copyrights, establish courts, declare war, raise and support military forces, and protect civil rights. Under the Tenth Amendment, those powers not specifically delegated to the federal government are reserved for the states or the people.

The structures of state governments mirror those of the federal government. Like the federal legislative branch, nearly all states have bicameral legislatures (that is, legislatures made up of two houses, such as a Senate and a House of Representatives).[1] Similarly, the federal courts have parallel entities in the various state judicial systems. Finally, at both federal and state levels the executive branch consists of a head of state (the president or governor), an appointed cabinet, and a cadre of civil servants who implement policy. Governments at county and city levels typically consist of two branches: legislative entities such as county

---

1. At the time of this writing, Nebraska is the only state with a unicameral legislature.

commissions or city councils, and an executive branch consisting of a mayor or city manager and the employees of various city or county agencies.

Overlapping areas of authority among the various levels of government can create confusion about which entity is responsible for addressing a given problem. A recurring theme in U.S. history has been the struggle to determine the nexus of authority for social policy. As we will see in Chapter 9, the civil rights movement called on federal authority to restrict state discretion. Nevertheless, the federal government enjoys no authority over state governments except that which pertains to constitutional violations. In a vivid example of this tension between federal control and state or local control, the Social Security Act of 1935 was subjected to court challenge on the grounds that it represented abuse of federal taxing authority (see Chapter 4). State officials frequently claim the federal government has exceeded its constitutional authority or placed unmanageable demands (such as "unfunded mandates") on state governments. This complaint is often lodged in relation to federal grant-in-aid programs.

A grant-in-aid or block grant extends the capacity of the federal government to pursue a social agenda. Through grants-in-aid, the federal government offers money to states on the condition that they abide by federal regulations governing these programs. In this way the federal government can expand social programs that might arguably extend beyond its constitutional authority. For example, states elect to participate in the Medicaid program and receive federal funding to provide medical care to low-income residents. The medical care provided must conform to the requirements of federal law. Thus federal law has expanded and regulated health care for the needy. At the same time, participating states must pay part of the costs of their Medicaid programs. As we will see in Chapter 6, the Medicaid match represents a significant proportion of state budgets, leading governors to protest that federal Medicaid requirements interfere with state authority. In the late 1990s, an emerging (or reemerging) states' rights movement exerted pressure to reduce the federal Medicaid regulations and to allow states greater discretion in allocating these funds.

In a process known as "devolution," responsibility for social programs is transferred from federal to state levels of government. Block grants are often the vehicle for these transfers. Such was the case in 1996, for example, when the federal entitlement known as Aid to Families with Dependent Children (AFDC) was converted to a block grant known as Temporary Assistance to Needy Families (TANF). State-level discretion over the program increased, and the federal financial contribution was capped. The same thing happened in 1981, when Title XX was converted to the Social Services Block Grant. Typically the rationale for devolution is that officials at the state level, who are closer to program clients, can better respond to their needs. Critics argue that devolution creates a problem known as "race to the bottom," in which states try to ensure that their social services and benefits are no more attractive than neighboring states to avoid in-migration by potential welfare recipients.

Just as there is often tension between levels of government, there is also dispute about the proper roles of the legislative, executive, and judicial *branches* of government in social policy development. For example, some argue that the *Roe*

B O X 2.1   Democracy in Action: The Electoral Process

George W. Bush became president in 2000 without securing a majority of the popular vote. How could this happen? Simply put, American presidents are not elected by the American people. They are chosen by the Electoral College. The College was not developed simply because the founding fathers thought the general public was unintelligent. It stemmed from their commitment to states' rights and their concern that citizens in isolated rural areas might be disenfranchised in a popular election. As it turned out, the Electoral College does support states' rights. It also gives voice to rural voters and sustains the major political parties. Each state has a number of electors equal to its two senators plus its representatives. So urban states have more electors, but not exactly in proportion to their greater populations. States develop the rules that determine how electors vote, and all but two states call for a "winner take all" system in which the person with a majority of popular votes gets support from all of the state's electors. The two exceptions are Nebraska and Maine. As a result, President Bush was able to win the election without winning a majority of the popular votes. For more information on the Electoral College, visit the Federal Election Commission at http://www.fec.gov/.

---

v. Wade decision that established a woman's right to abortion moved the Supreme Court into an "activist" role in which it legislated social policy rather than simply interpreting the laws. In the following section we will describe the operations of the three branches of government at the federal level and discuss the processes through which they establish social policy.

BRANCHES OF GOVERNMENT

Social workers—indeed, anyone interested in influencing policy—must be conversant with how the branches of government operate because each of these entities plays a role in social policy. Put simply, the legislative branch passes the laws. The executive branch issues regulations and executive orders that determine how laws will be implemented and, in many cases, directly implements social policy. The judicial branch issues opinions that interpret laws and create a body of case law that also constitutes social policy. Thus, comprehensive understanding of a social policy should address the contributions of all three branches of government: legislation (legislative branch), regulations (executive branch), and opinions (judicial branch).

The Legislative Branch

All Legislative Powers herein granted shall be vested in a Congress of the United States, which shall consist of a Senate and House of Representatives. Article I, Section 1, United States Constitution

The U.S. Congress consists of a Senate and a House of Representatives. The Senate has 100 members, two from each state. Members of the Senate serve six-year terms. The House of Representatives has 435 members, with each state's representation being proportionate to the size of its population. At the time of this writing, the most populous state is California, which has 53 members in the House. The smallest delegations come from the states of Arkansas, Delaware, Montana, North Dakota, South Dakota, Vermont, and Wyoming, which have one representative apiece. Members of the House serve two-year terms. The primary functions of the U.S. Congress are legislation (creation of laws) and budgeting (collection and allocation of public funds).

Legislation.   Legislation begins with a proposal in the form of a bill or a resolution.[2] A bill is used for most legislation. Bills originating in the House of Representatives are designated by the letters "H.R.," while those originating in the Senate begin with "S." These letters are followed by a number that the bill retains until it is enacted into law. Students interested in tracking the status or history of legislation will find an excellent source of information in the "Thomas" website maintained by the Library of Congress (http://thomas.loc.gov).

Any House member may introduce a bill at any time while the House is in session. Traditionally, a receptacle known as the "hopper" (beside the clerk's desk in the House chamber) is provided for this purpose; hence the expression "put it in the hopper" means to introduce an idea or proposal. The sponsor's signature must appear on the bill. A bill may have an unlimited number of cosponsors. It is assigned a number by the clerk and referred to the appropriate committee by the Speaker of the House. The bill is then printed.

The Speaker of the House enjoys some discretion in deciding which committee will receive a bill and thus can greatly influence its fate. For example, the Speaker can slow a bill's progress by forwarding it to a committee that is hostile to its intent. Consideration by committees is an important phase of the legislative process. It is the time when the public has an opportunity to be heard. Usually the first step in this process is a public hearing in which committee members hear testimony from witnesses representing diverse viewpoints. Each committee publicly announces the date, place, and subject of any hearing it conducts. A transcript of testimony taken at the hearing is frequently printed and distributed by the committee. These are available through the "Thomas" website or in government document departments at federal depository libraries.

After the hearings are completed, the bill is reviewed in what is popularly known as a "mark-up" session. Here members of the committee study the bill and review related testimony. Amendments may be offered, and committee members vote to accept or reject these changes.

When the committee has finished its deliberations, a vote is taken to determine what action to take on the bill. The bill may be reported, with or without amendment, or tabled, which means no further action will occur. If the commit-

---

2. Most of the information presented in this section is found in a congressional document called *How Our Laws Are Made,* available through the U.S. House of Representatives. It is also available through the Library of Congress: http://thomas.loc.gov/home/lawsmade .toc.html (accessed February 20, 2005).

tee has approved extensive amendments it may decide to report a new bill. This is known as a "clean bill," which will have a new number. If the committee votes to report a bill, the report is written by a committee staff member. It describes the measure and reasons for approval. Committee reports are excellent sources of information for students and policy members interested in studying congressional intent.

Although consideration of a bill generally occurs only after it is reported out of committee, some measures are brought directly to the floor by the Speaker. Consideration of a bill may be governed by a resolution that sets out the debate procedures for the specific measure. Certain aspects, such as the amount of time allowed for debate and whether amendments can be offered, may be determined at this time. Debate time for a measure is usually divided between proponents and opponents. Each side yields time to members who wish to speak on the bill. When amendments are offered, these are also debated and voted on. After debate is concluded and amendments are determined, the House votes on final passage. In some cases, a vote to "recommit" the bill to committee is requested. This is usually an effort by opponents to change or table the measure. If a vote to recommit fails, a final vote is ordered.

The standing rules of the Senate differ from those of the House in that they permit senators to debate at length. Debate cannot be ended by a simple majority. This right of extended debate permits filibusters that can be brought to an end only if "cloture" is invoked through a vote of three-fifths of all senators. Senators also enjoy the right to propose floor amendments that are not germane to the matter under consideration. Thus, individual senators can raise issues and subject them to vote even if they have not been reviewed by a standing committee.[3] Although it is within their rights, senators do not filibuster every measure they oppose. To do so would seriously impede the Senate's functioning. Filibusters are reserved for issues on which senators hold strong opinions.

After a measure passes in its originating chamber (either the House or the Senate), it passes to the other chamber. It must pass both bodies in the same form before it can be presented to the president for signature. If either chamber changes the measure, it must return to the originating chamber for concurrence or additional changes. This negotiation may occur on the floor of the House or Senate. Often a conference committee will be appointed with both House and Senate members. This group will resolve differences and report identical versions to both sides for a vote. Conference committees also issue reports outlining the final version of the bill.

After a bill has passed both the House and Senate, it is considered "enrolled" and is sent to the president, who may (1) sign the measure into law; (2) veto it and return it to Congress (where a two-thirds vote is required to override his veto); (3) let it become law without signature; or (4) give it a "pocket-veto" if

---

3. I am grateful to Stanley Bach, senior specialist in the legislative process, government division, for his discussion of the rights of senators and his introduction to Senate processes.

the bill arrives at the end of a session; that is, if Congress has adjourned and the president does not sign a bill, it is automatically vetoed.

Resolutions.   Generally speaking, a resolution differs from a bill in that it does not become law but is either an expression of the opinion of Congress or an administrative act governing the operation of Congress. Resolutions may originate in either the House of Representatives or the Senate. Like bills, resolutions are numbered sequentially, with a brief designation that reflects their origins. Those introduced in the House of Representatives are numbered with the designation "HRES," which stands for "House resolution." Those originating in the Senate are designated "SRES," for "Senate resolution." Joint resolutions (designated "HJRES" or "SJRES") become law in the same manner as bills. The only exceptions to this rule are joint resolutions proposing an amendment to the Constitution. Upon approval of such a resolution by two-thirds of both House and Senate, it is sent not to the president but to the administrator of general services for submission to the individual states for ratification. Such was the case with the Equal Rights Amendment, discussed in Chapter 12.

Budgeting.[4]   Budgeting is a gargantuan task in the United States, involving both executive and legislative branches. The calendar complicates public understanding of the process. The federal budget year, or fiscal year, extends from October 1 through September 30 (see Table 2.1). The president is required by law to submit his proposed federal budget for the next fiscal year to Congress by the first Monday in February. This proposed budget is prepared by the White House Office of Management and Budget (OMB), under the president's direction and with consultation from cabinet members and other senior officials. The president's budget typically consists of several volumes, covering thousands of pages. But it is only a proposal that is subject to congressional approval.

Congress first passes a "budget resolution" that outlines the framework for budget decisions. It includes total spending targets, revenue projections, deficit figures, and spending targets for two types of spending: discretionary and mandatory (OMB, 2001a). *Discretionary spending* represents about a third of all federal spending, the portion that the president and Congress may spend through 13 annual appropriations bills. *Mandatory spending,* roughly two-thirds of federal spending, is authorized by permanent laws. It includes entitlements, such as Social Security, Medicare, veterans' benefits, and food stamps. It also includes interest on the national debt. Changes in mandatory spending cannot be made without revising the laws governing these programs.

Congressional examination of the president's budget consists of hearings and meetings by scores of committees and subcommittees. It is important to remember that, despite a plethora of technical details, budgeting is a political process characterized by negotiation. Budget negotiations are carried out under time

---

4. Much of the content in this section is drawn from A Citizen's Guide to the Federal Budget, which is available through the Office of Management and Budget.

TABLE 2.1   **Major Steps in the Federal Budget Process**

Budget Step	Budget Activities	Time Frame
1. President formulates budget for fiscal year (Sept. 30–Oct. 1).	Agencies in executive branch develop budget requests for submission to Office of Management and Budget (OMB). President reviews requests and develops budget.	February–December (Year 1)
2. Budget is transmitted.	Budget documents are prepared and sent to Congress by OMB.	December (Year 1) February/March (Year 2)
3. Congress reviews and approves budget.	Congress reviews the President's Proposals, passes its "budget resolution," holds hearings, and approves annual appropriations bills.	March–September (Year 2)
4. The fiscal year begins.		October 1 (Year 2)
5. The budget is implemented.	Under supervision of the OMB and General Accounting Office (GAO) agencies use the funds appropriated.	October 1 (Year 2) September 30 (Year 3)
6. Actual spending and receipts are tabulated.	Agencies and OMB prepare reports on outlays and receipts.	October–November (Year 3)

pressure, and failure to reach compromise can produce massive disruption. Such was the case in 1995, when federal agencies closed temporarily because of the lack of an approved budget.

After the president and Congress approve a budget, it is monitored by agency managers and budget officials, the OMB, congressional committees, and the General Accounting Office (an auditing arm of Congress).

Where the Money Goes

Figure 2.1 illustrates the spending categories in the 2006 federal budget. The 2006 federal budget included approximately $2.7 trillion in expenditures. Mandatory spending described above accounted for just over half of federal spending—54 percent in 2006. The largest federal program was Social Security, which continues to exceed military spending in the U.S. In 2006, this program, which provided monthly benefits to more than 52 million Americans, accounted for $550 billion, about 20 percent of federal spending. The next-largest mandatory funding category, other means-tested entitlements, included the Food Stamp Program, Temporary Assistance for Needy Families, Supplemental Security Income, Child Nutrition, the Earned Income Tax Credit, and veterans' pensions. This category accounted for about 14 percent of federal spending in 2006. It was followed by Medicare, which accounted for 12 percent of the budget; while Medicaid and the Children's Health Insurance Program (CHIP) absorbed about 7 percent. In 2006, interest on the national debt represented about 8 percent of federal spending.

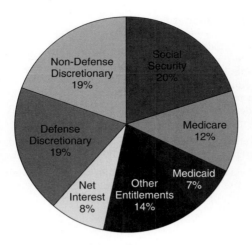

FIGURE 2.1 Major Categories of Spending: 2006 Outlays.

SOURCE: House Budget Committee (2006). http://www.budget.house.gov/budget_facts/Faq_june07.pdf.

Discretionary spending is divided into three categories. In 2006 about $510 billion, or 19 percent of the federal budget, was spent on defense. Another $32 billion was spent on Homeland Security. The remaining nondefense discretionary funding supported a wide array of programs, including education, training, science, technology, housing, transportation, and foreign aid, accounting for roughly 19 percent of the budget (www.gpoaccess.gov/usbudget/fy07/pdf/budget/tables.pdf, Table S–11, accessed September 29, 2007).

Trends in Federal Spending

Figure 2.2 illustrates broad trends in federal spending from 1940 to 2010, based on data provided by the OMB. The figure presents the proportion of federal outlays attributable to five broad functions: national defense, human resources, physical resources, net interest, and other functions.

Whereas national defense is readily understandable, the other categories deserve explanation. Human resources include education and social services, health care, income security, Social Security, and veterans' benefits and services. Physical resources include energy, natural resources and the environment, commerce and housing credits, transportation, and community and regional development. Net interest is payment on the debt. Finally, other functions include international affairs, general science, space and technology, agriculture, administration of justice, and general government.

The dramatic growth in human resource spending is largely due to Social Security expenditures. In 1940 the largest human resource expenditure category was education, training, employment, and social services. That year, the (inflation-

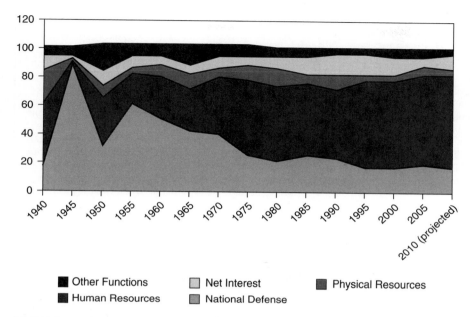

Other Functions   **Net Interest**   **Physical Resources**
Human Resources   **National Defense**

FIGURE 2.2 Trends in federal spending.

SOURCE (for data): http://www.gpoaccess.gov/usbudget/fy07/pdf/hist.pdf (accessed July 21, 2007).

adjusted) $28 million spent on Social Security represented 6.8 percent of human resource outlays, which combined took up a trivial fraction (4.3 percent) of the nation's GDP. By 2006, Social Security expenditures had exceeded $500 billion, accounting for a third (33 percent) of human resource expenditures. In 2006 human resource expenditures totaled 13 percent of the nation's GDP.

By contrast, defense expenditures reached an all-time high of 90 percent of the federal budget in 1945, and by 2001 had declined to an all-time low of 16 percent of the budget. Of course, this does not represent a decline in the absolute dollars devoted to defense. In 1945 defense expenditures were $82.9 billion in today's dollars. Even at its 2001 low, defense spending had grown to over $304 billion (in constant dollars). These figures might give defense contractors a moment's pause. In the height of World War II defense spending was literally hundreds of times the amount devoted to Social Security. By contrast, the twenty-first century opened with greater federal funding devoted to Social Security than to defense. We will see a parallel trend later in this chapter, as Social Security taxes have come to represent a larger share of federal revenues. Of course, the Bush years were good for defense contractors. By 2006, national defense absorbed nearly 20 percent of federal outlays or a total of nearly $536 billion (http://www.gpoaccess.gov/usbudget/fy07/pdf/hist.pdf, Table 3.1, accessed September 29, 2007).

B O X   2.2   Understanding the Federal Budget Deficit

The federal budget deficit, which is computed annually, represents the difference between revenues and expenditures in the General Fund. It differs from the national debt, which is money borrowed to cover the accumulated deficits. Each year that expenditures exceed revenues, more money is borrowed, which increases the national debt. On June 15, 2004, the national debt totaled $7.3 trillion. Interest on the debt is a large item in the federal budget, amounting to $434 billion in fiscal year 2006.

Government borrowing is much like personal borrowing in that it is affected by the prevailing interest rate, which is determined by the Federal Reserve.

Where individuals go to banks for loans, the U.S. Treasury borrows money from individuals when it issues notes and bonds.

There is no inherent danger in national debt, but the possibility of unlimited debt tends to undermine fiscal discipline just as the presence of easy money can lure consumers into bankruptcy. The challenge for our leaders is ensuring that the expenses for which we borrow represent investments that will improve the nation's economic well-being. When debt is incurred for purposes that do not contribute to future prosperity, it becomes a drain on future generations.

The Executive Branch

The executive power shall be vested in a President of the United States of America. Article II, Section I, United States Constitution

Headed by the chief executive (the president), the executive branch is organized into 15 departments, each represented by a member of the president's cabinet.

Among the cabinet-level departments, social workers are most familiar with the Department of Health and Human Services. This department includes the Administration for Children and Families, Administration on Aging, Health Care Financing Administration, Centers for Disease Control and Prevention, Food and Drug Administration, National Institutes of Health, National Institute of Mental Health, and National Library of Medicine. Social programs and programs with social implications are also housed in other departments, often for historical reasons.

For example, the Food Stamp Program (described in Chapter 5) is administered by the Department of Agriculture, which oversees the Forest Service, Natural Resources Conservation Service, Food and Consumer Service, National Agricultural Library, and National Agricultural Statistics Service. Other programs in this department with implications for social policy include farm subsidies, commodities distribution, and food price supports. A possible reason for the Food Stamp Program's position within the Department of Agriculture is its role in stabilizing the demand for agricultural products.

The Department of the Interior is also involved in the direct provision of social services and health care through the Bureau of Indian Affairs (BIA). This department also includes the Bureau of Land Management, U.S. Bureau of Mines, Bureau of Reclamation, Minerals Management Service, National Biological Service, National Park Service, Office of Surface Mining, U.S. Fish and Wildlife Service, and U.S. Geological Survey. Health and social programs for Native Americans are generally implemented by the BIA. Issues related to the BIA are discussed in more depth in Chapter 9.

B O X 2.3   **Democracy in Action: The Recall Process**

On October 7, 2003, California voters went to the polls and, in a historic election, voted an unpopular governor out of office. This event would not be surprising except for the fact that 2003 was not an election year. The now-infamous California recall was the result of changes to the state constitution made in 1911. It followed 31 previous attempts to recall governors, none of which ever made it to the ballot. To put a recall on the ballot, state law required a petition signed by 12 percent of the number of people who had voted in the previous election. Activists seeking the recall were able to meet this requirement after raising more than $7 million to support their efforts. They were outspent by their opponents, who raised more than $18 million to defeat the recall (http://www.recallmoney.com/money.php). California voters addressed two questions on October 7: first, whether or not they supported the recall, and second (regardless of their answer to the first question) what candidate should be the next governor. Anticipating success of the recall vote, 134 candidates ran (and 11 raised money) to defeat Democrat Gray Davis. Just over half (55 percent) of voters approved the recall, and in the end, the race went to the candidate with the biggest war chest. Arnold Schwarzenegger raised over $21 million to finance his successful bid. Pundits vary in their interpretations, with liberals arguing that "right-wing, conservative interests have purchased the governorship"—a position that is hard to support since opponents to the recall raised more than twice as much money as proponents. More moderate voices attribute the recall to the state's energy crisis and inadequate leadership from Davis.

Although military and social spending are often viewed as being separate from each other (a popular bumper sticker reads: "Won't it be nice when schools have plenty of money and the Army has to hold a bake sale to build a bomber?"), the Department of Defense provides a wide range of social and health services for military personnel and their dependents, and it is a major employer of professional social workers in many jurisdictions. The Department of Defense includes the Joint Chiefs of Staff, army, navy, air force, and Marine Corps. Similarly, the Department of Veterans Affairs, established as a cabinet-level agency to replace the Veteran's Administration in 1988, offers services (primarily health care) to veterans of the armed services.

The Department of Commerce includes the Census Bureau, Bureau of Economic Analysis, Economic Development Administration, Minority Business Development Agency, Patent and Trademark Office, and National Technical Information Service. Decisions made about the census often affect the nature of the information on which social policy is based. For example, the census treatment of ethnic minorities in the United States has changed in recent decades to reflect broader changes in our understanding of the role of culture in individual lives. Sampling techniques used by the census are often controversial because they may under- or overrepresent certain groups.

The Department of Housing and Urban Development (HUD) has a mandate to address issues related to community planning and development and fair housing, but increasingly finds itself addressing social policy issues through its attempts to meet the needs of residents of public housing. Programs under HUD are described in detail in Chapter 5. Its agencies include the Federal Housing Administration and the Government National Mortgage Association ("Ginnie Mae").

The Department of Education is charged with implementing national educational policy. The Department of Justice includes the Office of the Attorney General of the United States, Federal Bureau of Investigation, Drug Enforcement Administration, Federal Bureau of Prisons, Immigration and Naturalization Service, and U.S. Marshals Service. The Department of Labor includes the Bureau of Labor Statistics, Occupational Safety and Health Administration, Office of Small Business and Minority Affairs, and Women's Bureau.

A few of the cabinet-level departments have relatively little direct involvement in domestic social policy. The Department of State is charged with carrying out foreign policy and diplomatic efforts. The Department of Energy provides scientific and technical information and educational support to encourage efficient energy use and diversity in energy sources. The Department of the Treasury includes the Internal Revenue Service; Customs Service; Bureau of Engraving and Printing; Secret Service; U.S. Mint; and Bureau of Alcohol, Tobacco and Firearms. The Department of Transportation includes the Bureau of Transportation Statistics, Federal Aviation Administration, Federal Highway Administration, National Highway Traffic Safety Administration, and U.S. Coast Guard.

In response to the 9/11 attacks, the Department of Homeland Security (DHS) was established as a cabinet-level agency through the National Strategy for Homeland Security and the Homeland Security Act of 2002. By 2004, the DHS had more than 140,000 employees charged with the following mission: "We will lead the unified national effort to secure America. We will prevent and deter terrorist attacks and protect against and respond to threats and hazards to the nation. We will ensure safe and secure borders, welcome lawful immigrants and visitors, and promote the free-flow of commerce."

The Social Security Administration and the U.S. Postal Service are among 23 independent agencies that are not represented by a cabinet-level official.

The executive branch is far and away the largest employer in the federal system. As of September 2006 nearly 3 million (2,700,392) people worked as civilian employees of the federal government, of whom 63,246 worked for the legislative and judicial branches. Nearly one-third of these (28 percent) worked for the U.S. Postal Service. After the Postal Service, the Department of Defense is the second-largest employer, with a civilian workforce of 675,744 in 2006. The Department of Veterans Affairs comes next, employing 239,299 civilians. The Department of Homeland Security employed 154,100 in 2006. Health and Human Services pales by comparison, with 61,163 in its 2006 payroll, as does the Social Security Administration, with 63,615 employees in the same year (http://www.opm.gov/feddata/html/2006/september/table3.asp, accessed January 10, 2008).

The Regulatory Process.   While many assume that the executive branch simply "executes" but does not "create" policy, this perception is inaccurate. Through the regulatory process the executive branch translates legislation into services, resources, and decisions that directly affect individuals. Rules and regulations established by executive agencies have the force of law.

At the federal level,[5] rulemaking is primarily governed by the Administrative Procedures Act (APA), which has several provisions that allow for public participation. Usually rulemaking is initiated in response to legislative action, but the APA does allow for the public to petition an agency to begin rulemaking. Once the process begins, the APA requires that departments develop a rulemaking record that reflects both public participation and the factual conclusions on which the rule is based. Rulemaking must begin with a period of "notice and comment." Agencies provide public notice of their intent to begin rulemaking by publishing a statement in the *Federal Register*. Often this statement is accompanied by press releases as well as targeted electronic notices. Agencies must allow a reasonable period for public comment. Although the length of the public comment period is not specified by law, it usually lasts at least 60 days. At the end of this period, the agency prepares a summary of comments received and its response to those comments. This summary is followed either by a new cycle of notice and comments or by publication of the rule (Lubbers, 1998).

Since 1990, a procedure known as negotiated rulemaking (or "neg reg") has been allowed. This involves bringing interested parties into the process at an early stage and involving them in the drafting of the rule. Agencies that anticipate controversy over a regulation might use neg reg to reach a compromise among key players before the period of public comment.

An advocate's participation in rulemaking can take three forms. First, the advocate may petition an agency to begin rulemaking. Second, during the notice and comment period, an advocate can comment on a proposed rule and offer revisions. Finally, an advocate who is identified as an interested party can participate in negotiated rulemaking. Social work advocates naturally pay close attention to the legislative process. But failure to participate in the regulatory process can seriously undermine an advocacy effort.

The Judicial Branch[6]

> The Judicial Power of the United States shall be vested in one Supreme Court, and in such inferior courts as the Congress may from time to time ordain and establish. Article III, United States Constitution

There are two judicial systems in the United States: the Supreme Court and federal court system created by Congress under the authority of the Constitution and the state and local courts established by state governments.

The structure of the federal court system has varied throughout the nation's history. Under the Constitution, the only indispensable court is the Supreme Court, and Congress has established and abolished other courts over time. The current federal system includes the Supreme Court, 13 U.S. courts of appeals,

---

5. States have their own laws that govern rulemaking by state agencies. These laws are typically called Administrative Procedures Acts.

6. Much of the material in this section is drawn from *Understanding the Federal Courts*, available online at http://www.uscourts.gov/understand02/ (accessed February 6, 2008).

and 94 U.S. district courts and specialized courts. The U.S. courts of appeals serve 12 regions (in addition to the 12 regional courts, there is a federal court of appeals) and for historical reasons they are often referred to as circuit courts. In the nineteenth century, judges in courts of appeals rode the circuit on horseback, visiting courts in the region.

Most controversies are decided in the state courts because the power of federal courts is restricted. Under Article III of the Constitution, federal courts may decide "[c]ontroversies between two or more states; between a State and Citizens of another State; between Citizens of different States; [or] between Citizens of the same State claiming Lands under Grants of different States." Federal courts also hear cases in which the U.S. government or one of its officers is suing someone or being sued, as well as cases for which state courts might be biased or inappropriate.

Federal cases originate in district courts and may be reviewed by courts of appeals upon the request of one party. The final appeal in a few cases is heard in the Supreme Court. For example, the case of *Roe v. Wade* involved a class action suit challenging criminal abortion laws in Texas. A three-judge district court from the Northern District of Texas declared the state's abortion statutes void. The case was argued in 1971 before the Supreme Court, which also declared the Texas statutes unconstitutional. This case is discussed in more detail in Chapter 12.

The Supreme Court of the United States consists of nine justices appointed for life by the president with advice and consent of the Senate. In the nation's history, all but 27 Supreme Court justices nominated by a president have secured Senate confirmation. Each justice is assigned to one of the district courts of appeals for emergency responses (urgent appeals that cannot wait until the full court is in session), and the chief justice assumes additional administrative responsibilities. The Supreme Court convenes each year on the first Monday in October and usually remains in session until the end of June. During this period, the Court reviews about 5,000 cases annually. In most, a brief decision is offered, indicating that the case is not of sufficient importance to warrant review. Each year about 150 cases of great national importance are reviewed by the entire court.

While officers of the Supreme Court are called justices, those presiding over courts of appeals, district courts, and other courts are called judges. All federal judges are appointed by the president with the advice and consent of the Senate. Most judicial appointments are for life or, in the language of the Constitution, they "hold their Offices during good Behavior." These judges may be removed from office against their will only through "impeachment for, and conviction of Treason, Bribery, or other high Crimes and Misdemeanors." Between 1789 and 1992, 2,627 men and women served as federal judges. Of those, 184 (7 percent) resigned for reasons other than health or age. In the last 200 years, Congress has removed 7 federal judges following contested impeachment proceedings. Further, between 1818 and 1980, at least 22 judges have resigned or retired following allegations of misbehavior (Van Tassel, Wirtz, & Wonders, 1993).

The judicial system, like the executive branch, plays an important role in social policy development. For example, efforts to establish federal programs have often been challenged in federal courts. These efforts have included the Child Labor Act, which was twice declared unconstitutional, and the Social Security Act, which was successfully defended against a constitutional challenge. Disputes over federal entitlements such as Supplemental Security Income have typically been heard by federal courts. Indeed, some opponents of federal entitlements have argued that they clog the federal courts with disputes between citizens and states.

In this section we have examined the basic structure of the U.S. government in terms of both levels and branches. It takes only a basic level of understanding of human behavior to see that there are inevitable tensions among these levels and branches. The authors of the Constitution understood and anticipated these tensions and crafted "checks and balances" to prevent the concentration of power in any single individual or entity. As we saw in Chapter 1, some libertarian thinkers have argued that powerful private interests also serve as checks on the power of government. In the following section we will briefly examine privatization and its implications for the evolving role of government in the United States.

PRIVATIZATION: ENDING THE "ERA OF BIG GOVERNMENT"?

The term "privatization" refers to the private financing, production, development, and/or distribution of public assets or services. Privatization might involve international transactions, as when the City of Atlanta outsourced its water system to United Water, now a subsidiary of the French company Suez Lyonnaise des Eaux (Cotchett, 2004). Or it might include domestic transfers, such as the multistate movement to employ private firms such as Corrections Corporation of America in managing prisons. Often privatization is seen at the local government level, when basic city services such as garbage collection and ambulance services are provided through contracts with local companies. As we will see in Chapter 4, the past decade has seen numerous proposals to privatize our Social Security system.

Privatization—even of human services—is not a new concept. In the field of child welfare, state and local governments have employed private-sector organizations to deliver services since the early 1800s (Rosenthal, 2000). The term *private–public partnership* was once used to refer to the established practice of contracting services to private providers.

In the 1980s privatization received a major boost from the rhetoric and politics of the Reagan administration. Vowing to end "the era of big government," President Reagan introduced privatization as a strategy to increase efficiency of services and make them more responsive to local needs and concerns. Indeed, the 1988 report of the Presidential Commission on Privatization introduced the strategy as a means of reversing the expanded role of government that began with the Progressive Movement of the late nineteenth and early twentieth centuries (Karger & Stoesz, 2002).

The demise of the Soviet Union, seen by many as a definitive victory for capitalism, gave further impetus to the privatization movement. American enthusiasm for the free market seemed boundless, leading Nancy Jurik (then president of the Society for the Study of Social Problems) to observe, "We now live in a society characterized by a hyper-privatization that is reconstructing everything from non-profits and government, to community, family, and individual life— all in the image of the market" (2004, p. 1). Jurik invoked the term "new privatization" to describe the impetus to reinvent social institutions according to market principles.

The result has been an explosion in revenue for human service corporations and what Frumkin and Andre-Clark (1999) termed "the rise of the corporate social worker." Human services such as child care, nursing home care, hospital care, psychiatric care, and job training are increasingly carried out by for-profit corporations. For-profits are also major providers of welfare services. Frumkin and Andre-Clark identified three for-profit firms that have been important players in the privatization of welfare services: Maximus, Inc., America Works, and Curtis and Associates.

Construction and development of prisons is another growth area for private for-profit corporations. As Nicholson-Crotty (2004) noted, between 1987 and 1997, 26 states enacted legislation authorizing private management of secure correctional facilities. At year-end 2005, 33 states and the federal system reported a total of 107,447 prisoners held in privately operated prison facilities (Bureau of Justice Statistics, 2006, http://www.ojp.usdoj.gov/bjs/abstract/p05.htm, accessed January 10, 2008). The federal prison system and three states (Texas, Oklahoma, and Tennessee) reported the largest numbers of inmates in private prisons. Leading corporations in this area include the Corrections Corporation of America and Wackenhutt Corporation.

Of course, the trend is not entirely in one direction. As some services are contracted out to the private sector, others are brought back under the rubric of government. The latter process has been termed *reverse contracting* (Hefetz & Warner, 2004). The most well known recent example of reverse contracting is seen in airports. Prior to the 9/11 attacks airport security was handled by private companies. Despite clear documentation of ineffectiveness, this system remained in place, with devastating results. Amid public outcry the Transportation Security Administration (TSA) was established, and airport security officials are now employees of the federal government.

Theoretical and Practical Limits of Privatization

Proponents of privatization usually emphasize a perceived need to reduce the size of government. They exploit the popular stereotype of government workers as unresponsive and inefficient and invoke the stereotype of private-sector employ-

---

B O X 2.4   John Rawls on Justice

"Justice is the first virtue of social institutions, as truth is of systems of thought. A theory, however elegant and economical must be rejected if it is untrue; likewise laws and institutions no matter how efficient and well-arranged must be reformed or abolished if they are unjust."

---

ees as motivated and efficient. Unfortunately, decisions to privatize are typically based on sweeping political and ideological arguments rather than theoretical or practical considerations (Hefetz & Warner, 2004; Nicholson-Crotty, 2004).

Economic theory suggests distinct roles for the private market and public agencies, with government stepping in when the market "fails."[7] The private market fails when the conditions that support competition are not met. These include access to diverse providers, informed and able consumers, and assessable product.

Access to Diverse Providers.   Competition is the hallmark of a free market. For market efficiencies to obtain there must be multiple providers competing for a government contract or a consumer's business. Without competition (i.e., in the presence of a monopoly) there is no incentive to optimize cost-effectiveness, or even effectiveness in general! Without diverse providers, the market fails to deliver an efficient outcome.

Practically speaking, it is usually difficult to identify multiple providers in rural and inner-city locations. The unwritten history of privatization includes tales of public managers who have worked for months to prepare elaborate requests for proposals only to find that just one firm is interested in delivering the product.

Informed and Able Consumers.   Consumers must have the information and resources necessary to make intelligent choices among multiple providers. Consumers who are not competent to make their own choices, either because of limited capacity or because they are in state custody, cannot optimize their well-being. In this situation the market tends to favor the provider who can deliver the greatest cost-savings, irrespective of quality considerations.

Vulnerable populations are vulnerable consumers—unwilling or unable to distinguish among providers—so contracts for services to children, prisoners, the poor, and the mentally ill may be awarded to the lowest bidder and it can be years before quality failures come to the attention of decision makers.

Assessable Products.   To determine the value or the quality of a product or service it must be assessable—subject to objective assessment. Intangible aspects of a service (such as empathy or relationship) are difficult if not impossible to

---

7. For a more detailed discussion of the conditions necessary for market competition, see Lewis and Widerquist (2002).

objectively evaluate. If these intangibles are important, it will be difficult to determine the effectiveness of a contract with a private provider.

Petr and Johnson (1999) provided an example that illustrates the difficulty in assessing human services. They reported on the privatization of foster care service in Kansas. Contracts with private contractors stipulated that 90 percent of children in foster care would experience three or fewer moves. Contractors met this requirement by redefining a move to exclude "emergency" placements that lasted less than 30 days. If the term "moves" is subject to interpretation, imagine the difficulties in defining a concept like "care."

As we have seen, the absence of conditions that support competition should (theoretically) mitigate against privatization. Richard Titmuss offered another critique of privatization. He was one of the first to view privatization as part of a broad, dehumanizing trend. In his 1971 work, *The Gift Relationship,* Titmuss examines the privatization of America's blood banks. Comparing the commercial system in the United States with the voluntary system in England, he argues not only that the quality of the blood suffered but, perhaps more importantly, treating blood as a commodity undermined human bonds.

Under the right conditions privatization can improve the delivery of goods and services. When the market offers a competitive supply of contractors, when the consumer or recipient of the service is in the position to make choices and provide feedback, and when the product can be standardized, the private market can be an excellent allocation mechanism. For example, it is perfectly reasonable for the military to purchase food and even sophisticated weapons on the private market. Roads, electricity, and phone service are good examples of products that can be standardized and effectively delivered through privatization. The political and ideological climate of our times favors privatization. As a result, most professional social workers will be touched in some way by this trend. Yet, as we will see in later chapters, the privatization of human services such as child care, welfare, health care, and prisons has seldom lived up to the promises of its proponents.

THE U.S. TAX SYSTEM: A BRIEF INTRODUCTION[8]

Benjamin Franklin is often quoted as saying that only two things are inevitable: death and taxes. The two are sometimes approached with equal dread! No one likes to pay taxes. Indeed, public polls have revealed that a majority of Americans have cheated on their tax returns. Some of us spend more money on tax-avoidance schemes than the schemes ever save us in taxes. There is something intrinsically satisfying about avoiding taxes. Throughout the nation's history, pol-

---

8. This section draws heavily from the third edition of a law text by Michael J. Graetz
and Deborah Schenk, *Federal Income Taxation: Principles and Policies,* and the advice of a
singular tax attorney, Lawrence Barusch.

A HUMAN PERSPECTIVE Advocacy: Broad Coalition Proposes a Tax Increase

---

Contributed by Connie Ginsberg, Family Connection of South Carolina, Incorporated (retired executive director) and Leon Ginsberg, Appalachian State University, Boone, North Carolina

Confronted with severe Medicaid cuts in 2001, a coalition of organizations in South Carolina proposed to increase the state cigarette excise tax—then the lowest in the nation—and use the revenue to meet the health-care needs of low-income families and children. Connie Ginsberg was a leader in the coalition. She served on the steering committee, joined health providers in meeting with newspaper editorial boards throughout the state to explain the need for additional revenue, and organized a grassroots effort among families with children who had chronic illnesses or disabilities. The coalition, which included nonprofit organizations serving families and children, health organizations including physician specialty groups, lawyers' organizations, educators, and health insurance companies such as Blue Cross and Blue Shield, pressed its case in the state legislature and in public forums, including editorial boards of South Carolina's major daily newspapers, press conferences, and a rally on the grounds of the State House.

After months of work, the legislation to increase the cigarette tax failed in the SC House of Representatives by five votes. The incumbent governor, a Democrat who was facing a tough reelection campaign in 2002, which he ultimately lost, lobbied against the tax increase in the critical hours leading to the

vote. Coming so close to success, however, was a major victory in this tobacco state.

In 2002, a new governor, this time a Republican, opposed all tax increases and pledged to reduce those taxes that existed. Although an attempt was made to reintroduce the tax increase in his first years of office, for four years the cigarette tax proposal was essentially dormant.

The issue came up again in 2007, when the House of Representatives set forth a plan to increase the cigarette tax. Raising health-care coverage for low-income children was proposed as another item in the budget, not tied to the cigarette tax increase. This time, the governor supported a tobacco tax increase in his executive budget, but only as a basis for reducing other taxes.

The increased cigarette tax did not pass the state legislature in 2007. The Senate did not consider it, and South Carolina's cigarette tax remained the lowest in the nation. However, improving health-care coverage for children became a goal of the legislature and state funds were dedicated to increasing children's Medicaid coverage for the 2008 fiscal year budget. The governor vetoed the increase but a 100 percent vote of the legislature overrode his veto. So the main objective of the process was achieved without a cigarette tax increase.

From a political science viewpoint, the ultimate outcome of this effort was not surprising. Legislatures frequently resist dedicated taxes and prefer, instead, to appropriate funds overall, from whatever sources of revenue are available. Children's health services are popular, but a cigarette tax increase was controversial.

---

icy makers have tapped into this mind-set, using it to advance social agendas through the judicious use of tax credits and deductions. In this section we will first examine the basic structure of the U.S. tax system and then describe the use of taxation to accomplish social goals.

Structural and Philosophical Considerations

Americans pay taxes to each level of government. As with legislative processes, taxes at lower levels generally mirror those at the federal level. Sales taxes and property taxes are exceptions to this general rule as they are not applied at the federal level but are levied at the local levels. Occasionally proposals for a national sales tax or "value added" tax have surfaced, but to date none has been established in the United States.

There are few constitutional limits on the taxation authority of the federal government. Congress has the power to "lay and collect Taxes, Duties, imposts and excises, to pay the Debts and provide for the common Defence and general Welfare of the United States" (Article I, Section 8, Clause 1). Nonetheless, both income and Social Security taxes have been subjected to constitutional challenges. The Sixteenth Amendment, passed in 1913, affirmed the authority of the federal government to levy income taxes. Two Supreme Court cases upheld the constitutionality of the Social Security tax (see Chapter 4).

The utilitarian liberal philosophical perspective introduced in Chapter 1 emphasizes the distinction between regressive and progressive taxes. A regressive tax is one that falls most heavily on the poor. For example, a head tax exacts the same amount from each person. Since poor people have less money, the tax represents a greater proportion of a poor person's resources. The rate of a progressive tax increases as a person's affluence increases, and so the amount of tax paid is greater for the wealthy. Simply put, progressive taxes are based on the taxpayer's ability to pay. The federal income tax is a progressive tax, while sales and payroll taxes (described later in this chapter) are regressive.

The rationale for progressive taxation stems directly from a utilitarian liberal tradition. Under this philosophy, the goal of policy is to optimize well-being, or (since we're talking about taxes here) to minimize distress. For those individuals who are at, or very close to, a social minimum, taking 30 percent of their income will place them at a significant disadvantage. But for individuals who are well above a social minimum, taking 30 percent of their income will create much less distress. Or, to put it more simply, if you have two dollars and I take one of them, you will be unable to buy a half-gallon of milk. But if you have $200 and I take $100, or even $125, you will be able to buy much more than a half-gallon of milk. Under this view (which dominates federal, and to a lesser extent, state income tax structures), the community as a whole experiences less distress with a progressive tax than with a regressive one.

John Rawls's concept of a social minimum offers a second argument in favor of progressive taxation. Under this view, a regressive tax would put a larger proportion of the population below an acceptable minimum standard of living than a progressive tax.

Federal Income Tax.   The federal income tax is a progressive tax: the proportion of income subject to tax increases as a taxpayer's income rises.

Here is a simplified illustration: Consider six taxpayers. In 2007, taxpayer A had $6,000 in taxable income, taxpayer B had $25,000, taxpayer C had $50,000, taxpayer D had $100,000, taxpayer E had $200,000, and taxpayer F had $400,000. Taxpayer F would pay not only the highest absolute dollar amount in income tax but also a higher proportion of his or her income. Each person's tax would be assessed by dividing the income into steps or "brackets." The 2007 Tax Rate Schedule for individuals included six brackets, as illustrated in Table 2.2.

Federal income tax brackets are adjusted annually for inflation. From time to time, they are also changed through tax legislation. By the time you read this

TABLE 2.2   Computing Federal Income Tax (2007 Rates)

Taxable Income	Hypothetical Taxpayer (Taxable Income)*					
	A ($6,000)	B ($25,000)	C ($50,000)	D ($100,000)	E ($200,000)	F ($400,000)
$349,701 and over (35%)						$17,605.00
$160,851 to $349,700 (33%)					$12,919.50	$62,320.50
$77,101 to $160,850 (28%)				$6,412.00	$23,450.00	$23,450.00
$31,851 to $77,100 (25%)			$4,037.25	$11,312.50	$11,312.50	$11,312.50
$7,826 to $31,850 (15%)		$2,576.25	$3,603.75	$3,603.75	$3,603.75	$3,603.75
0 to $7,825 (10%)	$600.00	$782.50	$782.50	$782.50	$782.50	$782.50
Tax owed	$600.00	$3,358.75	$8,923.75	$22,110.75	$52,068.25	$119,074.25

*Figures under each taxpayer indicate the amount of tax owed

chapter, the brackets for federal income tax will no doubt be different. Nonetheless, these figures should help you understand the general concepts. In 2007, taxpayer A would have paid 10 percent of taxable income, or $600 in taxes. On the first $7,825 of income, taxpayer B would pay the same proportion as A. For income in the next bracket, B would pay the next higher rate, 15 percent. So B would pay $782.50 (10 percent of $7,825) plus $2,576.25 (15 percent of the remaining $17,175). Taxpayer B's total tax bill would be $3,358.75, or approximately 13 percent of the total income of $25,000. Taxpayer F would pay the most tax and the highest rate. Taxpayer F's tax is computed using all six of the income brackets listed in Table 2.2: $782.50 (10 percent of $7,825) plus $3,603.75 (15 percent of $24,025) plus $11,312.50 (25 percent of $45,250) plus $23,450 (28 percent of $83,750) plus $62,320.50 (33 percent of $188,850) plus $17,605 (35 percent of $50,300, the remaining income over $349,700). Taxpayer F's total tax bill would amount to $119,074.25, or approximately 30 percent of the total taxable income of $400,000. Thus, F's average rate of taxation, 30 percent, is the rate paid on each dollar of income. F's marginal rate would be 35 percent. In a progressive tax, the marginal rate (highest rate paid on the last taxable dollar) is higher than the average rate (rate paid on all taxable dollars).

Of course, in the real world, Taxpayer F would probably take advantage of various opportunities to reduce his or her taxes. Some kinds of income, such as the interest on bonds issued by cities and states, are not taxed at all. Currently dividends and long-term capital gains from sale of stock are taxed at a maximum rate of only 15 percent. Often tax can be deferred, thereby effectively reducing it. For example, high-ranking executives may receive "incentive stock options" that allow them to purchase company stock at a price that may be much lower than market at the time of purchase (thus reaping an economic gain) but defer paying any tax until they sell the stock.

In the United States a person's federal income tax obligation does not begin with the first dollar of income. Taxpayers are entitled to a standard deduction as well as personal exemptions for themselves and their dependents. In 2006, a single parent with one child would not incur federal income tax obligation for income below $11,750 (computed by adding the standard deduction of $5,150 to two personal exemptions valued at $3,300 each). The standard deduction is higher for people over 65 years of age and those who are blind. Like the tax brackets, the standard deduction and personal exemptions are adjusted annually for inflation.

The United States has not always had a federal income tax. George Washington and his secretary of the treasury, Alexander Hamilton, imposed the nation's first taxes on "distilled spirits and carriages." The money was needed to pay debts from the Revolutionary War. But, more importantly, Washington felt the tax was needed to establish the power of the new government. Like many of its successors, the nation's first "sin tax" met with protests. In 1794, protestors burned a tax collector's home, leading the president to send 13,000 troops into the area. This action suppressed the rebellion and secured the taxation power of the federal government.

The first federal income tax was proposed in 1862 by Abraham Lincoln to finance the Civil War. The tax affected relatively few Americans. It applied only to those with annual incomes over $600. Up to $10,000, these incomes were taxed at a rate of 3 percent. Income over $10,000 was taxed at 5 percent. The tax was subjected to a constitutional challenge, and in 1880 the Supreme Court upheld it (*Springer v. United States,* 102 U.S. 586). In subsequent years, the tax was raised and lowered, eliminated and reinstated. In 1895, the Supreme Court reversed its earlier decision and declared the income tax unconstitutional (*Pollock v. Farmers' Loan and Trust Co.,* 158 U.S. 601). This judicial decision led to the adoption of the Sixteenth Amendment, which allows Congress to tax income. Still, it was not until the World War II era that income taxes were applied to most Americans. The tax rates peaked at a marginal (not average) rate of 94 percent during this period, as funds were needed to cover wartime expenses.

Since the 1950s, individual income taxes have provided nearly half of the revenues collected by the federal government. In 1953, individual income taxes accounted for 42.8 percent of federal revenues. That figure ranged from 44.1 to 48.1 percent between 1983 and 1993 (Graetz & Schenk, 1995). In contrast, the contribution of corporate income taxes diminished during the same period, from 30.5 percent in 1953 to about 10 percent since 1986 (Graetz & Schenk, 1995). This trend can be expected to continue with the movement to cut federal taxes.

The Bush Tax Cuts

The second half of the twentieth century saw significant federal tax cuts, which have continued and expanded in the new century. To the layperson recent tax acts look like a bewildering array of changes in a complex and technical set of laws. For the present analysis we will focus on the impact of the 2001 and 2003 "Bush tax cuts" in three major areas: federal income tax brackets, treatment of capital gains and dividends, and the estate tax. Unless they expire or are repealed, these tax cuts will shift much of the nation's tax burden from the rich toward the middle class, increase the rapidly growing federal budget deficit, and reduce funding for public programs.

Federal income tax brackets saw the addition of a new 10-percent bracket and a one-to-two-point across-the-board reduction in the other brackets. The top bracket declined from nearly 40 percent to 35 percent.

Capital gains tax is paid on the sale of capital assets (stocks, real estate, bonds) that have been held for at least a year. Dividends are sometimes paid to stockholders as a way of distributing a corporation's income. In 2000, capital gains were treated as regular income, subject to a maximum tax of 39.6 percent. The maximum tax rate on capital gains is scheduled to drop to 15 percent by 2008 but may be restored to 20 percent in 2009.

The estate tax has also been the target of recent legislation. In 2000 the first $675,000 in estate value was exempt from federal tax. The maximum rate of 55 percent was paid by estates valued above $20 million. With the Bush tax cuts the exemption rose to $2 million in 2005, and is scheduled to increase to $3.5 million by 2009. The maximum rate drops to 45 percent. In 2010 the estate tax is repealed, but it is restored thereafter. Presumably in 2010 Congress will have a chance to reconsider this change.

The estate tax was established in 1916 to prevent the accumulation of massive fortunes and maintain the stability of our democracy. Many believed that inheritance encouraged sloth and that the estate tax would encourage charitable giving. But eliminating the estate tax, or as opponents call it, the "death tax," was a cause célèbre for the Bush administration. The PR campaign for this policy goal emphasized potential savings to family-owned small businesses and farms. Yet in 2000 the vast majority of family farms and small businesses were already exempt from the federal estate tax. The estate tax is probably the most progressive tax in America, drawing most of its revenues from estates valued in excess of $10 million.

The net effect of recent tax cuts has been to dramatically reduce taxes paid on "passive" or investment income. In 2004, the Institute on Taxation and Economic Policy (ITEP) reported that federal taxes on earnings averaged 23.4 percent while the tax rate for investment income was 9.6 percent. Taxes on earnings include Social Security and Medicare taxes, which, at an average of 12.7 percent, now exceed the average federal income tax, which is 10.7 percent. Income from investments does not support Social Security or Medicare. This represents a tax advantage for the affluent. ITEP noted that applying Social Security taxes to investment income would go a long way toward eliminating threats to these programs (see http://www.ctj.org/pdf/earnpr.pdf, accessed January 10, 2008).

Social Security Tax.   The 1935 passage of the Social Security Act financed the nation's retirement, disability, and unemployment insurance systems through a tax

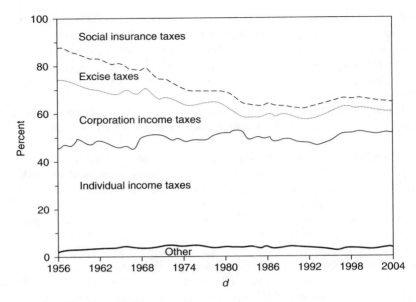

FIGURE 2.3 Sources of federal revenue.

Between 1956 and 1999, payroll taxes increased substantially as a percent of total revenues, and corporate income taxes declined, but individual income taxes remained roughly constant.

SOURCE: A Citizen's Guide to the Federal Budget, 2001. http://www.gpoaccess.gov/usbudget/fy01/guide02.html (accessed January 17, 2008).

on wages. This tax was originally set at 1 percent of wages and was expected to increase to 5 percent as the program grew. The payroll tax was equally divided between employees and employers. It was immediately subjected to a constitutional challenge, and the Supreme Court upheld the payroll tax (*Chas. C. Steward Machine Co. v. Davis*). Today the payroll tax amounts to 15 percent of the nation's wages, up to a limit called a cap. In 2007, income over $8,132 per month (above the cap) was not subject to the payroll tax. Half of the tax is taken directly from workers' paychecks, and half is paid quarterly by employers. It is usually listed on pay stubs as the "FICA contribution," with FICA standing for "Federal Insurance Contribution Act." In addition to the FICA tax, wages are taxed at 2.9 percent (again split between employer and employee) to finance Medicare's hospital insurance program. There is no wage cap on this Medicare tax.

The proportion of federal revenues drawn from payroll taxes has increased dramatically in recent decades. In 1953, payroll taxes contributed 10 percent of federal revenues. That figure had increased to 40 percent by 1994 (Graetz & Schenk, 1995) (see Figure 2.3).

State Taxes. As a result of the Bush tax cuts, most states are experiencing revenue pressures. These often lead to changes in state tax codes—changes that should be of immediate concern to social workers interested in social justice issues. Most state revenues are drawn from state income taxes, property taxes, and sales taxes. Among these, state income taxes are the most progressive. They generally mirror those at the federal level, except that state tax rates are lower. Property taxes are considered moderately progressive to the extent that those with the most valuable property pay the highest amounts. Sales taxes are the most regressive of the state tax alternatives. They are collected by vendors at the point of sale, and usually range from about 3 percent to 10 percent. Some states try to reduce the regressivity of their sales taxes by exempting essential items, such as food or medicine. (Please see the 1996 report by Citizens for Tax Justice and the Institute on Taxation and Economic Policy, "Who Pays? A Distributional Analysis of the Tax System in All 50 States," available at http://www.itepnet.org/wp2000/text.pdf, for an excellent discussion of the distribution of state tax burdens.) The notion of "race to the bottom," introduced earlier, applies to state income and sales taxes, as state officials worry that if their rates are higher than neighboring states, their more affluent residents (and corporations) will relocate or purchase big-ticket items elsewhere.

Local Taxes.   Traditionally, local governments have collected the bulk of revenues through property taxes. Tax rates on real property (e.g., land and some personal property, such as cars) can vary tremendously within a state, and from state to state. The tax is based on a formal appraisal of value. The timing of this appraisal can vary. Jurisdictions experiencing rapid changes in property values may conduct appraisals on a regular basis, such as three- to five-year intervals. In other areas property is appraised only when it is sold. The proportion of local revenues drawn from property taxes declined from 90 percent in 1960 to 74 percent in 1984 (Graetz & Schenk, 1995). The property tax is the primary source of funding for most public schools.

As Piven and Cloward (1997) noted, state and local governments are vulnerable to pressure from large businesses seeking tax reductions. Existing businesses threaten to relocate unless states exempt them from taxes—generally property taxes. Under the guise of "economic development," many cities spend public money trying to lure new businesses, often with promises of tax abatements. In this case, big businesses are generally the winners and public services are the losers. In some cases, businesses have taken tax breaks from local governments, only to renege on promises made and relocate. For example, officials in Galesburg, Illinois, gave Maytag over $2 million in tax breaks, only to have the company close its factory and move the work to Mexico. Maytag claims it paid all taxes that were due, but city representatives feel they were deceived (Egan, 2004).

With declining revenues from property taxes, local governments are relying more heavily on sales taxes for revenue. Local sales tax rates can vary from 1 to 3 percent. Local sales tax revenues may be used to finance specific services, such as parks or cultural activities, or may be applied to fund local government activities.

Tax Revolts.   In the preceding sections we noted some recent trends in U.S. government revenues. At the federal level, a growing proportion of revenue has been drawn from payroll taxes during the past five decades. The contribution of individual income taxes has remained fairly constant, and that of corporate income taxes has diminished. At the local level, we have seen a diminished contribution from property taxes, coupled with increased reliance on sales taxes. These trends reflect the influence of a popular movement known as the tax revolt.

While corporate lobbyists have worked quietly to reduce the corporate income tax burden, citizens' groups have publicly focused on reducing property tax obligations (Dworak, 1980). California has led the nation in tax protests. After nearly a decade of dramatic increases in property values (and property taxes), in June 1978 the state's residents voted to support Proposition 13, a constitutional amendment that would dramatically alter the state's tax system and set the stage for a new era of citizen involvement in tax policy. Proposition 13 limited residential property taxes to 1 percent of value and required a two-thirds legislative majority to pass tax increases. As a result, local revenues diminished by nearly a third, and the state's educational and municipal institutions suffered.

Other states followed California's lead, and during the late 1970s property tax limitation measures passed in Idaho, Nevada, Oregon, Michigan, Alabama, Massachusetts, and Missouri (Dworak, 1980). President George H. W. Bush took the tax revolt nationwide in his 1988 campaign when he issued the disastrous statement, "Read my lips: no new taxes!" Since then, few politicians have dared to suggest a tax increase. Antitax organizations, such as the National Taxpayers Union, are quick to oppose any measure that might raise taxes.

The irony of a tax revolt in the United States is not lost on our trading partners. U.S. citizens pay less in taxes than our competitors in the global market. Graetz and Schenk (1995) examined tax revenues as a percent of gross domestic product (GDP) for the United States and its trading partners. In 2004, U.S. tax revenues were about 25.5 percent of GDP. The average for countries in the Organization for Economic Cooperation and Development (OECD) was about 38 percent. Comparable figures for similar nations that year were as follows: Canada (33.5), France (43.4), Germany (34.7), Italy (41.1), Japan (26.4), and the United Kingdom (36.0) (http://www.oecd.org/dataoecd/8/4/37504406.pdf, accessed January 10, 2008).

Still, as Rubin (1998) pointed out, tax revolts are not about relative levels of taxation but about *the consent of the governed*. In the face of rapidly increasing government spending, citizens resist taxation. Uncontrollable economic events, such as inflation, also contribute to tax revolts. Finally, and perhaps most importantly, government spending on ineffective or unpopular programs can trigger popular resistance. Thus the challenge in a democracy is to maintain a level of consensus, both about the fairness of the tax system and about the social goals that it advances. Social workers are familiar with the social programs that are financed through tax revenues. We are less familiar with the direct use of taxation to accomplish social policy. This aspect of taxation is examined in the next section.

Taxation as Social Policy.   Taxes have long been used to influence social trends in the United States. As Graetz and Schenk (1995, p. 1) observed:

Today's income tax provisions, for example, favor new development of natural resources over recycling, tell people it is far better to own their own homes than to rent, give a break to families that have one spouse who stays at home rather than those that have both husband and wife in the job market, and make it cheaper for some people to marry, cheaper for others to divorce or remain unmarried. Federal alcohol taxes favor wine drinkers over beer drinkers, and both over those who prefer whiskey. Shortly after his inauguration, President Clinton proposed a new energy tax that would have given economic force to fathers' eternal admonitions to their children to turn off the lights, but Congress refused to enact it.

In addition, corporate income tax provisions favor companies that provide pension and health coverage to employees.

Tax policy attempts to influence social behavior through the imposition or the withdrawal of tax obligations. We are most familiar with the imposition of taxes to discourage or limit certain kinds of behavior. Thus, for example, we impose taxes on the purchase of tobacco, alcohol, and gasoline. On the flip side, desirable behavior can reduce a person's tax liability through tax deductions or exemptions. Home ownership is encouraged by laws that provide for a home mortgage interest deduction. More recently, tax deductions have been used to encourage home care of the elderly. The medical expenses associated with such care can be deducted from one's income. To encourage some kinds of investment, income from these sources can be declared tax exempt. For example, a state may declare that interest paid by municipal bonds will be exempt from state income tax.

Deductions and exemptions represent "forgone revenue" to the federal government and should be considered with the same deliberation as proposals for new expenditures. To encourage this view, the president is required to submit an annual "Tax Expenditure Budget" to Congress. Also known as "The Green Book," this budget is a useful document for policy analysts interested in the use of taxes for social policy.

Oddly enough, Americans seldom subject tax expenditures to the level of scrutiny that is applied to revenue expenditures. The nation's politicians find it easier to exempt someone from taxes than to establish a new social program. Tax exemptions and deductions are politically popular because Americans hate taxes. However, these exemptions and deductions favor the wealthy and do little or no good for the poor, because exemptions and deductions operate by reducing a person's income tax obligation. Given the progressive nature of the federal income tax, this reduction has the greatest value to those with the greatest tax obligation—the affluent (see Barusch, 1995).

This problem does not hold for tax credits, which can result not only in reduced taxes but in a refund from the Internal Revenue Service (IRS). A refund that is the result of a tax credit is not the same as a refund that comes because you have overpaid your taxes. The refund most people are familiar with is not based on their deductions per se, but on the fact that they have had more money withheld than they owed. A tax credit actually changes the amount that the taxpayer owes. For that reason, the Earned Income Tax Credit (EITC) provides significant benefits to the nation's working poor. The EITC, discussed in Chapter 14, provides a refund to low-income workers with children. In essence, it is an antipoverty measure embedded in the U.S. tax code.

Few of us make personal decisions on the basis of tax consequences. Taxes operate in the background, punishing and rewarding behavior in ways that may influence us without our awareness. But the U.S. tax system is an important tool for achieving social justice. It allocates billions of dollars every year and plays a significant role in distributing the costs and benefits of citizenship.

SUMMARY: THE ROLE OF GOVERNMENT IN PURSUIT OF SOCIAL JUSTICE

This chapter linked the philosophical perspectives outlined in Chapter 1 to contemporary American politics, offering a working description of political parties and labels and examining diverse views on the proper role of government. We suggested that govfernment is an important tool in the pursuit of social justice. Government evolved because we needed an organization to carry out this collective enterprise. The U.S. government can be seen as having both levels (federal, state, and local) and branches (legislative, executive, and judicial). Each plays an important role in the creation and implementation of social policy. We examined the movement to privatize government functions, and offered an approach for determining whether privatization of human services is appropriate. Finally, we examined the U.S. tax system and its role in social policy.

It is easy to become overwhelmed by the complexity of the U.S. government. By achieving a basic understanding of its structure, and remembering that in a democracy the central role of government is to carry out the will of the people, social workers can engage effectively in policy practice on behalf of their clients. Policy practice is the focus of Chapter 3.

KEYWORDS

Devolution	Liberals	Social policy
Political polarization	Libertarian party	
Conservatives	Domestic policy	

THINK ABOUT IT

1. List three arguments in favor of having the states, not the federal government, operate a major social program such as Social Security. Now list three

arguments opposing state management. We are all familiar with constitutional limits on the federal government. Does the Constitution limit the powers of the states?

2. What is the largest tax expenditure in the current Tax Expenditure Budget? What social goals does it serve?

3. Has your community used tax exemptions to attract business in the past year? What were the terms of those exemptions? Who benefited?

4. What is taxpayer C's average tax rate? What is his or her marginal rate?

WEB-BASED EXERCISES

For direct links to all the sites in these exercises, log on to the Student Companion Site for this book at academic.cengage.com/social_work/barusch, and choose Chapter 2.

1. Examine the trend in the national debt for the past 10 years at http://www .treasurydirect.gov/NP/BPDLogin?application=np. Now look at the 10-year trend in interest on the debt at http://www.treasurydirect.gov/govt/ reports/ir/ir_expense.htm. Describe the relationship between these two trends. Is it what you expected? How do you explain this relationship? (You will find a hint in Box 2.1.) What are the implications for social policy?

2. The judiciary has played a vital role in shaping social policy. Go to http:// supct.law.cornell.edu/supct/cases/historic.htm to view "Selected Historic Decisions of the U.S. Supreme Court" sponsored by the Legal Information Institute (LII). Under the LII's Collection of 631 Historic Decisions, choose "By Topic." Then search for the following Supreme Court cases:

Social Security
Steward Machine Co. v. Collector of Internal Revenue
Helvering v. Davis

Segregation
Plessy v. Ferguson
Brown v. Board of Education

Abortion
Roe v. Wade

Sterilization
Skinner v. Oklahoma

Marriage
Loving v. Virginia

Welfare Benefits
Saenz v. Roe

Read the court's opinion in each case and describe (a) the facts of the case, (b) the court's conclusion, and (c) the effect of this case on contemporary U.S. social policy.

3. Now, search for *Takao Ozawa v. United States* using your favorite search engine and do the same for this case. Why do you think Cornell Law School did not include this case among its historic cases?

4. Go to http://www.gpoaccess.gov/usbudget/index.html to view the budget of the U.S. government for the most recent fiscal year. Click on "Browse the FY08 budget" (there may be a more recent fiscal year, such as FY09). This will allow you to peruse the budgets of the federal departments. Download the budgets for the Department of Defense and the Department of Health and Human Services. Compare total outlays on the last page of each budget. Is the result what you expected? (Hint: Watch out for supplemental appropriations.)

SUGGESTED RESOURCES

Piven, F. F., & Cloward, R. A. (1997). *The Breaking of the American Social Compact*. New York: New Press. This book, particularly Chapter 3, "Welfare and the Transformation of Electoral Politics," is a must-read for anyone struggling to understand American politics in the twenty-first century.

www.gao.gov. The Government Accountability Office (GAO) is "the investigative arm of Congress." This site provides access to GAO reports and testimony, legal decisions and opinions, and presentations by the Comptroller General on a wide range of timely topics.

www.gpoaccess.gov. Maintained by the Government Printing Office, this site provides access to the huge array of government publications. And, best of all, their exhaustive Catalog of U.S. Government Publications is searchable! You can use it to locate the latest government publications on a subject of your choice.

www.thomas.loc.gov. This site is maintained by the Library of Congress "in the spirit of Thomas Jefferson." It provides a searchable database with the text and status of bills going back several years. It is an excellent source of up-to-date information on congressional proposals.

3

Policy Analysis and Policy Practice

We must complain, yes plain, blunt complaint, ceaseless
agitation, unfailing exposure of dishonesty and wrong—this is
the unerring way to liberty, and we must follow it.
W. E. B. DUBOIS, 1905

Aristotle systematically examines the dynamics of persuasion. In the second volume of his three-volume work *Rhetoric*, he describes three components of effective persuasion: *logos,* reason based on content and logic; *pathos,* reason based on passion and emotions; and *ethos,* reason based on the merits and character of the speaker. Aristotle argues for moderate use of all three components.

Aristotle also set the stage for a philosophy of policy practice based on the concept of a "marketplace of ideas." He saw rhetoric as a vital aspect of the life of a community, and believed that effective arguments would result in good decisions (Corbett, 1965). The marketplace of ideas can work effectively only when all voices are heard and all arguments are responsibly presented. Modern advocacy is influenced by Aristotle's views. We rely heavily on the three components of persuasion, and any advocate would do well to remember Aristotle's approach to the "art of argument."

The chapter begins with a human perspective, describing an advocacy effort on behalf of free public education in the state of Utah. Next, we introduce a definition of "policy practice." We then consider four established approaches to policy analysis: need assessment, Prince Policy Appraisal, product analysis, and cost–benefit analysis. We explore the contribution of a social justice perspective to policy analysis and then turn to the interactive aspects of policy practice.

A HUMAN PERSPECTIVE   Advocacy: Free Public Education

In 1895, when Utah became a state, its constitution guaranteed each citizen a "free" public education, at least until the end of the eighth grade. Initially the practice of charging fees for "extras" provided by the public schools, such as uniforms and supplies for special art projects, seemed perfectly compatible with the constitutional mandate. In time enrollment grew and educational funding fell behind. Schools relied increasingly on fees to bridge the revenue gap. By the early 1970s, the use of fees had extended to include not only the extras but basic necessities such as books and educational supplies. Local advocates became aware that the fees denied children from low-income families access to benefits available to those whose families who could afford to pay. Over the next 20 years, advocates from a statewide organization called Utah Issues employed a broad range of advocacy strategies to address the problem. Their efforts included careful analysis, individual advocacy, coalition building, careful research, and finally, litigation. The story of universal access to public education in Utah offers an instructive example of long-term advocacy for public policy.

Why are school fees a significant social justice issue? Irene Fisher, a key advocate in the early stages of the school fee effort, explained that the imposition of fees stigmatizes children from poor families by emphasizing class differences in a way that is personally and socially destructive. She explained, "When I grew up in South Dakota, no one knew we were poor. I was a cheerleader, and the school issued me a uniform just like everybody else. It may have been used in previous years, but so was everyone else's." In contrast, a low-income Utah parent wrote, "They threatened to withhold my daughter's grades and they always hounded her for money. I didn't have a job and we didn't have any money, but every couple of weeks they would pressure my daughter for the fees. She finally gave up and dropped out of school." Another parent explained that her son was arrested for shoplifting. He had stolen art supplies. His teacher had a special box of "poor kids' supplies" for children whose parents could not afford to pay the art supply fee. The boy stole supplies, rather than face the humiliation of using the supplies designated for "poor kids."

This account is based on interviews with advocates involved in the effort, and it draws heavily from a booklet by Bill Crim entitled *Sometimes You Need a Hammer: An Unfinished Story of Social Advocacy and Equal Educational Opportunity in Utah* (Salt Lake City: Utah Issues, 1994).

School fees were initially added to the funding equation of Utah's public schools as a way to fund enhancements to the educational and social experiences of students without requiring additional legislative appropriations. Once the seed was planted, the practice grew out of hand. Concerns surfaced as early as the 1930s, when the state legislature passed a bill requiring that public schools be free. Two years later, a state court interpreted the law, ruling that no fees could be charged for registration or tuition, and that all necessary supplies and books must be provided to students through grade 8. Although the law was clear, its enforcement mechanism was not. Schools continued to charge fees—sometimes in ways that were clearly illegal.

During the 1970s, the staff of Utah Issues began working on the school fee issue. With a mandate to advocate on behalf of the state's low-income population, the organization started working on a case-by-case basis, helping parents battle illegal fees. In time it became clear that individual advocacy efforts were insufficient, and the organization began holding workshops and conferences with affected parents, soliciting support from other advocacy groups, and preparing reports that the state legislature routinely ignored. The state superintendent of public instruction was concerned about the issue, however, and issued a memo to local districts urging them to develop clear policies allowing for waiver of school fees depending on family circumstances. This memo and related documents became the state's policy on school fees.

At this point, it became clear that three realities affected advocates' progress toward their goals. First, even though school fees were harmful and often illegal, decision makers believed their elimination was not feasible because of fiscal constraints facing the education system. Second, some policy makers felt that the availability of waivers effectively solved the problem. Third, those within the educational system who were most concerned about fees—the state superintendent of schools and the State Board of Education—were state, not local, officials. Utah's strong commitment to local district autonomy limited their power and authority over local decisions related to fees.

These circumstances strained the energies and resources of the Utah Issues staff. They had to operate not only at the state level but also locally with 40 individual school districts. Nonetheless, over the next several years, advocates held workshops with affected parents, helped parents plead their cases with local school personnel, and documented examples of continued harm.

Textbook fees emerged as a major target. Advocates tried during four state legislative sessions to obtain supplemental funding to permit elimination of textbook fees before finally getting a $2 million appropriation designated for that purpose in 1975. But local districts continued to charge textbook fees, and the State Board of Education continued to resist pressure to intervene. In 1981 there was a major setback when the Utah legislature passed a bill authorizing the sale and rental of textbooks to children in high school. A waiver provision was included in the law, but this was the first legislative sanction for fees for basic educational expenses. Advocates continued their efforts, but success seemed out of reach.

Perhaps as a result of this setback capping years of work, coupled with vital issues competing for the attention of poverty advocates, Utah Issues found itself in 1985 with progressively fewer collaborators on the school fee issue. Finally, no one else showed up at a key strategy meeting. The staff of Utah Issues decided to involve its board of directors in deciding how to approach an issue that mattered vitally but seemed to have lost its following. The board chair, an attorney, keyed into the challenging but obvious legal implications of the issue and volunteered to work with the staff to investigate strategic options. Over the next year, the board chair and staff developed and implemented a new phase of the school fee advocacy effort. The goal was to obtain statutory protections to reduce the harm done to low-income children through imposition of fees.

A legislative interim study committee was persuaded to investigate the school fee issue, and low-income public school students gained a handful of well-educated, committed legislators "on their team" who managed during the 1986 session to pass three laws. The first required that waivers be made available to low-income children for any fees associated with school-sponsored activities. The second law mandated parental notification of the availability of waivers and the application process. The third law provided for local school board review and approval of all fees in a public meeting. The State Board of Education, in turn, was required to develop rules implementing the new laws, and a low-income advocate was able to move closer to the policy-making process by gaining a seat on the board's school fee task force. The presence of

other child advocates on the task force offered the opportunity for successful coalition building on specific policy points.

A number of developments that year were less than positive, however. Other legislative action took a forceful step toward solidifying the state educational system's tremendous reliance on school fees as a funding source. The body passed a resolution to place a question on the ballot asking voters whether they would approve of ending Utah's constitutional guarantee of free public education for children in grades 7 through 12. Fearful that extracurricular activities would be eliminated if fees were not charged, voters passed the ballot measure the following November. Over the next seven years, a senator and two Speakers of the House attempted to repeat this action to remove free public education from the Constitution entirely, but these efforts were defeated. Public policy advocates and other legislators worked together to convince a majority that elementary school children were too young to face the painful experiences their older brothers and sisters endured.

The 1986 school fee law and resultant State Board policy provided new tools for advocates, who forged strong working relationships with State Office of Education staff charged with monitoring compliance over the next five years. Some parents reported success in securing fee waivers, but advocates continued to hear from parents that fees were not being waived and that inadequate or inaccurate information was presented. Children were still excluded from school activities and denied school supplies.

In 1991, advocates launched a three-pronged research effort to quantify the extent of the problem (i.e., the *need* for intervention). Committed to producing information that was both highly credible and reflective of the impact on children, they selected three approaches. First, a survey of low-income parents was conducted to assess their children's experiences with school fees and the fee waiver process. Second, all local district fee policies were systematically analyzed to gauge compliance with the 1986 laws and State Board policy. Third, a history of the school fee issue was prepared to place the issue within a clearer context. The resulting report, *School Fees in Utah: The Law and the Practice*, contained the advocates' findings and recommendations. The report was released to a broad audience and left no question that the majority of local school districts had, even after five years, failed to meet

Continued

Continued

the law's requirements and that parents had many concerns about the impact of the waiver's failure on their children.

At the time that this research was going on, a number of parents contacted Utah Legal Services, which had hired an attorney experienced in school law. As the attorney investigated these parents' circumstances, he approached the state superintendent of schools about the policies and practices of the individual school districts involved. After many discussions and further study, he concluded that the superintendent and State Board were caught in a dilemma. State appropriations for education were inadequate, leading local districts to rely on fees to cover the cost of their programs and activities. Although the State Board was aware of many violations, the philosophical principle of local governance was strong, the State Board had no relief to offer to districts if they waived fees for their many low-income, eligible students, and the State Board believed it had done all it could since 1986 to compel local districts to comply. When pressed, the superintendent admitted to the attorney that it would take a lawsuit to change these parameters.

Thus, in July 1992, Utah Legal Services filed a class action lawsuit against the Utah State Board of Education, the State Office of Education, and the state superintendent of schools in Third District Court. The lawsuit was commonly known as *Doe v. Utah State Board of Education*. The judge immediately granted a preliminary injunction requiring that the State Board enforce state fee waiver statutes. The Board was ordered to withhold funds from schools and districts that were out of compliance.

The preliminary injunction increased pressure to resolve the school fee issue. As the State Office of Education's legal staff worked to prepare effective materials to help local districts determine how to achieve compliance with a complex snarl of fees, local school boards struggled to react to their economic dilemma. They were suddenly faced with a choice between economic sanction and substantial reduction in revenue by granting waivers. Some turned to their legislators, calling for necessary, long overdue appropriations. Other districts mounted efforts to evaluate the impact of fees and to ascertain their role in fulfilling the mission of the public schools. Some student groups pledged to raise funds to support low-income students' participation. Conversely, in a few areas, teachers and students feared their favorite activities might be eliminated and lashed out at children known to be poor.

Attention in the education community turned in earnest to resolving the funding impetus behind school fees; low-income advocates, education administrators, parents, and teachers worked together on strategies to obtain legislative support during the 1994 general session. Backlash among some powerful legislators, resentful of the litigation and the assertive stance of the court, led to creation of a legislative school fee task force. Those selected for the task force were largely hostile to an appropriation to help districts cover fee waivers. The coalition of education advocates who supported waiver funding diligently attended six

---

Focusing on advocacy as a key element of policy practice, we consider specific tactics for advocacy, including preparing and presenting arguments, negotiation and compromise, and the use of relationship. Ethical considerations are examined next, as we ask whether social workers have an ethical obligation to engage in advocacy and we explore the ethical dimensions of common advocacy practices. The tactics described here can be applied in a variety of policy venues, from letters to the editor to testimony before Congress. Clearly this chapter can only begin to introduce you to the many perspectives and skills necessary for effective policy practice. You will find additional material in the books listed under "Suggested Resources" at the chapter's end.

months of difficult meetings with this hostile group of legislators. The task force was preparing legislation to water down the waiver laws before the judge's permanent injunction was finalized, but that injunction, which was stronger than the first order, was released in October 1994. The task force disbanded angrily.

Although the outcome of *Doe v. Utah State Board of Education* was a tremendous leap forward for low-income children, in social advocacy few victories are permanent. The underlying cause of schools' reliance on fees—limited state funding for education—still has not been addressed. Until it is resolved, school districts under financial pressure will be highly motivated to ignore waiver policies and impose fees in ways that are damaging and painful to low-income children.

A Social Work Perspective

This advocacy effort illustrates several basic principles of policy practice:

Persistence Is Vital

Victories and setbacks must be understood in the context of a struggle that may extend beyond the lives of those involved at any given time. When the state constitution was drafted, someone thought to include a guarantee of free public education. This provision suggests that the issue of educational equity has been around since statehood. Clearly those who hunger for a "quick fix" will be disappointed in the advocacy arena. This doesn't mean progress is not possible, but it may take a very long time—sometimes longer than we can bear.

Every Individual Counts

Despite—or perhaps because of—the magnitude of the struggle, each individual's efforts count. From the parents who called to complain and tell their stories, to lawyers who devoted their time to a class action lawsuit, every effort was integral to the process. Not all individual contributions receive public recognition, but all are vital to the success of an advocacy effort.

Advocacy Is Rarely About "Us Versus Them"

There is seldom a clear enemy to fight. Local districts in this example operated under impossible funding constraints. The State Board was hampered in its job by the overriding principle of local control of schools. The legislature struggled to stretch tax dollars as far as possible. At most, these entities can be accused of lack of consideration for vulnerable children, not of intentional evil. It is tempting, but counterproductive, to label an organization "them" and to dismiss its employees and volunteers as "the enemy."

Just as social policy includes laws, court opinions, and regulations, social advocacy takes place in all of these arenas. Many people think of advocacy as lobbying for legislation or program budgets. These efforts represent only one piece of the advocacy pie. Every bit as influential as the high-profile individual who testifies before legislative bodies and files lawsuits is the detail-oriented person who monitors the drafting of regulations and gently, but firmly, suggests revisions on behalf of vulnerable individuals.

WHAT IS POLICY PRACTICE?

Just as "individual practice" attempts to change individuals, "policy practice" focuses on changing policy. As Bruce Jansson said, "We define policy practice as efforts to change policies in legislative, agency, and community settings, whether by establishing new policies, improving existing ones, or defeating the policy initiatives of other people" (1999, p. 10). Although the two are closely entwined, policy practice does not *always* involve advocacy, but can encompass a range of activities.

Social workers engage in policy practice when they strive to master the laws and regulations that govern the services they provide to clients. This aspect of policy practice involves basic assessment. Social workers who critically analyze a court opinion to identify potential implications for their clients are involved in policy assessment at an advanced level. A policy practitioner who is engaged in advocacy might employ a wide range of tactics, from preparing an argument in favor of expanded services for the disabled to building a coalition of organizations concerned about child welfare. Finally, when community organizers educate residents in a low-income neighborhood about the problem of racial profiling, they are engaged in the "empowerment" aspect of policy practice. In this chapter we will explore tactics and considerations relevant to three central aspects of policy practice: assessment and analysis, advocacy, and empowerment.

ASSESSMENT AND ANALYSIS: RESEARCH FOR POLICY PRACTICE

While it is not possible for advocates to know *everything* about the policy or problem under consideration, it is vital that arguments include Aristotle's element of *logos*. At a minimum, advocates should be prepared to answer certain basic questions:

- How many people are affected by the problem or issue under consideration?
- What are they like (in terms of demographics such as age, race, sex, income, residence)?
- How long has this problem or issue been present?
- What is its history? Have there been previous efforts to address this concern? How well did they work?
- How do other jurisdictions (countries, states, communities) deal with this issue? What successes have they had?
- What are your recommendations or proposals to address the problem? Is there evidence that they will work?
- What do key authorities say about the issue? Who are potential allies and opponents?

Later chapters of this book offer material for the assessment and analysis of social policy in specific fields (poverty, health, mental health disabilities) and for specific populations (people of color, GLBT individuals, children, women, working people, and the elderly). Additional material can be obtained through a variety of sources, including books and professional journals, colleagues who have been working in the area, and Internet search engines. Some of the best policy analysis is done by professional public policy organizations such as the Urban Institute or the Center for Public Policy and the Budget. The best of these treat social justice as an integral component of their missions and conduct credible legal and social research.

Remember that there are some quality controls in professional books and literature—an editor, and in most cases other reviewers, have examined the material for accuracy and relevance. There are no such controls on the Internet. As a general rule, government websites provide the most reliable and valuable information. These can be identified by the ".gov" in the URL. Educational websites are usually reliable sources, but they should be viewed with caution. The URLs of educational sites end with ".edu." Material drawn from other types of sites should be used only with scrutiny. (For an excellent discussion of criteria for evaluating web sources, see Vernon & Lynch, 2000.)

Assessment and analysis are essential components of effective advocacy. In the following section we will examine several different approaches to policy analysis. Then we will consider the advocacy component of policy practice, drawing from the experiences of policy practitioners, as well as communication theory and research on persuasion.

POLICY ANALYSIS

Policy analysis is the systematic examination of a discrete aspect of social policy. Approaches to policy analysis vary in the extent to which they emphasize *description* as opposed to *interpretation*. As you study social policy, your awareness and understanding will expand. You will see social policy in new ways. First, you will become aware of the widespread impact of social policies—something that most people just take for granted. Second, your knowledge of the history of social policy will enable you to understand its purposes and effects more deeply. Finally, your focus on social justice will allow you to assess the contribution of policy to a more just society. In its most advanced form, your approach to policy analysis will represent your personal view of the meaning of the policy enterprise. It will reflect your perspective on what is just, as well as your awareness of the sources and assumptions behind your views. While it is always important to get your facts straight, your interpretation of social policy is neither "right" nor "wrong." At its best, it will be well informed and clearly reasoned. It will also be subject to change as your personal and career development progress.

This section will describe five techniques of policy analysis. They range from primarily descriptive methods, such as the "product" analysis described by Gilbert and Terrell (2002), to more interpretive approaches, such as Prince Policy Appraisal (Coplin & O'Leary, 1998). Sometimes the technical demands of policy analysis can obscure the fact that all analysis of this kind is inherently value-laden. Sometimes values are explicit. This is the case in cost–benefit analysis, for example, when we clearly state the benefits of a policy. Values are often implicit in the way a question is framed or the way data are treated.

The section closes by offering a distinctive social justice framework that can be applied to the analysis of social policy. A social justice framework for policy analysis makes explicit the values underlying a policy by carefully considering the impact of the policy on the distributive rules developed by a group of people. This framework can serve as an overlay for any of the methods described here by directing attention and interpretation to issues of fairness.

Approaches to policy analysis vary in the aspect of policy development that they address. "Process" techniques such as need assessment and Prince Policy

Appraisal help us understand the process of policy formation. "Product" approaches focus on describing the social programs that are typically products of policy once it has been developed. Perhaps the most well known of these product approaches is the framework described by Gilbert and Terrell (2002) that clearly articulates the dimensions of a social program. Finally, "performance" approaches such as cost–benefit analysis consider the impact of a particular policy. The choice of approach will, of course, depend on the purpose of the analysis. Any of these approaches can help inform social justice analysis, just as a commitment to social justice will change the way each approach is implemented.

Process Approaches

Several questions can be addressed in the process of policy development, including "Is there a need for this policy?" and "What is the likelihood that this policy will be established?" Each of these questions can be addressed using a distinctive approach to policy analysis.[1]

Need Assessment

Researchers apply a wide range of techniques to determine the need for a specific policy or program, including use of key informants, a community forum, social indicators, and community surveys (Rubin & Babbie, 2001). Here we will consider some conceptual issues that bear on the use of need assessment in public policy development. As is often the case, defining the key construct can be a challenge. In the public policy arena, "needs" represent an extremely complex social construct. Rubin and Babbie (2001) distinguish between definitions that use a "normative" approach and those that are based on demand. Using a normative approach, we would describe the objective living conditions of a target group in comparison to what society (or a large segment of society) would consider acceptable. On the other hand, when need is defined based on demands, only groups capable of perceiving and articulating their needs would be considered.

Normative Definition of Need.   The normative approach to need definition reflects the Rawlsian notion of a social minimum discussed in Chapter 1. The social minimum varies across societies. For instance, a common poverty threshold used in international research defines poverty as an income of less than one dollar per day. But in the United States we have general agreement that a person's "basic needs" should be met. Basic needs include the physical and social goods necessary to sustain life. Most days, the human body requires air, water, food, safety, and shelter. Beyond this, human infants cannot survive without affection-

---

1. This section will introduce you to some of the most interesting methods for the analysis of social policy. It offers a brief description that will enable you to use some of these methods but does not offer anywhere near the level of detail that is available elsewhere. Please see references throughout the section and suggested resources for books that can provide greater depth on any of these approaches.

TABLE 3.1   Social Policy and Basic Human Needs

Policy Goal	Basic Need	Programmatic Examples
Survival	Air, water, food, safety, shelter	Food stamps, public housing
Physical health	Clean environment, health care	EPA Superfund, Medicaid, Medicare
Psychological well-being	Belonging, self-actualization, meaningful engagement, intellectual development	Public education system, mental health system, volunteer opportunities

ate contact. In the arena of basic needs we distinguish between those necessary to sustain life and those necessary to maintain physical health. Physical health requires, for example, that air, water, and food be free of damaging pollutants.

Most social work scholars (i.e., Gil, van Wormer, Van Soest, and Garcia) include psychological well-being among the basic needs. Maslow's hierarchy of needs is commonly used to suggest that opportunities for belonging and self-actualization are necessary for human survival in complex societies. Erik Erikson's concept of meaningful engagement has also been treated as a basic need in our professional discourse. Any list of basic psychological needs should include the concept of intellectual development, since education is an important precursor to effective social participation.

Indeed, the presence of a large national program constitutes public recognition of the validity of a basic need. So, as we see in Table 3.1, it is not difficult to identify major programmatic efforts to address basic needs that have been identified.

Gil (1992) argues, "When the realization of basic needs is thwarted consistently, beyond a level of tolerance, by a society's way of life and social policies, constructive developmental energy tends to be blocked and transformed into destructive energy" (p. 19). This observation suggests that it is in society's best interest to ensure that all people have ways to meet their basic needs. Piven and Cloward (1971) argued that a central role of our profession is ensuring that basic needs are minimally met to prevent social decay and violence.

Demand-Based Definition of Need.   When we define need based on demand rather than social norms, the discourse becomes more political. Under this definition, need must be both perceived and expressed. Basic needs that are not expressed don't count. So if homeless people in the United States do not express their need for decent, affordable housing, that need does not come under consideration. By contrast, if the chamber of commerce expresses a need for sales tax relief, this need would be considered.

Some people question the legitimacy of expressed needs that are not basic needs. For David Gil, perceived needs can substitute for basic psychological needs that people believe cannot be fulfilled. So, for example, if opportunities for belonging are thwarted, an individual might substitute a perceived need for material wealth. Such people may become staunch advocates of policies that

A group of people with a banner at a peace and jobs rally, San Francisco, CA.

support their need to accumulate wealth. Highly sophisticated marketing efforts are used to generate perceived needs.

Nonetheless, the demand-based approach to defining need reflects some of the realities of policy development (and family life!). Unless someone expresses a need, it may go unmet. In policy practice, social workers can empower disenfranchised groups to express their basic needs in ways that can be understood by the majority or the powerful. And sometimes it falls to social workers to express needs on behalf of those who are unable to do this for themselves. As we will see, the legitimacy conferred by the basic needs of their clients can be a source of power for social work advocates.

Prince Policy Appraisal[2]

Niccolo Machiavelli wrote his best-known political treatise, *The Prince,* during the sixteenth century. Schooled in the political intrigues of Florence, Machiavelli focused on the effective use of political power. Aptly named for Machiavelli's work, the technique of Prince Policy Appraisal can be used to gauge the power dynamics that determine political support for a new policy initiative (Coplin & O'Leary, 1998). Offering a systematic approach to understand-

---

2. I am indebted to Emma Gross who introduced me to Prince Policy Appraisal, and to generations of Utah students who have implemented and refined this approach.

ing political processes that can seem mysterious to social workers, this technique consists of five steps:

1. Identify the *players* who are likely to affect the decision.
2. Determine a *position* for each player.
3. Estimate the *power* that each player brings to the issue.
4. Estimate the *priority* of the issue for each player.
5. Calculate the likelihood that the policy will be implemented.

Prince Policy Appraisal begins with a clear description of a policy proposal. It is important that the object of the analysis be a specific proposal, not a broad policy goal. Reducing poverty is a goal. Increasing child care for recipients of Temporary Assistance to Needy Families (TANF) is a specific proposal. Once the proposal has been outlined, analysis proceeds through each of the five steps outlined above (see Coplin and O'Leary, 1998, for more detail on how to conduct and apply this method).

Apart from providing an informed guess about the likelihood of implementation, Prince Policy Appraisal offers insight into the power dynamics behind the political process that can be used to inform advocacy strategy. By directing attention to the dynamics of political power, the method can help advocates set their intervention priorities for greatest impact. Results of Prince Policy Appraisal remind us, for instance, that it is more effective to change the position of a powerful player than of a less influential one; or that sometimes the most effective way to accomplish policy change is to increase the priority or salience of an issue for its less enthusiastic supporters.

Product Analysis

Product analysis is a detailed description of public programs that represent the "products" of social policy. Generally this approach considers five key aspects of a public program: the program goal or the social problem it addresses, the basis for entitlement (or eligibility), the nature of the benefit or service provided, the administrative structure used to deliver the program, and the program's financing mechanism. (Chambers, 2000, and Gilbert and Terrell, 2002, provide more detailed presentations of this approach.)

Goal or Social Problem.   Careful examination of a program's goal as well as the social problem it is designed to address sets the context for closer scrutiny of its specific components. Identification of the program's goal should refer to the best scientific knowledge available. This information should include a careful description of the affected population as well as known causes of the problem.

Some programs that were originally designed to address a specific problem have evolved over the years to focus on different concerns. Social Security is a good example. During the Depression unemployment was a primary concern. So the retirement program established by the Social Security Act of 1935 addressed this problem by requiring that those receiving benefits exit the workforce. A "retirement test" was instituted and measures were taken to discourage employment by older Americans. As we will see in Chapter 4, the problem of unemployment receded, which eventually led to elimination of the retirement test.

Public values and beliefs about the problem and about its relationship to other social problems can affect attitudes toward the program. The war on drugs reflects a widespread belief that people who buy illegal drugs are, first and foremost, criminals. This dictates a much different programmatic approach from that generated by the belief that people who purchase drugs are addicts. Our assessment of goals must include discussion of popular beliefs.

Basis for Entitlement.   Knowledge of eligibility criteria is central to understanding a program's intent and operations. Eligibility might be based on membership in a group assumed to be needy (e.g., HIV/AIDS victims, the elderly). It might be based on a carefully assessed need (e.g., disability, poverty). Program eligibility may be limited to people who work (e.g., Earned Income Tax Credit), or those who don't work (e.g., unemployment compensation). Finally, it may be related to prior social contribution, such as military service or payroll tax contributions.

Gilbert and Terrell (2002) examined the vital distinction between eligibility and access, noting that individuals who are eligible for a program do not necessarily receive the program's benefits. Barriers to access, both formal and informal, can make eligibility little more than a joke. The presence of such barriers is indicated when a program is "underutilized." As we will see in Chapter 4, only about a third of older adults eligible for Supplemental Security Income participate in the program. In mental health services, underutilization by people of color is common. While program staff may be inclined to blame nonutilizers for their failure to take advantage of society's offerings, a more productive stance might be to ask what features of the program constitute barriers to participation. The list of possible barriers is long and includes lack of minority personnel, publication of program documents in English only, lack of outreach to inform people about the program's existence, location of the program in areas that are not accessible to some groups, complex and stigmatizing eligibility procedures, and paltry benefits. Some argue that privatization results in "creaming," in which providers create barriers to access that eliminate difficult or less profitable clients.

Nature of the Benefit.   Public programs offer four types of benefits: services, goods, vouchers, and cash. Of course, some provide a combination of these. Benefits vary in the degree of choice (or power) afforded to the recipient. Services and goods provide the least choice. Social workers like to believe that our professional services empower the needy. But how many of the needy would choose to receive them? Even the way we deliver services can disempower recipients, since we usually make ourselves available from 9 to 5, a schedule that is convenient for the professional but not for the low-income working adult. In the TANF program, a client who chooses not to receive services risks losing her grant.

Goods offer a little more choice because clients can usually "take it or leave it." Distribution of food commodities is characteristic. In one community, low-income adults must stand in line at 6:00 in the morning, waiting for the "cheese truck" to arrive at the community center. Large slabs of cheese are passed out to eager recipients, along with a dose of humiliation.

Vouchers limit choice to a range of products. Still, recipients can usually select the time and place they will receive the goods. Food stamps are the classic example. The products that can be purchased are restricted, but shoppers can choose the store and shop at their own convenience.

Cash provides the greatest choice and flexibility to the recipient. It can be used anywhere, at any time, to purchase anything. As a result, programs that deliver cash are subject to criticism that their recipients are incapable of making rational decisions about money management.

Administrative Structure.   Several features can be considered in describing the administrative structure of a public program, including degree of centralization, types of staff, use of citizen participation, and availability of appeal procedures.

The principles of efficiency and access compete in decisions about the degree of centralization in public programs. Highly centralized programs have few offices and benefit from economies of scale. They are efficient but often hard to access. By contrast, satellite offices cost more but provide greater access. Sometimes the degree of centralization is an inverse function of the political power of program beneficiaries. Neighborhoods and groups with power advocate for convenient access to the public programs they use. Compare the number of fire stations in a middle-class neighborhood with the number of welfare offices in low-income neighborhoods.

The faces of staff speak volumes about the program. Lack of bicultural and bilingual staff in a program serving people of color represents a de facto barrier to access. Extensive reliance on paraprofessionals may reflect budget shortages or limited interest on the part of professional staff. Some programs employ former clients as a way to reach out to their target populations.

Echoes of the citizen participation movement of the 1960s and 1970s are still found in some public programs. Rather than reserve all important decisions for the experts, some programs use groups of involved citizens to ensure a democratic process. Of course, many citizen advisory groups and councils exercise little power in the important decisions that face a program. Nonetheless, the presence of such groups represents the potential for citizen participation. You never know when they will erupt and demand meaningful engagement!

Some public programs have established procedures for use by clients who are dissatisfied with staff decisions or services. These range from informal review processes to full-fledged administrative hearings. The presence and operation of these procedures are important factors to consider when describing a program. If all appeals are denied, the analyst has an inkling that all may not be fair and impartial when it comes to conflicts of this kind.

Financing Mechanism. In seeking to understand a program, we would do well to "follow the money." If we understand where the money comes from, we know a great deal about the importance and nature of a public program. Methods of financing vary from coercive to voluntary, along a continuum based on the experience of the giver. They also vary in the degree of separation from giver to program recipient.

No one voluntarily pays taxes, so programs that are funded using tax dollars are at the extreme end of the coercion continuum. Taxes weigh more heavily on some citizens than others. Some programs are financed through regressive taxes that bear most heavily on the working poor and middle class. So, as we saw in Chapter 2, in addition to knowing that a program receives funding from taxes it is important to understand what type of tax provides the source of the funds.

In a coercion-free world, all programs would be financed through voluntary contributions. Charity is an important source of program funding, particularly in the social services. Unfortunately charity is an unreliable funding source. Donors' preferences as well as their ability to give can shift without notice, so for vital social functions charity often falls short.

Programs also differ in the nature of the relationship between donor and recipient. In some cases there is no relationship. Other programs are at least partially financed through user fees paid by recipients.

Today many social service programs draw funding from an array of financing mechanisms. For instance, a meal program for older adults might be primarily supported through county taxes and funds authorized under the Older Americans Act, with a short-term federal grant providing supplemental funding and user fees covering the balance.

Performance Analysis

This section considers two evaluation methods that focus on program impact: cost–benefit analysis and social justice analysis. Whereas cost–benefit analysis can be predominantly technical, the social justice perspective offers a values-based approach to analysis of program impact. Combined, they represent a dynamic approach to determining the effects of proposed and existing social policies.

Cost–Benefit Analysis. What we broadly call cost–benefit analysis actually includes two specific techniques. The first technique, which is a narrower definition of the term *cost–benefit analysis,* involves estimating the monetary values of costs and benefits. In the second technique—called *cost-effectiveness analysis*—no attempt is made to assign a dollar value. Instead, the focus is on clearly describing costs and benefits. Social workers are generally more comfortable with the latter approach, although the discipline involved in assessing monetary values is sometimes worthwhile.

Costs and benefits may be immediate or long-term, and they may be either direct or indirect results of the policy under consideration. Sometimes costs and benefits—especially indirect or long-term ones—are open to dispute. Deriving the best possible estimate in each category can be an important challenge with

TABLE 3.2   Costs and Benefits of a Proposal to Expand Medicaid Coverage

	COSTS		BENEFITS	
	Immediate vs. Long-Term		**Immediate vs. Long-Term**	
Direct **vs.** **Indirect**	Increased tax on wages	Higher proportion of federal budget devoted to health care	Access to affordable health care	Lower incidence of preventable illness among low-income workers
	Drop in new hires	Greater demand and funding for health care raises cost of care	Less use of emergency room for primary care	Lower population risk of contagious disease

this approach. Table 3.2 offers examples of the possible costs and benefits of a hypothetical proposal to make Medicaid coverage available to low-income workers with financing through a payroll tax.

Costs and benefits are sometimes probabilistic—they are not always sure bets. This is especially true of long-term and indirect ones. In this example we might ask what the likelihood is that this program will result in higher prices for health care. Simple economics of supply and demand would predict that increased demand would raise the price of care. We would consult an economist (or the economics literature) to answer a question of this kind. Similarly, a public health expert might address the program's potential impact on the risk of contagious disease. The end result may be that the consensus view predicts little to no impact on pricing and a 15-percent drop in disease risk.

Cost–benefit analysis can be a useful way to organize and understand public debate about a policy proposal. The cost–benefit grid presented here can be used in public meetings to generate lists of potential costs and benefits in each category. It can also help students to understand public policy debates. Emotionally charged rhetoric can often be distilled into beliefs regarding possible benefits or costs. Laid bare, some of these beliefs can sometimes be dismissed as irrational, while others may contain a germ of truth.

Like any evaluation method, cost–benefit analysis has advantages and disadvantages. One advantage stems from its focus on *logos*. Cost–benefit analysis directs attention away from emotionality and partisan politics and toward the practical consequences of a proposal. It can be a splendid tool for organizing ideas and speculation into a useful form. It is, however, only a tool. Cost–benefit analysis says little about the morality of a proposal (Nussbaum, 2001). For this method, all policy proposals are morally equal. Yet, as we saw in the last chapter, perfectly "rational" decisions that violate human rights are unjustified regardless of their potential benefits.

Social Justice Framework for Policy Analysis

When justice is the goal of social policy, fairness becomes the target of analysis. So, for example, a need assessment that is conducted using a social justice framework would not pretend to be value-free or "objective." In the advocacy example that began this chapter, advocates for social justice provided a careful description of the problem to help make the case for legislation to protect low-income students' educational rights. Even the most technically sophisticated cost–benefit analysis is informed by a basic understanding of what is just, or beneficial. In this way social justice pervades policy analysis as a philosophy, a mission, and a goal.

Our understanding of social justice as the fair allocation of rewards and benefits of group membership generates a distinctive approach to policy analysis that has been called the social justice perspective. When this perspective is employed, we consider both the process of policy development and the impact of the policy itself. The steps of this approach are summarized as follows:

1. Assess the fairness of the policy development process.
2. Describe the allocation rules embodied in the policy.
3. Determine the net effect of the policy on vulnerable populations.
4. Reach a conclusion regarding the policy's impact on social justice.

Assessing the Process

The fair process principles introduced in Chapter 1 can be used to assess policy-making processes. The first question to consider is whether the parties involved have operated according to established rules. Whether the process takes place in the halls of Congress or the chambers of a city council, it should proceed according to written rules. Careful scrutiny sometimes leads to the conclusion that rules were not followed or were stretched. Decisions that should have been made in open meetings are made in closed caucuses, proper notice of a vote is not provided, people who are not qualified are allowed to vote, or (as in Florida's 2000 electoral process) legitimate voters are turned away. Sometimes these deviations are just mistakes, but often they reflect an attempt to derail democracy in favor of an individual or group.

Fair policy process not only follows established rules, it also includes the affected parties. But sometimes people whose lives will be changed by a policy do not have a voice in policy development. Voice and access are pivotal to effective democracy. When the voices of affected parties are silenced, the likelihood of an unjust result is high. If someone is treated as "other" and denied access to policy debates, basic principles of fairness are violated. Usually there is a rationale for declaring a person "other." He or she may be an undocumented immigrant about to be deprived of health care, a "union agitator" seeking a representation vote in a nonunion shop, or an "illegal combatant" seen as a threat to national security. In any case, the label of "outsider" is often used to exclude individuals from decisions that affect them.

The principle of "one person, one vote" is also vital to a working democracy. Yet this principle is violated when access to the policy development process is lopsided. At present, the campaign financing system used in the United States virtually guarantees wealthy people and organizations easier access to policy makers. Social workers can strive to restore balance by pointing out the problem and amplifying the voices of vulnerable people in the United States.

Describing the Allocation Rules

A first step in describing the allocation rules embodied in a policy is to ask, "What are the costs and/or benefits under consideration?" As we have seen, costs and benefits can be either immediate or long-term and either the direct or the indirect result of social policy. In this stage, the social justice perspective employs the tools of cost–benefit analysis. But this approach goes beyond cost–benefit analysis in its focus on the people involved. Here we ask *who* bears the costs, *who* receives the benefits, and what the justification is for this allocation. With this information we can derive the allocation rules, both informal and formal, that govern who receives and who pays. Understanding and articulating the allocation rules will reveal the philosophical underpinnings of a policy or policy proposal and illuminate its potential impact on social justice.

Table 3.3 takes the hypothetical example already discussed and outlines its human dimension.

In social justice analysis we can examine the allocation pattern in each type of cost or benefit. In the preceding example, the results would be as follows:

- Immediate/direct—A tax paid by all workers and employers funds health-care coverage for low-income workers and their families.
- Long-term/direct—Congress and the executive branch have less discretion in funding decisions so that low-income workers and their families can have fewer preventable illnesses.
- Immediate/indirect—Fewer jobs for the unemployed and new job hunters are the cost of lower use of ER services.
- Long-term/indirect—The price of health care for the general population rises and the population has lower risk of contagious disease.

This analysis illuminates some of the underlying dynamics in the policy. Immediate costs are borne by workers, employers, and the unemployed, while immediate benefits go to low-income workers in the form of greater access to care

T A B L E 3.3   Who Bears the Costs and Benefits of a Proposal to Expand Medicaid Coverage?

	COSTS		BENEFITS	
	Immediate vs. Long-Term		**Immediate vs. Long-Term**	
Direct **vs.**	Increased tax on wages (paid by all workers and employers)	Higher proportion of federal budget devoted to health care (Congress/ executive have less discretion in funding)	Access to affordable health care (for low-income workers/ families)	Lower incidence of preventable illness (among low-income workers/ familiies)
Indirect	Drop in new hires as employers absorb increased payroll costs (fewer jobs for unemployed and new job hunters)	Greater demand and funding for health care raises cost of care (for general population)	Less use of emergency room (ER) for primary care frees ER for patients with real emergencies, reduces budget needs for ER	Lower population risk of contagious disease (enjoyed by general population)

and less pressure to use emergency rooms for primary health care. Here the general working population pays for the care of its more vulnerable members. Over the long term, the discretion of federal budget makers is reduced and the health of low-income workers is improved. The population as a whole may experience rising health-care fees even as it enjoys less disease. Most of the costs we have identified are borne by broad segments of the population and groups who will not be unduly burdened. The only exception here is the cost borne by those who are not hired when employers tighten their belts to cover their share of the payroll tax. The benefits focus on low-income workers, a relatively needy group, as well as the general population.

Determine the Effect on Vulnerable Populations (Deserts, Needs, Rights, and Equality)

A social justice perspective in social work demands special attention to the potential impact of policy on vulnerable populations. These are people living with economic insecurity and groups who have historically been oppressed or underrepresented. Too often benefits to one such group come at a cost to another.

In Chapter 1 we examined the primary components of social justice as described by David Miller: desert, need, rights, and equality. We can return to these to pursue our conclusion regarding the social justice impact of a proposal. So we must consider: (1) the extent to which people will receive what we (and they) feel is deserved, (2) whether the proposed change violates anyone's rights, (3) whether a human need is being met (or ignored) in this proposal, and (4) the potential impact of the proposal on inequality. The relevance of each component will depend on the focus of the policy; nonetheless, each of these components has special relevance for vulnerable populations, and the social work profession has a mandate to ensure that these aspects are addressed in policy debates.

Taking these components into account lends a new dimension to the appraisal of costs and benefits in our example. Our proposed Medicaid expansion would help meet the health *needs* of low-income workers and their families. The costs would be borne by all workers and employers, who probably believe the increased tax deprives them of wages they *deserve*. The *needs* of unemployed workers and young people entering the labor force may be jeopardized if employers hire fewer workers. And, of course, in the United States, citizens do not enjoy a *right* to health care, even though some advocates argue that we should. If we focus on vulnerable populations, then to assess this proposal we must balance the health-care needs of low-income workers against the deserts of all workers and the needs of the potentially unemployed.

Reach a Conclusion

The outcome of a just act is a social world that is more just than it was prior to the act; and the outcome of a just policy is the same. Those of us who are not omniscient will be hard-pressed to anticipate the full impact of a policy (or, as chaos theory would have us believe, a butterfly's flight). So we do the best we can, keeping in mind our philosophical perspectives and personal biases.

Given any set of facts, diverse philosophical perspectives dictate various conclusions regarding the social justice impact of a given policy. By the time the analysis has reached this stage most people have reached a tentative conclusion about this impact. (Indeed, they may have *begun* with a conclusion.) The final challenge of social justice analysis is to present a conclusion and articulate its philosophical foundations. The perspectives we reviewed in Chapter 1 can prove helpful in this regard.

In our hypothetical example we may begin analysis with the belief that it is good to provide health care to people in need. This stems from our Rawlsian (contractual liberal) belief that health care is a social good that should be available to all. A utilitarian liberal perspective would support the redistributive aspect of this proposal, based on the belief that the well-being of society is enhanced when those who have more resources give to those who have less. Because this intervention does little to reorder the dynamics of our capitalist society, staunch socialists may find it uninspired. Still, the notion of meeting a need as basic as that for health care would be appealing to the socialist viewpoint. By contrast, libertarians and those who support oligarchy might view the proposal more critically. A libertarian perspective would weigh the imposition of a tax heavily, viewing redistribution or care of the needy as less important. An adherent of oligarchy might oppose any change in allocation as a threat to established order.

Policy analysis is fundamentally an intellectual process. The approaches outlined here can be used individually or in combination to improve our understanding of policy development, public programs, and the impacts of social policy. They can also be used to inform advocacy efforts—moving from thought to action. The following sections of this chapter focus on analytic and interpersonal skills that are essential for successful advocacy.

ADVOCACY SKILLS

Mark Ezell (2001) offers a useful definition of *advocacy* which, he argues, "consists of those purposive efforts to change specific existing or proposed policies or practices on behalf of or with a specific client or group of clients" (p. 23). Drawing on assessment and analysis, advocates use a variety of tactics to accomplish their goals. Four of the most widely held advocacy skills are examined here, including the use of arguments, compromise, relationship, and coalitions. Aristotle's three components of persuasion can help in each of these areas. Arguments must be based on careful reasoning and solid research (*logos*). They must be presented in a way that engages the audience's passions (*pathos*). Finally, in all areas, advocates must preserve their professionalism and credibility (*ethos*).

PREPARING, COMPOSING, AND DELIVERING ARGUMENTS

Persuasion, or argument, is central to advocacy. Three steps are involved in the use of argument: preparation, composition, and delivery.

Preparation: Speak to the Audience

"Speaking to the audience" sounds ludicrously simple but actually requires considerable analysis, empathy, and skill. Communication specialists describe this process as "constructing a receiver profile" (Johnston, 1994). Advertising firms spend millions of dollars building a profile of the targets of their persuasive efforts. Social advocates can increase their effectiveness by devoting time and thought to similar considerations. The advocate must identify the target audience and gear presentations to this group. The preparation process is complicated by the strong likelihood that any argument will be presented to multiple audiences. Several of these audiences, such as those charged with making a decision, are of primary importance, while others, such as fellow advocates, may have less importance. Nonetheless, effective persuasion demands that you win over as much of the audience as possible.

Constructing a receiver profile is an exercise in perspective-taking. O'Keefe and Shepherd (1987) identified four developmental levels in perspective-taking. At the first level, no attempt is made to determine the target's needs or interests; at the second, the advocate's needs are communicated without regard to those of the target; at the third level, the advocate is familiar with the target's position and has prepared counterarguments designed to change the target's mind; at the fourth level the advocate focuses on the target and elaborates on the advantages to the target of taking the desired action (Johnston, 1994).

Operating at the fourth and highest level of perspective-taking requires knowledge of the basic demographic characteristics of a target as well as the person's beliefs, attitudes, and values. The most effective persuasion optimizes the similarity between the persuader and the target on as many relevant dimensions as possible. Thus, for example, an advocacy team appearing before an all-male legislative committee might do well to include at least one man among the presenters. Further, the most persuasive presentations emphasize the similarity in beliefs, attitudes, and values between the advocate and the target.

Suppose, for example, that several discrete groups—the media, school board authorities, state legislators, the families themselves, and other advocates—will read a report on the effects of school fees on low-income families. The report must speak credibly to all of these groups, but the primary target may be state legislators considering a bill that will expand the use of school fees. The report should carefully address legislators' rather predictable needs. This calls for impeccable accuracy, concise but well-supported argument, avoidance of moralizing or blaming, and clear presentation of a solution to the problem. The report should acknowledge the constraints that legislators may face in adopting a solution, perhaps acknowledging that "no one wants to increase taxes, and we all want to support our schools." The next step is to help legislators understand that we can and must support schools without stigmatizing, discouraging, and damaging children from low-income families.

Advocates can tap into core American values to increase the likelihood that their audience will identify with them and be receptive to their message. Steele and Redding (1962) conducted a study of American values. Their results, which were remarkably similar to those identified in a 1940 study, are still relevant. The following list summarizes these core values.[3]

- *Puritan and pioneer morality:* Hard work, honesty, self-discipline, and cooperation
- *Individuality:* Personal integrity, the value of the life of even one person, personal rights
- *Achievement and success:* Personal success, money, self-made achievement, social status
- *Change and progress:* "New and improved," future and present always better than past, change for better
- *Ethical equality:* All equal before God; one person, one vote
- *Effort and optimism:* No problem too big
- *Efficiency, practicality, and pragmatism:* Getting things done
- *Rejection of authority:* Power of individual; freedom and rights over duties and obligations
- *Science and secular rationality:* Reason, control, prediction
- *Sociality:* Networking
- *Material comfort:* Happiness can be bought
- *Quantification:* Bigger, faster, more, longer, quantity over quality
- *External conformity:* Popularity, social status
- *Humor:* Leveling influence
- *Generosity and consideration:* Welfare, benevolence
- *Patriotism:* Loyalty to America and its values over loyalty to nation of origin

By appealing to these values, an advocate can generate agreement and identification in a wide range of target audiences. Of course, for a given argument, only some of the core values might apply, and audiences vary in the strength with which they embrace each value. Advocates should identify the most important core values held by their target audience. An advocate speaking before a group of social workers, for example, should include "appreciation for diversity" as a core value held by the audience. Someone appearing before the chamber of commerce might emphasize the contributions of free enterprise to our way of life.

---

3. From D. Johnston, *The Art and Science of Persuasion,* p. 227. © 1994. Reprinted with permission of the McGraw-Hill Companies.

It is important to be subtle and judicious in any appeal to the values of an audience. Any audience will be offended by manipulation or pandering. Condescension or an underlying message that the audience is ignorant or unfeeling is an immediate turnoff. An advocate's moral outrage on behalf of clients can alienate an audience by demonizing anyone who does not share the same fervor.

Composing the Argument

Three strategies can enhance the effectiveness of most policy-related arguments: anticipating opposing arguments, using authority, and integrating analytic material (facts and figures) with anecdotal material (stories and illustrations).

Anticipating the Opposition.   As a general rule, advocates should anticipate and address arguments that will be made by the opposition. In the field of communication this is referred to as a "two-sided" argument. Two-sided arguments present one perspective and then anticipate counterarguments. They are contrasted with "one-sided" arguments, which present only the perspective the speaker is advocating.

Some advocates believe it is simpler to offer one-sided arguments, noting that a risk in two-sided arguments is that you will work against yourself by presenting the opposing argument. But most summaries of communication research on this issue suggest that one-sided arguments should be used only under limited circumstances, such as when the audience is already in favor of your position, is easily confused on the issue, or is not aware of the opposition (Johnston, 1994; O'Keefe, 1992). The final case, in which the audience is unaware of opposition, should be treated with care. If a one-sided argument is presented and the audience becomes aware of the opposing point of view, an advocate can lose both credibility and the argument.

Generally an advocate should anticipate the opposition and present a two-sided argument or, at a minimum, acknowledge opposing views. Communication scholars recommend this approach when the audience is sophisticated, aware of contradictory positions, and not already in agreement with your position (Johnston, 1994). Effective arguments not only anticipate opposing arguments but present counterarguments that will effectively inoculate the audience against persuasion by the opposition.

B O X 3.1   An Approach to Avoid When Composing Arguments

We have all heard "slippery slope" arguments. When we were young, our teachers may have told us, "If I do this for you, I'll have to do it for *all* of the children." More sophisticated forms of this argument surface in contemporary debates such as the controversy over assisted suicide. Opponents argue that permitting assisted suicide for the terminally ill will lead to euthanasia of the disabled or even the unattractive. Slippery slope arguments have what my grandmother used to call "ear appeal." They sound good. They make sense at first blush. But upon careful consideration they are seldom persuasive. Indeed, a good debater can undermine an opponent's credibility by pointing out that the person has used a slippery slope argument.

In the school fees debate, advocates supporting waivers should anticipate that their opponents will argue that some parents will misuse the program, claiming waivers when they do not really need them. This argument might be defused by suggesting a simple certification process under which children eligible for free school lunches are automatically eligible for fee waivers.

Use of Authority.   Advocates rely on authority to persuade. Their authority might stem from the care and accuracy of their observations (*logos*) or their personal credibility (*ethos*). Thus personal or professional experiences, or even academic credentials, might contribute to an advocate's authority. Other sources are scientific, moral, or political authorities. Legal authority for an argument can stem, as we have seen, from a variety of sources, including the state and federal constitutions. Community leaders might also contribute authority to an argument.

Understanding the audience can influence an advocate's use of authority. The selection of authorities can either alienate or impress, depending on the audience. A group of secular humanists is likely to be more susceptible to the authority of definitive research than to religious authority. Colleagues might be impressed by the use of professional experience. State legislators in the Bible Belt might be persuaded by a well-chosen biblical passage.

Combining Analytic and Anecdotal Material.   A corollary to the observation that most arguments are presented before multiple audiences is the requirement that arguments speak to people using multiple communication approaches. Some members in an audience will be intrigued and impressed by the *logos* of an argument—the facts and figures. But others will find them dull or incomprehensible. Those who are either bored or intimidated by careful statistical analysis may perk right up when *pathos* is brought in through a strong, illustrative example.

Communications research underscores the importance of examples or stories. O'Keefe's (1992) review of research on the effectiveness of examples as compared to statistics suggested that examples are generally more effective with all but the most sophisticated audiences. This is consistent with Douglass's (1997) analysis of the nearly effective antihomosexual campaign of the Oregon Citizens Alliance (OCA) in 1993. Douglass wondered how such an unsophisti-

---

BOX 3.2   Another Approach to Avoid When Composing Arguments

Policy makers, representatives of the media, and the public at large have grown impatient with what I call "Ain't it awful?" arguments. These arguments outline, in exquisite detail, the horrible conditions an advocate has discovered—and they stop at that point. Although such a presentation can reflect a tremendous amount of effort and study, it leaves an audience feeling frustrated and impotent. Advocacy presentations should generally close with at least one specific recommendation that is likely to address the problem. At a minimum, the person presenting the complaint should recommend further study of the problem that has been identified. Beyond this, discussion of possible solutions —particularly those that have proven effective in different settings or with similar problems—is always advisable.

cated campaign could have led to the near passage of Measure 9, an effort to amend Oregon's constitution to define homosexuality as "abnormal, wrong, unnatural and perverse." After careful study, he concluded that the OCA's effective use of narrative (even without compelling analytic arguments) was the key to their success in securing a 47 percent "yes" vote on Measure 9. Fisher (1987) also provides evidence of the persuasive effectiveness of narrative.

The value of illustrations, such as graphics, should not be ignored. An effective presentation incorporates multiple approaches to communication: facts and figures, illustrative examples, and symbols. This multifaceted approach will engage a diverse audience and employ both *logos* and *pathos* to set the stage for persuasion.

Successful Delivery

Many social workers find oral presentation of their arguments stressful, particularly when it occurs in a formal setting such as a legislative hearing. We struggle with our fear, and we feel awkward dealing with some aspects of the setting, such as microphones and cameras. There are many self-help books available to help people overcome their fear of public speaking (e.g., Hoff, 1988).

I believe the essence of successful speaking is *intent*—knowing why you are there, and keeping your energy and your presentation totally focused on your message. Remember that everything else is peripheral. I like to develop presentations with three to five points and use the time prior to delivery to breathe deeply and review those points.

Organization of an oral presentation should be informed by research on memory. People remember what is said first and last, and they tend to forget what happened in the middle. A simple rule of organization is, "Tell them what you will say. Say it. Then tell them what you said."

A written script should be used only as a last resort. If you are going to be in front of television cameras or hundreds of people, the likelihood of severe stage fright is high and a script is a useful tool. Otherwise, an outline with key points and evidence should suffice. Use of a script often results in a lifeless presentation.

Any contact that acknowledges the audience's nonverbal communication enlivens your presentation. If the audience laughs or looks skeptical, a speaker should acknowledge their reaction and incorporate it into the presentation. This responsiveness will involve the audience and make the presentation more like a dialogue than a lecture.

Presentations can also be made in writing. Format is a vital component of all persuasive communication. Advocacy speeches and documents should be organized and concise. All policy reports should include a one- to two-page executive summary for use by members of the press who have limited time and need quotable material. The executive summary will also help legislators who are pressed for time and are simply unable to read every report they receive. Policy makers invariably appreciate a summary of key policies in the area, objective facts and figures, and clear recommendations. All audiences appreciate a table of contents and clear, jargon-free language.

Thus far, our discussion has focused on the more formal aspects of advocacy, such as public debate and presentation. Another element goes on "behind closed doors" and involves advocates in negotiation and compromise. A vital consideration in many advocacy efforts is when to hold out for an ultimate goal and when to accept a compromise. The decision to compromise is never easy, and it can be controversial. In the following section we will consider some factors involved in negotiation and compromise.

NEGOTIATION AND COMPROMISE

Politics has been called "the art of compromise." Effective compromises are crafted to provide each party something highly valued while asking that each give up something of lesser value. The net result is an increase in overall satisfaction. Preparation for compromise is an exercise in clarification of values. This exercise involves identifying one's own values (What is our "do-or-die" position?) as well as anticipating the values of the opposition (What is *their* "do-or-die" position?). Both questions deserve careful consideration.

Tedeschi and Rosenfeld (1980) offered a useful—if more technical—approach to analyzing positions in negotiation. They suggest that all parties have a status quo point, a resistance point, and a level of aspiration. If the negotiations fail, both parties will be at their status quo point and might as well not have engaged in the discussion. The resistance point is analogous to what I have called the do-or-die position. It is the minimum results required for the parties to reach an agreement. The distance between these two points, technically called the bargaining range, is the crux of the negotiation. If that distance is too great, negotiations will fail. If not, the outcome will depend on the skill and power of the negotiators. The level of aspiration is what each party hopes will come from the negotiation. Both will be satisfied if they come close to this level. These three potential outcomes have been called a bargainer's "utility schedule" (Tedeschi & Rosenfeld, 1980). In a compromise, both parties should clarify their positions and estimate the positions of other parties involved.

Unless an advocate has become familiar with the opposition, either through repeated exposure or through inside information, it will be difficult to anticipate their priorities. Therefore, a first stage in the process of negotiation is usually an exchange of information concerning goals and priorities. This exchange may not be framed as such, but a proposed "informational meeting" might have, as its hidden agenda, an opportunity to introduce a compromise.

USE OF RELATIONSHIP

Social workers have long understood the pivotal importance of relationship. As the advocacy experience described at the beginning of this chapter illustrated, advocacy is not about allies and enemies. It is about people, and today's opponent may be tomorrow's ally. While it is tempting, and sometimes emotionally gratifying, to cast the opposition as evil demons, this approach is ultimately detrimental. A dispute, debate, or disagreement is an opportunity to build a relationship with the opposition. Social advocates seldom have the financial resources to influence policy with money, but our capacity to establish and maintain relationships can be every bit as effective as the perks delivered by corporate lobbyists.

Social exchange theory offers a useful perspective for understanding relationships in the policy arena. Within this framework, reciprocity is the glue that holds society together. Reciprocity is simply give and take. It is the sense that a favor entails an obligation to reciprocate. Social workers are frequently given opportunities to do favors, as when a policy maker asks for information or advice, a candidate asks for a contribution or an endorsement, a colleague asks for moral support, or an administrator asks for supportive testimony. These requests are opportunities to build relationships.

Over the course of their professional careers, social workers give and receive assistance to the point where they and their contacts forget who owes whom. Some exchange theorists argue that friendship is simply a reciprocal relationship that has reached this point. Both parties feel vaguely indebted to the other, and each would help the other without hesitation—partly to fulfill a sense of obligation but partly because "that's what friends do."

In addition to this kind of exchange-based relationship, advocates enjoy the opportunity to build alliances based on mutual interests and shared respect. A long-term commitment to building supportive relationships will enhance an advocate's effectiveness. Sometimes this commitment requires separating the messenger from the message—acknowledging that, although you disagree with another's views, you are fond of each other as people. I have seen state legislators debate vigorously, almost to the point (I thought) of coming to blows. After the debate, in quieter quarters, the combatants checked in with each other, apologized for their excesses, and affirmed their commitment to the relationship. This capacity to sustain relationship through controversy is vital to effective advocacy.

BUILDING AND MAINTAINING COALITIONS

In a pluralistic democracy, coalitions can be quite powerful. The challenge for advocates is to identify potential coalition partners and then to establish clear guidelines for maintaining the coalition.

Potential coalition partners are groups and individuals who share an advocate's goal. A coalition is not a marriage—these groups need not necessarily be personally or philosophically compatible. Despite their differences they can work together to achieve a common goal. My first job taught me about unlikely partners in coalition. I was employed by the Oregon Environmental Council to organize a coalition of diverse interests that would focus on maintaining stream flows (keeping water in rivers). Our first task was to identify parties who shared our interest in keeping water in rivers. As it turned out, the Water Action Coalition, as it was eventually called, united the efforts of Native Americans, commercial fishermen, sports fishermen, and environmentalists. These groups were on opposite sides of the fence on other issues, but when it came to minimum stream flows they united to form a remarkably effective coalition. On a much grander scale, the civil rights movement involved a powerful coalition of religious and labor leaders from White and African American communities who demonstrated that they could transcend their differences and work together for a common cause.

Although common goals are an essential ingredient, a shared purpose is no guarantee of a smoothly functioning coalition. At some levels coalition building can become an intensely personal business. People who disrespect or loathe each other can make difficult coalition partners. An organization known for its confrontational tactics and extreme positions may not be able to build an effective coalition, nor can an individual advocate known for alienating or embarrassing the opposition. Coalitions are built and maintained by moderates whose positions and tactics are palatable to most potential partners—people who get along well with others. This does not mean that the more extreme personalities or groups cannot instigate a coalition, only that they may have a harder time facilitating ongoing operations or recruiting potential partners.

Coalitions require care and tending. Roles must be carefully defined. For example, it is vital that partners agree about how they will make decisions, what types of issues they will (and will not) address, how partners will be informed about developments, and who is (and is not) empowered to speak on behalf of the coalition. A general rule of coalition maintenance is "When in doubt, talk it out." Particularly in the early stages of their development, coalitions need both routine ways to communicate (e.g., monthly meetings) and emergency routes of conversation (e.g., e-mail, phone trees). The emergency routes are useful when a partner identifies the need for immediate action and can contact coalition members for their feedback and agreement prior to committing the coalition to a course of action.

Sometimes in the heat of an advocacy effort involving a coalition, a decision maker will approach one member of the coalition and offer a deal. The advocate is asked, on behalf of the coalition, to agree to a compromise. An advocate once told me, "This goes with the territory." Thus it is vital for all members of a coalition to understand who is and who is not empowered to negotiate on behalf of the coalition. Agreement on this point should be an early item on any coalition's advocacy agenda.

EMPOWERMENT IN POLICY PRACTICE

Empowerment is a vital component of policy practice and a crucial element of long-term social change. When we speak on behalf of others we are generally less effective than when we empower others to speak on behalf of themselves.

This is in part because our motives can be suspect when we claim to represent the interests of clients. Opponents argue, for instance, that when we advocate for increased program budgets or supports for the poor, we are actually trying to enhance our professional stature and line our own pockets.

When clients speak for themselves, they enjoy special credibility. As Pat Powers and others have noted (Hardcastle, Wenocur, & Powers, 1996), an advocate's credibility is greatest when the policy under consideration has directly affected either the advocate or a member of the advocate's family. For example, a former welfare mother or the sister of a person with a disability brings personal credibility to an advocacy effort. This credibility can be more influential than professional experience and degrees, moral and legal authority, and good science put together. Unfortunately, the same forces that generate personal credibility with regard to social problems (poverty, disability, prejudice, and discrimination) work against effective involvement in the policy arena.

We can empower people by helping them secure the knowledge, skills, resources, and opportunities to advocate for themselves. When Utah Issues held workshops to inform parents about the school fee issue and waiver regulations, it empowered parents by providing knowledge. When a social worker coaches a welfare mother through testimony before the state legislature, the client is empowered by acquiring new skills. When an activist hunts down a bus to transport children from low-income families to a march on the capital, he is empowering people by securing resources. When a bureaucrat suggests that clients be represented on an advisory committee, she empowers clients by securing an opportunity for them to speak out on behalf of themselves.

While direct advocacy places social workers on the firing line of controversial social issues, empowerment interventions allow them to operate in the background. Sometimes organizations and individuals who find the confrontational aspects of social advocacy unpleasant or abhorrent will find empowerment efforts perfectly acceptable. For example, a foundation that would never fund lobbying efforts may be willing to support client education. Similarly, a public official who would oppose expansion of welfare benefits may support a program to enhance the communication skills of welfare recipients, making it more likely that they will be able to secure jobs.

ETHICAL ISSUES IN POLICY PRACTICE

Some people think politics and policy practice are sordid activities. This perspective is sometimes used to justify deviating from ethical standards. In his now-classic work *Rules for Radicals,* Saul Alinsky (1972) offered another rationale for deviation. Alinsky argued that in social activism, as in war, the ends justify the means. He felt that the power differential between social advocates and policy makers was so huge that advocates were justified in suspending the rules of ethical conduct to achieve important policy victories.

It is important to keep in mind, however, that Alinsky was writing in a different era of social advocacy—a war truly was being fought, and advocacy was a life-or-death proposition. Further, Alinsky was writing for activists who were excluded from the realm of policy decisions. Unlike most of Alinsky's street-level activists, social work advocates are professionals. We have colleagues in most state legislatures, and to a great extent we are insiders in the policy arena. The power differential between social work advocates and some policy makers may be substantial, but it is never big enough to justify deviating from the rules of ethical communication.

In this section we will consider several ethical aspects of policy practice, first asking whether social workers have an ethical obligation to engage in advocacy, then exploring the ethical dimensions of two common practices: sharpening the message and using clients. We will then explore issues of confidentiality and conclude the section by describing the characteristics of ethical persuasion.

Is Advocacy an Ethical Obligation?

Mark Ezell (2001) observed that the National Association of Social Workers (NASW) Code of Ethics includes several statements that may support an ethical obligation to do advocacy:

- Social workers should advocate for living conditions conducive to the fulfillment of basic human needs and should promote social, economic, political, and cultural values and institutions that are compatible with the realization of social justice (Ethical Standard 6.01).

- Social workers should engage in social and political action that seeks to ensure that all people have equal access to the resources, employment, services, and opportunities they require to meet their basic human needs and to develop fully (Ethical Standard 6.04[a]).

- Social workers should act to prevent and eliminate domination of, exploitation of, and discrimination against any person, group, or class on the basis of race, ethnicity, national origin, color, sex, sexual orientation, age, marital status, political belief, religion, or mental or physical disability (Ethical Standard 6.04[d]).

The wording of these statements suggests that social workers are strongly encouraged, but not required, to undertake these activities and goals. The operative word here is "should." Had that word been replaced with "must" or "will," the Code could have been interpreted differently. Nonetheless, policy practice represents a powerful means for carrying out the professional mission of promoting social justice and human well-being.

Sharpening the Message

The practice of sharpening the message or "getting to the gist" is common in storytelling (Gilovich, 1991). We weed out extraneous details, narrowing our presentation to include only those critical facts that convey our message in the most efficient way possible. Dorothea Dix probably used this approach in her many presentations on the treatment of the insane. She "sharpened" her message, and as a result was (perhaps rightly) accused of exaggeration and outright lies.

Modern advocates often do the same thing, seeking and presenting information that supports their case while ignoring contradictory facts. This common practice has both ethical and practical ramifications for social work professionals. Social workers have a clear ethical prohibition against deceit. The NASW Code of Ethics includes several statements that emphasize the importance of truthfulness. Integrity is identified as a core value of the profession, and the Code requires that "social workers behave in a trustworthy manner."

Does this prohibition against deceit require us to present facts that do not support our position? The line between "sharpening the message" and deceit may be fuzzy, but both practices threaten the credibility of social advocates. In the advocacy arena, social workers have little to offer but professional and personal credibility. We do not give huge campaign contributions. We seldom control committee assignments or large numbers of votes. Instead, we strive to represent the disenfranchised and the vulnerable in a way that is credible, balanced, and persuasive. As professionals, social workers should emphasize balance and accuracy in our advocacy efforts, even at the risk of delivering a message that is less focused or dramatic than we might like.

Using Clients

Involving clients in advocacy also brings social work practitioners into delicate ethical territory. For some clients, like Annie Boone (Chapter 12), the opportunity to become involved in advocacy is empowering and transformative. For others, however, it may be terrifying, humiliating, and personally damaging.

How can a practitioner determine whether it is ethical (as opposed to advisable) to involve a client in an advocacy effort? The concept of self-determination, a core social work value, provides some direction here. When a client chooses to enter into an advocacy effort, with full knowledge of what this effort is expected to entail, that client is exercising the right to self-determination. The social worker's obligation is not to protect the client from discomfort or to promise immediate results but to inform the client—insofar as possible—what can be expected.

A typology proposed by Martin Buber offers another way to judge the ethics of client involvement. Buber suggests that we can hold two distinct attitudes toward other people, an "I–thou" attitude or an "I–it" attitude. An "I–thou" attitude recognizes the individuality of the other and treats the person as worthy of respect. An "I–it" attitude treats the other as an object designed to serve the communicator's selfish needs (Friedman, 1960). Ethical client involvement requires that clients be treated with respect and that communication be characterized by honesty and directness, without the use of power or subordination. Clients must never be treated as a means to an end. The advocacy effort must not "use" clients, but "engage" them in a mutual effort to achieve a shared goal.

A practitioner cannot always predict how the client will respond to advocacy experiences, but it is essential to make sure the client is as informed as possible about what to expect. A social worker who worries about "using" a client should consider whether the client was able to make an independent decision about involvement, and whether the client fully understands, based on the social worker's explanation, what to expect, both of the advocacy experience itself and of its potential results.

Keeping Confidences

Advocacy is a public act, in a public arena where one should assume that "there are no secrets." This may seem strange, since we know on its face that this assumption is probably not true. Nevertheless, it is a useful assumption to live by. Whenever an advocate begins to think the client will "never find out about it," the advocate is probably taking a risk that could jeopardize a relationship, or worse. In policy practice it is best to assume that every word you utter and every act you commit will become public knowledge. Advocates live in a fish bowl, and the more controversial the cause, the more transparent the bowl.

A corollary to "there are no secrets" is the danger of receiving confidences. When you are engaged in policy practice, people may offer to share confidences with you. They may offer secrets so tantalizing and interesting that it is hard to resist hearing them. Resist you must; however, simply as an act of personal protection. Consider this: If this person is willing to tell you this secret, how many other people have been told? And even if you are not the one who reveals it, how can you ensure that no one else will? Thus, unless you have a strong relationship with someone in the political arena, it is best to avoid these "dangerous confidences."

Of course, it goes without saying that if you do accept someone's confidence you must guard it carefully. Sometimes it is unclear that something is being told "in confidence." Most of us have had the painful experience of inadvertently revealing a confidence we thought was common knowledge. When someone tells us something that seems sensitive or newsworthy it is important to ask that person, "Am I free to pass this on and give you as the source? Or would you prefer that I hold it in confidence?" This practice will build trust in the relationship.

CHARACTERISTICS OF ETHICAL PERSUASION

In the marketplace of ideas, ethical persuasion is a two-way process, with expectations for both advocate and listener. Johnston (1994) offered a summary of the expectations of both communicators in an ethical exchange:[4]

1. Persuaders are clear, direct, and honest about their intentions.
2. Communicators promote mutual respect and mutual satisfaction of goals, rather than self-interests.

4. From D. Johnston, *The Art and Science of Persuasion*, p. 72. Copyright © 1994. Reprinted with permission of the McGraw-Hill Companies.

3. Communicators use strategies that confirm others and preserve the dignity of others.

4. Communicators seek input and elaboration from each other.

5. Persuaders avoid the use of active deception and the withholding of relevant information, except when the truth may cause significant harm to others.

6. Communicators listen and critically process each other's messages.

7. Communicators welcome and explore dissent.

8. Communicators analyze their own and others' biases without defending or threatening their own or others' egos.

9. All participants in the persuasion process share the ethical responsibility of persuasive outcomes and respond to each other with resoluteness and openness.

10. Communicators weigh opinions equally, rather than on the basis of individual power or status.

11. Communicators assess probable consequences of their message on others.

12. Communicators employ persuasion to celebrate the human qualities of diversity, personality, intelligence, passion for beliefs, humor, and reasoning.

13. Communicators encourage social discussion and social contact.

14. Communicators critically challenge claims of certainty and truth.

15. Decisions are subject to revision over time.

16. The relative power of the persuader and the receiver determines the degree of ethical responsibility.

17. Communicators maintain free speech, but the probability of harmful consequences guides the ethical decision to produce a persuasive message.

In an advocacy exchange, both advocate and listener are responsible for ensuring that the debate about social issues results in the best possible decision. Both parties share an obligation to ensure civil, fair-minded interaction.

Clearly, advocates cannot control the behavior of their audiences—and audiences sometimes misbehave. It takes only a short time in the advocacy trenches to encounter a listener who is more intent on humiliating the advocate than on hearing a new perspective. Indeed, most experienced advocates can tell horror stories of public attacks by legislators or elected officials.

It is difficult not to take attacks personally, but that is exactly what an advocate must do. I believe it is helpful for beginning advocates who are under attack to ask themselves why the official is behaving in this way. The person may be grandstanding or playing to a constituency that is hostile to your position. He or she may be threatened by your effectiveness or may just be in a bad mood. It also helps to recall that public attack is a violation of the "rules of engagement," and the attacker's colleagues probably view it that way. They may be embarrassed by the attack. Indeed, a virulent and irrational attack by an opposing legislator may advance an advocate's cause better than the advocate's own arguments![5]

LEGAL CONSIDERATIONS IN POLICY PRACTICE

Some readers of this book may be independently wealthy and engage in social work as philanthropy. The rest of us will be using other people's money. Such use imposes legal obligations. Technical rules are often difficult to understand, remember, and apply. You will find it useful to remind yourself, from time to time, who is providing the funds for your activity and what those persons expect of you. Social advocates often find themselves working for the government or for public charities. Some of the limitations on these groups are discussed in the following sections.

The Hatch Act

The Hatch Act is a federal statute passed in 1939 to regulate the political activity of civil servants. Its primary focus was ensuring that federal employees did not use the power or resources of their offices to promote political candidates. The act was amended in 1993 to allow some political involvement by federal employees. The Hatch Act also applies to employees of private, state, and local organizations whose activities are financed by federal loans or grants (e.g., Head Start employees). Most states have adopted provisions similar to the Hatch Act for state employees.

Employees who are covered by the Hatch Act are not permitted to do any of the following:

- Use their official authority or influence to affect an election
- Solicit or discourage political activity of anyone with business before their agency
- Solicit or receive political contributions
- Be candidates for public office in *partisan* elections
- Engage in political activity while on duty, in a government office, wearing an official uniform, or using a government vehicle
- Wear partisan political buttons while on duty

The key to Hatch Act compliance is avoiding misuse of the power or authority of government office. The act certainly does not rule out all political involvement by government employees. They can, for example, serve as candidates in

---

5. Sometimes a beginning advocate may feel under attack when legislators or officials are asking questions the advocate cannot answer. In such situations, it is best to admit ignorance and offer to find the answer and provide it to the questioner later.

nonpartisan elections (e.g., school board), register and vote as they choose, contribute money to political organizations, attend fundraising functions, be active and hold office in a political party or club, and campaign for or against candidates in partisan elections.

Preserving Tax-Exempt Status

Groups that rely on public support usually seek to qualify for tax-deductible contributions. Such groups are described in Section 501(c)(3) of the Internal Revenue Code and are therefore often referred to as "501(c)(3)'s" or "501(c)(3) organizations." Donors can usually make contributions to such organizations free of estate and gift tax as well as federal and state income tax.

These attributes "stretch" the donor's dollars. Suppose Mr. A is willing to part with $100 of his personal wealth to support your organization. If he makes a gift of $150 and receives a tax deduction of the same amount he may "save" $50 in taxes, so he is out of pocket only $100 while your organization receives $150 in revenue. Special provisions in the tax code can help stretch contributions in a variety of ways. These include special treatment for appreciated property, private foundations, charitable remainder and charitable lead trusts (including trusts established during life and by will), charitable annuities, and "endowment funds" (usually mutual funds) permitting current deductions for future contributions. If you become involved with the "development" (fundraising) side of your organization, you may need to learn more about these provisions.

The extra $50 from Mr. A, along with the other money and benefits, comes from the government in the form of taxes not collected. Naturally there are "strings attached." A few organizations are unwilling to accept the strings. They may still be nonprofit entities and often are tax-exempt—that is, they do not pay income tax per Internal Revenue Code Sections 501(c)(4) to 501(c)(22). However, unless the rules of Section 501(c)(3) are followed, there will be no deductions available to donors—no "stretching" of the donor dollar.

Perhaps the most famous example of a nonprofit organization that decided to forgo 501(c)(3) status is the Sierra Club. This group was formed for summer treks in the mountains and preservation of the lands visited. In the mid-1960s the Sierra Club found itself fighting to preserve the Grand Canyon from dams. The organization lobbied Congress to oppose reclamation projects proposed by state and local governments. Using government funds to influence legislation, particularly legislation supported by other governments, raises serious issues. The Sierra Club decided, in effect, to stop taking government handouts. It gave up its 501(c)(3) status and continued its advocacy efforts.

Social advocates are likely to find themselves in a similar position. You may be trying to persuade legislators or other policy makers to take actions opposed by other parts of government. Here are some of the rules that apply:

A 501(c)(3) organization is one in which "no substantial part of the activities . . . is carrying on propaganda or otherwise attempting to influence legislation . . . and which does not participate in, or intervene in (including the publishing or distributing of statements) any political campaign on behalf of (or in opposition to) any candidate for public office."[6] For public charities that wish to engage in limited political activities, Congress has provided what is known as a "Conable[7] election," or "safe harbor"[8] that may offer greater ability to act with less risk of challenge. The Conable election may be selected by filing a form with the IRS.[9]

Under the safe harbor (or Conable election) clause, certain activities are explicitly permitted without the need to report them as lobbying. The following activities are included:

- Making available results of nonpartisan analysis, study, or research
- Providing technical advice or assistance to a political body in response to a written request from such body
- Appearances before or communications to legislative bodies that affect the existence of the organization, its powers and duties, or its tax exemption
- Communication between an organization and its members with respect to legislation of interest to the members, other than efforts to encourage members or others to attempt to influence legislation

Under the Conable election, any communication with a government official or employee who is not a member of the legislative body considering action (e.g., a staff member or executive) is permitted as long as it is not intended to influence legislation.

Influencing legislation (lobbying) includes attempts to influence the opinion of the general public or any segment of the public or any legislative body. It includes matters before local government bodies and extends to any initiative, referendum, constitutional amendment, motion, resolution, or bill.

Under the Conable election, the amount of "influencing legislation" that can be done is clear, relatively easy to calculate, and once determined, allows the organization to make informed choices about its activities. The 501(c)(3) knows that when it is really critical to lobby (or influence legislation) it can do so without fear of jeopardizing its tax status. The amount that can be spent to influence legislation is based on an organization's total budget, not including fundraising expenses, and may not exceed $1,000,000 per year regardless of the budget. The amount of permitted expenditure for an organization is called its "lobbying nontaxable amount." If the limits on this amount are "normally" exceeded by 150 percent, the organization will lose its 501(c)(3) status.

The preceding discussion is a summary of current law, which may change. Details have been omitted. You may wish to consult Internal Revenue Service Publication 557, *Tax Exempt Status for Your Organization*. The Alliance for Justice,

---

6. Code §501(c)(3)

7. The Conable election, which is found in §501(h) of the Internal Revenue Code, is named after Barber Benjamin Conable Jr., a congressional representative for the state of New York from 1965 to 1985.

8. Code §§503(h) and 4911.

9. Currently made by filing Treasury Form 5768.

located in Washington, DC, also helps nonprofits understand laws governing their advocacy efforts. There are also separate laws in many states that govern these activities and require reporting by any entity that engages in lobbying.

While you should be aware of these laws, don't let them distract you from your mission. Laws are like the rules of a game. To some extent they may control how you advocate, but they need not and should not affect your long-term goals.

SUMMARY: QUESTION THE INEVITABLE AND CHALLENGE THE INVINCIBLE

David Gil (1998) criticized most frameworks for policy analysis, arguing "that major aspects of prevailing institutional and cultural realities tend to be treated as 'constants' rather than as 'variables'" (pp. 117–118). Gil urges social workers to question contextual factors that most people take for granted. Today these might include the "right" of corporations to make a profit or the inevitability of zero-sum budgeting.[10] Too often, social advocates are stymied by opponents who argue that their proposals would "cost too much money." Keeping their values in sight, social workers can question these constants, noting that failure to solve a social problem may ultimately prove more costly, or arguing that the amount spent on humanitarian values is dwarfed (as it is in most community budgets) by the amount committed to economic development or even transportation infrastructure.

This chapter offered several approaches to policy analysis. Each of these tools directs attention to a different aspect of social policy. The process-based approaches (need assessment and Prince Policy Appraisal) can be used to assess policy development. Product analysis can be used to systematically describe the "product" of policy development process—that is, the program itself. Performance-based methods such as cost–benefit analysis enable us to describe the impact of a social policy. Finally, the social justice perspective focuses our attention on the justice of a policy. This approach is new, and you may find it unsatisfying. We all want formulas for simple answers to whether a policy is good or fair. But in our complex world, simple answers are usually wrong. By addressing the questions in the social justice framework you will develop a deep, nuanced perspective on social policy. Informed by your personal philosophy, this perspective will represent your professional assessment of the impact of a policy on social justice.

---

10. Zero-sum budgeting assumes that increased funding in one human service area must be offset by reduced funding in another area. In some settings (such as personal budgeting), this approach is appropriate and necessary, but in the complex arena of federal (or even state) budgeting, it can artificially restrict the range of options available for advocates. Along these lines, it was astonishing to witness how quickly after September 11, 2001, Congress found billions of dollars to bail out the airline industry and mount a military response. Prior to the terrorist attacks, a budget request of such magnitude would have faced stiff opposition.

In this chapter we also provided tools for policy practice, perhaps best summarized as "questioning the inevitable and challenging the invincible." Our examination of the school fee controversy in Utah illustrated some important themes in policy practice:

- *The struggle is long.* Social advocates usually strive for extremely high goals such as "the elimination of injustice." We must celebrate the victories and acknowledge the setbacks without losing sight of our long-term objectives.

- *Every individual counts.* Each contribution to an advocacy effort is important and deserves acknowledgment.

- *"Us vs. them" does not apply here.* There is no evil conspiracy to deprive vulnerable Americans of the means to live. Sometimes people take opposing positions, but that does not mean they are enemies. The better you understand the reasons for their position, the more effectively you will be able to address their opposition.

- *Social policy is more than legislation.* It is easy for advocates to focus on getting a bill passed and forget that beyond passage of legislation they must consider regulations created by the executive branch, budgets that limit program services, and judicial opinions that may alter a bill's impact. Effective advocacy happens in all three branches of government.

Beyond these themes, this chapter introduced a philosophical view of policy practice as participation in a marketplace of ideas. We discussed Aristotle's suggestion that effective persuasion incorporates *logos, pathos,* and *ethos,* offering specific tactics for advocacy, coalition-building, and client empowerment. We considered five distinct approaches to policy analysis: need assessment, Prince Policy Appraisal, product analysis, cost–benefit analysis, and social justice analysis. We addressed ethical issues in policy practice and argued that responsibility for effective debate is shared by the advocate and the audience. The chapter closed with a brief review of major legal considerations governing policy practice by social workers, and with an exhortation to *question the inevitable, and challenge the invincible.*

KEYWORDS

Policy evaluation	Advocacy and social work	Social reform
Social policy analysis		Program evaluation

THINK ABOUT IT

1. You are the director of a small antipoverty organization, and you have been invited to join a well-established welfare-rights coalition. After agreeing to join, you find the coalition's tactics are so confrontational that your continued participation risks alienating some of the organizations that have given your organization money. What should you do?

2. A local bank that vigorously (and, you think, unethically) opposed your efforts to increase the supply of affordable housing last year offers to give your organization a significant amount of money for its organizing efforts this year. Would you take the money? Why or why not?

3. The homeless shelter in your town has hired you to do a study of "repeaters"—that is, people who come back to the shelter over and over but don't seem to change their lives. The shelter director sees these people as a problem and wants to identify them early and keep them out of the shelter. Your results suggest that these "repeaters" tend to have intractable problems such as substance abuse and mental illness. When you submit your report, the director calls and withdraws his previous invitation for you to present it before the board of directors. What, if anything, should you do?

4. The band director from an inner-city school asks for your advice. The band has been invited to compete in a prestigious contest. The director has enough money to buy new instruments. The band's current instruments are old and dented and cannot produce good music. However, she does not have funds to purchase new uniforms for everyone. She is thinking about asking students to purchase their own uniforms, except for those who cannot afford them. What are her alternatives? What factors should she consider in making her decision?

5. Describe how you would incorporate Aristotle's three components (*logos, pathos,* and *ethos*) into a policy presentation on school fees or some other topic of interest to you.

6. Violence often results when society consistently thwarts an individual's effort to meet basic needs. This perspective contrasts sharply with a punitive approach to those who perpetrate violence. Using the Palestinian intifada as an example, consider the advantages and disadvantages of this interpretation of violence.

WEB-BASED EXERCISES

For direct links to all the sites in these exercises, log on to the Student Companion Site for this book at academic.cengage.com/social_work/barusch, and choose Chapter 3.

1. Go to www.statepolicy.com, the website for a social work advocacy group called Influencing State Policy. Click on Newsletter Archives and read the latest news from rowdy social workers.

2. Go to www.iscvt.org, and subscribe to the newsletter of the Institute for Sustainable Communities. It's easy to unsubscribe, and the publication will give you news about the activities of social justice advocates around the world.

SUGGESTED RESOURCES

Cohen, D., de la Vega, R., & Watson, G. (2001). *Advocacy for Social Justice: A Global Action and Reflection Guide*. Bloomfield, CT: Kumarian Press.

Ezell, M. (2001). *Advocacy in the Human Services*. Belmont, CA: Brooks/Cole.

Fisher, R., Ury, W., & Patton, B. M. (1991). *Getting to Yes: Negotiating Agreement Without Giving In*. New York: Penguin.

Meenaghan, T. M., Kilty, K. M., & McNutt, J. G. (2004). *Social Policy Analysis and Practice*. Chicago: Lyceum Books.

Schneider, R. L., & Lester, L. (2001). *Social Work Advocacy: A New Framework for Action*. Belmont, CA: Brooks/Cole.

VeneKlasen, L., & Miller, V. (2007). *A New Weave of Power, People, and Politics: The Action Guide for Advocacy and Citizen Participation*. Rugby, U.K.: Practical Action.

www.afj.org. The Alliance for Justice strives to "strengthen the public interest community's ability to influence public policy and foster the next generation of advocates." Their website offers information about IRS regulations and laws governing nonprofits, access to their publications, advocacy alerts, and job announcements.

www.iscvt.org. Maintained by the Institute for Sustainable Communities, this site provides resources and networking opportunities for social justice advocates throughout the world.

www.osc.gov. This is the official site of the Office of Special Counsel, an excellent source for information about compliance with the Hatch Act (Reference: 5 U.S.C. chapter 73, subchapter III, as amended; 5 CFR part 734; PL 103-359 Section 501(k)).

www.policy.com. This site is operated by SpeakOut.com, a nonpartisan Internet activism portal. With a trendy appearance, the site has "activism centers" that provide news articles on a variety of topics, abstracts of articles, opportunities to chat, and some fun surveys. The site is updated daily.

www.statepolicy.org. This site is part of "Influencing State Policy," an initiative designed to help social work faculty and students become more involved in state policy. It includes a link to stateline.org, which provides policy-relevant news for each state, as well as inspiring descriptions of advocacy initiatives that have received awards.

PART II

Collective Responses
to Social Problems

© Neil Orloff. Courtesy Art Access Gallery, Salt Lake City, Utah

Must we face problems alone?

Problems come in many shapes and colors. In the early stages of intellectual development our problems are intensely personal and our ability to empathize with the problems of others is limited. One hallmark of maturity is the capacity to view problems from diverse perspectives and to empathize with those who experience problems that are foreign to us.

In our professional lives social workers are concerned with social problems, so the question of what constitutes a social problem has been the subject of much theoretical work in our field. In this section we will consider two approaches to understanding social problems. The first, developed by Abram de Swaan, a professor of social sciences at the University of Amsterdam, examines the conditions necessary for personal problems to become social problems. Policy is seen as the vehicle for organizing collective action to address these problems. The point here is not to evaluate policy but to determine when it might be mobilized to address a problem.

The second approach, which involves analyzing social problems, begins where the first leaves off, setting the stage for evaluating the effectiveness of social policies. It examines the values and beliefs that inform our understanding of social problems. One of the best examples of this approach was developed by Donald Chambers, a social work professor at the University of Kansas (Chambers, 2000). Chambers's method offers a great way to understand the underlying dynamics of social policies. Both of these approaches contribute to our understanding of social problems.

PREDICTING COLLECTIVE ACTION

During the Paleolithic Era, humans banded together to hunt mammoth. In the twentieth century, they paid Social Security taxes. Since the dawn of our species, humans have used collective action to meet personal needs; but no human society responds collectively to every personal problem. How can we determine whether a problem will be addressed collectively?

Abram de Swaan (1988)[1] identified three conditions that encourage collective solutions to personal adversity. First, the *external effects* of the adversity must be recognized. One person's suffering must affect another, and the "other" must recognize that effect. Second, *individual remedies* must be of limited effectiveness. Attempts by individuals to escape the external effects or to avoid the problem

---

1. De Swaan's book *In Care of the State* serves as the basis for much of this discussion. Drawing from two distinct intellectual traditions, welfare economics and historical sociology, de Swaan asks, "How and why did people develop collective, nation-wide and compulsory arrangements to cope with deficiencies and adversities that appeared to affect them separately and to call for individual remedies?" The result is a compelling work.

must prove ineffective. Finally, when adversity and/or its external effects can strike at any time with unpredictable magnitude (*uncertainty of moment and magnitude*), collective responses are more likely. The development of modern plumbing serves as an excellent example.

In the nineteenth century, cholera epidemics devastated many European cities. The 1832 wave of cholera took 18,000 victims in England and a comparable number in Paris. Nineteenth-century scientists quickly linked the infection to lack of fresh water and inadequate sewage removal. Those who could apply individual solutions (the rich) removed themselves to healthier (usually higher) quarters; but the disease was still established among the poor, and it began to invade the quarters of the rich. As de Swaan notes, "Mass epidemics provided a striking image of interdependency between fellow city-dwellers, poor and rich, established and newcomers, ignorant and cultivated alike" (p. 124). As the failure of individual solutions became evident, there was widespread agreement that a collective approach was in order.

Experts decided that citywide sanitation systems were the best solution, although they would be disruptive and expensive. Initially sewer lines were installed in wealthy neighborhoods and financed through what we now call user or connection fees. As soon as wealthy neighborhoods were saturated with pipes, the "venous-arterial system" of sanitation networks was extended throughout the city—a "public good" supported by compulsory taxes and fees. Sanitation departments were established to collect fees and maintain the systems.

Thus modern plumbing, the collective approach to supplying fresh water and removing sewage, developed because of the external effects of the adversity experienced by the poor (the wealthy were exposed to cholera); the failure of individual remedies (moving to higher ground did not protect against the disease); and uncertainty regarding the moment and magnitude of adversity (one never knew whether or how badly one might be affected by the disease).

The problems discussed in Part II are shared, to various degrees, by all Americans. Each meets de Swaan's three criteria for collective action (external effects are recognized, individual remedies are of limited effectiveness, and there is uncertainty of moment and magnitude); and each of these problems has mobilized governmental action to allocate benefits and resources. As a result, progress toward social justice has been achieved through collective action in the form of governmental policies and programs.

SOCIAL PROBLEM ANALYSIS

Social problem analysis sets the stage for evaluating the effectiveness of social policies.[2] It has four key components: problem definition, causal analysis, identification of ideology and values, and consideration of winners and losers. Here we

---

2. The interested reader will find a terrific discussion of problem analysis in Chambers (2000), from which I have drawn heavily in preparing this section.

will consider the problem of unemployment in relation to each of these components.

Problem definition begins with the premise that social problems are important problems. Their importance may be a function of two things: the status of the people experiencing or observing the problem and the sheer number of individuals affected by the problem. Often social workers begin to define a problem by describing the affected population. We might go further and consider demographic features and historic trends in the number of people affected.

In the case of unemployment we might begin with a description of who, exactly, we will consider unemployed. Because the Department of Labor regularly monitors the number of people who fit its definition, it is relatively easy to say whether the problem is increasing or decreasing. As you might expect, when the number of people experiencing a problem is increasing, it is easier to identify it as an important social problem. A concern for social justice might lead us to focus on groups, such as youth, women, and people of color, who are more vulnerable to unemployment than others.

In this early stage of problem definition, perspective comes into play. In the United States people who are not actively looking for work are not officially considered unemployed. Some dispute the government's definition, arguing that workers who have become too discouraged to search for a job should be counted among the unemployed. Generally these people seek to make the case that unemployment is important—possibly more important than the government would have us believe.

Causal analysis in social policy differs from research designed to identify causes. In social policy analysis we are less interested in objective reality than in public perceptions. The question is not "What causes this problem?" but "What do key participants in policy development believe causes the problem?" Of course, responsible policy makers should be aware of research that identifies causes of a problem. Good research should never be disregarded. But for the purposes of social policy analysis, our understanding of the problem must incorporate pervasive beliefs that lack scientific foundation. Beliefs about causes influence the design of social policies and programs to address problems. In fact, it is sometimes interesting to go backwards in this analysis—looking at the specifics of a program and deciphering what they imply about the perceived causes of the problem.

Identifying ideology and values embedded in popular definitions of social problems is an interesting exercise in itself. As Chambers (2000) noted, it is sometimes difficult to distinguish what we know from what we believe. He suggests that value statements generally reflect what we think *should* or *should not* be true. So the official definition of unemployment may reflect the belief that one should never give up trying to find a job. Someone who has ended a job search must be deficient and therefore unworthy of our consideration. An advocate might find it useful to challenge this belief by documenting and sharing the experiences of workers who have given up. As we saw in Part I, values are inherent in the design of social programs and social policies. As professionals, our challenge is to bring these hidden assumptions into the open for public examination and dialogue.

It is vital to acknowledge that, as Chambers (2000) noted, some people win from the presence of a social problem. Social workers tend to focus on the losers —people likely to become our clients—but winners can become obstacles to our efforts to ameliorate the problem. Returning to our case example, major employers might appreciate the presence of a large pool of potential workers. It might strengthen their ability to negotiate wage cuts and reduce the cost of discharging an employee. *Consideration of both winners and losers* enhances problem analysis. Beyond this, our description of losers should expand beyond those directly affected by the problem. Clearly unemployment affects the unemployed workers and their families. But the risk of unemployment can affect working conditions for those who are employed. It might also affect the tax base of local communities, reducing resources available for critical services such as "911" and police.

ABOUT PART II

It may be helpful to clarify the organizational structure of the book. Some may ask, "Aren't people living in poverty, experiencing mental illness, or suffering from physical illness or disability *vulnerable?*" and "Don't the vulnerable populations discussed in Part III have *problems?*" Certainly. The difference is that the problems discussed in Part II of the book represent risks that are widely shared by Americans. With some qualifications, *anyone* could become impoverished, mentally ill, physically sick, or disabled. Vulnerable populations are vulnerable by virtue of personal characteristics not shared throughout the population. Their vulnerability is typically the direct consequence of oppression and discrimination. This is an important distinction because the policy approach to broadly distributed risks differs from that used to protect vulnerable populations. Where social insurance programs may be designed to permit members of society to share risks, corrective policies such as civil rights or affirmative action are more typically designed to reduce oppression of vulnerable populations.

Part II begins with the legislative framework that defines our nation's collective response to many social problems: the Social Security Act. This is the focus of Chapter 4. Then we will trace the development of policies and programs to address four social problems: poverty (Chapter 5), physical illness (Chapter 6), mental illness (Chapter 7), and disability (Chapter 8). In each case, society's collective response can be traced to some of the conditions that de Swaan identified: external effects, failure of individual remedies, and uncertainty of the moment and magnitude of adversity. And in each case, our understanding is informed by Chambers's four analytic components: problem definition, causal analysis, identification of ideology and values, and consideration of winners and losers. Each chapter will focus on the problem under consideration, beginning from a human perspective with a case study and then examining definitional issues, the development of policies and services, and emerging policy issues. In each chapter, we will include the background material necessary for students to apply policy frameworks presented in Part I to emerging policy issues in the field.

4

The Social Security Act

We are moving forward to greater freedom, to greater security
for the average man than he has ever known before in the
history of America.

FRANKLIN DELANO ROOSEVELT, FIRESIDE CHAT,
SEPTEMBER 30, 1935

Most Americans think of Social Security as a retirement program for the nation's elderly. In fact, as this chapter will reveal, three types of programs are authorized under the Social Security Act: social insurance, public assistance, and health and social services. These programs serve Americans of all ages and income levels. The retirement program, known as Old-Age Insurance (OAI), was part of the original Social Security Act, along with unemployment insurance; public assistance programs for the aged, the blind, and dependent children; and health services for mothers and children. The titles of the 1935 act are presented in Table 4.1.

Subsequent amendments added survivors' insurance, disability insurance, medical insurance for the aged, and two means-tested programs: Medicaid and Supplemental Security Income (SSI). Other, less well known programs administered under the Social Security Act include the Maternal and Child Health Services Block Grant, the Social Services Block Grant, and the State Children's Health Insurance Program. The current titles of the Social Security Act are presented in Table 4.2. In this chapter we will trace the emergence of social insurance in Western Europe and the United States and then discuss the major programs authorized under the Social Security Act: old-age and survivors insurance, disability insurance, unemployment insurance, medical insurance, SSI, and health and social services. In each section we will consider the background of the

TABLE 4.1   Contents of the Social Security Act of 1935 Original

Preamble: An act to provide for the general welfare by establishing a system of Federal old-age benefits, and by enabling the several States to make more adequate provision for aged persons, blind persons, dependent and crippled children, maternal and child welfare, public health, and the administration of their unemployment compensation laws; to establish a Social Security Board; to raise revenue; and for other purposes.

Title I	Grants to States for Old-Age Assistance
Title II	Federal Old-Age Benefits
Title III	Grants to States for Unemployment Compensation Administration
Title IV	Grants to States for Aid to Dependent Children
Title V	Grants to States for Maternal and Child Welfare
Title VI	Public Health Work
Title VII	Social Security Board
Title VIII	Taxes with Respect to Employment
Title IX	Tax on Employers of Eight or More
Title X	Grants to States for Aid to the Blind
Title XI	General Provisions

program and then discuss its current status. Major reform proposals will be presented as well. Following a discussion of the program's treatment of women, the chapter concludes with a brief consideration of the philosophical underpinnings of Social Security in the United States.

SOCIAL INSURANCE IN WESTERN EUROPE

Early social insurance schemes developed in Western Europe addressed the "three fears" of industrial workers: poverty in old age, illness, and unemployment. As several historians have pointed out, the Social Security programs established during the nineteenth century were adopted by authoritarian, rather than democratic, regimes (Flora, 1983; Flora & Heidenheimer, 1981; Rimlinger, 1971).[1] An important motivation was undoubtedly the need to secure loyalty from the growing number of industrial wage earners.

---

1. Germany, Austria, Finland, Sweden, and Italy had established compulsory social insurance programs for workers by the end of the nineteenth century (de Swaan, 1988).

T A B L E 4.2   Titles of the Social Security Act

Title I	[Grants to States for Old-Age Assistance] (replaced in 1974 with SSI)
Title II	Old-Age, Survivors, and Disability Insurance Benefits (commonly called "Social Security")
Title III	Grants to States for Unemployment Compensation
Title IV	Grants to States for Aid and Services to Needy Families with Children (replaced with Temporary Assistance to Needy Families in 1996) and for Child Welfare Services
Title V	Maternal and Child Health Services Block Grant
Title VII	Administration of the Social Security Act
Title VIII	Employment Taxes (superseded by IRS Code)
Title IX	Miscellaneous Provisions Related to Employment Taxes
Title X	[Grants to States for Aid to the Blind] (replaced with SSI)
Title XI	General Provisions
Title XII	Advances to State Unemployment Funds
Title XIII	Special Benefits for Certain World War II Veterans (expired)
Title XIV	[Grants to States for Aid to the Permanently and Totally Disabled] (replaced with SSI)
Title XVI	Supplemental Security Income for the Aged, Blind and Disabled (SSI)
Title XVII	Grants for Planning Comprehensive Action to Combat Mental Retardation
Title XVIII	Health Insurance for the Aged and Disabled (Medicare)
Title XIX	Grants to States for Medical Assistance Programs (Medicaid)
Title XX	Block Grants to States for Social Services
Title XXI	State Children's Health Insurance Progam

Titles VI and XV have been repealed.

The regime of Otto von Bismarck is credited with establishing Europe's first social insurance program through a series of acts passed in the 1880s. Popular myth holds that Bismarck's motivation for establishing this program was a desire to force his political foes into retirement. A more likely explanation is that the social insurance program (*Sozialversicherung*) was established as part of an effort to strengthen the German state by securing the allegiance of the industrial working class. Sozialversicherung was successful in this regard. It offered workers a stake in the political order and gained enough popular support to survive two world wars, National Socialism, and foreign occupation to remain a central feature of the German welfare state (de Swaan, 1988).

Oddly enough, leaders of the German labor movement opposed the establishment of Sozialversicherung. Drawing on Marxist doctrine, labor leaders believed that workers should have global allegiance to other members of the proletariat rather than to a nation-state. Leaders of workers' parties may also have seen the program as another tactic in the government's ongoing repression of their organizing efforts. Despite their initial opposition, labor leaders were effectively co-opted by the program. As de Swaan (1988) notes, union leaders and Socialist Party officials were quickly "integrated into the state's fabric as executives of the national insurance system" (p. 188).

In England, the elaborate system for relief created by the Elizabethan Poor Law (see Chapter 5) was a barrier to the development of social insurance. Leaders of charity organization societies that provided aid to the indigent were adamant in their belief that poverty was the result of personal failings and that efforts to relieve it should focus on moral reform of individuals. But as industrialization advanced, local authorities were overwhelmed by the needs of older workers. With the 1906 election of a Liberal government, Lloyd George and Winston Churchill formed an activist regime that, with the support of organized labor, passed the Pension Act of 1908, establishing social insurance for retirement income.

The French social insurance system was established in 1930. Small property owners had successfully opposed social insurance for several decades. These members of the "petite bourgeoisie" feared that government control of the large sums of capital accumulated in national insurance funds would increase government control of the capital market, disrupting their businesses. They also argued that Social Security taxes would undermine workers' ability to accumulate personal savings. The establishment of the French program has been attributed to the erosion of the bourgeois power base and the support of moderate labor organizations (de Swaan, 1988).

France's position on social insurance was unusual, since most European nations had mandatory old-age insurance programs in place prior to World War I (1914–1918). Throughout the continent, these new programs served a state-building function, converting wages into accumulated capital through a mandatory system operated by a public administrative apparatus. The programs enhanced workers' loyalty to the state by giving laborers a stake in the government.

SOCIAL SECURITY IN THE UNITED STATES

Like the French, Americans established social insurance for workers later than most European nations. Despite growing recognition of old-age dependency as a social problem, the widespread belief that poverty was caused by individual inadequacies effectively precluded comprehensive federal legislation. Workers were expected to set aside personal savings for their retirement.

Many workers bought private insurance against accidents and illness. In 1910, roughly half of the workforce had such insurance (Achenbaum, 1986). These workers typically filed disability claims if old age forced them to retire. Those who failed to provide for their old age were left to the mercies of their families or to the limited public and charitable assistance that was available.

After the 1920s, large companies (public utilities, railroads, and manufacturing firms) established private pension plans for their employees. Retirement insurance was made available to federal employees in 1920 through the establishment of the Federal Employees Retirement Program. By 1931, 18 states had established compulsory old-age insurance programs for workers (Piven & Cloward, 1971). By 1933, 21 states and the territories of Alaska and Hawaii operated relief programs for dependent elderly people (Achenbaum, 1986).

In this context, proposals to establish social insurance against old-age dependency were unsuccessful. They surfaced periodically during the Progressive Era, promoted by advocates such as Abraham Epstein and I. M. Rubinow. Epstein founded the American Association for Old-Age Security in 1927 to advance his social insurance scheme. But for the most part, these proposals did not have the support of workers or federal politicians, and there was widespread belief that a mandatory social insurance program would be declared unconstitutional by the Supreme Court (Kingson & Berkowitz, 1993).

The Great Depression was not the first major economic upheaval in the United States, but its duration and intensity were overwhelming. Achenbaum (1986, p. 16) described the economic impact:

> Between October 1929 and June 1932, the common-stock price index dropped from 260 to 90. The nation's real GNP, which had risen 22 percent between 1923 and 1929, fell 30.4 percent over the next four years. Nearly 5,000 banks, with deposits exceeding $3.2 billion, became insolvent; 90,000 businesses failed. Aggregate wages and salaries in 1933 totaled only 57.5 percent of their 1929 value. The gross income realized by farmers was cut nearly in half; the farm-product index took a dive from 105 to 51 between 1928 and 1932. More than a thousand local governments defaulted on their bonds. . . . Insecurity pervaded the land.

The Depression overwhelmed local and state relief programs, and widespread insecurity undermined the popular belief that poverty was the result of personal irresponsibility. No longer could middle-class Americans feel confident that hard work would insulate them from poverty. Job loss and destitution, once seen as individual problems, now seemed to call for collective action. The external impacts of insecurity were evident in the domino effects of bank and business closures. Individual remedies, from personal initiative to private insurance, had little effect. Finally, no one really knew who would be singled out for unemployment.

A wide range of reform proposals came to the fore. Most involved the use of taxes to fund guaranteed incomes in old age. Francis E. Townsend, a retired doctor from California, organized "Townsend Clubs" to support his proposal that everyone over 60 who was unemployed[2] be given $200 a month on the condition that they spend the amount within 30 days. The program was to be funded

---

2. The requirement that Social Security recipients be unemployed was an integral part of the act. Some have argued that this "retirement test" evolved in an effort to reduce unemployment. It effectively moved the elderly out of the labor force to make jobs available to younger workers.

through a tax on business transactions. Others, including Upton Sinclair and Senator Huey P. Long, advanced similar ideas.

The 1932 presidential election brought Franklin Delano Roosevelt into office with a clear mandate to "do something." His opponent, incumbent Herbert Hoover, had argued that the market should be left alone to correct itself. Roosevelt and his colleagues supported the establishment of a government insurance program to protect the unemployed and the aged. Roosevelt established the cabinet-level Committee on Economic Security (CES), under the direction of Edwin E. Witte, to draft proposals for New Deal programs in collaboration with Frances Perkins, a social worker who was appointed Secretary of Labor. In January 1935, Roosevelt presented Congress with "the most comprehensive social welfare bill that any president had ever asked Congress to consider" (Kingson & Berkowitz, 1993, p. 35). It combined programs for the unemployed, children, and the elderly within a single piece of legislation, the Social Security Act. (Please see http://www.ssa.gov/history/ for interesting material on the history of Social Security in the United States.)

The act that passed in 1935 was only a skeleton of the Social Security Act as we know it today. Its old-age insurance offered benefits only to retired workers, not to their survivors or to workers with disabilities. Further, the original program covered only about half of the labor force, excluding many farm and domestic workers, state and local employees, and the self-employed.

"I came to Washington to work for God, FDR, and the millions of forgotten plain common workingmen." —Frances Perkins

---

B O X   4.1   Frances Perkins: An Architect of Social Security

Born in 1882, Perkins was the first woman appointed to a cabinet position in the United States. She served for 12 years as Roosevelt's secretary of labor and was one of the key architects of Social Security. As Perkins put it, "I came to Washington to work for God, FDR, and the millions of forgotten plain common workingmen." Perkins was an unforgettable figure in the Roosevelt administration. Arthur Schlesinger described her by saying, "She had a pungency of character, a dry wit, an inner gaiety, an instinct for practicality, a profound vein of religious feeling, and a compulsion to instruct." She remained in federal service until the death of her husband in 1952, and continued to lecture until her death in 1965. (For more information, see http://www.ssa.gov/history/fperkins .html.)

The Social Security Act was subjected to two constitutional challenges before the Supreme Court in 1937, both of which focused on its only compulsory element, Old Age Insurance. In the first case (*Chas. C. Steward Machine Co. v. Davis*), the Charles C. Steward Machine Company of Alabama sued to recover its share of Social Security taxes, claiming it was an illegal excise tax. The Court upheld the constitutionality of the tax, holding that the magnitude of the emergency presented by the Depression justified federal intervention. In the second case (*Helvering et al. v. Davis*), a shareholder with Edison Electric Illuminating Company of Boston argued that deduction of Social Security taxes from wages would produce unrest among employees and "would be followed by demands of increases in wages and that corporations and shareholders would suffer irreparable loss" (Supreme Court, 1937). In rejecting this argument, the Court relied on the concept of general welfare:

> Congress may spend money in aid of the general welfare. . . . The purge of nation-wide calamity that began in 1929 has taught us many lessons. Not the least is the solidarity of interests that may once have seemed to be divided. Unemployment spreads from state to state, the hinterland now settled that in pioneer days gave an avenue of escape. . . . *The hope behind this statute is to save men and women from the rigors of the poorhouse as well as from the haunting fear that such a lot awaits them when journey's end is near.* (Supreme Court, 1937, p. 640, italics added)

Having survived these challenges, the program was put in place. Retirement benefits were financed by employer and employee contributions of 1 percent each on a wage base of $3,000, with a maximum contribution of $30 per year. Benefits were paid out at age 65, and amounted to about $22 per month for single workers and $36 per month for couples. To allow a reserve to accumulate, no benefits were paid until 1940. The first benefit paid was $22 per month to Miss Ida Fuller, a retired secretary. Miss Fuller lived to be over 100. She paid less than $100 in Social Security taxes and collected about $21,000 in benefits (Schulz, 1995). As we will see later in this chapter, other women have fared less well under Social Security.

OAI was not the only program established through the Social Security Act of 1935. The act included 11 titles (see Table 4.1). In the following sections of this chapter, we will trace the development of five key programs authorized through the Social Security Act of 1935 and its later amendments: OASI; Disability Insurance (DI); Unemployment Insurance (UI); medical insurance; Public Assistance for the Aged, Blind, and Disabled (SSI); and health and social services.

OLD-AGE AND SURVIVORS INSURANCE
FOR WORKERS

In the 1936 election, Franklin Roosevelt roundly defeated the Republican contender for president. In its second term, the Roosevelt administration set out to expand the Social Security Act. The 1939 amendments expanded coverage by adding benefits for workers' survivors and dependents. Widows of both active and retired workers received a portion of the benefits to which the workers were entitled, as did other dependents of retired workers.

Subsequent years saw continued expansion of Social Security coverage. In 1950, farm workers and the self-employed were added, bringing coverage to about 90 percent of the labor force. Later, provision for early retirement was added, allowing workers to retire at the age of 62 with 80 percent of the monthly benefit they would have received at 65. In 1972, the cost-of-living adjustment (COLA) was established to raise benefits at rates linked to inflationary increases in the Consumer Price Index (CPI). In 1977, procedures for "indexing" earnings were put in place. Indexing adjusts earnings for inflation in benefit computations, resulting in more generous treatment of earnings from the early years of a worker's career.

The 1980s marked the beginning of a retrenchment period for Social Security. By this time, program expansions had eroded reserves, and the OASI trust fund was on the verge of bankruptcy. Anticipating the demands that would be presented by the baby boomer cohort, in 1981 President Reagan appointed a bipartisan commission, the National Commission on Social Security Reform, chaired by Alan Greenspan, to recommend measures to restore the program's solvency. The following measures were implemented in subsequent amendments:

1. *Revisions in the COLA.* These included a one-time delay of the COLA and a "stabilizer" on future COLAs. If the trust fund falls below certain measures, the COLA will be indexed, not to the CPI, but to the average increase in wages (if it is lower). This provision has not been applied to date.
2. *Taxation of benefits.* Up to half of benefits were made subject to federal income tax.
3. *Increased retirement ages.* Starting in 2003, the age for receipt of full retirement benefits was set to rise gradually. By 2027, the retirement age for full benefits would be 67. Early retirement would bring 70, rather than 80, percent of the regular benefits.
4. *Work incentives.* These provisions increased the amount beneficiaries could earn through employment before their Social Security benefits were reduced, and eliminated the reduction of benefits altogether for workers over the age of 70 years old.

The work of the National Commission became law in the 1983 amendments to the Social Security Act. The Commission's work was pivotal in two ways. First, its recommendations greatly enhanced the program's solvency; and second, the process of reform undertaken by the Commission reduced the influence of partisan politics and enhanced the quality of technical information that was used in the Social Security debate. These reforms also represented fundamental shifts in the program's approach. First, by subjecting Social Security benefits to income tax, the reforms introduced another progressive element into the program. As discussed in Chapter 2, the income tax draws a higher proportion of income from high-income Americans than it does from the poor. Second, the introduction of work incentives represented a significant departure from earlier policies under which retirement was a condition for receiving benefits. This change suggests that the policy goal of removing older workers from the labor force had become less compelling.

The 1983 amendments set the stage for subsequent revisions, primarily designed to maintain system solvency through the retirement of the nation's baby boomer generation. In 1999, President Clinton called for partial privatization of Social Security to increase trust fund income. This alternative was also considered by the Bush administration.

In 2000, in rare unanimous votes in both houses, Congress eliminated the Social Security retirement test altogether. Under PC 106-182, the Senior Citizens' Freedom to Work Act, beneficiaries at full retirement age can continue to work with no reduction in benefits. Beneficiaries who are under full retirement age were still subject to reductions in their benefits for earnings above the exempt amount. In 2007 this amount was $12,960 per year (Social Security Administration, "How Work Affects Your Benefits," http://www.ssa.gov/pubs/10069.html, accessed January 14, 2008).

How OASI Operates

OASI is the primary source of retirement income in the United States, supporting more than 40 million retired workers and their families in 2005 (http://www.ssa.gov/policy/docs/statcomps/supplement/2006/highlights.html, accessed January 14, 2008). Although it was not intended to be the sole support of elderly recipients (savings and pension income were seen as equal contributors), many low-income elders depend entirely on Social Security. In 2000, those whose income was in the lowest quintile (fifth) of the elderly population received 82 percent of their income from Social Security. This compared to 19 percent of the income received by the top quintile (Social Security Administration, 2000).

OASI is a carefully crafted compromise between two objectives, offering "welfare" to low-income seniors and "investment" to others. Thus the program integrates the principles of *equity* and *adequacy*. Equity is achieved when benefits drawn are based on contributions paid—in other words, when individuals receive a return that is proportional to their investment in the program. Under the principle of adequacy, benefits should be sufficient to maintain a decent standard of living, regardless of individual contributions.

To achieve equity, an individual's benefits are computed on the basis of prior contributions. Benefits are based on a person's "average indexed monthly earnings" (AIME). Earnings between ages 21 and 62 that were subject to the payroll tax (as of 2001, earnings under $80,400 per year) are adjusted for inflation. Then the five years with lowest earnings are dropped. The resulting total is averaged to produce the AIME. To be eligible to draw Social Security benefits, an individual must have worked in covered employment for at least 40 quarters (i.e., 10 years).

Adequacy refers to the guarantee of sufficient income for a modest existence in old age. The "replacement rate" under OASI is designed to ensure adequacy. Benefit computations replace lower earnings more generously than high earnings. As of 2007, the first $680 of AIME were replaced at the rate of 90 percent; earnings from $681 per month to $4,100 per month were replaced at the rate of 32 percent; and earnings between $4,101 and the maximum ($8,125) were replaced at 15 percent (http://www.ssa.gov/OACT/COLA/piaformula.html, accessed January 14, 2008). Thus individuals retiring with low lifelong earnings enjoy a higher replacement rate than those retiring with high earnings. This does not mean their Social Security check will be larger, but that the difference between working income and Social Security income will be smaller than it would be for someone with high earnings.

OASI is financed through a payroll tax authorized under the Federal Insurance Contributions Act (FICA). Originally this was set at 1 percent of earnings up to $3,000 (a maximum contribution of $30 per year). Today this tax totals 15.30 percent of wages up to a cap. In 2007 this wage cap was set at $97,580 per year. Half of the tax is paid by the employer and half by the worker. The largest portion of these combined contributions (12.4 percent of wages) is allocated to Old-Age, Survivors, and Disability Insurance (OASDI). The remainder (2.9 percent of wages) goes to finance Medicare. The Medicare portion is not subject to a wage cap. High-income workers pay more tax, and low-income workers receive more generous replacement income. This aspect is sometimes described as a "redistributive feature" of the Social Security program.

The "minimum monthly benefit," another redistributive feature, is now something of a historic relic. At the inception of Social Security, the minimum benefit was set at $10 per month (Achenbaum, 1986). Under the 1972 amendments to the Social Security Act, Congress indexed the minimum benefit to inflation. By 1981 it had increased to $170.31 per month for a worker retiring at age 65. Faced with rising Social Security costs, Joseph A. Califano, then secretary of health, education and welfare, proposed repealing the minimum benefit. The primary argument for repeal was that the 1974 establishment of Supplemental Security Income (SSI) eliminated the need for a minimum benefit. In 1981, the Reagan administration repealed the minimum benefit. The next year it was reinstated for current retirees. Today, the minimum benefit is provided only to workers who were 62 years old before 1982 (Schulz, 1995).

Social Security is a "pay as you go" program. That is, most of the revenue collected through payroll taxes is used to pay for the benefits of current recipients. The remainder goes into four separate reserve funds: OASI; Disability; Hospital Insurance (Medicare Part A); and Supplementary Medical Insurance (Medicare Part B). Until the early 1980s, revenue matched benefits paid, at approximately $200 billion per year. Since passage of the 1983 amendments developed by the National Commission on Social Security Reform, the OASI and DI trust funds have been accumulating reserves to pay for the retirement of the baby boom generation. In 2006, for example, these reserves increased by $206 billion, so that at the end of the year the combined trust funds held a balance in excess of $4.0 trillion (http://www.ssa.gov/OACT/TR/TR07/trTOC.html, accessed January 14, 2008).

Extensive (and sometimes misleading) discussion of the solvency issues related to Social Security threatens to undermine public confidence in the program. Challenges to the system reached the level of absurd in 1995, when a group calling itself The Third Millennium reported that more people aged 18 to 34 believed in UFOs than believed they would ever collect Social Security benefits.[3]

More credible (but certainly not definitive) information is available through the OASDI Trustees Report, which is issued annually and is available online (see http://www.ssa.gov/OACT/TR/TR07/ for the 2007 report). Under the trustees' "best guess" intermediate assumptions, the reserves in the OASI trust fund are projected to be exhausted in 2042. Reserves in the combined OASDI trust fund would, according to this projection, be depleted in 2041. Each year the estimate is adjusted to reflect contemporary demographic and economic conditions. The results have varied considerably. For instance, in 1998 the trustees projected the revenues would be exhausted in 2032.

Depletion of the trust fund reserves does not mean that the program would be unable to pay beneficiaries. The trustees project that under current tax rates, the fund will be able to pay about three-fourths of its costs in 2042. The remainder would require what the trustees refer to as "a flow of cash from the General Fund of the Treasury." Other alternatives for addressing the problem include an increase in payroll taxes, reduction in benefits, or restructuring the financing mechanism to increase revenues. Privatization proposals have dominated recent debates about how to maintain solvency.

"Privatizing" OASI.   Generally, efforts to reform OASI produce "winners" (those whose benefit status would be improved) and "losers" (those who would receive fewer benefits). Because reform is largely dictated by political considerations, the clout of the winners compared to that of the losers can give an indication of the probability that a reform will be enacted. As we review privatization proposals, it is useful to consider who is expected to benefit from proposed changes.

In 1979, Jose Pinera, then labor minister of Chile, oversaw the final stages of privatizing that nation's pension system. At the end of his term Mr. Pinera came to the United States to cochair a project funded by the conservative Cato

---

3. The Third Millennium was a group with about 1,700 members that claimed to represent the interests of younger workers, also known as "Generation X." In the early 1990s, this group organized a poll, conducted by Frank Luntz, that reported that more young Americans believe in flying saucers than in the future of Social Security. While the results of the poll have been widely disseminated, its methodology has been questioned (see McLeod, 1995).

BOX 4.2   Raiding the Trust Funds?

Highly charged political rhetoric about Social Security erodes public confidence in the system. To stop Congress from "raiding the trust funds," candidates promise to "put Social Security funds in a lock box." These arguments have little bearing on the realities of Social Security financing and a lot to do with the politics of fear.

Money paid into the Social Security trust funds, like the money you put in a bank, is not kept there. Just as the bank invests your money, the money in the trust funds is invested on your behalf. The safest investment in this country is U.S. Treasury notes. They do not provide high returns, but payment is guaranteed by the federal government. As we have seen, the national debt consists of outstanding Treasury notes. So

when the Social Security trust funds invest in Treasury notes, they are "for accounting purposes" reducing the deficit. This accounting approach has been in place since the 1970s and is known as the "unified budget." In other words, the budget takes the trust fund resources into account. Fundamental to the success of this system (and of the nation) is the federal government's commitment to honor its contractual obligations by paying off Treasury notes and paying Social Security benefits. The unified budget does not, in itself, jeopardize Social Security. But large deficits can reduce the government's financial stability. Thus the problem is not the unified budget itself but use of Social Security funds to mask irresponsible federal spending.

Institute to advance the case for privatizing the U.S. Social Security system (Dreyfuss, 1996). These efforts were successful in persuading President Clinton to include partial privatization of OASI on the policy agenda presented in his 1999 State of the Union address. Following the 2004 election, President George W. Bush made privatization a top priority. While the specifics of proposals vary, the basics of privatization are simple: moving Social Security funds away from government treasury bonds into the stock market.

Why has privatization become the subject of national debate? The rhetoric of the debate focuses on the system's impending insolvency and suggests that younger workers have no faith in the system. But an underlying cause may be found in the system's changing economics. As Quinn and Mitchell (1996) argue, "Social Security is newly vulnerable because it is no longer a good deal for all" (p. 78). In the system's early decades, all workers could expect to receive more in benefits than they would have received if they had taken the amount they paid in Social Security taxes and invested it themselves. But as the ratio of workers to beneficiaries has declined, payroll taxes have increased and benefits for upper-income retirees have been taxed. So for some workers (primarily high earners) expecting to retire in one decade or more, OASI benefits will be less than what they would have received had they put their payroll taxes in low-risk investments. One-earner couples and recipients with incomes in the bottom half of the earnings distribution continue to receive more from Social Security than they would have received from private investments. But, for the first time in the system's history, a sizable number of workers will not. This prospect not only has made the redistributive aspect of the program explicit but it has also undermined political support for Social Security among high earners (Kingson & Quadagno, 1997).

The similarities among privatization plans that have been proposed are striking. As Quinn and Mitchell (1996) note, "They all recommend the maintenance of a mandatory, universal, public social insurance program, with retirement, survivor, and disability benefits" (p. 80). Generally, privatization proposals establish a two-tiered system, under which minimal payments are supplied through a mandatory, universal program and a second tier is invested in the private market. There is some concern that a two-tiered system could result in eroded support for the flat-rate benefit and undermine the antipoverty function of Social Security.

Also striking in the privatization debate is the extent to which the redistribution function of Social Security is maintained. None of the plans advanced under the Clinton and Bush administrations suggested turning Social Security into a welfare system through means-testing of beneficiaries. Some of the plans called for modest increases in the payroll tax to maintain benefits at promised levels. One of the least-publicized aspects of some privatization plans has been the suggestion that a proportion of trust fund reserves be invested in the private market rather than in government securities.

Opposition to privatization came from a surprising source when Alan Greenspan, originally appointed by Ronald Reagan as chair of the Federal Reserve Board, testified before Congress in 1999. Greenspan argued that it would be impossible to keep politics out of the stock market if public funds were invested there by the Social Security system. He further suggested that moving Social Security assets into the stock market would diminish returns by reducing the efficiency of the market as a whole. (Greenspan's testimony is available at http:// www.federalreserve.gov/boarddocs/testimony/1999/19990303.htm.)

Another significant concern is the high cost of privatization. First, administrative costs of the present system are extremely low—Congressional Budget Office (CBO) estimates place costs at $11 per year per participant (CBO, 2004). These costs would clearly rise if the program were to manage an individual investment account for every worker. Second, even partial privatization would divert money away from the Social Security trust funds, further undermining the financial stability of the program. It is unclear how the deficit created by this diversion would be addressed. During the 2004 presidential debates, John Kerry repeatedly raised this concern, asking President Bush where the "transition funding" would come from.

Women and OASI

Early debate about the Social Security Act referred to "men and women" workers, lending an impression of gender neutrality. But in its original form, Social Security reflected the dominant family structure of the day, in which nearly all women depended on working men for income. In fact, as mentioned earlier, the program did not address the income needs of these non-wage-earning women at all until the 1939 amendments added coverage for dependents and survivors. Further, until 1977, men seeking to receive survivors' benefits were required to demonstrate financial dependency.

As a dependent, a woman is now entitled to 50 percent of the benefit her husband receives upon his retirement. As a survivor, or widow, she receives 100 percent of his benefit. Thus, during her husband's lifetime, a wife receives benefits as a dependent (half of the husband's benefit) so that a couple receives 150 percent of his benefit (100 percent for him and 50 percent for her); upon his death, she receives benefits as a survivor (100 percent of the husband's benefit).[4] Widows may not claim benefits until they reach the age of 60. If they do choose to draw benefits at that age, the benefit is reduced by almost one-third from what it would have been at full retirement age. Those who apply for benefits at the age of 62 experience a smaller reduction (Quadagno & Meyer, 1990).

With rising divorce rates, provisions for widows left out a growing category of women: divorcées who had been dependent on their husbands for support. Therefore, in 1965 provision was made for women who had been married for at least 20 years. In 1977 that period was decreased to 10 years. Today, a woman who was married to a worker for at least 10 years is eligible to receive half of her husband's (or ex-husband's) benefit, as long as she has not remarried. She cannot receive benefits until she reaches the age of 60. Further, she cannot receive her benefits until her former husband applies to receive his.

Women are more likely than men to rely on Social Security as their sole or primary source of income. For instance, in 2006 42 percent of women, compared to 28 percent of men, over 62 reported that Social Security benefits constituted over 90 percent of their income (American Academy of Actuaries, 2007; *Issue Brief: Women and Social Security,* www.actuary.org, accessed October 18, 2007). But the benefits paid to women are lower than those paid to men. In 2000, the average monthly retirement benefit paid to men was $951, compared to a mean of $730 for women (Nuschler, 2002).

The Social Security system is facing criticism for its treatment of dual-earner couples. Generally, because of departures from the workforce and lower lifetime wages, most working women receive higher benefits as dependents than they would have received on the basis of their own work histories. Thus they receive no benefit for the payroll taxes they paid during their working years. This violates the principle of equity, since these working women receive no return on their investment in the program.

Another significant inequity is the fact that dual-earner couples with low to moderate incomes receive lower retirement benefits than couples in which one partner earns a high income and the other is not employed. Benefits are based on the income of the higher-earning partner. Table 4.3 provides a simplified illustration of the effects on couples in three different situations. Each of the couples earns the same total monthly income, $6,000.

In Couple A, one partner earns a monthly salary of $6,000 and the other partner is not employed. The wage earner's retirement benefits are based on

---

4. While this may seem (and is intended to be) fairly generous treatment of widows, in essence it means they are expected to live on two-thirds of the amount they had been receiving while they were part of a married couple. For low- and moderate-income couples, this reduction often leaves the widow in poverty.

TABLE 4.3   Differential Treatment of Dual-Earning Couples

	Couple A	Couple B	Couple C
Monthly earnings 1	$6,000	$5,000	$3,000
Monthly earnings 2	0	1,000	3,000
Monthly OASI tax (12.4%)	744	744	744
Benefit base 1	6,000	5,000	3,000
Benefit base 2	3,000	2,500	3,000
Combined base	9,000	7,500	6,000

100 percent of earnings, and the spouse's benefits are based on 50 percent of the same earnings. Thus, the couple's combined retirement income is based on 150 percent of the wages earned, or a combined wage base of $9,000.

Dual-earning couples fare less well. In Couple B, both spouses are employed. The first earner makes $5,000 per month and the second makes $1,000 per month. The first earner is entitled to benefits based on $5,000. The second earner will draw retirement benefits based on 50 percent of the wages of the higher-earning partner. Thus, Couple B receives benefits based on a combined wage base of $7,500, even though their total income was the same as Couple A's.

Couple C includes two earners with equal monthly salaries. Each partner earns $3,000 per month. Their retirement benefits are based on 100 percent of each person's wages, or $6,000,[5] the lowest wage base of the three couples in our comparison.

Earnings Sharing. Proposals to establish "earnings sharing" would combine the earnings of a married couple and allocate half of the combined total to the husband and half to the wife for the duration of the marriage. This change would benefit divorced persons who had less than 10 years of marriage, giving them credit for their husband's (or wife's) earnings. It would also eliminate the inequities experienced by dual-career couples. To keep the system revenue neutral, the gains experienced by these two groups would be offset by losses to another group, in this case women (and a few men) who receive benefits as dependents without a work history.

Caregiver Credits. Another growing concern is lack of recognition for the unpaid labor of women caring for children and disabled or elderly family members. Women's caregiving responsibilities often force them to stop working, which jeopardizes their retirement benefits. Several proposals to allow Social Security credit for caregiving years have been introduced in the U.S. Congress. Typically, these proposals would allow credit for up to five years of no or mini-

---

5. For another explanation of this phenomenon, with benefit computations, see Schulz, 1995.

mal earnings while a worker is living with a young child or caring for a disabled family member. Caregiver credits attempt to address the difficulties experienced by women who leave work to care for family members. These proposals have been criticized as unfair, since they offer no benefits to those who take on double duty, meeting family care responsibilities without leaving the workforce.

In this section we have traced the development of old-age insurance in the U.S. Social Security system. In the following sections we will consider two other types of social insurance: unemployment insurance and medical insurance.

UNEMPLOYMENT INSURANCE

When the Social Security Act passed in 1935, unemployment was an overwhelming concern. An estimated 11 to 15 million workers were out of work, and the resulting pressure on relief programs was staggering. A few states, most notably Massachusetts and New York, had attempted to pass unemployment insurance legislation prior to the Depression. But, until the Depression, these bills had consistently failed in state legislatures (Altmeyer, 1963).

Unemployment Insurance (UI) was an integral part of the Social Security Act of 1935. It was one of two social insurance programs the president and his advisers felt should be enacted immediately; the other was old-age insurance. The CES debated whether Unemployment Insurance should be operated as a federal-state partnership or as a strictly federal program. Unlike OAI, UI was established as a federal–state partnership. Under Title III of the 1935 Social Security Act, the role of the federal government was limited to making grants available to states interested in administration of UI. Funds for these grants were provided through a federal payroll tax paid by employers. A tax credit was made available to employers whose states met federal guidelines for UI. Within two years, UI extended nationwide, with programs established in all states. Originally, UI applied only to workers in firms with eight or more employees. Later, coverage was extended to those in firms with at least four employees.

Financing for the state contribution to UI is provided through a tax on payrolls. The state unemployment tax rate varies, depending on the firm's use of unemployment compensation during previous years. This is known as "experience rating." Under this approach, firms that have had high rates of unemployment pay higher unemployment taxes than those with lower unemployment rates. The use of experience rating was designed to reduce unemployment by giving employers an incentive to stabilize their workforce. Alternatively, some considered it fair to allocate the social cost of unemployment so that companies producing the problem bore the greatest cost (Altmeyer, 1963). Funds for UI are placed in an unemployment trust fund. A state agency known as the State Employment Security Agency is charged with administration of the program.

UI was designed to provide temporary replacement of lost wages for workers who had strong attachment to the labor force. As a result, eligibility for UI is based on three factors: the worker's earnings history, the reason for unemployment, and the worker's availability for work. Within these categories, specific requirements vary from state to state. Most states require that a worker be in covered employment for the first four of the last five calendar quarters prior to filing a claim. Earnings must be above a minimum that is set by the state. Second, the job loss must be due to factors beyond the worker's control. Workers who choose to leave their jobs are not eligible for unemployment benefits. Finally, recipients of unemployment benefits must actively seek employment and must accept suitable employment if it is offered. Most states also require that workers be unemployed for at least one week before filing for UI benefits.

Like eligibility requirements, benefit levels vary from state to state. Most states provide half of a worker's salary for up to 26 weeks. Congress may extend this period to 39 weeks during economic recessions. Most states have maximum benefits, and some argue that inflation has eroded the value of unemployment compensation (Altmeyer, 1963; McMurrer & Chasanov, 1995). Another concern has been the disparity of benefits paid from state to state. Since state unemployment taxes are based on benefits paid, firms in states with high benefit rates suffer from a competitive disadvantage. This situation can lead to a "race for the bottom," in which states compete for the lowest unemployment tax rates. One way to succeed in this race is to keep benefits as low as possible.

Since UI's inception, the role of the federal government has expanded. In 1970, the Extended Unemployment Compensation Act was passed to allow the use of federal funds to provide benefits beyond state time limits during periods of high unemployment. Federal funds collected under the Federal Unemployment Tax Act finance 50 percent of the Extended Benefits Program. The other half is funded through state revenues. The Emergency Unemployment Compensation program was established in 1991 to supplement state coverage during times of high unemployment (McMurrer & Chasanov, 1995). The federal government finances all of the costs of this program through general revenues.

Financing for the federal share of the UI program is provided through a payroll tax paid by employers. In 2005, that tax amounted to 6.2 percent of the first $7,000 of covered employee wages (http://workforcesecurity.doleta.gov/unemploy/uitaxtopic.asp, accessed January 14, 2008). Employers in states with insurance programs that met federal requirements received credits against this tax of up to 5.4 percent of covered wages. The Department of Labor has administrative responsibility for the federal component of the UI program.

Nearly all U.S. workers are covered by UI. In 2000 the Department of Labor reported that 97 percent of employees were covered (OMB, n.d.). Only workers on "small" farms and the self-employed are not covered. Despite this growth in coverage, only a minority of unemployed workers receive UI benefits (Burtless & Saks, 1984). The proportion of unemployed workers who received unemployment compensation bottomed out in 1984 at 28.5 percent (McMurrer & Chasanov, 1995); nonetheless, by 2007 only 37 percent of the unemployed were receiving UI benefits (Stone, Greenstein, & Coven, 2007; http://www.cbpp.org/7-20-07ui.htm, accessed August 28, 2007).

Low rates of UI benefit receipt can be attributed in part to changes in federal and state policies. First, federal loans to states for their UI trust funds were changed in 1982, when states were required to repay the loans with interest. Prior to 1982, the loans had been interest-free. This change created an incentive for states to tighten their eligibility requirements, and many did so. Denial rates increased significantly, as did minimum earnings requirements. Many states have reduced both the amount and the duration of UI benefits. Federal laws also changed the value of benefits. In 1979, UI benefits were partially taxed, and in 1986 all UI benefits were subject to federal income tax. States were also required to reduce or eliminate UI payments to workers who received pensions or Social Security payments (Corson & Nicholson, 1988).

DISABILITY INSURANCE

The Social Security Act of 1935 did not provide for Disability Insurance (DI). Although there was some consideration for workers who lost earnings due to disability, the overriding concern was potential malingering. As one member of the Social Security advisory council put it, "You will have workers like those in the dust bowl area, people who have migrated to California and elsewhere . . . who will imagine they are disabled" (Berkowitz, 2000).

In 1956, the Social Security Act was amended to provide monthly benefits to "permanently and totally disabled" workers aged 50 to 64 and to adult disabled children of deceased or retired workers through the OASI program. With this addition, OASI came to be known as OASDI. Congress passed DI by "the barest of margins" (Berkowitz, 2000) despite opposition from the American Medical Association (AMA), private insurance companies, and employers' organizations. Even the Eisenhower administration opposed disability coverage (Altmeyer, 1963).

Opposition to DI stemmed from the fear that it would reduce a worker's incentive to work. In response to this concern, coverage did not extend to those with a temporary disability but to workers who were "permanently and totally disabled." The disability determination requirements were quite stringent. Eligibility for disability payments, like OASI eligibility, was based on a worker's past participation in covered employment.

In subsequent years, DI was liberalized. In 1958, benefits were provided for dependents of disabled workers. During the same year, coverage was extended to disabled workers of all ages; however, to be eligible a worker had to have completed at least 10 years in covered employment. Disability coverage is financed through the payroll tax, so with these additions the payroll tax (originally 1 percent) was increased to 2.25 percent each for employees and employers.

The liberalization of the program did not apply to disability determination, which, as we will see in Chapter 8, remains stringent. An estimated 19 million working-age adults have a disability that could limit their ability to work (Kaye, 2000). Among them, about 7.5 million received DI in 2005 (Social Security Administration, 2006, http://www.ssa.gov/policy/docs/statcomps/di_asr/2005/, accessed January 14, 2008). Recent years have seen increases in the number of female beneficiaries and individuals with mental impairments. In 2005 people who were disabled by mental disorders represented about a third of DI beneficiaries. The same year, DI beneficiaries received an average of $938 per month, resulting in an income well below the poverty threshold (ibid.).

Concern about the DI program's effect on work incentive has led to several initiatives. Under the Ticket to Work and Work Incentives Improvement Act of 1999, the Social Security Administration must offer recipients of Social Security disability payments or SSI the opportunity to participate in rehabilitative services designed to enhance their ability to be self-supporting. The act also removes two major disincentives to work. First, it allows participants who do enter the workforce to retain their Medicare or Medicaid coverage for an extended period. Second, it allows for an expedited eligibility determination if their effort to work is not successful. Thus, while disability beneficiaries who go to work would lose their cash payments, they would retain medical coverage and be assured that their cash assistance could be reinstated.

Recent years have also seen changes in the program's treatment of people who suffer from addiction. Prior to 1996, severe drug addiction or alcoholism was considered an appropriate basis for receiving disability benefits under OASDI or SSI. As the number of individuals whose disability stemmed from drug addiction or alcoholism increased, there was rising concern that they were abusing federal disability programs. As we will see in Chapter 8, the result was a series of initiatives that ultimately resulted in denial of OASDI and SSI benefits to anyone who is disabled primarily as the result of addiction.

MEDICAL INSURANCE

With the exception of the United States, all developed countries provide some form of national health insurance. In the United States, health insurance is available to the elderly through Title XVIII of the Social Security Act (Medicare).

The Development of National Health Insurance in Europe

Medical insurance originated with the "sickness insurance" that was initially provided to craftsmen in sixteenth- and seventeenth-century Europe. The craft guilds collected dues from members to establish funds to assist sick and disabled colleagues. With industrialization, sickness insurance was extended to factory workers. Industrial laborers joined *Krankenkassen,* or sickness insurance societies, often operated under the auspices of their unions. In 1854, Prussian legislators made sickness insurance compulsory for low-wage workers.[6]

Otto von Bismarck, once prime minister of Prussia, became chancellor of the German Empire in 1871. Bismarck viewed sickness insurance, like pension

---

6. Prussia was one of 30 German states at the time.

insurance, as a vehicle for cementing workers' loyalty to the German state. During a two-year period, from 1881 to 1883, Bismarck spearheaded the passage of a law that required low-wage workers in certain occupations to join a sickness insurance fund. Two-thirds of the cost of premiums was paid by the worker, with one-third contributed by the employer. As Roemer (1993) observed, "It is noteworthy that physicians raised no objections to this legislation; it ensured payment for their services to low-income patients; more affluent middle-class patients remained in the private market" (p. 92). Passage of this law set the stage for subsequent expansion of national health insurance throughout Germany and the rest of Europe.

In Britain, the National Health Insurance Act passed in 1911 under Prime Minister Lloyd George. Based on the German model, this legislation established compulsory health insurance coverage for low-wage workers. "Friendly societies" were established as the British equivalent of Germany's sickness insurance funds. They covered prescription drugs and general practitioner services, since hospital and specialist care were offered through public and charitable hospitals. After World War II, the British Labour Party enacted the National Health Service (NHS) Act of 1946, establishing the program of national health insurance that currently operates in Great Britain. Rather than simply covering drugs and general practitioner care, the NHS offered broad coverage to all British residents, with financing through general revenues. It became a model for post–World War II health insurance reform in other European nations.

France was the last major European nation to establish national medical insurance for industrial workers. As in most nations, autonomous sickness insurance societies had proliferated. French physicians were politically powerful, and they insisted that insurance operate on an "indemnity" basis, under which the patient pays the doctor's fee and then seeks reimbursement from the insurance provider. During times of economic hardship, physicians agreed to charge a negotiated fee schedule (Roemer, 1993).

Medical Insurance in the United States

Discussion of national health insurance in the United States began as early as 1912, with a proposal from Theodore Roosevelt's Bull Moose Party. In 1935, the designers of the Social Security Act were concerned about medical costs, but most believed that unemployment and old age were more immediate risks to workers than inability to pay for medical care. There was also the threat that physicians would oppose social insurance for health care.

In the 1940s, President Truman made national health insurance a legislative priority. But he was less effective than Roosevelt at working with Congress, and the American Medical Association (AMA) derailed his proposal. In addition, the post–World War II expansion in employee benefits meant that a growing number of workers were covered by private health insurance through their unions or employers. Consequently, Medicare was not enacted until 1964.

Pressure for Medicare came in part from the recognition by Social Security officials and others that the elderly had been left behind during the expansion of private health insurance. Retired workers were usually unable to obtain group insurance through a former employer; and insurance companies were reluctant to insure them as individuals, viewing the aged as bad risks. As President Johnson put it, "Many of our older citizens are still defenseless against the heavy medical costs of severe illness."

Robert Ball (commissioner of Social Security under Presidents Kennedy, Johnson, and Nixon) explained that advocates for Medicare saw it as "a first step toward universal national health insurance" (Ball, 1996). The AMA had favored national health insurance in 1916 but, by the time Medicare came up for debate, the organization vigorously opposed any government-sponsored health insurance. Most business groups, especially those in the insurance industry, joined the opposition to Medicare (Ball, 1996). Medicare's strongest advocates were leaders of the labor movement, who started to advocate for enactment in 1957 and made the final push during the expansion of Lyndon Johnson's Great Society programs.

As initially conceived, Medicare was to provide only hospital insurance. This limitation was intended to defuse AMA opposition by minimizing federal involvement in the patient–physician relationship. But the original legislation was amended in Congress to include doctors' services. The resulting program offered both hospital insurance (Part A) and optional coverage for physician services (Part B).

Parts A and B remain as they were originally conceived. Part A is provided to the beneficiary at no charge, and covers many services provided within hospitals and nursing homes, as well as home health services and some hospice services. Part B is purchased through a monthly premium. Unless beneficiaries notify Social Security that they do not want Part B, the premium is automatically deducted from each Social Security check. Under the 2003 Medicare Modernization Act, Part B premiums vary on the basis of income. In 2007, individuals with annual incomes below $80,000 paid the standard premium of $93.50 per month, while those with higher incomes paid an "income-related adjustment." The adjustment increased with income to a high of $161.40 per month for individuals with annual incomes in excess of $120,000 (http://www .ssa.gov/pubs/10162.html, accessed January 14, 2008). Part B covers doctors, therapists, ambulance, and diagnostic services as well as prostheses, medical equipment, and certain other medical services and supplies. Medicare offers limited coverage of nursing home care, paying some expenses associated with stays of up to 90 days. As originally conceived, Medicare operates the same as private indemnity insurance, paying "reasonable fees" for all covered services. This program is discussed in greater detail in Chapter 6.

In addition to these original programs, recent legislation has added two new "parts" to Medicare. Part C, known as Medicare + Choice, permits beneficiaries to enroll in managed care plans; and Part D provides limited coverage for prescription medications. These are described in Chapter 6.

MEANS-TESTED PROGRAMS UNDER
THE SOCIAL SECURITY ACT

The Social Security Act authorizes three public assistance programs: Aid to Dependent Children (now known as Temporary Assistance to Needy Families, or TANF); SSI; and Medicaid. These programs operate as federal–state partnerships and are means-tested, with eligibility based on income and assets. Funding is supplied by general revenues.

Public Assistance for Dependent Children

Title IV of the Social Security Act of 1935 provided federal grants to states that chose to provide public assistance to dependent children (ADC). In 1955, Nevada was the last state to provide ADC benefits. By that time, provisions of the Social Security Act of 1950 had taken effect. These allowed grants under the program to take into account not only the needs of dependent children but also those of the caretaker, usually the mother.

In 1962, the Kennedy administration proposed several revisions to ADC. Most noticeably, the program was renamed as Aid to Families with Dependent Children (AFDC) in an effort to emphasize the family context. The same year, amendments to the Social Security Act called for the delivery of social services to AFDC recipients. This change was to be the last major expansion of public assistance to dependent children under the Social Security Act.

During the 1970s and 1980s, growth in the welfare rolls exceeded population growth. At the same time, real wages eroded, and public support for welfare deteriorated. With the election of Ronald Reagan in 1982, the call to "end welfare as we know it" was popularized. Responding to this call, Congress and the president enacted the Family Support Act of 1988, which added a work requirement to AFDC. Harshly criticized as "work-fare" by advocates for the poor, this measure was only a hint of what was to follow.

The 1996 Personal Responsibility and Work Opportunity Reconciliation Act (PRWORA) effectively dismantled the New Deal guarantee of a minimum income for needy children. The act abolished the AFDC entitlement, substituting a block grant to the states. Federal guidelines required states to enforce work participation requirements and established a five-year lifetime limit for assistance under the new program, called Temporary Assistance to Needy Families (TANF). PRWORA also restricted noncitizens' access to SSI, although some of the more draconian measures were later softened. TANF is discussed in greater detail in Chapter 5.

Supplemental Security Income

The SSI program was established in 1972 (implemented in 1974) to provide a minimum guaranteed income to elderly, blind, or disabled persons. SSI combined several state-administered, categorical programs (Aid to the Blind; Aid to the Disabled; and Old–Age Assistance) into a single entity. Eligibility is based on categorical status (recipients must be either aged, blind, or disabled) and financial hardship. The program is administered as a federal–state partnership. State agencies manage eligibility determination and may supplement SSI payments, and the Social Security Administration manages federal contributions and regulation of the program. Since its inception, SSI has been remarkably unchanged, but it has seen considerable enrollment growth in recent decades (U.S. General Accounting Office, 1995).

In 1990 the commissioner of Social Security appointed the SSI Modernization Panel to review the program and suggest modifications. Chaired by Dr. Arthur Flemming (former Social Security commissioner), the panel undertook an exhaustive study of the program. The panel's report, released in 1992, identified major weaknesses in SSI and recommended a series of reforms. These included increasing benefits to 120 percent of the poverty threshold, adding staff to reduce delays in eligibility determination, eliminating the reduction in benefits for recipients who lived with family members, and increasing the program's asset limits (U.S. Department of Health and Human Services, Social Security Administration, 1992).

The recommendations of the Modernization Panel were largely ignored, yet SSI was revised, along with other welfare programs, through the 1996 Personal Responsibility and Work Opportunity Reconciliation Act. Under this welfare reform legislation, legal immigrants lost access to both SSI and food stamps unless they or their spouse had worked for 10 years and had not received benefits previously. Following implementation of the 1996 reforms, an estimated 500,000 immigrants (more than half of them elderly) became ineligible for SSI. Another 935,000 immigrants (many of them elderly) lost their eligibility for food stamps.[7] SSI benefits for most of these "pre-enactment" immigrants were restored by the Balanced Budget Act of 1997; however, this act did not restore benefits for "post-enactment" immigrants who arrived in the United States after August 1996 (Fix & Passel, 2002).

SSI has a strict means test. In 2006, income limits for eligibility were $603 per month for individuals and $904 per month for couples. In-kind income, including food, clothing, or shelter (or "something" that can be exchanged for food, clothing, or shelter), is considered when determining eligibility. If a person lives with a family member who provides shelter and food, the applicant's income is adjusted through addition of one-third of the federal SSI benefit amount. When this in-kind contribution is taken into account, some people become ineligible for SSI. Resource limits for SSI were subject to a one-time adjustment in 1984. Current asset limits are $2,000 for individuals and $3,000 for couples. Homes, adjoining land, and automobiles are not counted as assets in determining SSI eligibility, but life insurance policies with cash values in excess

---

7. Although states were allowed to prohibit legal immigrants from participating in Medicaid, most have consented to continue to provide Medicaid benefits to immigrants who were on the program before welfare reform as well as to new immigrants after five years of U.S. residency.

of $1,500 per person are considered (http://www.ssa.gov/policy/docs/statcomps/ supplement/2006/ssi.html, accessed January 14, 2008).

Benefit levels vary from state to state. Although the federal monthly benefit is fixed (in 2006 it was $603 for an individual and $904 for a couple), some states supplement this amount with contributions from state funds. All but six states (Arkansas, Georgia, Kansas, Mississippi, Tennessee, and West Virginia) provide a supplement. In 2006, some states (Hawaii, Oregon, and Utah) provided token amounts, whereas more generous supplements were found in Alaska ($362 for an elderly individual and $528 for an older couple living independently) and California ($233 for an elderly individual and $568 for an older couple) (http://www.workworld.org/ wwwebhelp/ssi_state_supplements_overview.htm, accessed January 14, 2008).

The SSI program, while "ideally suited to serve as a vehicle for reducing poverty among the elderly" (Zedlewski & Meyer, 1987, p. 14), fails to fulfill its promise for two reasons: nonparticipation and inadequate benefits. Only about half of the aged who are eligible for SSI benefits participate in the program, with those of greater education and health status more likely to participate (Zedlewski & Meyer, 1987; Davies et al., 2002). Concern over access problems led the U.S. Administration on Aging (AOA) to fund outreach demonstration efforts designed to raise public awareness of the program and to simplify the application process.

Those who do participate in SSI find that the program's benefits do not raise them above the poverty level. For example, in 2006 an elderly individual living in a state that did not supplement SSI would receive $604 per month, for an annual income of $7,248. The federal poverty threshold for that person was $817 per month, or $9,800 per year (http://aspe.hhs.gov/poverty/06poverty .shtml, accessed January 14, 2008). Moon (1990) based her critique of SSI on this difference between benefit levels and the poverty threshold and further argued that the program was unfair to women. Benefits for couples are more generous than those for individuals. Individuals are most often women living alone. In 2006, older individuals in states without supplements received benefits amounting to 74 percent of the poverty threshold, while older couples received 82 percent of the poverty level.

Medical Care for the Indigent: Medicaid

In 1950, the first federal program of medical care for indigent Americans was established as a grant-in-aid program. Authorized under the Social Security Act amendments of 1950, this program offered a federal match to states wishing to provide medical care to participants in other public assistance programs; however, not all states elected to participate.

In 1965, with an administration committed to medical insurance, Medicaid was established as Title XIX of the Social Security Act. Like the earlier program, Medicaid would operate as a federal–state partnership, with the federal match determined on the basis of poverty levels in the state; however, Medicaid was more generous than the previous program. It would be 17 years before all states had established Medicaid programs. Arizona was the holdout, waiting until 1982 to participate.

Medicaid differs from Medicare in both its administrative apparatus and its eligibility requirements. Medicare is administered by the Social Security Administration, whereas direct administration of Medicaid is carried out by each state. States vary in their eligibility requirements and in medical services covered, although coverage of some services is required by federal law. This mandatory coverage includes inpatient and outpatient hospital services; physician, midwife, and nurse practitioner care; laboratory and X-ray services; nursing home and home health care; and rural health clinic services. States may provide additional services. These commonly include prescription drugs, clinic services, hearing aids, dental care, prosthetic devices, and long-term care for the mentally retarded.

Medicaid funds health care for millions of Americans. Eligibility requirements are both means-tested and categorical. In addition to having limited income and assets, clients must belong to a covered group. These groups include children, pregnant women, the elderly, and people with disabilities. In 2002, the program served 51.4 million people at a cost of $248.8 billion (Kaiser Family Foundation, http://www.kff.org/medicaid/upload/7523.pdf, accessed January 14, 2008). Medicaid has absorbed a growing proportion of state budgets in recent decades, leading state and federal policy makers to focus on cost-containment strategies.

The elderly and disabled are a minority of those served by Medicaid, but they account for most program costs because of their more intensive use of health-care services. In 2002, for example, 10.5 percent (5.4 million) of Medicaid clients were elderly and 14.2 percent (7.3 million) were blind or disabled; yet these groups accounted for 68 percent of program spending (ibid.). Unlike Medicare, Medicaid covers custodial care in a skilled nursing facility. As a result, the program is the primary public financing mechanism for long-term care of the elderly. In 2005, Medicaid expenditures for nursing home care totaled $53.6 billion (Weiner, Freiman, & Brown, 2007). Chapters 5 and 6 provide further discussion of Medicaid.

HEALTH AND SOCIAL SERVICES

In addition to social insurance and public assistance, the Social Security Act allows for the use of federal funds to provide some health and social services. Four of the act's titles authorize services: Title IV allows for child welfare services, Title V establishes maternal and child health services, Title XX authorizes social services, and Title XXI creates the State Children's Health Insurance Program. Although federal staff are employed under these titles, they do not provide direct services because doing so is generally considered incompatible with constitutional limitations on the power of the federal government. Instead, federal staff members administer grants to the states. States then deliver services or arrange for their delivery in ways that are compatible with the federal regulations governing each program.

Child Welfare Services (Title IV)

Title IV of the 1935 Social Security Act established a program of grants-in-aid for states to set up their ADC programs. The title also allowed for child welfare services, allocating $1.5 million for that purpose (Social Security Administration, n.d.). An initial focus was on development of child welfare services in rural areas, though states had flexibility in using their child welfare allocations. Katharine Lenroot, director of the Children's Bureau in 1935, explained that

> [t]he basic principle followed in planning programs, especially in child welfare, was that of taking each state where it was, and encouraging initiative and flexibility, with great emphasis on local responsibility. . . . The term "child welfare service" was seen for the first time, in many states, as extending far beyond institutional care, or foster home care, or protective services, or cooperation with juvenile courts, to include a variety of measures, such as casework service, homemaker service and day care to strengthen and supplement the child's own home so that he could remain in it. (Social Security Administration, n.d., p. 2)

Just as the 1950s were a time of expansion for other Social Security Act programs, child welfare experienced tremendous growth and increased federal appropriations. With the shift from a rural to an urban emphasis, child welfare services reflected the broad social transition of the United States into an urban, industrialized nation.

Today, child welfare services under Title IV include federal payments for foster care and adoption assistance, preventive services designed to keep children in their homes, services to develop alternative placements for children for whom foster care or adoption are not feasible, and family reunification services. Family preservation services are authorized under Title IV to provide intensive support to maintain children in their homes. Funds are also provided for training of child welfare professionals and research in methods of improving services in the field. States receive fixed allocations under these statutes, although some must meet matching requirements. Child welfare services are discussed further in Chapter 11.

Maternal and Child Health Services (Title V)

Title V of the 1935 Social Security Act allowed for grants to states in support of maternal and child health services. This program enabled the U.S. Children's Bureau to continue the work it had begun in establishing clinics for mothers and children throughout the nation. Grants for maternal and child health did not require states to provide matching funds, but the program's regulations did stipulate that states had to use funds to extend or improve upon existing services (not to replace them) and that states were required to focus on needy areas (typically rural areas) and groups with the severest hardships.

Today, these services are provided in each state under the Maternal and Child Health Services Block Grant. With a focus on low-income mothers and those in rural areas, these block grant funds are used to meet the health objectives established under the Public Health Service Act of 2000. States have latitude in allocating these funds. Typical services provided include immunizations, visiting nurse activities, rehabilitative services for blind and disabled children, and case management for children with special health-care needs. In addition to the state allocations, federal funds are available under Title V for training health personnel and conducting research on health-care delivery, genetic testing and counseling, hemophilia, and early interventions.

Social Services Block Grant (Title XX)

Title XX of the Social Security Act was passed in 1975 to provide social services to vulnerable Americans. A funding cap of $2.5 billion was established, making the program a "capped entitlement." It was converted to the Social Services Block Grant (SSBG) through the Omnibus Budget Reconciliation Act of 1981. The SSBG provides funds to states for social services directed toward achieving economic self-sufficiency; preventing or remedying neglect, abuse, or exploitation of children or adults; preventing or reducing inappropriate institutionalization; and securing referrals for institutional care. Within these broad goals, states have flexibility to decide what services they will provide. SSBG funds are typically used to provide day care for children, home-based services for the elderly or disabled, and protective services. Each state's allocation is based on its population. The SSBG does not have a state matching requirement.

Children's Health Insurance Program (Title XXI)

In 1995, an estimated 10 million children, 13.8 percent of Americans under the age of 18, were not covered by medical insurance (Weil, 1997). Concern for these vulnerable children led to the creation, through the 1997 Balanced Budget Act, of the State Children's Health Insurance Program, known as SCHIP, or simply as CHIP. The program authorizes funding for states to provide health coverage to uninsured, low-income children. It targets children in families with incomes between 100 and 200 percent of the federal poverty threshold. These families are not eligible for Medicaid but generally cannot afford to purchase private insurance. States enjoy flexibility in designing their CHIP programs. They may either expand their existing Medicaid coverage or establish separate programs. The CHIP program limits enrollee costs by prohibiting deductibles and limiting co-payments to nominal amounts. Usually premiums are not allowed.

SCHIP detractors have argued that families are using it instead of private coverage, an argument that received support from a 2007 report by the Congressional Budget Office (CBO). The CBO concluded that somewhere between a quarter and a half of the 8 million children covered in 2007 were in families that dropped private insurance (CBO, 2007). This was clearly on President Bush's mind in 2007 when he vetoed the Children's Health Insurance Program Reauthorization Act. With a price tag of $35 billion, the bill would have raised income eligibility to 300 percent of the poverty level, extending coverage to an additional 4 million children. It passed the House and Senate with bipartisan support. But President Bush argued that it "would move health care in this country in the wrong direction," citing his concern that greater numbers of families would drop their private health insurance coverage to get their children enrolled in CHIP (CNN, 2007).

A TOOL FOR SOCIAL JUSTICE: THE PHILOSOPHIES OF SOCIAL SECURITY IN THE UNITED STATES

The Social Security Act is the foundation of America's safety net and a central vehicle for promoting social justice. It applies three broad strategies: (1) individual insurance financed through payroll taxes and user premiums, (2) public assistance financed through federal grants-in-aid using federal and state general revenues, and (3) health and social services financed through general revenues.

Social Security is a pivotal mechanism for allocating the costs and benefits of U.S. citizenship. Perhaps the most controversial of the act's provisions stem from the costs it has imposed on citizens. This controversy is seen, for example, in the constitutional challenges that were raised concerning the OAI program's compulsory payroll tax. The payroll tax has risen considerably in recent decades, from 2 percent of wages and a $3,000 cap to more than 15 percent of wages and an $89,700 cap in 2005. Thus, OAI absorbs a significant proportion of the incomes of low- and middle-income workers. Proposals to increase the payroll tax continue to fuel the controversy over this cost of membership.

Other costs imposed by the Social Security Act are tied less directly to the act itself but are every bit as controversial as the payroll tax. The public assistance and service programs funded under Social Security are financed through general revenues, often at both federal and state levels. As indicated in Chapter 2, these revenues are generated through individual and corporate income taxes. Since these taxes are progressive, Social Security's public assistance and service programs represent a significant redistribution of income from the affluent to the needy. Movements to dismantle these programs, most recently through the elimination of AFDC, combine with reductions in the tax burden of affluent Americans to redistribute the nation's resources from the poor to the rich.

Social Security represents a distinctly American approach to vulnerability and social justice. The program borrows little from oligarchic and socialist philosophies. Instead, it reflects the two philosophical perspectives on social justice most compatible with American political and economic thought: libertarianism and liberalism.

The Social Security Act was carefully crafted to minimize libertarian objections. The imposition of compulsory taxes was minimized, as was the role of the federal government in delivery of assistance and services. The increasing use of block grants to fund Social Security Act programs is part of the trend toward devolution, or moving decision making as close as possible to the individual level. This movement is an indirect outgrowth of the libertarian emphasis on personal freedom. The Social Security Act defers to the private market in several areas, as when it establishes benefit levels that are well below the poverty threshold. No able-bodied worker would be motivated to forgo employment with the promise of such minimal sustenance. This unwillingness to provide an alternative to private employment illustrates the principle of "less eligibility," which will be discussed in Chapter 5.

The contribution of liberal philosophies to Social Security in the United States is readily apparent. The act established a "social minimum" for income below which Americans in some vulnerable categories (the deserving poor) should not fall. Thus the SSI program delivers a minimum income for the aged, blind, and disabled. The public assistance and health and social service programs under Social Security may be viewed from a utilitarian perspective as optimizing social well-being. Financed through progressive taxes, they transfer income from those who can afford it most easily to enhance the well-being of those who are most in need of assistance.

SUMMARY: SOCIAL SECURITY PROGRAMS

In this chapter we have explored programs established through the Social Security Act of 1935 and its amendments. From a historical perspective, Social Security is seen not simply as a tool for improving workers' well-being but as a political vehicle for securing loyalty to a state. Even as it secures worker loyalty, it presents tremendous administrative demands, requiring the construction of an elaborate government administrative apparatus. Contemporary programs established through the act reflect three models: (1) social insurance programs financed through payroll taxes and premiums, (2) public assistance programs financed through federal and state general revenues, and (3) health and social service programs delivered through grants-in-aid to the states. Several proposals to reform the OASI program were reviewed here: privatization, earnings sharing, and caregiver credits. These proposals can be seen as efforts to shift the costs and benefits of citizenship, thereby directly influencing social justice.

KEYWORDS

New Deal   Great Depression   Social Security

THINK ABOUT IT

1. The Social Security Act of 1935 was carefully crafted to comply with constitutional provisions restricting the role of the federal government. Compare the act's insurance programs with its means-tested programs. Do they differ in the roles assigned to the states? How and why?

2. Social Security developed in Europe during the latter part of the nineteenth century. What was happening in major Asian countries during this period? What type of insurance did workers in these countries have against "the three fears" of poverty, illness in old age, and unemployment? What forms of social insurance are offered by Asian nations today?

3. What are the consequences should a state fail to adhere to federal laws and regulations governing a grant-in-aid program? Have these consequences ever been applied to your state?

4. Consider the redistributive function of Social Security as it is reflected in the funding sources for the three types of programs authorized under the act (social insurance, public assistance, and services). Which of these has the strongest redistributive function? Would this be changed under proposed "Social Security reforms"?

WEB-BASED EXERCISES

For direct links to all the sites in these exercises, log on to the Student Companion Site for this book at academic.cengage.com/social_work/barusch, and choose Chapter 4.

1. Go to the Social Security Administration website at http://www.ssa.gov/planners/calculators/htm. Use the quick calculator at the SSA site to estimate your retirement benefits based on the earnings you anticipate as a professional social worker. Now double your earnings estimate. What difference does that make in your estimated benefits? Investigate your "break-even date." Do you expect to live longer than this? If so, would you be better off retiring at 62, your full retirement age, or 70 years of age?

2. Go to http://www.ssa.gov/OACT/TR/ to view the current report of the Social Security Trustees. Have the projected dates of trust fund depletion changed in the past few years? Can you explain these changes? How do the trustees explain the situation? Do you find their explanation compelling?

SUGGESTED RESOURCES

Achenbaum, W. A. (1986). *Social Security: Visions and Revisions.* Cambridge: Cambridge University Press.

Kingson, E. R., & Berkowitz, E. D. (1993). *Social Security and Medicare: A Policy Primer.* Westport, CT: Greenwood Publishing Group.

www.ssa.gov. Maintained by the Social Security Administration, this site offers outstanding historical material on the act as well as the opportunity to subscribe to a free e-mail newsletter that gives updates on news affecting Social Security.

5

Poverty

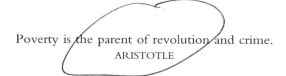

Poverty is the parent of revolution and crime.
ARISTOTLE

In the United States we tend to attribute poverty to individual flaws such as laziness, intemperance, or inability to defer gratification. This tendency to "blame the victim" is behind many of the nation's attitudes and interventions. The Great Depression demonstrated, however, that the risk of poverty is widespread and unpredictable. The conditions for collective action discussed in the introduction to Part II were present, and the New Deal was enacted. Social Security is probably the nation's most effective antipoverty program, providing income to millions. The Depression ended more than 60 years ago, and it is easy to forget the lessons of that difficult time. As we will see in this chapter, contemporary poverty policies increasingly rely on private market solutions, restricting public assistance to those who are clearly unable to support themselves through paid employment.

This chapter begins with a human perspective as we consider the experiences of Antonia Flores, a mother raising her son with support from the Temporary Assistance for Needy Families (TANF) program. Next, we will explore the problem of defining poverty and then move on to examine divergent values and beliefs about poverty and the poor. These include religious explanations of poverty, as well as economic and sociological theories about its causes. To provide some historical background, we will trace the development of interventions to prevent or alleviate poverty. The 1996 welfare reforms will be examined, along with other contemporary programs and policies. We then look at the contemporary realities of poverty in this nation, examining populations at

Driving away from my meeting with Antonia, I had an angry lump in my stomach. It was hard to parse the feeling, since Antonia herself was so cheerful and positive. In fact, the main advice she had for other women on TANF was "Stay positive. I know it's sometimes hard, but you have to stay positive." Besides, Antonia Flores does not fit the stereotype of a welfare mother. She is bright and articulate. Her home is immaculate. Her son and the niece she cares for are healthy and well-behaved.

Antonia lives with her mother, her brother, and her son in a modest three-bedroom home located in a working-class neighborhood within a stone's throw of the interstate highway. Walking up the drive I saw tulips blooming in flower beds of most of the little post-WWII brick bungalows. The neighborhood was well cared for, and I suspected that it had been a peaceful place to live until the interstate went in.

I rang the door and waited for a bit, noticing the lace curtains on Antonia's front window and the multiple locks on the front door. Antonia undid the locks one by one, then flung open the door and greeted me with a twinkling smile. At 34 years old, Antonia describes herself as square: "4 feet high and 4 feet wide." She is, in fact, less than 5 feet high and morbidly obese. The day we met, Antonia was dressed in a black tank top and slacks, with dark eye makeup and bare feet.

Antonia is the only member of her family who has ever received public assistance. Her father immigrated from Mexico and works as a mechanic. Her mother, who is of Irish descent, works as a registered nurse. Her siblings all work at "good" jobs. Antonia identifies as a Latina. She finished high school and got a good job with Discover Card, moving up through the ranks to become a senior account manager. Despite the impressive title, the job did not pay especially well. However, it did offer health insurance.

While working for Discover Card Antonia met her husband, Ted. They married in 1999, and the man who had courted Antonia abruptly disappeared. In his place was the "new Ted," an addict who promptly lost his job at a fast-food outlet and became verbally abusive. By the time Antonia fully realized what her husband was like, she was pregnant with her son Christopher. When Chris was born Antonia was the sole support of the family. Even when sober, Ted was not much of a companion, and when he was high, he could be downright abusive, calling Antonia names and criticiz-

ing her. One morning when Chris was 3 months old and she was late to work, Antonia made the mistake of asking Ted to change a diaper. When he blew his stack, she walked out on him and later walked out on the relationship.

That was five years ago. Antonia had a good job, and she moved in with her mother and brother. Family support provided a stable environment for her son, and life went smoothly until Antonia began to have health problems. After weeks of nighttime stomach aches, she learned that her gall bladder had to be removed. When that was done, her knee gave out, and she had surgery to repair it. She developed asthma and missed work for occasional attacks. With all this going on, people at work were getting fired. There were rumors that Discover was weeding out longtime workers to replace them with new employees at lower wages. Antonia tried to avoid missing work, but when her knee was reinjured in a car accident, she had no choice. She went in for a repeat surgery, never imagining it would cost her the job she had held for 14 years.

As Antonia explains, Discover sent a letter demanding physician certification of her injury. The letter went out via UPS and was left at a back door. By the time she found it, the deadline for submitting verification had passed. Nonetheless, she rushed to the doctor's office and watched as they faxed the certification to Discover. Despite multiple attempts, her employer never acknowledged receipt of the document, and Antonia was summarily terminated. Although she was eligible for unemployment benefits, the human resources people at Discover recommended that she go on TANF.

Although paperwork was a bizarre hassle at times, Antonia speaks highly of her experiences with TANF. The transition to Medicaid was smooth. All of her doctors agreed to accept Medicaid payments, and it was cheaper than COBRA benefits. Her caseworker was "great," as was the social worker. The program even gave her counseling to help her deal with "relationship issues." Her caseworker helped her apply for support from the WIC program, which she described as "great!" She applied for public housing but faced a waiting list a yard long. It would be years before Antonia and her son would be eligible.

Antonia felt that TANF benefits were insufficient to meet her needs. She received $640 per month, of which $300 went for child care and $250 went to her mother for rent. And the program had a 30-hour-per-week work requirement. The work was sometimes pointless, requiring Antonia to hang around the TANF office waiting for someone to give her a task. Day care was subsidized, but it was hard to find a provider willing to accept TANF rates.

But Antonia's greatest concern was the TANF limitations on schooling. She wanted to complete a college degree and learn to be either a counselor or a computer programmer. Given her people skills, Antonia thinks she could be a great counselor, but she thinks computer programming might be more marketable. Under TANF neither is possible. The program will only support approved Associate of Arts programs. And there seems to be a mismatch between available programs and Antonia's needs and abilities. For instance, on a list of approved programs was one that would train her to be a trucker. Antonia pointed out to her caseworker that this was "ludicrous." She couldn't even reach the pedals on a truck, and when would she get to see her son?

Antonia is not one to complain, but she was happy to offer recommendations on how TANF could be improved. In her state, Medicaid does not pay for dental care. So she and her son live without regular exams and routine cleanings. If a tooth becomes infected, Medicaid will pay for extraction but not repair. So one of the worries that keeps Antonia up at night is the fear that she will break a tooth and end up with an empty space in her mouth. Antonia recommends that Medicaid provide limited preventive care for dental needs—"maybe just once a year." She is also concerned about a mismatch between the training programs approved as work participation for TANF and the job market in her state. Despite great demand for computer professionals, no computer training is provided under TANF. Antonia sees this as a missed opportunity. She argues that fathers should be held accountable for their children's well-being. Her husband goes from job to job, quitting as soon as the state begins to garnish his wages for the back child support he owes.

After six months on TANF, Antonia decided that it wasn't worth it. She went off cash assistance, keeping her food stamps and Medicaid. I asked whether she did this because of the lifetime limit on cash assistance. Antonia said she had never heard of the lifetime limit. She asked for details with alarm, worrying that the deadline might apply to food stamps and Medicaid.

I asked Antonia about her worries, and she said they were all "American dream" worries: "Will I be able to own a home? Can I have a car? Will I be able to pay for my son to go to college? Will I ever be able to retire?" These and other concerns made sleep impossible until Antonia discovered Ambien. She takes the sleep medication every night, and it seems to make life easier. She takes six or seven other medications as well, and notes that Medicaid coverage is better than the insurance she had when she was working. Under private insurance those co-payments really mounted up.

Antonia's dreams focus on her son. "He's a *wonderful* kid. Sometimes sassy, but just great!" Since her state has just established a school voucher program, she would like to take Chris out of public school. Because their local school is under renovation, he is bussed for half an hour to a school with large classes where he has experienced some bullying. Antonia has talked with the local Catholic school, and they are willing to accept the voucher even though it won't cover all of his tuition. She will be allowed to work off the difference by providing assistance in the office. With a good education, Chris will be able to live the American dream, even if Antonia won't.

Reflecting on poverty in America, Antonia acknowledges that her income is below the poverty threshold but says she does not consider herself poor. She thinks she is fortunate because her family is so supportive and her son so terrific. She thinks the main problem is low wages, reporting that when she worked for Discover she sometimes had to call in sick because she didn't have enough money for gas. Commenting on rising inequality and the high cost of housing, Antonia asks, "Is profit really that much more important than people?"

Antonia provides day care to her 2-year-old niece, and the child calls her "mama." During our interview she alternately nestled in Antonia's generous arms and romped around the bare living room, flirting with me and showing off her tricks. This child care provides the only source of cash for Antonia and her son. I had offered to pay her $20 for our interview, and when I gave her the bill, she exclaimed, "Now we get to see *Spider-Man 3!*" The movie wouldn't be out for weeks, but she knew her son would love it.

A Social Work Perspective

Why did Antonia's experiences make me so angry? Antonia followed the rules. She finished high school, got a job, got married, and had a child. Lacking major

Continued

Continued

physical or mental disabilities, she should have had a good shot at the American dream. But this was not to be. Her employer had shifted into a twenty-first-century paradigm in which employees are dispensable. So when she began to have health problems after 14 years of low-paid employment, Antonia was "terminated." Evidently it was no longer profitable to employ her. Discover passed the buck to TANF, effectively avoiding the bur-

den on its unemployment insurance. Other major corporations such as Wal-Mart and McDonald's use public assistance to fill gaps left by the inadequate pay and nonexistent health coverage they offer to their employees. Then, through their politicians, they put the squeeze on these people, stigmatizing them as a "welfare problem." The result is lower personnel costs and higher shareholder profits.

risk, recent trends in inequality, and three "secondary risks" associated with poverty: homelessness, violence, and fraud. The chapter will close with a brief consideration of the future prospects of America's poor.

DEFINING POVERTY

Poverty can be understood in both absolute and relative terms. "Absolute poverty" is based on a fixed level of resources, or "threshold." A person whose resources fall below the threshold experiences absolute poverty. Eligibility requirements for public poverty programs such as TANF reflect the concept of absolute poverty. "Relative poverty" is based on comparison. A person whose situation is disadvantaged compared to someone else's, or compared to what it was in the past, experiences relative poverty. Compared to her siblings, Antonia experiences relative poverty, but because of her other babysitting income and family support she is relatively advantaged compared to other TANF recipients. Some have argued that relative measures of poverty are more informative than absolute measures because the self-images, experiences, and prospects of poor families are affected by the affluence in the broader culture, regardless of their actual level of deprivation.

The most common definition of poverty used in the United States, the Federal Poverty Threshold, is an absolute measure. It is used by the Census Bureau to gauge poverty, and serves as the basis of eligibility for several means-tested programs, including the Food Stamp Program, Supplemental Security Income, and TANF.[1]

---

1. Technically speaking, there is a difference between the poverty "threshold" and the poverty "guidelines." The guidelines are based on the threshold and are used to determine program eligibility, while the threshold is used for statistical purposes such as the measurement of poverty. The guidelines are issued by the Department of Health and Human Services, while the threshold is issued by the Bureau of the Census.

The Federal Poverty Threshold was developed in the 1960s by Mollie Orshansky, an economist who worked for the Social Security Administration. Charged by the Kennedy administration with developing an effective measure of poverty, Ms. Orshansky found that the only existing measure of family needs was based on food. This measure, called the "Economy (or 'Thrifty') Food Plan" had been developed by the U.S. Department of Agriculture. It estimated the cost of food required to sustain nutritional adequacy during a temporary emergency or shortage of funds. Since it was believed that food costs represented one-third of a family's budget, the total budget was set by multiplying the Economy Food Plan by three. Initially the poverty threshold for farm families, female-headed households, and the elderly was lower than the standard amount. These differences were based on consumption studies conducted by the Department of Agriculture that revealed lower food expenditures among women and the elderly. Farm families were believed to have access to inexpensive garden produce, and nutritional studies suggested that the elderly had lower caloric requirements (Orshansky, 1965).

The poverty threshold has been changed in two ways. In 1969 the measure was "indexed" to the Consumer Price Index (CPI) so that it rises annually with inflation. Then, in 1981, in response to political pressure and technical arguments, the thresholds for farm families and female-headed households were raised to the standard level (Fisher, 1997). For statistical purposes, the threshold for those older than 65 remains 8 to 10 percent below that of other households. This difference does not affect their eligibility for public programs, but it is reflected in Bureau of the Census poverty estimates.

Each year, the Department of Health and Human Services publishes the latest poverty guidelines in the Federal Register and on its website (go to www.hhs.gov and search for poverty threshold and year). The poverty guidelines for 2007 are listed in Table 5.1.

TABLE 5.1   **2007 U.S. Department of Health and Human Services Poverty Guidelines**

Persons in Family or Household	48 Contiguous States and DC	Alaska	Hawaii
1	$10,210	$12,770	$11,750
2	13,690	17,120	15,750
3	17,170	21,470	19,750
4	20,650	25,820	23,750
5	24,130	30,170	27,750
6	27,610	34,520	31,750
7	31,090	38,870	35,750
8	34,570	43,220	39,750
For each additional person, add:	*3,480*	*4,350*	*4,000*

SOURCE: U.S. Department of Health and Human Services (2007). *Federal Register, 72*(15), 3147–3148. http://aspe.hhs.gov/poverty/07poverty.shtml (accessed April 14, 2007).

CRITIQUES OF THE POVERTY THRESHOLD

Some people have argued that the federal poverty threshold overestimates the extent of poverty in the United States because it does not count "in-kind" benefits such as food stamps, housing assistance, and medical programs as income (Friedman & Friedman, 1979; Murray, 1994). According to this view, the in-kind benefits available to the poor should be counted as income, based on their market value. Charles Murray argued that the benefits available to poor people made it "possible for almost anyone to place themselves [*sic*] above the official poverty level" (Murray, 1994, p. 64). Going even further with this argument, Gilder (1981) suggested that the poor receive benefits every bit as valuable as a middle-class job because they have more leisure time and they work "off the books." Others have argued that the poverty threshold should be revised to include assets as well as income because some poor people own their homes (see Oliver & Shapiro, 1990).

Others argue that the federal poverty threshold underestimates financial hardship. Mollie Orshansky, the economist who developed the threshold, suggested that it was at least 40-percent too low because the "multiplier" used to estimate total budget at three times food costs was too small (Chambers, 1982). Recent estimates suggest that low-income families in the United States spend roughly one quarter of their income on food, compared to a national average of about 12 percent. This would suggest a multiplier of 4, rather than 3 (see Ruggles, 1990).

Other critics of the poverty threshold focus on the Economy Food Plan itself. Some note that it was intended as a *temporary* budget and is inadequate for sustaining health over an extended period. The plan also places heavy demands on homemakers. It requires that a shopper know where to buy the least expensive commodities; be able to transport and store large quantities of food; and have the time, energy, and ability to prepare meals from basic staples (Chalfant, 1985; Wilson, 1987).

Another problem with the federal poverty threshold is its failure to take into account regional differences in the cost of living. A family of four would be hard pressed to live on $20,650 (the 2007 poverty threshold) in New York City, but they might find it possible in rural Alabama.[2] The threshold does not take into account other circumstances, such as chronic illness or disability, that might affect a family's needs.

Several authors have suggested alternative approaches to the measurement of financial hardship in the United States. Holden and Smeeding (1990) identified five sources of financial vulnerability among the elderly: lack of health insurance, limited assets, Social Security benefits that preclude Medicaid eligibility, high housing costs, and chronic disability. They concluded that 35 percent of older people experienced at least two of these sources of insecurity. Robert Binstock

---

2. This issue is at least partially addressed when the threshold distinguishes between Alaska and Hawaii and the 48 contiguous states. The poverty threshold for Alaska is 1.25 times that used in the 48 states, while that of Hawaii is 1.15 times the mainland threshold.

(1985) suggested that measures of poverty incorporate household expenditure patterns as well as an individual's ability to cope with hardship. Either of these measures would involve a complex assessment process. In contrast, the federal poverty threshold is attractive because of its historic consistency and its administrative convenience. Thus it will probably continue to be the dominant measure of financial hardship in this country.

VALUES AND BELIEFS ABOUT POVERTY AND THE POOR

Values and beliefs about poverty influence the methods chosen to prevent or mitigate poverty. These values and beliefs can be grouped into seven broad categories: religious teachings about charity; punitive responses to the poor; poverty as motivation; "human capital" approaches; "culture of poverty" explanations; "restricted opportunity" explanations; and "pauperization" arguments. These ideas emerged in diverse historical contexts, each offers a distinct outlook on the individual and structural factors that contribute to poverty, and each supports a distinct approach to poverty interventions.

Religious Beliefs About Charity

Charity is an essential part of the teachings of most world religions. Buddhism teaches that "emancipation of the heart through love and charity" is the most important form of righteousness. Islamic teachings view charity not as a "favor done by the giver" but as "spending for the cause of Allah . . . as a means to purify the soul of the giver and to . . . unite him with his poor brother" (http://ourdialogue.com/charity.htm, accessed January 15, 2008).

Ancient Jewish doctrines moved care of the poor from the realm of charity to that of justice. They taught that not only did the well-off have a duty to give charity but the poor had a right (and even a duty) to receive it. The Talmud, a collection of biblical texts accompanied by rabbinical commentaries, prescribes in careful detail how relief is to be administered. Under Talmudic law, a poor man should receive "Sufficient for his needs in that which he wanteth . . . [if he is hungry] he should be fed; if he needs clothing, he should be clothed; if he lacks household utensils, they should be purchased for him" (Trattner, 1989, p. 3).

With roots in Jewish traditions, Christianity retained this emphasis on care of the poor. The New Testament emphasizes that the soul's entry into heaven depends on deeds of mercy and charity. Most telling in this regard is the description of Judgment Day in the Gospel of St. Matthew: "And the King shall answer and say unto them, Verily, I say unto you, Inasmuch as ye have done it unto one of the least of these my brethren, ye have done it unto me" (Matthew 25:40). Under Christian teachings, care of the poor is a matter of both justice and charity. The needy have a right to assistance; and the spiritual well-being of the rich depends on their providing charity. The Christian notion of salvation requires the faithful to care for the poor, not only for altruistic reasons but also for the benefit of their own souls.

As early as the sixth century A.D., care of the poor was an integral part of some Christian monastic traditions. Using income from land holdings and donations, monks cared for the needy who came to their doors, as well as those who lived in nearby communities. Medieval hospitals, many of which were attached to monasteries, also provided services to the needy.[3]

Later, during the Middle Ages, the Catholic Church organized the first comprehensive system of relief in Europe. From the twelfth through the fourteenth centuries, relief for the poor operated under the direction of the Medieval Poor Law, a set of policies developed by church leaders to specify relief measures for the indigent. Under this system, "a poor man was considered an honorable man, and the only test for aid was need" (Segalman & Basu, 1981, p. 60).

Thus religious approaches to poverty do not attempt to explain why some people are poor and others are not. Poverty is treated as neither individual nor societal failure, but as an integral part of the human condition, offering the opportunity, requirement, or possibility of personal charity. This view stands in sharp contrast to approaches that treat poverty as a crime.

Poverty as Crime

Punitive responses to poverty are based on the belief that at least some of the poor are lazy and need punishment to overcome their evil ways. Most obvious among these "undeserving" poor are individuals who are able-bodied but do not work. But their ranks also include people whose disabilities might be considered their own fault, such as alcoholics and spendthrifts.

One of Alexis de Tocqueville's remarks after visiting America was that in the new nation there was only one crime: being poor. But Americans were not the first to assume a punitive stance vis-à-vis the poor. Laws in sixteenth-century England assigned severe punishments to able-bodied beggars. As Trattner (1989) reported, "They were to be brought to the market place and 'there to be tyed to the end of a carte naked and be beten with whyppes throughe out . . . tyll [their bodies] . . . be blody by reason of suche whypping'" (p. 7).

Modern approaches to the poor are seldom as harsh as these but are nonetheless punitive. The poor are no longer subjected to whipping but to shame and indifference. Lengthy waits are one form of punishment. In *Tyranny of Kindness,* Theresa Funiciello noted a sign in a New York welfare office that said, "NO MATTER WHAT TIME YOUR APPOINTMENT IS, IF YOU ARE NOT HERE BY 8:30 A.M. YOU WILL NOT BE SEEN" (Funiciello, 1993, p. 3). This punitive approach is consistent with the needs of a capitalist economy, as we will see below.

---

3. This discussion draws heavily from Walter Trattner, *From Poor Law to Welfare State: A History of Social Welfare in America* (New York: Free Press, 1989).

Poverty as Motivation

Some have argued that in preindustrial nations there is no individual poverty. Families, communities, and even nations as a whole may experience deprivation, but individuals are not left to experience poverty alone, and the poor are not isolated as "other" or "different." Under this view, capitalist industrial economies require poverty because they need a large unemployed segment in their labor force. The hardship and embarrassment associated with unemployment are seen as necessary motivators that make workers willing to labor for low wages in difficult conditions and to leave their homes and seek employment in industrial centers. Herbert Gans noted that poverty could be eliminated if the wealthy chose to do so. The fact that they choose not to do so indicates their need for a reliable source of cheap labor (Gans, 1971).

Regulation of charity in the interest of maintaining a labor force predates the industrial revolution. As we will see when we examine poverty interventions, the British parliament enacted the Statute of Labourers in 1348 to ensure that all able-bodied people were forced to work. Later on, the Elizabethan Poor Law would require anyone capable of working to do so, if only to earn the right to receive assistance.

As Antonia noted, TANF benefits are quite limited. This illustrates the principle of "less eligibility" and reflects the belief that poverty is an important motivator. Under this principle, no one on relief should be as well-off as the lowest-paid laborer. Less eligibility is an integral part of poverty interventions. It is manifest in the low level of benefits provided by public assistance programs and by humiliating administrative practices such as those described earlier.

Human Capital Explanations of Poverty

Some explanations of poverty focus on the skills, education, and experience or "human capital" that an individual brings to the marketplace. According to this view, the poor simply have inadequate or outdated skills and work experience. Neither the individual nor the system is responsible for poverty, which is seen as the inevitable consequence of a dynamic economy. With rapidly changing technology, workers need to constantly develop new skills. If, for whatever reason, they do not bring the appropriate skills to the labor market, they will not secure the jobs necessary to keep them out of poverty. Further, workers in "dead end" low-paying jobs are those who did not receive the education or training necessary to get a better job.

Empirical support for a focus on human capital as an explanation for poverty is seen in the association between educational attainment and rates of poverty. Figure 5.1 illustrates that association using census data from a 2006 supplement. Clearly people with higher levels of education enjoy dramatically lower risks of poverty. Of course, that doesn't tell the whole story, since, for example, women in the United States generally have comparable educational attainment to men but their risk of poverty is higher; and access to education is at least partly determined by class.

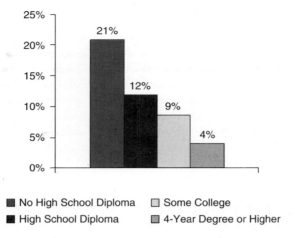

FIGURE 5.1 Educational attainment and poverty.

SOURCE (for data): U.S. Bureau of the Census (2006a). Current Population Survey, 2006 Annual Social and Economic Supplement. http://pubdb3.census.gov/macro/032007/pov/new29_100_01.htm.

Human capital explanations of poverty blame neither the individual nor the society, and they bring a (some would say simplistic) spirit of optimism to the task of reducing poverty. Interventions based on this outlook are likely to incorporate job training and education for the poor. They might also include subsidized employment designed to improve work skills. Federal job training programs, such as those funded under the federal Workforce Investment Act (WIA) of 1998 are examples of this approach to alleviating poverty. The WIA funds job training for dislocated workers and low-income youth to enable them to succeed in the modern labor market. The Ticket to Work program described in Chapter 4 is also based on this approach.

Culture of Poverty Explanations

The term "culture of poverty" was coined by Oscar Lewis, an anthropologist who studied poor families in Mexico and Puerto Rico. As he defined it, "The culture of poverty is both an adaptation and a reaction of the poor to their marginal position in a class-stratified, highly individuated, capitalistic society. It represents an effort to cope with feelings of hopelessness and despair which develop from the realization of the improbability of achieving success in terms of the values and goals of the larger society" (Lewis, 1965, p. xliv).

The culture of poverty is seen as a distinct set of values that arise in the context of hopeless disadvantage. These values include a present-time orientation that seeks immediate gratification and precludes long-term planning or deferred reward. According to this view, people raised in poverty prefer the instant rush of intoxication to the sustained effort of education. They may be seen as improvident or lazy, when in fact they have learned (or been taught) that effort is not rewarded, life is short, and pleasures are rare. Their behavior represents an effort to adapt to lifelong—even intergenerational—poverty. Drug addiction or teenage pregnancy can be understood as the natural consequence of growing up in poverty. Crime may be the logical reaction to repeated failure, and family breakup the inevitable result of a chaotic and unrestrained social milieu. Yet, as Segalman and Basu note, "The coping mechanisms by which the poor adjust to their state also serve to prevent them and their children from ever moving out of poverty" (1981, p. 13). An important component of this view holds that victims of poverty cannot make use of opportunities that present themselves later in life because they have been irreparably damaged by their culture.

Several authors have focused on describing the culture of poverty. In 1968, Edward C. Banfield of Harvard University argued that poverty creates a "present-orientedness" that leaves a person unable to plan for the future or to defer gratification. Acknowledging that some people become poor through accidents or misfortunes that are short-lived, he argued that others will be poor regardless of their circumstances. Such people lack the values and strengths necessary to succeed. Giving them money would be pointless because they would squander it on frivolous nonessentials.

Nicolas Lemann (1986) suggested that residents of black ghettos in inner cities inherited the values and traits of sharecroppers. Most of them, he noted, come from rural Southern roots, where sharecroppers could neither own property nor save money and thus failed to learn the values necessary to preserve family stability and accumulate financial reserves (see Segalman & Basu, 1981). In 1969, Senator Daniel Patrick Moynihan endorsed the culture of poverty argument in his controversial book *Maximum Feasible Misunderstanding,* which argued that poverty among African Americans reflected the failure of African American family life.

Apart from the question of their accuracy, culture of poverty explanations apply only to those who experience lifelong, intergenerational poverty. Interventions based on such explanations attempt to change the values of poor adults or to teach their children a different set of values. Historically, the latter objective was used to justify removing poor children from their homes and placing them in middle-class settings where they were expected to learn the values of thrift, abstinence, and productivity. Two striking examples of this practice are found in the history of U.S. child welfare practices. During the nineteenth century, Charles Loring Brace of the Children's Aid Society removed children from urban tenements and placed them with middle-class farm families. Well into the twentieth century, Native American children were removed from their homes on reservations and lodged with middle-class white families. Other interventions based on this viewpoint simply exposed poor adults to middle-class role models in the hope that they would absorb new habits and values.

Restricted Opportunity Theories of Poverty

Like culture of poverty explanations, "restricted opportunity" theories about poverty surfaced in the twentieth century. But where the culture of poverty explanation attributes poverty to personal attributes, restricted opportunity explanations focus on structural barriers that prevent individuals from securing the education or jobs necessary for financial success. Noting that "the playing field is not level," proponents of this view hold that institutional discrimination on the basis of gender, race, or other characteristics restricts opportunities and increases the risk of poverty.

Proponents note that poverty is not randomly distributed in the U.S. population. Female-headed households are more vulnerable than those headed by men; people of color are more likely to be poor at any age than Caucasians; people with disability experience high rates of poverty; and children who grow up in impoverished conditions face the strong likelihood of spending their lives in poverty.

This greater risk of poverty can be explained with reference to discriminatory practices in education and the workplace. Some of the programs established under President Lyndon Johnson's War on Poverty during the 1960s reflected this perspective, attempting to increase the educational, employment, and political opportunities available to the poor. Civil rights laws designed to increase opportunities for women and people of color also reflect the restricted opportunity explanation of poverty.

The Pauperization Argument

In 1994, President Clinton promised to "end welfare as we know it." He was certainly not the first U.S. policy maker to make this promise, which reflected a widespread belief that welfare did not relieve poverty but caused it by fostering dependence on a system that destroyed the incentive to work. Under this view, the welfare system created "paupers" (or permanently poor people) from those who might otherwise succeed. If there were no welfare, the pauperization argument holds, those who receive public assistance would be motivated to find jobs and pull themselves out of poverty.

In itself, this idea was not unique to the twentieth century. Nineteenth-century advocates of poorhouses raised the specter of pauperization to criticize the practice of "outdoor relief" (providing financial support to people in their homes, rather than requiring them to enter a poorhouse). Indeed, the pauperization argument has been used frequently to criticize systems of cash assistance for the poor.

PUBLIC INTERVENTIONS TO PREVENT
OR ALLEVIATE POVERTY

In most capitalist nations, poverty interventions engender deep-seated ambivalence. The allocation principle used in most programs ("to each according to his need") is incompatible with that of a capitalist economy ("to each according to his product"). Thus poverty programs are often criticized for their socialist underpinnings. Further, as we will see here and in Chapter 14, the history of poverty interventions reflects the demand for and attitude towards labor.

British Approaches

In 1348, an outbreak of bubonic plague decimated the populations of several European nations. In England a labor shortage led to the passage of the Statute of Labourers, which forbade giving charity to able-bodied beggars. The law also set maximum wages and imposed travel restrictions to ensure that laborers would stay within their home parishes and accept employment there, rather than traveling to pursue opportunities elsewhere. This law is a striking illustration of the use of poverty policies to control the labor force, based on the idea of poverty as a motivator. It also represented an early policy constraint on private relief efforts.

Two hundred years later, during the sixteenth century, a series of laws were passed in England to regulate begging. These laws established a clear distinction between the "deserving" and the "undeserving" poor. Severe punishment was allotted to able-bodied people who were not inclined to work, but those unable to work were assigned areas where they could beg. In 1536, the Act for the Punishment of Sturdy Vagabonds and Beggars elaborated both the punishments for undeserving beggars (which extended to branding, enslavement, and execution) and government relief for the deserving poor. The act directed local public officials to collect donations from the churches for poor relief. In this way, government poverty policy moved from the regulation of beggars to the administration of relief in partnership with the church. The act also reflected the human capital explanation of poverty because it provided for training of indigent youth and community service employment for unemployed adults.

Later in the sixteenth century the parish system became unable to collect sufficient voluntary donations to meet the demands for poor relief. A new statute called the Elizabethan Poor Law was passed to levy a tax for the care of the poor and create an administrative structure for the management of relief efforts.

Statutes passed during the sixteenth century established the basic principles that were later codified in the Poor Law of 1601 (also known as the Elizabethan Poor Law). This law remained essentially unchanged for 250 years and was the foundation of the measures European colonists put in place when they came to the New World. Its basic principles included the following.

- *Family responsibility.* Parents were legally responsible for supporting their children and grandchildren, and conversely, children were responsible for their aged parents and grandparents.

- *Local responsibility.* Aid was managed through local units of government called parishes, and strict residency requirements discouraged vagrancy. Indigents who did not meet residency requirements were returned to their home parishes. Community relief efforts provided for needy neighbors, not for wandering strangers.

- *Differential treatment.* The law distinguished between the deserving and the undeserving poor. Among the deserving, it established three major categories: children, the able-bodied unemployed, and those incapacitated by disability or age (the "impotent"). The undeserving included those who were too lazy, shiftless, or drunk to support themselves.

- *Preference for work.* Public relief was not intended as an alternative to paid employment. Those who could work were expected to do so. Children were employed in apprenticeships, the able-bodied unemployed were given jobs, and the undeserving were sent to workhouses for forced labor. Only the disabled were excused from the work requirement.

- *Public assistance through compulsory taxation.* Under the Poor Law of 1601, mandatory taxes were collected to finance the relief of poverty. Every household in a parish was taxed, and the money was collected by overseers of the poor. Those who did not pay the tax were threatened with imprisonment.

The Elizabethan Poor Law provided the foundation for later U.S. interventions designed to alleviate poverty and maintain social equilibrium. Its differential treatment set the stage for the categorical eligibility requirements seen in SSI and Medicaid, while work preference is manifest in TANF requirements that beneficiaries seek paid employment. Finally, in the U.S. public assistance is financed —as it was in the Poor Law—through compulsory taxes.

American Approaches to Poverty in the Eighteenth and Nineteenth Centuries

In the following sections we will trace the development of American relief from its origins in the colonies to the present. As we will see, relief in colonial times was a chancy affair—a person's care depended not only on the town in which he or she lived but also on good relationships with community leaders. The nineteenth century was marked by widespread intolerance for public relief and contempt for the poor. These attitudes led to diminished outdoor relief and the growth of poorhouses. Social work emerged in this period, with two contradictory approaches to poverty: the Charity Organization Societies and the Settlement Movement. It took the Great Depression to convince twentieth-century Americans of the need for a federal system of relief.

In recent years it has become important, and sometimes difficult, to separate rhetoric from reality and message from messenger. For example, President Lyndon Johnson declared an "unconditional war on poverty," yet his Great Society programs did little to expand relief for the poor. President Nixon spoke ardently against welfare, yet his administration was marked by significantly expanded benefits for the poor. Republican Presidents Reagan and George H. W. Bush were at the forefront of antiwelfare rhetoric, but it took a Democrat (Bill Clinton) to dismantle the federal relief entitlement for children.

Poverty Interventions in Early America.   America was not colonized as a refuge for Europe's poor. Instead, the New World was a haven for adventurers and religious minorities. The first permanent settlement was established at Jamestown in 1607. The Virginia Company sent a group of adventurers to identify ways of exploiting the region's natural resources. Women joined the settlement later, in 1608. The pilgrims didn't come to New England until the English civil war was imminent. Refugees from that conflict, the pilgrims were people of limited means—craftsmen, small shopkeepers, and farmers—but they were hardly destitute.[4] Later, colonists who could not pay for their passage financed their trips by selling their labor as indentured servants. While these servants entered the colonies without resources, the terms of their indenture were generous, and in at least one state (Pennsylvania) they received land grants at the end of their service.

During the early years of shared deprivation, government programs to alleviate poverty were a luxury the colonies could ill afford. Individual misfortune, such as disease or bereavement, met with neighborly kindness—or at least, assistance.[5] But the number of people living in poverty, including widows and orphans, those disabled by age or disease, and others, increased. By the mid-seventeenth century most of the colonies had initiated formal provisions that made local taxpayers responsible for the support of their poor neighbors. Measures adopted by the colonies were modeled on the Elizabethan Poor Law and included the principles of family and local responsibility.

Care of the poor was undertaken by the town in which they resided. Towns used three approaches. The most straightforward approach was to send poor individuals to live with their kin. Another involved placing the poor in private homes at public expense. The fee was usually set through an auction where those in need were offered to the lowest bidder, with the fee paid by the town. A third approach was sometimes used when people needed only temporary aid. In this practice, called outdoor assistance or outdoor relief, payments were given directly to the person in need.

The principle of local responsibility meant that people who were displaced or had left their original homes were not entitled to receive aid. Most towns discouraged needy strangers from staying. Some "warned away" visitors who might become a burden, prohibiting the sale of land to strangers without official permission, and requiring residents who brought in servants to support them if they became needy. Port towns, troubled by the arrival of needy immigrants, required captains of vessels to post bonds for each passenger they discharged. In some cases, the towns forced captains to return the destitute to their points of origin.

Despite these efforts destitute strangers kept arriving and ultimately, these "unsettled poor" proved to be the undoing of the principle of local responsibility.

---

4. During the nineteenth century the British shipped prisoners and beggars to Australia, but this practice was not widespread in North America. Nonetheless, it was a significant concern to the colonial leaders. In 1776, Benjamin Franklin was sent to England to protest the transportation of criminals to the colonies.

5. A possible exception to this neighborly assistance was the treatment of witches, who were usually single older women of limited means who violated community norms.

Wars and migration overwhelmed the towns' ability to provide assistance, as refugees from Indian wars arrived in towns with little more than the clothing on their back. Eventually towns asked colonial authorities for funds to provide relief for these strangers. Thus the colonial treasury began to reimburse towns for the care of the unsettled poor.

Relief in the New Nation.   The War of Independence left many of the new nation's residents widowed, orphaned, or disabled, and seriously disrupted economic ties to England and other European nations. Although private philanthropy supplemented public relief efforts, local relief organizations were overwhelmed by requests for assistance. Many of these came from people who did not meet local residency requirements. As a result, one of the first actions undertaken by the new states was the establishment of administrative structures for handling poor relief. New York was the first state to do so, setting up the Committee on Superintendence of the Poor.[6]

Despite the general welfare clause of the U.S. Constitution (Article I, Section 8), the United States did not pass national legislation governing the provision of relief. Responsibility for the relief of poverty was left to state and local governments.

Relief in Nineteenth–Century America.   The nineteenth century was a time of industrial expansion in England and the United States. The demand for industrial workers triggered new criticism of outdoor relief. Several arguments were made against outdoor relief. Economists argued that relief interfered with the natural relationship between capital and labor. By providing an alternative to industrial labor, it reduced the pool of available workers. Other critics argued that outdoor relief created dependency. Still others noted that the needy were embracing the idea that they had a right to relief. This ingratitude on their part, along with the compulsory taxation required to finance relief efforts, were seen as interfering with private charity.

These arguments were effective in both England and the United States. In England, the Poor Law Reform Bill was passed to eliminate outdoor relief and relegate the disadvantaged to almshouses and workhouses. Unlike their counterparts across the Atlantic, American poverty officials did not completely dismantle the system of outdoor relief. But they did expand "indoor relief," sending many of the nation's poor to institutions.

Most states assigned responsibility for poorhouses to the counties. For example, in 1824, New York enacted the County Poorhouse Act calling for the construction of one or more poorhouses in each county. These institutions proliferated. For most people they were not permanent addresses but temporary shelters in times of need. Families might move into poorhouses during an especially harsh winter or stay there during periods of temporary unemployment. Over

---

6. The state of New York was at the forefront of poverty relief for several decades. New York is the only state that addresses relief of poverty in its constitution, and it led the nation in establishing relief during the Great Depression.

A HUMAN PERSPECTIVE Advocacy: Historic Organization Continues Its Tradition of Advocacy and Support

Contributed by Saliwe M. Kawewe, Southern Illinois University at Carbondale, School of Social Work, and President, Delmo Housing Corp.

Sharecropping farm families in the 1930s had limited resources and few options, living in near-perpetual bondage to landowners. The Southern Tenant Farmers Union (STFU) was established in 1934 in Memphis, Tennessee, to seek better working conditions, freedom, and homeownership for the croppers in the Mississippi Delta. Leadership included Reverend Owen Whitfield, an African American sharecropper and lay preacher of socialist bent; H. L. Mitchell, a white man with links to New Deal agencies; and Thad Snow, a planter sympathetic to the cause. Over time, many leaders, organizations, and churches in St. Louis and beyond were appalled by the croppers' living conditions, including faculty and students from the George Warren Brown School of Social Work at Washington University, St. Louis.

The STFU used a variety of tactics, from demonstrations like the Roadside Demonstration of 1939 to media campaigns and consultations with leading politicians. Their efforts produced results. Between 1940 and 1941, the Farm Security Administration (FSA) built low-income rental houses for tenants and croppers. Organized as "villages," the houses were located on 10 plantations, with seven designated for whites and three for blacks.

When the FSA was phased out, planters hoped to take over the housing themselves and evict the tenants. Instead, in 1945 the Delmo Housing Corporation (DHC) was formed as a self-help project to help tenants

purchase their homes. As a result of the DHC's intervention, the villages continue to provide housing for low-income farm families.

The situation of tenant farmers who were the early beneficiaries of DHC services has changed, but the organization has survived, adapting its operations in response to human need, availability of resources, and changing political environments. It has established credit unions in the villages and made small loans to support home-based enterprises. Today, the DHC operates a thrift shop and conducts voter education and leadership development programs. For those in need of more extensive medical care, clinics have been established and transportation is provided. The DHC has advocated for improvements in local educational systems to make them more responsive to the needs of tenants' children, and it has established day care centers and recreational facilities.

Despite pervasive racial tensions, the DHC maintains its tradition of racial diversity, with representatives from diverse origins serving on its board of directors and among its volunteers. It is organized as a tax-exempt entity.

Economic conditions in Missouri's "Bootheel" are stagnant, and the region experiences a brain drain similar to that reported in many Third World nations. Promising young people migrate north in pursuit of career advancement. The DHC is working to stem this tide, providing scholarships and leadership to shore up regional opportunities. The work of the DHC is as relevant today as it was when the organization was founded 60 years ago—a testament to its strong leadership and community support.

time, more and more elders spent their final months in poorhouses, so these facilities were precursors for today's nursing homes.

The end of the Civil War saw a new population in need of assistance—newly freed African American men and women in Southern states. For several million former slaves, the abrupt change in status brought a need for education, employment, and assistance. To address these needs, a Bureau of Refugees, Freedmen, and Abandoned Lands was established in the U.S. War Department two months before the war ended. This agency, usually called the Freedmen's Bureau, took what today would be called a holistic approach to the relief needs of the freedmen. As Trattner (1989) pointed out,

[The Freedmen's Bureau] served as a relief agency on an unprecedented
scale, distributing twenty-two million rations to needy persons in the
devastated South. It served as an employment agency . . . a settlement
agency, leasing certain abandoned properties to black cultivators . . . it
employed doctors and maintained hospitals . . . it encouraged the
founding of black schools and then provided them with financial aid . . .
it served as legal agency, maintaining courts in which both civil and
criminal cases involving ex-slaves were dealt with in an informal and just
manner. (p. 79)

In its second year of operation, the Freedmen's Bureau became part of a
controversy between President Andrew Johnson (himself a Southerner) and the
U.S. Congress.[7] Congress voted to extend the Bureau, but Johnson vetoed the
measure, arguing that the Constitution did not permit a federal system of relief.
Congress overrode his veto, and the Bureau continued to operate for six years.
In 1876, the Freedmen's Bureau was closed, having demonstrated that the federal government could deliver comprehensive relief to needy individuals for
whom states either could not or would not provide.

By the end of the nineteenth century, the United States had been transformed from a small local economy to a world-class manufacturer. This industrialization brought an explosion of jobs in settings that can only generously be
described as sweatshops. The textile mills that moved into the newly recon-
structed South offered much-needed jobs to poor white Americans and African
Americans, but they were jobs with low pay and abysmal working conditions.
Dramatic economic growth created massive fortunes, such as those enjoyed by
William Henry Vanderbilt, John D. Rockefeller, and J. P. Morgan, and raised
the general standard of living. It also meant expanded demand for laborers who
were willing to endure periodic unemployment and difficult working conditions.
In this context public support for government relief efforts waned.

The dominant economic philosophy of the times was Social Darwinism.
According to this view, those who did not flourish in the booming economy
could only be inferior specimens. Public care for them not only undermined private charity but weakened the human race by permitting the "unfit" to survive
and reproduce. Members of the economic elite found in Social Darwinism a philosophy that was closely aligned with their interests. As a result, public relief efforts diminished.

The decline in public relief was not accompanied by a drop in destitution.
The nineteenth century saw a series of financial crises occurring at 10- to 20-year
intervals that led John Kenneth Galbraith to remark later that the times between
crises corresponded "roughly with the time it took people to forget the last disaster" (Strouse, 1998, p. 66). Panics disrupted the stock market and threw millions out of work. Private charities raced to respond to massive need, and the

---

7. Johnson's ongoing battles with Congress eventually led to the nation's first presidential
impeachment hearings.

result was a chaotic proliferation of organizations, all serving the same pool of indigents.

This disorganization horrified many charity workers, who argued that private relief efforts needed to be rationalized along "scientific" lines. Thus, when the Reverend Stephen Humphreys Gurteen proposed the creation of a charity organization society (COS) for Buffalo, New York, his suggestion met eager acceptance. Indeed, charity organization societies, going by names such as Society for Organizing Charity, Associated Charities, and Bureaus of Charities, proliferated.

Charity organization societies did not provide relief. Instead, they conducted detailed investigations to distinguish the worthy from the unworthy poor and then referred those deemed worthy to relief agencies. The goal was to raise the morals of the poor by exposing them to well-intentioned volunteers from middle- and upper-class backgrounds. Long before the term "culture of poverty" was coined, this intervention reflected the belief that upright role models could improve the values of the poor. Thus "friendly visiting" was born. Mary Richmond's 1917 book, *Social Diagnosis,* widely considered the first systematic description of social casework, grew out of the experiences of COS friendly visitors.

The movement was not without its critics. Jane Addams, the founder of Hull House, was one of the most vocal. She argued that charity organization societies were "cold and unemotional, too impersonal, and stingy . . . pervaded by a negative pseudo-scientific spirit." Their vocabulary, she argued, was one of "don't give," "don't act," "don't do this or that"; "all they have for the poor is advice, and for that they probably send the Almighty a bill" (Trattner, 1989, p. 91).

The COS movement fostered the development of social casework, and the settlement house movement set the stage for community organization. A contemporary of the COS movement, the settlement house movement differed in philosophy, approach, and goals. The COS philosophy treated indigence as the result of individual moral failure, while the settlement movement placed poverty in a broad social context. COS workers carefully investigated individual worthiness, while settlement workers focused their equally systematic research efforts on the social conditions of urban poverty. The primary goal of COS intervention, friendly visiting, aimed to improve the morals of the worthy poor. Settlement interventions did not distinguish between worthy and unworthy and aimed to reduce class divisions and enhance living conditions in urban slums. The testy relationship that prevailed between COS workers and settlement workers continues today in the tension between social work professionals committed to individual treatment and those who focus on social change.

At the end of the nineteenth century the relief of poverty was largely a private affair, involving the pioneers of the social work profession in two movements. The COS movement aimed to reduce poverty through individual change, while the settlement house movement used a community organization model to attain the same goal. Public involvement in relieving poverty was generally limited to institutional care provided in poorhouses and other settings for the "dependent, defective and delinquent" (Leiby, 1978). The role of government in poverty relief and amelioration would undergo dramatic changes in the next century.

American Approaches to Poverty in the Twentieth Century

In the beginning of the twentieth century huge personal fortunes were made through monopolies in oil and railroads. "Robber barons" like John D. Rockefeller (Standard Oil), Andrew Carnegie (steel magnate), and Cornelius Vanderbilt (New York railroads) controlled both government and the lives of thousands of industrial workers. Inequality reached heights that had not been possible in an agricultural economy. Care of the poor was left to private charities, and outdoor relief was minimal. In these conditions the Progressive movement was born.

The Progressive Era spanned the first two decades of the twentieth century and was marked by a sea change in the role of government. First, legislation was passed to reduce government corruption. These initiatives included civil service reforms and revised election procedures. Leaders of the Progressive movement also set out to ease the suffering of industrial laborers and the poor. Legislative initiatives included child labor laws, health and safety laws, antitrust provisions, and establishment of the progressive income tax.

The notion that government should play a role in care of the poor was accompanied by a more accepting stance vis-à-vis outdoor relief. Some date the changing attitude toward relief to the 1909 White House Conference on Children, convened by President Theodore Roosevelt. Conference participants, 200 of the nation's elite, concluded that children should be cared for whenever possible in their own homes, and that the "home should not be broken up for reasons of poverty" (Trattner, 1989, p. 200). Like their contemporaries, conference participants were strongly opposed to outdoor relief. They stated that widows' pensions should be provided by private charities under the direction and supervision of the charity organization societies. In actual practice, however, many private agencies refused to give funds to women who were capable of working. Widows were forced to work, often for long hours at low wages, to support children they were unable to supervise. The result was maternal illness and child delinquency.

Advocates of widows' or mothers' pensions argued that it was ultimately less costly, in both human and economic terms, to provide public assistance to women with dependent children. This approach would preserve children from neglect, prevent juvenile delinquency, and protect the health of mothers. Proponents noted that the boom and bust nature of the industrial economy exposed workers' families to financial insecurity that jeopardized the well-being of children. They believed that mothers were performing a valuable service in caring for their children. Not only were they the best possible caregivers but they did not belong in the workplace.

Social workers, especially those employed by private charity organizations, opposed widows' pensions. They protested against transforming voluntary per-

© Dorothea Lange/FSA/Getty Images

March 1936: The mother of a migrant family holds a baby while a young girl stands behind her and rests her chin on her shoulder under a lean-to, Nipomo, CA.

sonal charity into an impersonal entitlement, arguing—in terms remarkably familiar today—that entitlements would undermine the work ethic of the poor. These arguments proved unsuccessful.

In April 1911, Missouri became the first state to enact a widows' pension law that provided cash assistance to mothers with dependent children. By 1935, all but two states—South Carolina and Georgia—offered public assistance to widows with dependent children. Over time, these programs were extended beyond widows to include other mothers raising children without spouses. A few recipients were single mothers with "illegitimate" children. Others were wives of men who were incapacitated, imprisoned, or otherwise unavailable to support their families. Assistance was conditioned by a "suitable home" provision, requiring the mothers to maintain healthy and supportive environments for their children. These widows' pensions set the stage for Title IV of the 1935 Social Security Act, which would establish a grant-in-aid program known then as Aid to Dependent Children.

The Depression and the New Deal.   Prior to the Depression, only a few crusaders saw relief as a public responsibility. Some of these advocates sought a fundamental reorganization of the U.S. economy toward a socialist model. Others preferred mandatory social insurance to buffer the effects of capitalism. But these were minority views. It took an economic calamity to shake the antipathy most Americans felt toward public assistance.

For some, including President Herbert Hoover, it would take more than economic calamity. Despite his personal background in relief work,[8] Hoover was reluctant to intervene during the Depression. He felt the economy was basically sound, and as soon as confidence had been restored, prosperity would return. Thus, he repeatedly advised the public that the "worst was over." Hoover saw in federal relief the enslavement of the American people. Consistent with this philosophy, in December 1930 the president approved an appropriation of $45 million to feed the livestock of struggling Arkansas farmers but opposed an additional $25 million to feed the farmers and their families. While the president postponed federal action, private charities around the country folded.

State and local governments did their best to shore up the failing private relief effort. The most notable effort was undertaken in New York. Then-governor Franklin D. Roosevelt had commissioned studies of the situation by the state's charity organization societies. He called a special legislative session to discuss the crisis, and New York became the first state to provide unemployment relief. Millions of dollars were passed on to local governments to provide subsidized work opportunities and relief. Roosevelt appointed a New York City social worker, Harry Hopkins, to direct the effort as head of the new Temporary Emergency Relief Administration.

Roosevelt's philosophy stood in sharp contrast to President Hoover's. Roosevelt saw relief as a matter of public duty, not charity. With this viewpoint, Roosevelt accepted the Democratic Party's nomination for president and defeated Hoover by a landslide in 1932.

The first order of business in Roosevelt's "New Deal" was emergency relief for the unemployed. The Federal Emergency Relief Act, signed into law in May 1933, established a series of grants-in-aid that were provided to the states through the Federal Emergency Relief Administration (FERA) under the direction of Harry Hopkins. Hopkins and Roosevelt agreed that all federal relief programs were to be operated by public agencies. They felt that provision of public subsidies to private agencies resulted in corruption and inefficiency. Thus the relief and commodity distribution programs operated under FERA were administered by governmental units. Along with the FERA, a veritable alphabet soup of programs was created. Most emphasized work in exchange for relief, an approach that would prove popular with Americans.

In addition to emergency relief measures, Roosevelt sought to establish a system of social insurance for workers. In 1934 he created the Committee on Economic Security (CES) to develop a proposal. The committee included four cabinet members and Harry Hopkins. It was headed by the nation's first female

---

8. The president organized a flood relief effort in the Mississippi Valley and was a relief administrator during World War I. As secretary of commerce in 1921, he organized a conference on unemployment relief. As a result of this background, he enjoyed widespread support from social workers in the 1928 election.

cabinet official, Frances Perkins, secretary of labor. Edwin E. Witte, a professor from the University of Wisconsin, served as the CES executive director. In January 1935, after six months of intensive deliberation, the committee delivered its outline for a social security program to the president.

Public assistance programs established under the Social Security Act did not involve the federal government in the direct provision of relief. Instead, they established grant-in-aid programs under which revenue from the general fund was distributed to the states. The states then established relief programs that operated in accordance with regulations set at the federal level.

These grant-in-aid programs departed from the Poor Law principle of local responsibility in financing and authority, if not in distribution. Local authorities no longer used local funds to support local indigents. Financing came from federal revenues. Eligibility requirements and grant levels were determined by a federal agency. Local agencies were left to distribute relief under direction and guidance from federal authorities.

New Deal relief efforts touched millions but did little to end the Great Depression. All of the federal relief programs (FERA, the Civil Works Administration (CWA), and Works Progress Administration (WPA)) ended before the hardships had passed. Even the establishment of Social Security did not stimulate economic recovery. It took World War II to pull the United States out of its most devastating economic crisis.

World War II and the War on Poverty.   World War II brought prosperity to a nation weary of hardship. Employment opportunities expanded, and as a result personal incomes rose for all workers, including women and people of color. To reduce discrimination in the defense industry, President Roosevelt issued the famous Executive Order 8802, forbidding "discrimination in the employment of workers in defense industries or Government because of race, creed, or national origin" (Trattner, 1989, p. 279). Rosie the Riveter became emblematic of the need for women to work in support of national defense.

The war ended in 1945, and for many the postwar years proved unusually prosperous. There were recessions (1948–49, 1953–54, 1957–58), but the postwar boom, with its increased demand for labor, led many to believe that poverty would simply wither away in the growing economy.

By the 1950s many argued that poverty had already disappeared. John Kenneth Galbraith was among them when, in 1958, he called the United States "The Affluent Society." Acknowledging the existence of poverty at the fringes of this society, Galbraith and others contributed to the widespread perception that poverty in the land of plenty was the result of inadequate skills and faulty personal choices.

Meanwhile, the welfare rolls told a different story. Not only did the public assistance rolls grow but their composition changed. Prior to Social Security, the elderly made up a majority of public assistance recipients. They were replaced by a new class of unemployed people: former agricultural workers. Technological developments from 1940 to 1960 mechanized the nation's farms, increasing productivity and dramatically reducing the number of agricultural jobs. Most of these were located in the South, and African Americans were disproportionately represented in this group of the newly unemployed.

Some public programs for the poor were expanded during this era. In 1950 the Aid to Dependent Children (ADC) program (established with the 1935 Social Security Act) was amended to include "caretaker" grants for mothers of dependent children. Later, its name was changed to Aid to Families with Dependent Children (AFDC). Social services were added to AFDC, and the Department of Health, Education and Welfare was created. The Social Security Act was further amended to include a new categorical program, Aid to the Permanently and Totally Disabled.

With these expansions and the continued elimination of agricultural jobs, relief rolls continued to grow during the 1960s. Indeed, the number of people receiving public assistance more than doubled from 1960 to 1970, a period when the nation's population increased by only 12 percent. President Kennedy brought to his presidency a commitment to eliminate poverty, hunger, and unemployment. The young president inspired a belief that these ancient problems could be eliminated through determined intervention. But this spirit of optimism, like the Kennedy administration itself, would be short-lived. Under his administration the federal poverty threshold was established, enabling the nation to systematically monitor financial hardship. Figure 5.2 illustrates trends in poverty since the establishment of the threshold.

When Kennedy took office in 1961, AFDC was expanded to include low-income two-parent families headed by an unemployed member. This new program, called Aid to Families with Dependent Children—Unemployed Parent (AFDC-U), was designed to provide help to families who had been ineligible due to the presence of a "man in the home." AFDC-U was conceived as a temporary measure, and states were not required to participate.

The following year, the 1962 Public Welfare Amendments to the Social Security Act were signed into law. These measures provided federal support for state provision of social services (casework, job training, and other services) to AFDC recipients and echoed the belief of the COS movement that individual change was pivotal (perhaps even more important than material relief) in reducing poverty. Under the amendments, material relief and personal improvement were linked, and public assistance recipients found in their caseworker both an eligibility worker and a friendly visitor.

Public assistance was expanded through the 1964 passage of the Food Stamp Act, which provided for the distribution of vouchers to the needy for the purchase of food products. The Department of Agriculture was charged with administration of the program, seen by some as a way of reducing the impact of agricultural price supports on the poor.

During the mid-1960s riots erupted in the slums of major cities. Unlike the antiwar riots that would follow, these riots represented protests against social conditions such as discrimination, unemployment, inadequate housing, and poverty. In 1966, welfare rights demonstrations broke out in cities across the nation. In their classic work *Regulating the Poor,* Piven and Cloward (1971) argued that

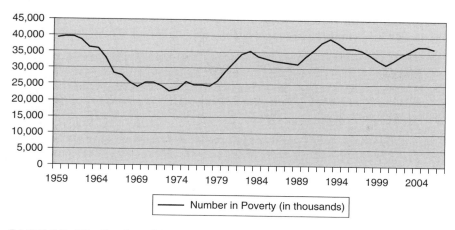

FIGURE 5.2 Number of Americans with incomes below poverty: 1959–2006.

SOURCE (for data): U.S. Bureau of the Census. Historical Poverty Tables. http://www.census.gov/hhes/www/poverty/histpov/hstpov2.html.

the subsequent expansion of public relief programs was a response to social unrest, and hence the role of public programs (and the social workers who staffed them) was to maintain a status quo that relied on the oppression of the poor and people of color.

In response to the riots, President Johnson established the Kerner Commission to investigate their causes and recommend ways to prevent future unrest. The commission recommended creation of a federal jobs program for the unemployed.

President Johnson declared "unconditional war on poverty" in his 1964 State of the Union address, calling on Congress to support his "Great Society" programs designed to vanquish "the most ancient of mankind's enemies." These programs were established through the Economic Opportunity Act, which created a federal Office of Economic Opportunity. They included the Volunteers in Service to America (VISTA), a domestic version of the popular Peace Corps; the Neighborhood Youth Corps, which provided jobs to unemployed teens; Operation Head Start, which offered preschool training to children; a community action program designed to mobilize low-income communities to fight the causes and manifestations of poverty; and a program for rural families and migrant workers.

The War on Poverty reflected the belief that poor families needed training and encouragement to better themselves. It did not offer money or jobs to the poor, but instead sent (middle-class) professionals to change their culture, values, and expectations.

The War on Poverty was minimally funded, due (as suggested in Harrington, 1984) to the competing demands posed by the war in Vietnam. It also faced opposition from both ends of the political spectrum. Radicals like Saul Alinsky opposed the Great Society programs as "a macabre masquerade" (Alinsky, 1972). Conservatives opposed the expenditures involved. Disenchantment with the programs would undermine the nation's brief confidence that interventions informed by social science could eliminate social problems. The failure of the War on Poverty eventually set the stage for the War on Welfare.

The War on Welfare.   In 1968 Richard Nixon won election by a wide margin. A staunch conservative, the new president saw in his election a mandate to dismantle the Great Society programs and criticize recipients of public assistance. This he did, with enthusiasm.

Although Nixon struck the first blows in the War on Welfare, reforms proposed and enacted during his administration did more to enhance the status of the poor than all the Great Society programs combined. He proposed to replace the federal–state AFDC program with a single federal program. His proposal, called the Family Assistance Plan (FAP), would have created a federally guaranteed minimum annual income for families with children. It called for strict penalties and strong incentives to ensure that everyone who was able-bodied (including mothers of children younger than three years old) worked in paid employment.

The FAP, while not generous in its benefits, would have increased the incomes of AFDC recipients in poor Southern states. It also represented a significant philosophical change in public assistance because it assigned primary responsibility to the federal government and provided a guaranteed minimum income for Americans.

These ideas were also reflected in the "Negative Income Tax" experiments, designed to test the impact of a guaranteed minimum income in four U.S. locations between 1969 and 1978. Although the impact of the income guarantee on work effort was minimal, the experiments' findings were widely interpreted as an indictment of this approach. (For more information about these experiments, please see http://www.irp.wisc.edu/research/nit.htm.)

Many liberals, including social workers, opposed the FAP. In part, this opposition reflected their distrust of Nixon, but in an era of high unemployment, the plan's work requirements (dubbed "workfare" by opponents) struck many as ludicrous. Welfare rights activists thought the guaranteed minimum was too low, and they were concerned that the plan would lower benefits to welfare recipients in more generous states. Conservatives were unhappy with the expanded federal role proposed under the FAP, and some objected to the notion of mothers with young children being forced to work. The president showed no commitment to the plan, and eventually it died in committee.

While AFDC remained unchanged, the Nixon era saw significant improvements in other public assistance programs. These included expansion of the Food Stamp Program, the establishment of cost-of-living adjustments (COLAs) for Social Security, the creation of an Earned Income Tax Credit (EITC), and the consolidation of three categorical assistance programs (Old-Age Assistance, Aid to the Blind, and Aid to the Permanently and Totally Disabled) into Supplemental Security Income (SSI). The Social Service Amendments (Title XX of the Social Security Act), also passed during this period, provided $2.5 billion to states to deliver social services to welfare recipients.[9] Notably, these expansions took place in an era of high unemployment (low demand for labor).

Following Nixon's resignation in 1974 in the wake of the Watergate scandal, Gerald Ford enjoyed a brief term as president. Best known for his unconditional pardon of Nixon, Ford presided over an era of economic "stagflation." Economic growth was stagnant, while unemployment climbed to its highest rate since 1941 (9 percent), and inflation was in double digits. The number of Americans living in poverty rose dramatically, and white American male-headed families emerged for the first time as a group at significant risk of poverty.

President Jimmy Carter contributed to the antiwelfare rhetoric of his day. In 1977, he proposed the Better Jobs and Income Program (BJIP), which would replace existing public assistance programs, such as AFDC, SSI, and food stamps, with a two-tiered system. For the able-bodied, the program would offer part-time subsidized jobs that paid the minimum wage or better. Those deemed unable to work included the aged, the blind, the disabled, and parents of children under 14 years old. They would receive a cash benefit more generous than that offered under existing public assistance programs. Unlike the FAP, Carter's proposal offered universal coverage (it was not restricted to families with children); benefits were more generous, and work exemptions extended to parents of children aged 3 to 14. But, perhaps most significantly, the BJIP proposed to guarantee jobs for those able to work. This work guarantee was the source of most of the opposition from conservatives. Industry representatives feared that publicly subsidized jobs would compete with those available in the private sector. Liberals opposed the work requirement, dubbing the plan yet another attempt to impose workfare on welfare recipients. After introducing his plan in Congress, the president encountered other challenges (such as the Iran hostage crisis) that undermined his ability to pursue significant domestic policy initiatives.

Ronald Reagan, a movie actor and former governor of California, swept into office with an overwhelming victory. Reagan declared that the War on Poverty had been won, and he labeled welfare recipients as "cheats" and "freeloaders." Reagan argued that the federal government should not be in the business of providing welfare, which he believed was best left to private charities in local communities. Thus began a 12-year period (two Reagan administrations, followed by one administration headed by Reagan's vice president, George H. W. Bush) marked by tax cuts for the wealthy, ever-expanding defense budgets, and reduced domestic spending.

Just before his reelection to a second term, President Reagan signed his "sweeping overhaul" of the nation's welfare system. The Family Welfare Reform Act, sponsored by Daniel Patrick Moynihan, had as its major provision the Job Opportunities and Basic Skills (JOBS) program. The program revised,

---

9. Title XX also marked the first time the federal government provided funding for social services to individuals with incomes above the poverty line. While welfare recipients received means-tested services, those with higher incomes could use Title XX services on a fee-for-service basis.

BOX 5.1   Legislating Morality

In the 1960s, states routinely cut off benefits for un-married women who had men in their homes. Social workers who learned of these relationships were charged with terminating benefits, a role some found incompatible with their professional mission of service to the poor. "Man in the house" regulations were based on the premise that these men were "substitute fathers" and should be responsible for the children's care. This premise was rejected by the Supreme Court in the 1968 case *King v. Smith*, and man-in-the-house rules became a thing of the past. But the impulse to use welfare to legislate the morals of poor people continues. TANF legislation expresses preference for married, two-parent families, and recent reauthorization attempts have evinced willingness to spend billions of dollars to promote this family form.

but did not fundamentally alter, the conditions of public relief. Under JOBS, all welfare recipients had to secure jobs or enroll in job training or educational programs. Mothers of children under age three were exempted from the work requirement. Those who did go to work were to receive support for one year to assist with child care and transportation expenses, and Medicaid coverage was extended for one year. The act required states to participate in the AFDC program for two-parent households, dubbed AFDC–Unemployed Parent (AFDC-U). It also included new procedures for collecting child support from noncustodial parents of children whose custodial parents received welfare assistance. The basic premise of JOBS was that welfare recipients needed little more than training and motivation to become self-sufficient.

Ending Welfare As We Know It.   Unlike his predecessors, President Clinton presided over an era of relatively low unemployment. Like his predecessors, Clinton came into office promising to "end welfare as we know it." Unlike his predecessors, he did it. Clinton authorized the most sweeping welfare reform since the Great Depression: the Personal Responsibility and Work Opportunity Reconciliation Act (PRWORA) of 1996 (HR 3734).

PRWORA was part of the "Contract with America" offered by Republican representatives to Congress in 1994. In the flush of victory, the new Republican majority took aim at a variety of federal entitlement programs, including food stamps, Medicaid, and AFDC, and proposed converting federal assistance into block grants. This conversion would allow for reduced federal allocations and greater state discretion over the programs. While the Food Stamp Program and Medicaid were left as federal entitlements, PRWORA converted AFDC to a state block grant known as Temporary Assistance for Needy Families (TANF).

States were permitted to undertake a wide range of activities, as long as they were consistent with TANF purposes:

1. To provide assistance to needy families so that children may be cared for in their own homes or in the homes of relatives

2. To end the dependence of needy parents on government benefits by promoting job preparation, work, and marriage

3. To prevent and reduce the incidence of out-of-wedlock pregnancies and establish annual numerical goals for preventing and reducing the incidence of these pregnancies

4. To encourage the formation and maintenance of two-parent families.

State activities under the first two purposes of the act were required to focus on needy families, while those addressing the last two purposes could be more broadly targeted.

PRWORA was a comprehensive piece of legislation expected to reduce federal welfare expenditures by $54.5 billion by 2001 (Welfare Policy Organization, 1997). It converted the open-ended entitlement under AFDC to time-limited assistance with a mandatory work requirement. It also reduced Food Stamp benefits, prohibited most legal immigrants from receiving either SSI or food stamps (a measure that accounted for much of the anticipated budget reductions), and established more stringent eligibility requirements for children under SSI.

Ending a 50-year-old entitlement for needy children and their families, PRWORA was the most far-reaching welfare reform legislation since the New Deal. It reflected several of the values and beliefs outlined at the opening of this chapter. PRWORA set lifetime limits on public assistance that could not exceed (but could be shorter than) five years. This reflected the belief that welfare promotes dependency (the pauperization argument). The legislation also established work requirements for welfare recipients, forcing them to develop job skills or enter the labor market. While these requirements may have reflected a desire to increase human capital available to the poor, the act also included restrictions on the type and duration of job training. The work requirements seemed tailor-made to ensure that welfare would not serve as an alternative to employment in a growing economy with high demand for laborers. PRWORA allowed states to exempt 20 percent of TANF recipients from lifetime limits, establishing a class of "deserving" poor, and leaving the states to define that group. Most states incorporated physical disability into their exemptions, suggesting that these individuals continue to be the legitimate focus of relief. At the same time, the act established new categories of "undeserving" poor, including individuals with drug-related felonies, teenage parents who leave home, and legal immigrants.

PRWORA was amended through passage of the Balanced Budget Act of 1997. This measure restored SSI benefits to most noncitizens, established a $24 billion program that allows states to expand Medicaid eligibility or directly purchase health coverage for uninsured children, and set up a $3 billion welfare-to-work program for long-term welfare clients.

PRWORA was enacted through 2002, and operated under a series of continuing resolutions and extensions until it was reauthorized in the Deficit Reduction Act of 2005. The reauthorized program allows states to use TANF funds, not only to provide benefits, but also to promote two-parent families.

T A B L E 5.2   Family Poverty Rates, 1996 and 2006

	1996 Rate (%)	2006 Rate (%)	Percent Change
All families	11.0	9.8	−11
Single-parent female	32.6	28.3	−13
Single-parent male	13.8	13.2	−4

SOURCE: U.S. Bureau of the Census. Historical Poverty Tables, Table 4. http://www.census.gov/hhes/www/poverty/histpov/hstpov4.html.

Indeed, the Deficit Reduction Act provided $150 million per year to promote "healthy marriage" and "responsible fatherhood" initiatives, including activities such as marriage education and training, advertising campaigns, and values education in high schools. Another $50 million per year is provided under PRWORA to support abstinence education (http://www.hhs.gov/news/press/2002pres/welfare.html, accessed October 27, 2007).

Following the inception of TANF the nation's welfare rolls shrank by 59 percent, the greatest caseload decline in American history. Over 4.4 million individuals stopped receiving benefits (U.S. Dept of Health & Human Services, 2006). The federal agency charged with administration of TANF reported increased that employment among low-income single mothers, particularly mothers with children under 6 years of age. As Table 5.2 indicates, poverty among female-headed families declined substantially between 1996 and 2006. Indeed, poverty among single-parent families headed by women dropped faster than that among families headed by single men. Nonetheless, these families continued to experience higher rates of poverty than those headed by men. In 2002 over 1 in 4 single-parent families (more than 3.6 million families) headed by women had incomes below the poverty threshold, compared with slightly over 1 in 10 (564,000) single-parent families headed by men.

Thus, employment among single mothers of young children rose, and poverty declined among single-parent female-headed families. This suggests that the well-being of low-income families is less dependent on the structure of government benefits and more dependent on the U.S. labor market. As we will see in Chapter 14, labor policy is becoming an important determinant of the opportunities and quality of life experienced by low-income Americans. It is incumbent upon social workers to become versed in labor policy, which has become as important as welfare policy in the lives of those struggling to make ends meet.

General social indicators tell only part of the story of the impact of TANF. Over 3.4 million people stopped receiving government benefits, and a growing body of research attempts to describe what has happened to them. Clearly a significant number of TANF "leavers" have lost both food stamps and Medicaid. Medicaid enrollment, in particular, has dropped since the welfare reform legislation (Ku & Garrett, 2000). Some entered employment, though it is unclear whether their job situations are stable or financially adequate. There is some indication that the child welfare system is experiencing greater demands associated with TANF leavers, and some parents have given up custody of their children due to their inability to provide financial support (Taylor & Barusch, 2004).

PROGRAMS FOR AMERICA'S POOR

In this section we will examine four programs that serve America's poor: TANF, food stamps, Housing Assistance, and Medicaid. The SSI program, which provides a minimal monthly benefit to the elderly, blind, and disabled, was discussed in Chapter 4.

But first we need to place the discussion in context. A simple description of the array of means-tested programs in the United States might give the impression that the needs of the poor are met. That might be true if everyone who was eligible to receive assistance did so. Instead, most means-tested programs serve only a fraction of the nation's poor. Table 5.3 presents the proportion of people in poverty-level households and households of all income levels who live with someone participating in a means-tested program. These figures underscore the importance of Medicaid, the only program that reaches the majority (slightly more than half) of the nation's poor. Medicaid is followed by food stamps, used by nearly a third of the nation's poor. Cash assistance reaches about one in five poor households, while public housing subsidies are provided to very few households. The presence of children raises program participation substantially. Winicki (2003) reports that 86 percent of poor households with children received some form of means-tested assistance.

Medicaid

Established under the 1965 Amendments to the Social Security Act, Medicaid provides health insurance to the nation's poor. Direct administration of Medicaid is carried out by each state, with federal matching funds meeting from 50 to 80 percent of program costs. States vary in their eligibility

T A B L E 5.3   Program Participation by the Nation's Poor, 2003

	Percent Below Poverty	Percent at All Income Levels
Persons in households receiving means-tested assistance	68.0	26.0
Medicaid	54.7	19.7
Food stamps	35.5	7.2
Cash assistance	22.6	6.4
Public housing subsidy	18.1	4.0

SOURCE: U.S. Bureau of the Census (2004). POV26: Program Participation Status of Household-Poverty Status of People: 2003—All Races—All Income Levels and Below Poverty Level. http://pubdb3.census.gov/macro/032004/pov/new26_001.htm.

requirements, though all cover recipients of TANF and SSI. States also vary in the services covered through Medicaid. Some services are required by federal law, including inpatient hospital services, outpatient hospital services, rural health clinic services, laboratory and X-ray services, skilled nursing facility (nursing home) services, and physician services. Optional services include prescription drugs, eyeglasses, dental care, diagnostic screening, and preventive care.

The majority of Medicaid recipients are mothers and children like Antonia and her son, but the bulk of the program's expenditures go to care for low-income elderly and disabled people because of their greater need for medical attention. As we will see in Chapter 6, Medicaid is an important source of funding for long-term care.

Under federal law, TANF recipients who leave the program by securing employment may retain Medicaid coverage for up to twelve months under a program called "transitional Medicaid." For some low-income Americans, like Antonia, medical coverage is even more vital than cash assistance. Of course, transitional Medicaid coverage proves insufficient for many low-income Americans, given the erosion of employer-based coverage. This topic is discussed further in Chapter 14.

Most metropolitan areas require that Medicaid recipients enroll with a managed care provider. This requirement is a cost-control measure that may also improve health-care access for the poor. On the other hand, the focus on cost control that is characteristic of managed care may introduce barriers that prevent the poor from accessing needed care. The advantages and disadvantages of Medicaid managed care are discussed further in Chapter 6.

Food Stamps

The Food Stamp Program has operated nationwide since 1974, with its current structure determined by the Food Stamp Act of 1977. It is operated by the Department of Agriculture (USDA) and provides vouchers for the purchase of food items by eligible households. The costs of the program are borne primarily by the USDA, which covers 100 percent of benefit costs and 50 percent of administrative costs. The remaining administrative costs are borne by the state and county agencies charged with administering the program.

Eligibility requirements established at the federal level are based on the USDA's Thrifty Food Plan (similar to the Economy Food Budget on which the poverty threshold was based), and are approximately 100 percent of the federal poverty threshold. In 2008, the maximum net monthly income limit for an eligible family of four was $1,721 (http://www.fns.usda.gov/fsp/applicant_recipients/eligibility.htm#income). Households may have up to $2,000 in countable assets, such as a bank account. A person's home and one vehicle may not be considered countable assets. Households in which at least one person is over the age of 60 may have up to $3,000 in assets and retain their eligibility for food stamps. The Food Stamp Program imposes work requirements on able-bodied adults without dependents (U.S. Department of Agriculture, 2000a).

The Food Stamp Program has been criticized for providing inadequate benefits. The maximum monthly allotment for a household of four in the 48 contiguous states was $518 in 2007. However, because the allotment is adjusted to reflect family income, the average monthly benefit is lower. In 2006, the average monthly allotment of food stamps was approximately $94 per person, or $214 per household[10] (http://www.fns.usda.gov/pd/18fsavgben.htm, accessed January 15, 2008). From time to time, politicians and other public figures attempt to draw attention to the problem of inadequate benefits by living on the food stamp allotment themselves.

Many Americans who are eligible for food stamps participate in the program (Castner & Cody, 1999). States' participation rates have varied tremendously. For example, in 1997, when national participation was at approximately 62 percent, only 45 percent of eligible residents of Nevada participated, compared to 92 percent of eligible residents of West Virginia (Mathematica, 2000).

Recent years have seen a decline in food stamp participation from 71 percent of eligibles in 1994 to 62 percent in 1997 (Mathematica, 2000). The USDA reported that participation in January 1998 dropped to 20.3 million participants, a decline of 14 percent from the previous year (Castner & Cody, 1999). This decline has also been observed among families with children whose incomes are below poverty. Winicki (2003) reports that 67 percent of these families received food stamps in 1995. By 1999 that figure had dropped to 54 percent, and, as Table 5.3 indicates, by 2002 less than a third of families with poverty incomes participated in the program.

Lower food stamp participation can be attributed in part to changes made as part of the 1996 welfare reform legislation (PRWORA). The 1996 act changed the Food Stamp Program in several ways: it reduced the level of benefits, denied benefits to most legal immigrants, and created time limits for receipt of benefits by able-bodied adults without children.[11] Approximately 6.73 million people have left the Food Stamp Program following passage of PRWORA. Declining participation may be an unintended consequence of the act (Winicki, 2003). Alternatively, some may just conclude that food stamps "aren't worth the trouble." It can take hours to complete an initial application, and some states require recertification every three months. Since most welfare offices are open only during the workday, low-income parents with jobs must leave work to secure and maintain their food stamps. For many, the benefits are not worth the time, effort, and humiliation involved (see Castner & Cody, 1999; Mathematica, 2000; Rosenbaum, 2000).

---

10. Benefits for Alaska, Hawaii, and the U.S. territories of Guam and the Virgin Islands are higher, reflecting higher food costs in these areas.

11. Able-bodied adults without children can receive food stamps for a maximum of three months in a three-year period, unless they meet certain work requirements.

Temporary Assistance for Needy Families

Serving over 2 million families, TANF consists of a federal block grant to the states. The program allows states to establish eligibility criteria, provided that their treatment of recipients is "fair and equitable," and that individuals convicted of drug felonies be excluded from participating. Key characteristics of the program include the following:

- Work requirements
- Lifetime assistance limits
- Maintenance of effort requirements
- Financial rewards and penalties to states
- Special requirements for teen parents
- Paternity determination and child support enforcement

Work Requirements.   Employment is a central focus of TANF. States are required to assess each recipient's skills and develop a "personal employability plan" that identifies barriers to employment and training needs. TANF recipients can be "sanctioned" if they do not participate in their plans. Participation can include vocational education (limited to 12 months), secondary education, up to six weeks of job search, community service, subsidized employment, unsubsidized employment, and providing child care for a recipient engaged in community service. Recipients may also comply with work requirements if they are working to eliminate barriers to employment, such as addiction or mental illness. With some exceptions, TANF recipients must work as soon as they are "job ready," which must happen no later than two years after they begin receiving assistance.

Lifetime Assistance Limits.   Under federal law, families that have received 60 months of TANF cash assistance are not eligible for further federally funded cash assistance. States may elect a shorter limit. They may also exempt 20 percent of their TANF caseload from the limit. Recipients who have been on TANF for longer than 60 months may be supported through state funds or through money from the Social Services Block Grant.

Maintenance of Effort Requirements.   TANF includes a cost-sharing requirement known as "maintenance of effort" (MOE), which requires that states spend a minimum amount on TANF activities. This amount is based on whether the state has met its required work participation rate in a given year. States that have met their rate requirements must devote 75 percent of the amount they spent on AFDC in 1994 to TANF. Those that have not must spend 80 percent of their 1994 expenditures. A contingency fund is available to states experiencing severe economic problems.

Financial Rewards and Penalties to States.   Special bonuses are provided to "high performance states" in which high proportions of TANF recipients exit the program for employment or in which rates of teen pregnancy go down. States are subject to financial penalties in a wide range of circumstances, including failure to meet work participation requirements, noncompliance with the five-year lifetime limit, failure to satisfy MOE requirements, neglecting to sanction recipients who do not meet participation requirements, failure to comply with requirements regarding paternity establishment and child support collection, not submitting required reports, and inappropriate use of funds.

Special Requirements for Teen Parents.   Teen parents are required to participate in training or school and may not receive assistance unless they live at home or in an approved adult-supervised setting.

Paternity Determination and Child Support Enforcement.   As was the case with AFDC, TANF recipients are required to assist in identifying and locating their children's fathers. Those able to document domestic violence (usually through a police report) are exempt from this requirement. Failure to cooperate can result in lower benefits or program termination. The state agency charged with administration of TANF operates a child support collection operation, and funds collected are used by the state to offset its TANF budget. While they are on TANF, mother and children do not receive this child support until the state has recovered its payments to the family. Even after the TANF benefit period ends, some states continue to collect money from the noncustodial parent until the state's TANF costs are recovered.

The transition from AFDC to TANF was fraught with controversy and ambiguity. Welfare advocates were horrified by the prospect of families being cut off abruptly from public assistance. Program recipients were often unaware of provisions that affected them, such as the measure that exempts victims of domestic violence from the requirement that they assist officials in collecting child support if doing so would present "undue hardship," or the 20 percent exemption that allows some recipients to continue receiving assistance after they have passed the lifetime limit. The work participation requirements have been interpreted either broadly (to include a wide range of activities such as participating in mental health or substance abuse treatment) or narrowly (to include only paid employment). The use of "sanctions" also varies. Some of this ambiguity results from the "devolution" process. Under TANF, decisions made at the state level have greater impact on recipients' lives than was the case under AFDC.

Housing Assistance

In the United States, housing is not an entitlement, but a private commodity to be traded for profit in the real estate market. As a result, budget allocations for assistance programs consistently fail to meet the need for housing, and low-income Americans who seek housing assistance confront waiting lists and complex bureaucratic requirements.

Federal housing assistance is provided through three programs that date back to the New Deal, when public housing was developed for low-income working families. The structure of current federal low-income housing programs was in place by the mid-1970s. Federal programs include public housing, which offers low-cost housing to the poor and the disabled; Section 202, which provides developers with incentives to build housing for the elderly and disabled; and Section 8, which provides rent subsidies to low-income families.

Public Housing.   Widespread federal involvement in public housing dates to the Great Depression. The National Industrial Recovery Act (NIRA) of 1933 provided federal funding for housing construction. But the focus of New Deal efforts was less on provision of housing for the poor than on creation of jobs for the unemployed. Public housing was made available to the working poor who lived in "intact" families. Unwed mothers were excluded from most housing units, and few (usually 10 percent) of the units were available to families on welfare.

World War II brought a serious housing shortage. The Federal Housing Administration (FHA) and GI home mortgage programs offered low-interest mortgages to middle-class Americans and veterans. Members of Congress and welfare authorities argued that public housing should be reserved for those in greatest need. As a result, new policies lowered income limits for eligibility and prohibited discrimination against welfare families and unwed mothers.

By the mid-1960s, public housing in the United States had become a "war zone," replete with drug dealing and violent crime. Mildred Hailey was one of several resident leaders who advocated for reform in public housing. Reasoning that federal indifference and resident apathy conspired to create hellish living conditions, Hailey and others argued for returning control (and even ownership) of public housing to the residents. She took over the project she lived in, Bromley Heath in Boston, and with an administrative board of fellow housing residents set out to manage and police the project. Since then, a growing number of public housing units have been purchased or managed by the residents themselves.

Section 202.   Section 202 of the Housing Act of 1959 was passed to provide low-interest construction loans to nonprofit sponsors (such as churches and civic organizations) who were interested in expanding the supply of low-cost housing for the low-income elderly and disabled. Once constructed, a Section 202 housing development is operated by the nonprofit sponsor with federal oversight. The elderly have probably been the greatest beneficiaries of this program. In 1990, 70 percent of new Section 202 units were designated for elderly residents, with the remaining 30 percent for the disabled (Sonnenberg, Budget Analyst, Department of Housing and Urban Development, personal communication, 1993). There has been a substantial increase in the proportion of existing public housing units intended exclusively for the elderly. In 1960, units for the elderly made up only 3.2 percent of public housing stock. By 1988 the figure had grown to 26 percent (U.S. Department of Commerce, 1992).

Section 8. The Housing and Community Development Act of 1974 included Section 8 to provide rent subsidies for low-income families. Families eligible for Section 8 benefits are given a voucher to cover part of their rent. Each family is expected to pay 30 percent of its income toward rent. The voucher covers the remainder up to a predetermined amount.

As Mulroy (1990) points out, Section 8 is frequently cited as "a great liberator," freeing low-income families from reliance on public housing and from exorbitant housing costs. Because of limited funding; however, Section 8 reaches only a small fraction of low-income households. In 1980, the Office of Management and Budget (OMB) estimated that only 8 percent of eligible households were receiving subsidies (U.S. General Accounting Office, 1980). The OMB report noted, "The Section 8 may be likened somewhat to a lottery in which only a few strike it big. For those families fortunate enough to get into the program, many can be expected to stay in it for a long time" (U.S. General Accounting Office, 1980, p. 12). Although the number of vouchers available under Section 8 was increased during the Clinton administration, the program still falls short of meeting the housing needs of low-income Americans (U.S. Department of Housing and Urban Development, 1993, 1999). Clients who do receive vouchers often find the program's procedures and regulations complex and difficult (Mulroy, 1990).

SUMMARY OF ATTITUDES AND INTERVENTIONS

A major thread that runs through the history of poverty policy in the United States is the close connection between the values and beliefs discussed earlier in this chapter and interventions designed to prevent or alleviate poverty. When the presence of poverty was seen as an opportunity for more comfortable people to secure their salvation, charity was given with an open hand and little concern for its impact. When poverty was viewed as a crime, the response was to impose punishment. If poverty serves to motivate the industrial labor force, it is important that relief not create a class of comfortable paupers. If poverty is the simple result of human capital limitations, the answer must lie in education and training for the poor. If there is a "culture of poverty," then the values and beliefs of children and adults with low incomes must be changed. If poverty is the result of limited opportunities, ensuring equal opportunity should relieve the problem. And, most recently, if poverty is caused by welfare, then "ending welfare as we know it" should reduce the suffering of the poor.

Another historical thread is the tremendous variety in Americans' beliefs about poverty. The poverty policies we live under reflect a combination of these beliefs. Indeed, Americans' beliefs about poverty are as heterogeneous as the poor themselves. The following section describes the current face of poverty in the United States, one that is increasingly made up of female-headed households with children.

REALITIES OF POVERTY IN THE
CONTEMPORARY UNITED STATES

In 2006, over 36 million Americans had incomes below the federal poverty threshold (http://pubdb3.census.gov/macro/032007/pov/new01_100_01.htm). While some of them received income assistance through public programs, a majority did not. As we will see in this section, the poor are a heterogeneous group, and the causes and consequences of their poverty are varied and complex.

Characteristics of America's Poor

If poverty is one of the risks, or costs, of membership in American society, its distribution reflects an important allocation principle. If the risks of poverty were randomly distributed, one might fairly argue that poverty is the result of personal idiosyncrasy or failure. John Rawls's "veil of ignorance" (discussed in Chapter 1) might then predict that the nation's policies would maximize the well-being of the poor. But Americans do not enter the world with equal risks of poverty. Indeed, one's risk of poverty is in some ways inversely related to the likelihood of serving in Congress. Several factors determine both probabilities, among them race, age, gender, residence, immigration status, and employment. Each of these factors is addressed in the following sections.

Race.   Although white Americans make up the largest group with incomes below the poverty threshold, they do not experience the nation's highest poverty rates. For example, in 2000–2002, non-Hispanic white Americans represented 75 percent of the total U.S. population but made up just under half (46 percent) of America's poor. Clearly white Americans are underrepresented among the nation's poor. The poverty rate for non-Hispanic white Americans was relatively low (7.9 percent) compared to Asian Americans and Americans from the Pacific Islands (10.2 percent), Hispanic Americans (21.5 percent), African Americans (23.2 percent), and Alaska Natives and Native Americans (23.2 percent) (U.S. Bureau of the Census, 2003d). These figures are presented in Table 5.4.

Gender.   Women experience a significantly higher risk of poverty than men, hence the phrase "feminization of poverty." In 2005, female heads of household had a 31.1-percent risk of poverty, compared with a rate of 10.8 percent for married couples. African American female heads of household had the highest rate (39.3 percent) compared to 39 percent for Hispanic American women and 22.6 percent for white American women (http://www.census.gov/hhes/www/poverty/histpov/hstpov2.html, accessed January 15, 2008). As we will see, women are much more likely than men to work for below-poverty wages in the United States.

Age.   In America, children experience the highest risk of poverty. Whereas the overall poverty rate in 2006 was 12 percent, 17 percent of children under 18 lived in poverty that year. Young children are especially vulnerable to poverty,

TABLE 5.4 **Poverty and Ethnicity in the United States: Three-Year Average, 2000–2002 (Overall Poverty Rate: 11.7 Percent)**

Race/Ethnicity	Percent Below Poverty	Percent of Poverty Population	Percent of General Population (2000)
Non-Hispanic White (only)	7.9	46.0	75.1
Asian and Pacific Islander (only)	10.2	4.0	3.7
Hispanic American (only)	21.5	25.0	12.5
African American (only)	23.2	25.0	12.3
American Indian and Alaska Native (only)	23.2	2.0	0.9

SOURCE: U.S. Bureau of the Census (2003d). Poverty Tables Based on Current Population Surveys. Poverty figures: http://www.census.gov/hhes/www/poverty/poverty02/pov2_and_3-yr_avgs.html; General population figures: http://www.census.gov/population/www/cen2000/briefs.html.

with 21 percent of those under the age of 5 living in households with incomes below the poverty threshold. Over half (54 percent) of children under 5 years in families headed by a single mother lived in poverty. In sharp contrast, only 10 percent of children of the same age in families headed by a married couple had incomes below the poverty threshold (U.S. Bureau of the Census, 2007).

The elderly—those aged 65 and over—had a substantially lower risk of poverty (10.4 percent) in 2002 than children. This does not mean that all of the nation's elderly are well-off. First, as mentioned previously, the poverty threshold for the elderly is lower than for other age groups. Second, a significant proportion (16.9 percent) of those over 65 years old had incomes below 125 percent of the federal poverty threshold. In 2002, 19 percent of individuals over age 75 who lived alone had incomes below the poverty threshold, as did more than a third (36.5 percent) of single African American women over 75 (U.S. Bureau of the Census, 2003c).

Residence.   Prior to 1994, the South led the nation in poverty. Now that distinction is sometimes shared with the West. In 2005, the South had a poverty rate of 14 percent, compared to 12.6 percent for the West. This compares to poverty rates of 11.3 percent for the Northeast and 11.4 percent for the Midwest (http://www.census.gov/hhes/www/poverty/histpov/hstpov9.html, accessed January 15, 2008). These regional trends are mirrored in the state-level rates.

The poverty rate in rural America once exceeded that in the nation's cities. Today that situation has reversed. The nation's highest poverty rates are found in the inner cities. In 2005, the poverty rate in principal cities was 17 percent, compared to a suburban poverty rate of 9.3 percent. Rural poverty, measured as that "outside metropolitan areas," was 14.5 percent (http://www.census.gov/hhes/www/poverty/histpov/hstpov8.html).[12]

---

12. It is worth noting that, until 1981, the poverty threshold for farm families was lower than for others. The rationale was that farm families had access to low-cost food.

Immigration Status.   American citizens who are foreign born have a slightly lower risk of poverty than those who are native born. The poverty rate for naturalized citizens was 10.4 percent in 2005, compared with 12.1 percent for native-born citizens. Foreign-born individuals who have not attained citizenship have a substantially higher poverty rate. In 2005, 20.4 percent lived in poverty (http://www.census.gov/hhes/www/poverty/histpov/hstpov23.html,   accessed January 15, 2008).

Employment.   As we will see in Chapter 14, having a job does not guarantee escape from poverty. Many Americans with incomes below the poverty level are employed. In 2002, a majority of poor families reported having at least one member who worked. But only 19 percent reported that one member worked full time, year-round. Within the general population, 54 percent of families report having at least one member who is employed full-time year-round (U.S. Bureau of the Census, 2003c).

Summary: Characteristics of Americans Living in Poverty.   America's poor and near-poor are a heterogeneous group, dominated by children in female-headed households. Many of the poor are white Americans, and nearly half are employed. But people of color and those with either part-time or seasonal employment are extremely vulnerable to poverty. The nation's poor are concentrated in the central cities, which in 1997 housed 42.2 percent of those with incomes below the poverty threshold. Most (73.7 percent in 1997) of the poor live in families related by blood or marriage. Finally, although immigrants experienced somewhat higher risk of poverty, the vast majority (85.3 percent) of the poor were native born (Dalaker & Naifeh, 1997). As we have seen, the risk of poverty is unevenly divided among U.S. population groups. The following section considers recent trends in inequality.

Inequality in the United States

Inequality has increased significantly in the United States during the last three decades. Between 1967 and 1973, income increased for most Americans, regardless of whether they were in the top income quintile (the fifth of the population with the highest incomes) or the bottom quintile (the fifth of the population with the lowest incomes). During this period, the Congressional Budget Office reports that the mean adjusted family income for those in the lowest quintile increased by 30 percent, while the mean adjusted family income for the highest quintile grew by 21 percent. Since then, the American economic situation has changed markedly. Income for the bottom quintile has declined, while income for the highest has risen dramatically. Put simply, for the past three decades, the rich have gotten richer and the poor have gotten poorer. While this growth in inequality slowed somewhat during the economic growth of the 1990s, it continued nonetheless (Bernstein et al., 2000).

Increases in inequality would be interpreted differently by adherents of each of the philosophical perspectives introduced in Chapter 1. The perspective of

---

B O X   5.2   Inequality Going to Extremes?

Between 1973 and 2000, inflation-adjusted incomes for 90 percent of Americans declined by 7 percent while inflation-adjusted incomes for the nation's most affluent 1 percent increased by 148 percent, and the top 0.01 percent saw their incomes rise by 599 percent (Piketty & Saez, 2003). An organization known as United for a Fair Economy reported that executives in

U.S. corporations average over 300 times the income of production workers. Some argue that this reflects social norms that favor private wealth over community assets or public responsibility. Others suggest that this concentration of riches is a consequence of America's campaign finance system. Is excessive wealth becoming a social problem?

---

oligarchy would suggest that inequality is a natural, perhaps divinely inspired, method for ordering the social classes. From a libertarian perspective, inequality is the inevitable and even desirable result of a competitive economy, and governmental efforts to reduce it are wasteful and inappropriate. Philosophical liberals tolerate a certain amount of economic inequality if it does not jeopardize political equality. John Rawls, a contractual liberal, suggested that inequality was acceptable as long as those who were least well-off did not fall below an agreed-upon social minimum.

In addition to lack of resources, poverty brings "secondary risks" that further deteriorate the quality of life available to disadvantaged Americans.

"Secondary Risks" of Poverty

America's poor are not just economically vulnerable. They are exposed to homelessness and violence to a much greater degree than other citizens of the United States. Further, they are accused of "fraud," despite the relatively small economic impact of their fraudulent activities. In the following section, we will examine these secondary risks that accompany poverty.

Homelessness.   In the United States a house is a commodity, developed and traded for profit. A house can provide shelter and protection. A "home" provides continuity and a social context for adults and children, and those who become homeless lose more than shelter. They lose connection with their past, friends, and schools, and their place in a community. Two developments in the U.S. housing market have increased the vulnerability of low-income people. The first is a diminishing supply of low-cost rental housing; the second is a reduced federal commitment to housing assistance.

As we mentioned earlier, the majority of low-income families do not have access to federal housing assistance, and they fare poorly in the private housing market. Since the early 1970s, the supply of low-cost rental housing has been diminishing. Analyzing data from the Annual Housing Survey, Sternleib and Hughes (1981) report the following.

More than a million units, which in 1973 rented for less than $150 a month, literally disappeared from housing inventory. . . . Low-rent housing units are literally being removed, and the potential renter who can only afford low rent finds the inventory available to him or her shrinking markedly. (pp. 111–112)

Urban renewal efforts have cost the nation more than a million rooms in "single-room-occupancy" (SRO) hotels. In recent decades, major cities such as New York have lost many of their SROs. Some buildings have simply been demolished. "Gentrification" has also reduced the supply of low-cost housing. In 1984, Harrington described gentrification as "the process whereby the middle class and the rich take over the physically sound and architecturally charming housing of the poor" (Harrington, 1984, p. 119). "Public subsidies, such as tax abatements for refurbishment, have often subsidized this process. But there has not been a commensurate subsidy to provide housing for the displaced" (p. 12). The supply of low-income housing continued to diminish during the 1990s. As the U.S. Department of Housing and Urban Development (HUD) reports, between 1991 and 1997 the number of affordable rental units in the United States dropped by an estimated 372,000, which amounted to 5 percent of the nation's supply (U.S. Department of Housing and Urban Development, 1999). As an inevitable result of declining supply, the cost of housing increased. In recent decades the Consumer Price Index for shelter has consistently increased at a rate higher than the general Consumer Price Index. This trend continued during the economic prosperity of the 1990s, requiring low- and middle-income Americans to devote an ever greater share of their income to housing (ibid.).

Federal housing interventions attempt to bridge the gap between the financial resources of low-income Americans and the cost of housing, but recent decades have seen erosion in all three programs. This erosion was especially marked during the Reagan administration, when funding for public housing was severely reduced. Funds allocated went from $32 billion in 1981 to $6 billion in 1989 (Burton, 1992). The number of Section 202 units dropped from a high of 39,381 in 1978 to 7,281 in 1990 (Sonnenberg, Budget Analyst, Department of Housing and Urban Development, personal communication, 1993). In a despairing note, Koebel complained in 1998 that "[t]he failure of government to directly provide decent housing for low-income families is now accepted as a given" (Koebel, 1998, p. 3). Coupled with a tight housing market, government inattention to the housing needs of the poor contributes to increased homelessness.

Michael Harrington (1984) suggests that people without homes be called "uprooted" rather than "homeless." Harrington notes that major economic transformations often create "a floating population" of people whose role in the old economic order has disappeared.

It is hard to estimate precisely the number of Americans who are homeless. Two methods yield very different results. The "point-in-time" approach asks how many people are homeless on a particular day (or night). Using this method, Burt (1992) suggests that at any given time approximately half a million people were homeless during the late 1980s. Generally point-in-time estimates of homelessness range from 500,000 to 750,000 people on any given night (McCallum & Bolland, 2001). The "period–prevalence" approach asks how many people have experienced homelessness during a longer period, usually either a lifetime or the past five years. A national telephone study completed in 1994 (Link et al., 1995) found that 7.4 percent of American adults (13.5 million people) had been homeless at some point in their lives. The Urban Institute (2000) estimated that about 3.5 million Americans, of whom 1.35 million were children, experience homelessness in a given year (http://www.urban.org/url .cfm?ID=900366, accessed January 15, 2008).

Who are America's homeless? There are three distinct groups: single adults, families, and runaway teenagers. Single adults are predominantly homeless men, among whom an estimated 20 to 25 percent suffer from severe and persistent mental illness (Koegel, Burnham, & Baumohl, 1996). The proportion who suffer from addiction disorders has been estimated at 22 percent (ibid.). Notably, studies have found that between 22 percent and 40 percent of homeless men are veterans (Humphreys & Rosenheck, 1995; Waxman & Trupin, 1997).

Families with children are the fastest-growing group, making up approximately 40 percent of the nation's homeless (Shinn, 1997). A study commissioned by the U.S. Conference of Mayors reported that children represented about one-fourth of the urban homeless (Waxman & Trupin, 1997). A 1990 Ford Foundation study found that half of homeless women and children were fleeing abusive situations (Zorza, 1991).

Thousands of teenagers flee (or are kicked out of) their homes each year to live on the streets of major cities. Children who "age out" of foster care are also at significant risk of homelessness (Russell, 1998). Estimates of the number of homeless youth range from 500,000 to 4 million (Klein et al., 2000). Only about half of these make use of homeless shelters, leading Slesnick (2004) and others to identify two types of homeless youth: "shelter kids" and "street kids." All homeless children are vulnerable to physical and sexual abuse, and many of their basic needs go unmet (Karabanow, 2004). The Runaway and Homeless Youth Act provides funding for outreach, supportive services, and shelters for runaway and "thrownaway" youth under auspices of the Department of Health and Human Services, Family and Youth Services Bureau.

Federal policy toward the homeless has been marked by reluctance. When the growth in homelessness first reached public awareness in the early 1980s, the Reagan administration took the position that it was not a problem that demanded federal intervention. In this period, advocates struggled to document the number of homeless people, and political debates about the extent of the problem raged. In 1983 a federal task force on homelessness was created, and in 1986 the Homeless Persons' Survival Act, later renamed the McKinney Homeless Assistance Act, was passed. Funding, as well as the type of programs that can be funded under the act, increased until 1995, when the budget reached a peak of $1.49 billion (National Coalition for the Homeless, 1999). Programs funded under the act have provided "safe havens" for the mentally ill who are homeless, ensured public education for children in homeless families, offered

health care to the homeless, and established emergency shelters and food programs. Since 1995 McKinney programs have been subjected to budget cuts,
and the legislation has been criticized as addressing the symptoms, but not the
causes, of homelessness.

Violence.   Michael Harrington (1984) argued that, "[c]ertain social and economic conditions—above all, the experience of becoming marginal, useless—
create not a fate, but a greater likelihood that some (a minority) will turn to
violent crime either as means to an end, a way of earning a living, or else as an
act of sheer rage" (p. 189). Poverty leaves people especially vulnerable to aggres-
sion and victimization.[13] Indeed, consideration of broad trends in violence in the
United States led Gurr (1989) to comment that increases in violence have typically been associated with "immigration, war and economic deprivation" (p. 12).
This may also be the case in France and Germany, where higher rates of violence
have been documented among marginalized groups of immigrants (Short, 1997).

Social dislocation and extreme poverty foster violence. There is also some
evidence that inequality is associated with higher homicide rates (Blau & Blau,
1982). Violent crime is concentrated where marginalized groups are restricted to
certain neighborhoods or communities, such as inner-city ghettos, and is often
gang-related. It is unclear why ghetto residents experience more violence.
Possible explanations include lack of opportunity, few role models for success,
higher residential mobility, family disruption, and cultural values that tolerate violence (Short, 1997).

According to the Department of Justice, more than 1.3 million violent
crimes (aggravated assault, robbery, rape, and murder) were reported in 2004,
and that year was the last of a 13-year decline in the rate of such crimes (U.S.
Department of Justice, 2006a). In 2005 and 2006 the rate of violent crime in the
United States increased substantially (U.S. Department of Justice, 2007).
Regional differences have also been observed, with the South and West report-
ing disproportionately high rates of violent crime, while the Northeast and
Midwest reported lower rates (ibid.).

Poverty and race interact to leave young African American men at tragically
high risk for violence. During the nineteenth and twentieth centuries, African
American men were more likely than white American men both to be murdered
and to commit murder (Short, 1997). In 2003, African American men aged 25 to
44 were more than 10 times as likely to die as the result of homicide than white
men the same age (www.kff.org/minorityhealth/upload/7541.pdf, accessed
October 27, 2007).

---

13. James F. Short (1997) argues, and I agree, that violent crime creates two victims: the
perpetrator and the identified victim. Both lives are either ended or permanently disrupted
by the experience.

Welfare Fraud

A popular urban myth holds that food stamp recipients use their coupons to buy guns and drugs, and hundreds of Americans have heard that "a friend of a friend" saw a woman drive to the welfare office in a Cadillac. In reality, welfare fraud is neither as prevalent nor as straightforward as many Americans believe.

The Food Stamp program distributes more than $22 billion worth of food vouchers each year. The USDA estimated that in 1990 less than 1 percent of participants defrauded the program (usually by lying about eligibility), and approximately 5 percent of funds were lost to fraud; a total that amounts to just over $1 billion. Those who benefit most from food stamp fraud are not participants but retailers. In the most common form of food stamp fraud, the retailer purchases the stamps for 65 to 85 percent of their face value and then turns them in for full reimbursement. While this practice frees participants to spend the reduced amount on whatever they like, the profit accrues to the retailer. In one of the largest cases, a retailer in Toledo, Ohio, improperly redeemed $7.2 million in food stamps. This individual had been previously convicted of food stamp fraud but evidently never quit the lucrative practice (Cook, 1989). It is dishonest retailers, not the poor, who profit most from food stamp fraud. The U.S. Department of Agriculture reports that the use of electronic benefits transfer (EBT) cards is an effective antifraud measure (U.S. Department of Agriculture, n.d.)

Public assistance payments seem designed to produce fraud. Cash assistance consistently fails to raise family incomes above the poverty threshold. For example, in 2002, the average TANF payment to a family of three ($355) was less than a third of the federal poverty threshold for the same family ($1,251) (http://aspe.hhs.gov/hsp/indicators04/apa-tanf.htm#ttanf6, and http://aspe.hhs.gov/poverty/02poverty.htm, accessed January 15, 2008). Even when in-kind assistance such as food stamps, Medicaid, and housing supports are included, families find it difficult to raise children with such limited resources. Many mothers secure other sources of income, a practice that (if unreported) constitutes welfare fraud (see Funiciello, 1993). Antonia's babysitting is one example of this widespread practice.

From a broader perspective, the economic impact of welfare fraud pales in comparison with that of middle-class offenses. Middle-class fraud includes practices such as health-care fraud and tax evasion that benefit members of the middle and upper classes, often at the expense of taxpayers. In 1992, the General Accounting Office (GAO) reported to Congress that health insurance fraud (including that in the Medicare and Medicaid programs) cost an estimated 10 percent of the total U.S. health-care dollars, as much as $170 billion in 2003 (http://www.nhcaa.org/eweb/DynamicPage.aspx?webcode=anti_fraud_resource_centr&wpscode=TheProblemOfHCFraud, accessed October 27, 2007). Common forms of Medicare fraud include billing for services not furnished, misrepresenting the diagnosis to justify payment, soliciting, offering or receiving a kickback, and "upcoding" (billing for more costly services than those actually delivered).

Tax evasion also takes its toll. Based on IRS data, the GAO reported that taxpayers ultimately pay about 87 percent of the taxes they owe. Groups vary in the extent of their tax evasion, with wage earners reporting 99 percent of their earnings, while self-employed workers report only 19 percent. The difference between taxes owed and those collected, called the "tax gap," has increased. In 1981, the tax gap amounted to $76 billion, or 1.6 percent of the nation's gross domestic product (GDP). By 1992, that figure had grown to $127 billion, or 2 percent of the GDP (U.S. General Accounting Office, 1994b), and in 2005, the IRS estimated the nation's tax gap somewhere between $312 billion and $353 billion, which is primarily attributed to underreporting of income by individuals (http://www.irs.gov/newsroom/article/0,,id=137247,00.html, accessed October 27, 2007).

America's energetic pursuit of welfare fraud can hardly be attributed to its drain on the public purse. Even when the amount lost seems large, it is a small fraction of the amount lost to health insurance fraud and tax evasion. Yet welfare fraud raises the public ire in a way that tax evasion never could. Why is that so? Is it more corrupt for a welfare mother like Antonia to be paid under the table for providing child care to her neighbors than it is for a businessperson to conceal income from the IRS? Or is the public furor over welfare fraud just another vehicle for humiliating recipients of public assistance?

SUMMARY: WHAT DOES THE FUTURE HOLD FOR AMERICA'S POOR?

This chapter began with the case of Antonia Flores, a bright, articulate woman who is struggling to ensure a brighter future for her son. Her success as a mother might in earlier eras have entitled her to public assistance. But under current welfare law, Antonia, along with millions of other welfare recipients, is encouraged to assume "personal responsibility" for her limited means. The nation's collective responsibility for low-income families and their children is limited. Upon reaching their lifetime limits, former welfare recipients may retain food stamps, Medicaid, and housing assistance. But they will not have money to pay for other basic necessities such as utility bills or clothes for themselves and their children.

Fundamental to current welfare policies is the belief that for most people work is the best antidote to poverty. This serves the needs of the capitalist economy, in which diminished work incentive represents a significant economic threat. Welfare reform reduces that threat, both by eliminating the choice between welfare and work, and by reducing the quality of life for those on welfare. Of course, as we will see in Chapter 14, many Americans like Antonia find that work does not provide the economic security they need for themselves and their families.

Walter Trattner (1989) ends his exhaustive survey of the history of the American welfare state by suggesting that "[p]erhaps a time will come anyway when most Americans will acknowledge—or be forced to acknowledge—what our colonial forebears simply took for granted, namely, that the poor will be with us, always, through no fault of their own, and that they, too, have a right to a healthy, happy, and secure life" (p. 342). Whether the poor will be able to live "a healthy, happy, and secure life" in the United States remains to be seen.

KEYWORDS

Elizabethan Poor Law

Great Society

Poverty

Welfare reform

Work standards

Aid to Families with Dependent Children (AFDC)

Temporary Assistance for Needy Families (TANF)

Homeless shelters

Housing policy

America's underclass

Income maintenance

Living wage

Public welfare

Rural poor

Food stamps

THINK ABOUT IT

1. Consider the three conditions that facilitate collective action to address individual problems, as outlined in the introduction to Part II. The events of the Great Depression led many Americans to see poverty as an individual problem with "uncertainty of moment and magnitude." Does this view still hold? Do any of these conditions play a role in contemporary debates about welfare reform? Should they? Does poverty in the United States have any "external effects"?

2. Which of the philosophical conceptions of social justice presented in Chapter 1 is most influential in the structure of the U.S. welfare effort?

3. Presidents Roosevelt and Bush differed significantly in their attitudes toward privatization. How would you characterize this difference? Can you explain why the two presidents approached the use of private organizations to deliver services so differently?

4. Compare your state's poverty rate with the rate nationwide. Is it substantially different? If so, how would you explain the difference?

WEB-BASED EXERCISES

For direct links to all the sites in these exercises, log on to the Student Companion Site for this book at academic.cengage.com/social_work/barusch, and choose Chapter 5.

1. Go to the poverty page maintained by the U.S. Bureau of the Census at http://www.census.gov/hhes/www/poverty/poverty.html. Click on "Small Area Income and Poverty Estimates." Then choose "State and county data." Here, you can compare the poverty rate in your state with that in other states and in the nation as a whole. Is your state's poverty rate higher or lower that the U.S. rate? How do you account for this finding?

2. Each year the Administration for Children and Families (part of the U.S. Department of Health and Human Services) prepares a report to Congress on the TANF program. Go to http://www.acf.hhs.gov/programs/ofa/indexar.htm, and review the most recent Annual Report to Congress on TANF. What issues are highlighted in the report? What are the characteristics of TANF families? Do you see any information describing the amount of the cash benefit?

3. If you are intrigued by the politics of welfare reform, go to http://www.theatlantic.com/issues/97mar/edelman/edelman.htm and read "The Worst Thing Bill Clinton has Done," a scathing critique of PRWORA, written by a leading welfare expert who worked for the Clinton administration.

SUGGESTED RESOURCES

Danziger, S., & Gottschalk, P. (1995). *America Unequal.* New York: Russell Sage Foundation.

Deparle, J. (2004). *American Dream: Three Women, Ten Kids, and a Nation's Drive to End Welfare.* New York: Viking Books.

Harrington, M. (1984). *The New American Poverty.* New York: Holt, Rinehart & Winston.

Katz, M. (1989). *The Undeserving Poor.* New York: Pantheon Books.

Kilty, K. M., & Segal, E. A. (Eds.). (2006). *The Promise of Welfare Reform: Political Rhetoric and the Reality of Poverty in the Twenty-First Century.* New York: Haworth Press.

Kozol, J. (1991). *Savage Inequalities: Children in America's Schools.* New York: Crown.

Specht, H., & Courtney, M. (1994). *Unfaithful Angels: How Social Work Has Abandoned Its Mission.* New York: Free Press.

Trattner, W. I. (1989). *From Poor Law to Welfare State: A History of Social Welfare in America* (4th ed.). New York: Free Press.

www.census.gov/hhes/www/poverty.html. Maintained by the Bureau of the Census, this site is a good starting point for up-to-date information on poverty in the United States.

www.ufenet.org. This site is operated by United for a Fair Economy (UFE), an organization devoted to policies that reduce inequality in the United States. UFE is "grounded in the belief that our country would be a far more democratic, prosperous, and caring community if we narrowed the vast gap between the very wealthy and everyone else." The UFE website offers an introduction to the organization and provides position papers on issues.

www.urban.org. Operated by the Urban Institute, a nonprofit organization, this site provides reports on social and economic problems.

6

Physical Illness

The health of the people is really the foundation upon which
all their happiness and all their powers as a state depend.
BENJAMIN DISRAELI, JULY 1877

The role of government in health care has long been the subject of debate.
Early public health reformers met vigorous opposition when they proposed
what we now consider the most basic public health measures. Today the role of
government in the financing and delivery of health care is again under dispute, as
Americans question the efficacy of private-market solutions to medical needs. At
issue is the extent to which illness should be addressed through collective, as opposed to individual, action.

Allocation of health care is clearly a social justice issue, as is the extent to
which a patient should be held responsible for his or her illness and the cost of
its treatment. America's reliance on private-market solutions to health problems
has created a multibillion-dollar health-care industry to serve economically productive and affluent members of society. In the same nation, millions are denied
access to basic health care. Should health care be treated as a social good, with no
one permitted to fall below a minimal standard? Is the private market the most
efficient means of distributing health care? Should individuals bear the risk (and
the cost) of catastrophic illness? Should the public bear the cost of illnesses caused
by personal behavior? These and related questions are considered throughout this
chapter.

We will begin by considering the case of Tanya Johnson, a young woman
who contracted human immunodeficiency virus (HIV) from her boyfriend.
Tanya's situation illustrates many of the dilemmas of health care in the United
States. We then trace the development of public health interventions in the

United States, focusing on three major federal health agencies: the Public Health Service (PHS), the Children's Bureau, and the Veterans Administration. Next, we will look at the federal role in financing health care through Medicaid and Medicare, exploring the impact of this legislation on the private health-care industry. The next section outlines the U.S. health-care investment (in the form of health expenditures) and its return (in terms of infant mortality and longevity). Returning to a national focus, we then consider the relationship between health status and class, race, and gender in the United States. Modern epidemics are examined in the next section, which offers a nod to microbial indifference for national borders. Issues of global governance come to the fore, along with the changing role of the World Health Organization, as we consider two global epidemics: HIV/AIDS (acquired immunodeficiency syndrome) and severe acute respiratory syndrome (SARS). In the final section we consider two fundamental policy dilemmas affecting health care in the United States: criteria for assigning risk and the use of the market to allocate health care. The chapter closes with brief consideration of health-care reform and the role of social workers in health-care policy.

HISTORY OF PUBLIC HEALTH INTERVENTIONS
IN THE UNITED STATES

Most of us are familiar with the major medical breakthroughs of the twentieth century: the development of antibiotics, immunizations, and advanced surgical techniques. Less familiar, but perhaps more significant, have been advances in public health. As we have seen, modern plumbing improved the health status of populations throughout the world. In this section, we will focus on the development of public health interventions in the United States.

The development of public health has been integral to the growth of the U.S. welfare state. Policy milestones include the 1912 creation of the Children's Bureau; the 1930 establishment of the Veterans Administration; the 1944 creation of the PHS; the 1946 establishment of the Centers for Disease Control and Prevention (CDC); the 1953 creation of the Department of Health, Education, and Welfare; and the 1965 passage of Medicare and Medicaid.

Public health reformers in nineteenth-century America drew from the English approach to community health, seeing (perhaps more clearly than we do now) the close link between poverty and disease. Just as this nation imported major elements of the Elizabethan Poor Law, we also inherited the perspectives of Britain's "Sanitary Movement." Edwin Chadwick and other leaders of the movement advocated national oversight of sanitation in urban areas, government tracking of vital statistics, and local regulation of waste drainage and purification of drinking water. When their suggestions were initially presented to Parliament

At the age of 24, Tanya Johnson is considered unin-surable due to a preexisting condition. Tanya is HIV-positive. She sees herself as living with, not dying from, AIDS and refuses to view herself as a "victim" of the epidemic. Her situation illustrates many of the tensions experienced by people coping with chronic illness in the U.S. health-care system.

A bouncy, attractive woman with long, curly auburn hair, Tanya describes herself as "perfectly healthy . . . I don't take medications, and I have good T cells, and I have a low viral load. I do have symptoms. My lymph nodes are swollen a lot and inflamed, and sometimes they ache. They don't hurt; they ache. And so I just take Motrin for it. I get fatigued very easily. I take Motrin for cramps, for chest pains, headaches. I'm a walking ibuprofen advertisement."

When she speaks to high school classes for the local AIDS foundation, she begins by saying, "My name is Tanya Johnson, and I've had HIV for four years that I contracted from a very lovely sociopathic IV drug user." "He *was* [sociopathic]," she assured me. "He's in prison right now, as a matter of fact, so he's proven it." Tanya met her boyfriend at a party one night. "We'd gone to a party, and this guy was there, and he was friends with us," and so they started going out. "It just kind of happened. I'd go to his place and party sometimes, and it just happened one night. It wasn't like we dated or anything."

Tanya's boyfriend knew he had AIDS, but didn't tell her. "I'm not angry about this. 'Cause I'm not. It's my own fault, you know? I knew what I was doing, you know? And you have to take your own responsibility for yourself. I knew about safe sex and I knew about AIDS. I lost my virginity when I was 14, so I knew about all the precautions to take. I wasn't stupid. I was just crazy, I guess. I was immortal, and I was on top of the world, and nothing bad was ever going to happen to me. I was go-ing to live forever—young, and beautiful, and thin."

After Tanya and her boyfriend broke up, she learned that he had AIDS. "So I went to go to get tested. I'd been tested before so I knew the drill. I waited past the 90 days 'cause I kind of really didn't want to know. I invented all the reasons in the world why it couldn't possibly be, and then all the reasons why it could possibly be, and I . . . you know? The flu-like symptoms that they tell you about. I didn't feel good for a whole month. I called for my test results, and I was getting off at 3:30 P.M. I says, 'Are my test

results in?' She says, 'Yes, they are.' I says, 'Great. I'll be in after work.' She says, 'No.' She says, 'Come in tomorrow.' I says, 'No, I can come in right now.' She says, 'No, come in tomorrow. How about 4:00?' And by now I'm panicked, 'cause I just know. And I says, 'What time do you open?' She says, '9 A.M.' I says, 'I will be there at 9 A.M.' I did not sleep that night. Did not have sex with my boyfriend that night, you know. And of course I hadn't told him about any of this. The next morning I go in. And you know when I go in, I have to sit and wait forever in the waiting room. And then I go in, and then . . . the lady that gave me the test took me into a room, and there was another lady sitting there. And I just started crying. They didn't even have to tell. And the lady that was in with her, she's a case manager for the state. And she's a wonderful lady. She says, 'What are you going to do when you leave here?' I says, 'I don't know . . . go home. . . .' She says, 'Call your mom right now. Make an appointment and meet her for lunch and tell her,' and I'm like, 'Okay.' She didn't want me to leave the office and have nowhere to go."

Tanya is an only child. She told her mother over lunch, and her mom responded, "So, do you want to live forever?" "I says, 'Well . . . yeah. I kind of would like to. You know? I'm 21 years old!' I couldn't tell Dad. She told Dad for me. I went home the next afternoon, and my dad came out of the bedroom, and my mom had told him, and he comes up to me and just gives me a big, huge hug, then went back to his bedroom. He couldn't stay with me because he was, you know, just too choked up. He says, 'I love you' and walked back in his bedroom. My family's been great. Except for my Uncle James, and he doesn't talk to me or won't come anywhere near me."

Tanya works as an office manager for a small firm with 10 employees. She likes her job. "The people are really nice, which is amazing, 'cause you know, usually at jobs, people are so cruel. And I like what I'm doing." The people at work don't know that Tanya is HIV-positive. It is important to her that her employers not know about her condition, because she was fired from her last job because of her HIV status.

When she was diagnosed, Tanya had worked as a computer operator for Homebase for four and a half years. She had health insurance and a 401(k). After careful deliberation she decided to tell the manager. "I thought he was a nice guy. I've never been a good judge of character. I thought maybe he could help me in case I needed some time off. I told him in confidence.

He then has a staff meeting. Tells all the staff managers, my supervisor, his office staff."

Tanya describes the result as "nightmarish." After a year, she was fired for failing to come in for a scheduled shift. The manager had scheduled her for back-to-back closing and opening shifts. Because it was too draining, she had frequently asked not to be given this kind of shift and had been accommodated. "I requested, two weeks in advance, that the schedule be changed. I told the general manager, and he refused to change the schedule. 'Look,' I says, 'I'm not going to do this to myself. I know what will happen to my body if I do it. . . . It'll make me sick. Do you want me to be sick?' He told me I would just have to work it. Everybody worked back-to-backs. He says, 'You know, I get tired too. You don't see me calling in sick.' My God! He has no clue what tired means. And so I told him I wouldn't show up for the shift. So I worked the night shift, and in the morning I set my alarm and I called him, and I called in sick. 'Well, Tanya,' he says, 'we have a problem.' The next day I went to work and they suspended me. I knew they were going to fire me. Before I went in to work, they had taken my picture off the computer room door."

Tanya experienced a health crisis shortly after she was fired, and she talked to her doctor about the experience. Her doctor referred her to "an ACLU attorney," who found someone to take her case. Tanya's lawyer took the case on a contingency basis and will receive payment only when Tanya does. Now, after mediation and two hearings before the state industrial commission, Tanya has a ruling in her favor. The judge ruled, in essence, that Homebase failed to provide the reasonable accommodation due to Tanya under the Americans with Disabilities Act. When Tanya received her notice in the mail, she was thrilled, not because of the money (back pay) she may receive, but because she had been vindicated. "They did something wrong and they hurt me, and so yeah, I'm fighting back . . . and if they'll do it to me, then they'll do it to someone else, you know? And I don't want someone else to go through what they put me through."

When she was fired, Tanya lost her health insurance. With her preexisting condition, getting new insurance was "a complete nightmare." In fact, she did without insurance coverage for four years. "I applied for it when my time came up. I filled out the paperwork and sent it in 'cause I wasn't going to give it to my employers. Well, at the same time my employer decided to change insurance companies. The gentleman that had sold us this insurance policy, I called him and I says, 'Norm, I'm gonna mail you my insurance application.' I says, 'When you get it, if there's a problem, call me. Not my supervisor.' He's all, 'Okay.' So about two days later he calls me. He goes, 'I got your application, and unfortunately we're gonna deny your entire group because of your application.'"

So Tanya's firm didn't include her in their group's applications. "'We're gonna do this,' he [her supervisor] says. 'If you can get insurance on your own, we'll pay 75 percent of the premium,' which he didn't do." Instead, Tanya went to the State Department of Health, which ran a Health Insurance Premium program for people with AIDS, funded under the Ryan White Act. To enroll in the program, Tanya needed to verify that the employer's insurance firm had reached its "cap." Under state law, health insurers are required to cover a certain proportion of "uninsurables" before they can begin denying coverage. But the insurance firm in this case had not reached its cap. As it turned out, "The insurance company just basically said, 'We're denying you,' but they hadn't really reached their cap." So the company was required to insure Tanya. "If I hadn't had to have verification, I never would have known, and I wouldn't have insurance."

Tanya must wait a year for coverage of her preexisting condition. For care, she relies on the services provided under her state's Ryan White program, which she describes in glowing terms. Her case manager is "absolutely amazing," her physician's assistant is "wonderful," and her physician walks on water. At present, her care needs are limited to biannual testing and periodic treatment of emerging symptoms.

Tanya teaches HIV 101 to high school classes. Her new boyfriend recently accompanied her to one of these sessions. "The teacher, instead of putting Matt (that's my boyfriend) over on the side of the room—he was just gonna sort of sit and listen—he put his chair right next to me up front. So, Matt's sitting here, like okay, you know? And I go through my story and one of the kids asked, he says, 'Well, what does your boyfriend think about this?' And I said, 'I don't know. Matt, what do you think about this?' He's like, 'What?' And then they start asking him questions, and I think it was a really good thing to have him there. He came off with this just suave, smooth answer. . . . That's why I like him."

Continued

Continued

Matt recently moved in with Tanya, and they are talking about buying a house (or maybe a ranch) together and getting married. Tanya would rather not have children. "I did a talk, and a girl was very . . . 'Well, can't you adopt?' I said, 'It takes a lot of energy to raise a child, and that's energy I need for myself if I'm going to stay healthy. My body works a lot harder than normal people's bodies, just at rest . . . and I've never had a craving to have kids.'"

Tanya is exceptionally motivated, with a positive attitude toward life and toward coping with HIV. As she puts it, "I don't understand depression. I don't get depressed. I get angry sometimes at people. I get pissy and whatever. But I don't get depressed." She has made lifestyle changes to maintain her health: drinking distilled water, avoiding rare meat, reducing her alcohol intake, carefully washing fruits and vegetables, and avoiding overexertion. "I figure it's easier to change my lifestyle now, while I'm healthy, than later, when I'm sick. *If* I get sick, God forbid."

But a lot of people Tanya knows through the AIDS Foundation don't take care of themselves. "They don't enjoy their life. They still do drugs; they still drink. I have one friend who's not supposed to take his medi-cation when he takes alcohol and drugs, so when he goes to parties, he doesn't take his medication." Tanya attributes her good health to lifestyle and attitude: "My basic frame of mind is to be happy."

When she was initially diagnosed, Tanya knew very little about what to expect from the disease. During the first few months she "wasn't thinking in terms of the future." She only thought she was going to die. But she has developed a new philosophy. "You know? It changes your whole outlook on life. I don't get upset about all the petty [things] . . . [like] who squoze the toothpaste on the wrong side of the tube. These things aren't important. My family and my friends, those are my priorities. Enjoying my life is my priority. Everyone's going to die. AIDS is not the only thing that people die from. People die from all sorts of cancers, and accidents . . . natural disasters. Everyone is going to die. I'd kind of like to die with dignity."

A Social Work Perspective
Tanya's experience as an American with a chronic illness has been influenced by several public policies. Federal policies that have affected her include Medicaid, the Ryan White Care Act, and the Americans

---

in 1844 and 1845, they met with shocked protest. Many saw them as violations of private property rights and individual liberties. Nonetheless, a staunch group of reformers, most of them from privileged backgrounds, persisted and in 1848 secured passage of the Public Health Act, which established local boards of health throughout the nation. Under the act, the establishment of a local board could be triggered either by petition of at least one-tenth of taxpayers in the area or when mortality over a seven-year period exceeded 23 people per 1,000. Local boards dealt with water supply, sewage, management of cemeteries, control of "offensive trades" (such as prostitution), and investigation of conditions affecting community health.

Like the British model, the American approach to public health focused on local, as opposed to national, efforts. Local boards of health assumed responsibility for a wide range of public health tasks, from regulating and inspecting public eating establishments to maintaining vital statistics and managing quarantines. Fee and Porter (1991) described their work as "a kind of rearguard action against the filth and congestion created by anarchic economic and urban development" (pp. 20–21).

But there was a role for the federal government. In his classic history of the field, George Rosen (1993) dates the U.S. government's first involvement in

with Disabilities Act (ADA). State policies, such as the state regulation that requires health insurance providers to serve the uninsurable, have also directly affected Tanya's care.

In some respects, Tanya's experience parallels that of anyone with a chronic condition who seeks care in the U.S. health-care market. She has gone for extended periods without health insurance. The care she receives is determined by the political will of Americans. Should she become unable to care for herself, Tanya will rely on family and friends as long as possible, hoping to delay or avoid nursing home placement. Should she need long-term nursing care, Tanya will probably apply for Medicaid. Of course, she would be required to "spend down" her personal resources to become eligible.

The stigma associated with AIDS creates hysteria and discrimination. When Tanya was fired, she had access to legal remedies provided by the 1990 passage of the ADA. Like most programs for people with disabilities, the ADA was not drafted with HIV/AIDS victims in mind. Nevertheless, disability policies such as the ADA and income supports like Old-Age, Survivors, and Disability Insurance (OASDI) and Supplemental Security Income (SSI) have become significant resources for this group, because HIV/AIDS is considered a disabling condition.

Tanya is distinctive in having access to effective drugs that mitigate the effects of HIV. She contracted AIDS after a tremendous increase in pharmacological research. She lives in an industrialized nation, which gives her access to treatment that is unheard of and a life expectancy that is unparalleled in developing countries. Her treatment will be expensive, however. At the time of our conversation, a three-drug regimen that included a protease inhibitor cost approximately $12,000 to $16,000 per year (Farmer, 1996, p. 264).

The United States is the only industrialized nation that does not offer universal health coverage. In this country we depend on a private market to provide health care and health insurance. Perhaps as a result of the failures of that market, new laws are enacted each year to regulate the operations of insurers and providers. Indeed, the year after I met Tanya, the Health Insurance Portability and Accountability Act restricted the use of preexisting conditions to deny coverage. But even today Tanya must remain employed to maintain private health insurance. If she becomes impoverished, she will depend on public care.

public health to the Marine Hospital Service. Established by Congress in 1798, the Service was designed to meet the health-care needs of seamen. Crews of merchant vessels were integral to the commercial success of the nation, but they were not residents of any parish or town, so the system of local responsibility left them without health care.

The Marine Hospital Service provided medical and hospital care to sick and disabled seamen, financed through a monthly tax of 20 cents on each man's wages. The result was the world's first prepaid, comprehensive medical and hospital insurance plan. The Treasury Department collected the fees, and the Service was placed under its jurisdiction. As a result, until 1935, most federal public health services operated under the Treasury Department.

Another federal health responsibility involved immigration. In America, as in Europe, human travel from infected areas was the primary vehicle for spreading epidemics. So early attempts to control epidemics of cholera, yellow fever, typhoid, smallpox, and other diseases focused on immigrants, who were seen as sources of foreign contagion, which then spread like wildfire through overcrowded urban slums. In 1878, the National Quarantine Act gave the Marine Hospital Service authority to inspect immigrants. At first this screening was intended to bar "lunatics and others unable to care for themselves" but it later extended to "persons suffering from loathsome and contagious diseases." Federal involvement in public health continued to expand. In 1879, a National Board of Health was established to collect information, advise the federal government on public health issues, and devise a plan for quarantine procedures.

Meanwhile, the development of immunizations expanded the responsibilities of local health authorities. From 1880 to 1898 scientists in Europe identified specific organisms responsible for most of the infectious diseases of the time. Even before these organisms were described, researchers had observed that a mild case of disease could produce lifelong immunity. This observation was accompanied by experiments (often conducted on poor children) that attempted to produce immunity through injection of blood from an infected patient. Louis Pasteur is credited with establishing and developing the principle of prophylactic inoculation.

These developments were observed by public health scientists and officials in the United States, and soon laboratories were added to local public health departments. Laboratory staff performed diagnostic tests, conducted research, and provided vaccinations to community physicians. Their practical importance was demonstrated, setting the stage for widespread acceptance of government involvement in public health.

FEDERAL HEALTH AGENCIES

Three types of federal health agencies emerged in the United States during the twentieth century (Hanlon & Pickett, 1979). These include the PHS, the only national agency concerned with broad health issues; agencies that serve specific groups, such as the Children's Bureau, the Women's Bureau, the Administration on Aging, the Bureau of Indian Affairs, and the Veterans Administration; and agencies that deal with specific problems or programs, such as the Office of Education, Food and Drug Administration, Department of Agriculture, and Bureau of Labor Statistics. We will briefly review the history of three of the largest federal health agencies: the PHS, the Children's Bureau, and the Veterans Administration.

Public Health Service

Public health specialists generally consider the PHS to be the most important federal agency in the field. The PHS grew out of the Marine Hospital Service. In 1902, Congress recognized its expanded responsibilities by renaming it the Public Health and Marine Hospital Service and placing the agency under the direction of a surgeon general. In 1912 the agency was again renamed, this time with the title it bears today: the U.S. Public Health Service. The 1935 passage of the Social Security Act charged the Service with providing grants-in-aid to states and territories to assist in establishing health services and training health personnel. In 1953, the Service moved from the Treasury Department into the newly established Department of Health, Education, and Welfare (HEW). In 1980, the Department of Education became a separate agency, and HEW was renamed the Department of Health and Human Services (HHS).

The Service involved the federal government in direct provision of medical care. Originally hospitals and clinics were established to serve those eligible for care (seamen, federal civilian employees who became ill in the line of duty, members of the Coast Guard, and anyone requiring immunization for yellow fever). Later, under the Indian Health Service, medical facilities for Native Americans and Eskimos were established. In time, however, direct operation of most hospitals and clinics was phased out.

Today the PHS supports direct care by providing grants to other organizations. Through its Health Resources and Services Administration (HRSA), the PHS finances the delivery of primary and preventive care to medically underserved residents in the United States and its territories. Some services funded through these programs include black lung clinics for coal miners, prevention and primary care delivery at the U.S.–Mexico border, medical services to migrant farm workers, health care for native Hawaiians, comprehensive care to residents of public housing, and primary care and substance abuse services for the homeless. The PHS also delivers primary health care to people who are detained by the Immigration and Naturalization Service.[1]

Children's Bureau

Establishment of the Children's Bureau was debated for six years before Congress finally authorized it in 1912. With support from the National Consumers League, the National Child Labor Committee, and many women's organizations and church groups, the Bureau was created to serve as a center of research and education for the general welfare of women and children. It was placed under the Department of Commerce and Labor, signaling an early focus on regulation of child labor. Under the direction of Julia Lathrop, the Bureau was authorized only to investigate and report on health issues affecting children and their mothers.

But even this charge involved Bureau staff in controversial activities, one of which involved maternal and child health. The Bureau's research indicated serious maternal and child health problems in rural areas, lending momentum to an emerging movement to establish maternal and child welfare programs through federal grants-in-aid. Opponents of this effort included the American Medical Association, anti-suffragists, the Sentinels of the Republic, and several other organizations who saw the Bureau's proposals as a violation of personal, family, and states' rights and a step toward socialized medicine.

Nonetheless, in 1921 (the year Grace Abbott took over as director of the Children's Bureau) the Sheppard-Towner Act was passed, with the Children's Bureau assigned to administer the grants-in-aid. It is easy to imagine the

---

1. For more information about HRSA programs, see http://hrsa.gov/.

enthusiasm with which Abbott and her staff of reformers set out to establish maternal and child welfare programs throughout the states. They moved fast, and in the two years following passage of Sheppard-Towner 15 states established programs.

The original act included what we now call a "sunset clause," which provided for review and extension of its programs after five years. This clause gave opponents another chance to attack the Bureau. As a result of their efforts, a bill to extend Sheppard-Towner for seven years failed, and a two-year extension passed. This defeat signaled the end of the program. After Sheppard-Towner expired, 35 states decreased appropriations for child hygiene, and nine states eliminated this funding entirely (Hanlon & Pickett, 1979).

This hiatus in child and maternal health programming did not last long, however. The 1935 Social Security Act not only restored the Sheppard-Towner programs but extended the Bureau's responsibilities to include maternal and child health as well as child welfare services and services for crippled children. These programs were administered by the Children's Bureau through grants-in-aid to the states.

Through subsequent decades the Children's Bureau continued to act on its original mandate to investigate and report on issues affecting children's welfare, and the programs and services under its auspices continued to expand. When World War II left wives and children of servicemen unable to pay for medical care, the Bureau alerted Congress to the situation and the Act for the Emergency Maternity and Infant Care for the Wives and Children of Servicemen was passed. In 1963 the Maternal and Child Health and Mental Retardation Planning Amendments (to the Social Security Act) provided federal support for state-run projects that offered comprehensive care for high-risk mothers and infants in low-income families. Two years later, the Social Security Act was again amended to allow for the development of comprehensive health services for children and youth. Funds were allocated for clinics, hospital care, and health education for low-income families.

The costs of the Vietnam War brought significant reductions in funding for these programs. Reorganization of the Department of Health, Education, and Welfare separated the health and social welfare functions of the Children's Bureau. Health functions, such as prenatal care for low-income mothers, primary health care for their infants and children, and disease prevention programs, were assigned to the newly created Maternal and Child Health Program that operates today in the PHS. The social welfare functions of the Bureau, including protective services and shelters for high-risk youth, child care for recipients of public assistance, and adoption services, are now lodged in the Administration on Children, Youth, and Families within the Department of Health and Human Services.

Department of Veterans Affairs

Government provision for veterans in the United States can be traced back to the Pilgrims. Following their war with the Pequot Indians, the Pilgrims passed a law providing that disabled veterans would be supported by the colony. Since then, expanded benefits for veterans have often been used as an inducement to join the military and as a reward for service. The first residential and medical facility for veterans was authorized by the federal government in 1811. After the Civil War, many states established medical and convalescent facilities for veterans. Treatment was provided for all diseases and injuries, whether or not they were service-related.

The current system of federal veterans benefits originated in 1917 when the United States entered World War I. Benefits included disability compensation, insurance, and vocational rehabilitation for the disabled. In the 1920s these programs were administered by three different federal agencies: the Veterans Bureau, the Bureau of Pensions, and the National Home for Disabled Volunteer Soldiers. These agencies were combined to form a single Veterans Administration (VA) in 1930, "to consolidate and coordinate Government activities affecting war veterans." The status of the VA was enhanced in 1989, when it became a cabinet-level department. Upon creation of the new department, President George H. W. Bush said, "There is only one place for the veterans of America, in the Cabinet Room, at the table with the President of the United States of America" (U.S. Department of Veterans Affairs, n.d.).

The VA system grew from 54 hospitals in 1930 to 158 hospitals, 854 clinics, 132 nursing homes, and 42 inpatient rehabilitation facilities in 2004 (Department of Veterans Affairs, 2004). (Facts about the Department of Veterans Affairs are available online at http://www.va.gov/.) These facilities provide a broad spectrum of medical, surgical, and rehabilitative care.

Like most health-care programs, the VA medical system has experienced dramatic cost increases in recent decades. Cost-containment attempts have included restrictions in the nature of medical coverage and in the population covered. For example, injuries and diseases that are not service-related are not always covered, and access to care is subject to a means test. Thus, VA health care has undergone a transition from being an entitlement for all veterans to a program that primarily serves low-income veterans. The transition has not been smooth, and in 1996 the General Accounting Office (GAO) and others called for "VA eligibility reform." The 1996 passage of the Veterans Health Care Eligibility Act was an attempt to clarify and simplify eligibility requirements for VA health care. Under this act, all veterans seeking health care can apply for enrollment in what the VA is calling a "Uniform Benefits Package." Health care will be allocated through enrollment priorities that are based on degree of disability and financial need.

The 2007 scandals at the Walter Reed VA hospital brought the system's weaknesses into sharp relief. More than 1.5 million Americans have served as volunteer soldiers in Iraq and Iran, and many returned with debilitating physical and mental wounds. In February 2007 a series of articles in the *Washington Post* exposed the appalling conditions in Walter Reed's Building 18. The problems of substandard housing and care had been raised in other venues for years, but this time the national outcry led to swift action by the Bush administration. Though he had only been on the job for six months, Major General George W.

Weightman, commander of Walter Reed, was quickly and publicly relieved of duty. A bipartisan commission was formed to hold hearings and issue recommendations.

FEDERAL FINANCING OF HEALTH CARE

While the PHS, the Children's Bureau, and the VA have all been involved in delivery of health care, the federal role now extends to health-care financing as well. Through Medicaid and Medicare, federal funding is used to pay for care that is delivered by other providers. Medicaid finances care for low-income Americans, while Medicare provides coverage for workers who have become elderly or disabled. Both programs are managed at the federal level by the Centers for Medicare and Medicaid Services (CMS) within the Department of Health and Human Services.

Health insurance coverage was not widespread in the early years of the twentieth century. Most Americans simply purchased their care. As late as 1963, for example, only 56 percent of the elderly had hospital insurance (U.S. House of Representatives, Select Committee on Aging, 1990). Those who lacked coverage and financial resources either did without treatment or used community health clinics and charity hospitals, which were few and far between. Some states provided limited support for meeting the medical needs of public assistance recipients and others deemed "medically needy" or "medically indigent."

Early reform efforts date to the Progressive Era, a period of economic prosperity and social reform lasting from roughly 1890 to the 1920s, when the American Association for Labor Legislation (AALL) campaigned for "sickness insurance" to cover workers and their dependents (Skocpol, 1995). The reformers' efforts were opposed by the American Medical Association (AMA) and business interests. Ultimately the campaign, and the organization itself, were defeated. Theodore Roosevelt's Bull Moose Party proposed a national health insurance program in 1912, but more than 50 years went by before any form of national health insurance was established in the United States. The 1965 passage of Titles XVIII and XIX of the Social Security Act established Medicare and Medicaid, despite the objections of the American Medical Association.[2]

There is some irony to AMA objections, because the passage of Medicare and Medicaid established reliable financing for many of the services provided by its members. Both programs provided "indemnity" coverage, also known as fee-for-service insurance. Under this model, providers were reimbursed by the program for all medically necessary services delivered to beneficiaries. While some restrictions on fees were put in place, both Medicare and Medicaid have become major sources of revenue for health and allied-health providers, setting

---

2. The American Medical Association did not always oppose national health insurance. Indeed, the organization supported early efforts in this area.

the stage for huge increases in public health-care expenditures. The establishment of Medicare and Medicaid financed tremendous growth in the health-care industry, even as the programs improved access to care for the poor, the aged, and the disabled.

Medicaid

When Medicaid was established, the federal government had only limited involvement in health care for the poor. Nonetheless, there was some precedent for federal intervention. The Hill-Burton Act of 1946 allocated federal funding for hospital construction and required that hospitals receiving these funds provide care to the indigent. Further, the 1950 amendments to the Social Security Act provided for some federal participation in meeting the medical needs of public assistance recipients.

Through Medicaid, "The poor were promised that they would soon have access to mainstream medical care and that health care was a basic right" (U.S. House of Representatives, Select Committee on Aging, 1990, p. 7). The program was established as a federal–state partnership, primarily funded through federal money, with a matching requirement for the states. Administration was carried out by the states, with federal regulation and oversight. Medicaid does not provide health care directly; instead reimbursing providers for the care of low-income patients.

During Medicaid's first 30 years, the population covered by the program expanded. Initially Medicaid eligibility was restricted to recipients of public assistance. Later, states were required to cover all pregnant women and infants living in households with incomes up to 185 percent of the poverty line, as well as low-income persons with disabilities.

Partially as a result of the expanded beneficiary pool, the costs associated with Medicaid increased dramatically. Total expenditures more than doubled from 1988 to 1992. Expenditures continued to grow. In 1991, Medicaid spent $88.6 billion to provide health care to 27 million low-income people. By 2006, total Medicaid spending had increased to $315.3 billion (Kaiser Family Foundation, n.d.). With these increases, matching funds for Medicaid consumed an ever-larger share of state budgets.

This growth in spending was not entirely due to new groups entering the beneficiary pool, however. As the Kaiser Commission on the Future of Medicaid (1993) argued, only one-third of the growth in cost was due to enrollment increases. Another third was attributed to medical price inflation and the remainder to state utilization of "Medicaid maximization strategies" designed to increase their federal Medicaid match. For example, states might transfer clients to Medicaid from state-funded programs for the medically indigent, effectively transferring a portion of the states' health-care costs to the federal government.

Medicaid Cost Containment.   Concern about rising Medicaid costs has fueled efforts at cost containment. The past two decades have seen draconian attempts to reduce Medicaid costs. These have included adoption of a prospective payment system, reductions in provider payments, eligibility restrictions adopted through welfare reform legislation, and managed care.

In 1983 the Hospital Prospective Payment System was developed to reduce Medicaid costs. Instead of reimbursing hospitals for all reasonable costs, this system provides payment at a set rate for diagnosis-related groups (DRGs). Under prospective payment, a hospital receives the same amount for every patient with a certain diagnosis, regardless of the services provided. Designed to promote greater efficiency, the use of DRGs has led to earlier hospital discharges. Advocates and service providers agree that the prospective payment system has led hospitals to discharge patients "quicker and sicker" (Fischer & Eustis, 1989). In 1989 the principle of prospective payment was extended to physician payments as well as hospital bills.

Cost-containment pressure has led to reductions and freezes in provider payments under Medicaid. By 1990, Medicaid payments to physicians averaged 50 percent of their charges and 60 percent of the Medicare rate (Physician Payment Review Commission, 1991). The result of provider cuts was a drop in the number of physicians who were willing to serve Medicaid patients (Derlet & Kinser, 1994).

On August 22, 1996, President Clinton signed the Personal Responsibility and Work Opportunity Reconciliation Act (PRWORA). In addition to replacing Aid to Families with Dependent Children (AFDC) with TANF, the act had significant implications for Medicaid. TANF beneficiaries who lost aid because they refused to work could lose Medicaid coverage. Further, states were no longer required to cover pregnant women and children with incomes between 133 percent and 185 percent of the federal poverty level. Finally, nonemergency care for legal immigrants was substantially reduced. States were required to provide Medicaid coverage to legal immigrants who had entered the country before January 1, 1997, as well as those who were veterans or on active military duty, refugees and some people granted asylum, and those with a 10-year work history. But legal immigrants who had entered the United States after January 1, 1997, were banned from Medicaid for five years.

These cost-containment measures are starting to bear fruit. For the past few years, the increase in Medicaid costs has slowed. Indeed, the Center for Budget and Policy Priorities (CBPP) reported that in 2002 the growth in health-care costs per Medicaid enrollee was lower than the growth observed in private insurance plans (Ku & Broaddus, 2003). This trend has been attributed to expanded use of managed care.

Medicaid and Managed Care. Medicaid beneficiaries were familiar with managed care long before it became a household word. In 1981, the Omnibus Budget Reconciliation Act permitted state-level experimentation with Medicaid managed care. Arizona was the first state to require all of its Medicaid clients to enroll in managed care through its "Health Care Cost Containment System." Other states followed, and by 1996, 40.1 percent of Medicaid enrollees were in managed care programs (Zuckerman, Evans, & Holahan, 1997). These were primarily AFDC clients. Today all of the states except Wyoming require that some

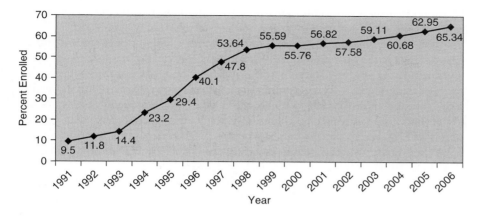

FIGURE 6.1 Medicaid beneficiaries enrolled in managed care.

SOURCE: U.S. Department of Health and Human Services, Centers for Medicaid and Medicare Services. 1991–1996: http://www.cms.hhs.gov/medicaid/managedcare/trends1.asp. 1997–2006: Medicaid Managed Care Enrollment Report. http://www.cms.hhs.gov/MedicaidDataSourcesGenInfo/04_MdManCrEnrllRep.asp.

Medicaid recipients enroll with managed care organizations. The growth in Medicaid managed care is illustrated in Figure 6.1.

In the most common approach to Medicaid managed care, the state contracts with a managed care provider—typically a health maintenance organization (HMO)—to provide care for Medicaid clients on a "capitated" basis. Under capitation, the HMO receives a fixed amount for each Medicaid enrollee, regardless of the services provided.[3] Although Medicaid beneficiaries must enroll in managed care, CMS's Freedom of Choice regulations require states to allow enrollees to choose among contracted managed care providers.

The key to an effective system of Medicaid managed care lies in negotiation and monitoring of each state's contract with providers. The central role of state health departments represents an opportunity for social work practitioners to ensure that the needs of consumers are addressed in these processes (see Perloff, 1996). As advocates and employees, social workers can ensure that the service mix, the provider choices, and the contract monitoring procedures address the needs of Medicaid clients (see Rosenbaum et al., 1988). Further, social workers can increase the voice of Medicaid recipients in decisions related to managed care. As Perkins, Olson, and Rivera (1996) observe, "Recipients have tended to take a back seat when it comes to consumer involvement with the Medicaid program and its services" (p. 3). Mechanisms for increasing the influence of Medicaid recipients include consumer surveys, grievance procedures, hotlines, and consumer representation on advisory boards. A few states have established

3. The term "HMO" was coined by analysts for the Nixon administration and initially stood for "health management organization." A last-minute change, solely for public relations purposes, created the more user-friendly "health maintenance organization." At the time, President Nixon was responding to what he announced was a "health care crisis" (Petchey, 1987).

Medicaid managed care ombudsman programs, which may encourage consumer involvement.

The impact of managed care on Medicaid clients appears to be mixed. Critics suggest that it represents a sacrifice in the quality of care available to low-income Americans. But, for some, managed care may improve access because providers under contract with state Medicaid programs are not allowed to refuse enrollment to an eligible client (Rowland & Salganicoff, 1994). A few studies have assessed Medicaid clients' satisfaction with managed care. In general, clients in HMOs reported higher satisfaction with their care than those in traditional fee-for-service arrangements (Sisk et al., 1996; Temkin-Greener & Winchell, 1991).

The growth in Medicaid managed care has not yet had a widespread effect on the program's elderly and disabled clients. A 1995 analysis estimated that of the $9.9 billion in Medicaid payments to managed care organizations, only 10 percent were for disabled beneficiaries and 1 percent were for elderly clients (Rowland & Hanson, 1996). Of course, the elderly and disabled have more complex health-care needs than other clients and thus may be less profitable for managed care organizations.

Long-Term Care.   The proportion of elderly people in the U.S. population is growing, and the life spans of people with disabilities have increased. During the 1980s and 1990s, these trends converged to increase the demand for nursing home care. This period saw dramatic increases in the number of older adults who lived in nursing homes, and rising demand for long-term care changed the role of Medicaid (Jobas & Kovner, 2002). Because Medicare offers only limited coverage for long-term care, many families turned to Medicaid, making it the nation's de facto long-term care insurance program.

The widespread use and high cost of nursing home care led many to advocate for the expansion of intermediate alternatives (Estes, Swan, & Associates, 1993). This push for alternatives reflected the observation that many nursing home residents did not require the intense level of medical care provided by a nursing home. Indeed, most people with disabilities prefer to be cared for in their own homes.

Today, long-term care alternatives include residential care as well as other arrangements such as in-home care and assisted living. Both Medicaid and Medicare offer limited funding for care provided in a patient's home, and many states fund community-based care using Medicaid's Home and Community-Based Waivers. We have also seen increased public recognition of the role played by family members in caring for people with disabilities. In 1999, the Administration on Aging introduced a National Family Caregiver Program as part of the reauthorization of the Older Americans Act. With a budget in excess of $165 million, this program provides support to family members who provide care to seniors.

Perhaps as a result of these developments, use of nursing facilities has gone down. From 1990 to 2000 the number of Americans living in nursing homes dropped from 1,772,030 to 1,720,500 (Centers for Disease Control, 2006;

Jonas & Kovner, 2002). This is especially noteworthy given that the number of older adults in the U.S. population increased during this period. Issues related to long-term care of older adults are discussed further in Chapter 13.

Medicare

The Medicare program differs fundamentally from Medicaid. It is not means-tested, and it provides health coverage to workers who are at least 65 years old or disabled and who are eligible for Social Security benefits. It is not operated as a federal–state partnership but is managed exclusively by the federal government. Medicare is not welfare for the disadvantaged but an entitlement earned through participation in the workforce. Despite these differences, the history of Medicare parallels that of Medicaid in many ways.

Prior to the 1980s, revisions to Medicare were characterized by expanded benefits and enhanced quality control. The 1972 Social Security Amendments added coverage for the disabled and people with end-stage renal disease. They also established professional standards review organizations (PSROs) as a vehicle for quality control. Benefit expansion was also part of the 1982 amendments, which added hospice coverage.

One effort to expand Medicare benefits was quickly repealed. In 1988, the Medicare Catastrophic Coverage Act (MCCA) provided for increased benefits (including prescription drug coverage), financed through a surtax on enrollees whose incomes were high enough that they owed federal income tax. Those who paid the surtax complained bitterly, arguing that they were being asked to do something required of no other segment of the population: pay for the care of others in their age group. Most MCCA provisions were repealed in 1989.

Recent decades have been marked by exponential increases in Medicare costs, coupled with repeated cost-containment efforts. The Hospital Prospective Payment System described earlier has been applied to Medicare as well as Medicaid. DRGs have successfully reduced Medicare's hospital costs, and prospective payment has since been applied to services provided by physicians and other health-care providers (Prospective Payment Assessment Commission, 1995).

In the case of Medicare, cost-containment measures have extended beyond reductions and freezes in provider payments[4] to include increases in premiums and deductibles paid by beneficiaries. Despite these increases, the proportion of Medicare Part B costs that is covered through premiums has dropped. In 1967, the Part B annual premium of $36 per enrollee accounted for 40 percent of that program's income. By 1991, the premium had increased to $359 per year but accounted for only about one-quarter of program income (U.S. House of Representatives, Select Committee on Aging, 1990). The remaining cost of Part B is paid through general tax revenues. As the proportion of costs covered

---

4. Freezes and reductions in Medicare's provider fees have led to a growing number of physicians declining to accept Medicare patients.

by beneficiary premiums has declined, the amount drawn from the general fund has grown—and with it, congressional opposition to the program (Rasell & Weller, 2001).

Under current law, premiums must cover 25 percent of program costs and contribute to the maintenance of a reserve in the trust fund. To support this goal, Part B premiums now increase for high-income beneficiaries. In 2007 the standard monthly premium of $93.50 applied to the vast majority of beneficiaries; however, for a minority (estimated at 4 percent of seniors) the premium increased to $106, $124.70, $143.40, and $162.10, depending on the extent to which the beneficiary's annual income exceeded $80,000. The highest premium applied to individuals with annual incomes above $200,000 (or $400,000 for couples) (U.S. Department of Health & Human Services, 2006, Medicare Fact Sheet: Medicare Premiums and Deductibles for 2007, available at www.hcca-info.org).

As we saw in Chapter 4, Medicare Hospital Insurance (Part A) is financed through a payroll tax. The late 1990s were marked by rising concern over the financial status of Part A. In 1996, the trustees predicted that unless radical changes were made, the Hospital Insurance Trust Fund (which funds Part A) would be depleted, and outlays would exceed revenue by 2001. The Balanced Budget Act of 1997 included measures designed to reduce Part A expenditures. Savings from these measures, along with the economic growth of the late 1990s, led the trustees to revise their estimate. In 2001 the date of projected depletion was moved forward to 2029 (Rasell & Weller, 2001). Despite this reprieve, the costs of Medicare continue to rise.

Medicare and Managed Care.   Some attribute Medicare's rising costs to unrestrained utilization by the program's beneficiaries. Managed care was widely perceived as an effective way to control utilization and reduce costs. So in 1995, the Medicare Risk Program (now called Part C or Medicare + Choice) was established to encourage beneficiaries to enroll in HMOs. HMOs offer Medicare recipients lower out-of-pocket costs while using managed care to control utilization.

HMOs are attractive to healthy elders, who take advantage of the preventive care offered and who do not need much specialty care. The result is a phenomenon called "favorable selection," which refers to factors that encourage low-risk individuals to seek insurance from a particular provider. It is favorable to the insurance company in that it reduces the financial risk to the company. A contrasting phenomenon, "adverse selection," refers to factors that encourage high-risk individuals to seek insurance from a particular provider.

The experiment with managed care has not significantly improved the fiscal status of Medicare. Some argue that Medicare capitation rates paid to HMOs are too high for such a healthy subgroup of the elderly population (Butler, Lave, & Reuschauer, 1998). Others note that the cost savings achieved through reduced utilization may be less than the high overhead rates charged by HMOs, resulting in no net savings to the Medicare program (Brown et al., 1993). There is growing concern that favorable selection results in a "creaming" effect in which HMOs enroll the healthiest Medicare recipients, leaving high-risk elders in the fee-for-service system. Recent efforts to lower capitation rates to reflect the relative health of elders who enroll in HMOs have led growing numbers of HMOs to simply withdraw from the Medicare market. Indeed, by 2000 approximately 1 million Medicare beneficiaries had seen their HMO coverage canceled (Hoffman, 2000).

Medicare Prescription Coverage: A Case Study in the Politics of Reform. For years the Medicare program has been criticized for failing to provide coverage for prescription medications. Since Medicare's inception, the practice of medicine has changed, and prescription medications have emerged as an important tool, with the potential to prevent or delay the onset of conditions that would be painful and costly to treat. The nation's seniors and their physicians recognized the efficacy of the new generation of prescription medications, and as a result their out-of-pocket expenses for drugs rose dramatically. Clearly there was high demand for prescription coverage under Medicare.

Meanwhile the cost of prescription medications in the United States was rising. Pharmaceutical companies argued that these price increases were necessary to support the lengthy and complex research and development process required to bring new drugs to market. Critics attributed the price increase to advertising by drug companies. In addition to adding to the drug companies' expenditures, this advertising triggered increased demand (and hence increased prices) for medications.

Unlike the United States, Canada regulates medication prices. A discrepancy surfaced, with Americans paying more for medications than their Northern neighbors. Canadian pharmacies discovered a new market for their wares, and soon Americans were purchasing their drugs in Canada through online pharmacies and bus trips across the border. Legislation was passed to allow Americans to import prescription medications from Canada (since they were doing so anyway), but the George W. Bush administration stalled implementation. Regulations were never issued because the Department of Health and Human Services refused to certify that any drug bought in Canada was safe and effective—certification that was necessary to begin development of regulations.

The issue remains contentious. In 2004, Vermont filed a lawsuit attempting to force the administration to act, but this effort was unsuccessful. Importation legislation in both the Senate and the House in 2007 contained a "poison pill" provision requiring administration certification of safety—certification that both Clinton and Bush administrations have refused to supply. In May 2007 the Senate passed legislation that, again, required certification of imported prescription drugs from Canada, Australia, Europe, Japan, and New Zealand. Opponents of importation have raised the specter of terrorism, and—perhaps as a result—there have been reports of Homeland Security officials seizing prescription medications at the border.

The pharmaceutical industry has become a major force in Washington. In 2001, the *New York Times* reported that the industry had 625 registered lobbyists and a budget for lobbying and campaign contributions that amounted to $197 million—the largest of any U.S. industry (Wayne & Petersen, 2001). Further, according to Public Citizen (a public-interest group founded by Ralph Nader), pharmaceutical companies spent a record $108.6 million in 2003 on lobbying activities and employed an army of 824 lobbyists (http://www.citizen.org/documents/MedicareDrugWarReportREVISED72104.pdf, accessed September 15, 2007). Of course, the American pharmaceutical industry has been extremely profitable, with the top 10 companies recording profits of $35.9 billion in 2002 (Public Citizen, 2003). In this context Congress undertook to develop a Medicare prescription drug benefit in 2003.

During the 2002 election cycle, President Bush announced that reforming Medicare would be a priority for his administration. The Republican Party (GOP) leadership had begun drafting legislation to add prescription coverage, with an estimated price tag of $400 billion over 10 years. Democrats criticized the legislation but offered little serious opposition. The Senate version of the bill passed with a narrow majority under the sponsorship of Bill Frist (R–TN), the Senate Republican leader, and four cosponsors. At the same time, a bill was working its way through the House under the sponsorship of Dennis Hastert (R–IL), Speaker of the House, and 20 cosponsors. By July 2003 bills had passed both houses, but negotiations to resolve the differences between House and Senate versions were lengthy and inconclusive. In November the American Association of Retired Persons (AARP) endorsed the legislation and began a $4 million advertising campaign in support. With this pivotal endorsement, the conference agreement was approved and the Medicare Prescription Drug, Improvement, and Modernization Act was signed by the president on December 8, 2003.

Prescription coverage under the voluntary program began on January 1, 2006, and is offered through private insurance companies with government subsidies. Medicare beneficiaries can purchase a Medicare discount card that provides a reduction in the costs of medications. The program established a formulary, or list of approved drugs, for specific conditions. Drugs that are not on the formulary would not count toward deductibles. The legislation includes a tax subsidy to insure that firms currently providing prescription coverage to their retirees continue their coverage. It also includes a little-known provision that prohibits private companies from offering prescription drug coverage that competes with the Medicare program.

Reactions to the legislation have been mixed, with some agreeing with Senator Ted Kennedy that it could destroy the 40-year-old Medicare program. Many fear that Part D coverage will crowd out other drug benefits. Others worry that the prohibition on competing drug coverage and the use of a formulary will restrict seniors' choices. Finally, critics note that the act does not allow the Medicare program to use its purchasing power to negotiate for reduced drug prices. Meanwhile, fiscal conservatives object to the program's price tag, arguing that the new program adds to the nation's record debt. The Congressional Budget Office estimated 2006 program costs at $32 billion, with projected cumulative outlays of nearly $800 billion by 2015 (Lichtenberg & Sun, 2007). The AARP has been sharply criticized for its endorsement, with some noting that the organization derives nearly one-fourth of its income from the sale of health insurance to its members. Thus, some argue, the AARP has a conflict of interest —on one hand charged with representing the interests of seniors and on the other drawing a profit from its insurance business.

GROWTH OF THE "HEALTH INDUSTRY"

Since the passage of Medicare and Medicaid, the United States has seen a dramatic concentration of private capital in what has come to be called the health industry. Before the 1970s, for-profit health companies were largely confined to the pharmaceutical sector. By the mid-1980s hospitals had entered the for-profit sector, with profits exceeding those of drug companies. In 1987, for example, the largest for-profit hospital chains—Hospital Corporation of America, Humana, National Medical Enterprises, and American Medical International— each exceeded the sales of most pharmaceutical manufacturing firms (in excess of $3 billion). This growth was not confined to acute care. By 1990, 12 nursing home chains with total sales of $4.5 billion dominated the market, and 80 percent of nursing home facilities in the nation were proprietary.

The expansion of for-profit health-care facilities left a shrinking role for nonprofits, the traditional providers for the poor and underserved. Nonprofit hospitals have typically provided a fuller range of health services than for-profits and may be more responsive to community need. For example, most AIDS units are run by nonprofits, as are the vast majority of trauma units. Yet in the 1990s nonprofits were rapidly taken over by for-profits who were "gaining market share by buying out competitors, reducing excess capacity in their markets" (Cerne, 1995, p. 44).

As J. Warren Salmon (1995) observes, "No other nation in the world has witnessed as absolute or rapid a growth in health expenditures as has the U.S., and no other nation has such a for-profit presence in its health sector" (p. 22). Even Wall Street analysts have expressed concern with this trend. An analyst with Morgan Stanley suggested that "[u]ltimately we're going to see the formation of oligopolies, where each market or state will have three or four major players, and that's it. We're heading toward a utility model by the end of the decade, and at that point the government will have to step in" (G. Wagner in Cerne, 1995, p. 42).

In the emerging for-profit health-care industry, the public policy goal of reducing tax expenditures for health-care conflicts with the private sector's drive for profits. This conflict might explain the limited success of cost-containment measures in health-care programs. For example, when DRGs were introduced, the Senate Finance Committee monitored their impact on hospitals and in 1985 reported that (1) 81 percent of hospitals made a profit on their Medicare accounts; (2) the average profit margin was 14.12 percent, compared with 3.3 percent in the rest of the service sector; and (3) the return on capital averaged 24 percent (compared with 14 percent elsewhere in the service industry). The Committee suggested that in one year alone, Medicare contributed $5 billion

---

B O X   6.1   About the World Health Organization

The World Health Organization (WHO) was founded in 1948 to improve health throughout the world and monitor observance of international health regulations. The WHO led the effort to eradicate smallpox, a project that took about 10 years. Polio has been eliminated in the Americas and should disappear from the globe within a few years. The WHO collects and publishes epidemiological data from around the world and combats newly emerging infectious diseases. Indeed, Noji (2001) noted that "The WHO is . . . uniquely positioned to play a leadership role . . . because it has both the mandate and the networks to enable countries of the world to intensify their efforts against emerging diseases in a coordinated manner" (p. 229). Of course, the WHO budget is dwarfed by funds the World Bank commits to health loans.

---

to company profits. Despite cost-containment policies, much of the dramatic growth in the nation's private health-care industry has been financed by Medicare and Medicaid.

PUBLIC HEALTH INVESTMENTS AND RETURNS

The twentieth century witnessed the expansion of public-sector programs to provide and finance health care. Agencies such as the PHS, the Children's Bureau, and the VA have provided care to vulnerable Americans. Two major programs were established to pay for the health care of the poor and the elderly: Medicaid and Medicare. Rather than providing direct care, they offered reimbursement to providers. The availability of public financing contributed to dramatic growth in the private health-care industry—growth that was marked by an increasing presence of for-profit companies. This public subsidization of the private health-care industry emerged in the latter half of the twentieth century. It is related to the conflict between the public sector's need to contain costs and the private sector's desire to maximize profits, which has surfaced in the past two decades as a tension in the U.S. health-care system. In this section we will examine health spending and health outcomes in America's hybrid public–private health-care system.

Health Expenditures and the GDP

Health expenditures are typically measured both on a per capita basis (cost per person) and as a percent of the nation's gross domestic product (GDP). Using either measure, the United States spends more on health care than any other nation in the world. In 2005 per capita spending on health-care services was more than double that of other industrialized nations. That year, the United States spent $6,401 per person for health care, while the average for the 29 industrialized nations belonging to the Organization for Economic Cooperation and Development (OECD) was $2,801 (OECD, 2007).

TABLE 6.1   Health Expenditures of Selected Organization for Economic Cooperation and Development (OECD) Member Nations

Nation	1960 Spending (Percent of GDP)	2005 Spending (Percent of GDP)
United States	5.2	15.3
Germany	4.8	10.7
France	4.2	11.1
Japan	3.0	8.0
Canada	5.5	9.8
Australia	4.9	10.2
New Zealand	4.3	9.0
United Kingdom	3.9	8.3
OECD Median	**3.9**	**8.6**

SOURCE: OECD (2007). OECD Health Data 2007—Frequently Requested Data. http://www.oecd.org/document/30/0,3343,en_2649_37407_12968734_1_1_1_37407,00.html (accessed October 30, 2007).

In 2005, CMS reported that U.S. health expenditures had exceeded 15 percent of the GDP (Heffler et al., 2005). By international standards these expenditures are exceedingly high. Table 6.1 compares health spending as a percentage of GDP for eight industrialized nations. In 2005, the proportion of the U.S. GDP that was committed to health care was nearly twice the median for 29 OECD nations.

From a global perspective, the United States ranks highest of the developed nations in health spending, both on a per capita basis and as a percentage of the GDP. Do these high expenditures translate to favorable outcomes in the population's health? In the following section we will compare U.S. health outcomes with those of other countries.

Health Outcomes: The Return on Our Investment

The twentieth century witnessed improvements in Americans' health status. Life expectancy, a key indicator of well-being, increased from 47.3 years in 1900 to 77.9 in 2004 (http://www.cdc.gov/nchs/fastats/lifexpec.htm, accessed January 20, 2008). This increased longevity is the direct result of improvements in public health and the decline of infectious diseases, improvements that have been especially helpful in reducing mortality among children under the age of 5. In 1900, child mortality accounted for nearly a third (30.4 percent) of all deaths. That rate had dropped to 1.4 percent by 1997 (Centers for Disease Control and Prevention, 1999). Thus longevity trends as well as child survival over the twentieth century suggest a substantial return on the nation's public health expenditures. By comparison with health outcomes of other nations, however, the U.S. return is less impressive.

TABLE 6.2   Infant Mortality Rates (IMR) in Industrialized Nations (Deaths per 1,000 Live Births)

Nation	1978 IMR	1998 IMR	2005 IMR
Canada	12	6	5
Germany	15	5	4
United Kingdom	14	7	5
Australia	13	6	5
Japan	9	4	3
United States	14	7	7
France	11	6	4
WHO Average	**87**	**57**	**46**

SOURCE: 1978/1998: *The World Health Report 1999*. World Health Organization, 1999. http://www.who.int.whr/1999/index/htm. 2005: WHO Core Health Indicators. http://www.who.int/whosis/en/ (accessed October 30, 2007).

Infant Mortality Rates.   Infant mortality is a widely accepted measure of community health. The infant mortality rate (IMR) is usually measured as the number of infants who die before reaching one year of age per 1,000 live births. Data from 195 members of the World Health Organization permit international comparisons. Table 6.2 compares U.S. IMRs in 1978, 1998, and 2005 with those of six other industrialized nations: Canada, Germany, France, the United Kingdom, Australia, and Japan.

Clearly the twentieth century saw improved infant health among these highly industrialized nations. Improvement in U.S. IMRs, however, is not commensurate with health-care expenditures. With seven infant deaths per 1,000 live births in 2005, the United States ranked highest in infant mortality among these nations, while Japan consistently reported the lowest IMR. Although the United States spends more on health care than the comparison nations, these expenditures have not translated into lower infant mortality rates.

Life Expectancy.   A second measure of the health of populations is life expectancy, which reflects how long, on average, an individual of a specified age (usually a newborn infant) can expect to live. In part due to lower infant mortality, people living in industrialized nations have a longer life span. This increased life expectancy is often accompanied by a greater gender differential—in other words, the gap in life expectancy between men and women is bigger. Industrialized nations all reported gains in life expectancy in the last few decades of the twentieth century, as shown in Table 6.3. Again, despite the world's highest health expenditures, the United States is at or near the bottom of developed nations in terms of life expectancy.

This discrepancy between expenditures and health outcomes could lead to two different conclusions. First, one might conclude that the U.S. health-care system is inefficient. This argument is often used in support of proposals to radically overhaul the system. A different conclusion is also possible, however. The

TABLE 6.3 Life Expectancy (LE) at Birth in Industrialized Nations

Nation	1978 LE		1998 LE		2006 LE	
	Males	Females	Males	Females	Males	Females
Canada	71	78	76	82	78	83
Germany	69	76	74	80	77	82
United Kingdom	70	76	75	80	77	82
Australia	70	77	75	81	79	84
Japan	73	78	77	83	79	86
New Zealand	69	78	74	82	78	82
United States	69	77	73	80	76	81
France	70	78	74	83	77	84
World Average	**60**	**63**	**65**	**69**	**65**	**70**

SOURCE: 1978/1998: *The World Health Report 1999*. World Health Organization, 1999. http://www.who.int.whr/1999/index/htm. 2006: UN World Population Prospects Report, 2005–2010.

United States is distinctive among industrialized nations in the diversity of its population. Rather than concluding that the entire system is inefficient, one might conclude that the system is inefficient with respect to disadvantaged groups. Before considering the health status of vulnerable groups in the United States, we will briefly examine health conditions in developing nations. This should help us keep in mind the privileged position enjoyed by residents of the industrialized world.

Health Outcomes in Developing Nations

The United States, like other industrialized nations, has much lower IMRs than developing nations. Nations reporting the highest IMRs are listed in Table 6.4.

TABLE 6.4 Infant Mortality Rates (IMR) in Developing Nations (Deaths per 1,000)

Nation	1978 IMR	1998 IMR	2005 IMR
Sierra Leone	192	170	165
Afghanistan	183	152	165
Malawi	177	138	78
Guinea-Bissau	176	130	124
Angola	161	125	154
Rwanda	133	124	118
Somalia	149	122	133

SOURCE: 1978/1998: *The World Health Report 1999*. World Health Organization, 1999. http://www.who.int/whr/1999/en/index.html. 2005: WHO Core Health Indicators.

T A B L E   6.5   Life Expectancy (LE) at Birth in Developing Nations

Nation	1978 LE		1998 LE		2006 LE	
	Males	Females	Males	Females	Males	Females
Sierra Leone	34	37	36	39	41	44
Afghanistan	40	40	45	46	44	44
Malawi	42	44	39	40	48	48
Guinea-Bissau	36	39	43	46	45	48
Angola	38	42	45	48	41	44
Rwanda	43	47	39	42	45	48
Somalia	40	44	45	49	47	49

SOURCE: 1978/1998: *The World Health Report 1999*. World Health Organization, 1999. http://www.who.int/whr/1999/en/index.html. 2006: UN World Population Prospects Report, 2005–2010.

While the 27-year period from 1978 to 2005 saw improvements in IMR among developing nations, these rates continue to greatly exceed those observed in industrialized countries. With the exception of Afghanistan, all of the nations with the world's highest IMRs are located in Africa.

Clearly, life expectancy at birth is influenced by IMRs. Nations with high IMRs, such as developing nations, also have shorter life expectancies. As in industrialized countries, women in developing countries enjoy greater life expectancies than men (see Table 6.5). The past few decades have seen improved life expectancies for most African nations.

In the distribution of health care, life itself becomes a social justice issue. As we have seen, survival can be a function of privilege. International comparisons demonstrate that longevity and infant survival are differentially distributed on the basis of national wealth. In the following section we will examine the extent to which personal status contributes to health outcomes for people living in the United States.

VULNERABLE GROUPS IN AN AFFLUENT NATION

To a large extent, health is socially allocated. Class, race, and gender can determine both a person's risk of becoming ill and that person's ability to secure needed treatment.

Poverty and Health

Throughout the life span, income can determine the likelihood that one will contract a disease. Among children, poverty has long been associated with low birth weight, increased infant mortality, and nutritional deficits (Rice, 1991).

Adults with poverty-level incomes experience significantly higher risk of AIDS and other infectious diseases. The effects of environmental insults and inadequate care compound in old age, when a history of exposure to health risks, environmental toxins, stress, poor nutrition, and limited care can undermine health in many ways. Income also contributes to mental health. The risk of depression, for example, has been linked to poverty (Amato & Zuo, 1992; Belle, 1984; Murphy et al., 1991).

Poor health outcomes among low-income groups may result partially from the stresses associated with living in poverty, but reduced access to health care certainly compounds these difficulties (Himmelstein & Woolhandler, 1995). Those living in poverty have limited access to preventive care (Kelly et al., 1993), and a combination of financial barriers, transportation, and cultural differences militates against their receiving treatment (Williams, 1993). The net effect in the United States is poor health outcomes for citizens living in poverty.

Health Disparities

The National Institutes of Health (NIH) define health disparities as "differences in the incidence, prevalence, mortality, and burden of diseases and other adverse health conditions that exist among specific population groups in the United States." These specific population groups are racial and ethnic minorities. In the United States, people of color are more likely to fall ill than whites. Higher prevalence is evident in a wide range of diseases. For example, African Americans have a higher incidence of hypertension, cardiovascular disease, stroke, diabetes, some cancers, and end-stage renal disease than white Americans (Johnson & Smith, 2002).

People of color are less likely than whites to have access to culturally appropriate, good-quality care. In addition, both African Americans and Hispanic Americans have lower overall five-year cancer survival rates than whites (Johnson & Smith, 2002). Further, both infant mortality and life expectancy vary on the basis of ethnicity. These outcomes are illustrated in Tables 6.6 and 6.7. Here we see that

T A B L E 6.6   **Infant Mortality in the United States, 2003**

Ethnic Group	Infant Deaths per 1,000 Births
All mothers	6.8
White	5.7
African American	13.6
American Indian/Alaskan Native	8.7
Asian/Pacific Islander	4.8
Hispanic or Latino	5.6

SOURCE: Centers for Disease Control (2006). QuikStats: Infant Mortality Rates by Maternal Race/Ethnicity—United States, 1995 and 2003. http://www.cms.hhs.gov/MedicaidDataSourcesGenInfo/04_MdManCrEnrllRep (accessed February 12, 2008).

T A B L E 6.7   Life Expectancy at Birth, 2004

	Projected Life Expectancy	
Ethnic Group	Male	Female
Total	75.2	80.4
White, not Hispanic	75.7	80.8
African American	69.5	76.3

SOURCE: Centers for Disease Control and Prevention (n.d.). Health, United States, 2007. http://www.cdc.gov/nchs/products/pubs/pubd/hus/older.htm (accessed February 12, 2008).

African American mothers are more than twice as likely to lose an infant as whites, and the life expectancy of African American men is six years less than that of white men. As Johnson and Smith (2002) note, "The evidence of racial and ethnic disparities in health outcomes is overwhelming" (p. 30).

In the United States, where race is closely associated with class, it is difficult to distinguish the effects of race from those of class. Indeed, health policy analyst Vicente Navarro (1991) argued that in the United States, socioeconomic status is a more powerful determinant of health than race (see also Fordyce, 1996). Observed differences among races in this country cannot be interpreted without reference to economic disparities and race-based oppression.

In some cases, race and class interact to produce higher risk of illness. The incidence of type 2 diabetes, particularly in later life, is strongly influenced by this interaction. The disease occurs more often among those with lower socioeconomic and educational levels (Overfield, 1995) and is concentrated among African Americans, Native Americans, and Hispanic Americans. In addition to inherited susceptibility, lifestyle considerations such as diet, lack of exercise, and limited access to preventive health care contribute to a person's risk of contracting diabetes.

Long-term oppression can undermine health, as well. For example, Tay-Sachs disease is more common among the Ashkenazi Jews, whose ancestors originated in Eastern Europe, than among other populations. This concentration has been attributed to the unique historical circumstances experienced by this group, including frequent migrations, numerous extermination attempts, dense concentration in urban ghettos, and periods of rapid population expansion and inbreeding (Fraikor, 1973). Tay-Sachs is an inherited condition, characterized by very early onset, which causes developmental retardation, paralysis, dementia, blindness, and death by age 3 or 4 (*Merck Manual,* 1992, p. 1051).

Oppression can also discourage members of minority groups from seeking treatment. Both cultural and personal history come into play. For example, the Tuskegee syphilis experiments were conducted over a 40-year period from 1932 to 1972. While the victims of these experiments have died, African Americans of all ages carry the memory of this extended period when black men with syphilis were told they were being treated when in fact researchers were just observing the progress of their disease. On a personal level, people of color commonly encounter health professionals who ridicule or disregard traditional health practices and treat them with disrespect and prejudice.

In 1998, President Clinton made a commitment to eliminate health disparities in six areas: infant mortality, cancer screening and management, cardiovascular disease, diabetes, HIV/AIDS, and immunizations. Since then, the NIH has assumed a central role in efforts to reduce health disparities. Research and educational efforts in this area have increased dramatically under this initiative, and health professionals are being trained to provide culturally appropriate care. Social workers in health-care settings frequently have the opportunity to contribute to this endeavor by serving as translators and mediators for people of color.

Gender and Health

As we have observed, men have consistently shorter life expectancies than women. This gender difference in mortality is projected to endure for at least another half-century (Grambs, 1989).

Gender also influences the likelihood of becoming ill, known as "morbidity." In later years, this translates into higher rates of acute illness among men and more chronic illness among women. So, for instance, arthritis is much more common among women, while coronary heart disease more often strikes men (U.S. Senate Special Committee on Aging, 1988). Women develop late-onset diabetes at twice the rate of men (Dolger & Seeman, 1985). Older women also report more colds, infections, and stomach upsets than older men (Verbugge, 1985). Finally, women are more likely than men to suffer from urinary incontinence (Mitteness, 1987). Our health system more effectively meets the acute care needs more commonly experienced by men than it does the long-term care needs more often experienced by women (Estes, Swan, & Associates, 1993).

Gender differences have also been observed with respect to mental health. Throughout life, women typically experience higher rates of both mild and severe depression (Herzog, 1989; LaRue, Dessonville, & Jarvik, 1985). This finding holds true regardless of the approach used to measure depression (Holzer, Leaf, & Weissman, 1985). Women's greater risk of depression has been linked to their greater risk of poverty (Belle, 1984; Feinson, 1991; Krause, 1986).

Although it is difficult to separate the effects of class, race, and gender on health outcomes, some generalizations can be made. Poverty brings increased risk of physical and mental health difficulties as well as diminished access to care. Oppression can make people more vulnerable to disease. Finally, in part because they live longer than men, women experience higher rates of chronic impairment and greater need for long-term care—an area long neglected by our health-care system.

The Uninsured

The United States is distinct among industrialized nations in the large number of residents who lack health insurance. In 2005, for example, 46.6 million Americans, or 15.9 percent of the population, had no private or public health insurance (U.S. Bureau of the Census, 2005, Income, poverty and health insurance coverage in the United States: 2005, http://www.census.gov/prod/2006pubs/p60-231.pdf, accessed January 20, 2008). An even higher proportion of the population has experienced sporadic lack of coverage.

Without health insurance, Americans lack access to both preventive care and routine treatment. Local health departments provide some preventive care, such as childhood immunizations, but preventive care for adults under the age of 65, such as mammograms, blood pressure screening, and cholesterol checks, is not routinely available. The routine treatment that insured Americans seek through their primary care physicians is also not available to the uninsured. This lack of access to preventive care and routine treatment contributes indirectly to the high cost of hospital care as hospital emergency rooms deliver primary care to uninsured persons and as neglected conditions deteriorate into costly illnesses.

At a personal level, those who are uninsured tend to ignore symptoms and delay treatment, sometimes with lethal results. We see this in the cancer statistics, which reveal racial and income disparities in diagnosis, treatment and—as a result—mortality rates. In recognition of this problem, the National Cancer Institute has established a "Center to Reduce Cancer Health Disparities," with a budget to establish community-based programs to address the problem (see www.cancer.gov).

Infant Mortality in Harlem

Fidel Castro visited Harlem in October 1995 and bragged that Cuba's IMR was not only the lowest in the Caribbean but was lower than that of Central Harlem. Castro and others argued that this difference demonstrated the failure of the U.S. economic system. Babies in Harlem, a low-income, primarily African American neighborhood in New York City, were at least three times as likely to die in their first year as those in the rest of the nation.

On August 11, 1998, the New York City Department of Health issued a press release reporting that infant mortality in the city had reached a "historic low." More specifically, the press release stated that "[i]n Central Harlem, the IMR plummeted by more than 56 percent, from 15.2 deaths per 1,000 live births in 1996 . . . to an IMR of 6.6 in 1997, below the Citywide average."

What could have produced this dramatic change? The mayor's office, along with advocates and professionals working in Harlem, attributed the change to a series of federally funded initiatives: new drop-in centers where pregnant women could receive health education, counseling, workshops, and case management from pregnancy through their child's first year of life; a program called Healthline that provided information and referrals; an Adolescent Parent Education program that trained young parents; Child Health Plus, a subsidized insurance program for children; and Healthy Start, an effort that began in 1991 and focused on decreasing mortality in high-risk neighborhoods. Social workers, advocates, politicians, and health workers focused to improve health outcomes in this area. Their impact reveals the power of sustained effort and reminds us that social and health indicators are amenable to intervention. Inequality in health status and health care is not inevitable but is the direct result of allocation decisions made every day, including policy choices made at various levels of government.

MODERN EPIDEMICS AND GLOBAL GOVERNANCE

In the twenty-first century epidemics have assumed greater ferocity and reach, lending new meaning to the term "globalization" and new complications to international relations. As Beck (2004) notes, "systems designed to enhance mobility of the factors of production facilitate the global spread of what decades ago would have been localized disease outbreaks." Lee and colleagues (2000) expand on this idea, identifying the mechanisms through which globalization contributes to pandemics: "socioeconomic instability, intensified human interaction and mobility, environmental degradation, and inequalities within and across countries" (p. 11). In this section we trace the social justice implications of the HIV/AIDS epidemic and consider the weaknesses in global governance that were revealed by the 2002 SARS outbreak.

HIV/AIDS: A Global Epidemic

The global epidemic of HIV brings the social justice implications of global epidemics into devastating focus. Since the disease was detected in 1981, more than 20 million AIDS victims around the globe have died, almost 3 million of them in 2003. Indeed, 2003 saw approximately 5 million new HIV/AIDS cases, more than any previous year (CDC, 2004). The spread of this infection has been linked to sociopolitical conditions. As with most communicable diseases, poverty plays a key role.[5] Stillwagon (2000) reported that "HIV prevalence is highly correlated with falling calorie consumption, falling protein consumption, unequal distribution of income, and other variables conventionally associated with susceptibility to infectious disease" (p. 985). The deprivations of severe poverty result in a compromised immune system, leaving a person vulnerable to infectious disease.

But the relationship between economic status and HIV/AIDS is not simple. Sometimes forces associated with economic development, such as the breakdown of traditional social structures, can support the spread of HIV/AIDS. In Africa, for example, the role of truckers in spreading HIV is well documented

---

5. Poverty clearly facilitates the spread of infectious diseases. This is seen not only in the HIV/AIDS epidemic but also in the resurgence of tuberculosis and the spread of diabetes.

B O X   6.2   When Did AIDS Become an International Trade Issue?

At the 15th International AIDS conference in Thailand in 2004, French president Jacques Chirac accused the United States of using bilateral trade agreements to "blackmail" developing countries out of producing inexpensive antiretroviral drugs for AIDS patients within their borders. In September 2004 the World Trade Organization rules were revised to permit developing nations to ignore foreign drug patents in times of health crisis. Subsequently, U.S. trade negotiators were accused of requiring that Thailand dismantle its highly successful drug program to maintain trade relations with the United States.

(Whiteside, 2002). The spread of HIV has also been linked to U.S. colonial expansion. In both Puerto Rico (Baronov, 2003) and Honduras (Altman, 1999) contact between local sex workers and U.S. military personnel has contributed to the spread of HIV/AIDS. Indeed, Altman (1999) argued that the spread of HIV in Southeast Asia and South America may be associated with the U.S. "war on drugs," which led to the substitution of injected drugs for smoked opium.

The treatment options available to victims of HIV also bring class differences into sharp focus.

Among the millions of people living with HIV worldwide, the vast majority are in the developing world where access to antiretroviral drugs is extremely limited (Gayle, 2000). Until recently, the drug combination necessary for keeping an HIV/AIDS victim alive cost as much as $10,000 to $15,000 per year—an amount well beyond the reach of most people in developing nations. Very few of the HIV/AIDS patients in developing countries receive these life-saving medications.

Drug companies argue that these prices reflect the high cost of developing the new wonder drugs. Patents afforded these companies the exclusive right to produce the drugs. In 1998, faced with the deaths of thousands of its citizens, the Brazilian government announced that it would disregard patents and produce generic versions of antiretroviral drugs. India and Thailand followed suit. By producing these drugs locally, they were able to reduce the cost of three key drugs to as little as $30 per month per patient.

Today, access to generic AIDS drugs has become an international controversy, pitting the Bush administration and U.S. drug makers against world health authorities and AIDS organizations. Under U.S. law, funds allocated for international AIDS relief cannot be used to purchase generic drugs. U.S. officials argue that this stems from their concern for quality, suggesting that generic drugs are less effective. The William J. Clinton Presidential Foundation has been active in negotiating reduced prices for name-brand drugs through selected manufacturers. By contrast, the World Health Organization has promoted the use of generic drugs, arguing that they are effective and life-saving. The WHO operated a "three by five" campaign, with the goal of providing HIV/AIDS drugs to 3 million people by 2005. The campaign succeeded in reaching only one million patients instead of the proposed three million (World Health Organization, 2005).

HIV/AIDS in the United States

By 2007, the cumulative total of HIV/AIDS cases in the United States had reached 1.7 million, and over 550,000 people had died of the disease (CDC, 2007). The epidemiology of HIV/AIDS in this country clearly highlights the role of race, gender, and class. As Table 6.8 illustrates, African Americans and Hispanics are overrepresented among HIV/AIDS patients, while whites and other groups are underrepresented. Indeed, AIDS was the fourth leading cause of death for African American men between 25 and 44 years of age, and the third leading cause for African American women in the same age group (CDC, Slide Set: HIV Mortality (through 2004) cited by Henry J. Kaiser Family Foundation (2007), *HIV/AIDS Policy Fact Sheet* (http://www.kff.org/hivaids/upload/3029-071.pdf, accessed November 3, 2007)).

The characteristics of AIDS patients in the United States have changed in recent decades to include a growing number of women, children, and heterosexuals. Women are the fastest growing subpopulation among AIDS patients (Diaz, 1991; Kaplan & Krell-Long, 1993). In 1985, 7 percent of AIDS patients were female, and by 2005 the proportion had jumped to 27 percent (Henry J. Kaiser Family Foundation, 2007). The homeless population also has a high rate of HIV/AIDS infection (Stoner, 1995). Most children with AIDS are infected in utero, so the growth in pediatric AIDS cases has been attributed to the spread of the disease among women of childbearing age (Ploughman, 1995/1996). In utero infection rates have slowed considerably due to antiretroviral treatment.

But epidemiological figures can obscure the social meaning of AIDS. As Peter Conrad (1986) suggests, "AIDS is an illness with a triple stigma: it is connected to stigmatized groups; . . . it is sexually transmitted; and, like cancer, it is a terminal wasting disease. It would be difficult to imagine a scenario for a more stigmatizing disease" (p. 53). Since its discovery in the early 1980s, the disease has been associated with marginalized populations: homosexuals, drug users, Haitian immigrants, and Africans. Its early designation as "gay-related immune deficiency syndrome" reinforced the notion that AIDS was the product of a deviant lifestyle. In contrast, some argue that AIDS is sustained and promoted by social and economic inequalities that force young women into prostitution and create the ghettos that serve as breeding grounds for infection (Farmer, 1996).

T A B L E 6.8   **U.S. HIV/AIDS Cases by Ethnic Group**

Ethnic Group	Proportion of U.S. AIDS Cases	Proportion of U.S. Population
White, not Hispanic	29%	67%
Black, not Hispanic	50%	12%
Hispanic	19%	14%
Asian Pacific Islander	1%	4%
American Indian/Alaskan Native	<1%	1%

SOURCE: CDC (2007). HIV/AIDS Surveillance Report, Vol. 17, Revised Edition, June. U.S. Bureau of the Census, 2005 Population Estimates.

B O X   6.3   Appropriate Diagnosis Brings ADA Protections

Although Congress has refrained from listing conditions that make an individual eligible for disability benefits and protections available under the Americans with Disabilities Act (ADA), federal regulations and case law have clearly included AIDS as a legitimate disability (Stein, 1995). Therefore, appropriate diagnosis can provide protection against discrimination in employment and education, as well as income supports available under both Supplemental Security Income

(SSI) and Social Security (OASDI). Yet complications in the diagnosis of AIDS can restrict patients' access to treatment and income supports. Symptoms of AIDS differ among affected subgroups. Children tend to display symptoms that resemble failure-to-thrive and developmental delays. Adults often develop rare cancers and infections. In women, AIDS may manifest as pelvic inflammatory disease, cervical dysplasia, and vaginal infections.

In 1990, the growing number of "blameless" victims (those who, as Kimberly Bergalis said in her 1991 congressional testimony, "didn't do anything wrong") moved U.S. policy makers to pay attention. The primary legislative mechanism for funding prevention, treatment, and research on AIDS is the 1990 Ryan White Care Act, named after a teenage hemophiliac who died of AIDS. Services provided by the states through the use of these funds include health insurance programs that cover premiums for patients able to secure private coverage, drug programs that provide access to medication, and home-based health care. As we saw at the beginning of this chapter, Tanya Johnson received health-care services and insurance funding through her state's Ryan White program.

Public spending on AIDS has increased. The FY2001 federal budget included $9.2 billion in discretionary spending on HIV/AIDS by the U.S. Department of Health and Human Services. This was up from the 1993 budget amount of $2.1 billion. In Medicare and Medicaid programs, spending for the care of HIV/AIDS patients increased from $1.6 billion in 1993 to $3.9 billion in 2001. By 2001, NIH funding for biomedical research on AIDS was $2.1 billion, and services provided through the Ryan White Care Programs cost an estimated $1.7 billion (U.S. Department of Health and Human Services, 2000).

Meanwhile, the epidemic has raised questions of civil liberties, as the nation debates mandatory testing, reporting, and partner notification. At present, AIDS testing is mandatory for prison inmates, prostitutes, immigrants, and military recruits (Hunter & Rubenstein, 1992). Mandatory partner notification has been debated, as has required testing of all pregnant women.

In sum, the global outbreak of HIV/AIDS has raised challenging domestic and international policy issues. Within the United States, the Americans with Disabilities Act has been a vehicle for fighting discrimination against victims of this disease. The epidemic has raised issues that touch on international trade relations. The WHO has emerged as a leader in both prevention and treatment activities. As we will see in the next section, another global epidemic—severe acute respiratory syndrome (SARS)—has brought issues of international governance to the fore.

BOX 6.4   Avian Flu

The 1918 flu epidemic killed more than half a million Americans and was followed by smaller outbreaks in 1957 and 1968. Given this history, it is not surprising that President Bush took action in 2005 following an overseas outbreak of avian flu. Bush requested billions of dollars to develop methods for detection and containment of the flu within the United States, as well as funding to stockpile a limited supply of vaccinations and antiviral drugs. Of course, tax dollars would be used to purchase the drugs from private companies.

UN Secretary General Kofi Annan suggested that patents to these drugs be suspended in the interest of saving lives, but the Bush administration would not support this option, preferring to contemplate the expansion of presidential powers to deploy National Guard troops in a military-enforced quarantine (see transcript of October 2005 Press Conference at http://www.whitehouse.gov/news/releases/2005/10/20051004-1.html).

Severe Acute Respiratory Syndrome (SARS)

"When a farmer sneezes in China, a fisherman goes bankrupt in Australia" (Beck, 2004, p. 64). The 2002 outbreak of severe acute respiratory syndrome illustrated how interconnected our world has become. SARS is believed to have originated in live-animal food markets in Guangdong, China. The first case appeared there in November 2002 and SARS quickly traveled around the world. As Beck (2004) reported, by May 2003 the WHO had identified 6,234 cases of the disease. About 257 were located in Toronto hospitals and were traced to a woman who arrived from Hong Kong in February 2003. On April 22, the WHO advised against nonessential travel to Toronto. The result was a significant loss in revenue, estimated by Ontario officials at $84 million (Canadian).

Many analysts have argued that the spread of SARS was worsened by what was described as "deliberate obfuscation of information by the Chinese government" (Beck, 2004, p. 64). In February 2003, when international health organizations began posting information about the disease, Chinese officials claimed SARS was contained. A CDC team sent to investigate was denied access to Guangdong until April 2003. Indeed, once inspections were granted, Chinese doctors reported that they were told to hide SARS cases by packing people into ambulances while the inspectors were in their hospitals.

Global epidemics call for effective global governance. Existing systems and policies are rudimentary. "International Health Regulations" were developed in 1951 to reduce the threat of disease. These are periodically updated, and they set out procedures designed to limit transmission of infectious disease through shipping, aircraft, and other methods of transportation. They call on nations to report to the WHO when certain diseases (cholera, plague, and yellow fever) appear within their territories. The WHO's surveillance of infectious disease depends almost entirely on international goodwill, and the temptation to withhold information is great. Reporting an outbreak almost guarantees loss of tourism income and related revenues, and China is not the only country that has been reluctant to share information with international authorities (Lee et al., 2000).

B O X 6.5   The Obesity Epidemic: Are Americans Getting "Fat and Lazy"?

In 2005, S. Jay Olshansky and his colleagues published an article in the *New England Journal of Medicine* suggesting that the United States could face a significant drop in life expectancy as the result of increasing rates of obesity. Their review indicated that the prevalence of obesity had increased by about 50 percent per decade since 1980. Paul Terry, an epidemiologist at Emory University, offered a concise explanation for the epidemic: "The U.S. has the resources that allow peo-ple to get fat and lazy" (MacAskill, 2007). But the distribution of obesity suggests that ample resources are hardly to blame. Obesity is most prevalent among low-income Americans and people of color. Seeking to contain the nation's obesity epidemic, analysts point to "lifestyle choices," suggesting that Americans need to be educated about nutrition and motivated to exercise.

FUNDAMENTAL DILEMMAS IN U.S. HEALTH-CARE POLICY

Two fundamental dilemmas mark contemporary debates about health care in America. The first, involving how risk should be allocated, is clearly a social justice question. The second—perhaps more fundamental—issue is the extent to which the private market can reliably and efficiently deliver health care. The latter question has philosophical undertones as well as pragmatic considerations.

Assigning Risk

In the context of health insurance, a primary issue is the question of who bears the risk and who pays the cost of care. Under federally operated social insurance programs, such as Medicare and Medicaid, the nation essentially self-insures. Those who pay taxes bear the risk. In Richard Titmuss's view (1971), these social entitlements establish a moral community in which assistance from strangers replaces the one-on-one assistance of earlier times. The state serves as an intermediary, collecting insurance premiums and allocating benefits.

When Medicaid recipients are required to enroll in managed care, in essence the nation transfers the risk to the health-care provider, typically a for-profit managed care organization or an HMO. Under capitation, the program limits its risk to the amount allocated for each client under the capitation agreement. In the event of a health catastrophe, the HMO pays any additional cost; and if the enrollee does not use health care, the HMO reaps the benefit.

Some managed care entities are passing the risk down the line to physicians through what is known as "physician incentive plans." In some cases, physicians are paid a capitated rate and required to cover any additional costs above the designated reimbursement. In other cases, physicians who provide or authorize high-cost care run the risk of salary reduction through penalties or loss of bonuses. When financial incentives or disincentives are used to regulate or influence physicians' decisions, the "fiduciary responsibility" of physicians is jeopardized. Fiduciary responsibility in this case refers to the doctor's obligation to put the patient's interests first. Editors of the *New England Journal of Medicine* (1998) argue that the financial risk borne by physicians should be limited to avoid potential conflicts of interest (Pearson, Sabin, & Emanuel, 1998). Although the CMS does require that managed care organizations report on their physician incentive plans, there are currently no regulations limiting physician risk under Medicare and Medicaid contracts.

In health care there are two types of risk: financial risks and health risks. Financial risks are borne by the entity that pays unanticipated expenses. Health risks, such as death or disability, are borne by the patient. Health insurance separates health risk from financial risk in a way that, some argue, leads to overutilization of health care. To minimize their health risks, patients consume services without even thinking about cost. Copayments and deductibles attempt to stem this tendency by assigning part of the financial risk to the patient. Allocating the financial risk of illness is clearly a social justice issue. It is vital that policy practitioners in this area be prepared to effectively debate the fairness and desirability of assigning risk to the various entities involved: the patient, the physician, the HMO, the state, and the nation.

Market-Based Solutions Versus Public Provision of Care

Fundamental to many debates about health care in the United States is the extent to which health care is a commodity amenable to delivery through the private market. Some, like Siminoff (1986), have argued that health care can never conform to the ideal of the competitive market. We saw in Chapter 2 that in order for the market to operate efficiently, consumers must be able to make informed choices among various providers. In these circumstances inefficient or inadequate providers will not be chosen and the process of selection will favor those who provide the best care for the best price. In the health-care market, however, purchase decisions are not made by individuals but by their employers. The values and priorities of employers do not mirror those of their employees. Another significant obstacle to rational consumer behavior is the difficulty of evaluating the quality of medical intervention. Few patients are able to consistently distinguish good from poor care. Finally, the life-and-death nature of health-care decisions complicates the process of choosing a provider.

Others argue that regulation of the private market can solve these problems. Because providers who fail to offer acceptable care are sanctioned by licensing and accrediting authorities, anyone offering medical care must meet minimal requirements. Since cost is a significant concern, the fact that employers may be more concerned about the cost of employee benefits than the quality of care may be an advantage. Several states have developed standardized "report cards" for HMOs and other managed-care providers to help consumers choose a provider that best meets their needs. Finally, public policy (through enforcement of antitrust laws) attempts to ensure that no single entity enjoys a monopoly in the health-care market.

Although a libertarian argument might hold that the private market, left unchecked, will efficiently provide health care for all Americans, experience has shown that this is not the case. Left unchecked, the market provides health care only for those with the means to pay for it. Further, even those with the means to pay for care may lack the technical expertise to shop for the best care. Failure of market-based solutions to provide health care equitably and efficiently is well established. The question is how to fix a system that is widely agreed to be broken.

HEALTH-CARE REFORM PROPOSALS

The debate over health-care reform incorporates both incremental and comprehensive proposals. Incremental efforts retain the basic structure of the system but attempt to modify some components—for example, by regulating the insurance industry or encouraging the use of managed care. In contrast, comprehensive proposals would revise the system itself, typically by removing either public or private elements. Some proposals would eliminate the governmental role in health care, but "single-payer" proposals (discussed below) would eliminate the private market's role.

Insurance Regulation

In 1996, Congress passed and President Clinton signed the Health Insurance Portability and Accountability Act (PL 104–191), also known as "Kassebaum-Kennedy" for the bipartisan team who introduced the bill. The law's best-known provisions limit preexisting exclusions and improve the portability of health insurance. Under these provisions, insurers may impose only one 12-month exclusion period for any preexisting condition treated or diagnosed in the previous six months. This limitation should ensure that employees who maintain continuous health coverage will experience only one exclusion period in their lifetime. The law introduces the notion of "creditable coverage," requiring that individuals be given credit for their prior coverage when applying for a new plan. This means that the new plan will be prohibited from enforcing a waiting period for coverage of preexisting conditions. Portability provisions allow people, under certain conditions, to purchase health insurance if they leave their job and seek coverage as individuals.

In a less familiar provision, the law provides for "guaranteed issue and renewability." If an insurer sells policies to small businesses, the law requires the insurance company to sell its products to any small business. It also requires that insurers renew coverage for any group plan regardless of the health status of members of that group. This provision is important for people like Tanya Johnson. When her employer applied for coverage, the entire group's application was denied because of her HIV status. Under the Kassebaum-Kennedy legislation, insurers can neither terminate nor deny coverage in this way. This provision was implemented in response to small businesses, like Tanya's employer, that found their coverage canceled because of one high-cost employee.

Kassebaum-Kennedy also established a small demonstration program testing the use of medical savings accounts (MSAs). This controversial program allowed people to maintain special savings accounts (MSAs) analogous to individual retirement accounts (IRAs). Contributions to MSAs could be made by workers or their employers and were tax deductible. Employees were required to purchase health insurance with high deductibles and could use their MSAs to cover routine health expenses. In 2004 the demonstration project ended, but as part of the Medicare Reform bill the tax benefits and basic structure of MSAs (also called health savings accounts) were continued. Opponents argue that these tax-free accounts will be used by wealthy individuals who are in good health. The resulting adverse selection would leave sicker people seeking insurance through traditional providers and increase the costs of their coverage. Supporters argue that they represent progress towards a more efficient, "consumer driven" health-care system.

Kassebaum-Kennedy represented a significant departure from the traditional approach to insurance regulation in the United States. Historically, insurance has been treated as a business to be regulated by the states. Each state has an insurance official (often called the insurance commissioner) charged with overseeing the solvency and market practices of companies doing business in the state. Observing the increase in insurer failures and the number of companies that do business in several states or even several countries, however, many have begun to question whether states have the capacity to effectively regulate this enterprise.

Managed Care

Widely perceived as the solution to escalating health-care costs, managed care is central to many incremental health-care reform proposals.[6] Definitions of managed care abound. Most reflect the professional training of the author. For example, one economist (Wells, 1995) explains that managed care is designed to "provide comprehensive health care for a defined population within an available budget." A physician, writing in the *Journal of the American Medical Association* (Miller & Luft, 1994), says, "Physician practice is what is managed in managed care" (p. 1512) and argues that selection and management of physicians is the single most important distinguishing feature. A researcher (Eisenberg, 1995, p. 1670) describes managed care as "a natural experiment in health care reform." Finally, Wall Street analysts view managed care as a promising investment option within the already profitable health-care industry.

Even as federal policy has expanded the use of managed care by Medicaid and Medicare beneficiaries, Congress and the president have found it necessary to regulate the medical practices of managed care providers. For example, in 1997, President Clinton signed an act prohibiting what he termed "drive-through deliveries." Under the provisions of this act, health-care providers are

---

6. Terry Peak collaborated in the original research and drafting of the section on managed care.

prohibited from discharging a new mother after a hospital stay of less than 48 hours. The Patients' Bill of Rights is another effort to regulate managed care.

Health-Care Reform in Massachusetts

In April 2006, Governor Mitt Romney of Massachusetts signed the Massachusetts Health Care Reform Bill into law. The new law can be characterized as a "comprehensive incremental" approach to health-care reform. Maintaining the basic structure of the health-care delivery system, the law includes a series of initiatives focused around a single objective: to ensure that nearly all of the state's residents would be covered by health insurance. The law combines mandates and subsidies, insurance market reforms, and redirection of health-care funds in a comprehensive approach that has shown considerable promise. By June of 2007, nearly 80,000 adults were enrolled in the new Commonwealth Care Health Insurance Program (C-CHIP) for those with incomes below 300 percent of the federal poverty threshold (Kaiser Family Foundation, 2007, http://www.kff.org/uninsured/7494 .cfm, accessed November 4, 2007).

The new mandates apply to individuals and businesses. First, all adults in Massachusetts are required to obtain health insurance or be subject to tax penalties and fees. Premium subsidies are available on a sliding scale basis to those with incomes below 300 percent of the poverty threshold. Second, businesses with more than 10 employees must contribute a "fair share" to employee health insurance premiums and make available to their workers Section 125 cafeteria plans that allow workers to pay their health-care expenses with pretax dollars. Businesses that fail to meet these requirements must pay penalties.

Insurance market reforms are an important aspect of the new law. Individuals and small businesses may purchase coverage through the new Commonwealth Health Insurance Connector, which will collect premiums for the purchase of approved plans. These are limited to managed care providers contracted to provide Medicaid care. The law does allow insurers to sell coverage exclusively designed for 19- to 26-year-olds, but it eliminates the costly "non group" or individual insurance plans, merging them with "small group" plans, a move that is designed to reduce premiums for those who formerly had to purchase insurance on their own. The Connector Board is charged with establishing minimum coverage standards, though coverage requirements will not be enforced until 2009. The Board will also determine affordability standards and premium amounts. As of March 2007, the Board had eliminated premiums for those with incomes up to 150 percent of the poverty threshold and reduced them to $35 per month for those with incomes between 151 and 200 percent of the poverty threshold.

Benefits under the state's Medicaid program were expanded, and the total estimated cost of the measure for 2007–2008 was $1.725 billion. Most of this came from redirection of federal and state funds. Medicaid funds cover the bulk of the expenses. In addition, money in the state "Uncompensated Care Pool," which reimbursed providers for unpaid medical bills, is redirected into a

Health Safety Net Trust Fund and used in part to subsidize coverage for low-income residents. The program is expected to draw an estimated $338 million in new monies from state General Funds in fiscal year 2007–2008.

The Massachusetts Health Care Reform Bill is a carefully crafted bipartisan compromise. Without fundamentally revising the delivery of health care, it calls for significant expansion of the government's role both in financing and in regulating the health-care market. Other states have considered implementing aspects of the plan developed in Massachusetts, suggesting a ripple effect of state-level reforms.

Single-Payer Proposals

Single-payer proposals advocate government provision of health care for all Americans. Advocates attribute the discrepancy between health "inputs" and health outcomes to the fundamental inefficiency of the American health-care system. They argue that elimination of private health insurance providers would reduce this inefficiency by cutting administrative costs and overhead.

As anyone who has used health insurance in recent years can testify, the administrative complexity of the U.S. health-care system is enormous. This complexity led the Office of Technology Assessment to conclude that conversion to a single-payer system could result in savings in excess of $47 billion 1991 U.S. dollars. These savings would result primarily from the simplified administrative procedures of a single-payer system (U.S. Congress, Office of Technology Assessment, 1994). The money saved would have been more than sufficient to provide health coverage to everyone in the United States (Chamberlain, 1994).

Representatives of the health insurance industry vigorously oppose single-payer proposals. The health insurance industry spends millions of dollars in campaign contributions to ensure access to the nation's policy makers, even as it conducts vigorous advertising campaigns to defeat reform proposals. These campaigns appeal to middle-class fears of losing access to high-quality care if the United States adopts a single-payer system. Despite evidence to the contrary, lobbyists suggest that a single-payer system would create a federal bureaucracy that would prove even less efficient than the current system. They argue that Canadians and Britons dislike their national health-care systems, offering examples of middle-class consumers who, frustrated with waiting lists in their nations, travel to the United States for complex procedures such as coronary bypass surgery and hip replacements.

Despite the efforts of these powerful financial interests, a movement to support the single-payer alternative is gaining strength in the United States. Several grassroots organizations promote this reform, including Single-Payer Across the Nation (SPAN), which was founded in 1994, and the Universal Health Care Action Network (UHCAN), established in 1992. From time to time, single-payer legislation is introduced in Congress. Given the nation's level of dissatisfaction both with managed care and with other forms of private health insurance, it seems likely that these reform efforts will continue.

SOCIAL WORK ROLES IN HEALTH-CARE POLICY

Although social work in health care has been termed "a neglected area of practice" (DeCoster, 2001), social workers have long been involved in U.S. health-care policy as advocates, administrators, and practitioners. As director of the Children's Bureau, Grace Abbott took part in the establishment of programs for child and maternal health. Advocates in organizations such as Families USA work to ensure that the needs of the poor are taken into account in health-care reform. On a daily basis, discharge planners struggle to find appropriate care arrangements for people leaving hospitals.

Today's health-care system presents new challenges and opportunities for advocates, administrators, and practitioners. In a variety of settings and a variety of roles, social workers strive to ensure that vulnerable populations receive the care they need. At the state level, social workers battle against benefit cuts and monitor Medicaid managed care contracts. In clinics, hospitals, and other settings, social workers inform patients and their families of their rights and responsibilities and serve as intermediaries between members of minority groups and health-care institutions. In community agencies they work with nurses to educate low-income and immigrant families in the use of new and established medical technology. In Congress and state legislatures, social workers continue in the tradition of the Children's Bureau, investigating and reporting the needs and concerns of vulnerable Americans. Finally, social work professionals find excellent opportunities for advocacy and community organization efforts in grassroots movements that promote health-care reform.

SUMMARY: HEALTH-CARE ISSUES
IN THE UNITED STATES

We began this chapter by discussing the life experiences of Tanya Johnson, a young woman living with HIV infection. Tanya's experiences were influenced by several federal policies. She received services through the Ryan White Care Act. When she was fired from her job, she sued her employer for not complying with the requirements of the Americans with Disabilities Act. Insurance regulations at the state level helped her secure coverage, while the Kennedy-Kassebaum Act ensures that others will not face the difficulties she experienced in seeking private health insurance.

We traced the development of the U.S. health-care system, viewing it as a hybrid combining public regulation and financing with private delivery. We examined the development of public-sector interventions as well as the growth of the private "health-care industry," observing the contribution of public financing to the growth of this private industry, and the tension between the public sector's need for cost containment and the private sector's drive for profits. We next discussed the nation's investment in health care, using international comparisons to assess health expenditures and health outcomes. We considered the impacts of class, race, and gender in health status and health care, as well as the experiences of uninsured Americans. We discussed infant mortality in Harlem as a case example of the impact of sustained intervention on this health indicator. Then we addressed two fundamental dilemmas in U.S. health-care policy: the problem of assigning risk, and implications of market-based delivery of health care. We briefly considered health-care reform and the role of social workers in health care.

The United States is the only industrialized nation in which health care is not a right. In the United States health insurance is associated with employment, and public health care is grudgingly provided to the needy. The resulting hybrid system has resulted in inefficiencies that increasingly affect not only the poor but the middle class as well. Rather than pursuing an increased public presence in health-care delivery, the United States has expanded the use of managed care. The result has been a consolidation in the health-care industry that alarms even some stockbrokers. Consumer concerns have led to an attempt to balance the power of managed care organizations through federal regulation. Medicaid managed care brings this concern to the state level as states struggle to ensure that the needs of these vulnerable Americans are met. By participating in state contracting, consumer advocacy, and care monitoring, social workers can contribute to the well-being of low-income Americans.

Health-care reform is a continuous (if not steady) process in the United States. With a general understanding of the structure of our health-care system and a clear commitment to social justice, social work professionals can influence health-care debates. By adding the profession's voice and supporting the client's voice on health-care issues, social workers can make a direct contribution to the social justice of our health-care system.

KEYWORDS

Health-care costs	Infant mortality rate	Health-care reform
Health-care financing	Managed care	Health policy
Health-care insurance	Rural health care	Medicaid
Indigent health care	Uninsured	Medicare

THINK ABOUT IT

1. The effectiveness of the immunizations developed and distributed by public agencies advanced public acceptance of government provision of health care. This technological advance enhanced the stature of public health tremendously. Has there been any comparable development in the field of social welfare?

2. What roles do social workers play in the debate over health care in the United States? How do you feel about single-payer proposals? Do your views reflect your own background? Do they take into account the needs of vulnerable groups in the U.S. population?

3. What ethical dilemmas are social workers likely to encounter when working in a managed care setting? How might they resolve them?

4. If you had a choice, how would you assign risk among these entities: a Medicaid client (think of someone with whom you are familiar), a physician, an HMO, your state, and the federal government? Who should bear the greatest risk? Why? Should the client bear any risk? Why or why not?

5. How would Tanya's experiences seeking health insurance have been different after the passage of the Health Insurance Portability and Accountability Act? Has the act solved all the problems workers face with respect to private health insurance? What, if any, problems remain?

6. In the case of SARS, lack of information hindered early response to the epidemic. What is more important: a patient's right to privacy or the public's need to be protected from disease? Use a case example to support your choice.

7. Review the discussion of conditions necessary for the free market to efficiently deliver goods and services (Chapter 2). Are these conditions present in the delivery of health care? What conclusions do you reach regarding the use of the market to deliver health care?

8. What social and economic factors do you think contribute to rising obesity in the United States?

WEB-BASED EXERCISES

For direct links to all the sites in these exercises, log on to the Student Companion Site for this book at academic.cengage.com/social_work/barusch, and choose Chapter 6.

1. Go to http://www.who.int/hpr/NPH/docs/declaration_almaata.pdf to help you answer the following questions about the Alma-Ata Declaration on Primary Health Care.
    a. When was the declaration established?
    b. What are the basic provisions of this declaration?
    c. Are these consistent with U.S. health policy?
    d. What does the Pan-American Health Organization see as the primary impact of Alma-Ata? (Hint: go to http://www.paho.org/English/DD/PIN/almaata25.htm, or search www.paho.org.)
    e. What do you see as the impact of this declaration?

2. Go to http://www.pccw.gov/ to review the July 2007 recommendations of the President's Commission on Care for America's Returning Wounded Soldiers. To what extent have these recommendations been implemented in your local VA health-care facility? Do you think they have or will make a difference in the quality of care received by veterans?

SUGGESTED RESOURCES

Estes, C. L., Swan, J. H., & Associates. (1993). *The Long-Term Care Crisis: Elders Trapped in the No-Care Zone*. Newbury Park, CA: Sage Publications.

Garrett, L. (2000). *Betrayal of Trust: The Collapse of Global Public Health*. New York: Hyperion Press.

Navarro, V. (Ed.). (2002). *The Political Economy of Social Inequalities: Consequences for Health and Quality of Life*. Amityville, NY: Baywood Publishing.

www.cms.hhs.gov. This is the site for the Centers for Medicare and Medicaid Services. Here you will find general information about these programs, as well as statistics and material on current policy developments.

www.cmwf.org. This site is maintained by the Commonwealth Fund, a foundation interested in health-care issues. It offers some excellent reports on current policy issues.

www.who.int. Maintained by the World Health Organization, this site is a good starting point for international comparisons.

7

Mental Illness

Insanity is often the logic of an accurate mind overtaxed.
OLIVER WENDELL HOLMES

The pursuit of mental health is a long-standing American tradition. As early as Colonial times, Americans turned to experts for guidance on this subject. Later, the "mental hygiene movement" of the 1930s offered specific methods for achieving mental health. More recently, social workers have joined the burgeoning "self-help" industry. Yet, with the possible exception of California, which once adopted mental hygiene as a public policy goal, few governmental jurisdictions are involved in the pursuit of mental health.

Public resources and policies in this area generally focus on people with severe mental illness. From a social justice perspective there are important parallels between mental illness and physical illness. Like the health disparities discussed in the last chapter, we see the legacy of oppression and neglect in both the distribution and the treatment of mental illness. In addition, widespread misunderstanding about the causes of serious mental illness and discomfort with its behavioral manifestations result in stigma. Until we are either directly or indirectly affected, many Americans still view mental illness as a personal problem for which collective action is not required. This perspective will be a recurring theme in this chapter.

We will begin the chapter by relating the experiences of Rachel Sanders, a woman coping with depression and anxiety. After addressing the challenges of defining mental illness, we will examine values and beliefs about insanity. In later sections, we will trace the development of interventions for people with mental illness and examine contemporary realities of mental illness in the United States. The chapter closes with a discussion of emerging policy issues, including treatment of mentally ill offenders in the criminal justice system, involuntary commitment, mandatory outpatient treatment, and insurance parity.

DEFINING MENTAL ILLNESS

Definitions of mental illness vary in their emphasis. Some underscore biology, defining mental illness on the basis of genetic configurations, neurological activity, or brain chemistry. Other definitions emphasize behavior, treating mental illness as a failure of personality or personal development. During the 1960s and 1970s, mental health professionals such as R. D. Laing argued that mental illness was essentially a failure to conform. Thomas Szasz, a vocal proponent of this view, argued that mental illness was a "myth" and that labeling someone "crazy" or "mentally ill" was a sanction for violating social norms (Szasz, 1960).

In 1952, the American Psychiatric Association released the first edition of the *Diagnostic and Statistical Manual,* now in its fourth edition (the *DSM-IV*). This authoritative document reflects an ongoing effort to standardize psychiatric terminology that began during the 1920s. It defines mental illnesses in exquisite detail, based on cognitive, emotional, and behavioral indicators. The *DSM* has become an important tool in the social construction of mental illness. Its first edition reflected the view that mental disorders represented reactions or adaptations to psychosocial stressors. The *DSM-II,* issued in 1968, focused on describing psychiatric diseases, and its authors systematically eradicated all mention of "reactions" or "adaptation" from the manual. In 1980, the *DSM-III* was issued. This version has been described as a "paradigm shift" in American psychiatry. It represented a rejection of etiological explanations and a return to the medical model of mental illness. Later versions of the *DSM* (the *DSM-IIIR* and the *DSM-IV*) are still dominated by the medical model. They elaborate upon the classification schemes developed in the *DSM-III* but do not focus on the causes of mental illness (LaBruzza & Mendez-Villarrubia, 1994).

LaBruzza and Mendez-Villarrubia (1994) describe the *DSM's* role in the social construction of mental illness as "diagnosis by consensus" (p. 38). The manual's treatment of homosexuality is illustrative. Homosexuality was listed as a mental illness in the first two editions of the *DSM*. During the 1960s and 1970s, gay rights groups opposed this nomenclature, arguing that the difficulties experienced by homosexuals were caused by society, not by underlying mental pathology. In 1973, the American Psychiatric Association's board of trustees voted to delete homosexuality from the *DSM*. As LaBruzza and Mendez-Villarrubia note, "With a single vote the APA cured millions of gay men and women in America of the 'mental illness' of homosexuality" (p. 21).

Addiction disorders also represent a definitional challenge in the field of mental health. Addiction to alcohol or illegal drugs, per the *DSM*, is considered a mental illness. Further, advocates for those who suffer from addiction emphasize its biological component, framing addiction as a disease. Nonetheless, the general public and many policy makers view addiction not as a disease but as a

A HUMAN PERSPECTIVE   Rachel Sanders

Rachel Sanders is a dynamic woman of 50-something. She works for her state's mental health authority, coordinating consumer advocacy efforts under a federal grant. Rachel describes her job as "fantastic," and she clearly excels in her work. Yet, as Rachel points out, had she lived in the seventeenth century, she probably would have been "burned at the stake" during an episode of her illness. Rachel has a condition known as "atypical bipolar disorder and panic disorder," which has presented as alternating bouts of severe depression with severe paranoia, mania, and acute anxiety attacks.

Rachel is the oldest of eight children. Her parents were devoutly religious, and family life revolved around her father's academic career, the children's artistic pursuits, and the family's religious activities. From the outside looking in, she said, theirs was a model family. But privately, the children struggled to withstand their father's violent rages. Rachel was the primary target of his brutal verbal and physical attacks. Rachel's mother didn't stop the abuse, possibly because she drew satisfaction from being the family comforter. When Rachel was 19, the family spent two years in South America, where Rachel taught English as a second language to adults in a large international center. The family lived luxuriously, with many servants. This lifestyle gave the siblings time to socialize and become closer emotionally. Then Rachel's mother developed cancer. Rachel nursed her mother around the clock for the final four months of her life, and she was the only child present at her mother's death.

After a six-month stint traveling in Europe as a companion to a wealthy French woman, Rachel reentered college as a fine arts major. She was an award-winning writer and watercolorist, a concert pianist, and a National Merit scholar. During college, she experienced long episodes of depression during which she would "hide and sleep" rather than attending classes. While still in college, she met and married a high-profile, good-looking entrepreneur from California, and the couple moved to Los Angeles. With the profits from their business they enjoyed first-class round-the-world travel and an opulent lifestyle in Marina del Rey. They kept two expensive foreign sports cars, two private planes, and a 40-foot sailboat. In a spirit of adventure, Rachel took flying lessons and learned to pilot the boat. After a decade, when this marriage failed, she went into real estate. During this period, Rachel began to experience panic attacks.

The first attack, which occurred when she was 32 years old, started on a Sunday afternoon and lasted for eight hours. Rachel called 911, screaming, "I'm dying! I'm dying!" She thought she was having a stroke or a heart attack. Shorter attacks continued daily, and Rachel's circle of activities began to shrink. Although she took Valium as prescribed, Rachel couldn't safely drive on the freeway, and eventually she could barely leave the house.

During this period she married an extremely kind, sensitive older man of independent means, but this marriage ended amicably after less than three years. Faced with daily panic attacks, Rachel returned to her hometown and the emotional support of her siblings.

There, her life revolved around visits to the emergency room. She found an entry-level job at a hospital and was on Valium for two and a half years. Then she learned about Xanax and found that it more effectively controlled her panic attacks. Later, she returned to California and, as she put it, "got very grandiose." Rachel set up a corporation for international arts festivals and, as she said, "went through over a quarter of a million dollars of other people's money in less than 18 months."

Hoping to control her rising anxiety, she increased her Xanax intake until she began to develop psychotic symptoms. She had never heard of psychosis, and firmly believed that people were trying to kill her. Finally, Rachel called a sister in Alabama and cried, "They're coming to get me." Within hours, her sister flew to California and, with a brother, committed Rachel to Long Beach General Hospital with severe depressive paranoid psychosis. She hadn't eaten or bathed in days. Rachel was put in restraints and spent five days on a locked ward. She recalls her hospitalization as a negative experience, remembering the crowded facility and aides who joked about her condition. She was put on Stelazine and, when that started to pull her out of the psychosis, she was transferred to a halfway house in Inglewood.

In retrospect, Rachel feels she was released to the halfway house too soon. There, she cowered in her room all night, peering out the window at people she thought were coming to kill her. For days, she refused medications, thinking they were poisoned. Finally, she said, a "big, boisterous black woman," who terrified Rachel, bullied her into taking her medication. What a difference it made! Soon Rachel was whistling in the halls, and she was transferred to a residential care center in Watts, where she stayed for six weeks. Rachel enjoyed the center, which had a grand piano in the recreation room that she played for hours on end. Nonetheless, she was eager to leave the institutional setting. She took her medication regularly and convinced her sympathetic second ex-husband to let her stay with him. This arrangement didn't work well. She was heavily medicated and severely depressed, not capable of much more than long walks by the ocean all day while her ex-husband was away. Finally, one of her brothers invited her to visit for Christmas. She ended up living with him and his extraordinarily supportive wife and children for a year and a half, working in a medical setting and learning to cope with her frequent bouts of extreme paranoid ideation.

Rachel eventually moved into an apartment of her own and found a stable position as a patient advocate in a clinic. She worked at the clinic for six years before recurrent panic attacks forced her to resign. She lived on her savings for a year and a half, caught in a downward spiral that she attributes to losing the validation and structure of work. This crisis led to her second hospitalization, which lasted five days.

When her health insurance ran out, Rachel asked to be referred to a public clinic. There, her new therapist helped her apply for Medicaid and recommended that Rachel join a local mental health clubhouse program. After a successful volunteer experience, Rachel entered a transitional employment program. She found a job as a receptionist with the state mental health authority. When a new administrative support position became available, Rachel moved into consumer programs, which set the stage for her current administrative job.

Rachel sees her therapist regularly at a community mental health center. After much adjustment of medication types and dosages, she takes what her therapist calls "a sprinkle" of Xanax daily as a prophylactic to ward off panic attacks, along with a small dose of antipsychotic medication and Prozac. Rachel has become confident, both in her therapist and in her pharmaceutical regimen, and describes her therapist, a nurse/MSW, as "extraordinarily deft." Her therapist is gifted with deep empathy, and Rachel thinks it helps that she is a woman of about her own age. With this level of care, Rachel is comfortable and happy. In fact, she describes this as "by far, the happiest time of my life."

Rachel occasionally has minor attacks of intense paranoia but she's able to recognize them as such. After each one recedes, she experiences a warm feeling, "like you're coming back from a cold hell into a warm reality."

Rachel says, "You even learn to love your disease, as strange as that may sound. It forces you to develop compassion and is a marvelous lesson." She is grateful for these lessons, and feels she wouldn't have been able to learn them any other way. The main problem she has encountered is the public's lack of knowledge about mental illness. She feels fortunate that she can remember every detail of her past psychotic episodes. Most consumers she works with don't have that degree of recall. For them, each episode is a new and terrifying experience.

As a leader among mental health consumers, Rachel has had the opportunity to discuss issues of concern at the state and national levels. She believes that in the consumer community she works with, there is support for forced medication. Some of the mental health consumers she encounters have expressed reservations about side effects and the impact of mandatory medication on self-determination, but they feel the benefits of psychotropic medications override these considerations. Rachel is confident that the coming years will see even more sophisticated medications for mental illness. Her state's consumers are also interested in gun control and housing. At least half of the people Rachel works with are upset about proposed restrictions on their ability to purchase guns. Arguing that they are statistically less violent than the general population, they believe such restrictions violate their rights. Those living on Supplemental Security Income (SSI) and Social Security Disability Insurance (DI) find affordable housing scarce and struggle to get by on meager benefits: "They want us to pay for the sin of having a mental illness." Mental health insurance parity is another big concern, which Rachel sees as a state issue.

A Social Work Perspective

Given the timing, it is tempting to attribute Rachel's first bout with depression to the loss of her mother. While this event may have acted as a precipitating factor, Rachel explains her illness with reference to a combination of genetic and situational factors. She notes that depression and bipolar disorder are found on both sides of her immediate family, and that she

Continued

Continued

suffered regular abuse during childhood that probably had an impact on her mental well-being. Her youngest brother was diagnosed with paranoid schizophrenia when he was 17 and tried to commit suicide. He is now in his early 40s, living on DI and contributions from his siblings. Unlike Rachel, he has consistently resisted mental health treatment.

Despite her struggles, Rachel feels fortunate. At times, she has lost most of her possessions, but she has never been homeless. She attributes this to the generosity of her siblings. Indeed, Rachel feels that without her family's enlightened support, she would not have survived her illness. Rachel has achieved an astonishing reconciliation with the father who traumatized her so badly in childhood. She feels they probably will never be emotionally close, but they now have a peaceful and supportive relationship.

It is interesting to speculate on what might have happened if her childhood abuse had come to the attention of public authorities. Would Rachel have been removed from her parental home? Would the foster care system have provided the kind of supports that have sustained Rachel through her episodes of illness? Would an experience with child welfare authorities have mitigated or exacerbated the impact of mental illness on her life? Without family supports, would Rachel have joined the ranks of the homeless mentally ill who now haunt the nation's towns and cities?

"Oh, worse than that!" Rachel sums it up emphatically. "I'm certain that without my artfully gifted professional treatment and enlightened support of my family and friends, I'd have been dead long ago!"

moral failure. As we see in Chapter 8, this view is reflected in social policies regarding addiction as a disability.

As the length and complexity of the *DSM-IV* illustrate, mental illness is as intricate and varied as physical illness. We think of mental illness as a long-term condition that produces extreme emotions and behavior, such as depression or schizophrenia. But, as Mechanic points out, "some psychiatric conditions are like the flu or a gastrointestinal disorder; they are relatively short-lived and do not greatly disrupt one's life" (1999, p. 39). Indeed, as the field develops, professionals are able to describe and define mental illness with increasing specificity.

VALUES AND BELIEFS ABOUT MENTAL ILLNESS

Just as the definitions of mental illness have changed, so have social attitudes toward people with psychiatric disorders. In this section, we will examine several perspectives on mental illness, suggesting that Americans have viewed it alternatively as eccentricity, sin, disease, and disability.

Mental Illness as Eccentricity

In some contexts, mental illness is viewed as a sign of eccentricity, or uniqueness. In artists this eccentricity may be tolerable—even a sign of creativity. This attitude is most evident in the public response to artists who have mental diagnoses.

Several of the nation's most creative artists have been diagnosed with depression or schizophrenia. (For a discussion of the relationship between creativity and insanity, and a list of artists who have been treated for mental illness, see Jamison, 1993.)

In politics, however, eccentricity is less readily accepted. At its extreme, a negative approach to eccentricity among politicians is seen when insanity is used by authoritarian regimes to silence political opposition. Thus, for example, political activists in China and other nations have been imprisoned, not as criminals, but as victims of mental illness, with their eccentric political views presented as evidence of insanity. The United States has limited tolerance for mental illness among its politicians. News of Thomas Eagleton's psychiatric treatment led to his replacement as McGovern's running mate in the 1972 presidential election. Thus it was courageous of Representative Lynn Rivers (D-MI) to publicly acknowledge her struggles with bipolar depression in 1998. The National Mental Health Association recognized her courage by presenting Representative Rivers with its Legislator of the Year award.

Mental Illness as Sin

During the early eighteenth century, mental illness was more often attributed to supernatural causes than to biological or social conditions. Cotton Mather, a Puritan minister, wrote prolifically on both mental and physical illnesses. As was typical at the time, he saw madness as a consequence of sin (Grob, 1994). Treatment took the form of prayer, repentance, and exorcism.

In this respect mental illness differs from physical illness. Physical illness is seldom attributed to sin, while mental illness is often linked to moral, personal, or familial failure. (Consider the "schizophrenogenic mother," for example.) When one is physically ill, treatment is provided as a matter of course, and (except in the case of severe contagion) incarceration is not even considered. But, as we will see, severe mental illness, with its problematic behavioral component, can lead to incarceration rather than treatment.

Mental Illness as Disease

Recent years have seen a growing awareness of the biological component of psychiatric disorders, and with it, a widespread view of mental illness as disease. This definition may be highly dependent on context.

David Mechanic (1962) examined the definition of behavior as "sick" or "bad." He argued that "if the behavior appears to be peculiar and at odds with the actor's self-interests or with expectations of the way a reasonable person is motivated, the evaluator is more likely to characterize such behavior in terms of the sickness dimension" (Mechanic, 1999, p. 38). But if the behavior is in some way self-serving, it is more likely to be evaluated as "bad." Thus a rich person who steals a loaf of bread is likely to be labeled "sick" or "crazy," while a poor person who does so will be labeled "bad."

Mental Illness as Disability

As we will see in Chapter 8, the notion of mental illness as a disability is significant to social policy because it determines eligibility for programs that serve the disabled. These entitlements include income maintenance as well as housing and rehabilitative services. Those whose mental illness renders them "unable to engage in any substantial gainful activity" (Social Security Administration, 2004) are eligible for monthly income through SSI and DI. Like Rachel, they also have access to medical coverage under Medicaid, and those who are on DI for 24 months become eligible for Medicare coverage. Disability also may entitle a person with mental illness to receive food stamps.

The label "disabled" cuts two ways. A mental patient who can persuade authorities that she is "permanently and totally disabled" will receive income support, in-kind benefits, and medical coverage. In order to secure rehabilitative services, however, she may need to demonstrate that she can be rehabilitated. That is, she may be "totally" but not "permanently" disabled. Thus, an individual with severe mental illness faces a quandary: is it better to give up hope of rehabilitation and gain a secure income, or to cling to hope and thereby gain access to rehabilitation? This quandary reflects the sophistication and fragmentation of the network of mental health interventions that have developed in the United States. The development of this network is described in the next section.

HISTORICAL DEVELOPMENT OF INTERVENTIONS FOR MENTAL ILLNESS

In this section, we will trace the development of public interventions for people with mental illness in the United States.[1] As we will discover, support for these interventions seems to ebb and flow, reflecting the fluctuating enthusiasm for available treatment methods. We will also trace the changing role of social workers in the mental health service delivery system.

Care of People with Mental Illness in Colonial America

Living in close proximity, American colonists were quick to recognize both the external effects and the unpredictability of mental illness. The impact of mental illness went beyond the victim's suffering, as Cotton Mather pointed out:

These melancholicks do sufficiently Afflict themselves, and are Enough their own Tormentors. As if this present Evil World, would not Really afford Sad Things Enough, they create a World of Imaginary Ones, and

---

1. Much of the material in this section is based on Gerald Grob's 1994 book, *The Mad Among Us,* and David Rochefort's 1997 work, *From Poorhouses to Homelessness.*

by Medicating terror, they make themselves as Miserable, as they could be from the most Real miseries.

But this is not all; *They Afflict others as well as Themselves, and often make themselves Insuportable Burdens to all about them.*

In this Case, we must bear one anothers Burdens. (Jones, 1972, pp. 129–137 [emphasis added])

Further, one never knew who might be the next victim. Thus, in 1651, when Roger Williams exhorted his fellow citizens of Providence, Rhode Island, to care for a widow who was "distracted," he reminded them that "we know not how soone our wives may be widowes and our children Orphans, yea and our selves be deprived of all or most of our Reason, before we goe from hence, except mercy from the God of Mercies prevent it" (Grob, 1994, p. 13).

In colonial America, mental illness became a public concern when it interfered with community safety or jeopardized personal survival. Indeed, one of the first laws governing care of the insane ordered the selectmen of Massachusetts to care for them "in order that they doe not Damnify others" (Grob, 1994, p. 7).

Public care of people with mental illness focused on meeting survival needs, but treatment was sometimes available. Therapies were eclectic, reflecting practitioners' varied notions about causes. Insanity was attributed to sin as readily as to extreme misfortune or digestive disturbances.

Richard Napier, an astrological physician of the era, treated thousands of patients for madness during his career. Treatments might include bleeding and purging. But Napier also used exorcism if he believed a patient was possessed, and environmental manipulation if he thought the trouble came from that source (Grob, 1994).

Depression was identified early in the nation's history, and its causes and treatments were outlined in Robert Burton's famous 1621 work, *Anatomy of Melancholy*. Burton, himself a frequent victim of melancholy, advised a range of treatments, including social contacts (avoiding solitude), music, prayer, and medicines. The latter might consist of "a decapitated head of ram . . . boiled with cinnamon, ginger, nutmeg, mace and cloves," or "living swallows, cut in two and laid reeking hott onto the shaved Head," and "blood of an ass drawn from behind his ear" (Grob, 1994, pp. 9–10).

These treatments, while often effective, were seldom part of public interventions. They were provided to those who could afford them, or in individual cases where charity dictated relief of suffering. The notion of a "right to treatment" was not part of the dialogue about public responsibility for people with mental illness.

The Promise of the Asylum

By the mid-eighteenth century, American understanding of mental illness focused more on personal and environmental influences and less on spiritual causes. During the age of enlightenment, belief in the potential for perfecting human beings—or at least improving their situations—increased general interest in curing mental illness.

With the growth of cities came the establishment of institutional settings for people with mental illness. Hospitals were available for those who could afford them, and almshouses were provided to the indigent. These almshouses initially combined the aged, young, infirm, and insane. Over time, however, efforts were made to separate the "distracted" from the rest of the population.

The nation's first public hospital designed exclusively for the insane, the Virginia Eastern Asylum, was established in Williamsburg in 1769. The rationale for its establishment included both the need for early intervention and the recognition of the external effects of madness. The act that allocated funds for the hospital stated in its opening clause that "several persons of insane and disordered minds have been frequently found wandering in different parts of this colony" and noted that "no certain provision" had "yet [been] made either towards effecting a cure of those whose cases are not become quite desperate, nor for restraining others who may be dangerous to society" (Hening, 1809–1823, Vol. 8, pp. 378–381).

During the latter part of the eighteenth century, public hospitals for people with mental illness proliferated, with a corresponding improvement in care. American institutions reflected a strong European influence. A Frenchman, Philippe Pinel, contributed to the expansion of the asylum by developing a new treatment approach. Based on exhaustive observations, he argued that bleeding and other practices generally were not effective. Pinel established what he called a *traitement moral* (moral treatment). Contrary to its name, Pinel's approach did not emphasize moral judgments or values. Instead, it offered a carefully structured environmental regimen in which the physician held complete authority. The goal was an institution in which physical abuse and neglect of patients were unheard of, and the environment was carefully structured to accomplish individual cures.

In England, William Tuke, a Quaker and merchant, applied Pinel's methods at the York Retreat. The Retreat was established by Quakers in 1792 to serve people with mental illness. It established a well-considered regimen that was remarkably effective. The success of the Retreat contributed to a widespread belief that hospitals for people with mental illness could accomplish cures. This optimism set the stage for expansion of mental institutions throughout England and the United States.

Of course, high-quality care was costly, and private institutions were forced to serve an affluent clientele in order to generate sufficient operating funds. Indigents were referred to public institutions, where they would receive custodial care but not the most sophisticated treatment.[2] The result was a class-based system of care in which the affluent were not forced to mix with members of the lower or immigrant classes.

---

2. Some public institutions did provide outstanding care. One of these was the Massachusetts State Hospital, established by Samuel B. Woodward, which served as a model of effective treatment under public auspices.

Dorothea Dix, "Apostle to the Insane"

Enter Dorothea Dix (1802–1887), who has been called the apostle to the insane. Ms. Dix was an educated woman from a middle-class family. Like many women from similar backgrounds, she found in social reform one of the few available outlets for her talents. Although she suffered illness and emotional trials, Dix was determined to contribute to society, observing that "life is not to be expended in vain regrets—self is not to be the object of contemplation—individual trials are not to be admitted to fill the mind to the exclusion of the sufferings of the *many*" (Brown, 1998, p. 76). When Dix was 39, she was invited to teach a Sunday school class at a jail outside of Boston. There, she found the insane housed with criminals in appalling conditions. Her outrage at this and similar conditions fueled a career in social advocacy.

Dix developed an effective methodology for her crusade to establish asylums for people with mental illness. She would travel to a state, visit prisons and almshouses, and prepare a petition or report outlining her findings. Dix then met with policy elites and members of state legislatures to encourage establishment or expansion of the institutions in each state.

Like many advocates, she was not above exaggeration or hyperbole if it helped her cause. Some, like her fellow reformer Samuel Gridley Howe, saw her dramatic presentations as necessary to convey the urgency of her mission. Officials who ran the facilities raised strenuous objections, however. The administrators of the Danvers almshouse argued that Dix was in the facility for only five minutes and had then described "the high wrought fancies of [her] imagination, instead of the practical realities of life" (Brown, 1998, p. 95).

Howe linked the causes of insanity to the failings of social institutions, arguing that society caused insanity, so should be held responsible for care of its victims. Dix, on the other hand, held that the causes were irrelevant. A deeply religious Unitarian, Dix argued the moral necessity of protecting the insane from the "predatory forces of society" (Brown, 1998, p. 93).

The expansion of public hospitals for people with mental illness continued for more than a century. Through the course of her career (1840–1860), Dix was instrumental in founding or expanding 31 asylums for people with mental illness (Brown, 1998). Within these institutions, a new specialty called "psychiatric social work" was born. Paul Stuart (1997) traced the roots of psychiatric social work to 1907, when Massachusetts General Hospital assigned a social worker (Edith Burleigh) to its neurological clinic. Burleigh served as a liaison between the hospital and the community, supporting treatment plans developed by the psychiatrist. Her work became a model for other hospitals, which began hiring social workers to assist in the care of people with mental illness. Within most mental asylums a rigid hierarchy prevailed in which psychiatrists enjoyed the highest status and the greatest decision-making authority. Second in status and authority were psychologists, with social workers a distant third.

The expansion of asylums for people with mental illness peaked in 1955, when they housed more than half a million Americans. Ironically, this growth destroyed the very feature that inspired it: the promise of a cure for insanity.

Moral therapy and similar approaches were costly and could not be sustained in overpopulated, underfunded institutions. The gap between the reality of life in asylums and the promise of effective treatment widened, even as institutional populations grew. Cures were not unheard of, but over time, intractable cases of chronic mental illness came to dominate the asylum population.

Thus began a vicious spiral. The growing proportion of chronically mentally ill living in institutions belied the promise that the environment could be used to effect a cure. Without that promise, patients with transient or acute problems did not seek treatment in the institutions. This increased the proportion of intractable cases, which included senile elderly patients as well as victims of syphilis. The asylum became a place of despair—a last resort for those with no other options.

Commitment as Incarceration

Even as Dorothea Dix was advocating for expansion of institutions, others argued that involuntary commitment of mental patients was incarceration without due process. The case of Elizabeth Packard provided a vivid example. As Gerald Grob tells it,

> Packard had been stricken at the age of nineteen with "brain fever" and spent six weeks . . . at the Worcester hospital in 1835. Four years later she married Theophilus Packard, a Protestant minister who was nineteen years her senior. An unhappy marriage was exacerbated by sharp religious differences. Elizabeth Packard adhered to a liberal theology, while her husband was a devout Calvinist who accepted the total depravity of humanity. When Packard refused to play the role of an obedient wife and expressed religious ideas bordering on mysticism, her husband had her committed in 1860 to the Illinois State Hospital for the Insane . . . where she remained for three years. After being released, she was confined by her husband in a locked room . . . a friend secured a writ of habeas corpus. In a trial that received national publicity, Packard was declared sane. She then spent nearly two decades campaigning for the passage of personal liberty laws that would protect individuals and particularly married women from wrongful commitment. (1994, p. 84)

Elizabeth Packard was instrumental in establishing the National Association for the Protection of the Insane and Prevention of Insanity in 1880. On behalf of people with mental illness, this group advocated stricter standards for involuntary commitment and protection of patients' rights within institutional settings. In 1908, Clifford W. Beers wrote *A Mind That Found Itself,* documenting the indignities of institutional life and fueling the mental hygiene movement.

Preventing Mental Illness: The Mental Hygiene Movement

Enthusiasm for "mental hygiene" flourished as the promise of the asylum faded. The mental hygiene movement treated mental illness as a problem of social and/or personal adjustment. Its rationale was similar to that of the public health movement of the same era, and its proponents shared comparable zeal. They felt that improvements in family life and social conditions would prevent the minor mental disturbances that, left untreated, could develop into incurable mental disorders (Richardson, 1989; Rose, 1996).

The National Committee for Mental Hygiene was founded in 1909 to foster the prevention of mental disorders, arguing that prevention is both easier and less expensive than treatment. Leading philanthropic agencies such as the Rockefeller Foundation contributed to efforts to find the causes of mental illness. Childhood problems came to the fore, and the mental hygiene movement began to focus on promoting healthy child-rearing practices. By 1930, the precepts of mental hygiene were widely accepted. That year's White House Conference on Child Health and Protection declared childhood "the golden period for mental hygiene" (Richardson, 1989, p. 107).

Truancy and delinquency were seen as precursors of mental illness, and participants in the mental hygiene movement soon came to see the classroom as an ideal setting for preventive psychiatric work. Visiting teachers and psychiatric social workers served as on-site trainers and demonstrators in the public schools, "educating teaching staff into a different attitude toward children" (Richardson, 1989, p. 89). With funding from the Commonwealth Fund, child guidance clinics were established in eight U.S. cities to apply the principles of mental hygiene to the problems of childhood.

The most successful child guidance clinic funded by the Commonwealth Fund was in Los Angeles. Its focus was not on referrals from the courts or schools but on children brought in by their parents or other relatives for adjustment problems. Children with mental retardation and established mental illness were referred elsewhere. Based on the popularity of the clinic, the state of California attempted to set up a statewide mental hygiene service (Richardson, 1989).

As mental health moved out of the asylum, the roles of mental health professionals changed. The field of community psychiatry was born, bringing psychiatrists out of mental institutions and into schools, courts, and even private homes. In child guidance and community education programs, social workers enjoyed higher status than they had been accorded in the rigid hierarchy of mental institutions.

The mental hygiene movement promoted the idea that childhood experiences were relevant to public policy because they contributed to mental illness in adulthood. Unfortunately, little research had been conducted on the precursors of mental illness. As a result, much of the work done by mental hygiene proponents, such as the campaign to reduce "bad mental habits," had a propaganda-like feel. Popular wisdom was promoted as the solution to complex psychiatric problems. As the idea of heredity surfaced as a popular explanation for insanity, proponents of mental hygiene became advocates for "eugenic" policies such as sterilization of people with mental illness.

The basic premise of the eugenics movement was that human characteristics and behavior were determined by genetics. So sterilization was seen as the ultimate means of preventing mental illness. Indiana passed the first law requiring sterilization of people with mental illness. Many states followed suit, and by

World War II, 30 had passed similar legislation. California was particularly active in pursuing this policy. Between 1907 and 1940, 18,500 mental patients were sterilized, half of them in the Golden State (Grob, 1994).

Mental Health Treatments During the Depression and World War II

The period from 1929 to 1945 was tumultuous for mental health care in the United States. Resources available for institutional care were decimated by the Depression. But treatment innovations, primarily from Europe, again promised hope of cure. Some of the treatments would strike us as bizarre today. For example, an Austrian psychiatrist, Julius Wagner-Jauregg, observed that mental symptoms sometimes disappeared in patients who had typhoid fever. He drew blood from a soldier with malaria and injected it into several patients. The results were promising, and he received a Nobel Prize in 1927 for this work. Fever therapy, or malaria therapy, became popular in U.S. institutions and generated hope that mental illness could be cured.

This optimism extended to other innovative approaches, such as insulin therapy, lobotomy, and use of electrical shock. The latter became popular, and between 1935 and 1941 more than 75,000 patients received shock therapy. Surgery was less popular. About 18,608 patients underwent psychosurgery between 1936 and 1951 (Grob, 1994). Together, these therapies improved release rates for mental hospitals.

Events during World War II changed the mental health field. The war graphically demonstrated both the extent of mental illness among Americans and the influence of environmental stress. Over 1.75 million inductees were rejected by the military for psychiatric reasons (Grob, 1994). Despite this screening, many of the men sent into combat developed psychiatric symptoms. Military practitioners treated these men at the front, demonstrating that even extreme cases of what we might now call posttraumatic stress disorder (PTSD) could improve outside an institutional setting.

Federal Involvement in Mental Health

The end of World War II saw variation in the quality of care available through the nation's mental hospitals. In Kansas, the influence of the Menninger Clinic was felt soon after its founding in 1944. The Menninger brothers established an outstanding facility that continues to provide leadership in mental health care. They also advocated for improved care in the state's public institutions.

Residents in other states were less fortunate. An exposé of Oklahoma mental institutions by Mike Gorman, "Oklahoma Attacks Its Snakepits," was published in *Reader's Digest*. It became the basis for a famous novel called *The Snake Pit*, published in 1946 by Mary Jane Ward. This novel was adapted for a popular motion picture that starred Olivia de Havilland.

Together, these media events increased concern for the quality of care in mental hospitals and triggered a call for increased federal involvement in mental health services. The mental hygiene movement had already found a home in the federal government in 1930, when the U.S. Public Health Service created a Division of Mental Hygiene. Near the end of World War II, Robert H. Felix took over leadership of the division. He is widely recognized as the leading force in the 1946 passage of the National Mental Health Act.

The National Mental Health Act of 1946.   The National Mental Health Act had three goals: to support research on psychiatric disorders, to train mental health personnel through fellowships and grants, and to provide grants to the states to establish clinics and demonstration programs. The act also required states to establish a single state agency for planning and administration of federal mental health funds. Under the act, the National Institute of Mental Health (NIMH) was established in 1949 as a branch of the Public Health Service. Robert Felix was its first director. One goal for NIMH leaders was to broaden the scope of mental health services beyond institutions. This community-based approach to treatment was more compatible with a public health approach to mental health. It served as the basis for the community mental health movement, which led to the discharge of thousands of mental patients from public facilities.

The Community Mental Health Movement
and Deinstitutionalization

The idea of alternatives to traditional mental hospitals was not entirely new. In the mid-nineteenth century innovators like John M. Galt had advocated community-based care for the chronically mentally ill. In Illinois a model facility, the Illinois Eastern Hospital for the Insane, later renamed the Kankakee State Hospital, was constructed in 1877 to house the chronically mentally ill. It featured a decentralized plan, with small out-buildings to house patients, and cost about one-third the budget of larger centralized facilities. In 1885, Massachusetts developed a small board and care program for the "harmless insane," and by World War II, eight states had similar programs. They proved less costly than institutional care, and advocates like social worker Edith Stern suggested that the quality of care was better in family-like settings.

In the 1950s, new treatment technologies increased Americans' enthusiasm for community-based care. These included psychotropic drugs that promised to control some of the most problematic symptoms of mental illness. One such drug was chlorpromazine, marketed as Thorazine, which helped control the symptoms of schizophrenia. It was followed by tranquilizers and antidepressants.

Psychotherapies were also developed during this period. The effectiveness of psychotherapies in combat situations set the stage for their eventual acceptance by the mental health community. Despite initial skepticism, community-based approaches grew in popularity, and with them the idea that treatment of mental illness could be effected outside an institutional setting.

These changes set the stage for state legislation in support of community-based care. In New York, the Community Mental Health Services Act was passed in 1954 to provide state reimbursement of local mental health expenses. In 1957 California passed the Short-Doyle Act, designed to increase community services by providing a state–local match.

The Kennedy administration advanced a federal plan for community mental health services. The first step in this plan was the 1961 release of the report of the Joint Commission on Mental Illness and Health. This report outlined the results of an extensive study of mental illness and its treatment. It offered the administration an Action for Mental Health program that was both ambitious and expensive. The program would involve the federal government in diverse phases of mental health treatment, from prevention through aftercare.

Kennedy established a task force on mental health under NIMH leadership. This group advanced the concept of a comprehensive mental health center in each community that would provide a range of services and would eliminate the need for mental institutions. The administration embraced this notion and held that the role of the federal government was not to operate the centers but to stimulate their establishment. Toward that end, the Mental Retardation and Community Mental Health Center Construction Act of 1963 provided a three-year authorization of $150 million for the construction of community mental health centers (CMHCs).

Americans were as enthusiastic about the construction of CMHCs as they had been about the establishment of mental hospitals. President Kennedy gave a special message to Congress describing this "bold new approach" to the treatment of mental health and mental retardation. There was evidence that self-help models, such as those demonstrated by Fountain House in New York and Thresholds in Chicago (Beard, Propst, & Malamud, 1982) might help meet the needs of former mental patients. There was great hope that people with mental illness would be integrated into a welcoming community, with supportive services at hand. Two factors militated against the realization of this dream: the limited funding available for CMHCs and the very nature of serious mental illness.

During the 1960s and 1970s, the nation's fiscal resources were increasingly committed to the Vietnam War (Harrington, 1984). Only limited federal funding was available to construct CMHCs. Instead of the planned 2,000 centers, by 1980 only 754 were in place. Further, those CMHCs that were established did not effectively serve individuals with "severe and persistent mental illness" (SPMI). The centers were outpatient treatment centers, not residential facilities. They were based on the premise that patients would live independently in the community, perhaps with family members. But many patients with SPMI did not have families to receive them. Family members were either unable or unwilling to cope with the challenges presented by their illnesses.

Nonetheless, the number of people living in public mental hospitals began to drop. In part, this reduction occurred because the 1965 passage of Medicaid created a reimbursement mechanism for the elderly to live in nursing homes. Many elders were simply transferred from state mental hospitals into nursing homes (Morrissey & Goldman, 1986; Roberts & Kurtz, 1987). During the 1960s the number of Americans living in nursing homes nearly doubled, from 470,000 to nearly 928,000.

The 1974 establishment of SSI as a federal entitlement provided further rationale for releasing mental patients into the community. It was believed that this federal safety net would provide the financial resources necessary for people with mental illness to live independently. But the 1980 disability amendments changed the definition of disability for SSI eligibility and called for a review of SSI recipients every three years. Those who were disabled by virtue of mental illness were especially hard hit. Although they represented 11 percent of SSI recipients, they constituted 30 percent of those deemed ineligible for the program after these reviews (Grob, 1994).

Later presidents did not share Kennedy's enthusiasm for expanding the federal role in mental health. Johnson's Great Society emphasized poverty and related ills. Nixon opposed the use of federal funds to establish CMHCs, and he unsuccessfully attempted to terminate the program. The Carter administration formulated the Mental Health Systems Act to create a framework for service delivery, but was unable to achieve full funding of mental health services. Reagan converted mental health and substance abuse programs into a block grant that was subsequently eliminated.

During the 1960s and 1970s, patients' rights advocates raised the argument that involuntary commitment to a mental facility was incarceration without due process. Involuntary commitment procedures were successfully challenged in federal and state courts. These decades saw several landmark events restricting involuntary commitment. In 1969, California passed the Lanterman–Petris–Short Act to discourage commitment and lengthy confinement. The 1972 *Lessard* decision (*Lessard v. Schmidt*) in Wisconsin established the due process rights of patients faced with commitment. Similar to the rights of individuals faced with criminal incarceration, they included the right to timely notice of charges, notice of right to a jury trial, aid of counsel, protection against self-incrimination, and use of an evidentiary standard "beyond a reasonable doubt." One of the most well-known cases resulted in the *Wyatt v. Stickney* decision, which in 1972 established patients' right to be treated in the "least restrictive setting" (Roberts & Kurtz, 1987).

Several advocacy groups, such as the National Mental Health Association, the National Alliance of Mental Patients, the Network Against Psychiatric Assault, and the Coalition to Stop Institutional Violence, emerged to support the civil rights of mental patients. One of the most enduring, the National Alliance on Mental Illness, was established in 1979 to advocate for patients' rights and reduce the stigma associated with mental illness.

Pressures to reduce public funding of mental hospitals, optimism about community treatment, and public aversion to incarcerating mental patients against their will converged in a movement to "deinstitutionalize" mental patients. Deinstitutionalization involved moving severely mentally ill patients out of public mental hospitals and then closing all or part of the hospitals. It has been termed "one of the largest social experiments in American history" (Torrey, 1997, p. 8). In 1955, the peak year for hospitalization of people with mental illness, 558,239 patients lived in the nation's psychiatric hospitals. By 1994 there were only 71,619 patients in public mental hospitals.

While the nation was transferring patients out of public mental hospitals, private psychiatric facilities were flourishing, as were the psychiatric wards of general hospitals. As David Mechanic (1999) noted, "Between 1970 and 1992, the number of nonfederal general hospitals with separate psychiatric services increased from 797 to 1,616" (p. 130). The growth of private facilities during this period was also dramatic. By 1992, these private facilities reported more than 1.7 million discharges for short stays (Graves, 1995). Private psychiatric facilities remain a growth industry, catering to patients with insurance coverage and organizing their services to optimize profits. The care they provide typically involves short stays, and their patients are more likely to have affective disorders such as depression. Public hospitals, by contrast, serve patients who need long-term care, including those with psychotic disorders, such as schizophrenia, and addiction disorders.

Clearly, deinstitutionalization did not represent a wholesale rejection of institutional treatment for mental illness. Low-income patients with intractable problems were released from hospitals, while those with private insurance and short-term difficulties had access to private institutional care. Indeed, some have argued that deinstitutionalization would be more accurately termed "transinstitutionalization," because it involved the transfer of people with chronic mental illness from public mental hospitals to nursing homes and criminal justice facilities (Torrey, 1997).

Mentally Ill Offenders in the Criminal Justice System

In a trend some refer to as the "criminalization" of mental illness, growing numbers of the mentally ill find themselves in U.S. jails and prisons. People with mental illness are overrepresented in prison populations, with a prevalence of mental illness estimated at four to five times that in the general population (Hartwell, 2003; Kupers, 1999). The U.S. Department of Justice reported in 2006 that over half of prison and jail inmates suffered from mental illness, with female inmates experiencing higher rates of mental health problems than males (U.S. Department of Justice, 2006b). In 2007, Fisher and Drake pointed out "the startling reality that more individuals with mental illness are now committed to jails and prisons than are admitted to psychiatric facilities" (p. 545).

A 2002 report by The Sentencing Project suggested that prisons had replaced psychiatric hospitals as institutions for the mentally ill, noting that jails and prisons housed more than 283,000 mentally ill inmates in 1999, and in 2002 public psychiatric hospitals had only 70,000 patients. Observing the growing number of inmates with mental illness, The Project report noted that Los Angeles County Jail, "reputed to be the largest *de facto* mental institution in the United States, holds an estimated 3,300 seriously mentally ill inmates on any given night" (p. 3).

BOX 7.1   The Insanity Defense

In 1981, John W. Hinckley Jr. attempted to assassinate U.S. president Ronald Reagan. Hinckley's attorneys entered a "not guilty by reason of insanity" plea, and proceeded to successfully demonstrate that Hinckley had biological and behavioral symptoms of schizophrenia. Hinckley would spend his life in a psychiatric facility rather than face prison. The *Hinckley* decision set the stage for the 1984 Comprehensive Crime Control Act, which requires defendants to prove by "clear and convincing" evidence that they are unable to "appreciate the nature and quality or the wrongfulness of the act." This legislation included the Insanity Defense Reform Act, which set out sentencing provisions for offenders suffering from mental illness.

People with mental illness do poorly in prisons. Their behavior can disrupt already tense conditions in these facilities, creating risks and demands that affect other prisoners as well as staff. Prison conditions are likely to exacerbate behavioral and affective symptoms of mental illness. A purely pragmatic outlook might conclude that mentally ill offenders should be diverted out of the criminal justice system.

As part of a trend known as "therapeutic jurisprudence" (Wexler & Winnick, 1996), diversion programs have been established to accomplish this goal. People with mental illness may be diverted at any point, from the "prebooking" stage (prior to formal charges), to "postbooking" interventions that attempt to prevent or reduce jail time. Most programs in the United States are postbooking diversions. Diversion is the focus of 2000 legislation called America's Law Enforcement and Mental Health Project Act. This act provided statutory authority for the establishment of Mental Health Courts (modeled on the successful "drug courts") to divert nonviolent offenders with mental illness out of the criminal justice system and into appropriate treatment. As of 2006, 38 states had established mental health courts (Erickson, Campbell, & Lamberti, 2006). Despite their popularity, there is no clear evidence that diversion programs improve outcomes for mentally ill offenders (Cowell, Broner, & Dupont, 2004; Lamb, Weinberger, & Reston-Parham, 1996; Steadman, Barbera, & Dennis, 1994; Torrey, 1997).

MENTAL ILLNESS IN THE UNITED STATES TODAY

As we saw in the last section, several threads run through the history of mental health interventions in the United States. The first is a tension between the goals of the mental hygiene movement (prevention and health promotion) and the needs of people with serious mental illness. This thread runs through the social work profession because many are attracted to practices and activities that promote mental health. Some, like Specht and Courtney (1994), argue that this attraction drains resources from programs that serve people with major psychiatric disorders. A second thread is the debate over the proper use of institutional or mandatory treatments for people with mental illness. Some argue that the use of these approaches should be minimized because they infringe on the civil rights of patients. Others note the vulnerability of (and sometimes the threat posed by) mental patients, and suggest that the public need for safety has priority over individual freedom. In this section we will assess the realities of mental illness in the United States today.

Like physical disorders, mental illnesses are not randomly distributed throughout the population. Cultural, social, and economic conditions influence a person's risk of mental illness. In the following sections we will look at the distribution of mental illness in the United States, exploring the association between mental illness, homelessness, and violence. We will survey the financing of mental health services and examine access to treatment. We will then examine policies affecting social workers in the mental health system, focusing on licensure and the duty to warn. We will conclude with three emerging policy issues: involuntary commitment, mandatory outpatient treatment, and insurance parity.

The Prevalence of Mental Illness

Two major national studies have been conducted under the auspices of the NIMH to determine the prevalence of mental illness among Americans. The first was completed in the early 1980s. Called the Epidemiological Catchment Areas (ECA) study, it examined lifetime prevalence of major disorders in five communities: Los Angeles, California; New Haven, Connecticut; Baltimore, Maryland; St. Louis, Missouri; and Durham, North Carolina. While not strictly representative of the U.S. population, the sample numbered 20,000 and represented more than 1.6 million people living in these communities. The ECA study used a diagnostic interview schedule based on the *DSM-III* to examine a wide range of disorders (see Robins & Regier, 1991).

The second prevalence study, conducted by the NIMH in the mid-1990s, was called the National Comorbidity Study (NCS). This study surveyed more than 8,000 people, aged 15 to 55, in a widely dispersed sample designed to be representative of the U.S. population. Interviewers used a revised version of the instrument developed for the ECA study (see Kessler et al., 1994).

Results from the NCS suggested that mental illness is a common experience among Americans. Nearly half of the sample (49.7 percent) reported having had at least one psychiatric disorder in their lives, and almost a third (30.9 percent) had experienced at least one disorder in the 12 months prior to the interview (Kessler & Zhao, 1999).

Results also suggested that the most common psychiatric disorders among Americans were major depression and alcohol dependence. One in 10 respondents reported an episode of depression in the 12 months prior to the interview, and 17 percent reported a bout of depression at some time during their lives. Similarly, 7 percent of the sample reported alcohol dependence in the 12 months prior to the interview, and 14 percent reported a history of alcohol dependence. When addictive disorders were combined, they were more common than depression, with one fourth of the sample reporting at least one addictive disorder during their lives. Similar results were obtained when all the anxiety disorders were combined. Nearly one in five respondents (19.3 percent) reported having had an anxiety disorder in the 12 months prior to the interview. Other diagnoses, such as antisocial personality disorders (2.8 percent) and schizophrenia (0.5 percent), were less common (Kessler & Zhao, 1999).

Comorbidity (the presence of more than one psychiatric disorder) is a significant concern for mental health practice and policy. As Kessler and Zhao (1999) noted, "Although a history of some psychiatric disorder is quite common among persons 15 to 54 in the United States, the major burden of psychiatric disorder in this age segment of our society is concentrated in a group of highly comorbid people who constitute about one sixth of the population" (p. 67). These individuals reported having had three or more severe psychiatric disorders. A typical pattern of comorbidity involved a combination of addiction with one or more other disorders.

Social Class and Mental Illness

From a social justice perspective, the distribution of mental illness among the population is of interest for two reasons. First, mental illness might be a symptom or result of social or economic disadvantage. Second, access to treatment (as a benefit of group membership) may be distributed on the basis of advantage rather than need.

There is strong evidence of an association between mental illness and social class. The first epidemiological study documenting this association was conducted in 1934 at Johns Hopkins University. Researchers examined agency and hospital records to identify individuals with symptoms of mental illness. They concluded that there was an "unmistakable association between personality problems and low economic status, with the lowest income groups having about six times the number of problems as the highest income groups" (cited in Perry, 1996, p. 19). Their results were replicated in a series of studies across the country.

More recent studies have also documented the association between social class and mental illness. These include both the ECA study and the NCS described earlier. Both suggest that low socioeconomic status (SES) is associated with increased risk of mental illness in general, and with increased risk of depression, alcohol dependence, and schizophrenia in particular (Holzer et al., 1986; Muntaner et al., 1998). Other studies have consistently reported higher rates of depression, schizophrenia, addiction, and other disorders among low-income populations (Dohrenwend, 1990; Eaton, 1985; Kessler et al., 1994; Robins et al., 1984).

Although the association between social and economic disadvantage and mental illness is well established, the underlying causal mechanism is under dispute. It is difficult to establish whether the stresses associated with low SES cause mental illness (the "social causation" argument) or the disabilities associated with mental illness cause a person to move down the SES ladder (the "natural selection" argument).

Many studies have documented the deleterious effects of economic, personal, and social stress on mental health. In 1973, Harvey Brenner published a famous study of the relationship between employment rates and mental hospitalization. He compared hospitalization rates for new cases of psychosis with employment rates in New York from 1910 to 1960 and found an inverse relationship. When the employment rate went down, admissions to treatment, especially among men, went up. When economic times improved, hospitalization rates declined. Of course it is not clear that the economic downturns actually caused mental illness. The economic stress may have simply exacerbated underlying conditions, overwhelming individuals' coping abilities. Nonetheless, the study did suggest an association between mental illness and economic conditions. Likewise, several studies have documented the adverse mental health consequences of unemployment (for example, Gray, 1985; Osipow & Fitzgerald, 1993).

More recent studies have also identified higher prevalence of mental illness in economically distressed populations. For example, Rand Conger conducted a series of studies of farm families in Iowa during the farm crisis of the 1980s. His results demonstrated a strong association between economic distress and psychiatric illnesses (Conger et al., 1994).

Homelessness and Mental Illness

The homeless mentally ill have become fixtures of America's urban landscape. They shuffle along city sidewalks, cutting a wide swath as they talk and gesture to companions who are invisible to others. Attempts to estimate the proportion of mentally ill among the homeless have generated remarkably similar results, leading a 1990 Task Force of the American Psychiatric Association to conclude that the prevalence of severe and persistent mental illness among homeless people "ranges from 28 percent to 37 percent" (American Psychiatric Association, 1990). When alcohol and drug addictions are included, the proportion jumps to 75 percent or more (Torrey, 1997). If anything, these estimates are probably low, as people with mental illness are likely to refuse to be interviewed for surveys of this kind.

Homelessness, in itself, exposes people to an increased risk of victimization. The homeless who are mentally ill are especially vulnerable. Few studies have systematically documented the increased risk that mental illness brings to the homeless, yet common sense suggests that impaired thinking would undermine survival skills. Indeed, every major city in the United States has a horror story to offer (see Kates, 1985). Freezing to death in the winter is, as Torrey observed, "all too common" among homeless persons who are mentally ill (1997, p. 19). Torrey links the increased incidence of homelessness among mentally ill persons directly to the deinstitutionalization movement, arguing that laws regarding civil commitment have become irresponsibly restrictive.

Violence and Mental Illness

Are people with mental illness more prone to committing violent acts than the general population? Perhaps the most definitive source of answers to this question is the ECA study mentioned earlier. The survey included questions about violent acts, such as hitting or throwing things at someone, causing bruises or injury, fighting, and using a weapon. Individuals with severe mental illness were compared with those with no mental illness on these measures of violent behavior. Results suggested that people with a severe mental illness were more likely than people with no mental disorder to commit all of the violent behaviors examined. People suffering from schizophrenia were especially likely to have committed a violent act (Swanson et al., 1990). Similar results have been reported in numerous studies (Hodgins, 1992; Link, Andrews, & Cullen, 1992; Straznickas, McNeil, & Binder, 1993), including a survey of family members conducted by the National Alliance on Mental Illness (see Steinwachs, Kasper, & Skinner, 1992).

Media coverage of violent crimes committed by individuals suffering from severe psychiatric disorders supports the general perception that people with mental illness are dangerous. In some communities acts of violence by individuals suffering from mental illness have triggered calls to forbid anyone with a mental diagnosis to purchase a gun. As advocates for people with mental illness have pointed out, such measures unduly penalize Americans with mental illness. As in the general population, mentally ill persons who commit violent acts constitute a small minority.

Among people with mental illness, as in the general population, excessive use of drugs and alcohol substantially increases the risk of violence (Link et al., 1992; Marzuk, 1996; Monahan, 1992). Those who commit violent acts usually fail to comply with their medication regimens (Torrey, 1997). Indeed, the most common scenario found in media coverage involves an individual suffering from active psychotic symptoms who is not receiving treatment. Thus, the violent act may be as much a result of limited treatment access as it is a consequence of mental illness *per se.*

The "De Facto" Mental Health Service System

A variety of mental health services and treatments is available in the United States. Together, they make up what some refer to as the "de facto mental health service system" (Regier et al., 1993; Surgeon General, 1999). The system has four components: the specialty mental health sector, the general medical/primary care sector, the human services sector, and the voluntary support network sector.

The specialty mental health sector is staffed by mental health professionals, such as psychiatrists, psychologists, psychiatric social workers, and psychiatric nurses. The bulk of services are provided in outpatient settings, with inpatient care delivered in special psychiatric units in general hospitals. Private psychiatric hospitals and residential treatment centers also provide care for troubled children and adolescents. Public-sector facilities include state and county mental hospitals as well as CMHCs. Just under 6 percent of adults and about 8 percent of children and adolescents use specialty mental health services in a year (Surgeon General, 1999).

Although it is not primarily designed to meet mental health needs, the general medical/primary care sector is an important component of the service delivery system. In 1999, the U.S. surgeon general reported that more than 6 percent of the adult population used this sector for mental health care. The general medical sector often serves as an initial point of contact for adults with mental illness, and for some it is the only source of mental health services.

The human services sector consists of social services, rehabilitation facilities, school-based counseling, prison-based services, and religious counselors. This sector is the primary source of mental health services for children, serving up to 19 percent of children. Adults are less likely to use human services for mental health treatment. The NCS revealed that 5 percent of adults had accessed this sector.

The voluntary support network includes self-help groups and peer counselors. The 12-step program offered by Alcoholics Anonymous is an example of this type of service. The surgeon general reported that this is a rapidly growing segment of the nation's mental health system. Nonetheless, it reaches few of those afflicted with mental illness. According to the ECA study, about 3 percent of U.S. adults used self-help groups in the early 1990s (Surgeon General, 1999).

In any given year, about 15 percent of the adult population and 21 percent of children receive mental health services through one or more of these sectors (Surgeon General, 1999). But many of those afflicted by mental illness do not receive treatment at all. In 1995, the National Advisory Mental Health Council estimated that of the 5.6 million Americans with severe mental illness, approximately 60 percent received treatment in any given year. That left roughly 2.2 million individuals with severe mental illness who did not receive treatment (Torrey, 1997). Fragmented mechanisms for financing mental health care leave many Americans without access to treatment.

Financing Mental Health Care.   In the United States, mental health care is financed through diverse public and private sources. In 2003, approximately $73.4 billion was spent for the treatment of mental illness and addiction. This amount represented about 6 percent of total health spending. Just over half (53 percent) of mental health expenditures came from public sources, primarily state and local governments. The remainder was paid by private insurance firms and individuals (Mark et al., 2007).

Public expenditures for mental health services have generally increased at a rate comparable to those for treatment of physical illness, with federal sources assuming a larger share of these costs, while the burden borne by state and local authorities has dropped. This trend reflects the rising importance of Medicare and Medicaid in financing mental health care. In 2003 Medicaid accounted for about 26 percent of mental health expenditures (Mark et al., 2007). Several new initiatives have also expanded the federal role in financing mental health care. These include the Community Mental Health Block Grant, Community Support Programs, the PATH program for the homeless mentally ill, and the Comprehensive Community Mental Health Services for Children and Their Families program (U.S. GAO, 2000). The role of private insurance in financing mental health care has diminished slightly, which may have inspired legislative

---

A HUMAN PERSPECTIVE   Advocacy: Restoring Care for People with Mental Illness

Contributed by Theresa L. Blakley, Union University, Jackson, Tennessee, and Emily Ann Hill, BSW, Union University Alumna

In 2006, when Tennessee cut 26,000 people with mental illness from its TennCare (Medicaid) program, Emily Hill and her fellow BSW students at Union University were outraged. As they investigated the situation their sense of injustice grew. Recipients who had both mental and physical illness were retained on the program but were limited to five prescription medications, forcing awful choices about whether to treat physical conditions such as diabetes or to purchase medication for the management of severe mental illness. Use of psychiatric emergency services spiked. Stories began to accumulate, like that of a man who was cut from TennCare and went into a manic episode. He drove a car into a building and died from severe head trauma. The police thought he must have been drunk, but instead he was suffering from the abrupt withdrawal of his psychotropic medications.

Vowing that they would "sleep when it's over," Emily and her classmates began an advocacy intervention with the support and direction of their social policy instructor, Dr. Theresa Blakley. Since their efforts focused on educating legislators, one of the challenges they faced was, as Emily explained, "translating student outrage into language legislators could understand." Another challenge was mastering the legislative process and learning to read complex legislation. The BSW students joined forces with established stakeholders in Tennessee's advocacy community, such as the AARP, NAMI, and business interests, and became part of an extensive lobbying campaign to reform the TennCare program.

Two important legislative changes resulted from their combined efforts. First, a joint resolution passed that called for a fiscal study of the program. Advocates were convinced that the study would reveal that TennCare cuts were ultimately more expensive than leaving the program's funding levels intact. The second result was passage of a bill promoted by the AARP that softened the five-prescription limit. Another important result was the lessons learned. Emily and her classmates came to understand the power of social work in influencing policy through establishing coalitions, lobbying with informed passion, and building respectful relationships with legislators.

---

efforts to mandate mental health coverage known as "parity" legislation (U.S. GAO, 2000). These initiatives are discussed below.

Medicaid has been described as "the single largest and most important medical program affecting persons with severe and persistent mental illness" (Mechanic, 1999, p. 194). The mental health services financed under Medicaid vary from state to state, with differences in both coverage and expenditures per Medicaid recipient. Expanded use of Medicaid waivers and increased state-level control of the program tend to exacerbate regional disparities in service access.

Access to Treatment.   Access to mental health treatment is clearly a social justice issue. Apart from the uneven availability of services already described, both income and race have consistently emerged as significant predictors of access. Individuals who have private insurance coverage for mental health care are more likely than those without coverage to receive treatment for a wide array of diagnoses. Moreover, people of color are less likely to receive treatment than members of the cultural majority.

For years, the racial disparity in service access has been explained by hypothesizing that minorities experience less mental illness. Recent studies (see Zhang & Snowden, 1999) have refuted this claim. Although people of color experience mental illness differently, their overall prevalence of mental illness is comparable. Underutilization may reflect a lack of people of color among mental health professionals, which results in language and cultural barriers to utilization. It may also reflect widespread economic disparities.

Managed Care and Mental Health Services.   Managed care has become a vehicle for controlling the cost of mental health services, and has been applied both to private insurance coverage and to Medicaid. Medicaid recipients in most states are required to enroll with managed care providers, but states vary in their treatment of mental illness under managed care.

Two managed-care approaches have been applied to treatment of mental illness: "carve out" and "capitation." Under a carve-out strategy, mental health services are treated separately from medical services. Either the health maintenance organization (HMO) or the state Medicaid authority contracts with local treatment providers for mental health care and substance abuse treatment in an approach known as Managed Behavioral Health Care (MBHC). State experiences with MBHC have varied, with some states such as Massachusetts showing cost reductions, improved access, and treatment innovations, while others, such as Tennessee, have experienced major implementation problems (National Conference of State Legislatures, 2007).

Under capitation, the managed care provider receives a fixed amount per year for each Medicaid enrollee with diagnosed mental illness. Capitation of mental health services is complicated by the unpredictable trajectory and complex treatment requirements of mental illness. Several studies of the impact of capitation have demonstrated cost savings; however, the impact on client outcomes seems to be mixed (Cuffel et al., 2002).

Social Workers in the Mental Health System

Throughout the twentieth century, social workers played an important role in the nation's mental health system, even as mental health practitioners constituted a growing proportion of social workers. Social work professionals were involved in most aspects of the service delivery system, from institutional treatment to community care. Indeed, in the 1990s the NIMH noted that social workers provided the lion's share of mental health care in the United States. This led to several initiatives that increased NIMH spending on the development of social work infrastructure in mental health (National Advisory Mental Health Council, 1991). Two policies have had a direct impact on social workers in mental health practice: licensing and the duty to warn.

Licensing.   Licensing of mental health professionals has had a significant impact on the availability of mental health treatment. Insurance reimbursement is typically available only for services provided by licensed professionals, and in most states a license is required for the use of professional titles such as "counselor" or "social worker." Physicians have generally resisted expanding the licensed activities of other professionals in the mental health field. Similarly, psychologists, social workers, and nurses often compete for the legitimacy afforded through licensing.

Social work licensing procedures vary from state to state. Usually candidates for licensure must demonstrate that they have completed educational and practice requirements, and they must successfully complete an examination. With a license they may practice independently or in agencies that are reimbursed by federal or private insurers. Few states accept licenses issued in other states, and there is no national license for social workers. The National Association of Social Workers (NASW) offers a national credential for clinical social workers known as membership in the Academy of Certified Social Workers (ACSW), but this is not a professional license.

Duty to Warn.   The duty to warn, with its attendant duty to protect, was established by the 1976 *Tarasoff v. Regents of the University of California* decision and subsequent rulings. Mental health practitioners whose patients present a significant threat of violence are required to take whatever steps are reasonably needed to protect the intended victims. Many view this requirement as a threat to confidentiality that can undermine patients' trust. Of course, in most settings, practitioners must inform their patients of this duty. After an exhaustive review of research on the duty to protect, Appelbaum (1994) concluded that "[t]he duty to protect has complicated life for some clinicians, but it may have made life safer for some potential victims; and it has by no means been the disaster some authorities feared" (p. 99).

Emerging Policy Issues

Several policy issues have emerged in the field of mental health care. Three of these are discussed in this section: involuntary commitment of people with mental illness, outpatient commitment for people with mental illness, and insurance parity for mental health care.

Involuntary Commitment.   In America, some people with mental illness have been confined against their will in institutions of various kinds since the nineteenth century. As early as 1806, the State of Virginia passed a law that permitted the involuntary commitment of mental patients. Justification for depriving these people of liberty stems from two sources: the police power of the state and the concept of *parens patriae* (state as parent). Under the latter principle, the state is responsible for the care of those who are unable to care for themselves. Commitment cannot, however, be undertaken lightly. U.S. law views the deprivation of liberty as one of the most serious applications of governmental power. A person who might be deprived of liberty has the right to due process, as outlined in the Fourteenth Amendment to the U.S. Constitution.

The due process rights of people with mental illness were not well established nationally until 1975, when the Supreme Court ruling in *O'Connor v. Donaldson* clarified the conditions under which a state might commit someone for psychiatric care. The court found that "a State cannot constitutionally confine . . . a non-dangerous individual who is capable of surviving safely in freedom by himself or with the help of willing and responsible family members or friends" (Stavis, 1995). This decision has been widely taken to establish dangerousness (imminent danger to self or others) as a standard for involuntary commitment. This strict standard has come under scrutiny lately as public concern for the untreated mentally ill has risen.

The National Alliance on Mental Illness (NAMI) and others have argued that this standard is too strict, preventing the state from protecting people with mental illness under the principle of *parens patriae* (see Torrey, 1997). NAMI has suggested that civil commitment should be used in the case of people who are "gravely disabled," regardless of their dangerousness (Stavis, 1995).

Mandatory Outpatient Treatment. While civil commitment uses state coercion to compel those with mental illness to accept inpatient treatment, several measures have been established to compel or encourage people with mental illness to follow with outpatient treatment regimens.

The use of involuntary outpatient commitment (IOC), or court-ordered treatment, has also been endorsed by NAMI. IOC procedures have been established in nearly all states, with North Carolina as the pioneer (Swartz & Swanson, 2004). Under IOC, a court orders a patient to comply with a specific outpatient treatment program. Thus, for example, a patient might be required to take medications and to participate in regular outpatient therapy. Proponents argue that IOC improves the quality of life for mental patients, protects the community from patients who fail to comply with their medication regimen, and reduces the amount of time patients spend in mental hospitals. Opponents note that IOC deprives patients of the right to refuse treatment, requires excessive state intrusion, and is subject to abuse.

National surveys of IOC suggest that its effectiveness varies. Perhaps the most significant barrier to successful implementation has been the reluctance of community mental health centers to assume responsibility for IOC patients, particularly those who are noncompliant (Torrey & Kaplan, 1995). Difficulties also stem from failure to specify what happens to patients who do not cooperate with their treatment plan, as well as concerns about liability and cost (Mechanic, 1999).

Conditional release and conservatorship/guardianship have also been used to encourage treatment compliance. Under conditional release programs, patients' release from mental hospitals is based on compliance with an outpatient treatment regimen. Unlike IOC, conditional release is administered by the hospital superintendent rather than the court. Conservatorship and guardianship are widely used in California (Torrey & Kaplan, 1995). Under these procedures, a third party is appointed by the court. As conservator or guardian this person can then legally compel the patient to comply with a treatment program or involuntarily commit the patient for institutional care.

Insurance Parity. Until the 1970s, most insurance companies covered mental illness on a par with physical illness. Over time, companies found that their mental health costs were rising nearly twice as fast as their health-care expenses. Mental health treatment looked like a "bottomless pit," with unreliable diagnosis and potentially unlimited demand. Insurers began to reduce both the number of psychiatric visits covered and the amount paid for the visits, and to establish "lifetime caps" on mental health care. By 1993, only 2 percent of private insurers offered parity for outpatient mental health treatment, and 20 percent offered parity for inpatient care (LaBruzza & Mendez-Villarrubia, 1994).

Private insurance coverage of mental health treatment is complicated by the difficulty of determining what constitutes "medical necessity." With respect to mental illness, medical necessity is hard to define. Is it medically necessary to provide psychotherapy to someone in the throes of divorce? What if the person suffers from schizophrenia? This problem is complicated by the unpredictability of mental illness. Some patients may recover spontaneously without any treatment, while a lack of treatment may produce tragic results in others.

Another complication in the parity debate is called the "moral hazard" problem. The term "moral hazard" refers to a tendency for consumers to over-utilize mental health services if they are covered by insurance. This concept has been applied to physical illness, but it has been a more significant concern for mental disorders. The argument here is that psychotherapy can be personally fulfilling and may require years of treatment. Insurance companies use co-payments and service limits to control over-utilization.

As private insurers have reduced mental health coverage, families and patients have reported difficulty securing care. NAMI has reported cases of individuals exhausting their lifetime mental health benefits in a single hospital stay. NAMI and others argued that differential coverage of mental health care represents a form of discrimination against people with mental illness. So, with support from professional organizations such as the NASW, NAMI launched a campaign to advocate for insurance parity.

Insurance parity involves the use of government regulation to require insurers to offer the same benefits for mental disorders as they would for physical disorders. Parity applies to annual or lifetime limits, service or dollar maximums, co-payments, and deductibles.

State legislatures took the lead in requiring mental health parity. As early as 1975, New Hampshire was one of the first states to mandate parity for certain diagnoses. By 2006, 42 states had passed some kind of mental health parity legislation. State laws vary in their definition of mental illness, coverage requirements, and exemptions (http://www.ncsl.org/programs/health/shn/2007/sn483c.htm, accessed July 31, 2007).

In 1996 the National Mental Health Parity Act was signed into law. The act represents a small step toward parity, requiring that insurance plans providing a mental health benefit apply equal annual and lifetime limits to mental and physical illnesses. So, for example, private insurers can no longer set a $1 million lifetime limit for cancer patients and a $50,000 lifetime limit for mental illness. The law applies only to businesses with 51 or more employees, so it covers only a small fraction of the U.S. labor force. It does not require that health plans cover or maintain coverage for mental illness. Substance abuse and drug addiction are excluded from the parity requirement. The law does not require parity with respect to visit limits or managed care provisions. It does not apply to insurance plans sold to individuals. Finally, if a company demonstrates that compliance results in an increased cost of at least 1 percent, their plan may be exempted from the parity requirement. Most state laws provide more benefits than the federal statute (NIMH, 2000).

Critics of mental health parity offer several arguments. Some take a libertarian position, arguing that parity requirements represent inappropriate intrusion of government regulation into the private market. More compelling arguments focus on the potential impact of parity on the uninsured. Some argue that by increasing premiums parity will move health insurance out of reach of the working poor. Finally, opponents have argued that parity requirements may lead companies to drop mental health coverage altogether.

SUMMARY: MENTAL HEALTH INTERVENTIONS AND ISSUES

At the beginning of this chapter we met Rachel Sanders and discussed her experiences coping with serious mental illness. We found several factors that contributed to Rachel's success. Her family has the resources and commitment to sustain her. While she has at times lost all of her financial resources, Rachel has always been able to rely on family support. Finally, Rachel has a strong mind, and insight into the nature of her illness and its treatment. Many people with serious mental illnesses are less fortunate. Lacking family, finances, and (at times) insight, they rely on what we have termed the de facto mental health system.

After considering Rachel's life experiences, we examined the challenges of defining mental illness, suggesting that the *DSM-IV* represents "diagnosis by consensus"—our best attempt to derive a working typology of mental illness. We then examined the values and beliefs that influence public reactions to mental illness and public policies for people with mental illness. We traced the development of mental health interventions in the United States, closing with a critical review of the deinstitutionalization of mental patients. In the final section, we examined contemporary realities of mental illness in the United States, including the association between class and mental illness, the financing and organization of mental health services, policy issues affecting social workers in the mental health system, the risks of homelessness and violence, and emerging policy issues.

Mental health policies bring several social justice issues to the fore. The allocation of mental health professionals is clearly a matter of distributive justice. When market forces determine this allocation, those who are most vulnerable may be left to fend for themselves. Clearly American mental health policy must distinguish between the seriously mentally ill (people with schizophrenia, manic–depressive illness, and other brain-related disorders) and the "worried well" (those who suffer from "quality of life" and emotional problems). The former would clearly fall under the rubric of "mental illness," and policies and services for them should be labeled accordingly. The latter are concerned primarily with "mental health." Torrey and others argue that mental health is a private, not a governmental concern, and scarce public resources should be reserved for mental illness.

Need-based allocation rules can be problematic, however. Those who are most in need of care may lack insight into their illness. The tension between the liberty rights of people with mental illness and the public interest in their treatment is manifest in struggles over involuntary commitment. Mental health practitioners and policy makers struggle to sustain a just balance between these competing goals.

The history of mental health interventions in the United States is marked by cycles of reform. The first cycle came with the development of moral treatment and saw the expansion of the mental asylum. The second, marked by a focus on prevention, was the mental hygiene movement. The third cycle, the community mental health movement, resulted in the deinstitutionalization of mental patients. As Morrissey and Goldman (1986) observe, "Each reform began with the promise that early treatment in the new setting would prevent the personal and societal problems associated with long-term mental disability" (p. 11). As each reform failed to fulfill its exaggerated promise, however, public disenchantment increased and Americans became less willing to finance programs for people with mental illness. Today prisons have become de facto psychiatric institutions, housing an estimated quarter of a million people with mental illness. This reality has occasioned a new wave of reform as advocates and criminal justice officials recognize that jails and prisons are inappropriate settings for mentally ill people. Perhaps diversion programs will trigger a new cycle of reform, expanding the nation's diminished community mental health service capacity.

These reform cycles obfuscate a fundamental reality in the field of mental health: the fact that some people cannot survive without institutional care. Without expanded support and financing for mental health programs, these individuals become like flotsam, drifting through the streets of American cities.

KEYWORDS

Community mental
    health movement
Drug abuse
Alcoholism
Mental health advocates

Mental health laws
Mental health policy
Mental health services
Mentally ill

Serious mental illness
Involuntary
    commitment

THINK ABOUT IT

1. Why does the handout of the National Alliance on Mental Illness entitled *Facts about Mental Illness* say that "[d]espite media focus on the exceptions, individuals receiving treatment for schizophrenia are no more prone to violence than the general public"? Is this statement true?

2. What mental health services are available to your state's Medicaid recipients? What is the average expenditure per Medicaid recipient? Is mental health a "carved-out" service in your state?

3. Should insurance companies be required to cover all mental diagnoses, or should parity requirements be restricted to severe diseases with organic components, such as schizophrenia or major depression?

4. What steps could a private or public insurer take to reduce the "moral hazard" problem without denying needed treatment to people with mental illness?

5. Use the social justice perspective presented in Part I to analyze a proposal to provide income supports to people with alcohol or drug addiction.

6. Consider whether mental illness meets the criteria for collective action outlined by Abram de Swaan (see Part II introduction). Do you think improved public understanding of mental illness would change this situation? Why or why not?

WEB-BASED EXERCISE

For a direct link to the site in this exercise, log on to the Student Companion Site for this book at academic.cengage.com/social_work/barusch, and choose Chapter 7.

Go to the website of the David L. Bazelon Center for Mental Health Law at http://www.bazelon.org. What is the current legislative agenda for this advocacy organization? What recent court cases are identified? Select one of these to discuss with your class. Consider subscribing to their e-mail alert system, which provides alerts on policy issues in mental health.

SUGGESTED RESOURCES

Appelbaum, P. S. (1994). *Almost a Revolution: Mental Health Law and the Limits of Change.* New York: Oxford University Press.

Mechanic, D. (1999). *Mental Health and Social Policy: The Emergence of Managed Care.* Boston: Allyn & Bacon.

Torrey, E. F. (1997). *Out of the Shadows: Confronting America's Mental Illness Crisis.* New York: John Wiley & Sons.

www.bazelon.org. This site is maintained by the David L. Bazelon Center for Mental Health Law. It offers advocacy and reports in support of the civil rights of people with mental illness.

www.macarthur.virginia.edu. Maintained by the MacArthur Research Network on Mental Health and the Law, this site is a good source of background information on developments in the area.

www.mentalhealth.org. Maintained by the Center for Mental Health Services (CMHS) in the U.S. Department of Health and Human Services, this site offers government reports and provides links to other mental health sites.

www.nami.org. This site is maintained by the National Alliance on Mental Illness (NAMI), the nation's foremost advocacy group for mentally ill persons and their families. It outlines NAMI positions on emerging issues in the field. The site is a great source for information on upcoming federal legislation.

8

Disability

But the great Master said, "I see
No best in kind, but in degree;
I gave a various gift to each,
To charm, to strengthen, and to teach."
LONGFELLOW, "THE SINGERS," 1849

The human race is distinguished by variety—in appearance, abilities, and desires we are more different than alike. Some of us can do things others only dream of, while some cannot do things that most people take for granted. In this chapter we will focus on public policies that affect people with disabilities. After considering the experiences and insights of Alexis Mondragon, we explore the definition of disability before turning to a brief review of the historic treatment of people with disabilities and the disability rights movement. We then examine contemporary realities, such as the prevalence of disability in the United States and the association between race and disability. We close with a look to the future.

A note on organization: Placement of this chapter was challenging. In the introduction to Part II, I argued that the policy response to risks we all share is development of social insurance, while the response to vulnerable populations is antidiscrimination and protective measures. Disability is a risk we all share (many Americans are "temporarily able"). Yet policies in this area include both policy approaches. As we will see, Disability Insurance is operated along a social insurance model. In contrast, the disability rights movement and the structure of the Americans with Disabilities Act focus on eliminating discrimination. This paradox is one of the distinguishing features of this area of social policy. I chose to place the chapter in Part II to emphasize our common bond in the shared risk of disability.

DEFINING DISABILITY

Strictly speaking, "disability" refers to the absence of ability. Over time, the label "person with disability" has become an accepted way to describe a large and diverse group. As Longmore and Umansky (2001) put it, "Some are blind and some are deaf. Some walk with crutches and some are missing limbs. Some are paralyzed; a few have multiple disabilities" (pp. 3–4). Some were born with a disability, some trace their disability to an accident or illness, and for some the process of aging has brought a loss of abilities. With all this diversity, people with disabilities share a collective identity and the common experiences of vulnerability, exclusion, and discrimination.

Public policy reflects four approaches to defining disability:

- *Medical model.* Under this view, disability represents an impairment that results from loss or abnormality of physiological or anatomical structure or function. The loss or abnormality is generally attributed to an underlying medical condition.

- *Economic model.* From this perspective disability is about lost productivity. A person is disabled to the extent that he or she is unable to work, and the challenge for social policy is to provide income.

- *Functional model.* This model focuses on specific activities, such as walking or talking, and the intervention focus is on physical rehabilitation or adaptation.

- *Ecological model.* Under this view, disability results from the interaction between individuals and their environments. This model calls for equal access to education, housing, services, and employment; and for community integration of people with disabilities.

These definitions operate to various degrees in the public policies that affect the opportunities and resources available to people with disabilities. Of these, by far the most extensive is Social Security Disability Insurance (DI), which was introduced in Chapter 4. For the purposes of DI,

> "Disability" means inability to engage in any substantial gainful activity by reason of any medically determinable physical or mental impairment which can be expected to result in death or which has lasted or can be expected to last for a continuous period of not less than 12 months. An individual shall be determined to be under a disability only if his physical or mental impairment or impairments are of such severity that he is not only unable to do his previous work but cannot, considering his age, education, and work experience, engage in any other kind of substantial gainful work. (Social Security Administration, 1999)

A HUMAN PERSPECTIVE Alexis Mondragon

I met Alexis in the office of the Disabled Rights Action Committee, located at the back of a one-story strip mall. As I walked toward the building, I found my anxiety surfacing. I was afraid of Alexis—afraid of myself really, of doing or saying something that would hurt or offend her, of failing to connect. I'd heard that Alexis was a powerful woman with little patience for social workers. The voice that greeted me as I entered the building could come from no one else. She was giving orders in the tone of someone accustomed to authority.

Alexis is a strong woman. She radiates vitality from her motorized wheelchair. That day she wore a green sweatshirt with a skeleton in a wheelchair and the words, "Not grateful and Not dead yet." It set off her thick white hair beautifully. We shook hands and quickly found space for me to sit in the office foyer.

I was ready for a tear-jerker story, but Alexis gave me laughter. She was born in Pasadena 75 years ago and trained for a career in nursing. She joined the army as a nurse, but caught polio in the early 1950s. The Salk vaccine was available. "It was there, but it wasn't there. Like the flu vaccine." She went to get it when she was pregnant and they were out. Later, she had her baby daughter vaccinated, but there wasn't enough for Alexis. So she made an appointment for the following week. In the interim she caught it. Laughing, Alexis said, "So you see! It was *meant* to be!" Since her husband was in the army, she spent nine months in the local army hospital, where she received good care. Though she was never in an iron lung, her husband told her that one was kept outside the door of her room, just in case.

Alexis's mother-in-law cared for her baby during the following year while she was in rehab. She could have gone to Warm Springs, a hospital founded by FDR for polio patients, but elected to stay. She didn't want to leave her husband. Her therapists had been trained at Warm Springs, and the care she received was outstanding. Alexis built her upper body strength and found the water therapy especially helpful. After rehabilitation, she spent most of her time in a wheelchair.

Alexis returned to nursing, doing triage for two years for a private doctor. Laughing, she said of this period, "I talked to my sister who was alive at the time. She said, 'What do you do?' and I said, 'Oh, I tell people where to go and what to do.' And she said, 'Well, that sounds like something you could do.'"

Alexis's husband stayed in the army. They had two more children, and life went on. In 1961, when he was in his fifties, he was discharged from the army and moved into administrative jobs in the private sector. When his employer "went belly-up," he found it hard to get a new job. Alexis said, "He was over 50 and they would look at him and who cares what the law says."

Alexis went to work as executive director for an advocacy group that focused on poverty issues. She explained that she was attracted to advocacy because she "always had a good sense of justice."

In 1990 Alexis got postpolio syndrome, which has challenged her functioning. She explained that postpolio "takes you back to where you were." She has lost much of her upper body strength. The fibers that relay impulses to her muscles have deteriorated, and rehabilitation is no longer an option. Alexis says about 65 percent of polio patients develop postpolio syndrome. For her it has meant going from a manual wheelchair to the motorized chair—a difficult, but not overwhelming, transition. As she said, "I'm never down for very long." For Alexis the antidote to feeling down is doing what needs to be done. That, and "a husband who makes me laugh."

Advocacy on disability issues has been central in Alexis's life since the mid-1970s. She recalled one of her first actions. The goal was to change policies in the Department of Education. After extensive negotiations an advisory committee was set up. Saying, "Be careful what you ask for," she explained that when representatives with disabilities serve on these committees "they are treated really nice." They get cookies and plaques and are asked their opinions. But since they never get to vote, and they don't change policy, Alexis avoids serving on advisory committees, seeing them as a waste of time. If the advisory committee is not run by people with disabilities, it's "just a token thing . . . all you can do is give advice."

Alexis works closely with American Disabled for Attendant Programs Today (ADAPT) (formerly American Disabled for Accessible Public Transit), a national advocacy group. ADAPT puts on a major action about twice a year, and Alexis has only missed four or five since 1983, during a time when she was caring for her mother. ADAPT puts on demonstrations and, as Alexis puts it, "We tell them what we want. . . . Civil disobedience is where it's at." The actions are great fun—"like a family reunion." And Alexis can cite many examples of policy victories ADAPT has achieved through demonstrations.

Transit is a recurring theme in advocacy for people with disabilities. When President Carter was in office, he issued an executive order calling for lifts on all public buses. The transportation authorities went to court and got an injunction prohibiting enforcement of the order. During the interim, the local busing authority had installed lifts on 23 new buses. When the court order came in, they bolted the lifts in place, making them useless. Responding to advocates' efforts, the busing authority did a test run in a very small community. Lifts were not used, so the authority claimed they were not needed. Tired of serving on committees and being ignored, advocates did a "crawl on." On Main Street they stopped buses, crawled up the steps, went to the next stop, and got off. They passed out leaflets. After two weeks with no results, people from neighboring states were invited to a conference, and at 5:00 P.M. advocates went out and stopped "every bus in the city." The media came, and Alexis had a much-publicized conversation with the transit director in which she said, "Everyone needs lifts on the buses. We don't want to be treated special." And so, she said, "We had the meeting, and the next thing we knew the lifts were ordered even before the ADA went into effect."

Now ADAPT is focusing on the Medicaid in Community Attendant Services and Support Act (MiCASSA) and implementation of the *Olmstead* decision. As we will see in this chapter, these efforts are designed to enable people with disabilities to live in the community, rather than in nursing homes.

Alexis remembers when Newt Gingrich agreed to sponsor the bill. He looked at the name and said, "Oh! My house! I understand that! Living in my house." ("Mi casa" means "my house" in Spanish.) MiCASSA will allow the federal and state money used to keep a person in a nursing home to follow the person into the community, "with no worries about waivers." It would be available to the person for life. This year, Alexis explained, "We finally got it heard by the Senate Finance Committee." ADAPT did a 144-mile march from Philadelphia to Washington, DC—the "We Are People" march. She described it:

> We charged 95 wheelchairs at night and marched all day long from 10 to 16 miles. It took us two weeks, and we made a DVD of the march. We went and passed it out to everyone in Congress. When we went in we said we were just delivering the DVDs. We didn't say anything about taking over the finance committee. For six hours ADAPT chanted and sang. The room was packed and I couldn't get in. I was outside the room. But they chanted and sang and our demand was that they hear the bill. Grassley's folks came and tried to negotiate and they refused to put it in writing. We'd been through this so many times, and they said, "You've got to trust us." They arrested us in the end. All they did was just cite us. Just downstairs in the cafeteria. Of course we knew we'd be out of there by 6:00 A.M. so they could serve breakfast. So they just gave us citations and released us. The fine was $50. I don't remember what the charge was—maybe failure to obey.

Alexis explained why people object to the term "handicapped." The origin of the term lies in the low status of people with disabilities in historic England. They spent their time begging, with "cap in hand." She also explained that in her state there is hierarchy even within the disabilities movement, describing a "pecking order" in which people who walk with crutches enjoy high status in comparison with paraplegics and quadriplegics. People with cognitive impairment and developmental disabilities hold up the lowest rung. She explained that people who bring their disability on themselves—for example, by having a car accident while driving under the influence—are sometimes considered and treated as an "unworthy" class.

She objects to social workers, explaining that to this profession, people with disabilities are just "a service industry" of individuals who "need to be taken care of." This patronizing attitude is disempowering. Instead Alexis wishes social workers would "listen."

I was surprised, at the end of our interview, to hear Alexis and her colleagues speak disparagingly of Christopher Reeve. She explained to me that people in the movement had hoped that Reeve would be a strong advocate. But he didn't fight on disability issues. Reeve fought "for a cure," and the improvements he made in his functional status were unrealistic for individuals without his wealth. So Reeve failed to convey the idea that disability can be a natural part of life. Alexis compares "disability pride" to "gay pride," mentioning the rich culture of the disability community.

Continued

Continued

Alexis argued that the real disability is attitude. She compared "ableism" to racial prejudice, arguing that people who are able-bodied feel both afraid of and superior to people with disabilities. Reeve, she explained, "set us back by keeping the fear [of disability] alive."

A Social Work Perspective

Like Alexis, approximately 1.6 million Americans use wheelchairs for mobility. The vast majority use manual wheelchairs, and about 155,000 have motorized devices (Kaye, Kang, & LaPlante, 2002). Among people who use wheelchairs, polio is an uncommon condition. The most common are stroke (experienced by 11.1 percent of wheelchair users) and arthritis (10.4 percent) (Kaye, Kang, & LaPlante, 2002). In some ways, Alexis's experiences may not be typical. Health care has not been a problem for her because as veterans she and her husband are eligible for services provided by the Veterans Administration. As we will see, this is not the case for many people with disabilities.

Alexis is a powerful representative for people with disabilities. She likes advocacy because, as she explained, "It works." She is optimistic, seeing the Fair Housing Act and the Americans with Disabilities Act as essential tools for achieving equality for people with disabilities.

The connection between attitudes and policy became clear as I talked with Alexis, and my own attitudes toward people with disabilities moved from fear and pity to respect and acceptance. With attitudinal changes come policy changes that allow for equal access to public spaces, employment, and housing.

The expression "temporarily able-bodied" has special meaning in the context of population aging. As more Americans live to be very old, the number of people living with disability will inevitably grow. And, as Alexis's experiences illustrate, most of us are just one accident or major illness away from our disabled selves.

A BRIEF HISTORY OF POLICIES AFFECTING PEOPLE WITH DISABILITIES

Long ago and far away, when we were a small nomadic race, people with severe disabilities simply did not survive. Babies born with serious impairments were subjected to infanticide, and others were abandoned because they threatened the survival of the group. As tribes became settled, people with mild disabilities could be integrated, performing what tasks they could do to help the collective. Industrialization brought a separation of home and workplace, and people

BOX 8.1   Stopped in My Tracks

Like many able-bodied Americans, I walked past empty "handicapped" spaces with resentment that could be stifling when I was loaded with groceries or pressed for time. One such day I rushed past a new row of empty handicapped spaces into a restaurant to meet a colleague who used a wheelchair. I told her I wanted a special sticker of my own, and she said, "Okay, here's the deal. I'll trade you my handicapped sticker for your legs."

disabilities were not welcome in factories. They were either kept in isolation at home or sent out to fend for themselves on the streets.

Some saw the birth of children with disabilities as divine punishment for their parents' sins. Superstitions arose to explain this phenomenon, generally placing blame on the mother. So, for example, maternal drunkenness, masturbation, attempted abortion, or anxiety were believed to produce children with deformity or disability. Remnants of these beliefs can be seen today in the guilt and ostracism often experienced by mothers of children born with disabilities (Hattersley et al., 1987).

In nineteenth-century America, people with developmental disabilities were labeled "idiots" or "lunatics." Their treatment paralleled that of the mentally ill, and they were seldom distinguished from people with mental illness. Institutions were established to house them, along with others seen as "dependent, defective, or delinquent." Some of these asylums offered education and rehabilitation, but many were strictly custodial.

Even at the dawn of the twenty-first century the United States does not have a single coherent disability policy. Instead, laws and programs have developed piecemeal over the decades, responding to human needs and reflecting public opinions with various degrees of success. Here we will consider four types of policies: income supports for workers and veterans who become disabled, vocational training designed to enable people with disabilities to enter the workforce, education of children with disabilities, and laws to promote the civil rights of people with disabilities.

Income Supports for Disabled Veterans and Workers

The first national disability program in the United States provided pensions to disabled veterans. As Scotch (2001) explains, these early pensions supported veterans of the Civil War who had fought for the North, along with their dependents. Veterans' pensions were justified not on the basis of need but of moral obligation. The nation owed support to young men who had sacrificed to defend it.

As industrialization progressed through the nineteenth century, factories became major employers, and job-related injuries increased. Workers who became disabled as the result of a job-related injury had to sue to receive compensation from their employer. But the courts allowed employers a wide range of defenses, and the burden of proof rested on the employee. Injured employees had to prove that the injury was not the result of their own carelessness (contributory negligence), that a fellow worker did not cause the injury (fellow-servant rule), and that the injury was not caused by a risk that the worker should have been aware of, given the nature of the job (assumption of risk) (Berkowitz, 1987).

As the hazards of industrialization progressed, the courts became jammed with injury cases. Both employers and employees suffered from extensive delays and unpredictable results. The only ones who could count on being paid were the lawyers!

The Progressive Era brought an attempt to reform this system through workers' compensation laws. To this day there is no national workers' compensation program in the United States. The first state program was established in Wisconsin in 1911, and by 1921, 45 states and territories had developed workers' compensation (Scotch, 2001). Workers' compensation was designed to introduce predictability and reduce the burden of litigation for both workers and employers. The basic structure remains unchanged. It is a system of compulsory insurance administered by local commissions, with awards predetermined by the nature and extent of the injury.

But disputes persisted, and they continue today. Some revolve around the extent of disability, as when a man with a back injury claims he is unable to work and the insurance company that denies his claim argues otherwise. Others question whether an injury was, in fact, job-related. One woman who slipped and fell 20 feet from her office was denied benefits on the grounds that her injury was not work-related (Berkowitz, 1987).

As we saw in Chapter 4, the 1935 New Deal offered insurance for some of the hazards faced by industrial workers, but disability coverage was not included due to objections from business and medical interests (Scotch, 2001). This coverage would be added in 1956 with the DI program. Although DI benefits were established as a federal entitlement, eligibility would be determined at the state level. Since its inception, the number of Americans served by the DI program has grown dramatically, as Figure 8.1 illustrates. As we saw in Chapter 4, this growth has led to pressures to limit coverage under DI and to encourage DI recipients to work.

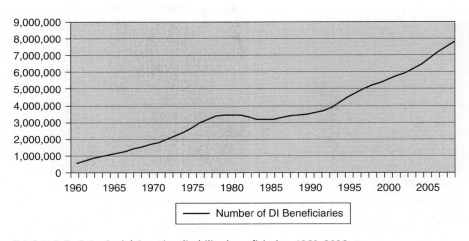

FIGURE 8.1 Social Security disability beneficiaries: 1960–2006.

SOURCE: Social Security Administration (2007). Annual Statistical Report on the Social Security Disability Insurance Program. http://www.ssa.gov/policy/docs/statcomps/di_asr/.

Addiction as Disability

Prior to 1972, people who were disabled by virtue of addiction had access to income support provided under DI and Supplemental Security Income (SSI), as well as food stamps and housing assistance. But increasingly punitive attitudes toward addiction, coupled with rising costs, led to erosion of these benefits.

First, the 1972 amendments to the Social Security Act required that SSI beneficiaries whose disability was caused by addiction receive payments through a representative payee and participate in treatment. These amendments included no restrictions on DI recipients. Twenty-two years later, the Social Security Independence and Program Improvements Act of 1994 placed a three-year time limit on both SSI and DI benefits to people who were disabled by virtue of addiction. The act also extended treatment requirements to DI recipients. It reflected what many in Congress saw as "inappropriately diverting scarce federal resources from severely disabled individuals" and "providing a perverse incentive, contrary to the long-term interest of alcoholics and addicts, by providing them with cash payments so long as they do not work" (Committee on Finance, 1995; Lewin Group, 1998).

From 1972 to 1996, people who were addicted to drugs and/or alcohol could only receive SSI or DI benefits through a payee, and they were required to participate in treatment. Nonetheless, during the early 1990s, the number of SSI recipients whose disability stemmed from addiction increased substantially, from 24,000 in 1990 to 131,000 in 1995 and more than 200,000 in 1996 (Gresenz, Watkins, & Podus, 1998).

Some of this growth was due to "cost shifting" by states. In the early 1990s, several states encouraged substance abusers who were on state-financed general assistance (GA) programs to apply for SSI benefits. In Illinois, for example, the state paid for psychiatric evaluations for substance abusers who applied for SSI, and financed a legal advocacy program designed to secure SSI benefits for this group (Katz, 1994). This strategy shifted the cost of income maintenance for this group from the state-funded GA programs to SSI, which is primarily funded by the federal government.

Growing numbers of beneficiaries brought concerns about possible misuse of both SSI and DI. An audit by the General Accounting Office suggested that, despite the treatment mandates, only a minority of people with addictions who received SSI were in treatment (U.S. General Accounting Office, 1994a). Representative payees were also scrutinized. These were the individuals charged with managing recipients' checks and ensuring that the recipients were in treatment. Audits revealed that many payees were not suited for these tasks, some being themselves addicts, and others being bartenders or liquor store owners (Cohen, 1994). This finding, along with the results of urinalysis of some cocaine addicts receiving SSI, strongly suggested that benefit checks were being used to purchase drugs and alcohol. Finally, rates of rehabilitation for substance abusers on both SSI and DI were extremely low (U.S. Department of Health and Human Services, 1994).

Ultimately, these findings supported the general notion that addicts were using public funds, not to secure rehabilitation, but to support their drug and alcohol habits. This belief, coupled with the popularity of a punitive stance regarding addiction, led to the 1996 passage of Public Law 104-121, which terminated SSI and DI benefits for individuals disabled by drug or alcohol addiction (see Sowers, 1998). Aid recipients with other disabling conditions were allowed to appeal the termination of their benefits.

Finally, all Social Security benefits to victims of addiction were cut off. The Contract with America Advancement Act of 1996 eliminated eligibility for DI, SSI, Medicare, and Medicaid for those whose drug addiction or alcoholism was material to their disability. Later, passage of the 1997 welfare reform act would permanently deny welfare assistance and food stamps to people convicted of a drug felony.

In 1997, just over 209,000 individuals received termination notices, and 141,000 ultimately were cut off from SSI and DI (Gresenz, Watkins, & Podus, 1998). For these people, termination meant more than the loss of monthly income. They were no longer subject to the treatment mandate, no longer had contact with their representative payees, and no longer had medical coverage. This was the first time in the history of the Social Security program that the cause (rather than the extent or duration) of disability was used to deny eligibility. While some returned to their states' GA rolls, others joined the ranks of the homeless and destitute.

Vocational Training

Apart from pensions and income supports, disability programs have historically offered training and rehabilitation to enable people with disabilities to reenter the workforce. Expanding on a post–World War I program for disabled veterans, the 1920 Smith–Fess Act established a vocational rehabilitation program for all Americans with disabilities. Through a federal–state partnership, the act authorized job placement, vocational training, and counseling services.

Clients were those aged 16 or over who had the potential for employment either in the labor force or in the home (Longmore & Umansky, 2001). As a result, the program engaged in creaming, screening out those whose disability, age, or other characteristics suggested little promise for employment. In addition, psychological tests were used to determine a person's potential for improvement.

Congress and some program planners expected clients of vocational rehabilitation to be referred from workers' compensation programs. But this did not happen. As Berkowitz (1987) explains, "At the state level, workers' compensation programs remained close to the 'labor' bureaucracy, and vocational rehabilitation became linked to the education bureaucracy" (p. 155). The cultures and procedures of the two programs were incompatible.

When DI was established in 1956, funds were made available to pay for vocational rehabilitation of program beneficiaries. But by the early 1960s it became clear that few DI beneficiaries could be effectively served by vocational rehabilitation. Berkowitz (1987) reports, "In fiscal 1978, the state vocational rehabilitation agencies served 154,541 Social Security and federal welfare beneficiaries. They rehabilitated 12,268 people at an average cost of $7,976. As a result of rehabilitation, 6,346 people left the benefit rolls" (p. 162). Nonetheless, when SSI was established in 1974, funds from Social Security trust funds and general revenues were allocated to rehabilitate program beneficiaries—this despite the fact that eligibility for the program called for "permanent and total disability."

In part, continued funding was supported by the popularity of rehabilitation over income supports. Vocational rehabilitation was presented as the antithesis of welfare, taking people who would otherwise be dependent and returning them to productive employment. This argument was buttressed by a series of cost–benefit analyses arguing that money spent on vocational rehabilitation was returned in tax payments and welfare savings (Berkowitz, 1987).

Facing a fiscal crisis in Social Security and guided by a philosophy of fiscal conservatism, the Reagan administration practically eliminated the link between DI and vocational rehabilitation. The Omnibus Budget Reconciliation Act of 1981 established a new program that would cost an estimated 3 percent of the previous one. Under the new program, funding would be provided only after a participant had been employed for nine months. Decoupled from Social Security, vocational rehabilitation programs continued to receive federal funding amounting to over $1 billion per year (Berkowitz, 1987).

Education for Children with Disabilities

In the nineteenth century, children born with developmental disabilities were considered "idiots" or "lunatics" and confined either to isolation in private homes or to the brutal conditions of the asylum.

As the concept of rehabilitation surfaced in the early twentieth century, some children were enrolled in "hospital-schools"—living environments that combined physical treatment with a moral, vocational, and academic curriculum. The Widener Memorial School for Crippled Children, established in Philadelphia in 1910, was a model of this type of institution (Byrom, 2001). These asylums became important innovators in the use of adaptive equipment, and they attracted significant philanthropic funding. But they continued the widely accepted practice of segregating children with disabilities.

The 1954 Supreme Court decision in *Brown v. Board of Education of Topeka* alerted Americans to the problem of segregation on the basis of race. But it would be 20 years before this principle was applied to children with disabilities. As we will see in the next section, the civil rights movement of the 1970s brought a new activism to disability advocacy. Parents and organizations concerned with the rights of children with disabilities brought lawsuits arguing that, although the Constitution does not promise every child an education, the Fourteenth Amendment does establish the right to equal protection.

Two lawsuits were pivotal. The Pennsylvania Association for Retarded Children sued the state of Pennsylvania in 1971, successfully arguing that under the Fourteenth Amendment states were required to provide all children who

---

B O X 8.2   Amy's Story

Amy Rowley was an elementary school student who had very little hearing. An extremely intelligent child, Amy was an "A" student in her mainstreamed classroom. The school provided a hearing aid, part-time interpreter, and tutors, which enabled her to succeed. But her parents felt Amy was not performing to her maximum potential and requested a full-time interpreter. In the 1982 case (*Hendrick Hudson Central School District v. Rowley*) the U.S. Supreme Court held against Amy's parents, interpreting the Individuals

with Disabilities Education Act (IDEA) to mean not that each child receive an education tailored to achieve his or her maximum potential, but that the state was responsible for providing an "adequate" education. R. C. Smith, who wrote a book about the case, observes, "Amy was cursed in being deaf and bright, because she would always get by and always be told she was doing fine." (*Ragged Edge,* listed under Suggested Resources, published several articles about this case.)

---

have mental retardation access to free public education. This principle was extended in *Mills v. Board of Education of the District of Columbia,* when the court held that each child was entitled to free public education regardless of the nature or extent of disability (Fleischer & Zames, 2001). In 1975, the Education for All Handicapped Children Act (renamed in 1990 the Individuals with Disabilities Education Act, or IDEA) required that states assess all children with disabilities and provide them "appropriate elementary and secondary education." States were required to develop "individualized educational plans" (IEPs) for children with disabilities and to deliver education according to these IEPs. In addition to the principle of individualized education, IDEA called for integration of children with disabilities into the mainstream by requiring that education be provided in the "least restrictive environment."

Implementation of this landmark legislation has been difficult, to say the least. Chronically short of funds, schools have balked at providing the supports and modifications necessary to fulfill the goal of appropriate education for children with disabilities in the least restrictive environment. Parents and associations have time and again resorted to litigation to force schools to comply with IDEA. While these efforts are not always successful, the tone of the debate is slowly changing from a focus on the "needs" to an emphasis on the "rights" of children with disabilities. As we will see in the next section, this shift is consistent with a growing movement supporting equal rights for people with disabilities.

The Disability Rights Era

During the last three decades of the twentieth century, civil rights became part of the national dialogue. Advocates for people with disabilities set out not to secure *help* but to redefine "disability" in American society. As a result, between 1970 and 1990, more than 50 pieces of disability legislation were passed (Longmore & Umansky, 2001) and a philosophy of independent living emerged to guide advocacy and service development (Hayashi, 2007).

B O X 8.3   Activism at Gallaudet

During the disability rights period, activism was not limited to national issues. In 1988 students at Gallaudet University, the premier institution for the education of the deaf, protested the appointment of (yet another) hearing person as president of the university. As Longmore and Umansky (2001) report, "They demanded a 'Deaf President Now!' and they won" (p. 11).

This legislation largely resulted from the efforts of advocacy groups, such as the American Coalition of Citizens with Disabilities, the Association for Retarded Citizens (ARC), ADAPT, and Not Dead Yet. Some of these groups lobbied for equal access, and filed suits in federal and state courts. Others, like ADAPT, used tactics that had proven successful in the civil rights movement— blocking buses, picketing, and conducting sit-ins. The National Council on Independent Living, founded in Washington, DC, in 1982, now serves as a focal point for advocacy, and local independent living centers throughout the nation provide services and advocacy in support of independence.

We have already discussed the major educational reform that marked this period, the Education for All Handicapped Children Act of 1975. There were several other significant pieces of legislation as well:

- *The Architectural Barriers Act of 1968.* The ABA requires that buildings designed, built, leased, or renovated with federal funds after 1968 provide access for people with disabilities. Uniform Federal Accessibility Standards were established as guidelines under the act, calling for accessible walks, ramps, curb ramps, entrances, elevators, and restrooms.

- *Section 504 of the Rehabilitation Act of 1973.* Section 504 prohibits discrimination on the basis of disability by employers and organizations that receive federal funding. This applies to the delivery of benefits and services, as well as employment opportunities.

- *Fair Housing Act of 1968 (as amended in 1988).* Title VIII of the Civil Rights Act, also known as the Fair Housing Act, prohibits discrimination on the basis of disability. The law applies to most housing, and among other things requires that landlords allow tenants to modify housing (at the tenant's expense) to accommodate a disability. Buildings constructed after 1991 that include four or more units must meet special access requirements. This law is enforced by the Department of Housing and Urban Development (HUD).

Americans with Disabilities Act of 1990.   The period culminated with passage of the Americans with Disabilities Act (ADA) in 1990. This law had origins in the National Council on Disability (NCD). Under the Reagan administration, the NCD held meetings with disability leaders in every state and issued recommendations that "Congress should act forthwith to include persons with disabilities in the Civil Rights Act of 1964 and other civil and voting rights legislation and regulations" (Fleischer & Zames, 2001, p. 89). Later the NCD agreed that disability bias was a distinct type of prejudice that called for a separate law. An early version of the ADA was introduced in 1988. This version defined disability more broadly and had stricter antidiscrimination provisions than the bill that was ultimately passed. Among these was a mandate that all buildings be accessible within two years.

As ultimately passed, the ADA bars discrimination by covered employers against qualified individuals, and calls for "reasonable accommodation" in employment (Title I); public services and transportation (Title II); public accommodation (Title III); and the National Telephone Relay Service. The ADA applies to companies that employ 15 or more workers. To be covered an employee must be qualified, either with or without accommodation, to perform the essential functions of the job. Under the ADA, disability is defined as "a physical or mental impairment that substantially limits one or more . . . major life activities." The term "impairment" refers to "any physiological disorder or condition, cosmetic disfigurement, or anatomical loss affecting one or more [body systems] or any mental or psychological disorder." The definition also applies to individuals who either have a record of impairment or are regarded as having an impairment, and is compatible with that used in the Rehabilitation Act of 1973 (Faillace, 2004).

Implementation of the ADA rests with the U.S. Department of Justice Equal Employment Opportunity Commission (EEOC) and the courts. The Department of Justice reviews complaints and may pursue litigation on behalf of those whose ADA rights have been violated. Alternatively, individuals may pursue remedies through lawsuits. Procedures for filing an ADA complaint are outlined in a booklet, *ADA Questions and Answers,* available through the ADA Information Line: 800-514-0301 (voice) or 800-514-0383 (TTY).

A growing body of case law has clarified (and at times confused) the definition of "disability." The U.S. Supreme Court has heard several cases that involved interpretation of the ADA. Generally these have focused on clarifying the definition of disability for the purposes of the act. For example, in *Cleveland v. Policy Management Systems Corp.,* the court concluded that receiving DI benefits did not automatically make a person ineligible for ADA protections. Carolyn Cleveland argued that for DI purposes she was "totally disabled" but with reasonable accommodation could perform the "essential functions" of her job. The court supported her argument, stating that "despite the appearance of conflict that arises from the language of the two statutes, the two claims do not inherently conflict" (Fleischer & Zames, 2001, p. 103).

Another case clarified what is meant by a "major life activity." In 2002 the Supreme Court ruled on the case of *Toyota Motor Mfg., Ky. v. Williams.* Williams was employed at a Toyota plant and requested accommodation for carpal tunnel syndrome. She later sued, claiming that she had been denied ADA accommodation. The Supreme Court found that, although her disability did limit her ability to perform some manual tasks, it did not limit her ability to perform major life activities such as household chores, bathing, and brushing her teeth, so she was not eligible for ADA protections. (See http://straylight.law.cornell.edu/supct/ for the Supreme Court opinion on this case.)

Two 1999 cases, *Sutton v. United Airlines* and *Murphy v. United Parcel Service,* introduced the notion of "corrective" or "mitigating" measures to narrow the definition of disability. In the *Sutton* case, two sisters who had applied for jobs as airline pilots were turned down because they did not meet the airline's uncorrected vision requirement. The court rejected their complaint, holding that with assistive devices (glasses) they could perform other jobs and so did not meet the ADA definition of disability. A similar finding in the *Murphy* case held that hypertension did not constitute a disability for ADA purposes because when corrected with medication it did not substantially limit important life activities.

The *Olmstead* Decision.   One of the most significant ADA cases resulted in a ruling known as the *Olmstead* decision. On June 22, 1999, the Supreme Court ruled in the case of *Olmstead v. L.C. and E.W.* that "[u]ndue institutionalization qualified as discrimination 'by reason of . . . disability.'" The case involved two patients (L. C. and E. W.) in a state psychiatric hospital in Georgia who successfully argued that they were inappropriately placed and could live in a community-based setting (Hayashi, 2004).

Implementation of the *Olmstead* decision remains an important project for ADAPT and other disability advocates. Nearly 2 million Americans with disabilities live in institutional settings (Kaye, 2000). With adaptive equipment, a barrier-free environment, and some supports many of these people could live in their communities.

Disability advocates are united in their support of the Medicaid Community Attendant Services and Supports Act (MiCASSA—sometimes called the "Community Choice Act"). This legislation would expand residential options for people with disabilities, allowing them to choose community care with attendant services over nursing home care. MiCASSA calls for the Medicaid money otherwise spent on institutional care to follow the individual and pay for services in the community.

As the result of consistent advocacy on the part of ADAPT and other organizations, the Deficit Reduction Act of 2005 provided for establishment of the Money Follows the Person Rebalancing Demonstration. In 2007, more than $1.4 billion was allocated to 31 states to move people out of institutional settings. Part of President Bush's "New Freedom Initiative," the program allows Medicaid beneficiaries in need of long-term care supports to receive them in a setting of their choice.

The ADA has generated a large body of case law, of which only a few cases are discussed here. Most of these cases focus on defining the terms used in the act. The primary contribution of the ADA is not open to dispute. The act represents a clear statement that discrimination on the basis of disability is not acceptable.

A HUMAN PERSPECTIVE   Advocacy: Thinking on Her Feet

Contributed by Jennifer Greenfield, Metropolitan Congregations United, St. Louis, Missouri, and Susan Tebb, Saint Louis University

Few MSW students have the chance to draft legislation, and when Jennifer Greenfield began her advocacy project she did not expect such an opportunity to come her way. In the spring of 2007, Jennifer was completing a practicum at Metropolitan Congregations United (MCU), an interfaith organization representing 62 congregations in metropolitan St. Louis. Her primary goal was to work on Medicaid reform during the 2007 state legislative session and to oppose a proposal known as the MO HealthNet that did not completely restore the 2005 Medicaid cuts.

Under the slogan, "MO HealthNet Is the Wrong Rx for Missouri," Jennifer's advocacy responsibilities included working with three disabled consumers who had been adversely affected by the 2005 cuts but who had never told their stories in public. She helped them prepare to give personal testimony at a rally. In addition, she wrote policy briefs and action alerts and testified before a House committee.

At the rally and at church services throughout the city, participants signed prescription slips calling for comprehensive Medicaid reform, which were then placed in mock prescription bottles. During a lobby day the following week, she joined volunteers who delivered these mock prescriptions, along with the policy brief she had prepared, to all the Missouri legislators. She spoke directly with several legislators and helped a Medicaid consumer prepare testimony for a committee hearing.

The next week, the committee released a new draft of the MO HealthNet legislation that failed to address their primary concern: eligibility for 400,000 people who had lost Medicaid coverage or services in 2005. So

Jennifer joined a Medicaid recipient to head back to the Capitol and deliver 10,000 petition signatures to the committee. Unexpectedly, the committee chair announced that testimony in support of full restoration of cuts would not be allowed that day. With just a few minutes to prepare, Jennifer identified a specific line item in the bill to target and proposed new language that reflected the MCU advocacy goals. She then presented the 10,000 signatures, in a stack of paper more than 1 foot tall, to the committee chair. Jennifer then went out to speak at a press conference. She was quoted in the *News Tribune* as saying, "We are concerned that despite weeks of hearings and debate, there is no discussion about restoring health care to the hundreds of thousands of people who are suffering because of cuts to Medicaid in 2005. Missourians want legislation that will insure people with disabilities, children, seniors and the chronically ill have the care they need." The story of one woman with a disability who was affected by the cuts was also included. A few days later, Jennifer received a follow-up e-mail from the chair, noting that her proposed language had been included in the final Committee version of the bill.

Jennifer's ability to think on her feet had direct results for people with disabilities who relied on Medicaid. The experience brought several important lessons. First, because the legislative schedule and process are highly fluid, it is not possible to plan advocacy strategies that will cover every contingency. Advocates must remain flexible and be skilled at making quick decisions if they want to be actively involved in developing legislation. In this case, the media served as a valuable ally, which suggests that cultivating relationships with reporters is an essential part of policy practice. Finally, by empowering and assisting those who are most vulnerable, social workers can have an important impact on policy decisions.

CURRENT REALITIES AFFECTING
PEOPLE WITH DISABILITIES

As is true of physical and mental illness, the likelihood of experiencing a disability is associated with social class and ethnicity. Low-income individuals and people of color have a higher risk of disability. And in the United States a cyclical relationship holds between poverty and disability, with each increasing the risk of the other. Further, as we see in the next section, the aging of the U.S. population has increased the prevalence of disability.

The Prevalence of Disability

The 2000 census identified 49.7 million Americans—19 percent of the civilian, noninstitutionalized population—as having some type of disability (http://www .census.gov/prod/2003pubs/c2kbr-17.pdf, accessed July 31, 2007). The most common causes of disability are heart disease, back problems, arthritis, and asthma (Kaye, 2000), although injuries remain an important factor in disability (Kaye et al., 1996).

Disability rates have risen in the United States since 1970 due to population aging and a rising incidence of disabling conditions among younger age groups. In 1996, Kaye and colleagues analyzed data from the National Health Interview Survey (NHIS) to report an upward trend in the proportion of Americans living with disabilities. In 1970, they reported 11.7 percent of the population experienced activity limitation, and by 1994 that figure had risen to 15.0 percent. To some extent this is due to population aging (as Table 8.1 illustrates, disability increases with age). But these researchers also reported that growing numbers of children and young adults were identified as having disabilities. Indeed, well over half of the population with disabilities (an estimated 68 percent) is under age 65 (Kaye, 2000).

Poverty and Disability

In 2001 the U.S. Department of Commerce reported that about half of adults with disabilities do not work, and 70 percent of people with severe disabilities do not work. These high rates of unemployment translate into poverty rates that are significantly higher than the general population. The 2000 census revealed a poverty rate of 17.6 percent among people with disabilities, compared with a rate of 10.6 percent for those without. Young people with disabilities had a poverty rate of 25.0 percent, compared with 15.7 percent for those without (U.S. Bureau of the Census, 2005). Of course, people with disabilities are

T A B L E 8.1 Disability Increases with Age

Age Group	Percent with Any Disability		
	Males	Females	Total Population
5–15 years	1.1	0.8	0.9
16–64 years	19.6	17.6	18.6
65 years and up	40.4	43.0	41.9
Total (5 and up)	19.6	19.1	19.3

SOURCE: U.S. Bureau of the Census (2000a). Disability Status 2000: Census 2000 Brief. http://www.census.gov/hhes/www/disability/disabstat2k.html.

categorically eligible for income support through SSI. But SSI benefits alone are not sufficient to raise their incomes above the poverty threshold.

Race and Disability

Disability is more common among some people of color. As Table 8.2 illustrates, African Americans and Native Americans have the highest disability rates in the United States. Nearly one in four (24.3 percent) people in these groups report having a disability, compared with 18.5 percent of those identified as "White, not Hispanic."

Further, there is evidence to suggest that in the U.S. labor market, people of color who also have disabilities experience multiple disadvantages. In work based on national and statewide samples, researchers from the University of San Francisco reported that disability status results in lower employment rates for people of color, and that the difference in employment opportunities between those with and without disabilities is greater among minority populations (Trupin, Sebesta, & Yelin, 2000; Trupin & Yelin, 2005).

SUMMARY: AN EMERGING AGENDA

In this chapter we have traced the progress of disability policies in the United States, noting a contemporary focus on redefining disability in America. This task has, by most measures, barely begun. Access continues to be a problem, and people with disabilities experience unusually high rates of poverty and isolation. Nonetheless, a clear policy agenda can be discerned.

Some see a "fundamental contradiction" in disability policy (Berkowitz, 1987). Most of the public money in disabilities is spent to support people outside the labor force, leaving few resources to support training programs and civil rights legislation that expand opportunities to enter the labor force. Concern about "paying people not to work" is a recurring theme.

T A B L E 8.2   Disability and Race

Race	Percent with Any Disability			
	5–15 Years	16–64 Years	65 and Up	Total Population 5 and Up
White, not Hispanic	5.6	16.8	40.6	18.5
African American	7.0	26.4	52.8	24.3
American Indian, Alaska Native	7.7	27.0	57.6	24.3
Asian	2.9	16.9	40.8	16.6
Hispanic/Latino	5.4	24.0	48.5	20.9
Native Hawaiian/Pacific Islander	5.1	21.0	48.5	19.0

SOURCE: U.S. Bureau of the Census (2000a). Disability Status 2000: Census 2000 Brief. http://www.census.gov/hhes/www/disability/disabstat2k.html.

Berkowitz offers a clear agenda for disability policy:

> If prejudices stand in the way of employment, then handicapped people must be protected by the vigorous enforcement of civil rights laws. If physical barriers prevent people from working or from taking part in other activities, then public policy must seek ways to remove the barriers. For those whose conditions make work impossible, public policy should promote independence and self-care. Being handicapped should not be equated with being helpless. We need to move disability policy beyond retirement and toward the participation of the handicapped in American life. (1987, p. 9)

Another significant concern is widespread prejudice against people with disabilities in America today. As Senator Edward Kennedy declared, "We must banish the patronizing mind-set that disabled people are unable. In fact, they have enormous talent, and America cannot afford to waste an ounce of it" (Fleischer & Zames, 2001, p. xvii).

Kennedy's comment acknowledges the benefits communities can derive from full participation by people with disabilities. Community integration has become a watchword for disability advocates throughout the developed world who seek to include people with disabilities in the lives of their communities. For instance, in the United Kingdom, an organization called the Promoting Social Inclusion Disability Working Group develops recommendations that will support integration in employment, transportation, housing, citizenship, and education. In Australia, the Royal Rehabilitation Center operates a Community Integration Program designed to promote the inclusion of people with a wide range of disabilities. At the University of Pennsylvania, the Collaborative on Community Integration promotes the inclusion of people with psychiatric disabilities. These and other advocates argue that all people, regardless of ability, have the right to full community participation.

KEYWORDS

Mainstreaming in education	ADA	Developmental disabilities

THINK ABOUT IT

1. The 1996 decision to deny SSI and DI benefits to addicts reflects a belief that they should assume personal responsibility for their disability. Can you think of other situations where the cause of a disability might be used to deny coverage (i.e., to enforce personal, as opposed to collective, responsibility)?

2. Why do you think the language of the ADA extends protections to people who are "regarded" as having an impairment? How would you determine

whether someone who is regarded as having a disability merits ADA protections? Have any complaints on this basis been successful in the courts?

3. Retirement policies have important consequences for people who become disabled during their working lives. Disability is an important cause of early retirement as well as unemployment in mid- to late-life. Consider the relationship between disability and race. How do you think people of color will be affected by increases in the age of eligibility for Social Security retirement benefits?

WEB-BASED EXERCISES

For direct links to all the sites in these exercises, log on to the Student Companion Site for this book at academic.cengage.com/social_work/barusch, and choose Chapter 8.

1. Go to the Ragged Edge website at http://www.ragged-edge-mag.com. Click on advanced search. Under the second heading, "Search our libraries and archives," make sure "Ragged Edge Archives 2001–present" is selected, and enter "Amy Rowley." Read the material presented, and consider the question of educational equity for children with disabilities. Do you agree with the Supreme Court decision in this case? Why or why not?

2. Go to the Centers for Medicare and Medicaid Services (CMS) website. Open the page related to the "Money Follows the Person Grants" demonstration projects (http://www.cms.hhs.gov/DeficitReductionAct/20_MFP .asp). Here you should find a downloadable copy of the Summary of State MFP Program Applications. Open this document, and read what (if anything) your state is doing as part of this new initiative.

SUGGESTED RESOURCES

Fleischer, D. Z., & Zames, F. (2001). *The Disability Rights Movement: From Charity to Confrontation*. Philadelphia: Temple University Press.

Journal of Social Work in Disability and Rehabilitation. Distributed by Haworth Press, this journal offers a look at major issues affecting social work with and for people who have disabilities.

Longmore, P. K., & Umansky, L. (Eds.). (2001). *The New Disability History: American Perspectives*. New York: New York University Press.

Swain, J., French, S., Cameron, C., & Barton, L. (2003). *Controversial Issues in a Disabling Society*. London: Open University Press.

www.ragged-edge-mag.com. *Ragged Edge* is an online magazine for the disability community, offering discussion of current issues and personal experiences. It's lively and always an interesting read.

PART III

Vulnerable Populations

Discrimination and Oppression

Will they find a level playing field?

In the mosaic of American life, each individual is in some sense a minority. Some groups in the United States have, however, been singled out to endure discrimination and oppression that members of the racial and cultural majority have been spared. Both "discrimination" and "oppression" have become "hot button" terms that are frequently misunderstood.

281

In a broad sense, "discrimination" means "the quality or power of finely distinguishing," but defined more narrowly, it means "making a difference in treatment or favor on a basis other than individual merit." Discrimination assumes policy relevance when it is based on *categorical* rather than *individual* characteristics, and when the difference in treatment occurs within a limited range of activities specified by law. Under U.S. law, several categories of persons are "protected," and discrimination directed toward individuals because of their inclusion in these categories is prohibited. In addition to race and national origin, protected categories include gender, religion, age, and disability.

As this part of the book will reveal, social policy in the United States has at times been a tool for discrimination and oppression of vulnerable populations. Only in the nation's recent history have we come to expect government not only to refrain from discrimination but to take steps to eliminate it. These changes have triggered a backlash marked by claims of "reverse discrimination."

Although the term "discrimination" has neutral or even positive connotations in some contexts, "oppression" is negative by definition. Adams, Bell, and Griffin (1997) offer a working definition: "Oppression fuses institutional and systemic discrimination, personal bias, bigotry, and social prejudice in a complex web of relationships and structures that saturate most aspects of life in our society" (p. 4). It constrains a person's opportunities and restricts development and self-determination. It creates a hierarchical society in which the privileged benefit from the subordination of other groups. It robs society of the talent and energies of thousands of people, even as it restricts individual opportunities for fulfillment.

Oppression leaves a group with limited or no access to resources or benefits. This is the case, for example, when the basic needs of children are neglected, when women's wages are consistently lower than men's, when elderly people's vulnerabilities are ignored, or when racial minorities, gays, and lesbians are denied employment opportunities.

Oppression can be subtle, as when a high school counselor discourages an African American student from enrolling in a college preparatory class, or when a girl cannot imagine herself becoming president of the United States. Oppression also takes more obvious forms, as when the nation's Congress, through the "Defense of Marriage Act," declares that gays and lesbians shall not have the right to marry, or a corporation routinely promotes white employees over qualified people of color.

In its most insidious form, oppression invades the hearts and minds of the oppressed, persuading them to limit their expectations and moderate their demands. When this "internalized oppression" is operating, we see members of oppressed groups perpetuating stereotypes and punishing or ignoring those who question the status quo. We see poor people blaming themselves for their need for assistance, Native Americans dismissing other Native Americans as lazy alcoholics, or gays rejecting other gays for behavior that marks them as "too queer."

Sometimes oppression in the United States has led to traumatizing events, such as the genocide of Native Americans, the internment of the Japanese during World War II, and the enslavement of African Americans. Several authors have suggested that these "cultural" or "collective" traumas[1] leave lasting marks, shaping expectations and worldviews for generations (Alexander et al., 2004; Erikson, 1976; Weaver & Brave Heart, 1999).

In Part III we will explore the experiences and status of vulnerable subgroups of the U.S. population: people of color (Chapter 9), gays and lesbians (Chapter 10), children (Chapter 11), women (Chapter 12), and elderly people (Chapter 13). Part III concludes with a focus on working Americans (Chapter 14). Although those of us who work for a living are not subject to systematic discrimination, the workplace can be exploitive, and in recent decades the vulnerabilities experienced by working Americans have become more pronounced.

In each of the following chapters we will focus in depth on the population under consideration, beginning with a human perspective and then examining societal norms and beliefs regarding the group. The development of relevant policies and services will be considered, as well as emerging issues and concerns. The material in these chapters will provide the background required for students to apply the social justice framework described in Part I to emerging policy issues affecting these populations.

---

1. I am indebted to Rita Takahashi, who provided background material on cultural trauma.

9

People of Color

E PLURIBUS UNUM

E pluribus unum—"of many, one"—historically referred to the union of the states. But it might apply equally well to the unity within diversity that has come to characterize the United States. Indeed, the United States is the most ethnically diverse country in the world—soon to be a nation with no clear racial majority. This diversity is a source of strength, vitality, and creativity. But intolerance mars the nation's fabric. Racial prejudice and hatred can be seen as a national plague, with periodic outbreaks and remissions. Recent years have seen a rise in hate crimes, particularly those that target Americans of Arab descent. But more insidious and pervasive than hate crimes is institutionalized racism: a subtle form of discrimination that denies access to basic necessities such as education, housing, and employment. The result of institutionalized discrimination is generally a higher risk of poverty, illness, and premature death among people of color.[1]

After considering the experiences and accomplishments of the Reverend France Davis at the beginning of this chapter, we will examine the roots of racism in the United States. Next is a brief overview of the history and status of people of color in the United States: African Americans, Hispanic Americans, Asian Americans, and Native Americans. The histories of these groups illustrate

---

1. A note regarding the politics of language: Many labels are offensive because (I think) the very process of labeling is inherently offensive. None of us chooses to be described first on the basis of our racial ancestry. We prefer to be known as individuals, not as categories. Yet categories are relevant to social policy. Resources are allocated and withheld using race-based categories. The language in this book has been selected to emphasize the value of diversity and support the goal of a racially just America.

both the role of government as an agent of racial oppression and more recent demands that it serve the interests of racial equity in the context of increasing diversity. Emerging policy issues are then considered, including hate crime legislation, English-only legislation, and standardized testing.

THE SOCIAL CONSTRUCTION OF RACE
AND ETHNICITY

Most scientists agree that race is a social construct with little basis in human genetics or biology (Cox, 1970; Fields, 1982; Wilson, 1996). The notion that there were "types" of humans, and the use of the word "race" to refer to those types, has been described as a European invention. Indeed, Wilson (1996) notes that "the word 'race'—meaning different human species—appeared in the English language at precisely the time when Britain began to colonize other lands" (p. 48).[2] Perhaps treating people who looked different as other races made it easier to justify their exploitation.

To say that race is a social construct is not to underestimate its impact. Race has profound meanings in the United States, even if they are primarily economic, historical, and political (see Goldberg, 1993; Gossett, 1965; Omi & Winaut, 1994). During the early part of the nineteenth century, Alexis de Tocqueville (1835) observed the persistence of racial prejudice and division in the United States, speculating that the nation would experience a race war at some time in its future.

Ethnicity has been used in several contexts to single out groups that may not be racially distinct but are characterized by shared culture, common history, values, attitudes, and behaviors. Thus, for example, ethnicity was used to marginalize certain groups of European immigrants, such as Italians and Irish, who were sometimes referred to as "ethnics." It was used by Nazis in their persecution of Jews. Today the term "ethnicity" has lost much of its pejorative flavor and is simply used to describe groups with distinctive cultural and historical traditions. Figure 9.1 presents the racial composition of the United States based on the 2005 American Community Survey.

Of course, the United States is not the only nation in which the construct of race serves as a tool for social stratification. Throughout the Americas, social and economic opportunity are still concentrated among those of European descent, leaving indigenous, immigrant, and mixed-racial groups at a disadvantage. This is the case in Brazil, for example, where people of mixed and African descent have shorter life expectancies, lower educational attainment, and diminished occupational opportunities (Fernandes, 2004; Reichmann, 1999). Similar patterns have been observed in other Latin American nations (Appelbaum, Macpherson, &

---

2. The beginnings of Britain's colonization of other lands can be traced to the late 1500s.

When I called the Calvary Baptist Church to schedule an appointment with Reverend Davis, his booming voice greeted me from the answering machine: "It's a great day at Calvary Baptist. We have services every Sunday at 11:00, and we would love to see you there." With that welcome, I went on to request an hour of his time for an interview that would go into a book on social policy. I knew he was a busy man and I couldn't expect a leisurely discussion. This would have to be a highly focused interview.

I met Reverend Davis at his church office, which was crowded with memorabilia from the Reverend's career. On the walls were beautiful drawings of African Americans, a birthday card made by one of his children, a few inspiring quotes, and a picture of Reverend Davis from 1974 when he became pastor of the church. Piles of books were stacked on the floor. The furniture was worn, but the computer was state-of-the-art. As I arrived his secretary was leaving, so he warned me he would have to answer the phone himself. During our hour together, Reverend Davis received a dozen phone calls, all of them important, and all brief and to the point. Sometimes he would answer with "Grand Central Station . . ." which aptly described his office—Command Central for his urgent and important calling.

France Davis was born in 1946 in Georgia, the eighth of nine children. He grew up on a cotton and corn farm and attended African American schools throughout his education. His parents were adamant that their children receive more education than they had received. Mr. Davis had completed third grade, and Mrs. Davis eighth grade. Both insisted that their children at least consider going to college.

Of his parents, Reverend Davis said, "Other people use celebrities as role models. I use my parents. . . . They modeled participation and involvement in the community and society in which I grew up." Although they were unable to register to vote during his early years, France's parents were always active in the affairs of their community, and when they were able to register, they participated in the electoral process. They set the stage for their son's success through their teaching and guidance. Reverend Davis recalled, "They taught us early to strive for balanced living; to get oneself academically prepared, but also spiritually prepared and then economically, socially, and politically

aware. The goal was always to be best, and as African Americans we were taught that to be the best you had to be twice as good as anybody else."

After finishing high school, he went to Tuskegee University in Alabama, the school founded in 1881 by Booker T. Washington. He started college in 1964 and became actively involved in the civil rights movement. He was part of Martin Luther King's Selma to Montgomery march and participated in student activities. He also wrote for the student newspaper, which gave him "a platform from which to talk about some of the issues."

Reverend Davis remembers his involvement in the civil rights movement as a great adventure. He had no support from his family; in fact, Reverend Davis believed that if his mother had known what he was doing, she "would probably have disowned me . . . [at least] she would have tried to get me to quit." There was some danger involved. "There was the Klan, and even the Alabama National Guard with their Confederate flag." But, as Reverend Davis put it, "I didn't have anything to lose. I didn't own anything, so no one could take anything away from me. I didn't have a job, so no one could fire me." Besides that, Reverend Davis was accustomed to the threat posed by hate groups, having grown up, as he put it, "in Klan country."

The greatest success Reverend Davis remembers from those days came in the march from Selma to Montgomery. The march "was a major achievement and undertaking in a place where the governor of the state had argued that admission to the white school would come over his dead body. So there was a sense of 'here we are, in his face' . . . we were right out in front of the capitol building. He was probably standing at a window looking at us. We were in his face and there was a real sense of accomplishment."

Other efforts were not always successful. Once Reverend Davis and some of his fellow students went into Mississippi to register voters. They were turned back at the airport in Mississippi, as outside agitators. "We were turned away because we were outsiders. . . . Someone had told them we were coming, so they were there and they just put us on a plane back out. . . . We were always considered outsiders. . . . One of the common strategies of the other side was to define certain people as outsiders and then to make them of no effect."

Overall, though, the civil rights movement was a deeply satisfying experience for Reverend Davis. "We had a great time at it, and got a lot done. . . . There was a sense of being part of that which was causing change of a major structural part of our society. What we were changing was the ways laws were interpreted from 1896 with the *Plessy v. Ferguson* Supreme Court decision. We were pulling down strongholds that were related to that [decision] so it was a sense of accomplishment, but also a sense of adventure."

Forced to withdraw from college due to lack of funds, Reverend Davis joined the U.S. Air Force and served for four years during the Vietnam conflict. Of this experience, he said, "Life in the service was exciting, and the travel in particular was educational. I probably learned more in four years of military travel and experience than I did in the previous years of college and high school. I saw the world in many ways and traveled to different countries. I saw the way people lived. So it was an opportunity to see people living all across the country and different places I never thought I'd be . . . to see how life was different, and as a result of that I concluded that there was no such thing as 'normal': everything is relative. . . . What's normal for me is just that—therefore no one is inferior or superior." Reverend Davis learned to speak Thai, and he made friends in every community in which he lived.

After leaving the service, Reverend Davis entered several colleges in California. He says he "took school seriously, and enrolled in four colleges full time." Somehow, Reverend Davis found time for involvement in the student movements at U.C. Berkeley. He also met his future wife during this period.

Then, in 1972, he was recruited by the University of Utah to serve as a teaching fellow. He describes his entry into the state as "difficult," reporting that he was "turned down for a place to stay . . . due to my skin color and cultural differences." His response reflected his personal commitment to social action. "As had been my custom before, I just decided to do something about it. I knew it wasn't right, and so I set about to take whatever action was necessary to get the person's attention." With the assistance of a university administrator, Reverend Davis "reminded [the landlords] that they were contractors with the university. Second, we reminded them that it was illegal to discriminate against a person because they were of a particular skin color or culture." Reverend Davis's efforts were successful, and he was offered housing. He took some

pleasure in turning down that offer. "The forces of the university were behind what I was talking about, and so with that understanding, they backed off. . . . They offered me, as a result of our pressure, any place that they had before it was done, but I, of course, refused." Reverend Davis accepted housing in the university's International House and enjoyed a congenial year there before he was married.

In 1974, the Reverend Davis was asked to "fill in" at Calvary Baptist when their pastor resigned and they were looking for his replacement. Reverend Davis said, "Since they haven't found anybody, I'm still filling in. . . . That's the way it is." His "filling in" has been marked by accomplishments and victories. The congregation has outgrown its current building, and construction of a new one is set to begin "any day." The church sponsors several important community-service projects, including a 30-unit housing project for the elderly and a preschool reading program. His own volunteer activities have included organizing to establish a Martin Luther King holiday in the state and a Martin Luther King Boulevard in its capital city, as well as serving on numerous boards and commissions.

As a member of the Board of Corrections, Reverend Davis has worked to reduce racial profiling by police departments. He is stopped by an officer once a month or more, usually in the daytime and sometimes at night. When the officers find out that the black man they just pulled over is a Baptist minister, they apologize. "They apologize when they find out that I have a name, credentials. But the unfortunate thing about that is that it suggests that people who don't have the credentials get a different kind of treatment. That's why I'm concerned about it." He says, "One of the problems with it [profiling] is getting anybody to admit that they're doing it. . . . There aren't any hard facts being collected." Reverend Davis hopes for passage of a bill that will require police to collect data on the racial backgrounds of people they pull over and cite for traffic violations.

I asked Reverend Davis about the role of the church in social change. His reflections could equally apply to the social work profession:

> I think first and foremost the role of the church is a spiritual role. It's designed to help people be all they can be from the inside out—to help them to

Continued

Continued

come to grips with who they are themselves, to understand their own heritage and their own being. That's first and foremost the role of the church in any community. But in addition to that, whatever it is that causes people to hurt is where the church ought to be. So if people are hurting spiritually, if they hurt physically, or with regard to housing or economically or socially or politically. . . . Fairness and justice issues are at the top of the table, and it is the role of the church to be the voice for the voiceless—to represent the lost, the least, and the last. Those three groups tend to have not much voice in the community, so it is the role of the church to help them be represented and to give them voice.

Reverend Davis feels that education is the best tool for combating racial prejudice. "I think much of what people do in terms of racial hatred and the problems of discrimination is based in ignorance." In his role as church leader and advocate for the African American community, Reverend Davis has been the target of racial hatred. He has a folder with vile hate mail that has come to the church, and the church building has been defiled with racist graffiti. These actions have led him to conclude that "some folk are just filled with meanness and hatred, and we have to find another way to deal with those. I don't know what that is."

Coping with racial hatred requires learning not to take it in and let it devour you. I asked Reverend Davis whether the hate mail enraged him. He replied, "I'm

accustomed to it, so it doesn't enrage me. I expect this horror—it's life as I've learned it. . . . It's upsetting, though. As long as they leave it here at my office [it's not as threatening], but every now and then somebody finds out where I live and they take it to the house, leave it at the door . . . but I've lived with this since I was born. I was born in Klan territory."

His experiences with racial hatred do not influence the way Reverend Davis feels about people. "I've learned to just consider the source of events, and I rationalize that the person that does that sort of thing is just probably angry and frightened, so what they direct toward me is what they feel toward themselves. They just hate themselves, so they need the hate of somebody else. I refuse to participate in their games." Indeed, Reverend Davis believes that this is an important skill for African American children to learn. In the church preschool program children are taught "not to take things personally, to rise above them."

Reverend Davis takes a long-term view of race relations in the United States. When I asked what it would take to heal race relations, he replied, "I think it's going to take a few generations passing off the scene, first of all. I think people of my generation and older are not likely to change much. So we're going to have to, as did the children of Israel in the Bible, die before we get to the Promised Land." He does not expect race issues to be resolved during his lifetime but hopes "we can get more young people understanding that difference does not mean 'less than'; it's just difference. 'Variety,' as my Daddy would put it, 'is the spice of life.'"

Rosemblatt, 2003; Wade, 1997). Some see this inequality as the enduring legacy of colonialism (for example, Avalos, Affigne, & Travis, 1997; Wilson, 1996).

THEORIES ABOUT RACISM

Racism is based on the idea that some racial groups are inferior to others. As a "fundamental lens" through which members of privileged groups view the world, it incorporates beliefs that justify racial oppression. Social scientists have speculated for decades concerning its roots. Like Reverend Davis, some attribute racism to lack of familiarity, or ignorance. Critical theorists focus on economic institutions; and, as we will see, these differing perspectives offer divergent views

Reverend Davis sees education as a top issue for the African American community. His advice for advocates interested in race issues is to "help to ensure that everyone learns to read and write—that they have a fair chance to get a good education." He is concerned about discrimination in education and employment, noting that policies must "ensure that people who have been discriminated against, who have been left out, are no longer." He argues that "some creative mind has got to come up with something that does not create as much backlash as affirmative action." Another critical issue for the African American community, in his opinion, is securing adequate, affordable housing.

By the end of our hour together, I knew Reverend Davis needed to move on to his next commitment. It was time for me to get out of the way so he could get back to the important work at hand. It is the work of a lifetime preparing for a time when racial hatred, discrimination, and bigotry are historical anomalies rather than daily experiences.

A Social Work Perspective

The Reverend France Davis is a role model and community leader. His parents raised him and his siblings in a loving, stable environment with high expectations and clear commitments. Like many parents who come from disadvantaged backgrounds, they told their children, "You have to be much better than the others for your abilities to be recognized." They also taught their son to understand racial hatred in ways that were constructive rather than self-defeating. They prepared their son not only to survive in a racist world but to strive for a better world. The result is a committed activist who has become indispensable to his congregation and his community.

Social policies have had a profound impact on Reverend Davis's life, even as he has influenced them. As he noted, his parents were unable to vote when he was small, and he attended segregated schools. The civil rights movement, of which he was an integral part, not only established African American electoral rights but tore down the "separate but equal" farce that resulted from the *Plessy v. Ferguson* decision. Housing policies also affected Reverend Davis. In retrospect, he felt that he would have been unable to secure housing as a young African American man in a predominantly white town without the assistance and support of a university vice president.

Racial profiling has touched Reverend Davis's life as it has touched the lives of many people of color. Profiling may not seem as noble a cause as voter registration, but we vote only once a year. In some communities, people of color going about their business may be stopped by police several times a day. Each time, they risk being cited or even arrested for something they didn't do.

Reverend Davis devotes his professional career to spiritual leadership and his civic volunteer career to social justice. Equal access to education and employment ranks high on his list of priority issues, as does housing access. But equally important, if less tangible, is his desire to work toward a society in which "difference is just that: difference."

on the future of racism, with some arguing that it will naturally disappear and others suggesting the need for intervention.

Those who use ignorance to explain racism argue that it is simply an early stage in the historical process of cultural assimilation—the inevitable result of early contact between disparate groups. For example, Park (1974) argues that racial conflict surfaced in the early stages of cultural contact and receded with the process of assimilation. He identifies four stages in the assimilation process: initial contact between racial or ethnic groups, competition between these groups, accommodation, and assimilation. The first two stages are marked by conflict and racism, which fades away in the later stages. Gordon (1964) elaborates on the later stages, arguing that assimilation proceeds in three stages: cultural assimilation (the minority culture is accepted or tolerated by the majority culture), marital

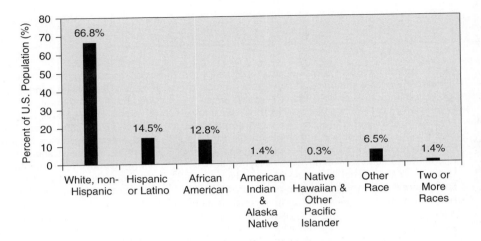

FIGURE 9.1 Racial composition of the U.S. population: 2005.

SOURCE: U.S. Bureau of the Census (2005). United States Demographic Characteristics 2005. http://factfinder
.census.gov/servlet/ADPTable?_bm=y&-geo_id=01000US&-ds_name=ACS_2005_EST_G00_&-_lang=en&-_caller=
geoselect&-format= (accessed December 11, 2007).

assimilation (interracial marriages occur in large numbers), and prejudice-free assimilation (the final stage, when notions of racial superiority disappear).

Market theorists, who analyze the impact of competitive forces on discriminatory practices, share the view that racism will simply disappear. For example, Sowell (1981) argues that, in a free market, firms that discriminate against talented minorities pay a higher price for a less productive labor force. In a competitive market, this inefficiency should ultimately either eliminate these firms or force them to change their discriminatory practices. Of course, Sowell assumes a perfectly competitive market in which those of all races enjoy equal access to training and educational opportunities that will increase their human capital.

Noting a significant decline in racism during World War II, Willhelm (1970) argues that when the demand for labor increases, racism diminishes, and when jobs are scarce it increases. This argument does not explain the intense racism that marked the antebellum South, when slave labor was in high demand; nor does this labor-based approach explain this nation's efforts to exterminate Native Americans.

In a contrasting view, other critical theorists attribute racism to economic exploitation, arguing, as Wilson (1996) does, that

> [r]acism is a modern historical phenomenon, grounded in alienating, exploitative, and oppressive economic arrangements. It arose in a particular stage in history, after the dissolution of feudalism, after the Protestant Reformation, and with the rise of a new economic order undergirded by the intense drive to accumulate wealth . . . it [this drive] fueled the genocide against Native Americans and propelled the Atlantic

slave trade. Modern racism emerged out of slavery and colonialism. These economic institutions created clear demarcation lines between the oppressed and the oppressor, which overlapped with color lines. The oppressed were not only separated from the oppressors, the oppressed were primarily people of color. The notion that people of color were of a different species and were inferior to the oppressors functions to legitimize the oppressive arrangement and to desensitize the dominant group to the plight of the oppressed. (p. 37)

Wilson argues that racism evolves as the result of oppressive economic arrangements. It provides justification for the suppression of one group for the benefit of another. Support for this argument is found in the history of both African slaves and European immigrant groups in the United States. Most of us understand that the notion of Africans as subhuman served to justify the brutal exploitation of slavery. But is easy to forget that when both the Irish and European Jews immigrated to the United States, they were characterized as inferior.

Class conflict theorists also attribute racism to economic sources, but instead of focusing on oppressive economic relationships they focus on competition between classes. This competition might take place between company owners and working classes or between managers and laborers, with the privileged classes using racist attitudes to maintain their advantaged positions. Under this view, racism will persist as long as inequality and the accumulation of wealth and privilege are tolerated.

THE ROLE OF GOVERNMENT: RACISM AND PUBLIC POLICY

Today some look to government to heal racial divisions and ensure equal opportunity for all. But for much of its history the U.S. government was itself the agent of racial oppression. Even leaders who professed belief in equality and liberty supported racist institutions. Stephen A. Douglas, a Democratic senator in 1858, stated the prevailing view clearly when he said, "[T]his government of ours is founded on the white basis. It was made by the white man, for the benefit of the white man, to be administered by white men" (Loewen, 1995, p. 154).

From its very foundation, the U.S. government was an agent of race-based oppression. Even the most cursory review of U.S. history reveals centuries of government-sponsored and government-supported racism. The question is not whether the U.S. government has been a racist institution, but what occurred to reverse this long trend. The same question applies to many state governments. This transition in the role of government did not occur magically or overnight, nor is it complete. Its development is chronicled in the following sections.

PEOPLE OF COLOR IN THE UNITED STATES:
A HISTORICAL OVERVIEW

Although immigration is a major theme in their history, people of color in the United States today are not all immigrants or the children of immigrants. Some, like Native Americans and "Californios," have ancestors who predated the arrival of Europeans. Most, like African Americans, some Mexican Americans, and Asian Americans, originated in other countries; arriving in the United States after the early European settlers. Historically, African Americans have made up the largest of these groups, but this has changed. Early in the twenty-first century the number of Americans identified as Hispanic or Latino exceeded the number who reported that they were African Americans (U.S. Bureau of the Census, 2005b). Beginning with African Americans, in the following sections we will briefly consider the histories of people of color in the United States.

African Americans

Slavery and Its Aftermath.   During most of the seventeenth century, laborers on plantations in colonial America were indentured servants from Europe. Indeed, legal distinctions between these indentured servants and African slaves did not develop until the 1660s (Stampp, 1956). As Morgan (1975) noted, interracial marriages were common in the first half of the seventeenth century.

In time, the supply of indentured servants diminished, and the slave trade accelerated to the point where the population of African slaves exceeded the European population in southern colonies. Public policies of the late seventeenth century began to distinguish European servants from African slaves, meting out differential punishment for offenses. For example, in 1705, a Virginia law required dismemberment of "troublesome" slaves, while at the same time prohibiting masters from whipping European servants, naked, without a court order (Morgan, 1975). In one of the most brutal public policies recorded in the United States, several colonies enacted legislation mandating castration of slaves who made repeated attempts to escape.

With the American Revolution came revolutionary ideas of freedom and equality. While some were able to restrict their notions of freedom to white men, other revolutionary leaders found this more difficult. Thomas Jefferson was deeply opposed to slavery, authoring legislation in Virginia that allowed for the gradual emancipation of slaves. Yet, among his slaves, the only ones he freed were his children—and he did so upon his deathbed. He left their mother, Sally Hemings, enslaved for the rest of her life.

In states with the least economic investment in slavery, an abolitionist movement began and legislatures enacted laws to restrict or abolish slavery. These laws were enacted in New York, Massachusetts, New Jersey, Pennsylvania, Connecticut, and Rhode Island. Meanwhile, Southern leaders seized on the notion of property rights and individual liberty to argue that the government had no right to deprive them of their slaves (because they were property). In the South, black slavery was seen as a prerequisite to white freedom.

After the Revolution, the new Constitutional government was designed by men of property. Enumerating the wealth of the members of the Constitutional Convention, Dye and Ziegler (1996) estimate that nearly a third were plantation owners and slaveholders. In deference to their economic interests, the Constitution did not prohibit or restrict slavery. In fact, it included measures that reinforced the institution. For example, in population counts designed to determine congressional representation, each slave was to be counted as three-fifths of a person. The Constitution also required that runaway slaves who reached free states be returned to their owners upon demand. Article IV, Section Two, stated that "No Person held to service or Labor in one State, under the Laws thereof, escaping into another, shall, in consequence of any Law or Regulation therein, be discharged from such Service or Labor, but shall be delivered up on Claim of the Party to whom such Service or Labor may be due." Since slaves were recognized as property, the Fifth Amendment, which protected property from arbitrary governmental seizure, helped to sustain the institution of slavery. Finally, under the Naturalization Act of 1790, U.S. citizenship was defined in terms compatible with the European worldview. The act required applicants for citizenship to be of good character and "white."

The first federal involvement in abolitionist efforts came in 1808 when the international slave trade was banned. Even then, Congress did not alter the terms of domestic slavery. The Fugitive Slave Act of 1850 and the Dred Scott decision of 1857 established an obligation to return escaped slaves and denied equal citizenship to African Americans.

State laws in the South not only treated slaves as property; they also restricted the activities of white residents in order to sustain the institution of slavery. Thus, for example, state laws prohibited whites—even slave owners—from teaching slaves to read or write. Owners were also prohibited from freeing their slaves unless the slaves left the state. Finally, interracial marriage, even between free adult blacks and whites, was strictly prohibited.

While the Civil War (1861–1865) did bring an end to slavery, it was not fought for that purpose. It was a war of independence for the South, and a struggle to maintain the Union for the North. Lincoln is reported to have said that slavery was acceptable, if that was what it took to sustain the Union. Because the war brought the promise of an end to slavery, hundreds of thousands of African Americans contributed energetically to the Northern war effort. For military and political reasons, the North's victory in the Civil War had to result in the end of slavery.

The postwar period was hardly one of racial equality. Southern landholders maintained their control over county and state governments and with the end of federal reconstruction, passed "Jim Crow"[3] laws designed to "keep Negroes in their place." The first Jim Crow law was passed in 1888 in Louisiana, declaring that African Americans could not be seated with whites on railway cars. In addition to laws that sharply enforced racial segregation in public facilities, state and county laws established other oppressive practices, including the credit system used in sharecropping, debt peonage, convict leasing, segregated schools, and voting restrictions.

Credit and Sharecropping.   Under sharecropping, those who worked the land owned very little, not even their tools. They paid a percentage of their crops as rent, and borrowed tools and animals from the landowner. The credit system used in sharecropping was particularly onerous. Under this system, croppers received advances for their seed, supplies, and household goods. The interest rates charged on these advances were outrageous, ranging from about 53 to 71 percent (Mandel, 1992). In addition to interest, landowners charged inflated prices for goods they sold to the croppers, who often had no alternative to the planter-owned stores.

Debt Peonage.   Under sharecropping and related practices, a landowner could virtually ensure a lifetime of debt for his tenants. Early in the twentieth century, nearly every southern state had a system of "debt peonage." Under state laws, the act of leaving the land without paying debts was defined as a form of labor fraud punishable by imprisonment. This legislation provided landowners with a pool of forced labor—tenants who could not leave the land because of their debts. The extent of debt peonage has been disputed. Some argue that the practice was rare and had died out by the Depression. But Daniel (1972) reports that it was not rare and cites cases as recent as the 1960s.

Convict Leasing.   The practice of convict leasing has been described as "comparable to the worst horrors of slavery" (Wilson, 1996, p. 88). Under this system, landowners and other employers would bid on contracts to use convicts on chain gangs for their labor. The convicts, the vast majority of whom were African Americans, had virtually no protection from abuse and lived in appalling conditions (Lichtenstein, 1996). They labored under the supervision of armed guards. Convict laborers had extremely high mortality rates. Camejo (1976) reports an annual mortality rate for convict laborers in the 1880s of one out of nine in

---

3. Jim Crow was not a real person. The term is a pejorative way of characterizing African Americans that was coined by a white minstrel named Daddy Rice. He would blacken his face and dress in rags, and then dance and sing while purporting to imitate African Americans. His most popular song, "Jump Jim Crow," was an insulting parody of African American culture.

Mississippi and one out of four in Arkansas. The practice died out by the 1940s, but chain gangs have been revived in several states, including Florida, Alabama, Arizona, and Iowa.

Segregated Schools.   Education is widely seen as a tool of empowerment, and thus race-based oppression has historically focused on denying educational access to African Americans and other people of color. Prior to the Civil War, southern states enforced laws that prohibited teaching an African American to read or write. During reconstruction, federal efforts did not address equal access to education, and the Supreme Court became an ally of oppressive forces through its *Plessy v. Ferguson* decision.

Homer Plessy was a light-skinned African American who purchased a first-class ticket on the East Louisiana Railway. When he tried to take his seat, he was ordered to go to the "colored" section. He refused to do so and was jailed. The case was reviewed by the Supreme Court in 1896, and in its decision the Court held that "if Plessy be a colored man and be so assigned, he has been deprived of no property, since he is not lawfully entitled to the reputation of being a white man" (quoted in George, 2000, p. 7). The Court introduced the idea that "separate but equal" facilities were lawful, a principle that would have an enduring impact on the educational opportunities of African American children.[4]

Until the middle of the twentieth century, the nation's segregated educational system relegated African American children to ill-equipped classrooms with outdated textbooks. Transportation and meal services available to white children were not provided in the "colored" schools. Access to higher education and professional training was severely limited. It was in this seriously under-funded system that Reverend Davis's parents were educated.

It was not until 1954 that the Supreme Court finally rejected the principle of separate but equal in its *Brown v. Board of Education* decision. On behalf of the National Association for the Advancement of Colored People (NAACP), Thurgood Marshall (later to become a Supreme Court justice) argued that segregation produced enduring damage in African American children, scarring them for life with a sense of inferiority (an example of the "internalized oppression" discussed in the introduction to Part III). Chief Justice Earl Warren delivered the Court's unanimous decision to order desegregation of the nation's schools.

Desegregation was not a simple matter. Three years passed before the school board in Little Rock, Arkansas, reluctantly concluded that they would have to desegregate their Central High School. Nine African American children were handpicked to attend the all-white high school. On Wednesday, September 4, 1957, the high school was surrounded by members of the National Guard and an angry mob. Eight of the children entered the school as a group under police

---

4. The *Plessy v. Ferguson* decision was not unanimous. Justice John Marshall Harlan wrote an eloquent dissent, stating that "The arbitrary separation of citizens, on the basis of race, while they are on a public highway, is a badge of servitude wholly inconsistent with the civil freedom and equality before the law established by the Constitution. It cannot be justified upon any legal grounds" (quoted in George, 2000, p. 8).

B O X 9.2   Dr. Charles Richard Drew (1904–1950)

Dr. Charles Richard Drew became world-renowned for perfecting the technique for separating blood plasma from whole blood so it could be used more readily. Countless lives were saved. At the age of 45, Dr. Drew was injured in an auto accident in North Carolina. He was taken to a local hospital, which refused to treat him. The hospital was for whites only. Dr. Drew was African American. He died from loss of blood.

---

protection. The ninth child, Elizabeth Eckford, did not have a phone and was not informed of the group's plans. She approached the school alone. Eckford vividly describes the painful experience in her book *Growing Up Southern* (Mayfield, 1981).

Voting Restrictions.   Southern states established voting restrictions that disenfranchised large blocs of African American voters. These included annual poll taxes that had to be kept current by anyone wishing to vote. Under these tax laws, an adult would be required to pay poll taxes for previous years as well as the current year before being allowed to register. Some jurisdictions required property ownership for voter registration, while others established complex literacy requirements. Some areas established poll taxes that applied only to African Americans. African Americans who did show up to vote were subject to harassment, intimidation, even violence. These measures kept millions of African Americans, like Reverend Davis's parents, out of the voting booth until the civil rights movement of the 1960s.

The New Deal.   The New Deal, seen by many as a progressive movement toward equality, incorporated several provisions explicitly designed to maintain racial privilege. Roosevelt faced a solid bloc of white southern congressmen who refused to support any Social Security legislation that included blacks (Duster, 1996). As a result, the Social Security Act of 1935 excluded domestic servants and agricultural workers—jobs predominantly filled by African Americans. The Wagner Act of 1935, which established the right of unions to collective bargaining, was revised to permit racial exclusion. Similarly, the 1934 National Housing Act exacerbated racial segregation in housing by permitting the use of race as a criterion for granting loans.

B O X 9.3   Ralph Bunche (1904–1971)

Ralph Bunche, African American, negotiated the first cease-fire in the Middle East, for which he received the 1950 Nobel Peace Prize.

Current Realities. The progress of U.S. policies affecting African Americans has been significant. Nonetheless, economic and health indicators show continuing race-based disadvantages.

African Americans have lower median incomes and higher rates of poverty than other groups. As Figure 9.2 indicates, from 2003 to 2005 the median household income for African Americans averaged $31,140, compared with $50,677 for non-Hispanic white households. Similarly, in 2005, the poverty rate for African Americans was 24.9 percent, compared with a rate for non-Hispanic white Americans of 8.3 percent. Further, as we will see in Chapter 14, African Americans continue to earn lower incomes than whites, even at comparable levels of educational achievement, and they tend to be underrepresented in highly paid occupations.

Household income for African Americans is also influenced by household composition, as this group has more female-headed households than other groups in the United States. For example, in 2006, 48 percent of African American households were headed by a single woman, compared with an overall rate of 30 percent for the nation. The rate for non-Hispanic whites was 28 percent; for Asian Americans, 21 percent; and for Hispanic Americans, 28 percent (U.S. Bureau of the Census, 2007).

In Chapter 6 we saw that African Americans experience significant health disparities, with higher infant mortality rates, greater cancer morbidity and mortality, and lower life expectancies than the general population. Apart from its obvious disadvantages, reduced life expectancy translates over a lifetime into lower Social Security benefits. So, one effect of these health disparities is that, for African Americans, the return on payroll taxes is diminished.

As Reverend Davis's experiences with the police illustrate, Africans Americans are disadvantaged by the criminal justice system, where race-based

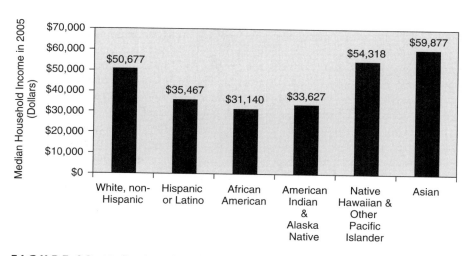

F I G U R E 9.2 Median household income by race: 3-year average, 2003–2005.

SOURCE: U.S. Bureau of the Census (2006). Income, Poverty and Health Insurance coverage in the United States: 2005. http://www.census.gov/prod/2006pubs/p60-231.pdf (accessed December 11, 2007).

disparities have been well documented. Generally, African Americans receive longer sentences than whites (Mustard, 2001). This situation has been exacerbated by the "war on drugs" under which Congress has passed statutes that mandate stiff sentences for some drug offenses. Perhaps as a result, recent years have seen a dramatic increase in the proportion of African Americans incarcerated in federal prisons. The Department of Justice reported that in 1930, 22 percent of the population of federal and state prisons was African American, and 1 percent was other people of color (U.S. Department of Justice, 1994). By 2006, African Americans and other people of color represented 65 percent of state and federal prisoners, with African American men more than six times as likely to be imprisoned as white men (U.S. Department of Justice, 2007b).

The role of sentencing guidelines in creating this disparity becomes clear when we consider the different approaches to prosecuting users of crack and powder cocaine. Less expensive than powder, crack cocaine is more widely used by people of color, while powder cocaine tends to be used by white people. For instance, in 2006, 82 percent of those sentenced for crack offenses were African American, while 66 percent of those sentenced for powder offenses were white (U.S. Sentencing Commission, 2007). Until 2007, sentencing guidelines for crack were considerably more severe than those meted out for other drug offenses. Indeed, crack was the only drug for which a first possession offense generated a mandatory five-year federal prison sentence. The U.S. Sentencing Commission has recommended that this disparity be eliminated, advice that has been ignored by Congress as inconsistent with its "get tough on drugs" stance.

Hispanic Americans

The term "Hispanic" refers to a person's ethnic and cultural origins. Hispanic Americans come from Spanish-speaking countries. Their history and culture reflect the global influence of Spain during its imperialist period. The Spanish (like other colonial powers) married members of the indigenous populations of their country's colonies. In Mexico, children of these mixed marriages were considered *mestizos,* with features of both the Spanish and the indigenous peoples. The population of indigenous Taino-Arawak in Puerto Rico was quickly decimated by war and disease, which led the Spanish to bring in slaves from Africa. Subsequent interracial marriages led some Puerto Ricans to identify themselves as black. Thus, "Hispanic Americans" may have different racial identities and different experiences of U.S. racism. Puerto Ricans immigrating to New York may find themselves identified as black, whether or not they self-identify in this way. Their access to housing and jobs may more closely resemble that of African Americans than it does other Hispanic groups.

The nation's Hispanic population has diverse origins and backgrounds. Some lived in the southwest before it was part of the United States. Others emigrated from Spanish-speaking areas—initially Mexico, and more recently Latin America, Puerto Rico, and Cuba.

This diversity complicates our understanding of Hispanic claims on U.S. social policy. Should they be considered an indigenous group that has experienced disadvantage and oppression (and is therefore entitled to affirmative efforts to remedy past injustices)? Or should they be viewed as a group that, like other immigrants, can be expected to achieve economic and social parity in the process of assimilation? (See Chavez, 1991, for a discussion of this question.) Is policy needed to improve the status of Hispanic Americans in the United States? Or will the process of assimilation mitigate the need for public intervention? In the following sections we will consider the diverse histories of Hispanic Americans in the United States, looking at the experiences of immigrants from Mexico, Puerto Rico, Cuba, and Latin America.

Mexican Americans. While other European nations were colonizing the northeastern region of what is now the United States, the Spanish government established its colonial presence in the southwestern region and in Mexico. The Spanish encouraged the settlement of California, recruiting settlers from Mexico who were willing to move north, so by the late eighteenth century the Mexican presence in California and the Southwest was well established.

Like Britain, Spain lost its American colonies, and the Mexican Revolution achieved that nation's independence in 1921. At that time, the land area of Mexico was about twice what it is today, including the current states of California, New Mexico, Arizona, Texas, Colorado, Arizona, and Utah. Mexican society was rigidly hierarchical, with those who possessed Spanish land grants, the "dons," enjoying a pastoral and aristocratic lifestyle for which those at the bottom, the indigenous peoples, supplied labor.

American visitors, and even settlers, were initially welcomed. As their numbers grew and their intent to claim territory became clear, Mexico outlawed American immigration. Nonetheless, Americans continued to arrive in violation of Mexican law, leading one commissioner in Texas to declare, "The incoming stream of settlers is unceasing" (Takaki, 1993, p. 173).

This influx lasted until the Mexican–American War was declared in 1836. Conflict first broke out in Texas, where the Mexican government had outlawed slavery. This new policy enraged slaveholding Texans who, under the leadership of Sam Houston, forced the Mexican government to cede the state. The "Lone Star Republic" was established as an independent nation, with Houston as its leader.

The Texas victory was widely interpreted as an advance for the Anglo-Saxon race. Stephen Austin had declared war with Mexico inevitable, viewing it as a conflict between a "mongrel Spanish-Indian and negro race" and "civilization and the Anglo-American race." Similarly, Sam Houston declared the Lone Star Republic would reflect "glory on the Anglo-Saxon race" (Takaki, 1993, p. 174).

For Mexico, the war was devastating. The United States annexed Texas in 1845 and extended U.S. borders to the Pacific. In the 1848 Treaty of Guadalupe Hidalgo, Mexico lost Texas and the Southwest Territories.

U.S. control of the area led to several measures designed to make life difficult for those of Spanish or Mexican descent. California passed a series of "Greaser Acts," declaring that those Spanish and Indian people who were not "peaceful and quiet" were vagrants subject to imprisonment. The acts also imposed a "Mexican Miners Tax" that required fees of all Spanish-speaking miners. Although the treaty's provisions afforded Mexicans the vote, poll taxes, language restrictions, and intimidation were used to reduce their political participation. Even the dons were subject to oppression. Landholdings that derived from Spanish land grants were challenged by American squatters. The U.S. court review was a lengthy and expensive process, and even if their title was declared legitimate, owners frequently had to sell their land to pay legal expenses.

As a result of these and similar policies, Mexicans in California and the Southwest lost their property and their social standing, and those who stayed were often reduced to the status of menial laborers. Even in these jobs, they encountered discrimination. Mexican workers in most industries (such as mining and railroads) were systematically paid less than "Americans" (whites) in the same jobs. A system of debt peonage was instituted, similar to that used to tie African Americans to Southern farms. Living in company towns, many were forced to buy clothing, food, and other supplies from company-owned stores. The high price of these goods charged by these stores left workers so deeply in debt that they essentially became slaves to the company. In Chapter 14 we will examine the history of Mexican laborers in the United States.

There was tension around the education of Chicano children. Employers wanted to restrict access to education to ensure a continuous supply of cheap labor. Parents longed for their children to become educated so they would enjoy a better standard of living. Most school districts restricted educational opportunities of Chicano children, channeling them into technical and domestic classes. Some of the larger districts established separate schools for Chicanos similar to those to which African Americans in the South were relegated.

Meanwhile, the nature of Hispanic immigration into the United States began to change, as residents of Puerto Rico, Cuba, and Latin America relocated to this country.

Immigrants from Cuba, Puerto Rico, and Latin American Countries. Cubans are the second-largest group of immigrant Hispanic Americans in the United States. Generally regarded as "elite" Hispanic immigrants, their ranks have included many landowners, professionals, and businesspeople. Since the 1960s, Cubans have immigrated in waves. Unlike Mexican immigrants, who seek economic improvement, Cubans tend to be "political" refugees looking for a different political system.

Puerto Ricans are, in fact, citizens of the United States. Their island was ceded by Spain in 1898 and, although they cannot vote for president, they have been citizens since 1917. Migration from Puerto Rico swelled during the 1940s and 1950s as young men left to serve in World War II and became aware of economic opportunities on the U.S. mainland. Today, nearly two-thirds of Puerto Ricans live on the U.S. mainland, primarily in New York (Chavez, 1991).

Latin American immigrants, primarily from the Dominican Republic, El Salvador, and Nicaragua, have increased the diversity of the U.S. Hispanic population. Many have fled political instability caused by the collapse of regimes (such as that in El Salvador) that were supported by the United States. In this situation, many immigrants had to struggle to secure refugee status because recognition of their oppression implied indictment of the U.S.-supported regime.

Current Realities.   The nation's Hispanic population has changed. Today it is more heavily composed of immigrants than it was only three decades ago. Chavez (1991) reported that in 1970 barely one in five Hispanic Americans was foreign-born, while by 1990 that figure had risen to more than a third. Where early Hispanic immigrants came almost exclusively from Mexico, more recent waves have brought migrants from Cuba, Puerto Rico, and Latin America (primarily El Salvador and Nicaragua). Mexican immigrants were primarily economic refugees, seeking to escape poverty. Refugees from Cuba and Latin America are primarily political refugees. They tend to include more professionals and members of landed classes. Nonetheless, these immigrants typically experience greater economic deprivation than second- and third-generation Americans of Hispanic descent (Bean & Tienda, 1987; Chavez, 1991).

Although the Hispanic American population in the United States has grown increasingly diverse, broad economic and health indicators suggest the group as a whole continues to experience disadvantages. For example, as Figure 9.2 indicates, during the period from 2003 to 2005 the median income for Hispanic households was $35,467, compared with a median for white non-Hispanic households of $50,677. Similarly, the poverty rate among the nation's Hispanic households was 21.8 percent in 2005, substantially higher than that of white non-Hispanic households, for which the poverty rate was 10.6 percent.

Health indicators reflect the diversity of the Hispanic American population. The National Center for Health Statistics reported that in 2004, 6.8 of 1,000 infants born in the United States died before their first birthday. Among Puerto Ricans, infant mortality was slightly higher, at 7.8 per 1,000. But rates for other Hispanic groups were lower. Mothers from Cuba enjoyed the lowest rate, at 4.6 per 1,000, while those from Central and South America had a rate of 4.7 per 1,000, and Mexican Americans, 5.5 per 1,000 (National Center for Health Statistics, 2007) As we saw in Part I, life expectancy for Hispanic Americans as a whole is generally comparable to or better than that of the white population.

Asian Americans

Asian immigrants traveled across the Pacific in response to the demand for labor in the rapidly expanding economy of the western United States. The Chinese came first, entering California just before the Gold Rush of 1849. They were followed by large numbers of Japanese, whose emigration was carefully managed by their government. Immigrants from Korea, the Philippines, and other Asian and Pacific Island locations came in smaller numbers. In the following sections we will consider the experiences of Chinese and Japanese immigrants to the United States.

Chinese Immigrants. Chinese immigrants came to this country in search of the "Gold Mountain," a land of beauty and wealth. Their native land was suffering from poverty and chaos caused by the "opium wars" with the British. To finance these wars, and to pay the large indemnities charged by Western imperialist powers, the Chinese (Qing) government imposed high taxes. Many farmers lost their land, and food shortages led to widespread famine.

During the latter half of the nineteenth century, hundreds of thousands of young Chinese men—primarily illiterate laborers—came to America. They were attracted by stories of countrymen who had spent a few years working in America and returned with fabulous wealth. These and related stories were propagated by labor brokers—entrepreneurs hired by American firms to recruit Chinese laborers. There is no evidence that Chinese men were kidnapped and brought to America as "coolies" (Takaki, 1993). Most stayed in California, but some made their way to southern states, where they served as an alternative to African American labor.

Initially the Chinese were welcomed and their contributions appreciated. They did not represent a political threat, since the Naturalization Act of 1790 reserved citizenship for whites, and the Chinese immigrants did jobs that no white person wanted to perform. Chinese laborers worked in the mines under cramped and dangerous conditions. When mining became less profitable, they were hired by the railroads. As Chinn and colleagues (1969) explain, the Central Pacific Railroad line was a Chinese achievement. Again, Chinese workers labored under extremely difficult conditions, laying track through Donner Summit during the winter of 1866.

Thousands of Chinese (nearly one-fourth of California's Chinese population in 1869) settled in San Francisco, where they established a thriving community known as Chinatown and helped the city to become a leader in manufacturing. Chinese were also successful as agricultural laborers in California's Central Valley.

Their conspicuous effectiveness and relative success led to resentment on the part of white labor organizations, which lobbied for passage of the Chinese Exclusion Act in 1882.[5] The act prohibited immigration by Chinese laborers. It was the first piece of immigration legislation that expressly forbade immigration from a specific nation.

Chinese continued to be targets of resentment and eventually moved into self-employment, opening small businesses such as restaurants, grocery stores, and laundries. Chinese laundries represented an especially good niche for former laborers. Few white men saw this occupation as an economic threat because it was incompatible with their view of the male role. Yet laundry required only a minimal investment and did not demand high levels of skill or literacy—an excellent alternative to facing the racial tensions of the labor market.

Racial tension persisted in other venues, however, and Chinese were seen as potential threats to the purity of the white race. In 1880, California passed a law prohibiting marriage between a white person and a "negro, mulatto, or

---

5. The Chinese Exclusion Act was renewed in 1892 and extended indefinitely in 1902. Its effect ended with the passage of the Immigration and Naturalization Act of 1924.

Mongolian" (Osumi, 1982). These "antimiscegenation" laws remained on the books in some states as late as 1998.[6]

Chinese immigrants were primarily male. For economic and cultural reasons, women did not emigrate from China. They had no value in the labor market and were accustomed to living within the narrow confines of their homes. Well-born Chinese women were nearly unable to walk due to the practice of binding their feet into "rosebuds." A few Chinese men were able to bring their wives to the United States, and thousands of Chinese women were sold into prostitution. Nonetheless, the population of Chinese immigrants was predominantly male.

Japanese Immigrants.   The Japanese immigration experience differed from that of the Chinese in several respects. First, it began later. The initial wave of Japanese immigrants came to the United States in 1885, roughly 40 years after the beginning of Chinese immigration. Second, their country of origin was not a relatively undeveloped region but an emerging world power. Japan had defeated the Russians in 1905 and commanded a measure of respect for its military and economic potential. Third, while the Chinese government was not involved in emigration, Japanese emigration was carefully orchestrated and monitored by the Japanese government, which was ready to intercede diplomatically if its citizens were abused by the U.S. government (Daniels & Kitano, 1970). These differences led to a less difficult immigration experience for the Japanese, particularly as it was affected by federal policies.

These advantages did nothing, of course, to reduce the impact of American racism or mitigate the demands of the American economy on Japanese immigrants. Like the Chinese, the Japanese fled economic deprivation and, like the Chinese, they sought a better standard of living. Another similarity was the widespread belief, if not expectation, that Japanese emigrants were only temporarily residing in the United States.

Like the Chinese, the Japanese came to the United States as laborers. Thousands worked in the sugar cane fields of Hawaii, and others became agricultural laborers in California. The agricultural skills of the Japanese were considerable, and they introduced new techniques and crops to the fast-growing agricultural economy of California.

Unlike the Chinese, Japanese women came to the United States to work alongside their husbands. In Japan they had already become accepted members of the industrial labor force, and a wife was an asset in the immigration process. As a result, the first generation of Japanese immigrants (the *Issei*) settled and raised a second generation (the *Nisei*) of U.S.-born Japanese Americans.

Like the Chicanos, Japanese immigrants saw education as the key to their children's advancement. Also like the Chicanos, the Issei encountered resistance in their attempts to secure a public education for their children. In San Francisco

---

6. South Carolina and Alabama were the last states to eliminate statutes prohibiting interracial marriage. South Carolina did so in 1998, and Alabama in 1999. These laws had been declared unconstitutional by the U.S. Supreme Court in 1967.

the resistance was especially strident. In 1906, in the middle of an anti-Japanese campaign by the *San Francisco Chronicle,* the board of education ordered all Japanese students (both native- and foreign-born) to attend the segregated "Oriental School" that had been established in Chinatown. Daniels and Kitano (1970) note that the furor was disproportionate to the number of Japanese children in San Francisco schools: "Only a very few students were involved—at the time of the order there was a grand total of 93 Japanese students distributed among 23 different public schools, and 25 of them were native-born citizens" (p. 48).

The school board's order created international uproar. The U.S. ambassador to Japan received official protests from the Japanese government, which maintained that the action violated treaties protecting the rights of Japanese citizens in the United States. President Theodore Roosevelt summoned the school board to Washington and, "with a combination of threats, pleas, cajolings, and promises, succeeded in having the school board rescind the offending order" (Daniels & Kitano, 1970, p. 48). Roosevelt also succeeded in persuading the California legislature to refrain from passing anti-Japanese legislation.

In return, Roosevelt exchanged a series of notes with the Japanese government that have come to be known as the Gentlemen's Agreement. The Japanese agreed to limit emigration of laborers and farmers to the United States. This concession quieted calls for national legislation to restrict Japanese immigration on the model of the Chinese Exclusion Act. The Gentlemen's Agreement did allow for wives to join their husbands in the United States, and as a result thousands of "picture brides" made up the last of the Japanese immigrants. These women had long-distance arranged marriages to men with whom they had exchanged only photographs prior to meeting as husband and wife in the United States.

Of course, the Japanese government's protection of its citizens in the United States did not pave the way to U.S. citizenship. In a telling example of judicial racism, the U.S. Supreme Court denied the citizenship petition of Takao Ozawa. In 1922, Ozawa (a graduate of the University of California and a young man of good character and light complexion) petitioned for citizenship. The Court ruled that his complexion, however light, did not qualify as "white," and thus he did not meet the criteria for naturalization, which limited applicants to "free white persons" and "persons of African descent." The Court ruled, in *Ozawa v. United States,* that "white" meant "Caucasian." As Daniels and Kitano (1970) report, however, the same Court ruled "shortly thereafter, that an applicant from India, who was ethnographically a Caucasian although his complexion was of a mahogany hue" was not, in fact, entitled to citizenship because "White did not mean Caucasian at all, but meant, rather, 'white' as commonly understood" (p. 54). This court served as what Daniels and Kitano called "the last bulwark of racism" until its membership changed in the 1930s and 1940s through appointments by President Franklin Roosevelt.

Current Realities.   Asian and Pacific Islanders are typically grouped together by the census, despite their heterogeneity. Economic indicators provide limited support for the popular notion that Asian Americans represent a "model minority." For example, as indicated in Figure 9.2, the median household income of Asian households during the period from 2003 to 2005 was higher than that of white households: $59,877, compared with $50,677. Nonetheless, as we saw in Chapter 5, the risk of poverty for Asian and Pacific Islanders remains somewhat higher than that of white households. The poverty rate for Asian/Pacific Island households was 11.1 percent in 2005, compared with a rate of 8.3 percent for white households. Clearly, while most Asian/Pacific Island households have attained economic parity, a few continue to experience economic disadvantage.

Several factors contribute to the higher median household income among America's Asian population. First, it has been attributed to this group's higher likelihood of having more than two workers within a household. Second, as we will see in Chapter 14, workers of Asian descent tend to be overrepresented among the ranks of managerial and professional workers. Finally, Asian Americans have a relatively high rate of business ownership. The rate among whites, measured as businesses per 1,000 in the population, is 80. The rate for Asian/Pacific Islanders is 68. Rates for other groups were considerably lower. Hispanic Americans had a rate of 32 businesses per 1,000 in the population, African Americans 20, and Native Americans 19 (Population Reference Bureau, 1999).

As we saw in Chapter 6, life expectancy and infant mortality among Americans of Asian and Pacific Island descent are generally favorable in comparison with the general population and with white Americans.

Native Americans

The history of U.S. policy in relation to indigenous peoples can be divided into five stages: initial contact and treaty making (1532–1828); removal and relocation (1828–1887); forced assimilation (1887–1945); termination (1945–1961); and self-determination (1961 to present) (Deloria & Lytle, 1983). Each stage has been marked by a powerful desire on the part of some European immigrants to appropriate communal lands and natural resources for personal economic gain.

Initial Contact and Treaty Making. When Columbus encountered Native Americans,[7] he is quoted as having remarked:

---

7. Some tribes object to the term "Native American," feeling that it is too broad and includes Native Hawaiians and other indigenous people in land now occupied by the United States. Today, many prefer to use "Native American" when referring to indigenous tribes of the continental United States, and "Alaskan Native" to describe native peoples of Alaska. Michael Yellow Bird argues that the terms "Indian," "American Indian," and "Native American" are "counterfeit identities," and advocates the use of "First Nation" and "Indigenous Peoples" (Yellow Bird, 1999); however, these terms have not been widely accepted.

BOX 9.4   The Great Law of Peace

Contrary to popular views of Native Americans as savages, some of the English colonists recognized that they had developed effective methods for governance. Indeed, historians agree that the U.S. Constitution drew as much from the Native Americans as it did from the Europeans (Schaaf, 1990). Their argument is compelling in part because neither Britain nor other major originating nations had faced the challenge of uniting disparate political entities. In creating their new nation, the colonists faced just that challenge. Each colony had a distinctive history and culture, yet all needed to work together if the nation was to succeed. This challenge had been effectively addressed by tribal confederacies on the eastern seaboard of North America.

The Great Law of Peace governed a confederation of Iroquois tribes (also called the Haudenasaunee Six Nations). For centuries, these tribes strove for balance of power and supported the idea of the inherent rights of people, including freedom of speech and religion. Their council-based system of governance was of great interest to colonial leaders, including George Washington and Benjamin Franklin.

While serving as Indian Commissioner for Lancaster, Pennsylvania, during the mid-1700s, Benjamin Franklin studied the Iroquois system of governance. In 1744, minutes of the Lancaster, Pennsylvania, Provincial Council reported that Onondaga leader Canasatego advised the council to form a league similar to the Iroquois confederacy, saying, "[O]ur Wise forefathers established Union and Amity between the Five Nations. This has made us formidable; this has given us great Weight and Authority with our neighboring Nations. We are a powerful Confederacy; and by your observing the same methods our Wise Forefathers have taken, you will acquire such Strength and power. Therefore whatever befalls you, never fall out with one another" (Friends Committee on National Legislation, 1987). Further, Schaaf (1990) notes that the "Albany Plan of Union," proposed by Benjamin Franklin in 1754, reflects the structures of the Iroquois confederacy's Grand Council. (Dr. Paul Wallace, an ethnohistorian, wrote extensively about the governance structures of the Iroquois and Algonquian peoples. See also Parker, 1916, and Weatherford, 1988.)

On the 200th anniversary of the signing of the U.S. Constitution (September 1987), a concurrent resolution to the 100th Congress set out to "acknowledge the contribution of the Iroquois Confederacy of Nations to the Development of the United States Constitution and to reaffirm the continuing government-to-government relationship between Indian Tribes and the United States established in the Constitution." Senator Daniel Inouye and colleagues introduced the resolution.

I am indebted to Russ Redner for introducing me to this material.

> They [Native Americans] are the best people in the world and above all the gentlest—without knowledge of what is evil—nor do they murder or steal. They are very simple and honest . . . none of them refusing anything he may possess when he is asked for it. They exhibit great love toward all others in preference to themselves. They would make fine servants. With 50 men we could subjugate them all and make them do whatever we want. (Phillips & Phillips, 1992, p. 166)

When Europeans established their first colony in Virginia, the area was inhabited by an estimated 14,000 members of the Powhatan tribe (Takaki, 1993). For these agricultural people, corn was a dietary staple, as it was for many of the tribes encountered by the European immigrants. During what John Smith later called "the starving time" (winter of 1607), the Powhatans shared their food with the immigrants and taught them principles of survival. Later, the Iroquois

Federation would teach the colonists important principles of governance by sharing "the Great Law of Peace" (see Box 9.4).

In return, the Europeans declared Native Americans "heathens" and promoted their view of the race as "backward" and "savage." This view helped to justify atrocities committed by the Europeans, who were eager to steal the land under cultivation by Native Americans.

European interest in Native American lands initially stemmed from the popularity of tobacco in England. In 1613, the colony in Virginia sent its first shipment of tobacco to London. Within seven years, tobacco exports had increased to 60,000 pounds (Takaki, 1993). The Native Americans' already-cleared fields would, when converted to tobacco, produce riches for the immigrants. Europeans' lust for land and their capacity for declaring other races "inhuman" set the stage for well-documented brutalities.

With the passage of the Naturalization Act of 1790, Native Americans were classified as "domestic foreigners" and denied citizenship. The task of working with these internal nations was assigned to Congress through the Constitution and affirmed later in the 1802 Indian Trade and Intercourse Act, which provided that no Native American land would be ceded to the United States except through treaties with Congress.

Removal and Relocation.   European demands for cotton led to expansion into the southeastern part of the country. The states of Alabama, Mississippi, and Louisiana were carved out of Native American territory for cultivation of cotton. Between 1814 and 1824, 11 "treaties of cessation" were negotiated, forcing tribes in this area to relocate to land west of the Mississippi. A popular justification for the appropriation of Native American lands was the argument that the Native Americans did not fully "use" the land.

Faced with the threat of extermination, the Native American nations fought back. The "Indian Wars" progressed, and violence by Native Americans was seen both as evidence of their "savagery" and as justification for their annihilation. President Andrew Jackson (a veteran of the Indian Wars) encouraged this view, allowing states to appropriate Native American lands for distribution to white settlers in contradiction to the Indian Trade and Intercourse Act as well as an 1832 Supreme Court Ruling.[8] One example of Jackson's practice of ignoring federal law came when the state of Mississippi abolished the sovereignty of the Choctaw nation. The federal government then collaborated in the state's effort to deprive Choctaw of their land through the "Treaty of Dancing Rabbit Creek." Tribal leaders, threatened with extermination, had no choice but to approve the treaty, which required that Choctaw cede their land (10,423,130 acres) to the federal government and move west of the Mississippi.

Alexis de Tocqueville described the exodus of the Choctaw from Mississippi:

---

8. Jackson is quoted as having responded to objections that he was acting in opposition to the Supreme Court by saying, "Let the Supreme Court enforce its ruling."

B O X 9.5   Blanche K. Bruce (1841–1898)

Blanche K. Bruce was the first African American to serve a full term in the U.S. Senate. Born a slave, Bruce was an ardent supporter of extending civil rights to Native Americans. Of the American experience, he said,

"As a people, our history is full of surmounted obstacles. We have been scaling difficult problems for more than a hundred years."

It was then the middle of winter and the cold was unusually severe; the snow had frozen hard upon the ground, and the river was drifting huge masses of ice. The Indians had their families with them, and they brought in their train the wounded and the sick, with children newly born and old men upon the verge of death. Three or four thousand soldiers drive before them the wandering races of the aborigines; these are followed by the pioneers, who pierce the woods, scare off the beasts of prey, explore the courses of the inland streams, and make ready the triumphal march of civilization across the desert. (de Tocqueville, 1835, pp. 352–364)

The federal government made a profit from the sale of the Choctaw lands. Since this sale was in violation of their treaty, the Choctaw sued in federal court. In 1890 they were awarded a settlement of nearly $3 million, most of which went to pay their lawyers (Wright, 1928).

In one of many similar incidents, one-fourth of the Cherokee Nation died on the "Trail of Tears" as a direct result of betrayal and manipulation sanctioned by the president and Congress. Cherokee lands covered what is now called Georgia. In 1829, the Georgia state government passed a law extending their authority to Cherokee lands. Aware that this action was a violation of federal law, Chief Ross of the Cherokee Nation wrote to President Jackson pleading for his protection. Jackson instructed his Indian commissioner, J. F. Schermerhorn, to negotiate a treaty to move the Cherokee. Schermerhorn presented the treaty to a Cherokee council that was carefully crafted to include only those Cherokee who were inclined to approve it. (Chief Ross was jailed for the occasion.) A tiny fraction of the Nation attended the Council. None of the tribal leaders was present. The treaty was ratified. Even some federal officials acknowledged it as a fraud. Nonetheless, Congress ratified the treaty, and the president approved it. And, as a result, most of the Cherokee Nation set out, in the middle of one of the worst winters on record, to resettle west of the Mississippi on land they had never seen.

As the Western expansion progressed and railroads were built, the lands west of the Mississippi captured the imagination of the U.S. government and its citizens. The railroads made extensive use of public policy to advance their interests, securing the rights to millions of acres of land that lay adjacent to their tracks and fostering passage of the 1871 Indian Appropriation Act. This act declared that "hereafter no Indian nation or tribe within the territory of the United States shall be acknowledged or recognized as an independent nation, tribe, or power, with whom the United States may contract by treaty" (Walker, 1874, p. 5). The act denied the very existence of tribes as legitimate political units, eliminating the need to negotiate treaties and paving the way for the railroads' expansion. This act was accompanied by federal policy that forcibly placed Indians on reservations, where they could be trained to become agricultural workers and eventually assimilated into the broader society.

Forced Assimilation. Under the reservation system, land was assigned to the tribes with the assurance that they would not be subject to attack by U.S. military forces as long as they were within reservation boundaries. Of course, the problem with the system was whites' insatiable appetite for Native American lands. Thus, in 1887, the Dawes Act, also known as the Indian Emancipation Act, was passed to eliminate the reservation system. White reformers believed that true assimilation would come only with private, not tribal, ownership of land. Under this act, each Native American head of household who was at least one-half Native American would be given a 160-acre parcel. If a reservation had more parcels than households, the "surplus" parcels would be sold to white settlers. The net effect of the act was removal of thousands of acres from the reservation system. Not only were "surplus" parcels sold, but individual settlers purchased or stole property from individual tribal owners. Tribal leaders recognized the threat the Dawes Act posed to tribal survival, and some, like Chief Lone Wolf of the Kiowas, went to court to argue that the parceling out of land was in violation of previous treaties. In 1903, the Supreme Court declared that the federal government could abrogate treaty provisions. This allotment procedure reduced Native American lands from 138 million to 48 million acres (Limerick, 1987).

In 1924, U.S. citizenship was conferred on all tribal members. Later, as part of Roosevelt's New Deal, Native Americans were offered an opportunity to regain tribal control of what remained of their reservation land through the 1934 Indian Reorganization Act (also known as the Howard–Wheeler Act). This law restored the political legitimacy of tribes (in the eyes of the U.S. government) and encouraged the maintenance of Native American culture on reservation lands. Reorganization meant that tribes would enjoy self-government on their lands, and that some funds would be allocated for purchase of additional tribal lands. The law included a provision that required ratification by a majority of tribal members. Most tribes did approve reorganization, but some (most notably the Navajo) chose to remain outside the system.

General Richard Pratt's motto, "Kill the Indian, Save the Man," was the watchword of a movement to assimilate Native Americans by removing children from their homes and placing them in boarding schools, run either by the government or by messianic Christian denominations. Pratt founded the first Native American boarding school in 1879, the Carlisle Indian School, in Pennsylvania. Three years later, U.S. Indian Commissioner Thomas Morgan supported the effort, commenting that it was "cheaper to educate Indians than to kill them" (Kelley, 1999).

Tens of thousands of Native American children were placed in these schools. The children were subjected to a harsh daily schedule, with only limited time devoted to education and the remainder to hard labor. They were strictly punished for revealing any evidence of their culture, such as carrying a medicine bundle or speaking their native language. The children were trained to be domestic servants and agricultural laborers.

This assimilation program peaked in the United States in 1931, when nearly one-third of Native American children were in boarding schools. It continues today in 52 boarding schools operated by the government. Most of these are located on the Navajo reservation. The schools are now managed primarily by Native Americans, many of whom are alumni. As a result, students can expect a less punitive, more culturally congruent experience (Limerick, 1987).

Termination.   The horrors of Native American removal, the reservation system, and the Native American boarding schools are well documented, as is the duplicity with which U.S. officials treated Native American tribes. Between 1778 and 1871, some 370 Native American treaties were ratified by the U.S. Senate.[9] Many of them were later abrogated or ignored. This duplicity is well remembered by Native Americans, and it colors their view of federal services and policies.

Federal recognition is critical for tribes seeking to establish services and provide benefits to their people. There are 562 federally recognized tribes in the United States, and about 148 groups seeking federal recognition. The process of attaining federal recognition is difficult and arbitrary. During the 1950s and 1960s the federal government pursued a policy of "termination," discontinuing recognition of several tribes (Churchill, 1998; Yellow Bird, 2001). At the same time, a program of relocation dispatched Native American people from reservations to cities with the goal of forcing them to assimilate into mainstream society.

A direct result of this policy is seen today in the numbers of Native American people living off reservations. In 1900, over 99 percent of federally recognized Native Americans lived on reservations. By 1970, nearly half (44.5 percent) lived off reservations. Current estimates suggest that over half of Native Americans—from 55 to 70 percent—live off the reservation (Churchill, 1998; Walters, 1999).

The betrayals committed by government representatives were not seen as "wrong" by most white U.S. citizens at the time they took place. Intelligent, well-meaning people had been persuaded that Native Americans were less human than whites—that they were "savage." The whites' insatiable greed for Native American land stemmed from an economic system that allowed for the creation of immense private wealth at the expense of communal and environmental values. It was reinforced by religious values that emphasized the superiority of

9. These treaties are compiled in a volume entitled *Indian Treaties, 1778–1871,* available through the Diplomatic Branch of the National Archives and Records Services, Washington, DC.

BOX 9.6   Wilma Mankiller (1945–)

Wilma Mankiller organized the residents of the impoverished and demoralized 300-family town of Bell, Oklahoma, to develop a clean water supply that was connected to every house. She went on to be elected chief of the Cherokee Nation.

Christianity. Finally, it was fostered by a failure to see, as Reverend Davis said, that "difference is just that: difference. Not better or worse, just different."

Current Realities: Self-Determination.   Today, U.S. Native American policy is administered by the Bureau of Indian Affairs (BIA). Figures from the 2000 census estimate a Native American population of 2.4 million (U.S. Bureau of the Census, 2001). For census purposes, a Native American is someone who reports that he or she is a Native American. The BIA recognizes 562 tribes, including hundreds of village groups in Alaska. The process of tribal recognition is lengthy and often contentious.[10] Native Americans speak 250 different tribal languages, and for most English is a second language.

Under current law, some 56 million acres of tribal lands are held in "trust" for Native Americans by the secretary of the interior. The federal government collects income on some Native American lands, through grazing and mineral leasing. This money is returned to the tribes as "trust income." It is not subject to federal income tax.

Tribes that are officially recognized by the federal government are considered "internal, dependent nations." As a result, most transactions on reservations are not subject to state income tax or sales taxes. Residents of reservations do not pay local property taxes. Native Americans living on a reservation do have the right to vote in state and local elections, though several western states (including Arizona and Utah) have attempted (so far unsuccessfully) to disenfranchise reservation residents within their jurisdictions.

Tribes are (understandably) sensitive about efforts to undermine their sovereignty, particularly by state governments. State efforts to regulate gaming on reservations were seen in this light. Accordingly, Native American advocates were alarmed by passage of the 1988 Indian Gaming Regulatory Act by Congress, which allowed for state regulation of gaming on reservations.

Another area that has been touched by sovereignty issues is child protective services. The 1978 Indian Child Welfare Act (ICWA) was designed to prevent removal of Native American children from their tribes and families. Under the ICWA, tribes have primary jurisdiction over Native American children who

---

10. The BIA bases recognition decisions on a group's continued cultural existence. But some tribes do an end run around the BIA, seeking recognition through a direct act of Congress. Given the high value of gambling for tribes, recognition decisions have significant commercial implications.

enter the child welfare system, and state authorities are required to give preference to kin and tribes in finding homes for those who are removed because of abuse or neglect. Advocates complain that states are reluctant to designate children "Indian," claiming that even enrolled children living off-reservation are "not Indian enough" to be subject to ICWA provisions. Further, the Multiethnic Placement Act (passed in 1994) is seen as weakening the federal mandate to seek Native American homes for Native American children. (These acts are discussed further in Chapter 11.)

Prior to the 2000 census, the last careful count of the nation's Native American population was that mandated by the Dawes Act in 1887. Census counts during the interim undercounted the Native American population, and as a result much was written about the so-called "vanishing race" (Churchill, 1998; Johansen, 2002; Thornton, 1987, 1996). Using a strategy familiar to social work since the Settlement House days, the Census Bureau hired Native American people to collect data for the 2000 census, and Native Americans were encouraged to participate in the census at powwows and other cultural events, urban Native American centers and clinics, schools and universities, and other settings.

As a result of these efforts, more than 4.1 million people told the 2000 census takers that they were at least part Native American, which is double the 2 million who reported Native ancestry in the 1990 census and 14 times the official figure of about 300,000 a century ago. Most of this growth was due to a change in census procedures. Census 2000 was the first in which respondents were allowed to choose more than one race. A total of 1.6 million Americans identified themselves as part American Indian/Alaska Native, which accounted for most of the increase. But even when those identifying as part American Indian/Alaska Native are not included, Census 2000 documented a 25-percent increase in the number of Americans identified as Native American people since the 1990 census (Johansen, 2002; Thornton, 1987, 1996, U.S. Bureau of the Census, 2002).

Available data provide a stark portrayal of the economic status of the first Americans. As indicated in Figure 9.2, the median household income for Native American and Alaska Native households during the period from 2003 to 2005 ($33,627) was about two-thirds of the median for white households ($50,677). Finally, in 2005 over a quarter (27 percent) of Native American households had incomes below the poverty threshold, compared to 13 percent of the overall U.S. population.

Native Americans live in diverse settings—in *hogans* in the deserts of Arizona, Utah, and Nevada, in concrete block houses on reservations, in urban apartments, and in suburban homes. Current estimates suggest that over half of Native Americans—between 55 and 70 percent—live off the reservation, many in urban centers such as New York and Los Angeles (Churchill, 1998; Ogunwole, 2002; Walters, 1999). Urban Native Americans generally enjoy greater income and better health than those living on reservations, although urban settings do not permit access to Indian Health Service facilities.

Reservations offer better access to tribal community and Indian Health Services, but living conditions can be difficult. Many homes have no electricity, refrigeration, or indoor toilets. Transportation can also be problematic, and many rely on poorly maintained dirt roads that become impassable in rain or snow. Finally, communication is a challenge, as many do not have telephones, receive newspapers, or have television sets (Bane, 1991).

Under the Indian Self-Determination and Educational Assistance Act of 1975 tribes are permitted to manage health programs formerly under the purview of Indian Health Service. Many have taken advantage of this opportunity and as Roubideaux (2002) reports, "approximately half of the IHS budget is now managed by tribes" (p. 1402). But access to health care is problematic, even on reservations. As the National Indian Health Board (2004) notes, funding for the Indian Health Service (IHS) has lagged behind need and even basic fairness. Indeed, the federal government spends nearly twice as much on each federal prisoner's health care as it does on a per capita basis for Native Americans and Alaska Natives. Per-person Indian Health Service expenditures were approximately $1,900 in 2003, a figure that, when adjusted for inflation, represents a net decline compared with budgets of the mid-1970s (National Indian Health Board, 2004). Limited access to health care, coupled with poverty and harsh living conditions, have contributed to higher rates of morbidity and mortality and reduced life expectancy for indigenous peoples in the United States (Centers for Disease Control and Prevention, 2007a).

POLICIES AFFECTING PEOPLE OF COLOR

The history of people of color in the United States is rife with examples of prejudice and government-sponsored oppression. Has the nation moved forward in recent years? Has racism become a thing of the past? In this section we will examine some policy developments in this area.

Hate Crime Legislation

Under current federal law, crimes committed because of a person's membership in a protected group (based on race, ethnicity, religion, or national origin) can result in more severe penalties. These crimes, called "hate crimes," are seen as more grievous than others because they not only harm the immediate victims but also instill fear in people with similar characteristics. Although a 1969 statute offered federal prosecution of crimes against racial, ethnic, or religious minorities engaged in federally protected activities (such as voting or attending public school), most federal legislation in this area dates to the 1990s. During the Clinton administration several bills were introduced to apply hate crime designation to crimes based on gender, disability, and sexual orientation. These did not become law. Recent federal initiatives in this area include

- The Hate Crimes Statistics Act of 1990, which requires the Justice Department to gather and publish statistics on crimes motivated by prejudice based on race, ethnicity, religion, or sexual orientation

- Portions of the Juvenile Justice and Delinquency Prevention Act of 1992, directing the Office of Juvenile Justice Delinquency Programs to study hate crimes and develop prevention and treatment programs for perpetrators

- The Hate Crimes Sentencing Enhancement Act of 1994, which calls for increased penalties when the crime is proven to be a hate crime

- The Church Arson Prevention Act of 1996, making damage to religious property a federal offense

- The Hate Crimes Prevention Act of 1998, which expanded federal jurisdiction to violent hate crimes and offered grants to state and local prosecutors to reduce hate crimes

Nearly all states have passed hate crime statutes that mirror federal law, allowing harsher penalties for crimes targeting people based on their race, ethnicity, religion, or national origin. About half of the hate crime statutes at the state level include sexual orientation.

Hate crime legislation is controversial. Proponents argue that harsher sentences for hate crimes are fair because these crimes are more damaging than similar offenses not motivated by hate. They suggest that stiffer penalties may deter potential perpetrators. Opponents compare hate crimes to "thought" crimes, arguing that it is impossible to demonstrate reliably that a crime was motivated by hatred and that efforts to do so infringe on the right to freedom of speech (see Troy, 1998).

In the wake of the attacks of September 11, 2001, hate crimes against Americans who are (or are perceived to be) of Arab descent increased dramatically. The FBI reported that anti-Muslim hate crimes increased from 28 in 2000 to 480 in 2001 (Federal Bureau of Investigation, 2002). Human rights organizations have documented thousands of incidents, ranging from murder to airport harassment and destruction of property. In a 2004 report, the Council on American–Islamic Relations (CAIR) reported increased harassment of people perceived to be Muslim, with a growing number of incidents involving government officials acting under the purview of the Patriot Act (CAIR, 2004).

English-Only Legislation

English-only proposals surfaced in this country as early as 1780, when John Adams proposed that the Continental Congress establish an official academy to "purify, develop, and dictate usage of English" (ACLU, 1996). His proposal was rejected as undemocratic. With the 1803 purchase of the Louisiana Territory, President Jefferson tried to impose an English-only policy on French speakers in that territory. The uproar from the territory led to a quick retreat, and Louisiana entered the Union in 1812 as the only state with a non-English-speaking majority (Kloss, 1998). The Californios (Spanish speakers who resided in California when it was conquered) were much less successful. Although the state's constitution recognized Spanish language rights and guaranteed bilingual publication of state laws, the following year saw the Gold Rush. Spanish-speakers became a minority, and "greaser laws" were passed to harass them (Leibowitz, 1969). "English only" became the law of the land in the new state of California. Finally, the forced assimilation of Native Americans into the English-only world involved taking Native American children to boarding schools far from home, where they were punished for speaking their own language.[11]

The English-only movement resurfaced in the 1980s, with proponents arguing that the English language needed legislative protection from the encroachment of other tongues and that "creeping bilingualism" threatened the very foundations of American culture. Legislation was advanced at the federal and state levels to restrict the use of other languages for government business.

Proponents of official English are generally political conservatives—the same people who favor immigration restrictions and would deny services to legal immigrants. In the early 1980s, a constitutional amendment was proposed that would have banned the use of languages other than English by federal, state, and local governments. It never reached a vote. Later, in 1994 Republican leadership in the House of Representatives passed a measure that prohibited the use of languages other than English by the federal government. Threatened with a presidential veto, the measure died without Senate action (Crawford, 1992). Since then there have been several unsuccessful attempts to pass federal English-only statutes. English-only proponents have been more successful at passing state legislation, and as of this writing, official English requirements have been established in most states.

Proponents of English-only legislation offer several arguments. First, they suggest that bilingual education delays or prevents acquisition of English by immigrants. They assert that immigrants today, unlike those of the past, refuse to learn English and insist on government-sponsored bilingual programs. Second, they argue that the United States is at risk of becoming balkanized like Quebec or India. Idaho Senator Steve Symms introduced an English-only amendment to the U.S. Constitution, arguing that "countless hundreds of thousands have lost their lives in the language riots of India. Real potential exists for a similar situation in the United States" (Crawford, 1992, p. 395). Finally, proponents suggest that English is a "common bond" holding Americans of diverse backgrounds together.

None of these arguments is based on evidence, and most are designed to appeal to anti-immigrant and racist feelings. Educational studies consistently demonstrate that non-English-speaking students do better in school and learn English more quickly in bilingual or structured English immersion classrooms (Ramirez, Yuen, & Ramey, 1991). There is no evidence of language-based political organization (aside from the English-only movement) in the United States. Finally, national pride in the United States tends to be more strongly associated

---

11. English-only efforts were also initiated in the U.S. territories of Puerto Rico and Guam. Less successful in Puerto Rico, these policies nearly eradicated the indigenous language of Guam.

BOX 9.7   Navajo Code Talkers, World War II

In a vivid illustration of the benefits of language diversity, Navajo Marines in World War II used their language for top-secret communications. It was the only code the enemy was unable to break. The Navajo Code Talkers took part in every assault by the U.S. Marines between 1942 and 1945. They are recognized in a permanent exhibit on the Pentagon Concourse. The 1990 Native American Languages Act (PL 101-477) recognized the right of indigenous peoples to use their native languages as mediums of commerce and instruction.

---

with ideals such as individual freedom and achievement than with the English language. As James Crawford, who has studied the English-only movement for a decade, notes, "English-only arguments are so value-laden in their distaste for diversity, so crude in their analogies with other nations, so credulous about the power of social engineering, and so bereft of factual evidence that they are difficult to take seriously" (Crawford, 1996, p. 4).

Millions of Americans do take these arguments seriously, however. Scholars differ on the reasons for this phenomenon. Some argue that the movement attracts people with racial prejudices and anxieties about cultural change (see Schmid, 1992). Others suggest that support for English-only legislation reflects an upsurge in national pride (see Citrin et al., 1990).

The effects of English-only legislation vary, depending on whether the laws simply declare English the official language or bar the use of other languages. The official declaration of the prominence of English has had little practical effect, but some legislation passed by the states has banned bilingual ballots and bilingual instruction in public schools, some cities have passed ordinances prohibiting the use of other languages in private signs, and some have eliminated the use of courtroom translation. These practices have all made life more difficult for non-English-speaking immigrants (ACLU, 1996).

Standardized Testing

On the surface, standardized tests appear race-neutral. Designed to measure general aptitude, most are not intended to promote discrimination. But the consequences of standardized testing consistently operate against people of color.

The intelligence tests used today are based on the Stanford-Binet test, which emerged during the heyday of the "eugenics movement." This movement advanced the view that high intelligence, like other desirable traits, was genetically based and less present in "inferior" races. The creator of the Stanford-Binet test, Lewis Terman, used it to provide support for the notion that northern Europeans were superior to other races. He argued that high scores were correlated with moral behavior, and that the higher IQs of northern Europeans explained their economic dominance.

As mentioned earlier, employment testing was frequently used during the 1960s in hiring and promotion decisions. In addition to measuring proficiency in specific skills, these tests often purported to measure general aptitude or intelligence. Because of limited educational opportunities, people of color did poorly on the tests. When the "intent" of the testing process was examined, the process appeared race-neutral; however, the "consequences" of the testing were disadvantageous to racial minorities. In 1966, the EEOC issued guidelines stipulating that tests with these consequences were in violation of Title VII of the 1964 Civil Rights Act unless the employer could demonstrate that they accurately predicted job performance.

SUMMARY: FUTURE PROSPECTS

In this chapter we have traced the history of and current realities experienced by four groups: African Americans, Hispanic Americans, Asian Americans, and Native Americans. A major thread in these histories is a shift in the role of public policy from the active promotion of race-based oppression to serving as an agent (to various degrees) of equal opportunity. Emerging debates about hate crimes, English-only legislation, and standardized testing have been explored. What remains is a brief discussion of the role of race and ethnicity in the world's most diverse nation.

Over the past few decades, and particularly during the economic boom of the 1990s, many people of color have moved into the middle class. For example, by 2006, about one-third of Hispanic, Native American, and African American households had incomes over $50,000 (U.S. Bureau of the Census, 2007). In 2005, nearly 6 percent of African American households had incomes in the nation's highest quintile (U.S. Bureau of the Census, 2006).

These statistics reflect a significant accomplishment, both for the United States as a whole and for the individuals involved. Economic advancement also tends to divide communities along class lines, fueling arguments that people of color who are not economically successful are personally flawed. Some people of color, frequently second- and third-generation members of successful families, have become vocal opponents of public income supports and affirmative action (see, for example, Linda Chavez's 1991 work, *Out of the Barrio*). These advocates argue, in essence, "If I could make it, so can they." While race-based disadvantage is very real today, coming years may see erosion in the cohesiveness of racial and ethnic communities as class, rather than race, becomes the great dividing line for American society.

KEYWORDS

Cultural diversity	Hispanic Americans	Assimilation
Affirmative action	Minority	Native Americans
African Americans	Multiculturalism	Immigration
Asian Americans	Racism	Slavery
	Hate crimes	

THINK ABOUT IT

1. Use the history of racial oppression in the United States to evaluate the major theories of racism discussed in this chapter. Does history support the idea that racism is the result of ignorance or of market competition? What do you see as the roots of racism? Do you think racism will be eliminated in your lifetime?

2. Do you think past injustices (such as the internment of the Japanese during World War II) entitle people to some kind of remedy? Is an apology in order? Economic reparation? To whom is it due? Should descendants of former slaves receive some kind of reparation? Why or why not?

3. Do you think a class-based society is more or less just than one in which race is the basis of social allocations?

WEB-BASED EXERCISES

For direct links to all the sites in these exercises, log on to the Student Companion Site for this book at academic.cengage.com/social_work/barusch, and choose Chapter 9.

1. Go to the website of the Southern Poverty Law Center (www.splcenter .org). Click on the "Legal Action" tab to learn about the cases the center has brought forward. Consider recent developments in the SPL's battle against hate groups.

2. Go to the website of the U.S. Bureau of the Census (www.census.gov). Click on "Poverty" (under People and Households); then go to the "Detailed Poverty Tables" (under Current Poverty Data). Under the most recent year, select "Official Poverty Tables," and find a table that includes the word "race." This will enable you to compare poverty rates for people of different races. Compare the most recent racial differences in poverty with those from the earliest year available. Have conditions improved or deteriorated?

SUGGESTED RESOURCES

Davis, K. E., & Bent-Goodley, T. B. (2004). *The Color of Social Policy*. Alexandria, VA: Council on Social Work Education.

Deloria, V., & Lytle, C. M. (1983). *American Indians, American Justice*. Austin, TX: University of Texas Press.

Mayfield, C. (Ed.). (1981). *Growing Up Southern: Southern Exposure Looks at Childhood, Then and Now*. New York: Pantheon Books.

Takaki, R. (1993). *A Different Mirror: A History of Multicultural America*. Boston: Little, Brown.

Wilson, C. A. (1996). *Racism: From Slavery to Advanced Capitalism*. Thousand Oaks, CA: Sage.

www.airpi.org. The American Indian Policy Center is a nonprofit organization that was founded in 1992 for the purposes of research, policy development, and education on Native American issues. The site offers some outstanding policy papers written from a Native American perspective.

www.doi.gov/bureau-indian-affairs.html. This is the official website of the Bureau of Indian Affairs, which is part of the Department of the Interior. It offers some useful background information, written from a somewhat defensive posture.

www.naacp.org. The National Association for the Advancement of Colored People describes itself as the nation's "largest and strongest civil rights organization." The NAACP's site offers information about the organization, as well as news briefs and access to their magazine, *Crisis*.

www.splcenter.org. The Southern Poverty Law Center is a nonprofit organization whose mission is to "combat hate, intolerance and discrimination through education and litigation." At the site, you will find information on current events and projects, "intelligence reports" on hate groups in the United States, and educational material for teaching tolerance.

10

Gay, Lesbian, Bisexual, and Transgendered Individuals

I will scatter myself among men and women as I go.
I will toss a new gladness and roughness among them,
Whoever denies me it shall not trouble me,
Whoever accepts me he or she shall be blessed and shall bless me.
WALT WHITMAN, "SONG OF THE OPEN ROAD"

The struggle for equal rights for GLBT (Gay, Lesbian, Bisexual, or Transgendered) Americans came to public awareness in 1969, when the New York City police raided a gay bar (Stonewall Inn) in Greenwich Village. The ensuing rebellion marked the beginning of the gay rights movement. Since that time, most Americans have seen television coverage of annual Gay Pride parades held in major cities throughout the country. These parades support a view of GLBT Americans as colorful, if eccentric, figures in the national land-scape. Such vivid images can obscure the reality of daily life for Americans of minority sexual orientations, those who are GLBT. These realities can include violence, employment discrimination, legal barriers to family formation, and lim-ited access to health and related benefits.

In this chapter, we will examine social policies that affect GLBT individuals in America. After reviewing the life experiences of Mike, a gay man who is pursuing a career in social work, we will briefly outline the history of the gay rights movement in the United States, paying special attention to political initiatives that deny civil rights to lesbian and gay citizens. Next, we will consider legal barriers to marriage, adoption, and child custody and explore discrimination against gays and lesbians by employers and organizations. We will take a look at hate crime legislation as well as social policy related to human immunodeficiency virus/acquired immunodeficiency syndrome (HIV/AIDS). We will then turn to policies and issues unique to transgendered individuals. The chapter concludes by considering the role of social workers and our professional Code of Ethics in the struggle for gay rights.

DEFINING HOMOSEXUALITY

Attraction between members of the same gender has probably always been an aspect of human sexuality. Homosexual activity (particularly among men) in ancient times is well documented, and cultures have varied in their response to same-sex attraction.

Homosexuality has been variously defined as "sin," "psychopathology," "preference," and "orientation." The term "homosexuality" was first applied in the mid-nineteenth century by the Viennese author Karoly Maria Benkert to refer to the "Uranians" described by Karl Heinrich Ulrichs in the 1860s. Ulrichs was a biologist in Hanover, Germany. Fascinated by findings of androgyny in early stages of human embryonic development, he concluded that homosexual attraction had congenital roots and identified what he called a "third sex," people who were attracted to members of their own sex. In 1864, Ulrichs issued a pamphlet calling for legalization of same-sex marriage. In deference to the stigma attached to his theories about a third sex, Ulrichs used a pen name (Greenberg, 1988).

Public understanding of the causes of homosexuality has considerable influence on social policy. The notion that homosexuality has a congenital cause has two implications: first, it leaves homosexuals "blameless." The tolerant views espoused by Ulrichs stemmed from his belief that homosexuality was an inborn trait and that people who couldn't help being attracted to same-sex partners should not be punished. Second, it suggests that children (and other innocents) cannot be "converted" to homosexuality. The fear that children will be corrupted by exposure to homosexuals is frequently used in persecution campaigns. Advocates of more tolerant public policies generally adhere to the notion that homosexuality is an inborn trait rather than an acquired characteristic.

Freud explained homosexuality in psychological rather than biological terms, placing its origins in early childhood experiences (Osborne, 1993). By attributing homosexual attraction to parenting, Freud helped expand the stigma of homosexuality beyond the individuals themselves to encompass their parents and families. Further developments in psychiatric theory would result in homosexuality

A HUMAN PERSPECTIVE Mike Dixon

Born during the early 1950s in northern California, Mike has known he was gay since the age of 8 or 9. He said, "I always felt 'different' from other kids, but I didn't really have a word for it. I did know that I shouldn't talk about it with anyone, and so I just kept whatever it was to myself." He has a vivid memory of the moment he realized he was gay. "I looked down and saw this older kid. He was swimming and only had shorts on. I got this overwhelming urge to grab him around the middle and hug him. . . . From that point on, I realized that I wasn't like the other boys I knew, but I didn't dare say why—even to myself."

Life in elementary school was rugged. Mike hated team sports, gym, and recess. Recess was especially awful "because that is when I would routinely get beat up by the bullies in school." But he loved working with his father and uncle in their heating business. "I used to go to work with them when I was a kid. I really loved doing this, and especially loved getting to 'do something' like rolling out pipe, soldering, digging holes for water pipes."

Mike said "things were a little better" when he got to high school. "The teachers were more intelligent, and I didn't feel like I was going to be picked on all the time . . . there were other kids like me—sort of brainy and withdrawn—and we hung out together." Still, he "got into drugs" in high school and nearly flunked out. Teachers identified him as an "underachiever," and eventually he graduated with a low C average. His sexual identity was not an important issue during high school. "I never had sex with anyone while I was in high school. I never even really thought about it. It never dawned on me that I could actually act on my desires—it was a hetero world, but even that was something that was taken for granted, and I didn't question why it was so." In retrospect, Mike said, "I have to say that I thought high school was a waste. I hated that place, and the conformist attitudes they tried to shove down my throat."

Mike graduated in 1968. After leaving home to attend college, he came out "to myself and a few other people I knew. I never came out formally to my parents." He felt that his mother "got it" without being told, but she never said anything. He said, "My father was kind of oblivious, and it turned out that he was completely cool about it when I came out to him around 1979, after my mother died." Mike's father liked all of his boyfriends and took care to include them in invitations and celebrations. Of his only sibling,

Mike said, "I came out to my sister around this time, and she didn't give a shit." Later his sister told him she resented his lifestyle, "like being queer was about partying, spending money, and having a good time."

During college, Mike "met this guy in a class" and they moved in together. They didn't really consider themselves a "couple" because they were so different. "He was a real political hippie and I was a sort of brain-nerd-sass-ass-intellectual." Still, he had "a pretty good life for an 18-year-old," and they found jobs in a printing plant. Mike worked there for almost nine years, putting himself through college.

Mike enjoyed college very much. "I really liked the atmosphere of college and was far more interested in what was going on in class and in talking to the people I met there." But the prospect of being drafted and sent to Vietnam threw a shadow over this period of his life. When his deferment was changed and Mike received a new draft card, he had a horrible fight with his parents. He told them he planned to go to Canada if he was called to Vietnam, and "They did not understand that I didn't think it was my 'duty' to go off and get killed in Johnson's war. That was a confusing, almost psychotic time in my life. I went to work four nights per week, studied like mad so I wouldn't get kicked out of school, and just prayed that the draft board didn't call me."

Time passed, and the draft was replaced by the "lottery." Mike's number was 332. "That did it," he said "I was free!" He graduated the next year and moved to Holland with a friend he had met in school. The year in Holland was great. "We lived in Delft, I learned Dutch, and just spent all day hanging out and drawing pictures of old buildings. I lived on my 'retirement' check—some paltry union pension rebate—that they gave me when I quit the printing company." Then Mike got a call that his mother was dying. He flew back, and "she was dead within a week."

Mike stayed in the United States and enrolled to do graduate work in art. Here he met his "first boyfriend." He "met this kid in one of my drawing classes . . . we had a torrid affair that lasted about nine months . . . then he left me for a younger guy. . . . I was devastated. I spent the next year in an alcoholic isolation that only snapped when I got arrested for drunk driving . . . that sort of shocked me out of my swoon, but I never forgot that kid for 10 years." Mike got into therapy, an experience that changed his life and his outlook on himself.

Nonetheless, he said, "I think I was still in love with him [first boyfriend] when I moved in with my 'second' boyfriend, after I moved to San Francisco in 1980." He met "Bob" through a mutual friend, and they hit it off right away. "He had this idea that we should start a catering company—I was a good cook and he had worked in hotels and knew the business, somewhat. We borrowed $5,000 from a friend, bought a used van and a couple of cases of cocktail glasses, had some cards printed at my old printing company, and we were in business. . . . We moved in together in 1981 and worked like dogs until he died in 1990."

The business was very successful. "We had the reputation of being one of the top five caterers in San Francisco, and we did it at the right time (the '80s) when people were spending money like it was water. We bought a huge house in the East Bay, with a pool. We went to Europe twice, went on long trips to New England and the South, went to Hawaii every winter for three weeks and generally lived as if there were no tomorrow."

But Mike's partner had AIDS. "When I think back on it, he must have had AIDS when we met. Then, in about 1985, he started to get 'opportunistic infections.' He got weaker and weaker, until finally he could not get out of bed without help. I kept the business together through his illness, and when I got a call during some job that he was not expected to make it through the night, I went and sat with him until he died. I went to Hawaii with his ashes . . . then I came back home. I put the house up for sale, sold the catering business, and just withdrew again."

Mike described the impact of AIDS on the San Francisco gay community, saying, "During this time about every male I knew died. I went to eight or ten 'memorials' (funerals were considered un-PC) during that year and a half period. It was one month for a while. I kept thinking, 'I'm next,' but kept testing negative. One after another, everyone I knew died of AIDS. That period in San Francisco gay history is famous now—people started calling it the Plague, but that seemed too lighthearted, somehow. It was just awful. Everyone anyone knew was dying these hideous deaths. The gay community was trying to mobilize, but there was not a lot of organization. We were all grieving—no one's story was any more heartbreaking than anyone else's. We were all wrecks. Most people I knew got through a few deaths, and then they died themselves. Mayor Feinstein came and spoke at Bob's funeral. They were business friends, and she couldn't believe that "even

Bob" would die. Straights just didn't get it. They seemed to just be unable to conceive of how huge it was, and of what it felt like to have your whole world die grisly deaths with only medical help and no social support other than that which we gave to one another. When we catered cocktail parties and dinners, I would overhear well-heeled straights saying things like, 'We have to do something about this! Pretty soon we are all going to get it if we aren't careful.' Little did they know—if some of those ladies knew what we knew about their husbands and sons, they would have been a little more respectful, I think."

After three years of "onslaught," Mike decided to move to the South with a friend, Tom. They bought a Civil War–era house in Tarboro, North Carolina, where, as Mike said, "We experienced no discrimination . . . in fact, it was the opposite. We got along with everyone, and even did some cooking—I wouldn't call it catering—around town. We knew everyone, and our house was a sort of central meeting place because it was right in the middle of town." Then, in 1995, Tom got really sick. "He knew what it was all about, and having seen dozens of his friends get sick too, he decided to forgo treatment and just let things 'take their course.' He was dead in two months, of acute sepsis and an encephalitic HIV infection. In other words, he went crazy, and then died of blood poisoning."

When Mike met his current partner through mutual friends in 1996, it was "love at first sight . . . we had everything in common except our age—he is 10 years younger than me. He and I felt like we had found the people we had been looking for all along. We still feel this way and never get tired of each other's company. We are in love with each other, and that has a way of making the past make sense. I certainly don't regret a second of my past, and if our relationship now is the result of all that living I did, then it was well worth the wait. I cannot imagine being so lucky as to be living with someone so wonderful in such a mutually complementary way. Believe it or not, we have never had a major fight, nor have we ever even had a negatively charged emotional exchange."

Rather than oppressed or victimized, Mike feels that gay men are lucky and enjoy tremendous freedom. "I think society expects little of us, as a group. We don't have that onus of having to have kids if we don't want it, and we aren't expected to join that work-and-spend

Continued

Continued

cycle that most heterosexual families are in. There is little outside pressure on our family—of the two of us and two dogs. We live our lives, pay our taxes, and take care of the yard. The cars are in good repair, and once in a while we go on vacation to some nice place. We cook our own food, clean our own house, and maintain pretty good relationships with our neighbors."

He can cite very few experiences of discrimination. Once, after they knew Bob had AIDS, he and Bob applied for health insurance. "We knew he had AIDS, but the world hadn't caught up with the idea that it was truly a fatal disease. We applied for a small business policy, and they came over and interviewed us. The agent got it right away that we were a 'couple,' and they turned down the application with no explanation. I called and asked them why, and they gave me some gobbledygook about being too small a business. I called the state office of consumer affairs, described the situation, and asked for their advice. They said that we were definitely discriminated against—in the City of San Francisco, insurance companies were not allowed to discriminate on the basis of sexual orientation, even then—but they said that we would have an almost impossible time proving it. They knew that insurance companies were trying to weasel out of policies they had already written to gay businesses because of the fear of AIDS claims, and there wasn't anything they were willing to do about it."

Discrimination has not been an important influence in Mike's life. "I have bought and sold houses, lived in a small southern town, lived in a conservative suburb in the East Bay, traveled all over the place with other men, in short, done everything everyone else does, and I have never felt discriminated against personally."

In his late 40s, Mike decided to pursue a career in social work because, as he puts it, "It is one of the very few things we can do for each other that truly makes a difference in our lives—both the social worker's and the client's." In the MSW program he had what he describes as his first real experiences of feeling discriminated against. He said that "judgmental marginalization would be a better way to put it." In one class, a fellow MSW student announced that he would have trouble working with gay men, "because that would be like asking me to work with child molesters or rapists." Mike said he couldn't believe his ears. When the school administration did not respond appropriately, Mike took matters in his own hands. "I confronted the student later, and we had a meeting of the minds. In short, I told him that if he and his buddies made it uncomfortable for me in class, I was going to get an attorney and make it very uncomfortable for them and the school . . . that ended it."

His advice to a gay person dealing with discrimination is simple: "Get a lawyer. Even though we don't have the law on our side, the public humiliation of having everyone know that you bash fags is probably enough of a deterrent in this day and age. Especially at a university. I would tell them not to bother with the 'let's get together and talk about this' routine. Bigotry is bigotry and ought to be dealt with accordingly. You can be friends after you have a level playing field. For homosexuals the field is never level. We are a particularly hated minority, and it is an uphill battle . . . better to get the big guns right away and save yourself the trouble of mediation in a world that does not really count you as a whole person anyway."

For Mike and his partner, the lack of a legal sanction for marriage is not a significant issue. "Who would want any authority regulating their material life, let alone their emotional life? We are together because

being considered a form of psychopathology. This view was pivotal in the persecution of homosexuals, particularly by the Immigration and Naturalization Service. It persisted for decades, waning only with the 1973 decision by the American Psychiatric Association to remove homosexuality from its *Diagnostic and Statistical Manual.*

Contemporary theories of the causes of homosexuality incorporate aspects of biological determinism, childhood experiences, and culture. Recent biological

we love each other, not because a state or a church has sanctioned our commitment. We are two men who choose to unite, and we are not trying to 'be like' the straight world because we are not straight." The same applies to restrictions on adoption and custody by gay and lesbian parents.

Possibly as an aftereffect of the trauma of the AIDS epidemic, Mike feels that the "mainstream" gay community is attempting to "normalize" their experience. "It is as if they are saying, 'We're just like you, but with this one tiny difference.' Neither Peter nor I believe that. We believe that we are not like the rest of the American culture—we are very different from it."

He believes homophobia is inevitable, and he attributes it in part to individuals' lack of clarity about their own sexuality and groups' need to define themselves as "right" by defining others as "wrong." His critique of social work education is biting. "I am shocked, almost on a weekly basis, at how little attention is paid to problems involving (or potentially involving) sexual orientation. I have sat through class after class and heard next to nothing about how things might seem from a sexual orientation other than heterosexual. Day after day, we tackle heterosexual family problems, heterosexual child problems, and heterosexual individual problems. All the intervention models seem to be constructed around heterosexual ideals and thinking. The sexual orientation angle has just been completely ignored. It is conservatively estimated that 8 to 10 percent of the population is lesbian, gay, or mostly homosexually oriented bisexual . . . this is a huge minority. The 'out' representatives are perhaps less than a quarter of that—maybe 2 to 3 percent at most. This minority crosses all ethnic, cultural, and racial lines—it is a minority of everyone. Certain occupations and avocations have a larger-than-average representation of homosexuals. I think social work is one

of them, and perhaps this accounts for the collective silence—lots of closet doors in this profession are tightly shut."

Mike says he "cannot envision a day when I, and those who come after me, will feel the real freedom of not being hated by someone—not for anything I have done or said, but simply because of who I am."

A Social Work Perspective

Mike's life underscores the uniqueness of human experience and the difficulty of making broad generalizations about the homosexual population. As a member of the gay community of San Francisco, Mike experienced the overwhelming grief and pain of the HIV/AIDS epidemic. He drew strength and creativity from that experience, even as it brought repeated personal losses. His experiences with the AIDS pandemic were shared by many GLBT Americans.

A self-professed "libertarian," Mike asks only that public policy not intrude on his personal life. For him, experiences of discrimination and laws that declare his lifestyle unacceptable have little relevance. Yet, as Mike readily acknowledges, these laws have a much different impact on members of the homosexual community who are attempting to raise children and who would like to pursue legal marriage. Mike sees hatred of homosexuality as inevitable and expects little from public policies that strive to eliminate it.

But in some ways Mike's experiences are unique to his race and gender. As a white male, he has had access to privileges and resources unavailable to women and people of color. For many—particularly women of color—experiences of discrimination are intensified by multiple jeopardies.

Following a brief discussion of definitional issues, we will focus on U.S. policies related to homosexuality.

studies have identified possible genetic precursors (see Murphy, 2005), and described embryonic developments associated with transgender sexual identity (see Qazy, 2006). Psychological theorists have focused on childhood experiences and young-adult socialization (see Friedman & Downey, 2002). Others have pursued an integrative approach, arguing for the interaction of biology, culture, and individual development (see Frank, 2007). Meanwhile, advocates of both gay rights and gay persecution continue to base at least part of their rhetoric on categorical (frequently inaccurate) statements about the causes of homosexuality.

B O X   10.1   Gay Rights in South Africa

Despite widespread public opposition to same-sex re-lationships, in 1996 South Africa became the first na-tion to prohibit discrimination on the basis of sexual orientation in its constitution. As a result, the nation now permits same-sex marriage and protects gay and lesbian citizens from discrimination in employment. South African Bishop and Nobel Laureate Desmond Tutu has spoken ardently in support of equal rights for homosexuals.

Ultimately, the causes of homosexuality are irrelevant to the case for or against gay rights. Persecution of individuals on the basis of any personal identity (gender, race, religion, or sexual orientation) is antithetical to democratic values, to the guarantees of the U.S. Constitution, and to some international perspectives on human rights.

A Sexual Minority

GLBT individuals are clearly a minority within the U.S. population. Mike men-tioned a widely used estimate that gay and lesbian men and women constitute 8 to 10 percent of the U.S. population. This figure probably comes from two Kinsey reports, *Sexual Behavior in the Human Male* (Kinsey, Pomeroy, & Martin, 1948) and *Sexual Behavior in the Human Female* (Kinsey et al., 1953). Based on his studies, Alfred C. Kinsey estimated that 13 percent of men and 7 percent of women engaged in sex primarily with same-gender partners for part of their lives. He went on to estimate that about 4 percent of men were exclusively ho-mosexual throughout their lives. Although Kinsey's methods have been ques-tioned (his study surveyed only volunteers, and thus he did not have a random sample), his figures were later duplicated in other studies (see Barnett, 1973; Michael et al., 1994).

Nonetheless, it is difficult to estimate the number of people who are homo-sexual. In 1992, Michael and colleagues surveyed a random sample of Americans about their sexual behavior. With a response rate above 80 percent, theirs is probably (as they claim) the most recent definitive study of the topic. Their re-sults underscore some of the difficulties inherent in an effort to count homosex-uals. Results varied depending on whether attraction, behavior, or identity was considered. For example, about 6 percent of men in their study said they were attracted to other men; about 5 percent said they had had sex with another man since turning 18; and about 3 percent of men said they considered themselves homosexual or bisexual. Similarly, about 10 percent of women said they were attracted to other women; about 4 percent said they had had sex with another woman after age 18; and about 1.4 percent of women said they thought of themselves as homosexual or bisexual (Michael et al., 1994).

B O X 10.2 UN Human Rights Commission Rules on Sodomy Laws

In 1994, nine years before the U.S. Supreme Court overturned the nation's sodomy laws, the UN Human Rights Commission ruled that such laws were in violation of the International Covenant on Civil and Political Rights (ICCPR). The Commission held that the term "sex," in Articles 2(1), 17, and 26 of the ICCPR, must be interpreted to include sexual orientation and, therefore, laws that criminalized same-sex contacts between consenting adults are in violation (see *Toonen v. Australia,* Communication No. 488/1992, U.N. Doc. CCPR/C/50/D/488/1992–1994).

LEGAL ISSUES

A review of legislation affecting GLBT Americans reveals the oppressive role of some state and federal government authorities. In sharp contrast to its policies concerning people of color and even women, the government seems to have adopted a much more hostile posture toward homosexuals. This hostility is manifested in the issues considered here, which include sodomy laws; state initiatives to limit rights of people who identify as gay or lesbian; the Defense of Marriage Act; legal issues in family formation, including child custody and adoption; discrimination in employment and volunteer work; treatment of gays in the military; hate crime legislation; and policies related to HIV/AIDS.

Sodomy Laws

Sodomy laws specifically forbade some physical expressions of affection between people of the same sex, even in the privacy of their homes. The nation's first sodomy law was enacted in Virginia in 1610 and carried the death penalty (Galas, 1996). Only 50 years ago, every state in the Union had sodomy laws on its books. Although some states still have such laws, they have been declared unconstitutional by the U.S. Supreme Court.

In 1986, sodomy laws were challenged in the *Bowers v. Hardwick* case. Michael Hardwick was arrested on sodomy charges after police entered his house to serve a traffic warrant and found him in bed with another man. Hardwick was convicted of sodomy and jailed. His lawyers appealed to the Eleventh Circuit Court of Appeals, arguing that the conviction violated Hardwick's right to privacy. Citing the importance of privacy in previous cases such as *Roe v. Wade,* they succeeded in overturning the verdict in the Eleventh Circuit. The State of Georgia appealed to the U.S. Supreme Court, which ruled against Hardwick. In a closely divided opinion (5–4), the Court held that the right of privacy did not apply to homosexual conduct.

In the 2003 case of *Lawrence v. Texas,* the Supreme Court overruled a Texas sodomy law in broad terms, and in effect apologized for the 1986 decision. The vote was 6 to 3. Justice Anthony M. Kennedy said that gays are "entitled to respect for their private lives. The state cannot demean their existence or control their destiny by making their private sexual conduct a crime." In a sweeping victory for the rights of Americans who experience same-sex attraction, the decision clearly established that state sodomy laws were unconstitutional.

State-Level Initiatives to Limit Rights of GLBT Americans

During the early 1990s referendums seeking to limit the rights of gays and lesbians were introduced in several states. These included Arizona, Maine, Michigan, Missouri, Nevada, and Washington, where supporters were unable to secure enough signatures to get them on the ballot. Antigay organizers were more successful in Colorado and Oregon.

Colorado Amendment Two.   In 1992, a campaign to pass the Colorado initiative known as Amendment Two was spearheaded by a right-wing organization called Colorado for Family Values, an offshoot of the Traditional Values Coalition of Anaheim, California, and the Eagle Forum (O'Rourke & Dellinger, 1997). Amendment Two was designed to repeal existing state and local laws that protected gay people from discrimination and to ban all future laws that would have recognized claims by GLBT individuals. Activists on both sides agreed that passage of Amendment Two would have historic impacts on the rights of GLBT Americans. Proponents argued against granting "special rights" to homosexuals. Opponents of the initiative argued that the issue was not about *special* rights, but protection of basic civil rights.

The initiative passed by a margin of 53 to 47 percent in November 1992. Many observers felt the public was ill informed about the amendment. They suggested its passage reflected voters' opposition to "special rights," not their desire to deny gay and lesbian citizens basic civil rights. The amendment did not go into effect. Nine days after it was passed, gay rights activists filed suit and sought an injunction against its enforcement. The injunction was granted in January 1993.

Amendment Two was declared unconstitutional by the U.S. Supreme Court in 1994, in a 6-to-1 decision that is frequently cited as evidence of progress in gay rights. In *Romer v. Evans,* the Court ruled that Amendment Two violated the equal protection clause of the Fourteenth Amendment to the Constitution. Justice Kennedy wrote the opinion (echoing the dissent in *Plessy v. Ferguson*) that the Constitution "neither knows nor tolerates classes among citizens." The opinion found the argument that Amendment Two simply denied homosexuals special rights "implausible," saying,

> The amendment imposes a special disability on those persons alone.
> Homosexuals are forbidden the safeguards that others enjoy and may
> seek without constraint. They can obtain specific protection against
> discrimination only by enlisting the citizenry of Colorado to amend the
> state constitution. . . . We find nothing special in the protections
> Amendment Two withholds. These are protections taken for granted by
> most people either because they already have them or do not need
> them; these are protections against exclusion from an almost limitless

number of transactions and endeavors that constitute ordinary civic life in a free society. (*Romer v. Evans,* p. 1627, cited by O'Rourke & Dellinger, 1997, p. 137)

The Court found that Amendment Two inflicted "immediate, continuing, and real injuries that outrun and belie any legitimate justifications that might be claimed for it." Further, justices inferred that "the disadvantage imposed is born of animosity toward the class of persons affected" (O'Rourke & Dellinger, 1997, p. 138).

Oregon Initiatives. While the Supreme Court considered Amendment Two, another anti-gay rights measure was under development in Oregon. It was not the first effort of this type. As Douglass (1997) notes, "During a three-year period from 1991–1994, Oregon voters considered state and local ballot measures dealing with homosexuality on thirty separate occasions" (p. 17). The antigay measures introduced in Oregon were developed by an organization called the Oregon Citizens Alliance (OCA).

The alliance had considerable success passing local initiatives. OCA introduced two statewide initiatives. In 1991, Ballot Measure 9 proposed to amend the Oregon constitution to define homosexuality as "abnormal, wrong, unnatural, and perverse." The measure would have prohibited local and state governments from encouraging homosexual behavior and, like Colorado Amendment Two, would have prohibited state and local governments from extending civil rights protections to GLBT Americans. OCA's campaign suggested that homosexuality posed a threat to the state's children and argued that gays and lesbians should have "no special rights." In this progressive state, opponents to the measure were many, and they were organized. Measure 9 was defeated by a 57-percent majority (Galas, 1996). Three years later, in 1994, OCA put Ballot Measure 13 before the Oregon voters. A toned-down version of the earlier initiative, Measure 13 was defeated by a 51-percent majority (Galas, 1996). The Oregon defeats coincided with voters in Idaho rejecting a similar measure, entitled variously "Stop Special Rights" and "Proposition One" (Levine, 1997).

B O X 10.3   Domestic Partners

The term "domestic partner" has been developed to describe a committed relationship that is not characterized by either marriage or a civil union. It may be applied to either same-sex or heterosexual relationships and, depending on the context, can confer access to benefits. Hundreds of U.S. businesses provide employee benefits to domestic partners, as do some jurisdictions. San Francisco became the first U.S. city to recognize domestic partnerships after the murder of Harvey Milk in 1979. Other cities, including West Hollywood and Berkeley, followed suit. Today several states, including California, Oregon, Washington, and New Jersey also recognize domestic partnerships. Of course, under DOMA, federal benefits such as Social Security may not be extended to domestic partnerships.

Since the Supreme Court decision in *Romer v. Evans,* antigay activists have focused their attention on initiatives such as the Defense of Marriage Act, described in the next section.

Defending Marriage

Mike is not alone in feeling that his inability to marry does not represent a disadvantage. Rimmerman (2000) notes that "same-sex marriage is not a crucial issue for many [gay] movement members" and suggests that those for whom it is central represent the more conservative elements of the movement (p. 51).

But for many GLBT Americans, the lack of legal sanction for a relationship has direct (and sometimes devastating) consequences. This is the case, for example, when a gay man's partner is critically injured in an accident and he is not permitted access to the intensive care unit because he is not a family member. It occurs when a lesbian who has lived with her partner for 30 years dies without leaving a will, and the partner is disinherited. It complicates the lives of GLBT individuals, who cannot secure health insurance or Social Security benefits for their partners.

Legal marriage confers access to a wide range of rights and benefits. Its importance was recognized by the Supreme Court in 1967, when Chief Justice Earl Warren wrote a landmark opinion that said, "The freedom to marry has long been recognized as one of the vital personal rights essential to the orderly pursuit of happiness by free men. Marriage is one of the 'basic civil rights of man,' fundamental to our very existence and survival" (*Loving v. Virginia,* Supreme Court of the United States, 1967). This opinion struck down laws in 16 states that prohibited interracial marriage and confirmed a "fundamental right" to marry.

Twenty-seven years later, three same-sex couples in Hawaii appeared in the local Department of Health to apply for marriage licenses. When a health official denied their requests, they filed suit. The case, known as *Baehr v. Lewin,* made its way to the Hawaii Supreme Court, which sent the case back to the lower court after ruling that under Hawaii's Equal Rights Amendment a standard of "strict scrutiny" must be applied to any measure depriving people of basic civil rights. The court found that the outcome in *Baehr v. Lewin* could not stand this level of scrutiny. The favorable decision did not establish a fundamental right to same-sex marriage, and it was invalidated through a subsequent amendment to the Hawaii constitution banning same-sex marriages.

Vermont was more responsive. In 1997, several gay and lesbian couples filed a lawsuit after they were denied licenses to marry (*Baker v. State of Vermont*). Two years later, in 1999, the Vermont Supreme Court decided that state law discriminated against homosexual couples and ordered the legislature to correct the problem, either by allowing same-sex couples to marry or by establishing a parallel "domestic partnership" status in which couples could register their relationship and enjoy the same rights as heterosexual couples. The state legislature drafted a bill to establish "civil unions" for same-sex couples. After extensive hearings and debate, the bill was signed into law by Governor Howard Dean in April 2000. Dean was reelected in November 2000 after what he described in his inaugural address as a "contentious" campaign.

Under the "full faith and credit" clause of the U.S. Constitution, states are required to recognize and enforce (give "full faith and credit" to) contracts established in other states. Antigay activists were concerned that civil unions registered in Vermont might be "exported" throughout the United States. They initiated legislation at both the state and federal level to prevent this possibility. The federal legislation was called the Defense of Marriage Act of 1996.

The Defense of Marriage Act (DOMA) was introduced during an election year (1996) by Representatives Steve Largent (R-OK) and Bob Barr (R-GA) in the House and Senator Don Nickles (R-OK) in the Senate. The bill passed both houses by overwhelming majorities and was signed into law (in the middle of the night) by President Clinton on September 21. DOMA does two things. First, it defines marriage for purposes of federal law as "a legal union between one man and one woman as husband and wife" and defines "spouse" as a "member of the opposite sex who is husband or wife." These definitions deny federal benefits, such as Social Security income, to partners in same-sex marriages. DOMA does not interfere with states' decisions about same-sex marriage, but it indicates that no state will be required to recognize a same-sex marriage that is legitimate in another state. Since the passage of the federal DOMA, nearly half of the states have passed their own versions banning same-sex marriages.

Advocates questioned the constitutionality of DOMA, arguing that the "full faith and credit" clause of the Constitution cannot be superseded by federal legislation. Still others have held that the law is incompatible with the Supreme Court ruling in *Romer v. Evans*. There have been several legal challenges to DOMA at the state level, which may eventually bring the matter before the Supreme Court for clarification. Meanwhile, those who seek to ban same-sex marriage have shifted their focus to the states.

One of the first antigay marriage initiatives at the state level took place in the nation's most populous state. In California, Proposition 22 was known as the Knight Initiative after state senator Pete Knight, one of its ardent proponents. The initiative said, "Only marriage between a man and a woman is valid or recognized in California." This deceptively simple phrase sounds almost like a simple statement of fact. Its proponents argued that the initiative was not "antigay" but "pro-family," suggesting that it was possible both to support gay rights generally and to vote for this marriage initiative specifically. Their efforts were effective. The Knight Initiative passed in 2000 by a wide margin (61 to 39 percent). Later in 2004, city officials in San Francisco openly challenged the law, performing hundreds of marriages before opponents won a court injunction forcing them to stop and nullifying the marriages. In March 2005, Judge Richard Kramer of the Superior Court of California reversed this ruling, and as of this writing the matter appears to be stalled in California courts.

In 2005, the California legislature became the nation's first to pass a statute that permitted same-sex marriage. Arguing that Proposition 22 indicated public opposition, Governor Schwarzenegger vetoed the legislation, along with a similar bill passed in 2007.

Across the country in Massachusetts the policy climate was more favorable for same-sex marriage. In February 2004, the Massachusetts Supreme Court ruled that there was no constitutional basis to deny gay and lesbian couples the right to marry. The court gave the state legislature six months to rewrite the state's marriage laws to make them consistent with the Massachusetts constitution. The legislature voted to ban same-sex marriages but allow civil unions, making theirs the second state in the Union to offer this alternative. But the court rejected the concept of civil unions, holding that they did not satisfy the requirements of the state constitution. So in a contentious session the state legislature approved a constitutional amendment that would prohibit marriage by same-sex couples but would allow for civil unions. Massachusetts law required that the amendment be approved by two subsequent legislative sessions before it could be presented to the public for a vote (Liptak, 2004). In 2006, the amendment was defeated. Following the defeat of a referendum to amend the state constitution, same-sex marriage remains legal in the state of Massachusetts at least until 2012 (Philips, 2007).

Constitutional amendments have rarely been used to deny civil rights to minority groups. But in recent years opponents of gay marriage have pursued a strategy of amending state constitutions, and in the 2004 election President Bush called for an amendment to the U.S. Constitution. The state-based strategy proved effective. Prior to the 2004 election, state constitutions in five states—Alaska, Louisiana, Missouri, Nebraska, and Nevada—had been amended to ban same-sex marriage. In 2004 amendments were approved by voters in 11 more states: Arkansas, Georgia, Kentucky, Michigan, Mississippi, Montana, North Dakota, Ohio, Oklahoma, Oregon, and Utah. As of this writing, roughly half of the states have enacted constitutional amendments that prohibit same-sex marriage.

Civil rights issues frequently involve protecting a vulnerable minority from the discriminatory views of the majority. The politics of same-sex marriage are similar to other civil rights battles in that a majority of Americans oppose the rights of a minority group. In 1967, when the Supreme Court struck down laws against interracial marriage, a majority of Americans opposed interracial marriage (Richards, 1999). As David Richards argues, "The prohibition of racial intermarriage was to the cultural construction of racism what the prohibition of same-sex marriage is to sexism and homophobia" (Richards, 1999, p. 163).

In the United States a majority of the population is opposed to same-sex marriage. This opposition undoubtedly reflects deep-seated beliefs. In such battles, political victories typically go to the majority, leaving the minority to resort to courts for protection of their fundamental rights, including the right to marry and raise their children.

Legal Issues in Family Formation

Child Custody and Visitation.   Unlike Mike and his partner, many gay and lesbian Americans are, or would like to be, involved in raising children. It is dif-

---

B O X 10.4   **Same-Sex Marriage in International Perspective**

In 1989, Denmark became the first nation to offer legal recognition to same-sex unions. Other Nordic countries followed suit, and in 2001 the Netherlands became the first nation to legalize same-sex marriages. Since then Belgium, France, Germany, Canada, Luxembourg, the United Kingdom, South Africa, and Slovenia have recognized same-sex commitment, either through civil unions or through marriage. On the other hand, some countries, such as Australia, Uganda, and Latvia, have officially banned same-sex marriage. (See www.ilga-europe.org for information on the status of same-sex unions in European nations.)

---

ficult to estimate how many gay and lesbian parents live in this country, in part because many hide their sexual orientation. Estimates that have been offered suggest the number of children with gay or lesbian parents ranges from 6 million to 14 million (Harvard Law Review Editors, 1990).

Like marriage, parenting is widely considered a "fundamental right." The right to raise one's children has been affirmed in several Supreme Court cases (see *Meyer v. Nebraska*, 1923; *Pierce v. Society of Sisters*, 1925; *Lassiter v. Dept. of Social Services*, 1981). Yet discrimination against gay and lesbian parents is evident in decisions regarding child custody and visitation following divorce proceedings, as well as adoption.

This discrimination reflects widely held beliefs that gays and lesbians are inadequate or inappropriate parents. Testimonials are frequently used to support this belief. Antigay activists ask unhappy children of gay and lesbian parents to elaborate on the difficulties they experienced while growing up. It is impossible to conduct a perfectly controlled and representative study comparing the parenting effectiveness of homosexuals and heterosexuals, but there is a growing body of evidence in the social science literature that sexual orientation predicts neither parenting ability nor children's sexual orientation (see Flaks et al., 1995; Gottfried & Gottfried, 1994; Patterson, 1995; Tasker & Golumbok, 1997). Nonetheless, the belief that homosexuals are unfit parents remains widespread, even among the nation's judiciary. Sodomy laws were frequently used as justification for denying parenting rights of homosexuals, with the illegality of a couple's presumed sexual conduct used as evidence of moral failure. As we have seen, the Supreme Court declared these laws unconstitutional in *Lawrence v. Texas*.

Three distinct approaches have been used by the courts to decide disputes regarding custody and visitation by gay and lesbian parents. These have been termed the "per se" approach, the "presumptive" approach, and the "nexus" approach (Patterson & Redding, 1996; Stein, 1996). The per se approach is no longer applied. Under this method, gay and lesbian parents were considered unfit per se, as a matter of law (Patterson & Redding, 1996).

The presumptive approach is more common. Under this approach, a homosexual parent is presumed to be an unfit parent unless he or she can demonstrate that the child will not be exposed to any homosexual influences. In jurisdictions that take this view, a parent need not have a partner to be judged unfit. Any kind of homosexual connection might be sufficient to deny custody. Simply be-longing to a gay rights organization might result in loss of a child (Patterson & Redding, 1996).

The most common approach, known as the nexus approach, begins from the position that a parent's sexual orientation is irrelevant to custody and visita-tion decisions. Before homosexuality can be discussed, a nexus, or connection, must be established between parenting and sexual orientation (Patterson & Redding, 1996).

Adoption.   Gays and lesbians become involved in two types of adoption pro-ceedings: "stranger adoption" and "second-parent" adoption. Stranger adoption occurs when a homosexual couple or individual offers to provide a permanent home to a child whose biological parents are unable or unwilling to do so. Such adoptions typically involve children in state custody who become available for adoption. Second-parent adoptions arise when the partner of a child's biological parent seeks legal recognition of his or her relationship with the child.

Despite growing numbers of children in state custody, some states do not allow cohabiting homosexual couples to adopt. In these states, gay and lesbian parents who live alone do adopt children, often by disguising their sexual orien-tation from authorities. A few states prohibit adoption by openly gay parents. In these jurisdictions, even private, second-parent adoptions by homosexuals are not allowed.

As is true of same-sex marriage, parenting by homosexuals taps into deep-seated prejudices among the American public. Most Americans believe homo-sexuals should not raise children (Patterson & Redding, 1996). Once again, the attitudes of an ill-informed majority deny members of a minority access to what many take for granted as a fundamental right.

DISCRIMINATION BY ORGANIZATIONS
AND EMPLOYERS

The federal government openly discriminated against homosexuals in its civil ser-vice system until 1975. Gay men and lesbians could not work for the federal government, period. This meant that homosexuals who did have federal jobs were forced to conceal their sexual orientation. Disclosure meant immediate dis-missal. Frank Kameny was the first federal employee to question this policy (Galas, 1996).

In 1957, Mr. Kameny worked as an astronomer with the U.S. Army map service. He held a Ph.D. from Harvard and was well qualified for the position. But within a year after starting, he was fired because his supervisor suspected that he was gay. As Kameny told it,

I was called in by some two-bit Civil Service Commission investigator and told, "We have information that leads us to believe that you are a homosexual. Do you have any comment?" I said, "What's the information?" They said, "We can't tell you." I said, "Well, then I can't give you an answer. You don't deserve an answer. And in any case, this is none of your business." I was not open about being gay at the time . . . but I was certainly leading a social life. I went to the gay bars. . . . They issued a letter: They said they were dismissing me for homosexuality. I was in shock. (Galas, 1996, p. 62)

Kameny waged a three-year battle to get his job back. His appeals to the Civil Service Commission, U.S. District Court, and U.S. Court of Appeals were all denied, and the U.S. Supreme Court refused to hear his case. These defeats mobilized him for a lifetime of activism. In the early 1960s, he began organizing gays in Washington, DC, to battle employment discrimination. These efforts paid off in 1975, when the U.S. Civil Service Commission reversed its policy on homosexuals.

With the exception of those states that include sexual orientation in their human rights statutes, employment discrimination against homosexuals is perfectly legal. A man or woman can be denied a job or a promotion, or be fired, for being homosexual. It is difficult to document the extent of employment discrimination against homosexuals; nonetheless, survey results suggest that between 16 and 44 percent of gay and lesbian workers have experienced some form of employment discrimination (Badgett, Donnelly, & Kibbe, 1992; Human Rights Campaign, 2000). Gays and lesbians who work with children as teachers, counselors, and coaches are especially vulnerable. Job discrimination against homosexuals also takes the form of verbal harassment. Nearly a third of lesbians and gay men surveyed in 1991 reported experiencing verbal harassment on the job (Comstock, 1991).

Laws governing employment discrimination on the basis of sexual orientation vary across the nation. Some openly homosexual teachers enjoy the protection of non-discrimination clauses that include sexual orientation, and others are subject to dismissal.

To address the problem of discrimination by employers, gay rights activists have sought federal protection through the Employment Non-Discrimination Act (ENDA). This bill would prohibit employment discrimination on the basis of sexual orientation. ENDA was first introduced in 1994 by Senator Edward Kennedy, with about 30 cosponsors in the Senate. It has had the support of the nation's largest labor union, the AFL-CIO, as well as numerous business interests (Sweeney, 1999). Hearings held in 1997 documented the effects of employment discrimination against gays and lesbians, and the bill was reintroduced in 1999. ENDA prohibits discrimination in hiring, firing, promotion, compensation, and other employment decisions on the basis of sexual orientation. It would not apply to the military, religious organizations, or businesses employing fewer than 15 people. It specifically does not establish affirmative action for sexual minorities. The bill has been introduced repeatedly, most recently in 2007, when the House of Representatives passed HR 3685, which may end employment discrimination based on sexual orientation in the United States. The bill passed by a wide margin, marking the first time that either chamber of Congress had passed such a bill. The act does not address discrimination based on gender identity and expression. As of this writing, it remains legal in most states for an employer to terminate an employee based on sexual orientation or gender identity.

Unlike homosexual marriage and parenting, most Americans oppose employment discrimination on the basis of sexual orientation. A survey conducted by the Human Rights Campaign found that 70 percent supported protections for gays and lesbians in the workplace. Similarly, an Associated Press poll conducted in 1996 indicated that 85 percent of Americans support equal rights in the workplace for homosexuals (Human Rights Campaign, 2001). This level of support suggests that a solution to employment discrimination could be pursued in the political arena, and that ENDA will eventually become law.

In addition to employment discrimination, homosexuals are subjected to discrimination in volunteer activities, most notably those sponsored by the Boy Scouts of America.

Exclusion of Gay Men and Boys from the Boy Scouts of America

The Boy Scouts' decades-long effort to exclude gay men and boys from the ranks of its volunteers culminated with the 1990 expulsion of James Dale by a New Jersey branch of the organization.[1]

Dale had been a Boy Scout since 1978, when he was 8 years old. As a high school senior, he had attained the rank of Eagle Scout. Before leaving for college in 1989, he applied for an adult membership. As a college student he was openly gay and became involved in gay rights activism. In 1990 his Boy Scout membership was revoked because the Boy Scouts "specifically forbid membership to homosexuals."

The Boy Scouts had a long-standing tradition of excluding gay men and lesbians, but New Jersey law prohibited discrimination on the basis of sexual orientation by public agencies and businesses. Arguing that they were a private organization, the Boy Scouts took the case all the way to the Supreme Court, which ruled in their favor in June 2000 (*Boy Scouts of America v. Dale*).

Although the Supreme Court's decision was widely held as a defeat for gay rights, communities throughout the nation have expressed their outrage by withholding support from the Boy Scouts. Several towns have held that, since the Boy Scouts are a private organization, they may not make use of public resources, such as educational and recreational facilities. Further, United Way chapters in some communities have either reduced or eliminated their support for the Boy Scouts. Perhaps in response to these community initiatives, the No Child Left Behind Act prohibited schools receiving federal funds from denying the Boys Scouts (or other "patriotic organizations") access to their facilities.

---

1. Mr. Dale's was one of several cases that resulted from the Boy Scouts' practice of denying membership to homosexuals.

Gays in the Military

In 1778, Lt. Gothold Frederick Enslin became the first man to be dishonorably discharged from the military for homosexuality. As testament to his shame, his sword was broken in half over his head. He marched out of Washington's camp at Valley Forge to the tune of a slow melancholy drumbeat (Galas, 1996). The U.S. military had a clear policy of dishonorable discharge of homosexuals until the early months of the Clinton administration.

That policy was based on the view that homosexuality was a mental illness and that homosexuals were therefore "unsuitable for military service" (Shilts, 1993). In addition, the presence of homosexuals was believed detrimental to troop morale. These beliefs conflicted with a 639-page report prepared for the navy in 1957. Known as the Crittenden Report after the chairman of the panel that wrote it, this document concluded that homosexuality did not interfere with effective military service. The report was not widely publicized until it "resurfaced" in 1976 (Shilts, 1993).

Prior to the Clinton administration, literally thousands of people were forced out of the military because they were gay (Shilts, 1993). Until the 1970s these discharges were private affairs. Then, in 1975, Sergeant Leonard Matlovich decided to mount a challenge. A decorated Vietnam veteran, Matlovich was serving as a race relations instructor for the air force. He noted similarities between previous discrimination against blacks and current discrimination against homosexuals. In both cases, military authorities argued that the minority soldiers would prove untrustworthy and would threaten the morale of other soldiers. Matlovich felt his outstanding service record was proof against this assertion. The air force disagreed, and when Matlovich informed them of his sexual orientation, discharge proceedings began. Matlovich challenged the discharge in federal court but was unsuccessful. He appealed the adverse ruling to the U.S. Court of Appeals, which ruled in his favor and called for the air force to reinstate him. The air force was reluctant to do so, offering him a $160,000 cash settlement instead. Matlovich accepted the settlement, feeling that his case would not fare well in the U.S. Supreme Court. He died of AIDS in 1988. Matlovich's tombstone bears this inscription: "A Gay Vietnam Veteran—When I was in the military they gave me a medal for killing two men, and a discharge for loving one" (Galas, 1996).

Following Matlovich's lead, a growing number of young gay men and lesbians fought their military discharges. When Bill Clinton campaigned for president, he promised to issue an executive order rescinding the ban on homosexuals in the military. After the 1992 election, the religious Right began organizing, with strong support in the Senate Armed Services Committee, veterans' groups, and the Pentagon. The political costs of overturning the ban appeared overwhelming. The resulting compromise established "Don't ask, don't tell, don't pursue" as the military's policy on homosexuality (Rimmerman, 2000).

The compromise allows gays and lesbians to serve in the military, but it places restrictions on their behavior. They may not tell anyone they are homosexual, or engage in hugging, kissing, or dancing with someone of the same sex, even when they are off duty. In 1994, the policy was challenged by six military personnel who were discharged. They argued that the policy violated their rights of free speech and equal protection. A U.S. District Court judge agreed with them and ordered the military to reinstate them (Galas, 1996).

The armed forces are one of the nation's largest employers. Probably thousands of gays and lesbians are members of the military, devoting years (and even risking their lives) to protect this nation. Current policy allows them only a tightly closeted existence. Challenges to this policy will undoubtedly continue, and eventually a case may reach the Supreme Court.

ANTIGAY VIOLENCE AND HATE CRIME LEGISLATION

In 1978, Harvey Milk, San Francisco's first gay city supervisor, was murdered by Dan White. White also killed Mayor George Moscone, presumably for his support of gay rights. White had campaigned on an antigay platform for his position on the board of supervisors, and had been the only member of the board to vote against the city's antidiscrimination ordinance.

Milk was one of the nation's early victims of antigay hate crimes. The FBI reports that violence against gays has escalated in recent decades. Only a few of these crimes come to public attention; one example was the 1998 murder of Matthew Shepard in Wyoming. Nevertheless, more than a thousand "bias-motivated incidents" against gays and lesbians are documented each year. In 2003, of the 9,100 bias-motivated incidents documented, 1,510 were based on sexual orientation (FBI, 2004).

Not all of these incidents represent severe violence, but the Southern Poverty Law Center (SPLC) noted an increase in murders of homosexuals at the end of the 1990s. The SPLC reported that figures from the National Coalition of Anti-Violence Programs documented 14 antigay murders in 1996 and 33 in 1998. These statistics led the SPLC to conclude that "gay men and lesbians suffer from extraordinarily high levels of violence based on their sexual orientation" (SPLC, 1999).

The upsurge in violence against gay men and lesbians triggered an effort to include sexual orientation in federal hate crime legislation. In 1999, Senator Edward Kennedy, along with 39 Democrats and 5 Republicans, sponsored legislation that would have added gender, disability, and sexual orientation to federally protected categories. Known as either the "Matthew Shepard Act" or the "Local Law Enforcement Hate Crimes Prevention Act," a version of the bill has been reintroduced in each successive Congress. In 2007, the bill passed both the House and the Senate but was vetoed by President Bush. Hate crime statutes in about half of the states include reference to sexual identity or orientation.

Opponents of expanded hate crime legislation cite concerns about freedom of speech, arguing that hate crimes are "thought" crimes—invasive and hard to prove. This argument has been central to the objections of conservative religious organizations and the American Civil Liberties Union (ACLU). Supporters argue that stricter hate crime legislation will reduce violence and harassment, if not hate itself.

HIV/AIDS AND SOCIAL POLICY

As Mike's story illustrates, the HIV/AIDS epidemic was devastating for the gay community. In addition to multiple losses, it spawned a wave of antigay sentiment that sometimes manifests itself in the very policies that have emerged in response to AIDS.

The Centers for Disease Control and Prevention reported that between 1981 and 2003, a total of 929,985 Americans were diagnosed with AIDS. During the same period, over half of a million (524,060) died of the disease (Avert, 2005). Most of those infected and killed were gay men, though heterosexual transmission accounts for a growing proportion of HIV/AIDS cases in the United States (Kaiser Family Foundation, 2007).

Fear of contracting AIDS intensified discrimination against gay men. Many gay men who worked in food services and other fields that involved contact with other people were summarily fired. Others were denied housing or health care. Indeed, as we saw in Chapter 6, the discrimination spawned by AIDS extended beyond gay men to include anyone affected by the disease. Because of this discrimination, the Americans with Disabilities Act of 1990 (ADA) provides specific protections for people with HIV/AIDS. The ADA prohibits discrimination in housing, health care, and employment, and it requires workplace accommodation for those who are ill.

Despite ADA protections, the fear of discrimination persists, and the issue of AIDS testing has become controversial. Indeed, there is cause for concern. Extremists such as antigay activist Paul Cameron and former Ku Klux Klan leader David Duke have advanced outrageous proposals for responding to the AIDS epidemic. Cameron, for example, suggested a mandatory nationwide testing program for AIDS, with those testing positive either confined to their homes or detained in camps. Duke suggested that AIDS patients be tattooed (Galas, 1996).

HIV/AIDS testing evokes a tension between those committed to protecting the rights and privacy of patients and those worried about controlling the spread of the disease. Like California, most jurisdictions have responded by providing ready access to voluntary testing, with measures to ensure complete confidentiality of the results. Until recently, mandatory testing was applied to organ donors, prison inmates, prostitutes, immigrants, and military recruits. But in 2007, New Jersey enacted legislation requiring that HIV testing be conducted on pregnant women and infants. Mothers may opt out of testing, but all infants whose mothers' HIV status is unknown or positive must be tested. This was the first statute that required testing of both mothers and infants, though several states addressed testing of either mothers or infants.

Programs for prevention and treatment of AIDS have also been controversial. Prevention efforts such as needle exchange and safe sex educational programs have drawn opposition for a variety of reasons, and thus they must rely on private sources for most of their funding. Funding for treatment and care of people with AIDS primarily stems from the Ryan White Care Act, which was discussed in Chapter 6.

TRANSGENDERED INDIVIDUALS

The term "transgendered" is not a medical or psychiatric diagnosis. Rather, it is an umbrella term that refers to people whose sexual identity or expression differs from conventional expectations of masculinity and femininity. The appearance, behavior, and characteristics of transgendered individuals often do not match popular gender stereotypes. Usually, transgendered individuals find that their personal gender identity is not compatible with their physical gender. Many (but not all) seek medical treatment that includes the use of surgery and/or hormones to bring their bodies into alignment with their identities. Others engage in cross-dressing and other nontraditional means of expression. The terms "gender variant" and "gender nonconforming" are sometimes used to describe this population. These terms do not describe a person's sexual orientation, which may be homosexual, heterosexual, bisexual, or asexual.

Nonetheless, the movement to support civil rights of gay, lesbian, and bisexual people has direct relevance to many who identify as transgendered. Indeed, some of the most highly visible members of gay, lesbian, and bisexual communities are transgendered. Because they more visibly threaten traditional gender norms, transgendered Americans are frequent victims of discrimination and even violence. Indeed, the National Coalition of Anti-Violence Programs reported that hate crimes against transgendered people tend to be especially brutal (Church & Minter, 2000).

Advocates for transgendered individuals have worked to include the phrase "gender identity or expression" in antidiscrimination language and hate crime legislation. They have succeeded in several U.S. jurisdictions. Some states have language preventing discrimination on the basis of gender identity or expression, while others include such language in their hate crime laws (Transgender Law and Policy Institute, 2005).

A HUMAN PERSPECTIVE   Advocacy: Victory in Washington State After 29 Years of Effort

Contributed by Janice Laasko, University of Washington, Tacoma, and Forrest Robert Stepnowski, BASW, University of Washington, Tacoma

Many Americans are not aware that, in the absence of state legislation to the contrary, it is perfectly legal to discriminate on the basis of sexual orientation in employment, housing, public accommodations, and other arenas. Yet gay and lesbian Americans have been terminated from employment, evicted from housing, denied access to health care and financial credit, and refused access to public areas because of their sexual identity. Twenty-nine years ago the GLBT community in the state of Washington began advocating for the addition of sexual orientation to the state's non-discrimination statute.

BSW student Forrest Robert Stepnowski and his colleagues took up the effort in 2005, lobbying for passage of House Bill 2661, which would add the words "sexual orientation" to the state's antidiscrimination law. They felt their efforts were consistent with the NASW Code of Ethics and supportive of their personal values. A significant part of the campaign was educa-tional. The students developed fact sheets on HB2661 and distributed them widely. Each student resolved to contact at least 12 people, asking for their support. They set up a table on campus for three days to distribute the fact sheets and seek support. A phone chain that was developed in the early stages of the lobbying effort proved vital when one legislator announced that she was reconsidering her previous support for the bill. The phone tree was mobilized and her office received nearly 100 calls urging her to stand firm in her support. The students participated in a lobby day at the capitol and attended committee hearings.

On January 27, 2006, while the students were in their social policy class, word came that the bill had passed. Their group's only GLBT member burst into tears, reflecting on the wide impact of their actions.

The students reported that the experience taught them about the legislative process and how best to utilize their personal strengths to influence legislators. Most importantly, they learned that they could make a real difference on behalf of disenfranchised and vulnerable populations. (Forrest was a 2006 winner in the Influencing State Policy contest.)

SOCIAL WORKERS, SOCIAL JUSTICE, AND GAY RIGHTS

In the United States sexual orientation is still used as the basis for denying a wide range of benefits, from marriage to employment. As we have seen in this chapter, GLBT individuals risk being denied benefits that many heterosexuals take for granted. The NASW Code of Ethics is clear on the profession's attitude toward discrimination on the basis of sexual orientation, stating that "Social Workers should not practice, condone, facilitate or collaborate with any form of discrimination on the basis of . . . sexual orientation."

Mike's experiences during his social work training were, sadly, not unusual. For some social workers the struggle for gay rights presents a dilemma. Their strong personal or religious beliefs against homosexuality may be in direct conflict with their professional obligation. (For more information on religious views of homosexuality, please see www.religioustolerance.org.) This professional obligation goes beyond prohibiting active involvement in discriminatory conduct. It discourages "condoning" discrimination on the basis of sexual orientation. The

TABLE 10.1   Prominent Gays, Lesbians, and Bisexuals

Leonardo da Vinci (1452–1519) A gifted artist, da Vinci is acclaimed for the beauty of his paintings and the novelty of his inventions. Little is known of his private life except that he was devoted to beautiful young men.

Mutsuo Takahashi (1937–) Internationally renowned poet and playwright.

Walt Whitman (1819–1892) Whitman's poetry is widely interpreted as homoerotic, though he was silent on the topic of his own sexuality.

Peter Ilyich Tchaikovsky (1840–1893) Tchaikovsky's lasting compositions include *Swan Lake, The Nutcracker,* and *The Sleeping Beauty.* He was reportedly tormented by his homosexuality, but in his will Tchaikovsky named his companion, Bob, as his sole heir.

Oscar Wilde (1854–1900) Wilde's literary legacy includes *The Picture of Dorian Gray* and *The Importance of Being Earnest.* Wilde was prosecuted for sodomy and died in exile.

Jane Addams (1860–1935) A pioneer in the field of social work, Addams founded Hull House in Chicago. Her most intimate relationship was with Mary Rozet Smith, her companion for 40 years. The two traveled and lived together. Addams won the Nobel Peace Prize in 1931 for her leadership in the international women's peace movement.

Gertrude Stein (1874–1946) Stein's lifetime intimacy with Alice B. Toklas led her to personify lesbian identity for many during the early twentieth century and beyond. An author and critic, Stein enjoyed considerable influence within the artistic community.

Virginia Woolf (1882–1941) The author of literary criticism, novels, and plays, Woolf is probably best known for her collection of essays, *A Room of One's Own.* After suffering several nervous breakdowns, Woolf committed suicide by drowning herself.

Ruth Benedict (1887–1948) Benedict was a cultural anthropologist. Her partner and collaborator, Margaret Mead, may be a more familiar figure. Mead and Benedict worked closely together, and Benedict left a lasting mark on her field.

Barbara Jordan (1936–1996) Lawyer, politician, and congresswoman, Jordan was awarded the Presidential Medal of Freedom in 1994.

Alan Turing (1912–1954) Turing was a mathematician whose research and theoretical formulations set the stage for the development of the digital computer. Turing died of cyanide poisoning in a possible suicide.

James Baldwin (1924–1987) Author of *Notes of a Native Son, Nobody Knows My Name,* and *The Fire Next Time,* Baldwin benefited from the support of his lover, Lucien Happersberger.

Andy Warhol (1928–1987) Best known for his painting of a Campbell's soup can, Warhol left a lasting mark on American contemporary art. Warhol was open about his sexuality, if reclusive in general.

Rev. Peter Gomes (1942–) Current Harvard University chaplain who came out as a gay man in 1991. Nationally known lecturer and advocate for gay rights.

Harvey Milk (1930–1978) Known as the first openly gay official elected in the United States, Milk was a strong advocate for small business and minorities during his tenure as a San Francisco supervisor. Milk was murdered by Dan White, an antigay activist.

TABLE 10.1 *Continued*

Barney Frank (1940–) In 1987 Frank was serving his fourth term in the U.S. House of Representatives when a reporter asked him whether he was gay. Frank answered in the affirmative and braced himself for the end of his political career. Instead, he was re-elected in 1988 by a strong majority.

Elton John (1947–) Elton John identified as bisexual until the late 1980s, when he came out as gay. His first marriage to another man ended in divorce, and he subsequently married his long-time partner, filmmaker David Furnish, in a 2005 ceremony in the United Kingdom.

SOURCE: Russell (1996); BBC (2005); Robinson-Lynk (2008).

challenge for these social workers is to limit the scope of their personal biases to ensure that these beliefs do not intrude into their professional lives.

SUMMARY: CURRENT AND FUTURE STATUS OF GAY, LESBIAN, BISEXUAL, AND TRANSGENDERED INDIVIDUALS

Some have argued that GLBT individuals need not suffer from discrimination because their sexual orientation is "invisible." If they did not disclose that they were GLBT, the argument goes, they would not be subject to oppression or persecution. In essence, if they would just go back into the closet, all would be well. Eskridge (1999) has called this "the apartheid of the closet." But life in the closet is stifling, lonely, and scary.

GLBT people have made outstanding contributions to our nation's culture and our daily lives (see Table 10.1). In this chapter we have documented the role of federal and state policy in the oppression of homosexuals. Today, because of majority opinion, this group continues to be denied fundamental rights, including in some cases the right to life itself.

Public opinion has been shifting, however. Growing numbers of Americans have voiced their objection to discrimination in employment and antigay violence. People with HIV/AIDS are no longer denied care on the grounds that, as Senator Jesse Helms said in his 1995 fight to reduce federal funding for HIV/AIDS, their "deliberate, disgusting, revolting conduct" was to blame for their illness (Galas, 1996, p. 84). These are signs of progress. Whether it will continue depends in part on the will and ability of social workers to support the struggle for equal human rights for all.

KEYWORDS

Homophobia	Marriage	Civil rights
Sexual orientation	Gay	

THINK ABOUT IT

1. Roughly half of the states have constitutional amendments banning same-sex marriage, and nearly half have passed statutory bans. What is the difference between these two approaches? Is one more binding than the other? What is the status of DOMA in your state? Has there been any litigation challenging the ban? If you were a gay rights advocate, how would you approach the issue of marriage equity?

2. Why do you think the California legislature passed two bills that would have permitted same-sex marriage after the voters have passed an anti-gay marriage referendum by a resounding margin? Was this political bravery on their part?

3. If you were advocating for gay rights, what would be your top-priority issue today? Why?

4. Does your university include sexual orientation and gender identity/expression in its non-discrimination policy? Does your city? Your state?

WEB-BASED EXERCISES

For direct links to all the sites in these exercises, log on to the Student Companion Site for this book at academic.cengage.com/social_work/barusch, and choose Chapter 10.

1. Does the UN recognize a fundamental right to marry a member of one's own sex? Go to http://www.un.org/Overview/rights.html or Google "Universal Declaration of Human Rights," and read Article 16 carefully. What do you think? Now review Article 2. Does this change your mind? What about material presented in Box 10.2?

2. Visit the website for the Transgender Law and Policy Institute (www.transgenderlaw.org), and choose the "Litigation/Case Law" page. From the page menu, choose an area of litigation and review the cases listed. Do you think case law in this area is moving toward or away from supporting the civil rights of transgendered individuals? Why?

3. Go to the website of the National Gay and Lesbian Task Force (www.ngltf.org). Go to the site's "Activist Center," and click on "Act Locally." Click your state on the map to check on policy initiatives that might be of interest.

4. Go to the website for Lambda Legal (lambdalegal.org), and click on the U.S. map under "In Your State." Now, select your state in the map and read about the current status of relationship recognition, employment protections, and parenting laws that affect GLBT residents. Are there any pending cases that might change these policies?

SUGGESTED RESOURCES

D'Emilio, J., Turner, W. B., & Vaid, U. (2000). *Creating Change: Sexuality, Public Policy, and Civil Rights.* New York: St. Martin's Press.

Richards, D. A. J. (1999). *Identity and the Case for Gay Rights: Race, Gender, and Religion as Analogies.* Chicago: University of Chicago Press.

www.hrc.org. The Human Rights Campaign is dedicated to promoting gay and lesbian rights. Their website offers action alerts and a searchable index of HRC publications.

www.indiana.edu/~glbtpol/. This site is maintained by Steve Sanders of the College of Arts and Sciences at Indiana University. It is updated regularly and offers excellent background material on issues of interest to sexual minorities in the United States. It also has links to other major sites.

www.ngltf.org. The National Gay and Lesbian Task Force is a leader in the struggle for gay rights. Their site provides news and issue alerts, as well as publications that offer useful background material on target issues.

www.transgenderlaw.org. The Transgender Law and Policy Institute engages in advocacy and policy analysis on behalf of transgendered Americans. Their site provides an introduction to policy and legal issues and an update on current initiatives.

11

Children

When the voices of children are heard on the green
And laughing is heard on the hill,
My heart is at rest within my breast
And everything else is still.
WILLIAM BLAKE
"NURSE'S SONG"

Children have played divergent roles in American society, from menial laborers to conscientious students, from dangerous villains to innocent victims. Once considered the private responsibility of their parents, children's welfare is now widely recognized as a matter of public interest. The well-established principle of *parens patriae* (state as parent) reflects government's compelling interest in the welfare of children. Indeed, many now feel that "it takes a village" to raise a child and that parents should not be expected to shoulder the responsibility alone.

In this chapter we will consider social policies that affect children in the United States. Following a case study of Lorenzo, a 15-year-old Hispanic boy, we will examine the treatment of children in their diverse roles. First, we will consider children as assets, outlining adoption policies that touch many families in the United States. In the next section, we will focus on their student role, considering the development and reform of U.S. educational policies. Next, we will address children as victims of poverty and violence. In the fourth and final section, children as villains, we will explore juvenile justice and policies related to misbehavior by children. The chapter closes with a discussion of the role of social workers in programs that serve the nation's children.

CHANGING CONCEPTIONS OF CHILDHOOD: FROM "LITTLE MEN" TO "FUTURE CITIZENS"

Social views of childhood have changed over the centuries. Perhaps the most well-known work on the topic is *Centuries of Childhood* by Philippe Aries (1962). Our discussion in this section draws heavily from his comparative study of modern and medieval families.

There was no place for childhood in the medieval world, where artists simply portrayed children as small-scale adults. This perspective prevailed throughout most of the ancient world as well. Aries observes that "the realistic representation of children or the idealization of childhood, in grace and rounded charms, was confined to Greek art" (p. 34). Aries suggests that this lack of distinctive representation indicates that "childhood was a period of transition which passed quickly and which was just as quickly forgotten" (p. 34).

From the twelfth through the fourteenth centuries, artists began to portray children, first in religious art and later in secular art. They were shown mingling with adults in a variety of settings depicting work, play, and relaxation. According to Aries, this mingling indicates that the world of children was not separated from that of adults.

But children were not treasured as individuals. Observing that portraits of children were rare, Aries notes that "childhood was simply an unimportant phase of which there was no need to keep any record." High mortality rates discouraged strong attachments to young children. "The general feeling was, and for a long time remained, that one had several children in order to keep just a few" (p. 38). The death of a child was considered "necessary wastage," and it was not until the eighteenth century that this idea disappeared from Western thought.

Aries dates the transformation in attitudes toward childhood to the seventeenth century, when children began to appear in portraits, and family portraits began to be organized around them. Further, children's dress changed in this century, from imitation of adult clothing to a distinctive, childlike style. This change was particularly evident for boys, as Aries notes: "The idea of childhood profited the boys first of all, while the girls persisted much longer in the traditional way of life which confused them with the adults" (p. 61). With this transformation came two distinct approaches to children. The first, practiced within the home by children's caregivers, involved "coddling" and "playing" with the children—enjoying their antics and giving them pleasure. The second, encouraged by public authorities and moralists, took children more seriously and encouraged discipline and direction. Thus children became not only sources of amusement[1] but future

---

1. As sources of amusement, prepubescent children were often caressed and teased about their sexual organs in a manner that would be unacceptable today. An example comes from the diary of a sixteenth-century physician who wrote of Louis XII's childhood. When the child was one year old, the physician reported that "[h]e laughed uproariously when his nanny waggled his cock with her fingers." Later the child copied the trick. He called a page and "shouted, 'Hey, there!' and pulled up his robe, showing him his cock" (Aries, 1962, p. 100).

Lorenzo is a vivid child, with jet-black hair and sparkling dark eyes. He has seen more of life than most 15-year-olds and often has trouble understanding or interpreting his experiences. Lorenzo lives with his paternal grandfather and his grandmother (whom he affectionately calls Nini), his 14-year-old sister, and her 4-month-old baby.

Lorenzo's family is of Mexican descent, and his grandparents speak both Spanish and English. They celebrate traditional Mexican holidays and watch Spanish stations on television. Lorenzo considers himself Mexican but does not believe he has ever faced discrimination because of his heritage.

Lorenzo is the oldest of six children born to Margaret and Garcia Martinez. His mother was 14 years old when he was born, and his father was 16 years old. Both parents have been convicted on drug charges, and over the course of several years all six of their children have been removed from their home. Lorenzo blames his mother for his parents' drug problems, saying that his father tried to quit from time to time, but his mother was deeply embedded in a drug culture and made her living by selling drugs. He remembers his parents' home as "always filled with drugs." He said he used to eat the seeds as his parents sat at the kitchen table sorting and bagging marijuana for sale. He remembers an uncle making him "take a hit" off a joint when he was 4 but says he didn't begin smoking regularly until he was in the sixth grade.

Lorenzo has not lived with his parents since he was in the third grade, when he moved in with his paternal grandparents. He says he doesn't know why he was moved. "It's just always been that way." A few years after he moved in with them, his grandparents became his legal guardians. Lorenzo thinks this measure was required by his school. Like all of his siblings, Lorenzo is only supposed to visit his mother under supervision. He says he feels "pretty close" to his mom, however, and he goes to see her whenever he wants, with or without supervision. But she still has problems. A few months ago she had a baby with another man. The baby was born with drugs in his system and was removed from her custody.

Lorenzo is outgoing and enjoys being with his friends. He moved frequently during elementary school but always had friends to hang out with. Since his fa-

ther had been involved in a gang, he "courted" (jumped) Lorenzo into the same gang. Lorenzo was courted when he was 13 but has known this gang since early childhood. His girlfriend is the sister of one of his homeboys, and Lorenzo sees the gang as a way of life. He says all of his cousins, nephews, and acquaintances are involved in the gang and that one of his favorite things to do is "hanging out with my homeboys" and smoking marijuana.

In 1996, Lorenzo's father was murdered. Lorenzo is not sure why but believes it was not gang-related. His father was involved in the gang, but a policeman told Lorenzo the murder was drug-related. This distinction seems important to Lorenzo, who is still a gang member but not involved in selling drugs. Lorenzo was close to his dad and misses him. He remembers that his dad sometimes worked odd jobs in construction and attended technical school for a while. His mom used to work at fast-food restaurants sporadically.

In sixth grade Lorenzo came to the attention of the local law enforcement authorities. He says he used to "get blazed" daily with his friends and began to commit crimes. He has been convicted for shoplifting, carrying a weapon in school (brass knuckles), possession of a stolen vehicle, and probation violations (dirty urinalysis, breaking curfew, running away). He has been in a youth detention center on three separate occasions for one week each time, has spent five days doing community service (shoveling snow from sidewalks), and narrowly escaped a youth work camp when his uncle pled in front of the judge to have him sent instead to an inpatient psychiatric facility. He spent three weeks there in the winter prior to our interview, followed by a week in an outpatient program.

Although Lorenzo feels that he has been treated reasonably by the juvenile justice system, his grandmother disagrees. She said, "The system is a joke. . . . These kids that have just minor offenses are treated worse than animals." Upon reflection, Lorenzo decided that the police don't give gang kids a second chance. "Once the police connect you with a gang you are automatically guilty of a crime. They seem to think that kids can never change."

Lorenzo strongly believes that kids could be kept out of the juvenile justice system if they knew more about "how awful it is." He thinks elementary school children should be taken on field trips to youth detention facilities and that guest speakers should show slides of children there. He feels pictures or videos of "the bad stuff" will work: "Get the kids at their sad times, when they're crying. . . . When you're in that cell, that's when it really hits you."

At the time of our interview, Lorenzo was on probation. He felt responsible for his behavior, saying, "Everything I did I chose. . . . I had a good home, good teachers at school . . . the only problems I had were ones I created." He also resolved to "stay clean" and leave the gang. Of course, Lorenzo knew that leaving the gang would be difficult. He expected to be given a hard time and to eventually get "jumped out." He was enrolled in an alternative high school and planned to finish school there, where he hoped it would be easier for him to stay away from gang activities and drugs. He planned to stay with his girlfriend and had just begun a job in the fast-food business. Lorenzo's long-term goal was to be a therapist: "Once I saw that cool office I decided I wanted to kick back and eat M&M's all day!" He thought he might be able to get a football scholarship and attend college.

A Social Work Perspective

Lorenzo's extended family is clearly a strong resource in his life. His placement with grandparents is an example of "kinship care," an emerging practice in the child welfare system. Whenever possible, children who enter state custody are placed with members of their extended family. Lorenzo's grandparents had the resources and were willing to take him in, and his uncle argued on his behalf in juvenile court. He describes his grandparents' place as "a good home," and his grandmother appears deeply concerned about his experiences with the juvenile justice system.

On the deficit side of his equation are Lorenzo's parents. Clearly a troubled couple, they combined teenaged parenthood, a gang lifestyle, and serious drug abuse in one dysfunctional package. One can only speculate about Lorenzo's experiences during the eight years when he was in his parents' care. But it is striking to note that his experience with counseling seems to have led Lorenzo not to attribute his situation to childhood trauma but to assume personal responsibility for following in his parents' footsteps. Perhaps this perspective reflects the attitudes he has encountered in a juvenile justice system that is increasingly inclined to blame (and punish) children for their misbehavior.

Lorenzo's life has been touched by two major components of the nation's child welfare system. First, child protective services intervened on behalf of Lorenzo and his siblings to remove them from their parents' home. In Lorenzo's case, the preference for kinship care brought him to a stable, supportive environment—his grandparents' home. Lorenzo's situation illustrates a potential advantage of kinship care. It afforded him access to the support of other members of his extended family, such as the uncle who intervened on his behalf in court.

The second child welfare component Lorenzo encountered was the juvenile justice system. Children of color, like Lorenzo, are disproportionately represented in all phases of the juvenile justice system, but particularly in detention facilities. Both Lorenzo and his grandmother felt that the system treated children—particularly those in gangs—like criminals and that the police did not believe in a child's capacity to change. This treatment may reflect a growing tendency on the part of the justice system to emphasize punishment over rehabilitation when dealing with serious youth offenders. It may also reflect increased fear on the part of the public and the police that criminal acts by youth gangs are spiraling out of control.

Why did Lorenzo join the gang? Was it for a sense of belonging? For structure and a role? For economic advancement? For access to drugs? Because of his father's involvement? Specialists in gang behavior have identified each of these factors as potential reasons for youth involvement in gangs. Children in gangs commit roughly twice as many crimes (especially violent crimes) as similarly "at-risk" children who do not belong to gangs. They are, therefore, more likely than others to be labeled "villains" and to be subjected to the worst punishment the system has available.

In Lorenzo we see multiple problems: substance abuse, child abuse or neglect, gang involvement, and criminal behavior. His future, like that of other children in similar situations, will depend on the capacity and willingness of his family and community to invest resources in him, as well as on his own ability to change.

citizens to be given direction and education. The family became a vehicle not only for the transmission of names and estates but also for the education of children. The concern of public and religious authorities of this era represents the early manifestation of *parens patriae,* which recognizes that the government has a significant interest in children's upbringing.

In time, the family and schools removed children from adult society, creating childhood as we know it—a sort of hiatus, a time of preparation and (for some) a time of fun. Given its emotional, moral, and intellectual importance, the modern family has much greater demand for privacy than the medieval one, and the distinction between private and public in modern life is more clear.

CHILDREN AS ASSETS

Throughout U.S. history, children have often been viewed as assets. The idea of children as economic assets prevailed during colonial and postcolonial times, when they performed labor for their families and employers. Policies in the United States have diminished this role through the regulation of child labor. These laws are discussed in Chapter 14. But modern children still constitute assets, most notably as the linchpins for family-building.

Childhood in Colonial America

The Europeans who settled in North America during the seventeenth century brought with them European views of children as little adults. Indeed, childhood in colonial America brought few special protections from family or government. Because of the contrast between the attitudes we now hold and those that prevailed in colonial America, many people have the impression that children were treated as property during that era. It probably would be more accurate, however, to say that they were viewed as economic assets.[2] Children's labor contributed to the family's well-being, and their fathers or masters (in the case of indentured servants and apprentices) had the legal right to their custody and control. Fathers and masters had legal control over children. They were also legally responsible for the education and moral upbringing of children in their custody. Mothers had no legal rights to their children if the father was alive, and only limited rights after his death. The rights afforded to children themselves were limited as well. Misbehavior was severely punished. Some children found their way into poorhouses, and others were sold as indentured servants (Mason, 1994).

State involvement in the lives of children was limited but not unheard of. Criminal charges brought against adults for child abuse were recorded as early as 1655 (Watkins, 1990). During that year, a master in Massachusetts was found

---

2. The exception to this statement is children born into slavery, who were treated as property to an extent not permitted with biological children and indentured servants.

guilty of maltreatment that resulted in the death of his 12-year-old apprentice. He was punished severely. Bremner (1970) reports on other cases in which children were removed from homes that had been deemed unsuitable. It was more common to bring criminal charges against masters to whom children were apprenticed than against parents. Parents were charged only in cases of grievous abuse, described by Thomas as "punishment that was grossly unreasonable in relation to the offense, when the parents inflicted cruel and merciless punishment, or when the punishment permanently injured the child" (Thomas, 1972, p. 304).

Colonial America had no established authority charged with protecting children. Those responsible for enforcing criminal laws responded to crimes against children. Similarly, there was no systematic procedure for identifying children who were abused or neglected. No laws required reporting of child maltreatment. Cases came to the attention of the authorities through accidents of fortune: a visit from an especially public-spirited neighbor, the arrival of a census-taker, or a complaint from a teacher. This lack of a structure or a system of child protection persisted until the establishment of the New York Society for the Prevention of Cruelty to Children during the nineteenth century (this topic will be discussed later in this chapter).

Today, few see children as economic assets; but they are still sought after for other purposes. Many adults derive satisfaction from being a parent, and some resort to adoption in their efforts to add children to their families. In the following sections, we will consider adoption policies in the United States.

Building Families Through Adoption

Once stigmatized as the foundation of "abnormal" families, adoption has become widely accepted, both as a method for providing loving homes to needy children and as an approach to creating or expanding families. National policy controversies have erupted around two types of adoptions, however: those in which the children and adoptive parents are from different racial backgrounds and those in which the adoptive parents are gay or lesbian.

Transracial Adoption.   In 2001, 14 percent of all U.S. adoptions were transracial, usually involving white parents and children of color (Vonk, 2001). Most of these were international adoptions, but another significant proportion involved African American children adopted by white parents.

Adoption of African American children by white parents was rare prior to the 1964 Civil Rights Act. These adoptions increased to a peak in 1971, when 2,574 African American children were adopted by white parents (Cox, 1994). The following year, the National Association of Black Social Workers (NABSW) expressed vehement opposition to the growing practice. They saw it as "an insidious scheme for depriving the black community of its most valuable resources: its children" (Day, 1979). There was also concern that white parents might be unable to prepare African American children to cope with discrimination and prejudice.

Three years later, the number of transracial adoptions of African American children dropped to 831 (Cox, 1994). Committed to the needs of the black community, the NABSW argued that adoption agencies, both public and private, applied white middle-class norms in evaluating prospective adoptive parents. As a result, they argued, African American families were denied the opportunity to adopt, and African American children were unnecessarily placed in white homes.

Despite the fact that African American families adopted at a rate 4.5 times greater than white families, the number of African American children available for adoption continued to exceed the number of African American families available as potential adoptive placements. Most of these children were available for adoption because they had been removed from their biological families by the public child welfare system. Several studies demonstrated that African American children who were raised by white parents developed healthy racial identities and did not experience unusually high rates of adjustment problems (Simon, 1994). As a result, during the 1990s a consensus formed among child welfare professionals that agency policies and preferences against transracial adoption were denying African American children permanent homes.

In 1994, President Clinton signed the Multi-Ethnic Placement Act (MEPA) (PL 103-382). The law is designed to "prevent discrimination in the placement of children in foster care and adoption on the basis of race, color, or national origin; to decrease the time children wait to be adopted; and to ensure agency recruitment of a pool of foster and adoptive parents who reflect the racial and ethnic diversity of the children available for adoption" (Pecora et al., 2000, p. 41). It established penalties for states that did not comply. Unfortunately, federal funds are not available to assist in recruiting minority families, either as foster or adoptive parents, and significant barriers persist. Among them are the lack of minority professionals within the child welfare system; the high proportion of single-parent, low-income families within the African American community; rigid requirements and fees; and pervasive institutional racism (Crumbley, 1999).

In 1994 (the year that MEPA passed), the NABSW revised its position on transracial adoption:

> We believe that too many children are placed in foster care unnecessarily and that often they remain in foster care too long. . . . When all reasonable efforts have been made to keep the child and family together, and when family preservation, family reunification, and relative placement have failed, then, and only then, should we seek adoption.
> Adoption should be within the same race. Transracial adoption should only occur after clearly documented evidence of unsuccessful same-race adoption. (Crumbley, 1999, p. 96)

While acknowledging the benefits of adoption over time in foster care, the NABSW does not accept the argument that suitable adoptive families are not available in the African American community. They argue that when an agency makes special efforts to recruit African American families, same-race placement of African American children can be as high as 94 percent (NABSW, 1994).

Recent years have seen some progress in the placement of African American children. The number of children waiting for adoption has gone down, as has the proportion of African Americans in this population. In 1998, most (52 percent) of the foster children available for adoption in the United States were African American (Administration for Children and Youth, 2006). By 2005, among the 115,000 foster children available for adoption, 36 percent were African Americans (Administration for Children and Youth, 2007).

Adoption by Gays and Lesbians.   With the exception of the few states whose statutes specifically forbid the practice, child welfare authorities throughout the nation confront thorny issues as they consider gays and lesbians as prospective adoptive parents. Ann Sullivan (1995) suggests that policy in this area be informed by two major trends in adoption. The first is the trend toward more inclusive adoption policies. Whereas several years ago only married Caucasians between 21 and 35 years of age who had no biological offspring were considered suitable adoptive parents, the opportunity to adopt children has gradually been extended to include unmarried women and men, people of color, disabled people, older individuals, and families with children. In each case, adoptions have been controversial, with opponents questioning the suitability of the adoptive parents. The second trend is the growing awareness that thousands of children in foster care are eligible for adoption. As we saw, these children numbered 115,000 in 2005.

Adoption by gay and lesbian persons runs counter to several myths: the idea that homosexual parents are likely to molest children sexually, that children adopted by homosexuals will be pressured to become homosexual, and that the children will be living in "immoral" environments. There is no empirical literature to support any of these claims. Indeed, perpetrators of child sexual abuse are predominantly heterosexual, and there is no evidence that the sexual orientation of a child is determined by that of his or her parent(s). Other opponents of gay/lesbian adoptions argue that the children will be teased by their peers from more traditional families due to the stigma attached to homosexuality. Of course, proponents of this argument can usually find anecdotal evidence of teasing or rejection by peers. Nonetheless, the social science literature shows no evidence of negative developmental effects. Indeed, the intolerance reflected in harassment of children in nontraditional homes may reflect dysfunction on the part of the harassers, rather than their victims.

The controversy that arises over transracial and gay/lesbian adoptions illustrates the powerful role that ideology and values can play in social policy debates. Both supporters and opponents of these less traditional approaches to family foundation can cite studies or cases in support of their positions. Of course, because it is not possible to randomly assign children to adoptive homes, social scientists cannot provide a definitive answer regarding the effects of transracial and gay/lesbian adoptions. As a result, these debates are slow to resolve, reflecting political compromises and changing views about what constitutes a good family. We can inform the debate by shifting our lens to consider what constitutes a good society—whether "the problem" may be lodged, not in these new family forms, but in the intolerance and prejudice they encounter in the broader society.

CHILDREN AS STUDENTS

Philippe Aries (1962) discusses the establishment of schools as a force that defined and extended childhood for western Europeans during the twelfth through seventeenth centuries.[3] Girls were excluded, but boys of various ages and classes were allowed to participate. Less formal and structured than modern schools, these institutions provided basic literacy skills and a smattering of Latin over periods that might extend as long as four or five years. The most well established were religious schools designed to prepare young boys for clerical careers. Another significant educational institution, dating back to the medieval period, was apprenticeship. Many boys learned crafts through lengthy periods of apprenticeship under masters. Indeed, in 1562, England passed the Statute of Artificers, designed to force poor children into apprenticeships. This statute represented an early poverty prevention policy designed to reduce the children's subsequent need for public assistance.

European immigrants brought the practice of apprenticeship to colonial America as a means of replenishing the skilled labor force. The first compulsory education law in colonial America involved apprenticeship. It was passed in 1642 by the Massachusetts Bay Colony. The act required that the selectmen of each town attend to the "calling and employment of children" and "especially of their ability to read and understand the principles of religion and the capital laws of the country" (Good, 1962, p. 28). This education was to take place not in schools but primarily in homes and shops.[4] Schools were established in a haphazard fashion that reflected the many competing demands on communities. They operated irregularly, with terms seldom lasting more than three months. Their curricula were organized around whatever reading and writing materials were at hand.

The Massachusetts Bay Colony passed an act in 1647 that attempted to establish educational consistency throughout the colony. The act required that towns with at least 50 families maintain an elementary school (then called a "dame" school because it was operated by a woman, often a widow). Towns numbering at least 100 families were required to provide a secondary school. Towns that failed to comply with the act were fined. Evidently some towns found it easier to pay the fine than to establish a school (Good, 1962). Similar laws eventually spread throughout the colonies. As towns grew, they were divided into school districts, each with its own governing board and elementary school. The practice of establishing local school districts continues to this day.

---

3. Most of the material in this section is drawn from H. G. Good's seminal work *A History of American Education*.

4. Good argues that this law represented the beginnings of public involvement in children's upbringing in the New World.

Many of the great thinkers of revolutionary America (Thomas Jefferson, Benjamin Rush, Samuel Knox, and Noah Webster) saw education as a fundamentally political endeavor. Education could secure liberty and democracy and set the stage for the nation's economic expansion. As Thomas Jefferson said of education's role,

> The object is to bring into action that mass of talents which lies buried in poverty in every country for want of means of development, and thus give activity to a mass of mind, which in proportion to our population, shall be the double or treble of what it is in most countries. (U.S. Commission on Civil Rights, 1967, pp. 94–95)

Education would help unite the states into a nation, but there was much debate over the form it should take. Should education be centralized at the federal level or treated as a local endeavor?

The Tenth Amendment to the Constitution left education to the states and discouraged federal interference.[5] As a result, the nation's earliest statutes involving education are found in state constitutions. Six of the new states included educational provisions in their constitutions. The most detailed was in Section 44 of the constitution of the state of Pennsylvania:

> A school or schools shall be established in every county by the legislature, for the convenient instruction of youth with such salaries to the masters, paid by the public, as may enable them to instruct youth at low prices; and all useful learning shall be duly encouraged and promoted in one or more Universities. (Good, 1962, p. 88)

In this early stage of the nation's history, state efforts could supplement private schools, and some states provided free education for the poor; but the notion of universal, free public education had not yet caught hold.

Free and universal public education was a uniquely American invention. It was more compatible with the nation's democratic ideals than the class-based systems that were in place in England and Europe. Because there was no model to follow, the establishment of the American school system was neither quick nor smooth. Indeed, during the nation's first few decades, there was no organized constituency that supported the concept.

The unionization of factory workers created the nation's first organized force for free public education. In 1828 (following the depression of 1819) the Workingmen's Party was organized in New York and Philadelphia. In Philadelphia, the party's initial advocacy efforts focused on the establishment of independent newspapers, libraries, and public lectures and debates. In 1829 the organization issued a report that addressed public education. It rejected the idea of providing free instruction only to the poor and argued for free and universal elementary schools "in which teaching was not to be restricted to 'words and figures' but would also attempt to form rational self-governing character"

---

5. This does not prevent Congress from authorizing funds for educational endeavors.

(Good, 1962, p. 120). The report proposed the establishment of local school boards that were elected by and answerable to the people they served. The Workingmen's Party in New York had a socialist wing, and in 1825 party members proposed the establishment of free public boarding schools for all children as a vehicle for eliminating class differences in the new republic. Ultimately, the movement for public education expanded beyond the laboring classes to include advocates from diverse walks of life.

Opposition to public education came primarily from the privileged classes. Some argued that apprenticeship made universal education both impossible and unnecessary. Others suggested that the laboring classes should work so that the rich could cultivate their minds. Many objected to the use of taxes to finance schools, seeing it as "an arbitrary division of the property of the rich with the poor" (Good, 1962, p. 122). Public schools, it was also argued, would be corrupt and inefficient.

Despite opposition, the public education movement grew, and after 1830 several states had expanded public education and retreated from their funding of private schools. Several cities (Philadelphia, Baltimore, and Cincinnati, for example) established public schools through special legislation passed prior to state action. Eventually, however, state constitutions were amended (or established in newer states) to direct legislatures, as the Illinois document does, "to provide for a thorough and efficient system of free schools whereby all the children of this State may receive a good common school education" (Good, 1962, p. 143).

States' public educational systems developed individually, in piecemeal fashion. As a result there was considerable variation. The most striking variation involved the segregation of African American children and Caucasian children in Southern educational systems (to be discussed later in this chapter). Over time, these regional differences have blurred, and a national pattern of public education has emerged (Good, 1962). One aspect of the national pattern that we now take for granted is compulsory attendance.

Compulsory Attendance Laws

Massachusetts passed the first compulsory attendance law in 1852, requiring that children between the ages of 8 and 14 attend school for 12 weeks each year. The law permitted exceptions for children of poor families, those who were ill, and those who were being "otherwise educated." Children were also excused from the 12-week requirement if local schools were not open that long. The law called for fines if parents did not comply, but punitive action was rare. It was not until 1900 that compulsory attendance laws were enacted in a majority (32) of the states, and it would be 68 years before the movement for compulsory schooling would reach all of the 48 contiguous states.

Compulsory education was controversial for two reasons. First, many objected to government interference with parental authority. Several attendance laws were subjected to constitutional challenges. They were upheld consistently, with arguments reflecting the view that the state had a compelling interest in the education of children. The second objection was that these laws prevented children from working in industrial and farm settings at a time when many parents relied on the labor of children to support their families.

Nonetheless, by 1918 all states had passed statutes requiring school attendance. Over subsequent years these laws have expanded the duration of required schooling and become more similar. Today most states require about nine months of regular attendance annually for children up to the age of 16.

An Expanded Federal Presence

During the twentieth century the federal government began to exert more influence over public education. Federal involvement included the forced desegregation of Southern schools, subsidized higher education for veterans, and financial supports such as the National School Lunch Program. Federal education programs are typically administered or supervised by the Department of Education, established by Congress in 1867 to provide educational information to state and local education authorities. Congress later reduced annual appropriations for the department and downgraded it to an Office of Education, later a Bureau of Education within the Department of the Interior. There it remained until 1929, when Herbert Hoover's National Advisory Committee on Education recommended the establishment of a cabinet-level Department of Education.

Desegregation.   Late in the nineteenth century, after Reconstruction, 17 southern states required that black and white children attend separate schools. Four other states permitted districts to engage in segregation. The U.S. Supreme Court supported the practice in an 1896 case. The case, known as *Plessy v. Ferguson,* did not directly involve school segregation, referring instead to a Louisiana law that required separate railroad cars for African Americans. The Court's opinion brought in the schools, however, stating that "separate and equal" facilities did "not necessarily imply the inferiority of either race," and cited "separate schools for white and colored children" as an illustration of the principle (Good, 1962, p. 577). With this judicial blessing, districts in the South and the North developed racially segregated schools.

In time it became abundantly clear that the separate schools for African American and white children were hardly equal. African American teachers were poorly paid, facilities were inadequate, and children's educational attainment suffered accordingly. On May 17, 1954, in its decision on *Brown v. Board of Education,* the Supreme Court reversed its earlier position, declaring that racial segregation in public education was unconstitutional. The Court said, "We conclude that in the field of education the doctrine of 'separate but equal' has no place. Separate educational facilities are inherently unequal" and concluded that segregation violated the equal protection guarantees provided by the Fourteenth Amendment.

Citizens' (sometimes violent) opposition to the Court's decision has been well documented (see Bouma & Hoffman, 1968; Crain, 1968; Damerell, 1968; Rubin, 1972). Opponents of desegregation argue that (1) it does not significantly improve academic achievement of minority children, (2) it effectively denies children access to neighborhood schools, and (3) schools play an insignificant role in the reduction of racial inequality (Scott, 2003).

© Carl Iwasaki/Time Life Pictures/Getty Images

African American student Linda Brown (front, center) sitting in her segregated classroom at the Monroe School. A case brought before the Supreme Court on her behalf resulted in the decision to make school segregation illegal.

The nation's progress toward school desegregation has been halting and remains incomplete. Twelve years after the Supreme Court decision, the U.S. Office of Education concluded that "the great majority of American children attend schools that are largely segregated—that is, almost all of their fellow students are of the same racial background as they are" (U.S. Commission on Civil Rights, 1967, p. 2). Decades later, Jonathan Kozol (1991) documented abysmal conditions in the inner-city schools that served children of color. A continuing challenge for U.S. educators has been the effort to ensure equal access to education for children of all races. The Head Start program represents an early-intervention approach to reducing inequality in American education.

Head Start.   One of the most significant federal investments in education has been Head Start. Established as part of the 1965 War on Poverty programs, Head Start is managed by the Administration on Children and Families within the U.S. Department of Health and Human Services. Head Start offers comprehensive

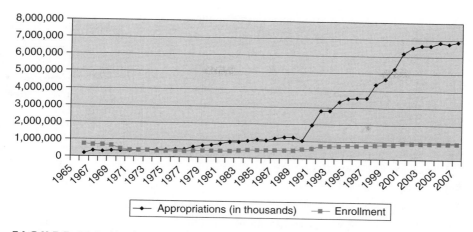

FIGURE 11.1 Head Start enrollment and appropriations: 1966–2007.

SOURCE: Administration for Children and Youth, DHHS. *Head Start Enrollment History.* http://www.acf.hhs.gov/programs/hsb/research/2003.htm. 2005, 2006, 2007 figures: http://www.caheadstart.org/HeadStartHistory.pdf (accessed December 27, 2007).

child development services for preschool children from low-income families. The program operates by extending grants to nonprofit and community organizations that administer the individual programs. Eligibility requirements vary, but most spaces are reserved for children who meet federal income guidelines. Programs also vary in the types of services they offer. Head Start programs have some required components, including educational and social services for families. Most establish links with social service providers serving low-income families in their communities. Parental involvement is a hallmark of Head Start programs.

Head Start is extremely popular, and its budget has grown from $96.4 million in 1966 to over $6.8 billion in 2007 (see Figure 11.1). In 2007, Head Start programs served more than 909,000 children between the ages of 3 and 5, a significant increase over the 733,000 served in 1965. Evaluation of the program has traditionally focused on the cognitive and academic achievements of the children involved. A congressionally mandated Head Start Impact Study demonstrated significant gains for children in the program across a range of areas, including pre-reading skills, social–emotional development, and physical health (Administration for Children and Families, 2005). Funding for the program increased dramatically during the two Clinton terms but remained flat under the George W. Bush administration.

Educating Children with Disabilities

Most of us are aware that the 1954 Supreme Court case *Brown v. The Board of Education of Topeka* affected school segregation in the United States.[6] But the case

6. I am indebted to Elizabeth LaMont, doctoral candidate at the University of Utah, for providing background information for this section.

also had implications for the education of children with disabilities since it established the principle of equal access to educational opportunity (Yell, Rogers, & Lodge Rodgers, 1998). As we saw in Chapter 8, it would be 20 years before Gerald Ford would sign the Education for All Handicapped Children Act requiring states that received federal funds to provide "free and appropriate public education" to children with disabilities. In 1990, this act was incorporated in the Individuals with Disabilities Education Act (IDEA). Under current law, states must provide

- Free and appropriate public education for all children with disabilities, regardless of the severity of the disability
- An individualized education program (IEP) for every eligible child
- Access to education in a regular classroom if possible
- Related services necessary to support the child in an educational environment (such as counseling, therapy, health services, and rehabilitation)
- Parental rights to participate in planning and consent to any change in educational programming
- Due process procedures to allow parents to appeal placement and other decisions
- Confidentiality of records

Nonetheless, state and federal resources for education are limited, and parents of children with disabilities must exercise vigilance (and sometimes engage in litigation) to secure the "free and appropriate public education" to which their children are entitled.

Modern Educational Reforms

Recent educational reforms have addressed two aspects of public education in the United States: school financing and school choice.

School Financing.   Throughout their history, American public elementary and secondary schools have been financed through local and state appropriations. Federal contributions typically represent only a small fraction of education budgets. State money comes from either general tax revenues or property taxes. The U.S. Department of Education reported that total funding for K–12 public education in the United States in 2003–2004 was $511 billion, about 4.7 percent of the Gross National Product (National Center for Education Statistics, 2007). Most of that amount comes from a combination of state funds (about 45 percent) and local taxes (another 45 percent). About 7 percent comes from federal sources and 2 percent from private sources (National Center for Education Statistics, 2004).

Inequality has been a hallmark of school financing in the United States. In his landmark work, *Savage Inequalities,* Jonathan Kozol (1991) notes "a certain grim aesthetic in the almost perfect upward scaling of expenditures from poorest of the poor to richest of the rich within the New York City area: $5,590 for the children of the Bronx and Harlem, $6,340 for the nonwhite kids of Roosevelt, $6,400 for the black kids of Mount Vernon, $7,400 for the slightly better-off community of Yonkers, over $11,000 for the very lucky children of Manhasset, Jericho and Great Neck" (pp. 122–123).

The nation's approach to educational funding supports this inequality. The "foundation program" was introduced in the early 1920s to balance local control with state support for education. Under this approach, the initial funds required to operate public schools are drawn from a local tax based on the value of homes and businesses within the district. In affluent districts this amount is sufficient to meet the schools' needs. In less affluent districts, where the tax rate is the same, lower property values result in less revenue. State funds are then allocated to bring financial resources of the poorer districts up to the "foundation" level—a level that, in theory, is roughly equal to the amount used in the wealthy districts. Of course, the needs of poorer districts are often greater because children experience higher rates of family dysfunction and community stress. Needs aside, poorer districts receive less funding because states set the "foundation level" to provide a bare minimum, not to establish an adequate educational foundation.

Kozol (1991) vividly documents the educational minimum provided for children in poor districts:

> Christopher approaches me at the end of class. The room is too hot. His skin looks warm and his black hair is damp. "Write this down. You asked a question about Martin Luther King. I'm going to say something. All that stuff about the dream means nothing to the kids I know in East St. Louis. So far as they're concerned, he died in vain. He was famous and he lived and gave his speeches and he died and now he's gone . . . don't tell students in this school about the dream. Go and look into a toilet here if you would like to know what life is like for students in this city." I do as Christopher asked. . . . Four of the six toilets do not work. The toilet stalls, which are eaten away by red and brown corrosion, have no doors. The toilets have no seats. One has a rotted wooden stump. There are no paper towels and no soap. Near the door there is a loop of wire with an empty toilet-paper roll. (p. 36)

Disparities in school finance have resulted in lawsuits against states. One of the earliest was filed in Texas in 1968. In a class action suit (*Rodriquez v. San Antonio Independent School District*), plaintiffs charged that the unequal financing of education violated the equal protection clause of the U.S. Constitution. After years of litigation, the state was forced to change its method of school financing. Similar outcomes have been observed throughout the nation. Since 1972, more than 40 school finance cases have been heard in state supreme courts (Center for Education Reform, 1999).

Title I of the Elementary and Secondary Education Act of 1965 is designed to address the difficulties experienced by schools in low-income neighborhoods. Title I is the largest single source of federal funding for education. Funds are used to provide teachers, tutoring, labs, parent involvement activities, prekindergarten programs, and other resources for schools with at least 40 percent of children on free or reduced-price lunch programs.

The No Child Left Behind Act of 2001 was designed to hold public schools accountable for their students' mastery of core subjects, particularly reading and mathematics. It included special provisions that targeted Title I schools, though its testing requirements applied to all public schools. Under the act, each state must test student progress in reading and math in each of grades 3 through 8, and at least once during grades 10 through 12. Title I schools must demonstrate "adequate yearly progress" across several student groups. Those failing to make progress are placed on the dreaded "Schools in Need of Improvement" list. Those on the list for two years or more face sanctions, including a requirement that Title I funds be used to transport students who elect to transfer to different schools, a requirement that Title I funds be used to tutor students who do not transfer, and corrective action such as staff replacement. Schools that fail in the same subject for four years must implement a restructuring plan that may include state management or reorganization as a charter school. Appropriations under the act amounted to a significant increase in federal funding for education. The act also included requirements for teacher qualifications and protections for school prayer.

Reauthorization of the No Child Left Behind Act was not completed in 2007, but at the time of this writing, it remains in effect. The law has done little to ease the nation's educational disparities. It has been controversial, and implementation has challenged many school districts. Teachers object that the act has forced them to "teach to the test," rather than focus more broadly on the subject matter (National Education Association, n.d.). In 2004, the General Accounting Office reported that districts are sometimes unable to provide viable alternative schools to students from Title I schools that have been sanctioned with school choice. In this situation, the district must provide transportation to alternative schools. Unfortunately, some districts do not have the capacity to absorb students into other schools. Others cannot offer schools that are substantially better than the students' original school (U.S. General Accounting Office, 2004).

Lotteries.   No doubt, nineteenth-century educational reformers would be astonished by the current relationship between gambling and the public schools. In 1964, New Hampshire became the first state in the union to establish a state lottery. Since then, 36 more states and the District of Columbia have established lotteries (NASPL, 1999). Most states devote part of their lottery proceeds to education. In Georgia, lotteries support college funds called "Hope" scholarships. The practice of allocating some proceeds to education has increased public support for the lottery.

In no case does lottery funding provide a substantial portion of the educational budget. In California, less than 2 percent of the 2006–2007 budget for public schools was drawn from the lottery (Education Data Partnership, 2007). As the government has moved into the gambling business, social workers and other helping professionals have become aware of gambling's toll. Compulsive gamblers have been compared to alcoholics in their capacity to ignore the costs of their problem behavior. Apart from the growing problem of compulsive gam-

Props from President Bush's press conference to promote No Child Left Behind legislation await demolition in front of the U.S. Department of Education building.

bling, professionals are concerned that those who participate in the lottery (the vast majority of whom lose money) come primarily from poor and working–class backgrounds. Thus the lottery is a regressive way to finance public education.

School Choice: Tuition Vouchers and Charter Schools.   Traditionally, children in the United States have been assigned to the school serving their neighborhood. School choice reforms give parents the opportunity to select the school that their children will attend. At its most basic level, school choice permits parents to send their children to any public school within the state. More complex and controversial school choice reforms include tuition vouchers and charter schools.

Under existing tuition voucher programs, the state or local school district provides parents with a portion of the educational funding allotted to their children and allows them to use these funds to enroll their children in the school of their choice. In some states, tuition vouchers can be used only for secular schools, while in other jurisdictions parents may use the vouchers to send their children to religious schools.[7] Voucher programs have been vigorously opposed by teachers'

7. The use of public funds to send children to religious schools has been subject to several court challenges. In a 1998 case, the Wisconsin Supreme Court ruled in favor of the practice.

unions at local and federal levels. Opponents of the programs argue that they damage public schools by diverting needed funds and by draining away the most academically motivated students. As a result, they argue, schools in poorer districts will deteriorate even further.

Proponents argue that giving parents in low-income areas the opportunity to send their children to schools outside their neighborhood equalizes educational opportunities and gives neighborhood schools the motivation to improve. School choice is the educational reform of preference for libertarians, most notably Milton Friedman (Friedman, 1955). According to Friedman, "A society that takes freedom of the individual, or more realistically the family, as its ultimate objective, seeks to further this objective by relying primarily on voluntary exchange among individuals for the organization of economic activity" (p. 1). Libertarians argue that parents should be given vouchers and allowed to use them to purchase an education in any licensed school, public or private.

Whereas tuition vouchers address the "demand" side of the education equation, enabling parents to shop for schools, charter schools address the "supply" side. Charter schools are expected to play a significant role in the No Child Left Behind Act. State legislatures provide for the establishment of special schools through a charter or contract that sets specific academic goals that must be met. These schools receive an allotment from the school district for students who choose to attend. Charter schools are, therefore, public schools. Exempt from district curriculum requirements and governance, they are managed by a charter board. The charter school concept was enthusiastically endorsed by the Clinton administration. President Clinton called for the establishment of 3,000 charter schools by 2000. Of course, the per-pupil allotment for charter schools is either the same amount as the established public schools or a lesser amount, and charter schools often face large start-up expenses to acquire buildings and purchase equipment. Therefore, their financial situation may be unstable. Opponents of charter schools argue that they are not feasible alternatives for low-income families and that they siphon affluent and academically motivated students away from the traditional public schools. A 2004 report released by the American Federation of Teachers (Nelson, Rosenberg, & Van Meter, 2004) argues that student achievement in charter schools lags behind that in traditional public schools.

CHILDREN AS VICTIMS

Public response to child victimization in the United States has been marked by episodes of high interest, followed by extended periods of indifference or inattention. Children have been victims of both poverty and violence. In this section, we will first consider the victimization of children through poverty and then examine violence against children.

Poverty and Children, Past and Present

In colonial times, children who were impoverished through parental death or other circumstances often were sold as indentured servants. In theory, this practice was designed to teach children a trade or skill, but more often indentured servants were assigned menial tasks and functioned essentially as slaves until they reached the age of release (21 or 24 for boys; 18 for girls). During indenture, parents lost their custody rights, so children were sold only under dire circumstances. During the nineteenth century, institutional alternatives were established in major cities. Instead of being indentured, impoverished children were sent to orphanages, almshouses, or poorhouses.

A harbinger of change came in 1909, when James E. West, a friend of President Theodore Roosevelt who had been raised in an orphanage, persuaded the president to convene a Conference on the Care of Dependent Children. The conference brought the needs of these children to national attention, setting the stage for the development of a public child welfare system (Trattner, 1989). Its keynote statement proclaimed, "Home life is the highest and finest product of civilization. . . . [C]hildren should not be deprived of it except for urgent and compelling reasons" (Trattner, 1989, p. 194). The conference led to a reduced emphasis on institutionalization and an increased use of adoption and foster homes for children in need. It also was the first in a series of conferences of its kind, held every 10 years until 1981, when it was canceled by the Reagan administration.

The U.S. Children's Bureau was established in 1912, three years after the first White House Conference on Children, despite fierce opposition from business interests who feared it would signal the end of child labor. They were prescient. Child labor eventually would become a significant issue for the Children's Bureau.

Julia Lathrop, a former Hull House resident and member of the Illinois State Board of Charities, took over as director of the agency. She chose infant mortality as the agency's initial focus. It seemed to be a relatively noncontroversial issue. After all, if the federal government spent $1.25 million dollars a year for the Bureau of Animal Husbandry, shouldn't it devote some of its resources to care for the nation's children?

The matter quickly became controversial, however. In 1918, based on research by the Children's Bureau, Jeanette Rankin (the first woman to serve in Congress) introduced the Sheppard-Towner Bill. The bill called for the federal government to offer grants-in-aid to states that would provide health care and education to disadvantaged mothers. Opponents accused Lathrop of being part of the recent Bolshevik Revolution and charged that the state was taking over the raising and medical care of children. Medical societies attacked the bill, its sponsor, and the staff of the Children's Bureau. In one of the debate's more vitriolic statements, Senator Thomas Reed of Missouri argued that if the bill passed, "female celibates would instruct mothers on how to bring up their babies" (Trattner, 1989, p. 199). Despite these views, after three years of debate and the ratification of the Nineteenth Amendment granting women the right to vote, the bill passed in 1921 and was signed by President Warren G. Harding.

Under the bill's mandate, between 1921 and 1929 nearly 3,000 maternal and child health centers were established in 45 states (Trattner, 1989, p. 199). State health departments were strengthened, and infant and maternal mortality rates dropped significantly. Despite the act's effectiveness, Congress refused to renew funding in 1929, bowing to the energetic opposition of both medical professionals and the new president, Herbert Hoover. Later, Title V of the 1939 Social Security Act would again establish federal grants-in-aid that enabled the Children's Bureau to resume its work in maternal and child health. This program operates today under the auspices of the Department of Health and Human Services.

Today, children in the United States face a higher risk of poverty than any other age group. Whereas in 2006 the general poverty rate was 12.3 percent, the rate for children under 18 years old was 17.4 percent, and for young children (those under 5) the probability of living in poverty was 20.7 percent. Some children of color face even higher risks of poverty. In 2006, one-third (33 percent) of African Americans under 18 years old lived in households with poverty level incomes, as did 27 percent of Hispanic children (U.S. Bureau of the Census, 2007b). Modern policies regarding child poverty in the United States reveal deep ambivalence. On the one hand, the notion of children suffering is unacceptable to most adults. Thus the development of educational programs, health care, and even social services for children in poverty seldom encounters serious opposition. On the other hand, the nation has long been inclined to blame adults for their indigence. Most children in poverty are intimately linked to an adult in poverty. Therein lies the ambivalence that fuels controversies regarding income maintenance programs. If what it takes to move a child out of poverty is financial assistance to a member of the undeserving poor, the nation balks.

This ambivalence is evident in the history of income maintenance programs funded under the Social Security Act. Initially, Title IV of the act established a federal–state grant-in-aid program called Aid to Dependent Children (ADC). In 1962, the name of the program was changed to Aid to Families with Dependent Children (AFDC). This change reflected growing awareness of the role of the family in children's lives, and it also underscored the reality that aid was provided to families, not directly to children themselves. In 1996, the federal entitlement provided under AFDC was converted to a block grant called Temporary Assistance to Needy Families (TANF). As discussed in Chapter 5, the name change is the tip of the iceberg of the changes initiated by the TANF program. Nonetheless, it is important to note that the word *children* has, for the first time since 1935, been eliminated from the name of the income maintenance provision of the Social Security Act.

The implications of poverty for children are far-reaching. Children in low-income families face higher health risks, in part due to substandard housing and limited access to health care. Their educational opportunities are also severely truncated. Finally, children in households with poverty-level incomes experience significantly higher rates of violence than those living in more affluent settings.

Violence Against Children, Past and Present

The latter part of the nineteenth century was a time of outcry for public intervention in cases of child abuse and gross neglect. In 1875, the case of "Mary Ellen" brought child abuse to public attention and led to the creation of the New York Society for the Prevention of Cruelty to Children (NYSPCC). The case has become the stuff of myth, based on the false belief that in the absence of laws to protect children, those designed to protect animals were applied to protect a child. This myth has been repeated in several social work texts (e.g., DiNitto, 1995; Kadushin, 1974). Yet, as Watkins (1990) demonstrated, laws to protect children were on the books as early as the seventeenth century. What was lacking was an entity to assume responsibility for their enforcement. The NYSPCC became that entity, and during the first 20 years of its existence it intervened in more than 230,000 cases, with enough impact to provoke criticism of its aggressive efforts to protect and rescue abused and neglected children.

Sallie Watkins (1990) presented the facts in the Mary Ellen case. In 1864, the infant was left with the Department of Charities by a woman who claimed to have no knowledge of how to reach her parents. Mary Ellen was indentured to a family at the age of 18 months. Mary Connolly was her mistress and her abuser. In 1873, Mrs. Etta Wheeler was visiting in poor neighborhoods when she heard complaints about a child being horribly abused. She posed as a census taker and investigated the situation in December 1873. Appalled by the child's condition, Mrs. Wheeler sought help from police and several charitable organizations before finding an ally in Mr. Henry Bergh, president of the New York Society for the Prevention of Cruelty to Animals (NYSPCA). Mr. Bergh intervened in the case as a private citizen, not as a representative of the NYSPCA. The laws he invoked to remove Mary Ellen were those designed to protect people in custody. A judge issued a special warrant that led to Mary Ellen's removal from the home and the subsequent trial of her guardian, Mrs. Connolly. When searches for her parents proved unsuccessful, Mary Ellen was placed in the care of Mrs. Wheeler. She married at the age of 24, had two children, and lived into her 80s. Her abuser, Mrs. Connolly, was sent to a penitentiary for one year. Mary Ellen's experiences were important, not because they changed the laws regarding abuse of children, but because they raised public awareness of the problem and led to the establishment of the NYSPCC.

The NYSPCC was the first organization of its kind in the world and the beginning of an "anticruelty" movement that spread throughout the United States and Europe. By 1910 more than 200 such societies had been established (Costin, 1992). The movement soon encountered a tension that to this day pervades the field of child welfare: the conflict between family privacy and child protection. The NYSPCC operated by aggressively removing children from homes and placing them in institutions. Institutionalization of children placed the organization in direct conflict with the deep-seated American preference for parental authority and family life. (This value was articulated in the famous resolution from the 1909 Conference on the Care of Dependent Children on home life mentioned earlier.) This conflict, coupled with social and economic conditions in the post–World War I period, drew attention away from the problem of child abuse. The ensuing period of indifference to the issue would last for several decades.

In the 1960s, child abuse was "discovered" yet again. A pediatric radiologist named John Caffey reported a new "syndrome" in infants that included subdural hematomas along with atypical fractures of limbs and ribs (Caffey, 1946). In 1962, C. Henry Kempe gave this condition a name: "battered child syndrome." With this label, child abuse resurfaced as a public concern (Kempe et al., 1962).

In its rediscovered form, child abuse was considered more a medical than a social problem. Responding to the advocacy of medical professionals, states quickly passed legislation dictating a public response to the abuse or neglect of children. Legislation was also enacted at the federal level. The Child Abuse Prevention and Treatment Act of 1974 established mandatory reporting procedures under which health and human service professionals were required to notify state authorities of suspected or known cases of child abuse or neglect. The act also established the National Center for Child Abuse and Neglect, and it provided some funding to serve troubled families.

As a direct result of federal and state legislation, more cases of abuse and neglect came to the attention of authorities, and greater numbers of children were removed from their homes. In the case of Native American children the situation became especially egregious. As part of a campaign to "acculturate" Native American children, the U.S. government and other authorities developed a program of placing them in boarding schools.[8] These schools forced the children to wear the clothes, eat the food, speak the language, and practice the customs of the dominant culture. In the United States, this practice continued from the late nineteenth century until the middle of the twentieth century. Although most boarding schools were closed by the 1960s and 1970s, the child welfare system continued a similar practice, as Native American children who were removed from their homes were often placed with Caucasian foster families. Critics saw foster placement as another attempt to eradicate the Native American culture—a practice that harmed the children whom the system was supposed to protect. In response to these concerns, the Indian Child Welfare Act of 1978 (PL 95-608) established tribal jurisdiction over Native American children who enter the child welfare system. Tribes exercise their jurisdiction in varying ways, but at a minimum the act calls for the placement of Native American children in foster and adoptive homes that reflect the Native American culture, and for assistance (financial and educational) to enable the tribes to administer their own child welfare and family support services.

As the child welfare system matured, the practice of removing children from abusive and neglectful homes brought more children into foster care. Policy makers became concerned about this increase, noting that decades of research had

---

8. Enrollment of Native American children in boarding schools was remarkably similar to the nineteenth-century practice of "placing out" developed by the Children's Aid Society, a topic that will be introduced in the section on children as villains.

illuminated flaws in the nation's foster care system. In the late 1950s, Henry Maas and Richard Engler (1959) had suggested that extended stays in foster care could produce behavior problems. Support for their view was offered at a 1963 conference sponsored by the Child Welfare League of America and the National Association of Social Workers. At this "Institute on Child Welfare Research," social scientists suggested that separating children from their parents and placing them in foster care was not always in the best interests of the child (Fanshel & Shinn, 1978). They documented an alarming phenomenon called "foster care drift," observing that children often languished for years in foster care, with little stability or planning for their future.

To address this problem, the 1980 Adoption Assistance and Child Welfare Act (PL 96-272) established clear procedures and timelines for the management of children who enter into state custody. Within 18 months of the child's placement, a dispositional hearing was to be held to place the child in the least restrictive, most family-like setting that was available and appropriate. States were required to make "reasonable efforts" to reunify families. Funds were provided for reunification services, which included a wide range of supportive activities, from parenting education and stress management to budgeting and case management. If progress toward reunification was not made, the law required states to begin "permanency planning" on behalf of the child. That is, the state agency was required to develop a plan for the permanent placement of the child in long-term foster care, guardianship, or (if parental rights were terminated) adoption. The law was codified as Titles N–B and IV–E of the Social Security Act and is still in force.

The 1980 law forced child welfare workers to make painful decisions. No longer could they wait and hope that abusive parents would change. Instead, for a limited time, workers became active partners with biological parents in an effort to preserve the family unit. Researchers and program administrators began to develop services and methods that would accomplish reunification. The Homebuilders program in the state of Washington was one model effort to support "family preservation"—that is, the reunification of children with their biological parents. This program developed a model that offered intensive services to families to prevent foster placement. Initial research on family preservation efforts was promising. Families were reunified and parenting was improved (Pecora et al., 1995).

The growing enthusiasm for family preservation led to the 1993 passage of the Family Preservation and Support Services Act (PL 103-66), which provided increased funding for reunification services. Each state received an amount of money based on the number of children receiving food stamps. Unfortunately, the Homebuilders model has proved hard to duplicate in other settings (Littell, 1995). Perhaps as a result, the nation's enthusiasm for family preservation seems to have reverted to an inclination toward child removal.

The Adoption and Safe Families Act of 1997 (PL 105-89) emphasized that the first priority for child welfare is the safety of children. While authorizing limited funding ($305 million in 2001) for family preservation, the law contains several provisions designed to encourage adoption, including incentive payments for states that exceed their average number of adoptions; expanded health coverage for adopted children with special needs; new, shorter, 12-month timelines for permanency hearings and filing for termination of parental rights; and modifications in provisions requiring reasonable efforts to preserve and reunify families. Under these modifications, states need not make such efforts in cases that involve "aggravated circumstances" (including but not limited to abandonment, torture, chronic abuse, and sexual abuse); cases in which parents committed (or aided, abetted, or attempted to commit) either murder or manslaughter of a child; cases involving felony assault that resulted in serious bodily injury to a child; and cases in which the parent's rights to the child's sibling have been involuntarily terminated. In essence, this law has established several categories of "undeserving" parents and excused states from the responsibility to try to preserve their families. In these cases, states must hold permanency hearings within 30 days (not 12 months) of a child's removal.

Children of color, especially African American children, are overrepresented in the public child welfare system (Chipungu & Bent-Goodley, 2004). This simple observation stems from underlying racial injustices in the U.S. economy, the criminal justice system, and the child welfare system itself. As we saw in Chapter 9, children of color (particularly African Americans) are more likely than other children to live in poverty. Due to racial disparities in the criminal justice system, children of color are more likely to have a parent who is incarcerated. As a result, these children are more likely to come to the attention of authorities due to allegations of child abuse or neglect. Once children of color enter the child welfare system, they are more likely than white children under similar circumstances to be removed from the home, and as a result children of color, who make up one-third of the general population of children in the United States, make up over 55 percent of children in foster care (Chipungu & Bent-Goodley, 2004).

The history of the U.S. child welfare system also reveals profound ambivalence toward the parents involved—a tendency to see them as either victims or villains. The nation puts no restrictions on procreation.[9] Americans must complete more training to become drivers than to become parents. This would suggest a "right" to raise children—one that many would intuitively endorse. Some, due to mental illness, substance abuse, or poverty, are unable to fulfill their parental obligations. Motivated by enthusiasm for biological parenting, child welfare agencies have undertaken what in some cases has amounted to heroic measures to achieve "family preservation." On the other hand, some view abusive or neglectful parents as villains, not victims. This view supports prompt removal of children from abusive homes, as well as punishment of the perpetrators. In some ways, it represents a return to the nation's nineteenth-century approach exemplified in the case of little Mary Ellen. Today, more children in the United States are dying because of violence than ever before. Many take their own lives,

---

9. China is probably the only nation in the world in which most people seek government approval before becoming biological parents. Even in China, the practice is extremely unpopular.

bringing youth suicide rates to unprecedented high levels. Still others are the victims of homicide, too often at the hands of those charged with their care.

Homicides against children peaked during the 1990s. In 1996, homicides of children aged 5 and under—most committed by parents or caregivers—reached a 40-year high (Wingfield, Petit, & Klempner, 1999). Homicide became the second leading cause of death for 15- to 19-year-olds and the leading cause for African American males in this age range. The homicide rate for male African American teens more than doubled between 1985 and 1996, from 46 per 100,000 to nearly 100. The rate for teenaged white men was 12 per 100,000 (Wingfield, Petit, & Klempner, 1999). Though homicide rates declined by 2005, the racial disparity persisted. That year, 26.4 per 100,000 African American teens aged 14 to 17 died as the result of homicide. This compares to a rate of 4.4 per 100,000 for white teens (U.S. Department of Justice, 2005).

From an international perspective, the United States has had an unusually high rate of homicide against children. In 1994, the World Bank compared the rate of homicide against youth in 26 high-income nations. The rate in the United States was five times higher than the total rate in all of the other nations combined. Among the 26 nations studied, homicides accounted for 1,995 deaths of youth under 15, of which 1,464 (73 percent) occurred in the United States (World Bank, 1994). Indeed, Dr. Paul Holinger et al. (1994) reported that a comparison of World Health Organization countries revealed the nation's youth homicide rate was "at the top of the list." Only Mexico and the former USSR had comparable rates.

Suicide and homicide rates tend to be parallel (Holinger et al., 1994). Suicide rates for American children have quadrupled since 1950 (National Center for Health Statistics, 1998a). In 2007, suicide was the third leading cause of death among Americans aged 10 to 24, accounting for 4,500 deaths. Suicide rates among girls aged 10 to 19 have risen in recent years, although boys remain at greatest risk of suicide (Centers for Disease Control and Prevention, 2007b).

Attempts to explain youth suicide and homicide tend to focus on individual pathology. Studies have identified risk factors such as substance abuse and mental illness (Blumenthal & Knupter, 1988; Davidson & Linnoila, 1992; Klerman, 1987). Although these risk factors have clear implications for social work practice, they say little about the potential role of public policies in addressing these parallel trends. Yet research on the contribution of economic factors suggests an important role for social policy. As Holinger et al. (1994) and others have noted, "Poverty appears to be the most consistent underlying risk factor in communities with high homicide rates" (p. 150). Economic factors such as unemployment are among the most important in determining both youth suicide and homicide rates. Clearly efforts to reduce poverty and economic vulnerability will have the secondary benefit of reducing the violence experienced by America's children. In addition, improved psychiatric treatment and reduced access to guns have been cited as social changes that might reduce the likelihood of suicide (World Health Organization, 2002).

CHILDREN AS VILLAINS

The Industrial Revolution brought overcrowding to U.S. cities, whose slums were notorious for producing "the dangerous classes" (a term Charles Loring Brace used to describe the children of urban slums). In 1853 Brace founded the Children's Aid Society and developed the practice of "placing out" poor urban children. Thousands of these children (most of whom were Roman Catholic) were sent to live on farms and work for families with "strong Christian (i.e., Protestant) values." This practice was harshly criticized. Brace attributed the criticism to "ignorant Roman Catholics" who spread rumors that the children were sold as slaves, given new names, and converted to Protestantism (Brace, 1872, p. 234). As a result, said Brace, the poor themselves opposed the practice. In his 1872 treatise on his work, Brace said, "Most distressing of all was, when a drunken mother or father followed a half-starved boy, already scarred and sore with their brutality, and snatched him from one of our parties of little emigrants, all joyful with their new prospects, only to beat him and leave him on the streets" (p. 235).

Opponents noted that the Children's Aid Society did not carefully investigate the foster homes, that the foster families sometimes mistreated the children, and that many of the children were never heard from again.

Over the course of 25 years, the Society removed 50,000 children from the streets of New York. Poor families protested the practice. The Roman Catholic Church charged the agency with using this practice to convert Catholic children to Protestantism. Later, many of the receiving states objected to having indigent youth dropped within their borders. Eventually, the practice of placing out was abandoned in favor of asylums.

Child Villains in Modern America

Today, many Americans still view some children as members of the dangerous classes, and the nation's treatment of youth who commit crimes has cycled from a severely punitive approach to an emphasis on education and rehabilitation and back to punishment.

Courts in early America did not differentiate between juvenile and adult offenders. The juvenile court movement of the nineteenth century (which coincided with emerging awareness of children as victims of abuse) led to the creation of separate courts and institutions for children that emphasized education and rehabilitation. Of course, given the widespread belief that the blame for delinquency lay with the individual child, these institutions often meted out severe punishment and extremely difficult living conditions.

Eventually the limitations of punishment as a deterrent became clear, and these institutions came to emphasize rehabilitation through the use of indeterminate sentences, probation and parole, and training and counseling. When offenders were released, they usually went straight into employment that had been arranged for them and remained on parole so that their reentrance into the community was carefully controlled. This system was applied in the New York State

Reformatory at Elmira in the 1870s. Studies found four out of five of their "graduates" did not return to a penal institution. Soon other states established similar juvenile facilities.

The world's first full-fledged juvenile court was created in Cook County (Chicago) in July 1899 (Denver, Colorado, established its juvenile court a year later). The aim was to reduce the stigma of juvenile crime and create new mechanisms for dealing with offenders. Hearings were informal, with no lawyers, oaths, or robes. The judge was in the role of a "parental guide," as defined by statute: "The care, custody, and discipline of the children brought before the court shall approximate as nearly as possible that which they should receive from their parents, and . . . as far as practicable they shall be treated not as criminals but as children in need of aid, encouragement and guidance" (Trattner, 1989, p. 118). Clearly this system depended heavily on the confidence of the public and legislators in the benevolence of juvenile court judges. The authority of these judges greatly exceeded that of judges in adult court. Later this approach was criticized as stripping children of their constitutional rights and placing them at the mercy of not-so-benevolent judges.

The *Gault* case, decided by the U.S. Supreme Court in May 1967, dramatically changed the operation of juvenile courts. On January 8 at about 10 A.M., 15-year-old Gerald Gault and a friend were taken into custody by the sheriff of Gila County, Arizona. They were accused by a neighbor of making phone calls "of the irritatingly, offensive, adolescent, sex variety" (*In re* Gault, 387 U.S. 1; 18 L. Ed. 2d 527; 87 S. Ct. 1428 (1967). At the time, Gerald was on probation as a result of having been with another boy who had stolen a wallet. Gerald's parents, both at work, were not notified that their son had been arrested. Gerald was taken to a detention facility. When the parents came home, they sent his older brother to look for Gerald and learned that he was in custody. The parents went to the detention facility and were told a hearing would be held the following day. There was no record of the hearing, and three to four days later Gerald was released, with no explanation. A note from the arresting officer indicated that the judge had set a date a week later for "further hearings on Gerald's delinquency." Gerald's mother requested that the woman who complained about her son be present at the hearing, but she was told that the complainant's presence was not necessary. At the end of the hearing, the judge committed Gerald as a delinquent to the State Industrial School "for the period of his minority [that is, until age 21]." The child was to be confined for years for making lewd phone calls, an offense that for an adult would result in a fine of $5 to $50 or not more than two months' imprisonment.

Concluding that "unbridled discretion, however benevolently motivated, is frequently a poor substitute for principle and procedure," the Supreme Court held that "neither the Fourteenth Amendment nor the Bill of Rights is for adults alone" and set forth procedural requirements for juvenile cases. These included timely notice of charges, the right of the child to legal counsel, the right to confront and cross-examine complainants, and protection against self-incrimination. At the same time that it imposed these due process requirements on juvenile courts, the Supreme Court upheld the constitutionality and desirability of other measures: the separation of juveniles from adult offenders, the practice of "seal-ing" juvenile records so they will not affect adult eligibility for civil service and other privileges, and the informality of juvenile court proceedings. These proce-dures remain in place today.

The Juvenile Justice and Delinquency Prevention Act of 1974. The Juvenile Justice and Delinquency Prevention Act of 1974 (JJDP) (PL 93–415) has become the vehicle for significant reforms of the juvenile courts. First, the act changed the courts' treatment of youth convicted of less serious offenses called "status offenses." Status offenses are behaviors that can be regulated be-cause of a youth's "status" as a minor. They vary from state to state but typically include curfew violations, truancy, and failure to respond to parental authority. Until 1974, children who committed status offenses were incarcerated in deten-tion facilities with those guilty of more serious crimes. The JJDP Act required states to separate status offenders from those guilty of criminal acts. As a result, as many as 40 percent of youths who were status offenders have been diverted from detention facilities (Clement, 1997).

In 1988, the JJDP Act was amended to address the disproportionate repre-sentation of minority youth (like Lorenzo, the subject of this chapter's case study) in the juvenile justice system. Unlike the diversion of status offenders, this initia-tive has been relatively unsuccessful. Both African American and Hispanic youth have been disproportionately represented in the nation's detention centers. In 1991, 43 percent of those in detention centers were black, 35 percent were white, and 19 percent were Hispanic. Training schools are the most restrictive juvenile detention facilities. There, African American youth represented 47 per-cent of the population. The general theme, as articulated by the Office of Juvenile Justice and Delinquency Prevention (OJJDP), was that "[i]n every state studied, minority males had a higher probability rate of incarceration before age 18 than their white peers" (Roscoe & Morton, 1994, p. 1).

People of color continue to be overrepresented in the juvenile justice sys-tem. For example, in 2003 African Americans had the highest youth incarcera-tion rate. That year, 754 African American youth out of every 100,000 were detained. This compares to rates of 496 for Native American youth, 348 for Hispanic youth, 190 for Caucasian youth, and 113 for Asian youth (U.S. Department of Justice, 2007c). As several studies have demonstrated, the over-representation of minority youth reflects the way they are "processed" in the juvenile justice system. People of color are more likely to be arrested, more likely to be charged, and more likely to be detained. Jeffrey Butts, of the Urban Institute, explains, "At each stage of the process, there's a slight empirical bias. And the problem is that the slight empirical bias at every stage of the decision-making accumulates. . . . [B]y the time you reach the end you have all minorities in the deep end of the system" (Center on Juvenile and Criminal Justice, 2007). These remarks echoed several previous studies of the treatment of minority youth (see, for example, Leonard, Pope, & Feyerherm, 1995).

Other Forms of Child Villainy

American children are still the "dangerous classes" when they engage in behavior that is threatening to the broader society. Behaviors identified as problematic include teen pregnancy and membership in youth gangs. When children become extremely threatening, the response of the nation's juvenile justice system is to "certify" them as adults so they can be tried and punished accordingly.

Teen Pregnancy.   Teen pregnancy creates two high-risk children: a child-mother and an infant. The mother is less likely than older mothers to receive adequate prenatal care (National Center for Health Statistics, 1998c). She is also less likely to finish high school: only one-third of teen mothers receive high school diplomas (Maynard, 1996). Finally, teen mothers are likely to receive public assistance: nearly 80 percent of teen mothers rely on welfare at some point in their lives (Congressional Budget Office, 1990). Children born to teenaged mothers have lower birth weights, are more likely to perform poorly in school, and experience greater rates of abuse and neglect (George & Lee, 1997; Maynard, 1996; Wolfe & Perozek, 1997). Sons of teen mothers are more likely to spend time in prison, while daughters of teens are more likely (like Lorenzo's sister) to become teen mothers themselves (Maynard, 1996).

The teen pregnancy rate in the United States peaked in 1991, at 116.5 pregnancies per 1,000 teens aged 15 to 19. It has declined in recent years, reaching a record low of 65.0 pregnancies per 1,000 teens in 2002. Seeking to understand this decline, the Guttmacher Institute reviewed data and surveys regarding teen sexual behavior and concluded that it is primarily due to increased use of contraception, although greater abstinence is a contributing factor (Guttmacher Institute, 2002). Teen pregnancy among Hispanic and African American women remains higher than among Asian and Caucasian Americans (Guttmacher Institute, 2006).

Teen birth rates have dropped along with pregnancy rates. Births to American women aged 15 to 19 peaked in 1957 at 96 births per 1,000 (Guttmacher Institute, 2002). In 2004 the National Center for Health Statistics reported a rate of 41 births per 1,000 teens (NCHS, 2004).

Like many issues in child welfare, the problem of teen pregnancy challenges the division between private familial matters and matters of public interest. Most Americans believe teenagers should abstain from sex, but they also feel that sexually active teens should have access to contraception (Princeton Survey Research Associates, 1997). Most also believe that teens should seek information about sex and reproduction from their parents, but sometimes this does not happen. Teen pregnancy has consequences, not only for the family involved but for the broader community. Recognizing the public interest in preventing teen pregnancies, public schools typically provide rudimentary education on sex and reproduction. These educational efforts often generate controversy. When they are coupled with proposals to educate teens about contraception—or even further, to provide them with contraceptive devices—the controversy can become overwhelming. Another delicate policy issue that bears on teen pregnancy involves abortions. Abortion is legal in the United States, but in most states teenagers seeking abortions must have parental approval (Robinson, 1999).

The United States reports higher rates of teen pregnancy and teen births than other developed countries. A 2002 study compared pregnancy rates and teen sexual behavior in the United States, Canada, Sweden, France, and England and Wales. The study concluded that the primary reason for higher pregnancy rates in the United States is lower rates of contraceptive use (Guttmacher Institute, 2002).

Youth Gangs.   Once confined to the urban core of a few major cities, youth gangs have been reported in every state in the nation. The OJJDP conducted Youth Gang Surveys in 1995, 1996, and 1997. The surveys were designed to gather general information about the prevalence of gangs, and they required the participation of thousands of police and sheriff's departments across the nation. In 1995, respondents reported a total of 23,388 youth gangs in the United States, with an estimated 664,906 members (Moore, 1995). By 2004, the National Youth Gang Center had identified over 24,000 gangs with 760,000 members. Youth gangs tend to concentrate in larger cities, with 99 percent of law enforcement agencies in cities of 100,000 or more reporting multiple years of gang difficulties (Institute for Intergovernmental Research, 2004).

Experts have identified several different reasons that youth join gangs. Observing that most of the nation's gangs originated in inner cities, some emphasize the role of poverty and hopelessness, suggesting that gang enterprise offers a chance for economic advancement. The recent expansion of gangs in affluent suburbs has led some observers (e.g., Monti, 1994) to emphasize the role of family dysfunction in gang involvement, noting that gang members often come from families affected by divorce, substance abuse, and abuse or neglect of children. The gang, they suggest, becomes a surrogate family—one with clear roles, loyalties, and responsibilities.

Regardless of the reasons for joining, once children are part of a gang, they are widely feared. There is a rational basis for that fear. As the OJJDP reported, "Gang members account for a disproportionate share of delinquent acts, particularly the most serious offenses" (Thornberry & Burch, 1997, p. 1). This observation stems from the Rochester Youth Development Study. Researchers followed a sample of 1,000 seventh- and eighth-grade boys and girls, primarily from high-crime areas. Interviewing children over a four-year period, they found that about 30 percent reported being a member of a street gang at some point prior to finishing high school. The same 30 percent committed 65 percent of the delinquent acts carried out by the entire group, including 70 percent of drug sales and 69 percent of violent crimes (Thornberry & Burch, 1997).

Often gang members commit delinquent acts while engaging in "gang enterprise": income-producing gang activities. A review of gang structure and activities prepared by Urban Dynamics (1999) indicated that the availability of cocaine and the ease with which it can be converted into "crack" has created an extremely lucrative business for gang members. Traditional gang enterprises, such as extortion, robbery, and burglary, have been replaced by drug sales. The net effect for a hard-core gang member without a high school diploma can be a high tax-free income that makes the minimum-wage job he or she might be able to perform in the legal economy seem laughable. As Barry Feld (1999) explains, "For many urban black youths, employment in the illegal economy provides an alternative to joblessness and poverty" (p. 197).

The nation's gang prevention efforts, largely orchestrated through law-enforcement authorities, have included the expansion of Community Oriented Policing Services (COPS). Often police focus on "hot spots," such as public housing units, assigning extra patrol officers there. Other programs have mobilized community organizations to strengthen efforts to keep children in school. Still other communities have established physical blockades to prevent traffic from moving through areas with a high incidence of drive-by shootings. At the same time, youth convicted of serious gang-related offenses face extremely punitive treatment in the justice system.

Certification of Serious Youth Offenders as Adults

The violent crimes committed by hard-core gang members have fueled public fear of serious youth offenders and given momentum to a movement to "get tough with these kids." One policy response has been the "waiver of juvenile court jurisdiction," or the "certification" of some youth offenders as adults. These processes remove the offender from the juvenile court system and place the youth under the jurisdiction of adult correctional authorities. Prosecution of youths as adults is based partly on a belief that these youthful offenders are not amenable to rehabilitation through the juvenile justice system, and partly because (in conjunction with the growing emphasis on "victim's rights") the idea of retribution has gained popularity in recent years. The net result is a series of policy decisions, beginning in the late 1980s, designed to move serious young offenders out of the juvenile justice system and into the criminal courts.

Typically a prosecutor will ask the juvenile court judge to "waive jurisdiction" in the case of a serious young offender who (1) is not amenable to rehabilitation and (2) represents a threat to public safety. States vary in the amount of discretion allowed the judge. In some cases, the age and seriousness of the offense might require that juvenile court jurisdiction be waived. For example, if a 15- or 16-year-old were to commit a murder, the case would automatically be referred to the criminal (adult) court. Other states provide for "prosecutorial discretion," in which the prosecutor, not the judge, may decide whether to try the case in juvenile or adult court. An emerging focus in these procedures has emphasized not the age of the offender but the nature of the offense. As a result, children charged with heinous crimes have been tried in adult courts and sentenced to adult prison and to death.

International observers were appalled by the willingness of U.S. courts to impose the death penalty on children. The practice went against provisions of the United Nations Convention on the Rights of the Child and several other

TABLE 11.1   Juveniles on Death Row at the Time of the 2005 Supreme Court Decision

Race	Number	Percent
African American	29	41
Caucasian	24	34
Hispanic	15	21
Asian	1	1
Native American	2	3

SOURCE: Death Penalty Information Center (2004). Juvenile Offenders Who Were on Death Row. http://www .deathpenaltyinfo.org/article.php?did=204&scid=27 (accessed January 1, 2008).

international treaties. Nonetheless, prior to a 2005 Supreme Court ruling, the laws of 38 states and the federal government authorized the death penalty for murders committed by individuals between the ages of 16 and 18. Between 1973, when a Supreme Court ruling revived the death penalty, and 1999, 180 juvenile death sentences were imposed. Thirteen people were executed during this period for crimes they committed between the ages of 16 and 18, with the states of Texas and Florida reporting the most executions.

Racial disparities in the criminal justice system were reflected in death sentences given for juvenile crimes. Young people of color were disproportionately represented among those receiving the death sentence. Among 71 people on death row in 2004 for juvenile crimes, nearly two-thirds were people of color. The victims of their crimes were typically white adults (Death Penalty Information Center, 2004). This is illustrated in Table 11.1.

Citing "evolving standards of decency," the Supreme Court held in the 2005 case of *Roper v. Simmons* that the Constitution bars capital punishment for crimes committed before the age of 18. An opinion drafted by Justice Anthony M. Kennedy described the rationale for the 5-to-4 ruling. The opinion noted that "it is fair to say that the United States now stands alone in a world that has turned its face against the juvenile death penalty." In his scathing dissent, Justice Antonin Scalia wrote, "I do not believe that the meaning of our Eighth Amendment, any more than the meaning of other provisions of our Constitution, should be determined by the subjective views of five members of this court and like-minded foreigners." The ruling will affect the fate of 71 inmates on death row (Greenhouse, 2005).

Victims or Villains?

In both child welfare and the juvenile justice system, children of color and those from low-income families are overrepresented. This preponderance suggests that victim and villain are not polar opposites, but flip sides of the same coin—a coin molded by institutional racism and economic deprivation. From a social justice perspective, abusive parents and youthful criminals can be seen not as victims or

B O X 11.1   John Lee Malvo

John Lee Malvo was arrested October 24, 2002, in connection with a series of sniper attacks on the Washington, DC, beltway that killed 10 people. He was 17 years old at the time. His first trial was held in Virginia, one of seven states that executed juvenile offenders. Malvo's lawyers used a plea of "not guilty by reason of insanity" to introduce evidence suggesting that Malvo had been brainwashed by John Allen Mohammad, the other perpetrator in the attacks. A jury convicted Malvo of capital murder and recommended life imprisonment without parole.

John Lee Malvo's childhood has been described as "miserable, impoverished, and lonely." His case raises the question of childhood culpability and underscores the dilemma faced when children commit atrocious acts. Does a horrible childhood justify murder? Are children subject to the same moral expectations as adults?

villains but as the inevitable result of systemic failures that may ultimately be corrected through social policy. In the following section, we will consider the role of social workers in social policies affecting the nation's children.

POLICY PRACTICE IN CHILD WELFARE: THE ROLE OF SOCIAL WORKERS

In some ways, twenty-first-century perceptions of children mirror nineteenth-century views. Children are once again viewed as part of the nation's "dangerous classes." At the same time, many of America's children face poverty, neglect, and abuse—even murder. Throughout the field of child welfare, there is a growing awareness that these phenomena are intertwined. In a monograph called *Breaking the Link between Child Maltreatment and Juvenile Delinquency,* the Child Welfare League of America noted a growing body of research documenting the close association between victimization of children and violence exhibited by youth (Child Welfare League of America, 1997). When society fails children, the results—for both the children and the society in which they live—are devastating.

Social work pioneers were aware of this relationship, and many focused their efforts on child welfare issues. Julia Lathrop, the first head of the Children's Bureau; Jane Addams, founder of Hull House; and others intervened on behalf of children who were victimized by the social conditions that impoverished their families. Today's social workers have the opportunity to continue the profession's long tradition of progressive advocacy on behalf of the nation's children. In the areas of child protective services, education, and juvenile delinquency, reasoned advocacy is needed as much today as it was in the nineteenth century.[10] In some ways, the

---

10. There is a tendency to pit children's needs against those of the elderly. The nation has roughly twice as many citizens under the age of 18 as it does over the age of 65 (Pecora et al., 2000). Yet our financial commitment to the elderly (through Medicare, Social Security, and related programs) dwarfs our investment in children's education and care. See for a discussion of the politics of intergenerational equity in the United States.

tools for this advocacy effort remain the same: state-of-the-art research that documents conditions and evaluates programs, and passionate advocates who can communicate the implications of that research to policy makers and the public. Contemporary child welfare advocates have also used class action lawsuits to direct attention to child welfare needs.

Advocates throughout the nation have discovered the power of litigation for improving the policies and programs that affect the nation's children. The use of the courts for social advocacy was alluded to in the discussion of school finance, in which inequalities have been challenged by a series of class action lawsuits. These suits have also been used to improve services for abused and neglected children. Several state agencies in this field have been the targets of class action suits, and a few have come under judicial supervision. This represents a new role for the judiciary, involving them in direct oversight of executive functions. It also frequently has the effect of increasing the financial resources available for child welfare services.

SUMMARY: THE CURRENT OUTLOOK
FOR AMERICA'S CHILDREN

The United States is a dangerous place for children. The nation's children face greater risks than their age peers in other industrialized nations. Nearly one in five American children lives in a family with poverty-level income—the highest child poverty rate in the developed world. The nation's infant mortality rate is also high compared with that of other developed nations. Finally, American children face an unparalleled risk of neglect, abuse, suicide, and murder. This vulnerability represents a major thread in the nation's response to its children—the irony of children suffering these hazards in a nation of such wealth.

George Henry Payne observed that "the general history of the child . . . moves as from one mountain peak to another with a long valley of gloom in between" (Costin, 1992, p. 194). This description is particularly apt in relation to policies affecting America's children. Social workers in this field have long attempted to harness the energy and commitment of the peak periods to sustain the nation's children through extended periods of indifference.

Today, social workers in child welfare confront Herculean tasks. Aware of broad social trends that might preclude effective parenting, they help troubled people learn to raise their children. In a system that seems increasingly punitive toward low-income parents, they help judges, administrators, and policy makers understand that the interests of a child frequently overlap with the rights of the child's parents. Aware of the educational failures that lead poor children to drop out of school and the economic transformations that have left them without viable employment options, they strive to keep disadvantaged youngsters out of gangs. Facing public skepticism about the effectiveness of "throwing money at education," they sustain local, state, and federal support for Head Start.

In child welfare, social workers are the physical embodiment of the principle of *parens patriae*. They are the arms of the state, reaching out to remove children from dangerous settings. The broader challenge now is to convert those settings into communities and homes capable of nurturing healthy human beings—to go from removing children from impoverished and neglectful settings to enriching homes and communities for children and their families.

KEYWORDS

Adoption assistance	Juvenile delinquency	Youth gangs
Child abuse laws	Teenaged pregnancy	Youth offenders
Child labor	Transracial adoption	Head Start
Child welfare agencies	Youth crime	

THINK ABOUT IT

1. What does your state constitution say about education? Has the state fulfilled its commitment in this area?

2. Do you think public child welfare agencies should allow gay and lesbian adoptions? If so, how should the agency manage public debate around the issue? Should it quietly allow a few qualified gay and lesbian couples to adopt? Would it be better to hold public forums on the topic? If agency policies prevent adoption by gay and lesbian couples, is the agency vulnerable to lawsuits?

3. Do you think school choice programs undermine public education? Who uses these programs? Are they serving low-income families? Why do you think the teachers' unions oppose vouchers?

4. What macroeconomic and social trends do you think contribute to youth violence in the United States? Have social policies contributed?

5. How have issues of diversity influenced child welfare policy in the United States?

6. Is there an established "right to parenthood" in the United States? Should everyone have the right to bear and raise their biological children?

WEB-BASED EXERCISES

For direct links to all the sites in these exercises, log on to the Student Companion Site for this book at academic.cengage.com/social_work/barusch, and choose Chapter 11.

1. Go to the website of the Child Welfare League of America (www.cwla.org), and do a search for material on "international adoptions." What are the trends in international adoption? From the CWLA's perspective, what are the domestic and international policy issues affecting this type of adoption? Now do a Google search on "policy issues in international adoption." What organizations are posting material on this topic? How do their perspectives differ from that of the CWLA?

2. Visit the website of the Children's Defense Fund (www.childrensdefense .org), and list the policy concerns mentioned on the home page. This will give you an idea of the Fund's advocacy priorities. Do they match your view of the most pressing problems affecting the nation's children? Why or why not? What sort of advocacy steps does the Fund want you to take? Do you think these will be effective? Why or why not?

SUGGESTED RESOURCES

Feld, B. C. (1999). *Bad Kids: Race and the Transformation of the Juvenile Court*. New York: Oxford University Press.

Illick, J. E. (2002). *American Childhoods*. Philadelphia: University of Pennsylvania Press.

Kellerman, J. (1999). *Savage Spawn: Reflections on Violent Children*. New York: Ballantine.

McAuley, C., Pecora, P. J. & Rose, W. (Eds). (2006). *Enhancing the Well-being of Children and Families through Effective Interventions: International Evidence for Practice*. London & Philadelphia: Jessica Kingsley Publishers.

O'Connor, S. (2001). *Orphan Trains: The Story of Charles Loring Brace and the Children He Saved and Failed*. New York: Houghton Mifflin.

www.childrensdefense.org. The Children's Defense Fund considers itself "America's strongest voice for children." This website offers CDF reports and summaries on topics ranging from child care to gun control.

www.cwla.org. The Child Welfare League of America is the nation's oldest and largest nonprofit organization, committed to "developing and promoting policies and programs to protect America's children and strengthen America's families." Their website offers a list of publications that can be browsed by subject, as well as current news on a wide range of issues related to child welfare.

www.ed.gov. The home page of the U.S. Department of Education offers a tremendous array of publications with an excellent search engine. A good source of general information and a good way to become familiar with the current administration's position on issues affecting education.

www.teenpregnancy.org. This site is maintained by the National Campaign to Prevent Teen Pregnancy. It offers current reports on topics related to teen pregnancy in the United States, as well as links to related sites.

12

Women

If I were asked . . . to what the singular prosperity and growing
strength of that people [Americans] ought mainly to be
attributed, I should reply: To the superiority of their women.
ALEXIS DE TOCQUEVILLE
DEMOCRACY IN AMERICA, III, 12

The status of women in the United States is neither singular nor static. A woman's situation is determined by factors apart from gender, such as culture, class, and sexual orientation. Therefore, it is probably more appropriate to speak of the "statuses" of American women. These statuses evolve and change in response to social movements and economic trends. Despite this diversity and flux, gender is pivotal in the allocation of resources, rights, and responsibilities in the United States and abroad. Thus, it is an important consideration in the pursuit of social justice.

After considering the life experiences of Annie Boone, we will examine the role of gender in the United States. Women's roles—as wives and mothers, as workers, as members of the military, and as citizens—serve as the organizing framework for the chapter. For each of these, the chapter traces the development of U.S. policies that have affected women, and then examines contemporary issues. The chapter also discusses emerging issues, including violence against women, the abortion debate, and child support. The chapter closes with a look at women in the social work profession.

A HUMAN PERSPECTIVE   Annie Boone

Annie Boone works for a grassroots organization called Justice, Economic Dignity, and Independence for Women (JEDI Women) (the same organization that helped Melissa in Chapter 1). Walking into its store-front offices, a visitor enters a beehive of activity. Men and women bustle through the main hall from office to office, displaying a sense of purpose and commitment. Annie serves as JEDI Women's lead organizer, a full-time (and then some) position that carries health benefits but no pension coverage. Her office is in the middle of all the activity, and she found it challenging to carve out time for our interview.

Annie is energetic and capable, with a rapid-fire manner of speaking. Her face framed by bouncy brown curls, Annie dresses in jeans and looks much younger than her age (late thirties). She has testified before the state legislature and the U.S. Congress and spoken to audiences numbering in the hundreds. She is frustrated by the insensitivity of lawmakers and shows contempt for women who don't understand life outside of their "Cinderella stories."

Hers is not a Cinderella story. Annie has experienced abuse at the hands of her father, her husband, and her sons. She has raised four children on public assistance. Annie wrote an article about her experiences called "A Wedding Band Is a Never-Ending Circle, and So Is Abuse" for the *Georgetown Journal on Fighting Poverty* (Vol. 3, Fall 1995, pp. 13–16). In it she relates that "I grew up thinking my only role in life was to become Betty Crocker—a good wife and a caring mother for my children. This message was inbred in me from the day I was born. A wife and a mother were all I ever wanted to be. I was never informed that . . . I should get as much schooling as I possibly could so that if something happened between my husband and myself, I could always take care of myself. The husband was the breadwinner of the family, and what he said went, whether you liked it or not. Women were to stay home, take care of their children, cook, and stay pregnant" (p. 13).

Annie's father was illiterate. Although he never abused his wife physically, he was very abusive with the children. His desire to control Annie was so powerful that he nailed her bedroom window shut and installed a lock on the outside of her bedroom door. As Annie said, "If he really wanted me in my bedroom, I was in my bedroom." She described one incident:

You know, he loved me to death, but his violence was, like, out of control. I can remember when I came home late one time from school and . . . he was upset because I didn't clean my room. . . . When I came in the door he started yelling at me, so I went up to my room and I slammed my bedroom door. He came in there and he was just irate, and he started pulling all my clothes out of the drawers and . . . kicking me in the back, you know, with his steel-toed boots. . . . Abuse was pretty much the norm, you know.

Annie met her future husband, Jim, when she was 14. He wasn't violent before they married. "He was a sweetheart, you know, a charmer." The tension between Annie and her father escalated until "just about a half a year before I turned 16, I came home and all my stuff was on the front porch, and my dad said, 'I have just had enough. I don't want you around our house until you learn to abide by my rules.'" Annie decided to move in with her boyfriend. When her father threatened to file statutory rape charges against Jim and tell the police she had run away, Annie decided to get married. Annie said she "fit into being a wife rather easily." Jim wanted to have 12 kids. Annie worked, but Jim was unable to hold a steady job. He didn't enjoy work. He was "into drugs and alcohol too. So that kind of takes away your motivation to want to do things."

The first hint of trouble was Jim's desire to control Annie's contacts with her friends. He didn't want her to have friends, and the tensions between Annie and her parents escalated. His eventual physical abuse was no secret to Annie's parents. Annie relates, "I was pregnant with my oldest, and my ex-husband had beaten me up pretty bad, and I called home and I said, 'I need to come. I just need to come home.' . . . I didn't know at the time I was pregnant. . . . I knew I was feeling really sick. I'm sure it was just morning sickness, but on top of him assaulting me and being in a strange environment . . . they sent me a plane ticket. . . . When I came back here, I had so much makeup on to cover up all the bruises, you know. I was just totally embarrassed by that and, um, I walked in the door and my mom said, 'You know, it'd be a really good idea if you'd go wash off that . . . makeup so we can see how bad you've been assaulted this time.'"

Annie's parents did not encourage her to escape the abuse. She explains, "They [imposed] a lot of their religious beliefs on me. . . . Women's roles in life were to stay married and have kids." In her article, Annie describes the pivotal incident that led to her divorce: "One message my parents taught me well was that marriage is a commitment for life to be faithful. I was faithful, but was always accused of cheating with other men. I found out that my husband had gotten my roommate pregnant and that they were having an affair in my own home. After I confronted my husband about this and he admitted to having an affair with her, I was determined to leave. The violence was out of control. . . . [T]he next morning my family had five trucks out to my home and I was out of his life in less than one hour." Annie lived with her parents, briefly, and regretted bringing them into the "war zone." Jim stalked the house, picking fights with family and friends. Finally Annie applied for public assistance to secure a home for herself and her children. She did not tell the caseworker that she was a victim of domestic violence, and the caseworker did not ask.

Of course, Jim was not (and still is not) completely out of Annie's life. Over the years he has told the children that if it weren't for their mother, they could live as a family. This has been especially hard on the boys, generating resentment that translated into destructive behavior. Annie's second son, Jacob, has an attention deficit disorder and hyperactivity, as well as a conduct disorder. Annie feels some personal responsibility: "Watching my children and the pain they've gone through and kind of feeling like I inflicted some of that, you know. I made some bad choices about, you know, my life and having kids so young. . . . I was never taught any of that."

Once she did leave, Annie found another source of stress in the caseworkers who entered her life. "Caseworkers, even though they want to sometimes help, they're not so helpful, you know, and I got so tired of all the caseworkers that wanted to make my life better and really what they were doing was creating more hassles for me, you know. . . . I asked the courts for help because my son was just out of control. Cops were at my house all the time. I felt like I was losing my sanity. I felt like I had to be around him 24/7, you know. And I was really striving for a better life. . . . I'd get a job and I'd get laid off because, you know, he kept gettin' in trouble at school and I'd have to go and take care of his problems, you know . . . so I always kind of felt like we were a family at war, and it was something that always bothered me because I spent so much energy trying to diffuse all that anger, you

know, and I felt like it was created by all the anger they'd seen at such a young age. And it just escalated as they got older. . . . I mean, my sons had abused me quite a few times. . . . I did everything in the community that I could . . . because this was just becoming too overwhelming.

"Well, finally they appointed me this caseworker and she came out to my home. . . . So on her first appointment with me she comes to my house, and you know, I've cleaned everything from top to bottom because I'm afraid . . . you know, the system here is . . . to cause more havoc. . . . When you walked in my house you smelled Pinesol and bleach. . . . And my girlfriend was sitting on the couch and this caseworker from hell walks in the door and says, 'I want you [to the girlfriend] to leave. This is a private meeting between me and Annie. And I really, Annie, want you to put that incense out, it's making my sinuses just go crazy.' And I thought, 'Oh God!' you know. 'I'm asking for help, not more destruction.' So, anyway, she sets up this plan for me and Jacob to abide by."

The plan required that Annie spend all her time with her children, with no opportunity to get respite or continue her education. Annie finally convinced the caseworker that she needed to go to school.

Annie worked to become self-sufficient. "Even back when I left my husband, there were certain things that I'd do to try and become self-sufficient. Like, I didn't have a car at the time. . . . The day care was 10 blocks from me. That's a lot to walk with a 4-year-old and little kids. So I had to take a bus that went from my house to downtown and then came back, for 10 blocks. It took me two hours to get to school and two hours to get back every night." Ultimately, Annie received her GED and completed a clerk-typist program with straight B's. "That's not bad with four kids, you know."

On public assistance Annie received $563 per month to support her family of five. Among the continuing challenges she faced was difficulty laundering clothes. Usually she washed them in the tub and hung them "all over the house" to dry. On the few occasions that she could afford to use a laundromat, she walked, pushing a borrowed shopping cart full of her family's clothes. "That was so humiliating, you know?"

While on assistance, Annie had two destructive relationships. The first was with a man who bought her a car. He claimed that a case of malaria from his tour of duty in Vietnam had left him sterile. When Annie

Continued

Continued

became pregnant, he insisted the child was not his. He was violent with Annie and one day took her car out and torched its interior. He finally moved out, and when Annie moved, she lost touch with him. The second relationship lasted eight years. Bob was physically abusive, but as Annie explained, her self-esteem was so low that she thought she "deserved" the abuse. It was not until her work with JEDI Women had convinced her of her own worth that Annie was able to agree that Bob should leave.

Why didn't she just leave him? Annie believes that as long as benefits are inadequate, public assistance will leave women vulnerable to predatory men. A man who can contribute transportation, food, and even a little cash to the household may enable a woman who would otherwise become homeless to pay the rent or give her children a few "extras" like new clothes or a day at the movies. As a result, women on welfare tolerate abuse that others would find unacceptable.

> One day I heard about JEDI and I called Deeda and I talked to her. . . . I said, "You know, there's gotta be something wrong with this whole scenario." She affirmed that I'm not the only woman out there that's going [through these difficulties]. . . . See, I'd tell myself that for years, is that I really felt like I was just born from hell or something because my whole life had been hell, you know . . . and Deeda's like, "Uh-huh. . . . There's a lot of injustice that happens to women; you know." . . . My first thing I ever did with JEDI was a protest. . . . I was just told that they were doing a news conference at the Capitol and that I should come. . . . I went to the Capitol and I was

standing in the group and they were doing like a skit. And it all related to my life, and it was like, "Whoa! This group's awesome. This is what I need!" . . . and at the same time I kept thinking, "God, I hope I don't get arrested out here being in this" . . . but the more involved I got, the more issues that I found that weren't just me, and that's when I decided that women really needed to be more vocal about what's going on with their lives.

Annie told her children about her plans to speak out about the domestic violence she had experienced. At first her boys were angry, but the girls have participated in JEDI Women events and were pictured in a recent newspaper article about their mother's activism.

Annie is optimistic about her family's future. Her oldest son is showing signs of new maturity. During his senior year in high school, he has been attending school more regularly, and Annie hopes he will graduate. Jacob is in a juvenile facility, "locked up for things that are really not his fault." But he has announced to members of his gang and opposing gangs that he isn't going to be involved in gangs anymore. Her oldest daughter called her father, "and she said, 'I'd never marry a man like you. I want somebody that's gonna be responsible and pay their child support if we ever got a divorce. . . . I just don't think there's a man qualified to meet my expectations, so I don't think I'll ever get married. I'll just go to school.'" Annie's youngest daughter is "hanging around girls that are sexually active," but Annie plans to enroll her in a program this summer that educates teenagers about the harsh realities of single parenting. Annie hopes none of her children experience violence. "I just have a lot of ex-

WOMEN AS WIVES AND MOTHERS

A recurring thread in policies that affect women as wives and mothers is the fear that government intrusion will violate the sanctity of the home. Americans have always distrusted government intervention, and the notion that "a man's home is his castle" often runs counter to public policy efforts on behalf of women. To a great extent, early American public policy treated wives and mothers as the wards of their husbands. In this section, we will examine the impact of this perspective in several areas: property rights and credit, divorce, reproductive rights, and legal approaches to domestic violence and rape.

pectations for my children, and I hope that being with me has taught them something. If nothing else, to be vocal about what's going on."

For herself, Annie dreams of going to law school and working with victims of domestic violence. She has some money for college coming from her two years as a VISTA volunteer, and she anticipates that when her youngest child turns 18 she will be free to pursue this dream. Annie is enjoying a measure of financial security and independence for the first time in her life. She is dating a very nice man who doesn't drink, shows no signs of violence, and pays child support for his three children. Although she would certainly not rush into it, marriage is a possibility. But, as she points out, the relationship would have to be strong to endure the schooling she envisions for herself.

A Social Work Perspective

Like Annie, most women on public assistance have been victims of domestic violence. Estimates of the proportion of mothers receiving public assistance who have experienced domestic violence range from roughly half (Curcio, 1996) to more than two-thirds (Allard et al., 1997; Raphael, 1996). Violence forces many women and children to leave their homes and places them at the mercy of public and private service agencies. Further, as Annie suggested, women experiencing abuse are at greatest risk of injury and death after they have left home (Fleury et al., 1998; Owens, 1999).

Annie's experience with public assistance would not be possible today. She was on Aid to Families with Dependent Children (AFDC) for 11 years. With current work requirements and lifetime assistance limits,

women now must secure employment as quickly as possible (see Chapter 5). Further, all states stipulate that mothers who are seeking public assistance must identify their children's father(s). This requirement enables the state to collect child support on the children's behalf. Sometimes mothers are allowed to keep a portion of the payments, and the rest is used to offset the cost of the family's welfare benefits (Garfinkel, 1992a). Although "good cause" exemptions to this requirement may be granted, they are rare (Pearson & Griswold, 1997). Thus, the state's interest in collecting child support from noncustodial fathers may further endanger women leaving abusive relationships.

Annie's training in clerical services prepared her to join the majority of employed women. Continued occupational segregation leaves most female workers in the service sector, often in jobs without benefits or pension coverage. Unlike millions of Americans, Annie has health insurance. Like approximately two-thirds of working women, however, she does not have pension coverage. At the moment, Annie is enjoying the support and relative security of employment in a nonprofit advocacy organization. She also has a long-term plan for financial security. Despite fears that going back to school may cost her the first healthy relationship she has ever had with a man, Annie is determined to earn the credentials necessary to secure her long-term financial well-being.

To understand the current status of women in American society, we will trace major policy developments that have affected women in three major roles: as wives and mothers, as workers, and as citizens.

Property Rights and Credit

From the seventeenth through the early nineteenth century, married women were subject to a common-law doctrine called "coverture." This principle was based on biblical notions of the unity of spouses and simply held that a man and his wife were "one person in the law" (Rhode, 1989, p. 10). The "one," of course, was the husband. Wives could not hold, acquire, control, bequeath, or convey property; enter into contracts; or initiate legal actions. Indeed, they could not legally withhold their wages from their husbands. The gender-based division of activity that was enforced by coverture had as its rationale a set of norms that have been described by historians as the "doctrine of separate spheres." According to this view, women were best suited to private roles within the

---

B O X   12.1   Female Heads of State

Suhbaataryn Yanjmaa, Mongolia, 1953

Maria Estela Martinez de Peron, Argentina, 1974

Lydia Guelier Tejada, Bolivia, 1979

Vigdis Finnbogadottir, Iceland, 1980

Agatha Barbara, Malta, 1982

Corazon Aquino, Philippines, 1986

Ertha Pascal Trouillot, Haiti, 1990

Sabine Bergmann-Pohl, German Democratic
Republic, 1990

Violeta Barrios de Chamorro, Nicaragua, 1990

Mary Robinson, Ireland, 1990

Chandrika Kumarantunge, Sri Lanka, 1994

Ruth Perry, Liberia, 1996

Mary McAleese, Ireland, 1997

Janet Jagan, Guyana, 1997

Ruth Dreifuss, Switzerland, 1998

Vaira Vike-Freiberga, Latvia, 1999

Mireya Elisa Moscoso de Arias, Panama, 1999

---

home, while men's character traits prepared them for public roles. Accordingly, women were legally barred from higher education, most professions, and public office. There were individual exceptions to these rules, such as women who operated taverns or were active in business. Often these women were viewed as "agents" for their husbands.

As it turned out, strict restrictions on married women's property rights impeded commerce in the emerging nation. This was the case, for example, when a deserted wife could not sell her property or enter into contracts. Thus, beginning in 1839, state legislatures began to remove the most blatant restrictions on women's legal capacity. Several jurisdictions enacted married women's property acts, which granted wives certain powers. Nonetheless, even as late as 1970, men continued to be given preference over women in the selection of guardians, trustees, and executors of estates (*Reed v. Reed,* 404 U.S. 71 (1971)).

Limitations on women's property rights contributed to restrictions on their ability to borrow money. As long as married women could not enter into contracts, they could not take out loans. Just over 30 years ago, many divorced women lacked credit records and thus were unable to borrow money. The Equal Credit Opportunity Act of 1974 prohibited discrimination in lending on the basis of sex. The Federal Trade Commission issued "Regulation B," which spells out the procedures for implementing the act's provisions. Among these is the requirement that credit records for husbands and wives be maintained separately, each reflecting the experiences of the couple. Further, organizations must disclose the reasons whenever credit is denied. Although some women continue to have trouble securing credit to which they might be entitled, legal recourse is now available to them.

Divorce

Historically, the federal government has not been a major force in the development of family law in the United States. As a result, divorce statutes vary from state to state. Further, many of the hard decisions in a divorce are made by individual judges using state law as a reference point. In this section, we will consider three aspects of divorce: the grounds under which it is granted, the division of marital resources, and the assignment of child custody. Divorce laws have undergone substantial changes in each of these areas.

The grounds under which divorce is granted have come full circle. Under Roman and early Anglo-American doctrine, consensual divorce (now known as "no-fault" divorce) was granted. Later, as divorce came to be seen as an ecclesiastical matter, the grounds for divorce were restricted. Early nineteenth-century American courts identified bigamy, impotence, and adultery as grounds for divorce. By mid-century, desertion and cruelty were added, although most courts did not identify "domestic chastisement" as cruelty. Although there was some liberalization over the years, most states applied these norms until the 1960s.

Class was a significant determinant of a couple's access to divorce. In New York, for example, where adultery was the only legal ground for divorce until 1966, wealthy couples either established residence in other states (like Nevada) that offered more liberal grounds or conducted elaborate courtroom charades to meet New York requirements. Less affluent couples were left with separation as the "poor man's divorce."

Procedures for dividing marital assets, assigning alimony, and awarding child custody have reflected the social norms governing gender relations both within and outside of marriage. Most states are "common-law" property jurisdictions, in which spouses' earnings during marriage are treated as separate property rather than joint assets. This practice stands in contrast with "community property" jurisdictions, which hold that all property is jointly owned by both spouses. Until 1970, divorce within "common-law" jurisdictions significantly disadvantaged wives who did not work.

In 1970, the Uniform Marriage and Divorce Act was developed by the National Conference of the Commission on Uniform State Laws (NCCUSL), a deliberative body that develops and disseminates model legislation for consideration by state legislatures. Although the legislation has seldom been adopted in its entirety (Schneider, 1991), many provisions of the act were incorporated by state legislatures. These included provisions requiring "equitable division" of marital resources. In many cases, this equitable division reflects the "one-third rule," in which wives are entitled to one-third of the property accumulated during the marriage. The husbands' greater share reflected their larger monetary contribution to the marital assets and ignored the wives' homemaking contributions.

In theory, a divorcing woman who did not receive substantial property might enjoy the security of lifetime alimony. In practice, however, as DiFonzo (1997) notes, "The most striking aspect of alimony was its scarcity" (p. 62). Data accumulated by the Census Bureau suggest that, around the turn of the century (1897–1906), alimony was requested in 13.4 percent of cases and awarded in only 9.3 percent. Nationwide data from the turn of the century to 1922 suggest that the proportion of divorcing wives receiving alimony was consistently below 15 percent (Jacobson, 1959).

The divorce rate in the United States doubled during the 1960s and 1970s, and courts increasingly used female participation in the labor force to avoid awarding alimony. Indeed, a stated goal of the Uniform Marriage and Divorce Act is to "minimize alimony as well as acrimony." As a result, alimony is seldom awarded except for brief rehabilitative periods.

Children and Divorce.   The principles by which courts award custody of children reflect changing views of the roles of both fathers and mothers. Early Anglo-American doctrine gave custody to the father, who essentially had a property right in the child. During the Industrial Revolution, the monetary value of a child's labor diminished, and American doctrine gradually evolved from "paternal preference" to "maternal presumption." Rather than giving priority to the father's rights, courts focused on the "best interests" of the child. Courts became unwilling to remove children "of tender years" from their mothers. For older children, the tendency was to focus on parental fitness. By the 1980s, two-thirds of states had officially abolished maternal preferences in favor of a more gender-neutral family law. Most had established some form of joint-custody legislation, and in contested cases, men were winning custody one-third to one-half of the time (Weitzman & Maclean, 1992).[1] During the early 1980s some states began adopting "primary caretaker presumptions," which grant preference to the parent who has been primarily responsible for attending to a young child's daily needs. Over time, then, custody provisions have gone from viewing children as the property of the father to viewing them as the developmental charges of the mother, to a more gender-neutral approach that emphasizes the caregiving function of the parent. Nonetheless, in the vast majority of divorces, primary custody of children is awarded to the mother.

Reforms that have made divorce law more gender neutral ironically may have also reduced women's bargaining power. Today, wives can no longer threaten to contest the grounds of the divorce or reveal proof of the husband's infidelity to get a better settlement. Similarly, the elimination of the presumption in favor of maternal custody may lead women to give up their property claims to avoid a stressful and protracted battle for custody of their children (Weitzman & Maclean, 1992). The loss of maternal preference has left women vulnerable when they do not conform to traditional stereotypes of the "good mother." Women who have had extramarital relationships or who are lesbian risk losing their children. Further, some courts have been hostile to "overly ambitious" women whose careers absorb much of their energy and time, while others have refused custody to women without work interests on the grounds that they lack financial means. Nonetheless, in 90 percent of divorces custody is awarded to the mother, supporting the popular maxim: "In a divorce, men become single and women become single parents."

---

1. As Deborah Rhode (1989) notes, a significant number of fathers who are denied legal custody of their children obtain de facto custody by abducting them.

A HUMAN PERSPECTIVE   Advocacy: Defeating the "Meth Moms" Bill

Contributed by J. R. Seaman, Lewis-Clark State College, Coeur d'Alene, Idaho, and Sarah Knott, Walsh and Associates, Coeur d'Alene, Idaho

In 2006, the Idaho legislature was debating a bill that euphemistically came to be called the "Meth Moms Bill," written to make drug use by pregnant women a felony. Stating that "it is a permissible inference that a pregnant female has consumed a controlled substance if during the pregnancy the female tests positive for the presence of a controlled substance or if the female or her newborn child tests positive for the presence of a controlled substance upon the birth of the newborn child," the bill explicitly allowed for incarceration but offered no guarantee of treatment. Indeed, punishment rather than rehabilitation was the sponsor's goal. Across the state, coalitions formed to oppose the legislation. Despite intense lobbying by the human service community in opposition to the bill, it passed the Senate. The only hope for defeating the bill was to convince members of the House to vote against it.

BSW student Sarah Knott set out to do just that. First, she completed a research project on the etiology of female substance abuse, the effects of incarceration on substance-abusing pregnant women, and whether pregnant women would forgo prenatal care to avoid the threat of imprisonment. With these facts in hand,

Sarah educated other students and encouraged them to speak with any legislators they could buttonhole at the Capitol. "Talking points" were developed and students were encouraged to get key points across within two minutes of conversation. Some legislators were so impressed with the facts that Sarah and her colleagues had diligently researched that they wrote back to the students. One student, for example, received a note back from Senator Phil Hart stating "as of yesterday, we held SB 1337 in our Judiciary Committee of the House. . . . In plain language, that means we killed the bill for the year." He went on to thank her for informing him of the issues and noted that "we just don't have the time or staff to handle too many issues at once." The student effort was a small victory for women that was won by committed students, human services advocates in Idaho, and informed legislators.

Sarah and her fellow students learned that legislation often addresses derivative problems, rather than their root causes. In this case attention was directed to punishing mothers addicted to methamphetamines, rather than to alleviating the problems that led to their addiction. The success of their efforts persuaded students that an informed advocate who can intelligently address decision makers can make a difference. Research was vital to this process, and the students' ability to marshal facts and communicate them effectively contributed to a successful advocacy intervention.

As single parents, most divorced women cannot rely on their children's father for support. Even when support is awarded, most divorced men fail to meet their obligations. Irwin Garfinkel (1992b) reports that "of women with children potentially eligible for child support . . . only six out of ten even have a child-support award. . . . [O]f those with child support awards, only half receive the full amount to which they are entitled, and over a quarter receive nothing. All told, more than half of the women potentially eligible for child support receive nothing" (Weitzman & Maclean, 1992, p. 207). In recognition of this problem, legislation was enacted in 1975 that established the Federal Office of Child Support Enforcement and provided federal funding for states to establish offices for support enforcement. Further, the 1984 Child Support Amendments and Family Support Act of 1988 require states to implement child support guidelines and automatic withholding of wages.

These and other measures have increased the amount of child support collected in the United States. The economic burden of child support is regressive, absorbing a greater proportion of the incomes of low-income fathers than of those who are well off. Nonetheless, stricter support enforcement translates into greater financial resources available to the children of divorce. (See Chapter 5 for discussion of child support collection and welfare benefits.)

Reproductive Rights

Humans have used measures to control fertility for several millennia, and only in modern times have birth control and abortion become emotionally charged political and moral issues. In the United States, increased use of abortion and contraception coincided with the shift from a rural to an industrial economy. With this shift, children became less an economic asset than a potential impediment to a family's economic advancement.

The Debates over Abortion and Birth Control. According to Deborah Rhode (1989), early opposition to abortion and contraception stemmed from two concerns: first, that when sex was separated from procreation the result would be widespread promiscuity, venereal disease, and social instability; and second, that if the "better" classes were able to control their fecundity while immigrants and working classes were not, the result would be an "inferior" race. Spearheading the opposition to abortion were physicians, who secured the high moral ground by arguing that abortion was unsafe for mothers, despite the fact that during the late nineteenth century (as today) abortion was considerably safer than childbirth. Physicians' opposition to abortion may have had an economic incentive. At the time, they had significant competition from midwives, in both reproductive health and obstetrics. Physicians' campaign against abortion included the myth that these "nefarious acts" were most often committed by midwives. Thus their opposition may have been part of a larger effort to discredit lay health providers (Reegan, 1997).

In 1873, Congress passed the Comstock Law, which prohibited the distribution of information about contraception and abortion. Most states also passed statutes making abortion a felony. These statutes remained unchanged until the late 1960s. It is interesting to note that key actors in today's abortion debate were considerably less involved in the nineteenth century. For example, the Catholic Church did not begin to actively oppose the practice until late in the century. Some feminists of the era did not consider the issue of significant importance and were reluctant to jeopardize the fight for suffrage over an issue they viewed as "too narrow . . . and too sordid" (Rhode, 1989, p. 204). During the early years of the twentieth century, some feminists openly opposed abortion, and most considered abstinence the appropriate measure for controlling fertility.

Margaret Sanger was the founder of a campaign for increased access to birth control during the early twentieth century. She was inspired to her advocacy efforts when she witnessed the death of an impoverished New York woman from self-induced abortion. Sanger's arguments for birth control did not emphasize feminist principles, focusing instead on hygiene and the prospect for "improving the race." She enlisted support from medical professionals by focusing on methods that could be controlled by physicians. In 1940, the term "family planning" was coined to shift the focus away from women's anatomy and sexual activity (Rhode, 1989, p. 205).

During the 1960s, members of the women's movement identified reproductive freedom as an essential right. At the same time, women had become more sexually active and were more often employed outside the home. The net result was an increase in the numbers of unwanted pregnancies and illegal abortions. Most estimates indicate that about 1 million abortions occurred annually, often performed under unsanitary conditions by unskilled practitioners. Thousands of women died each year, and many others suffered permanent injury. Their experiences served as the catalyst for efforts to liberalize abortion statutes.

In this context numerous polls attempted to weigh public sentiment regarding abortion. Results varied, but there was widespread public support for legalization of abortion, with varying figures depending on the circumstances. For example, support for abortion tended to be greater when respondents were asked to consider cases of rape or incest than when they were asked about its use as a method of birth control. In 1973, the Supreme Court heard *Roe v. Wade,* a case involving the constitutionality of a law prohibiting abortion except to save a mother's life. Justice Blackmun wrote the majority opinion that now governs women's access to abortion. That opinion concluded that during the first trimester of pregnancy the Fourteenth Amendment's guarantee of personal liberty implied a right to privacy "broad enough to encompass a woman's decision whether or not to terminate her pregnancy." Restrictions on that right required a compelling state interest in protecting either maternal or fetal life. At the time, the risk of abortion exceeded the risk of childbirth during the second and third trimesters, and fetal viability occurred during the third trimester. Thus, the Court permitted regulation of late-term abortion based on the state's interest in protecting life.

The decision, which satisfied neither feminists nor fundamentalists at the time, serves as the foundation for existing law governing women's access to abortion. It also set the stage for continuing debate.

The past two decades have seen a backlash against *Roe v. Wade.* Steady erosion in women's access to abortion probably began with the 1980 election of Ronald Reagan. During his tenure, President Reagan appointed half the federal bench and made three appointments to the Supreme Court, in each case attempting to select individuals who did not support *Roe v. Wade* (Melich, 1998).[2]

These appointments set the stage for two major Supreme Court decisions on the issue. In 1989 the Supreme Court upheld a restrictive abortion statute enacted in Missouri (*Webster v. Reproductive Health Services*). Then in 1992 the Court ruled that the usual standard applied to protection of constitutional rights ("strict scrutiny") did not apply to women's right to abortion. Instead, the court ruled that states could restrict access to abortion as long as the restrictions did not

2. Two of Reagan's appointees (Kennedy and O'Connor) did not prove to be as strongly opposed to *Roe v. Wade* as had been anticipated.

"unduly burden" the woman (*Planned Parenthood of Southeastern Pennsylvania v. Casey*).

A spate of restrictions have been passed by state legislatures, including mandatory waiting periods, parental notice and consent requirements, counseling requirements, and bans on "partial birth" abortions. In 1997, for example, 33 states enacted restrictions on abortion. In a few cases, these states have also expanded funding for programs that increase women's access to contraception, a measure seen by some as a practical approach to reducing the need for abortion. But public funding for contraception is itself controversial. Particularly controversial has been funding of programs that provide birth control education and contraceptive devices to teenagers.

Women's access to abortion has been further restricted by Congress. These restrictions usually involve the use of federal funding for abortions, and they are generally waived if the procedure is necessary to save a woman's life or if the pregnancy is the result of incest or rape. As of this writing, restrictions have been applied to the following groups of women: federal employees (whose insurance plans may not cover abortion); servicewomen stationed overseas (who may not obtain an abortion in a military medical facility); women in federal prisons (who may not use prison funds for abortion); women residing in the District of Columbia (who cannot use federal or local funds for abortion); and Medicaid recipients (who, under the "Hyde Amendment," may not use their health coverage for abortion). In each instance, the prohibition does not apply if the pregnancy is the result of rape or if the woman's life is endangered. Efforts to apply criminal sanctions to physicians who perform "partial birth" abortions were passed repeatedly in Congress and vetoed by President Clinton between 1996 and 2000. In 2003 Congress passed the Partial Birth Abortion Ban, and it was signed into law by President Bush. The bill did not include an exception for cases in which the mother faced a medical emergency, so was subjected to a Supreme Court challenge in the 2006 case of *Gonzalez v Carhart*. The closely contested 5-to-4 ruling upholding the ban has been attributed to the replacement of Sandra Day O'Connor with Justice Samuel Alito.

Debates over reproductive rights are emotionally charged and typically leave little room for compromise. Opponents of legal abortion argue that a fetus of any age should be seen as an innocent human being. They view abortion as murder, and a few go so far as to advocate violence against clinics and physicians. The notion of fetal rights leads not only to the view that abortion is murder but also to the argument that maternal behavior that is damaging to the fetus should be prosecuted. So, some suggest, maternal drug use during pregnancy might be treated not only as a crime in its own right, but as an assault on a human being. This viewpoint has become an integral part of the platform of the Republican Party and serves as a key point of difference between most Republicans and most Democrats in the United States (Melich, 1998).

Involuntary Sterilization.   The success of the family planning movement fueled a campaign for involuntary sterilization of thousands of poor and developmentally disabled women. With the development of relatively safe surgical ster-

> **BOX 12.2   Women in Leadership: Sima Samar, Minister of Women's Affairs, Afghanistan**
>
> Sima Samar serves as a minister and deputy chair of the interim administration in Afghanistan. Trained as a physician, she has turned to politics as a way to advance the interests of women in her country. Samar describes this as her primary mission. Since 1989 she has defied authorities by operating schools and health clinics for women. In 2001, Samar received the John Humphrey Freedom Award for her work on behalf of women.

ilization techniques, states passed a wave of compulsory sterilization laws. These laws were reviewed and sustained in a 1927 decision by the Supreme Court (*Buck v. Bell*). The case involved the sterilization of Carrie Buck, the supposedly "feeble-minded" daughter of a "feeble-minded" mother. Buck had just given birth in an institution to a feeble-minded child. Concluding that "three generations of imbeciles are enough" (Rhode, 1989, p. 205), Justice Holmes wrote the majority opinion supporting sterilization. As it turned out, evidence that Buck was "feeble-minded" was equivocal because the girl had been institutionalized to conceal her pregnancy, which was the result of a rape. Although the Supreme Court later cast doubt on the legality of the practice, it was used extensively by welfare officials who required "voluntary consent" to sterilization as a condition of receiving aid. Sterilization, particularly of poor minority women, continued until the 1980s, when it was curtailed by federal regulation.

Prescription Equity.   For years, private health insurance companies that provide coverage for prescription medications have denied coverage for contraceptives. In recent years, possibly owing to insurance coverage for the purchase of Viagra, the issue has come to the fore. Women's organizations, advocates, and several members of Congress have argued that companies that provide prescription coverage should not be allowed to exclude contraceptives.

There has been some progress toward prescription equity. In 1998, Congress extended contraceptive coverage to federal employees enrolled in the Federal Employees' Health Benefits Program. The following year, Senator Barbara Boxer and her colleagues introduced the Equity in Prescription Insurance and Contraceptive Coverage Act. The text of the bill noted that "[p]rivate insurance provides extremely limited coverage of contraceptives: half of traditional indemnity plans and preferred provider organizations, 20 percent of point-of-service networks, and 7 percent of health maintenance organizations cover no contraceptive methods other than sterilization" (sec. 112, Findings (9)). The act did not reach the floor for a vote that year, but prescription equity has been "an issue to watch" at both state and federal levels.

Violence Against Women

Murder and assault of women have long been recognized as unacceptable, but only during recent decades have wife abuse and acquaintance rape been viewed

---

B O X   12.3   **Women in Leadership: Naeela Al-Mulla, First Arab-Muslim Woman Representing Any Country as an Ambassador to the United Nations**

Naeela Al-Mulla, Kuwait's ambassador to the United Nations, presented a required report in January 2004 to the Committee on the Elimination of Discrimination Against Women. Ironically, the report indicated that

Kuwaiti women lack the right to vote or run for office, yet it was presented by the first Arab-Muslim woman representing any country before the UN.

---

as acts of violence. In this section we will look at domestic violence and rape as issues that continue to affect American women.

Domestic Violence.   Today wife beating is condemned as domestic violence, but it was referred to as "domestic chastisement" in nineteenth-century America. Wife beating was explicitly sanctioned by some early Christian ecclesiastics, who noted that "[i]t was preferable for husbands to punish the [wife's] body and correct the soul than to damage the soul and spare the body" (Rhode, 1989, p. 238). Since husbands were legally responsible for their wives' behavior, common law recognized a husband's right to discipline his spouse, provided that he "neither kill nor maim her." A few American courts defined the boundaries of that right: a husband was permitted to whip his wife as long as he used a switch no thicker than his thumb. (The phrase "rule of thumb" comes from this stipulation.)

Divorce was an option only if the abuse was extreme and unprovoked. It was not available to women who continued to live with an abusive husband or who were judged to have "provoked" the abuse either through "passionate language" or refusal to have sexual relations. Because women had few formal or legal avenues for dealing with spousal violence, their best recourse was community disapproval. When the beating exceeded locally acceptable standards, a wife might seek assistance from family members or community leaders. This situation continued fundamentally unchanged until the late twentieth century.

The battered-women's movement of the early 1970s focused on providing refuge for victims and raising public awareness of the problem. For years, organizations such as the Salvation Army had provided shelter to battered women, but their primary focus was on the problems caused by alcoholism rather than on abuse. In 1973 women's advocates succeeded in opening the first shelters specifically designed for battered women: Transition House in Boston and Rainbow Retreat in Phoenix (Dobash & Dobash, 1992).

With these beginnings, a social movement to address domestic violence was born. Emerson and Russell Dobash (1992) have identified three general goals of the movement: "assisting victims, challenging male violence, and changing women's position in society" (p. 29). The number of organizations working to assist battered women grew exponentially. In 1977 there were 163 groups operating 130 shelters, and by 1989 the number of programs had reached 1,200, with shelters housing 300,000 women and children per year (Dobash & Dobash, 1992).

BOX 12.4   Francine Hughes

On March 9, 1977, Francine Hughes was arrested for setting fire to her house while her ex-husband was sleeping. He died in the blaze, and she was charged with murder. During her trial she recounted her 12-year experience with an abusive husband, and the jury found Hughes not guilty by reason of temporary insanity. Her case, resulting in both a book (*The Burning Bed* by Faith McNulty) and an NBC movie, contributed to a growing recognition of domestic violence as an issue of national concern.

The battered women's movement grew from local and regional efforts to national initiatives in 1977, when a White House meeting was held to bring together activists and federal representatives. Within six months, the Commission on Civil Rights held hearings to consider whether battered women received equal protection under the law. Activists argued that because the legal system and police did not protect women, they were deprived of their liberty and property when forced to flee from abusive homes. More than 600 people attended the hearings, listening to presentations from 30 speakers. Among the issues discussed were law enforcement handling of domestic violence cases, oppression of women as a root cause of the violence, the potential for treating battering men, the incidence of husband abuse, and federal funding for shelters.

The National Coalition Against Domestic Violence (NCADV) focused on attempting to secure federal funding for shelters. They encountered opposition in Congress from representatives who argued that government had "no business intruding into family disputes" (Rhode, 1989, p. 243). The coalition secured the support of Representative Barbara Mikulski, who introduced the Family Violence Prevention and Treatment Act in 1978. Despite support from the Carter administration, the bill failed, and after the 1980 election of Ronald Reagan its chances for passage diminished. Finally, during the 1983–84 congressional session, Mikulski condensed the bill and introduced it as an amendment to the Child Abuse Prevention and Treatment Act. It passed, providing states with $65 million over three years for abuse prevention and victim services, as well as $2 million each year for police training.

Today, the NCADV reports that at least 4 million incidents of domestic violence are reported and more than 3,500 women are killed by their batterers each year. The 1990s saw a dramatically increased federal response. The 1994 Violence Against Women Act expanded the funding available for training law enforcement officials, established interstate domestic violence as a federal crime, and confirmed that sex-based violence violates a woman's civil rights.[3] In 1996 President Clinton established the National Domestic Violence Hotline (1-800-799-SAFE) through executive order. In the first year and a half of its operation, the hotline received more than 120,000 calls.

---

3. The Violence Against Women Act was declared unconstitutional by U.S. District Judge Jackson Kiser in Virginia, leading the National Organization for Women to argue that the judge's "bad" ruling is further evidence of the need for an Equal Rights Amendment.

Rape.   Unlike domestic violence, rape has long been recognized as a legal offense. However, it was primarily seen not as an offense against a woman but as an affront to the men in her life—her father or husband. Based on a view of rape as a threat to the patrilineal system of inheritance, U.S. rape law "builds on a history of class, race, and gender biases" (Rhode, 1989, p. 245). The social status of both victims and assailants has traditionally been influential in determining the legal consequences of the crime. Thus, in the United States, the rape of black women by white men was scarcely treated as a crime, while hundreds of black men were lynched when they were accused of raping white women (NAACP, 1969). Between 1945 and 1965, a death sentence was 18 times more likely for convicted black rapists with white victims than for any other combination (Rhode, 1989).

Women who charge strangers with rape have traditionally been subjected to a high level of scrutiny and a requirement that they demonstrate their resistance. Until the passage of "rape shield" laws in the late 1970s, a woman's sex life was considered permissible evidence in court. Defendants used accounts of past behavior to establish that a woman was "unchaste" and probably had incited the rape through her behavior. Further, failure to energetically resist a rapist was interpreted by some courts as an indication of consent. Thus, women were victimized twice: once by a rapist and once by a legal system that insisted on putting rape victims on trial. Rape shield laws prevent material regarding a woman's sexual history from being introduced by the defense during a rape trial.

Acquaintance rape does not correspond to the common understanding of the crime. Indeed, many women do not view forced sexual intercourse with a husband or date as a crime, so acquaintance rape often goes unreported. Nevertheless, under laws that are in effect in most states, sexual intercourse that is "accomplished forcibly, or by the threat of force without consent" (California penal code) is considered rape. The application and interpretation of this law often depends on the nature of a woman's relationship with the offender as well as her sexual history. Rape shield laws do not apply if a woman has had previous sexual relations with the offender (Horney & Spohn, 1991).

For years, spousal rape simply did not exist as a crime. Under the principle of coverture, man and wife were one—and how could a man rape himself? Later arguments held that, by getting married, women consented to intercourse upon demand and thus could not charge their husbands with rape. Opponents of prosecution of spousal rape continued to argue that the event itself was exceedingly rare and prosecution would involve the state as meddlers in "normal sexual relations" or voyeurs "behind the bedroom door" (Rhode, 1989, p. 250). Nonetheless, by 1990, 48 states had reformed their laws to include spousal rape. Successful prosecutions, while rare, have been reported (Wiehe & Richards, 1995).

During the past 25 years, the nation's laws have become less tolerant of violence against women. Two important reforms have been the rape shield laws passed in the states in the 1970s and the 1994 Violence Against Women Act. Of course, these laws serve women who have already been victimized. Rape and the threat of violence hurt not only the women who are direct victims but also women who constrain their movements and activities to avoid becoming victims.

American social policy has clearly influenced the costs and rewards incurred by women in their roles as wives and mothers. These laws reflect and influence broad changes in the social consensus about what constitutes justice in a family context. Today women can enjoy property rights and secure credit independently, regardless of their marital status. Divorce is available to more women than ever before. Public policy and public opinion have rejected the notion that a married woman should submit to "domestic chastisement" or rape. Women enjoy greater control over their reproductive futures than at any time in the past, and public policy has taken initial strides toward reducing the tensions experienced by mothers in the workplace.

WOMEN AS WORKERS

Today, most American women combine marriage, motherhood, and work. As a result, many policies and practices that affect women at work influence their other roles, just as resources to support their other roles affect women's ability to succeed in the labor market. Of course, a significant and growing minority of women do not marry and do not have children. A recurring challenge for U.S. public policy has been not only to enable the majority to combine family and work roles but to do so without disadvantaging the minority who are pursuing a different life path. Contemporary issues affecting women in the labor force are discussed further in Chapter 14.

Progress toward equal employment rights in the United States has been uneven at best. Attempts to expand government regulation of private employers confront deeply ingrained American beliefs about the fairness of the free market and the integrity of the entrepreneur. Public policy in this arena is often marked by ambivalence, reluctance, and denial. Nonetheless, our conceptions about what constitutes justice in the workplace have changed considerably. While pay equity may remain a distant goal, working women are no longer paid less simply because of their gender. Steps are being taken to reduce the career sacrifices that working women undergo when they become mothers. During retirement, many women enjoy the benefits ensured by the nation's pension reforms. Finally, the costs of labor force participation need no longer include the risk of being subjected to unwanted sexual advances.

WOMEN IN THE MILITARY

Operation Iraqi Freedom has brought the role of the U.S. military to the forefront of many debates, including those about the role of women in the military. Throughout the history of the United States women have served in the military. Sometimes women disguised their gender, pretending to be men in order to serve their country. As of this writing, more than 30,000 women are serving in Iraq, some in combat roles.

B O X   12.5   Women in Leadership: Yehudith Naot, Israel's Minister of the Environment

---

Born in 1944, Professor Naot completed her army service in 1962–1964. She is married, with three children, and is an associate professor of immunology.

Serving as Israel's eighth minister of the environment, she was recognized during her tenure in the Knesset as a passionate environmentalist.

The use of women in combat is controversial in the United States. Opponents argue that women are unable to manage the physical demands of combat and that their presence will undermine cohesion of the forces. Few dare to mention aloud the underlying belief that combat service is inconsistent with culturally accepted gender roles. Supporters note that, according to most studies, women who are properly trained and conditioned are able to meet the physical demands, and they suggest that restricting women from combat roles is a form of discrimination. Policy has moved toward permitting women to serve in combat roles. In 1992, the Defense Authorization Act repealed the long-standing combat exclusion applied to women pilots in the navy and air force. In 1993, the combat exclusion for women on combat ships was ended. Finally, in 1994, Defense Secretary Aspin approved a general policy to allow army women to serve with ground combat units during fighting.

The drafting of women is also controversial. In 1980 President Carter reinstated the draft registration process, recommending that Congress amend the Military Selective Service Act to permit registration and conscription of women. Congress declined to amend the act and allocated funding for registration of men only. Several men sued, challenging the constitutionality of the act, and their case went all the way to the Supreme Court. In June 1981 the Court held in *Rostker v. Goldberg* that Congress had acted within its constitutional authority in allowing for registration of men and not women. Congress may have the opportunity to reconsider its position. The Universal National Service Act was introduced in 2003, 2006, and 2007. This bill calls for all young people, including women, to perform a period of military service or a "period of civilian service in furtherance of the national defense and homeland security." This bill was introduced in the House by Representative Charles Rangel of New York. It had 14 cosponsors and was referred to the Armed Services Committee. In the Senate it was introduced by Senator Ernest Hollings of South Carolina and referred to committee.

WOMEN AS CITIZENS

Initially, women were not considered "citizens" or even "persons" under the Constitution of the United States. As Rhode (1989) notes, "When the framers of America's founding documents spoke of men—of 'men . . . created equal' and 'endowed . . . with certain unalienable rights'—they were not using the term

| BOX 12.6 | Women in Leadership: Masoomeh Ebtekar, Vice President of Iran's Environmental Protection Organization |

Dr. Masoomeh Ebtekar holds a Ph.D. in immunology. Born in 1960, she is married with two children. She has headed the communication network of women's non-governmental organizations in Iran and served as act- ing head of the National Committee of the 4th World Conference on Women in 1985. Dr. Ebtekar has published numerous articles and addresses the concerns of women whenever possible in her governmental role.

generically" (pp. 19–20). Women were not alone in this regard, sharing this exclusion with Native Americans (a Native American man was counted as two-thirds of a man in early censuses) and with African Americans, who were then held in slavery. Women's progress toward full citizenship in the United States has manifested itself in two major reform efforts. One effort was successful and the other was not. The first was the campaign for women's right to vote, and the second was the campaign for passage of the Equal Rights Amendment (ERA).

Suffrage

The right to vote, or suffrage, which is considered the defining characteristic of full citizenship, was denied American women until 1920. Women's suffrage was a long time coming. Signs of discontent surfaced as early as 1848, when the first convention to discuss women's rights convened in Seneca Falls, New York. Two years later, the National Women's Rights Convention, planned by Lucy Stone, Lucretia Mott, and Abby Kelley, drew 1,000 people. Sixteen years later, suffragists presented petitions bearing 10,000 signatures to Congress, asking for an amendment prohibiting disenfranchisement on the basis of sex. During the same year, 1866, the American Equal Rights Association was formed to pursue voting rights for women and African Americans. In 1868, when the Fourteenth Amendment was ratified, the word "male" was used for the first time to define a citizen for the purposes of voting. That same year, the first federal women's suffrage amendment was introduced in Congress.

During the years between introduction and passage of the Nineteenth Amendment, suffragists mounted a campaign that included marches and picketing, hunger strikes, fiery protests, and parades. At one especially clever protest in 1919, the National Woman's Party established a "watchfire for freedom" in which they burned every speech President Wilson had given about democracy. Suffragists were arrested by police, attacked by mobs, and reviled from many pulpits. Anti-suffragist organizations were formed to prevent women from securing the right to vote.

Opponents of suffrage (many of whom were women of means) argued that it would jeopardize traditional values—allowing women to vote would run "counter to the dictates of biology, the experience of evolution and the will of the Creator" (Rhode, 1989, p. 14). They argued that domestic disaster would ensue. In a version

> **B O X 12.7   The Nineteenth Amendment to the Constitution**
>
> "The right of citizens of the United States to vote shall
> not be denied or abridged by the United States or by
> any state on account of sex."

of the "slippery slope" argument, anti-suffragists suggested that, once women had the vote, they would want to enter the workplace, where mingling of the sexes would result in promiscuity. Thus, women's suffrage would pave the way to anarchy and free love. Others suggested that involvement in the public sphere would be hard to reconcile with the demands of the private sphere. Finally, some argued that either wives would vote the same way their husbands did—in which case their votes would make no difference—or wives would vote differently from their husbands, which would lead to domestic strife.

The suffrage movement found fertile ground during the settlement of the western part of the country. Wyoming granted women voting rights in 1869, while it was still a territory. Colorado followed 24 years later, adopting women's suffrage in 1893. Colorado was followed in quick succession by the states of Utah (1896), Idaho (1896), Washington (1896), and California (1911). By the end of 1914, women had voting rights in nine western states and Kansas. Six years later, the Nineteenth Amendment was ratified by 36 states and signed into law.

The Equal Rights Amendment

Three years after the right to vote had been secured, the National Women's Party (NWP) began working to establish a constitutional amendment protecting the civil rights of women. The ERA was authored by Alice Paul, head of the NWP. Its text read simply, "Equality of rights under the law shall not be denied or abridged by the United States or by any state on account of sex." In 1923, the ERA was introduced in Congress by Senator Curtis and Representative Anthony, both Republicans;[4] Anthony was the nephew of suffragist Susan B. Anthony. In response to dogged lobbying by the NWP, the ERA was introduced in each subsequent session of Congress.

The ERA was opposed by most moderate women's organizations, including the League of Women Voters, the Women's Trade Union League, the National

---

4. Members of the Republican Party supported the ERA well into the 1970s. The amendment was endorsed by the party in its 1940 platform. Indeed, Republican support for women's concerns historically exceeded that of the Democratic Party. The reversal on the part of Republicans dates to the Reagan era, when systematic efforts by conservative Republicans effectively silenced the party's progressive element. The transformation of the party's positions vis-à-vis women is well documented in Tanya Melich's 1998 book, *The Republican War Against Women*.

B O X 12.8	**Equal Rights Amendment**

"Equality of rights under the law shall not be denied or abridged by the United States or by any state on account of sex."

Consumers League, and the newly created Women's Bureau within the Department of Labor. Opponents feared passage would void protective legislation that restricted the number of hours women could be required to work and established minimum pay requirements for women.

The amendment was revived in 1967 with the establishment of the National Organization for Women (NOW), which pledged to battle for passage. Four years later, the ERA was approved without amendment by the House of Representatives. It had the endorsements of the National Education Association and the United Auto Workers. In 1972 the amendment passed the Senate. Although it passed both houses with substantial margins, two senators (Sam Ervin and Emmanuel Celler) were successful in setting a time limit of seven years for ratification.

With the clock ticking, NOW's campaign began. In light of Congress's overwhelming endorsement, the amendment seemed headed for early state ratification. Within months, 20 state legislatures had ratified it, often with minimal debate. It received a boost in 1973 with the endorsement of the AFL-CIO. During the late 1970s, however, the ERA lost its momentum. Anti-ERA groups began to surface, such as Phyllis Schlafly's National Committee to Stop ERA.

Schlafly, herself a lawyer, worked for a right-wing organization and devoted her considerable energies to defeating the amendment. Flying throughout the nation, she became the spokesperson for traditional values. Arguments against the ERA held that women would lose their preferential treatment with respect to family and military obligations. Wives would be legally required to work; divorcing women would lose presumptions in favor of awarding them custody of small children; and women would be subject to the draft and forced into combat. The ERA, it was argued, would permit homosexual marriage and require unisex public bathrooms. Finally, the states' rights argument was raised by some who believed the amendment represented unwarranted intrusion of the federal government into the prerogatives of state governments.

In response to anti-ERA efforts, NOW organized a convention boycott of unratified states that was supported by more than 450 pro-ERA organizations. Participating organizations refused to schedule meetings or conventions in states that had not ratified the ERA. It was at this point in the struggle, on July 9, 1977, that Alice Paul, author of the ERA, died at the age of 92. In 1978, with intense lobbying by women's organizations, the House of Representatives approved an extension of the ERA deadline to June 30, 1982.

BOX 12.9   Female Prime Ministers

Sirimavo Bandaranaike, Sri Lanka, 1960; 1970; 1994

Indira Gandhi, India, 1966; 1980

Golda Meir, Israel, 1969

Elisabeth Domitien, Central African Republic, 1975

Maria de Lourdes Pintasilgo, Portugal, 1979

Margaret Thatcher, United Kingdom, 1979; 1983; 1987

Mary Eugenia Charles, Dominica, 1980

Gro Harlem Brundtland, Norway, 1981; 1986; 1990

Milka Planinc, Yugoslavia, 1982

Benazir Bhutto, Pakistan, 1988; 1993

Kazimiera Prunskiene, Lithuania, 1990

Edith Cresson, France, 1991

Khaleda Zia, Bangladesh, 1991

Hanna Suchocka, Poland, 1992

Kim Campbell, Canada, 1993

Tansu Ciller, Turkey, 1993

Sylvie Kinigi, Burundi, 1993

Agathe Uwilingiyimana, Rwanda, 1993

Reneta Indzhova, Bulgaria, 1994

Chandrika Kumaratunga, Sri Lanka, 1994

Claudette Werleigh, Haiti, 1995

Sheikh Hasina Wajed, Bangladesh, 1996

Janet Jagan, Guyana, 1997

Jenny Shipley, New Zealand, 1997

Helen Elizabeth Clark, New Zealand, 1999

Irena Degutienë, Lithuania, 1999

Nyam-Osoriyn Tuyaa, Mongolia, 1999

Mame Madior Boye, Senegal, 2001

Maria das Neves Ceita Baptista de Sousa, Sao Tome and Principe, 2002

Chang Sang, South Korea, 2002

Anneli Tuulikki Jaatteenmaki, Finland, 2003

Beatriz Merino Lucero, Peru, 2003

Luisa Dias Diogo, Mozambique, 2004

Radmila Sekerinska, Macedonia, 2004

Angela Merkel, Germany, 2005

Maria do Carmo Silveira, Sao Tome and Principe, 2005

Yuliya Tymoshenko, Ukraine, 2005

Portia Simpson-Miller, Jamaica, 2006

Han Myung Sook, South Korea, 2006

SOURCE: http://www.terra.es/personal2/monolith/00women3.htm (accessed February 4, 2008).

The ERA battle extended (as many do) from legislatures to the courts, when in 1978 the attorney general of Missouri filed an antitrust suit against NOW's boycott. A year later a federal judge ruled that NOW's activities were protected by the First Amendment and did not violate antitrust laws. This decision was upheld by the U.S. Court of Appeals, and the Supreme Court declined to hear Missouri's appeal. In the late 1980s the legality of NOW's boycott was established. In other court action, legislators from Idaho, Arizona, and Washington filed suit challenging the legality of the ERA extension and seeking to validate states' right to rescind their earlier approval of the amendment. The case was assigned to Judge Marion Callister, who held a high office in the Church of Jesus Christ of Latter-Day Saints (the Mormons). The church actively opposed the ERA, and Judge Callister ruled the ERA extension illegal and rescission legal. Seventeen days later, the Supreme Court granted a unanimous stay, prohibiting enforcement of the Callister decision.

On June 30, 1982, the ERA was stopped three states short of ratification. Since then the amendment has been reintroduced in each session of Congress. Debate over the amendment continues, with opponents emphasizing that legislation of the past three decades has made the ERA unnecessary. Under this view, statutes such as Title VII of the Equal Rights Act of 1964, the 1963 Equal Pay Act, and the Equal Credit Opportunity Act of 1974 have provided remedies for the most glaring acts of discrimination against women. ERA supporters, including NOW, argue that the amendment is needed, if only for symbolic purposes, to put women squarely into the Constitution.

In this section we have considered two constitutional battles that have affected the status of women as U.S. citizens. The first, a fight for the right to vote, was a hard-fought victory; the second, a fight for the ERA, was an equally hard-fought defeat. In the final section of this chapter, we will consider the status of women in the social work profession.

WOMEN IN THE SOCIAL WORK PROFESSION

Many social workers devote themselves (like Deeda Seed in this chapter's case study) to the advancement of women. Within the profession itself, however, women experience the very discrimination that advocates struggle to eliminate. Most social workers are women. In 1995, 78.3 percent of the NASW's 113,352 members were women (Gibelman & Schervish, 1997). But women social workers are consistently paid less than men. Results of a 1995 report mirrored earlier studies going back 20 years. With over 37,000 NASW members reporting, male social workers earned more than female social workers (Gibelman & Schervish, 1995). On average, women earned 89 percent of men's salaries. This difference holds at all levels within the profession. Men earn more than women even when they hold the same degree, share comparable job titles, and have the same number of years of experience. Indeed, a 1991 survey of social work faculty found that men with doctorates who held the rank of full professor earned more than women, even when rank, degree, publications, experience, and ethnicity were all controlled (Sowers-Hoag & Harrison, 1991). Clearly, as Gibelman and Schervish (1995) and others have noted, it is time for the profession to "get its own house in order" (p. 628).

SUMMARY: THE STATUS OF WOMEN
IN THE UNITED STATES TODAY

Advertisements for Virginia Slims cigarettes used to annoy many women by declaring, "You've come a long way, baby." Apart from the irritating "baby," the slogan has a ring of truth. Women in the United States have come a long way in a protracted struggle that has taken its toll. Progress has been achieved largely through the efforts of thousands of women and men who participated in one of the great social movements of our time, the "women's movement." This chapter began by recounting the experiences of Annie Boone, who survived abuse to raise her children and build her own economic security. We chronicled the historical developments related to women's roles as wives and mothers, as workers and citizens. We outlined the contemporary issues that face American women and ended the chapter with a brief look at the position of women in the social work profession.

American women have achieved tremendous progress as wives and mothers, as workers, and as citizens. Today we can scarcely imagine being unable to vote, and the notion of coverture is inconceivable. Further, as we will see in Chapter 14, the past half-century has seen progress in the rights of working women. Like women in many other industrialized nations, American women have come a long way, but they continue to be overrepresented among the nation's disadvantaged and victimized. Clearly, we still have a long way to go.

KEYWORDS

Equal Rights Amendment	Gender equality	Sexism
	Divorce	Abortion policy
Feminism	Rape	

THINK ABOUT IT

1. To what extent do you think genetic or physical differences between men and women contribute to their different roles and rewards in the U.S. workplace?

2. Is the notion of equal pay for comparable work compatible with your view of social justice?

3. Are low-income mothers among the "deserving poor"? Why or why not? Consider the U.S. welfare system—under what circumstances would low-income mothers be considered deserving in this context?

4. Why do you think women in the military would be interested in serving in combat roles?

WEB-BASED EXERCISES

For direct links to all the sites in these exercises, log on to the Student Companion Site for this book at academic.cengage.com/social_work/barusch, and choose Chapter 12.

1. Women in combat: Go to www.americanrevolution.org (a Revolutionary War site maintained by the History Channel). In their "Scholar's Showcase" you'll find an essay by Tina Ann Nguyen on the role of women in that war.

It's titled "American Athenas: Women in the Revolution" and offers some interesting and seldom-told stories about women's roles in the revolution. They weren't just wringing their hands and keeping house!

2. Women in leadership: Use Google to learn more about one of the women listed in the "Women in Leadership" boxes in this chapter. Just search for her name and country of origin.

SUGGESTED RESOURCES

Bernikow, L. (1997). *The American Women's Almanac: An Inspiring and Irreverent Women's History*. New York: Berkeley Books.

Dobash, R. E., & Dobash, R. P. (1992). *Women, Violence and Social Change*. London & New York: Routledge Press.

Hoff, J. (1991). *Law, Gender, and Injustice: A Legal History of U.S. Women*. New York: New York University Press.

Rhode, D. (1989). *Justice and Gender: Sex Discrimination and the Law*. Cambridge: Harvard University Press.

www.dol.gov/wb/. Maintained by the Women's Bureau in the U.S. Department of Labor, this site offers information of interest to working women, not only in the United States but around the world.

www.now.org. The National Organization for Women provides an astonishing array of information through its website. Visitors to the site can sign up to receive NOW action alerts.

www.owl-national.org. This site is home to the national office of the Older Women's League. It is an outstanding source of information on policy issues of importance, not just to older women but to women of all ages.

www.pay-equity.org. This site is maintained by the National Committee on Pay Equity (NCPE), which acts as a clearinghouse for pay equity news and information. The site offers NCPE publications and updates on data and activities having to do with fair wages.

13

The Elderly

Our society must make it right and possible for old people not
to fear the young or be deserted by them, for the test of a
civilization is the way that it cares for its helpless members.

PEARL S. BUCK

The aging of the world's human population is unprecedented. Never before
have so many people lived to be so old. Of course, old age itself is not unheard of. A few noteworthy individuals have always survived to advanced age,
but mass aging is a new phenomenon. Today's elderly and their families have
been described as "modern pioneers" (Shanas, 1980), and nations throughout
the world are seeking the best ways to provide for their needs and tap into their
expertise. At the same time, we face an alarming tendency to blame the elderly
for social and economic problems and view their presence among us as a threat.
Robert Butler coined the term "ageism" to describe the negative stereotypes and
attitudes towards older adults and the process of aging. Ageism is widespread,
even among elders. Stereotyping and denigrating advanced age is a relatively
new form of oppression—a departure from more traditional appreciation of
old age.[1]

As more people survive into old age, the population of older adults is becoming more heterogeneous. The health status of older adults reveals great variety. Many suffer from debilitating chronic conditions, but others compete in the

---

1. A note on language is in order. Some object to the use of the words "elderly" and
"old" to refer to "people of advanced age." Yet these terms are widely used in policy discourse and in the lexicon of daily life. I cling to the hope they will one day have the
honorable connotations they deserve.

Senior Olympics. The same is true of economic well-being. Some of the nation's elderly (predominantly women, the very old, and people of color) live in abject poverty, but others number among the world's most affluent and powerful. This diversity complicates the task of program and policy development, bringing into question the continued use of age as the basis of eligibility for public programs.

In this chapter, we will look at the treatment of the elderly in colonial America, then trace the development of public policies affecting this age group. The section on contemporary issues will begin with an examination of current attitudes toward the aged. Changing demographic realities are considered next, followed by a discussion of programs and policies for the elderly. Finally, we will consider the role of social workers in serving the nation's elderly.

DEFINING OLD AGE

Demographic and social changes have had a tremendous impact on the role and status of older adults in the United States, changing even what we *mean* by "the elderly." Like so many human categories, old age is socially constructed. Prehistoric people who survived past their reproductive prime may have been considered "old." During the colonial era, Americans had short life expectancies, so the few who survived beyond 40 years were seen as aged. At the beginning of the twentieth century, U.S. life expectancy at birth had increased to 48 years, pushing up the definition of old age (Brody, 1971). By the dawn of this century, the nation's definition of "advanced age" had extended by several decades.

Today's definition places the onset of old age between the ages of 50 and 80. Senior organizations influence our concept of old age. Eligibility for membership in the American Association of Retired Persons (AARP) begins at 50 years of age. Age-based policies and programs clearly influence this definition, as well. At 62 Americans are eligible to begin collecting Social Security benefits. Eligibility for programs funded under the Older Americans Act begins at age 60. Medicare eligibility begins at age 65. Observing the growing proportion of Americans who were reaching the age of 65, Bernice Neugarten (then in her 60s) coined the term "young old" to describe those from 65 to 75 years of age and "old old" to refer to those over 75. More recently, the term "oldest old" has been used to describe people over the age of 80. Perhaps someday centenarians (one of the fastest-growing age groups) will be termed the "incredibly old."

Have you heard that "today's 60 is yesterday's 40"? How about "You're only as old as you feel"? These popular maxims reflect the improvements in health and functional status enjoyed by many older adults. Although, as we will see, physical vulnerability remains a hallmark of later life, growing numbers in their 60s, 70s, and 80s enjoy vigorous health. This new reality influences our definition of old age as well, and many consider themselves "old" only when they begin to experience mental and physical declines, coupled with functional,

Mrs. Sylvia Johnson, an 80-year-old African American woman, lives 12 blocks from the White House in a DC public housing unit. I met her through a volunteer organization serving the elderly in her neighborhood. Wilma, the outreach worker, took me for an initial visit two days before my scheduled interview. At that time, Mrs. Johnson's one-room apartment was crowded with her homemaker, Wilma, Amy (a volunteer with a housing advocacy group), and me.

On the day of the interview, Wilma gave me detailed directions, including where to cross the street, and instructed me to "call in" as soon as I arrived so she wouldn't worry. I was one of few white people in the area. Homeless young men shuffled by, deciding not to bother asking me for money. Young men in cars zoomed down the street, making as much noise as possible. A few old people passed, walking as quickly as they could. Apartment units in the area were surrounded by wire fences, with bars on the windows at street level.

Entering the building, I was scrutinized by three men who had been in the foyer during my first visit. The security guard remembered me. Still, he reviewed my ID and told me to write my name, agency, destination, and arrival time on his sign-in sheet. After signing in, I took the elevator to the fourth floor, where the hall was deserted. Mrs. Johnson's apartment, like most in the building, bore evidence of years of neglect. There were large holes in the walls where plaster had come off. Water ran continuously from the kitchen and bathroom faucets. Closet doors had come off their hinges and were propped against the wall. Walls carried several layers of grime, and cockroaches had the run of the place. The heating system worked, though, and the apartment was usually warm enough to keep a visitor in a light sweat.

Mrs. Johnson was heavy and had lost both legs and much of her eyesight to diabetes. She spent her time in a hospital bed, with blinds drawn. I entered the darkened room to find her lying in bed, the stumps of her legs against the foot of the bed, her head cocked to the side of her pillow, her eyes staring at the wall. She nodded slowly when I asked if she was okay.

Mrs. Johnson asked for some water. When I found a chipped mug and brought her water, she said it was too cold. I offered some ginger ale I'd seen on the counter. She drank five cups and then said she was hungry. After inspecting the refrigerator, I offered a bologna sandwich with mayonnaise. The bologna was open and dry in the refrigerator, not sealed in plastic. I found a plate and fixed the sandwich, while a half dozen cockroaches explored the counter. She ate eagerly, consuming all but the last corner of crust.

Mrs. Johnson did not have the strength to lift herself out of her bed. The mattress was covered with plastic, and she lay on the type of disposable absorbent towel called a "chuck" that is used in hospitals. Under her bed two of these had been discarded, along with a crumpled hospital gown.

Mrs. Johnson had a homemaker who came four hours a day from Monday through Friday. Funding for this service was provided by Medicaid and the Older Americans Act. On weekends her son Louis gave what care he could. Louis drank too much, and some said he used crack. A few days before the interview he had been barred from the building for a year because he had assaulted a resident. Louis had no place else to sleep and had clearly spent the preceding night on Mrs. Johnson's sofa. The morning before I came he left, locking his mother in. When I called in, Wilma warned me not to stay too long because there would be trouble if Louis showed up. With Wilma's advice in mind, I put my tape recorder at the foot of the bed and began to talk with Mrs. Johnson about her life.

Sylvia Johnson was born in 1913 in Camden, South Carolina. She told me that she was the fourth of 12 children, all of whom were "mean." No one in town picked on them because they were all so mean. Her daddy was big—over 200 pounds. He worked in the construction trade. Her mother was pretty nice, but if you misbehaved she would "get Daddy on you." What Daddy would do was never clear because Sylvia never dared find out.

Sylvia went to school and finished the eighth grade. While she was visiting her sister-in-law in DC, she met her future husband, a much older man. She decided to quit school and marry him. People teased her about marrying someone old enough to be her grandfather, but Mrs. Johnson thought he was a good man to marry. He gave her money, and she'd never had money before. She was happy with her choice. "I had a good husband. . . . Well, like he know better than to try to beat me, you know."

Mrs. Johnson had four sons. Her children knew better than to make her mad because she was "mean as a dog." People didn't bother her much because she was so mean. "Mean as a dog." It's a phrase she used often to describe herself. Her sons grew up mean, and they protected their mama. She never worked. But her husband had jobs and "things like that." They lived in a house on the edge of town. Then he died of "asthma, something like that." It made Mrs. Johnson cry to see him in such pain. Two of her sons died too.

Midway through the interview I was startled by a loud knock on the door. Two police officers wanted to look in the closet for Louis's coat. I didn't think to ask for a search warrant. They found the coat, examined it, and left. The closet was jammed full of men's clothes, with no women's clothes in sight.

Several people wanted Mrs. Johnson moved to a nursing home. I asked her whether she would like to go someplace where people could take care of her and bring her food. She said, "No." As we talked she often mentioned that people didn't "bother" her. I asked whether they had bothered her in the hospital. "Oh no. They were nice." One woman brought her food, and when Mrs. Johnson didn't like it, she brought in some country food. Would Mrs. Johnson like to go someplace like a hospital? "No, because this is more like a home." Not that it was a home, just more like one. Mrs. Johnson clearly preferred the apartment over a nursing home.

Because Louis had been violent, several people had accused him of abusing his mother. This she denied. No one had ever hurt her, because she was so mean and her sons were so mean. "Louis? He wouldn't hurt his mama. He's a good boy."

Mrs. Johnson used to watch TV for the stories, but as her eyesight deteriorated she found it harder to follow the plots and just watched the pictures—despite their being out of focus.

What did Mrs. Johnson like best about herself? "I'm alive." Many people she knew were dead, but she wasn't, and she felt there must be a reason for that. Maybe because she helped people when she could. "Maybe there's . . . one star got in my hat . . . I was always . . . you know, nice to people. I used to take children, take care of 'em."

Mrs. Johnson considered herself neither unfortunate nor poor. "You know, I'm the richest somebody in the world. . . . I thank God for bein' here, you know. I'm proud . . . a lot of folks . . . they're dead and gone." Reflecting on her life, she said, "It's all right, you know, like I've gotten married and everything and had a good life. . . . I'm knowin' folks, you know, they're getting

married and they're just messed over and they get on welfare; but I did not go for none of that."

Did she think about death? "Hush your mouth." Did she worry about it? "No." Mrs. Johnson didn't worry about anything. Nor did she need anything. If she had more money she'd probably buy something but she wasn't sure what, because she hadn't bought anything in a long time. Mrs. Johnson didn't long for anything. But she would love to go back to the country with its cool, clean air.

A Social Work Perspective

At the time of our interview, Mrs. Johnson seemed to be in dire straits. With severe functional limitations, an extremely low income, and limited family support, she depended on public services to meet her most basic needs. Most people who knew her—neighbors, the building security guard, and her outreach worker—would have felt more comfortable if Mrs. Johnson lived in a nursing home where she could receive 24-hour care. Medicaid would cover the costs of institutional care. But Mrs. Johnson did not want to go into a nursing home. She wanted to stay in the apartment.

Five months after our interview, Mrs. Johnson was still in the apartment. No steps had been taken to admit her to a nursing home. Her outreach worker doubted that this was even an option, given severe limitations on Medicaid beds in the area. Repairs to her apartment had not been made because funding for public housing in the District was limited. As her building manager explained, residents could enter all the repair requests they liked, but when there was no sheet rock, no plumbing supplies, "no nothing" in the warehouse, repair personnel could not do much.

Mrs. Johnson's situation combined lifelong poverty, family dysfunction, and severe health problems. But integral to her self-esteem was the fact that she had never been on "welfare." Her living circumstances made others uncomfortable. She lived in public housing in an impoverished neighborhood. We became aware of her situation because her neighborhood was served by an active home visiting agency. Surely other elders, equally dependent and equally neglected, were invisible because there was no outreach worker to knock on their doors twice a week.

social, or economic dependence. This presents a challenge to public policy, which seeks measurable and "objective" criteria for the allocation of resources and services.

CULTURAL PERSPECTIVES ON OLD AGE
IN COLONIAL AMERICA

Even as public policy relies on "objective" definitions of old age, it reflects popular beliefs and attitudes about the elderly. Before turning to the development of contemporary programs and policies for the elderly, we will briefly consider the status of the aged in early America, focusing on three groups: Native American elders, African American elders, and European American elders.

America's colonial era extended from the arrival of the Mayflower on November 11, 1620, well into the next century. Short life expectancies defined the experiences of the three main subgroups, all of whom faced hostile environments. For Native Americans the arrival of European immigrants radically decreased life expectancy by exposing them to diseases and war. African Americans under slavery had extremely short life expectancies. The usual lifespan of a slave during this period has been estimated at 28 to 32 years (Mintz & Kellogg, 1988). Short life expectancies also marked the lives of early European immigrants. Life expectancy was particularly short in the South.

As a result, there were few old people. Benjamin Franklin lived well into his 80s, but when he died in 1790 he had few age peers. Even as late as 1830, those over age 60 made up only 4 percent of America's population (Haber, 1983). Shorter life expectancy did not mean that *no one* reached extreme old age. Indeed, there are recorded cases among Native American tribes of individuals who reached 95 to 103 years (Simmons, 1945), but they were the exceptions, not the rule. As we will see, culture was (and continues to be) a strong determinant of values related to age.

Native Americans

Respect for advanced age was an integral part of many Native American cultures. Legends illustrate the powers enjoyed by Native American elders, who were central figures in many stories of creation. Among the Hopi, two aged goddesses were believed to have created all living things, and an old Spider Woman is said to have invented arts and crafts (Simmons, 1945). The Menomini, Creek, and Omaha all have held that old men were the first recipients of magic powers and healing arts.

Tribal food taboos often served the interests of the elderly, reflecting their influence on this important aspect of the culture. The most choice, nutritious tidbits were withheld from the young. Elders often enforced and, some claim, manipulated these taboos. Among the Omaha, for example, the tender part of buffalo intestine was considered harmful to youths, and young people were warned against eating bone marrow. Old men warned that it would cause sprained ankles in the young and could only be eaten by those past their prime (Simmons, 1945, p. 27).

Native American groups varied in their response to those of advanced age. The Omaha Indians retained their elders in leadership positions long after they began to fail physically. For them, knowledge and experience were pivotal in determining an elder's status (Simmons, 1945).

Nevertheless, honor for the aged did not preclude abandoning those who became helpless. In times of need, some tribes were forced to euthanize or abandon their elders. As Simmons (1945) observes, "Among all people a point is reached in aging at which any further usefulness appears to be over and the incumbent regarded as a living liability. 'Senility' may be a suitable label for this. . . . All societies differentiate between old age and this final pathetic plight. Some do something positive about it. Others wait for nature to do it or perhaps assist nature in doing it" (p. 87). Native Americans, particularly nomadic tribes, were forced to abandon those who reached the "helpless stage" of life. Typically an elder would be left with a cache of supplies and fuel. The Omaha, for example, did not abandon their aged on the open prairie but left them at a campsite with the promise of return. Less common than abandonment was euthanasia. Sometimes the Hopi, who placed a high premium on the elderly, would "help them to die" in an honorable, if violent, act of mercy.

Personal wealth often determined the quality of old age. Among the Navajo some elders accumulated wealth in the form of both tangible goods (horses, sheep, cattle, and goats) and intangible property, such as knowledge of medicinal herbs, healing ceremonies, and magic. Knowledge and healing powers could be exchanged for gifts or fees.

In most Native American tribes the aged poor were cared for. Among the Crow, for example, Edward S. Curtis reports that "[s]ometimes one man killed as many as fifteen buffalo in a run. He would then cry, 'I do not take the arrows back, nor the skin'; it was then known that all but a few, which he kept for himself, were for the use of the poor old people who had come hurrying out from the camp when the butchering began. . . . After a hunt a broad, level stretch of land was dotted with dead buffalo, men butchering, old men hurrying to and fro receiving a piece of meat from this one and that" (Simmons, 1945, pp. 21–22).

The willingness of a tribe or clan to support dependent elders often depended on the availability of food. As Simmons notes, "[A]mong the Hopi no aged person needed to fear starvation *as long as his many relatives had food to spare and he was able to go to their houses to eat*" (italics added, p. 23). It seems that a tribe's care of needy elders depended at least in part on the resources available to the group.

Gender also influenced the status of older adults. Across tribes, gender differences in prestige tended to mirror those observed in relation to wealth. Where women had access to wealth they enjoyed high status. It was more typical, though, for men to control wealth and have greater status than women. As Simmons notes, "[P]roperty rights of aged women show greater variations and seem to be more strongly influenced by the prevailing type of social organization" (p. 49). Women accumulated more property in groups characterized by matrilineal patterns of inheritance and descent. Women also fared better among groups that relied on collection, hunting, and fishing than among farmers and herders. Based on these observations Simmons concludes, "In the simpler beginnings aged women seem to have had a more nearly equal chance to acquire property, but with the development of society their mates and brothers have found it possible to get and to control more property" (p. 49).

Despite a general cultural disposition toward honoring age, the status of individual elders in Native American tribes was determined by knowledge and skill, wealth, and gender. Further, the treatment of needy elders was influenced, at least to some extent, by tribal resources.

African Americans

The brutalities of slavery dictated short life expectancies for African Americans who were kidnapped as young adults. Although those born in the colonies lived longer, slaves who survived to advanced age had no assurance of comfortable retirement. As Andrew Achenbaum (1986) reports, "If the law did not forbid it, some slave owners 'emancipated' superannuated blacks, thereby 'freeing' *themselves* of caring for elderly slaves. Others heartlessly banished their worn-out slaves like old horses to eke out an existence on their own" (p. 29, italics added).

Young African Americans generally treated their elderly "aunts" and "uncles" with deference and support. As Frederick Douglass recounted,

> "Uncle" Toby was the blacksmith, "Uncle" Harry the cartwright, and "Uncle" Abel the shoemaker . . . these mechanics were called "Uncles" by all the younger slaves, not because they really sustained any relationship to any, but according to plantation etiquette as a mark of respect, due from the younger to the older slaves. Strange and even ridiculous as it may seem, among a people so uncultivated and with so many stern trials to look in the face, there is not to be found among any people a more rigid enforcement of the law of respect to elders than is maintained among them. (Gutman, 1976, p. 218)

Older slaves often exercised near-absolute authority over the younger members of their communities. Herbert Gutman tells of an incident that illustrates this authority: "A white met an elderly man on a Mississippi plantation and learned from his owner that Uncle Jacob was a regulator on the plantation; . . . a *word* or a *look* from him, addressed to younger slaves, had more efficiency than a *blow* from the overseer" (p. 219). Older women were often appointed to care for children, teaching them prayers, hymns, and lessons along the way. As Leslie Owens explains, "A beginning lesson was to respect slave elders, particularly the aged" (1976, p. 204).

The respect accorded to elderly members of slave communities may be traced in part to West African traditions, in which elders were repositories for information about family and community history, folklore, and ritual traditions

(Gutman, 1976). The practice of referring to unrelated elders using familial terms was also adaptive. It helped create a "fictive" kin system among slaves that could help them to survive separation from blood relatives (Owens, 1976).

It is unclear what status differentials were observed among elderly African Americans. Possibly because of severe external oppression, there is no evidence of greater status being awarded on the basis of either possessions or gender.

European Immigrants

One persistent myth holds that European immigrants who reached advanced age in early America enjoyed high social status and strong family ties. Instead, as Carol Haber (1983) points out, "In early America . . . the relationship between age and honor was neither direct nor simple. For some, great age contributed to their high status; for others it led only to ridicule and neglect" (p. 9). Lacking programs and policies to define them as "old," nineteenth-century elders were judged by their individual attributes. Among Europeans, property, gender, and occupation were critical in defining a person's social status.

Elderly people who held sizable estates enjoyed commensurate prestige. Historians have studied seating in early American town halls as a measure of social status. The best seats, those closest to the front, typically went to senior landholders. In an agricultural economy, where the primary means of securing a living was through the land, control of property implied social stature as well as authority over family members. Thus, for example, an aged father might determine the timing of his son's or daughter's marriage. He might even select his child's spouse. But authority did not necessarily translate into affection. As Fischer (1977) notes, veneration "is a cold emotion." Younger generations may have respected the elderly, but the generations preserved an emotional distance.

A mother's authority and power derived almost exclusively from her spouse, and aged widows found themselves at the mercy of their children. To reduce mothers' vulnerability, some jurisdictions passed laws giving widows one-third of their husband's estates. Some husbands went to great lengths to specify precisely what property was to be included in their wives' shares. For example, when Adam Deemus of Allegheny County, Pennsylvania, made a will in 1789, he left his wife "the privilege to live in the house we now live in until another one is built and a room prepared for herself if she chuses [sic], the bed and beding [sic] she now lays on, saddel [sic] bridle with the horse called Tom: likewise ten milch [sic] cows, three sheep . . ." (Haber, 1983, p. 20). Some went further, stipulating that children would receive their inheritance only after providing acceptable support and care to their mothers. Such was the case in Timothy Richardson's 1715 inheritance. He did not receive his father's estate in Woodburn, Massachusetts, until he agreed to "give, sign, and pass unto his mother, the widow of the diceased [sic], good and sufficient security" (Haber, p. 20).

Many elderly Americans did not own large estates. In the absence of pensions or mandatory retirement laws, workers were expected to labor as long as they could. The loss of occupation meant not only the loss of a livelihood but also a decline in prestige as the retired worker gave up a principal means of social integration. Far from being an opportunity for leisure, retirement was the sign of impending poverty and possibly death.

Status differentials among European American elders are fairly well documented and seem to have been determined by gender, wealth, and occupation. Nonetheless, like Native Americans and African Americans, European immigrants had a general norm that supported respect for the aged. This norm would erode in subsequent years as attitudes toward the elderly shifted.

CHANGING PERSPECTIVES ON OLD AGE IN AMERICAN SOCIETY

Attitudes toward elderly *individuals* varied in colonial America as they do today. Nonetheless, most historians and social critics agree that values and attitudes were generally more positive toward the elderly *as a group* during the nation's formative years than they are today, suggesting a transformation in cultural values related to age. Some trace diminished respect for the elderly to the American Revolution (Fischer, 1977), while others date it within the last half of the nineteenth century (Achenbaum, 1978; Haber, 1983).

Signs of the transformation were apparent in several developments during the late eighteenth century (Fischer, 1977). First, seating in town meetinghouses was revised. Age was no longer taken into account. Instead, desirable seats were assigned solely on the basis of wealth. Second, the nation's first compulsory retirement law was passed in New York in 1777. Third, census takers observed a shift in what is referred to as "age heaping." This process results in higher-than-expected population counts in certain age groups and is the cumulative result of individuals lying to census takers about their age. In early America people tended to report being older than they were, but after the revolutionary period census data revealed a bias toward reporting younger ages. Finally, some argued that the fashion in clothing during this era came to favor youth (Fischer, 1977).

Other signs date the transformation to the late nineteenth century, when popular and scientific writing came to describe the elderly as ugly and disease ridden, rather than as stately and healthy. Paradoxically, the medical advances that contributed to longevity also focused attention on age-related disease and decline. As a result, instead of exalting their moral and practical wisdom, commentators began to equate age with illness and conclude that older people had nothing to contribute to society (Achenbaum, 1986).

What caused this transformation in attitudes? Many have concluded that industrialization lowered the status of elders in today's society (Achenbaum, 1986; Shanas, 1968). New practices in business and manufacturing technology stressed speed and efficiency, traits incompatible with the aging process. The industrial workforce had few jobs that could accommodate the elderly, and thus between 1851 and 1861 the old experienced the greatest decline in both economic and occupational rank of any age group (Haber, 1983). Further, rapidly changing technology made the knowledge and skills of elderly workers obsolete. Younger workers no longer looked to their elders for training and advice.

But industrialization alone could not account for the reduced status of the elderly. As Fischer (1977) points out, in Japan—a nation that underwent rapid industrialization—the status of the elderly has remained quite high. Further, signs of diminished respect for elders appeared in the United States before the Industrial Revolution.

Several other factors may have contributed. The war of independence may have brought not only a political revolution but a revolution in ideas as well. Rejection of the old political order entailed rejection of traditional ideas that held age as the basis of prestige (Fischer, 1977). The accumulation of wealth may also have disrupted the practice of stratifying society by age. Wealth may have replaced age as a way of discriminating among people. And, as we have seen, advancing medical knowledge may also have contributed. As diseases and physical losses associated with age were documented, older people began to be seen as incapacitated and worthless (Achenbaum, 1986).

Finally, the diminished status of older adults may have been caused by changed relationships with their children (Haber, 1983). Parents in colonial times were seldom without children. The birth of the first grandchild followed closely or even preceded that of a couple's last child. As women limited their family sizes and planned the timing of childbirth, the line dividing generations grew more distinct and the "empty nest" became more common. With no children to raise, the older generation no longer had a central function. Urbanization tended to limit family size and diminish parental authority. In a city an older son who resisted his father's authority could simply leave home and find a job—an option that had not been available when the sole source of income was the family farm.

In sum, age alone did not determine the status or well-being of adults in early America. All three of the cultural groups considered here showed evidence of a general norm of respect for the elderly. Native Americans typically expressed their veneration through myths and food taboos, providing care for needy elders as resources permitted. Elders served as fictive kin among slave communities, assisting in the education and direction of younger slaves. Among European immigrants, the status of the elderly was closely tied to their control of property, and landed elders wielded authority over their offspring. The status of European American elders showed signs of decline as early as the latter part of the eighteenth century. Historians hold different opinions regarding the causes of that decline, attributing it to revolutionary ideas, accumulated wealth, industrialization, urbanization, and changing family roles.

EARLY PROGRAMS AND POLICIES
FOR THE ELDERLY

The programs and policies developed for indigent elders in the new nation reflected both American attitudes toward age and the nation's beliefs about poverty. European immigrant elders who fell into poverty were treated as poor, not old.

Public Relief for Needy Elders

To be old and poor in America has always been a precarious position. The township records of early colonies illustrate the status of indigent elders. In these documents, the wealthy are listed by both first and last names and the poor are called by their last name with the prefix "old." Thus, while "Thomas Moore" might be a man of means, his poor cousin would be referred to as "Old Moore."

Public relief for indigent elders in the United States was initially modeled on England's Elizabethan Poor Laws. These laws did not allow for differentiation on the basis of age. Indigent elders were treated the same as any other group of poor people. Their sustenance was the responsibility of the parish or local community, which provided either "outdoor relief" (money to pay rent or buy goods) or "indoor relief" (lodging in a poorhouse).

With urbanization, the population of cities increased, as did the number of indigents within a city's borders. Philadelphia, for example, saw dramatic growth in its poorhouse population. Prior to 1750, fewer than 50 paupers per year were admitted, but by 1815 this number had risen to 2,250. Roughly a third of these were destitute by virtue of old age (Haber, 1983), but age was not yet used to distinguish among the poor. Older adults were lodged in the almshouse or poor-house among other worthy poor—people who were disadvantaged through no fault of their own.

Beginning in the 1830s the notion of a homogeneous class of indigents was challenged. Reformers who served the urban poor became interested in more efficient use of resources and decided to focus their efforts on those most capable of reform, the "redeemable poor." The elderly were not included in this category. In 1855, for example, the New York Association for Improving the Condition of the Poor (NYAICP) declared that it would assist only five groups: industrious laborers, indigent widows and deserted wives with children, educated single females, the sick and the bereaved who would improve, and mechanics who suffered temporary loss of employment (NYAICP annual report, 1855, p. 37, cited by Haber, 1983). The association resolved "to give no aid to persons who, from infirmity, imbecility, *old age,* or any other cause are likely to continue unable to earn their own support and consequently to be permanently dependent" (italics added, p. 38). Urban charity organization societies (COSs) took the same position. In 1892, Amos Warner expounded on the hopelessness of work with the aged: "In work with the aged one is conscious that for the individuals dealt with there is no possibility of success" (Haber, 1983, p. 40).

Thus, while COSs and other philanthropies were sending young laborers back to rural areas and attempting to retrain or rehabilitate others, the elderly were confined to public almshouses. In time they made up a growing proportion of the almshouse population. By 1904, 53 percent of the residents in almshouses throughout the nation were over 60 years old (Haber & Gratton, 1994).

Over time, age came to be associated with destitution (particularly by charity professionals).[2] In 1902 Homer Folks, New York City's commissioner of charities, announced a new name for the city almshouse: the Home for the Aged and Infirm. He intended to send the message that the residents of this facility were not the lazy able-bodied, but those who were simply too old or sick to earn a living. Institutional care was less expensive than outdoor relief for the aged, and so the almshouses came to be seen as the most appropriate setting for needy elders.

As "homes" or "asylums" were populated by the elderly and infirm, they took on a more medical focus. The line between hospital and almshouse blurred and "old-age homes" began to offer medical care in addition to room and board, setting the stage for the development of facilities we now call nursing homes.

Informal Assistance Among African Americans

During the antebellum era many African American elders lived in abject poverty. Unable to access the relief provided to European elders, African Americans relied on informal community supports. Organizations known as benevolent societies were organized in collaboration with homes for the aged. These mutual-aid societies worked to keep African Americans off public relief and to provide for a decent burial. Society members paid annual dues and in return were given sickness and death benefits, which could then be turned over to a home for the aged. For example, in 1864, Quakers and African Americans founded the Home for Aged and Infirm Colored Persons in Philadelphia to provide care for "worthy" and "exemplary" African Americans "who in their old age from sickness or infirmity have become more or less dependent upon the charities of the benevolent" (Pollard, 1980, p. 231). For at least 27 years, the Home provided lodging and care to members of Philadelphia benevolent societies and, in return, the societies turned members' benefits over to the Home. The number of these societies mushroomed. Philadelphia alone had more than 100 societies serving more than 7,000 members (Pollard, 1980). During the latter part of the nineteenth century, the resources of benevolent societies were strained by the longevity of their members. Ultimately, these societies were replaced by insurance firms with greater financial reserves. Nonetheless, benevolent societies represented a significant resource for elderly African Americans, serving as a hallmark of the community's response to need.

Public Pensions for Veterans

The nineteenth century set the stage for many of our current approaches to the care of needy elderly. Agencies that focused on the redeemable poor gave up on elders, reserving their energy and resources for young people with some hope of

---

2. Three classic books illustrate this tendency to associate age with poverty: *Pauperism and the Endowment of Old Age* and *The Aged Poor in England and Wales,* both published in the 1890s and written by Charles Booth, and *Old Age Dependency in the United States,* published during the same era by Lee Welling Squier.

employment. Poor elders increasingly found themselves "warehoused" in institutional settings—precursors of today's nursing homes. One class of elders was favored by public policy initiatives, however: military veterans.

Public pensions for veterans were the nation's first federal retirement programs. In 1829 (over 100 years before the passage of the Social Security Act) federal legislation awarded pensions to veterans of the Revolutionary War. Notably, this act was passed 46 years after the end of the war, ensuring that few would collect the pensions and that those who did would be very old. Later, provisions were made for survivors of the War of 1812, the Indian conflicts, and the Mexican War to receive federal pensions. These pensions were funded through general tax revenues and did not represent a significant drain on the public purse.

This changed when Civil War veterans were added to the federal pension program. Their addition (only 25 years after Appomattox), meant thousands of potential recipients might receive pensions, placing a huge drain on public revenues. Faced with this potential drain, the U.S. Pension Bureau stressed that the money was only for those in dire need, establishing severe restrictions on eligibility. Applicants had to prove they were "suffering from a mental or physical disability of permanent character, not the result of their own vicious habits, which incapacitates them from the performance of manual labor in such a degree as to render them unable to earn support" (Haber, 1983, pp. 110–111).

Administration of these restrictions was complex. Physicians disagreed about the character and cause of disabilities, and many decisions were appealed and reversed. In 1904, Theodore Roosevelt officially included every aged veteran in the pension program and declared that those who reached the age of 62 would be considered half disabled; at age 65 they would be considered two-thirds incapacitated, and those over 70 would be considered totally disabled. Thus chronological age replaced functional ability in determining who would receive a pension. This change dramatically eased the administration of the program, replacing physician examination with a simple review of birth records (Haber & Gratton, 1994). By establishing the ability of the federal government to operate a pension program, federal pensions for veterans set the stage for Social Security.

Contemporary policies affecting older adults reflect several of the themes introduced in this brief history. Among them are a tendency for publicly funded services to focus on the majority population, a willingness to make special provisions to meet the needs of veterans, the administrative complexity of using functional status as a measure of need, an inclination to apply institutional solutions to economic and social problems, and the impact of economic resources on community willingness to sustain indigent elders.

MODERN ATTITUDES TOWARD THE ELDERLY

International visitors to the United States often subscribe to the stereotype that Americans do not value or care for the elderly—that we put them in "warehouses." But American attitudes toward older adults are complex, rooted in cultural norms that dictate respect for the aged and distracted by contemporary pressures to shunt elderly people aside. In this section we will consider two divergent views of the nation's elderly: "intergenerational equity" rhetoric that paints the elderly in negative terms, and a "productive aging" approach that does just the reverse.

Intergenerational Equity

The past few decades have seen strident debate over "intergenerational equity." The term has become a catchword for political commentators predicting an "age war" or a "generational conflict" over the allocation of scarce resources. According to this view, "greedy geezers" have taken up more than their share of public funds, and America's youth have been deprived as a result. This argument is largely confined to the United States and has not been seriously advanced in any other nation (Kingson & Quadagno, 1997). It surfaced in a context of relative economic scarcity as U.S. economic growth slowed considerably during the 1970s, with limited increases in productivity and rising inflation.

Notably, the intergenerational equity argument was advanced, not by advocates for children, but by an elite group of political and business leaders. In 1984, Senator Dave Durenberger (R–MN) founded an organization called Americans for Generational Equity (AGE). This organization's goal was "to promote the concept of generational equity among America's political, intellectual and financial leaders" (Quadagno, 1989). Financial support for AGE came primarily from "banks, insurance companies, defense contractors, and health care corporations" (Quadagno, 1989, p. 360), and with that support the organization mounted an effective campaign of inflammatory propaganda that included articles with titles such as "Older Voters Drive Budget," "U.S. Coddles Elderly but Ignores Plight of Children," and "The Tyranny of America's Old" (Cook, 1996). AGE staff members also wrote books, such as *Born to Pay* by Phillip Longman (1987). Although AGE no longer exists, it had a dramatic influence on the debate about public support for the elderly (Quadagno, 1989). Similar work is carried out by the Concord Coalition, founded by Pete Peterson (former chair of President Clinton's Tax and Entitlement Reform Commission).

Robert Binstock offers an explanation for the popularity of the intergenerational equity argument. He observed a broad shift in the portrayal of the elderly around 1978, and suggests that prior to then the elderly were described using a "compassionate stereotype" that presented them as poor, frail, and needy. Older adults appeared as vaguely pathetic figures, clearly in need of assistance. During the 1980s, however, the media, public commentators, and scholars began describing elders as rich, healthy, and politically powerful. Their need for public resources became open to dispute. This shift served as the foundation for an emerging stereotype that Binstock (1983) calls the "aged as scapegoat," in which a wide range of political, social, and economic problems is blamed on senior citizens.

Productive Aging: An Attitude Shift

During the 1990s, a growing number of professionals and academics in the field of aging began to advance the concept of "productive aging." Their efforts, in part designed to counter the effects of the "greedy geezer" rhetoric, underscore the potential and the actual contributions of older adults. According to this view, the "new aged" are more healthy and more financially secure than any previous generation, and as a result, they are in a better position to contribute to the well-being of their families, their communities, and their society. Within this tradition, the elderly are portrayed as vital individuals who are eager for meaningful involvement (Perlmutter, 1990; Rowe & Kahn, 1998).

Central to this viewpoint is the notion that societal barriers, such as age discrimination in employment or inaccessible public buildings, make it difficult for elders to provide meaningful contributions. Thus advocacy in the field of productive aging would focus on removing those barriers and increasing opportunities for engagement. This more positive view of the aged offers a sharp contrast to the critical view presented in the intergenerational equity rhetoric (Bass, Caro, & Chen, 1993; Butler, Oberlink, & Schechter, 1990; Morrow-Howell, Hinterlong, & Sherraden, 2001).

DEMOGRAPHIC, SOCIAL, AND ECONOMIC REALITIES AFFECTING OLDER ADULTS

Modern public policies reflect social and demographic realities as well as attitudes. In this section we will examine several factors that have influenced policies and programs for older Americans.

The Graying of America

The twentieth century has seen unprecedented growth in the number and proportion of older adults. The United States is not alone in the "graying" of its population. Nations throughout the world are seeing similar growth and in many, like the United States, the situation is exacerbated by unusually high post–World War II birthrates.[3] The U.S. "baby boom" cohort consists of individuals born between 1945 and 1964. This group has moved through the system of age-based public services like a "pig in a python," and during the first half of the twenty-first century this generation is expected to accentuate the underlying growth in America's senior population. Figure 13.1 illustrates the growth in this age group.

---

3. As the austerity of the Great Depression and the war years was replaced by economic security and in some cases affluence, many nations in Europe, North America, and Oceania had baby booms. The dates vary, but each nation saw dramatically increased birth rates.

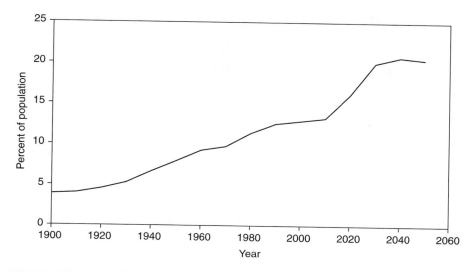

FIGURE 13.1 Percent of population 65 and older: 1900–2050.

SOURCE: Data from U.S. census reports and projections.

The baby boom was a temporary aberration in the long-term trend of declining fertility in the United States. It was followed in the 1970s by a new and more enduring demographic reality: the "baby bust." Fertility rates in the United States appear to have stabilized in the past three decades at levels well below those seen previously. The nation's current population growth has been partly due to improved life expectancy.

More Americans are surviving childhood, and greater numbers are living to advanced ages. These two trends have dramatically increased life expectancies. It has been estimated that in colonial America, life expectancy for the population as a whole was less than 40 years. As we saw in Chapter 6, life expectancy in the United States had risen to 77.9 years by 2004. This trend is largely the result of public health measures that have reduced infant mortality.

Declining fertility and increased longevity have caused unprecedented growth in the nation's elderly population. In 1830 only 4 percent of the U.S. population was over 60 years of age. This figure slowly rose to 6.4 percent in 1900. In 2003, 35.9 million Americans aged 65 and over represented 12 percent of the nation's population (U.S. Bureau of the Census, 2005c). By 2030, that number is expected to nearly double, to 69.4 million elders, who will represent 20 percent of the population. In other words, by 2030 one in five Americans is expected to be over age 65. This will place unprecedented demands on programs that serve the elderly.

Rising Diversity

The aging population has increased not only in numbers but in diversity as well. The numerical growth has been dramatic. Between 1930 and 2000, the number

T A B L E   13.1   Subgroups of U.S. Elderly Population

Year	Nonwhite (#)	Nonwhite (%)	Women (#)	Women (%)	People over 75 (#)	People over 75 (%)	Total 65 or Older
1930	422,222	6	3,308,000	50	1,913,000	29	6,634,000
1940	639,983	7	4,614,000	51	2,643,000	29	9,020,000
1950	895,000	7	6,472,000	53	3,855,000	31	12,270,000
1960	1,256,000	8	9,057,000	55	5,563,000	34	16,560,000
1970	1,701,000	9	11,605,000	58	7,530,000	38	19,973,000
1980	2,388,000	9	15,244,000	60	9,969,000	39	25,550,000
1990	2,638,000	10	18,587,000	60	13,034,000	42	31,082,000
2000	3,947,000	11	20,364,000	59	16,574,000	48	34,709,000

SOURCE: U.S. Bureau of the Census (1998).

of Americans 65 years of age and older increased by 414 percent. The fastest-growing subgroup within the elderly population has been the very old (75 and older). During the same period, the number of Americans in this group grew by 733 percent. Other fast-growing groups among the aged population have included people of color (624 percent increase) and women (506 percent).

As a result of these increases, growing proportions of the elderly population belong to these three subgroups (very old people, people of color, and women). In 1930, people 75 and older made up only 29 percent of the aged population. By 2000, that proportion had increased to 48 percent. Similarly, in 1930 women were 50 percent of the elderly, and by 2000 they represented 59 percent. Finally, people of color made up only 6 percent of the elderly in 1930, but by 2000 they amounted to 11 percent. Thus, not only has the number of elderly people in the United States been growing, but the elderly population itself has become more diverse. This is illustrated in Table 13.1.

Income and Age

In 1959, more than 1 in 3 (35 percent) of Americans aged 65 or over had incomes below the federal poverty threshold. By 2006 that figure had dropped below 1 in 10, or 9.4 percent (U.S. Bureau of the Census, 2007c). This decline is illustrated in Figure 13.2.

Yet Americans continue to experience financial vulnerability in their later years, and subgroups of the elderly population have high rates of poverty. In this section we will first consider poverty in late life before turning to a more general look at the income status of older Americans.

Poverty in Late Life.   With respect to the proportion of elders living in poverty, this country fares poorly by international comparison. In 2007 international research-ers studied the economic status of older adults in seven industrialized nations.[4] They

---

4. Nations studied included Canada, Sweden, France, Italy, Germany, the United States, and the United Kingdom.

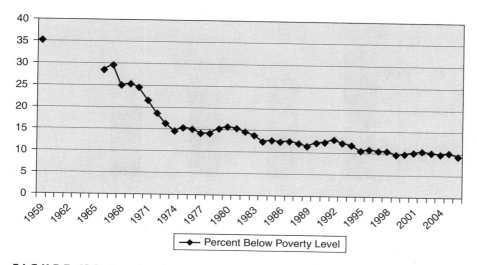

FIGURE 13.2 Poverty rates among Americans 65 and older: 1959–2006.

SOURCE: U.S. Bureau of the Census (2007). Historical Poverty Tables, Table 3: Poverty Status of People by Age, Race, and Hispanic Origin: 1959 to 2006. http://www.census.gov/hhes/www/poverty/histpov/hstpov3.html.

used 50 percent of median income as a poverty measure and concluded that the United States had the highest rate of poverty (Sierminska, Brandolini, & Smeeding, 2007). Their findings are summarized in Table 13.2. Within the United States the elderly subgroups that are growing fastest—the very old, women, and people of color—also face the greatest risk of poverty.

The very old continue to have higher rates of poverty and lower median incomes. The change in median income with age is illustrated in Figure 13.3. When the Department of Health and Human Services conducted a study of the economics of aging, they found that, whereas 35 percent of those aged 65 to 74 had low incomes, *two-thirds* of those over 85 were financially vulnerable (Alecxih & Kennell, 1994). This economic vulnerability persists. Americans aged 75 or older had a poverty rate of 11.6 percent in 2003, and nearly one in

TABLE 13.2 **Poverty Among Older Adults: International Comparisons**

Nation	Proportion "Income Poor"
United States	23.2
United Kingdom	14.9
Italy	11.7
Germany	10.8
Sweden	7.3
Finland	6.1
Canada	5.2

SOURCE: Sierminska, Brandolini & Smeeding (2007).

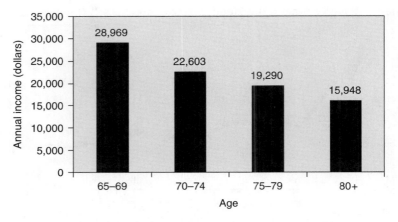

FIGURE 13.3 Median income by age: 2004.

SOURCE: Social Security Administration (2006). *Income of the Aged Chartbook: 2004.*

five (19.4 percent) lived on incomes at or below 125 percent of the poverty level (U.S. Bureau of the Census, 2005c). Of course, women make up the majority of the nation's very old people.

Older women have a higher risk of poverty than older men. In 2003, older women over 65 had nearly twice the poverty rate of men in the same age bracket. The rate for women that year was 12.5 percent; for men, 7.3 percent. Further, nearly a quarter (23.6 percent) of women aged 75 and older had incomes at or below 125 percent of the poverty threshold (U.S. Bureau of the Census, 2005c). Older women living alone in the United States are consistently the poorest group among the aged, faring worse than older couples.

Finally, people of color experience higher rates of poverty in their later years. In 2003, the highest risk of poverty among the elderly was experienced by African American women, among whom more than a quarter (27.4 percent) had incomes below the poverty threshold (U.S. Bureau of the Census, 2005c). African American elders overall have the highest rates of poverty among the elderly. In 2003, the poverty rate for African Americans over the age of 65 years was 23.7 percent compared to an overall rate of 10.2 percent for older adults of all races. Hispanic elders also experience elevated risk of poverty, with an overall rate of 19.5 percent in 2003. Gender and race differences in poverty rates among the elderly are illustrated in Table 13.3. Clearly, those who are most at risk of poverty are most likely to benefit from antipoverty programs.

Social Security has been termed the nation's most effective antipoverty program. Its impact was demonstrated in a seminal study by the Center on Budget and Policy Priorities (Porter, Latin, & Primus, 1999). Researchers analyzed five years of census data (1993–1997) to determine the number of elders in each state who would have been poor if they had not had Social Security benefits. Results indicated that Social Security lowered the number of elders in poverty from 15.3

TABLE 13.3 Poverty Among the Elderly: Gender and Race Differences

	Men (%)	Women (%)	Overall (%)
White	5.4	10.0	8.0
Hispanic	16.6	21.7	19.5
African American	17.7	27.4	23.7
Other	7.3	12.5	10.2

SOURCE: U.S. Bureau of the Census (2005c).

million to 3.8 million in 1997. Without Social Security, nearly half (47.6 percent) of the U.S. elderly population would have been poor. The study also revealed that 60 percent of those lifted from poverty by Social Security were women. Because women live longer than men, the fact that Social Security benefits are indexed to inflation is especially important to women.

Retirement Income for Older Americans. The importance of Social Security to the nation's elders becomes even more clear when we consider the sources of income for this age group. Sources of "aggregate" income (for all seniors) in 2005 are presented in Figure 13.4. As we can see, Social Security was the largest single source of retirement income, providing 40 percent of the income received in 2005.

Using data from 2004, the Social Security Administration reported that nearly 9 in 10 seniors (89 percent) received income from Old Age, Survivors, and Disability Insurance (OASDI), and the program was the only source of income for one-fifth (21 percent) of Americans over the age of 65, and over 90

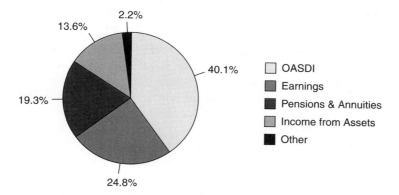

FIGURE 13.4 Income sources of the elderly: 2005.

SOURCE: Employee Benefit Research Institute (2007). Income of the Elderly Poulation Age 65 and Over, 2005. *Notes, 28*(5). www.ebri.org/pdf/notespdf/EBRI_Notes_05-2007.pdf (accessed January 8, 2007).

percent of income for another 13 percent. For one-third (34 percent) of the nation's elders, then, Social Security was the primary source of retirement income. It supplied over 50 percent of income for another 32 percent of seniors. Thus, Social Security supplies at least half the income for about two-thirds (66 percent) of older adults in the United States (Social Security Administration, 2006).

Here, we have considered the attitudes and conditions that make up the context of policy making in relation to older adults. That context is rather complex. American attitudes towards older adults reflect traditional values and contemporary tensions. The result can be paradoxical, alternating between resentment (of greedy geezers) and hope (for productive aging). At the same time, we face challenging material conditions: unprecedented growth in an older population that is becoming increasingly diverse, and economic conditions in which some enjoy affluent retirement while others live in abject poverty and many depend heavily on Social Security. In the following section we will consider the current status of programs and policies for older adults in the United States.

MODERN PROGRAMS AND POLICIES
FOR ELDERLY AMERICANS

Current programs for the elderly that are woven into the Social Security Act were introduced in Chapter 4. These include OASDI, Medicare, Medicaid, and Supplemental Security Income—programs that are integral parts of the nation's safety net for the elderly. In the following sections we will consider the Older Americans Act and public policies governing private pensions. We will also look at health policy issues, including assisted suicide.

The Older Americans Act and Age-Based Services

The Older Americans Act (OAA) was passed just prior to the escalation of the Vietnam War and the economic downturns of the 1970s. It represented a national commitment to meeting the needs of the elderly. Although its goals were exalted, OAA funding was limited. Nonetheless, the act established a national network of providers and governmental authorities charged with the care of the elderly. The history and structure of this network and some tensions inherent to OAA programs are discussed here.

Prior to the 1965 passage of the OAA, the elderly received limited social services through programs that had not been specifically designed for them. As early as 1950, President Truman initiated the first National Conference on Aging. Participants called for greater government involvement in meeting the needs of the elderly. Continuing interest led President Eisenhower to create the Federal Council on Aging in 1956 to coordinate federal activities related to aging. Successful passage of the OAA has been attributed to the 1961 White House Conference on Aging. The Conference brought experts on aging and advocates for the elderly to Washington, DC, from across the nation, raising awareness of issues affecting the elderly. In 1962, Representative John Fogarty of Rhode Island and Senator Pat McNamara of Michigan introduced legislation to establish an independent U.S. Commission on Aging. The Kennedy administration objected to creation of an independent agency. In 1963, the act was reintroduced, this time proposing an Administration on Aging (AOA) under the Department of Health, Education and Welfare. Again, the proposal was defeated.

The 1965 proposal reflected the 1963 version, but this time the bill received bipartisan support and the OAA was signed into law by President Johnson on July 14, 1965. In his remarks upon signing the bill, the president suggested the legislation would provide "a coordinated program of services and opportunities for our older citizens" (U.S. House of Representatives, 1988, p. 2). Of course, the goals of the OAA were considerably more lofty. They are presented in Box 13.1.

By means of partnerships between federal, state, and local authorities, the OAA established a network of 57 state offices on aging and 670 area agencies on aging that effectively blankets the United States. OAA programs were placed under the jurisdiction of the Administration on Aging (AOA), a federal agency within the Department of Health, Education and Welfare (HEW) (now Health

---

B O X 13.1   Older Americans Act of 1965: Declaration of Objectives

"[I]n keeping with the traditional American concept of the inherent dignity of the individual . . . the older people of our Nation are entitled to, and it is the joint and several duty and responsibility of the governments of the United States, the several states and their political subdivisions, and of Indian tribes to assist our older people to secure equal opportunity to the full and free enjoyment of the following objectives:

(1) An adequate income in retirement in accordance with the American standard of living.

(2) The best possible physical and mental health which science can make available and without regard to economic status.

(3) Obtaining and maintaining suitable housing, independently selected, designed and located with reference to special needs and available at costs which older citizens can afford.

(4) Full restorative services for those who require institutional care, and a comprehensive array of community-based, long-term care services adequate to appropriately sustain older people in their communities and in their homes, including support to family members and other persons providing voluntary care to older individuals needing long-term care services.

(5) Opportunity for employment with no discriminatory personnel practices because of age.

(6) Retirement in health, honor, dignity—after years of contribution to the economy.

(7) Participating in and contributing to meaningful activity within the widest range of civic, cultural, educational and training, and recreational opportunities.

(8) Efficient community services, including access to low-cost transportation, which provide a choice in supported living arrangements and social assistance in a coordinated manner and which are readily available when needed, with emphasis on maintaining a continuum of care for vulnerable older individuals.

(9) Immediate benefit from proven research knowledge which can sustain and improve health and happiness.

(10) Freedom, independence, and the free exercise of individual initiative in planning and managing their own lives, full participation in the planning and operation of community-based services and programs provided for their benefit, and protection against abuse, neglect and exploitation."

and Human Services). Originally the head of the AOA was a commissioner on aging who reported to the secretary of the HEW, but in 1993 Fernando Torres-Gil received a presidential appointment as the first assistant secretary for aging. This appointment established the AOA as a more autonomous federal agency. The act has been amended numerous times (Gelfand, 1988; U.S. House of Representatives, 1988).

Initial funding under the OAA was modest. In 1966, total appropriations amounted to $6.5 million. By 1988, this figure had grown to more than $1 billion, and the appropriation for fiscal year 2007 was more than $1.3 billion (Administration on Aging, 2008; U.S. House of Representatives, 1988).

A comparison of the 1966 and 2007 appropriations reveals the increasing complexity of programs operating under the OAA. The 1966 appropriations funded two categories: Title II, Grants for State and Community Programs on Aging ($5 million), and Title IV, Training, Research and Discretionary Projects and Programs ($1.5 million). The 2007 appropriations are detailed in Table 13.4.

OAA Programs Today. The OAA established the administrative structure for the delivery of social services to the elderly. Under the authority of the Administration on Aging (AOA), each state and territory operates its own "state office on aging." The network is further divided into area agencies on aging. Thus, every jurisdiction in the United States has a designated authority responsible for programming for the elderly. This tremendous accomplishment can be attributed to (and is dependent on) a partnership of federal, state, and local governments. Eligibility for services funded under the OAA is based solely on age. Anyone aged 60 or over may participate, regardless of income or assets.

Under the act, Area Agencies on Aging must avoid providing services themselves. Whenever possible they must contract with private and public entities. The funding formula for OAA programs is based on the proportion of the nation's elderly who reside in each state. As a consequence, states with large senior populations, such as Florida and California, enjoy higher OAA appropriations than states with relatively young populations, such as Alaska and Utah.

Funded by their appropriations, states sustain a network of OAA services, including those described in Title III of the act:

1. *Access services.* Transportation, outreach, information, and referral
2. *Supportive services.* Health (including mental health), transportation, housing repair, community-based services to prevent institutionalization, legal assistance, exercise programs, health screening, preretirement counseling, and "any other necessary services for the general welfare of the older people"
3. *Nutrition services.* Congregate meals in senior centers and home-delivered Meals on Wheels. In addition, a National Caregiver Initiative was passed in 2000 to provide services to family members caring for the nation's frail elderly.

Tensions Surrounding OAA Programs. Targeting of OAA services has been a source of tension in recent decades. As indicated earlier, the act requires that

T A B L E 13.4   2007 Appropriations Under the Older Americans Act

Activity	2007 Appropriation (dollars in thousands)
State- and community-based services	
Home- and community-based supportive services	350,595
Congregate nutrition services	398,919
Home-delivered nutrition services	188,305
Nutrition services incentive program	147,846
Preventive health services	21,400
Family caregiver support services	156,167
Total for state- and community-based services	*1,263,232*
Services for Native Americans	
Native American nutrition and supportive services	26,134
Native American caregiver support services	6,241
Total for Native Americans	*32,375*
Protection of vulnerable older Americans	
Long-term care ombudsman program	15,010
Prevention of elder abuse and neglect	5,146
Total for vulnerable older Americans	*20,156*
Program innovations	24,058
Aging network support activities	13,133
Alzheimer's Disease demonstration grants	11,668
Program administration	18,379
Health care fraud and abuse control	3,128
Total 2007 program funding	*1,386,129*

SOURCE: U.S. Administration on Aging. http://www.aoa.gov/about/legbudg/current_budg/legbudg_current_budg.asp.

services be made available to all Americans over the age of 60, regardless of their income or assets. Yet funding for these services amounts to less than $50 for each potential recipient (Americans aged 60 or over). Clearly, OAA services cannot meet the needs of *every* older American. Allocation of scarce resources is an ongoing challenge.

Congregate meals delivered in senior centers illustrate this tension. These meals provide important socialization opportunities as well as a nutritional supplement. They have consistently been one of the Administration on Aging's most well-funded programs. Yet congregate meals have been criticized as failing to serve cultural minorities and frail elders. The climate in most senior centers reflects the majority culture in the area.[5] While not overtly hostile, the activities, food, and atmosphere may not be familiar or welcoming to people of color. Similarly, frail elders—those who are most in need of assistance to maintain their independence—are unable to participate in congregate meals or senior center programs.

In response to this tension, the 1987 amendments to the OAA added Section 305 of Title III to require that states "(E) Provide assurances that preference will be given to providing services to older individuals with the *greatest economic or social need, with particular attention to low-income minority individuals*" (italics added). Subsequent appropriations have revealed an increased emphasis on cultural minorities and vulnerable individuals. Between 1986 and 2001, grants to Indian tribes more than doubled, going from $8.3 million to $23.5 million (Administration on Aging, 2001; U.S. House of Representatives, 1988). Programs serving frail and vulnerable elders were also initiated, including in-home services for frail elderly, elder abuse prevention, and long-term care ombudsman services. Most recently, the National Caregiver Support Program has been added to OAA programs. With funding in excess of $150 million, this program offers assistance, training, and respite to family members caring for the frail elderly. Since the 1987 amendments, OAA programs have shifted resources and focus to those in greatest need.

This creates a new tension. Seniors in greatest need are also those least likely to vote and offer the political support necessary to support increasing program budgets. The popularity of OAA services has been linked to their ability to serve mainstream, middle-class seniors. An ongoing challenge for OAA programs is sustaining political support while targeting populations most in need.

OAA programs are affected by changing perceptions of the nation's elderly. When seniors are perceived as "greedy geezers," Americans become more critical of programs that use age-based eligibility criteria, particularly if these programs fail to meet the needs of the most vulnerable elders. The challenge for the OAA network will be to respond credibly to this criticism while maintaining the integrity and political viability of programs funded under the OAA.

Public Policies and Private Pensions

Many Americans are familiar with public programs such as those operated under the OAA, but they may be unaware of the laws governing the establishment and operation of private pensions. Yet these policies affect the financial security of millions of older adults. The term "private" is a misnomer when applied to pensions. Few personal assets are as profoundly affected by public policy as pensions.[6] Although the first company pension plan was established in 1875 (by

---

5. In some areas an entire catchment area might serve predominantly minority residents. This is the case, for example, when a city's African American neighborhood has its own senior center. These centers tend to serve an African American clientele, and congregate meals reflect the predominant culture in the surrounding neighborhood.

6. See Schulz (1995) for a detailed discussion of private pensions.

the American Express Company), most were developed after passage of the Revenue Act of 1921. This law encouraged the development of private pensions by exempting both employer contributions and pension fund income from federal income taxes.

During the 1940s and 1950s private pensions mushroomed. The number of workers covered rose from about 4 million in the late 1930s to 10 million in 1950. This expansion was the result of wage and price controls imposed to control inflation during World War II. With wages capped, one of the few ways companies could attract qualified workers (themselves in limited supply) was to offer generous fringe benefits such as pensions and health insurance. Thus two public policy initiatives—wage controls and tax deductions—set the stage for the expansion of private pensions.

There were several problems with the early pensions: (1) they tended to treat top executives more favorably than regular employees; (2) workers often lost their benefits as a result of mergers, closures, and bankruptcies; (3) in some spectacular scandals, pension reserves were mismanaged and lost; (4) some workers were fired just months before they became eligible for a pension; and (5) workers' survivors (most of them widows) received no income from pensions upon the death of the worker.

In 1974 Congress addressed these problems by passing comprehensive legislation to regulate pensions. The Employee Retirement Income Security Act (ERISA) limited the number of years of employment an employer could require before a worker had the legal right to receive pension benefits—before the worked became "vested." It strengthened standards governing the management of pension funds. It restricted the extent to which employers could use pensions only to reward "key employees"—that is, highly paid executives. As we will see in Chapter 14, ERISA was amended in 1984 by the Retirement Equity Act to require that plans provide the option of a Joint and Survivor Annuity. This stipulation provides a modicum of income security to survivors.[7]

Another major public policy affecting pensions was the 1974 establishment of the Pension Benefit Guarantee Corporation (PBGC). Created through Title IV of ERISA, the PBGC manages a mandatory insurance program for pension benefits so that in the event of bankruptcy, workers do not lose all of their pension rights. Prior to the establishment of the PBGC, workers lost their pension if their employer went out of business. For example, when Studebaker terminated its pension plan in 1963, more than 4,000 auto workers lost part or all of their pensions (PBGC, 2001). When Braniff Airlines went out of business in 1982, however, the PBGC insured vested employees and provided benefits up to a maximum of about $1,500 per month (Schulz, 1995).

Although business representatives opposed each of these regulatory reforms, the laws did not slow the growth of pensions. Twenty million workers were covered in 1960 and 35 million in 1979. By 1995, an estimated 42 million

---

7. ERISA also enabled some employees to establish Individual Retirement Accounts.

workers, roughly half of the labor force, were covered by pension plans (Schulz, 1995).

Of course, many workers are still not covered. Most of these are employed in trade and service industries. Key factors determining whether workers will be covered are their union status and the number of people employed by the company. Workers without pensions are usually not union members and work for firms with relatively few employees. Women and minorities are overrepresented among workers who do not enjoy pension coverage. In the case study for this chapter, it is clear that Mrs. Johnson and her husband did not have pension coverage. (Women's experiences with pensions are discussed further in Chapter 14.)

The nature of pensions has changed since the 1980s. Most of those set up prior to 1960 were "defined benefit" programs. That is, they promised monthly benefits based on earnings and years of service. These plans offer workers a measure of security. Workers are insured by the PBGC, and most know how much retirement income they can anticipate. But they impose financial demands on employers, who are legally obligated to deliver pension benefits. During the 1980s, many employers began to offer "defined contribution" pension programs, under which a specified amount is deposited into a tax-sheltered retirement account for the worker. The 401(k) account is an example of a defined contribution plan. Such plans are not insured by the PBGC, and the retirement income they will generate is influenced by fluctuations in financial markets.

In 1980 defined benefit plans covered the vast majority (80 percent) of workers who had pension coverage. But their numbers have declined markedly. The PBGC reported a 63-percent drop in the number of defined benefit plans between 1985 and 1998, and by 1998 less than half of covered workers had pensions of this type (PBGC, 1998).

The spectacular failure of the Enron Corporation in 2002 illustrated the risks of defined contribution plans. Like many companies, Enron offered employees a 401(k) plan that was heavily invested in company stock. When the stock plummeted in value, employees lost their retirement savings. The resulting litigation and controversy led to passage of the Pension Protection Act of 2006.

Described as a "sweeping reform" of the nation's pension laws, the act regulates, to some extent, employers (such as Enron) who offer company stock as an investment in defined contribution plans. Through its financial provisions, the act reduces the extent to which companies can "under fund" their defined benefit pensions. The act also makes it easier for companies to automatically enroll employees in defined contribution plans, requires greater disclosure about the performance of retirement accounts, and regulates the extent to which employers can advise employees about investment of their pension contributions. Finally, the act permanently increased contribution limits for IRAs and 401(k)s. While the act contains a number of helpful technical improvements, it does little to extend coverage to workers who most need to save for retirement.

B O X 13.2   New Pension Insecurities?

In July 2004, United Airlines announced that it was halting all payments into its defined benefit pension plans, subject to bankruptcy and reorganization. United proposed to jettison its pension obligations by transferring pensions to the Pension Benefit Guarantee Corporation (PBGC). On behalf of the union that represented United ground workers, Robert Roach Jr. suggested that "Instead of terminating pensions, maybe we should explore terminating the employment of United's top management, who have mired the company in bankruptcy for more than two years"

(*Washington Post,* March 12, 2005). If successful, United's action could set the stage for similar moves by established airlines coping with increased competition from new airlines (without significant pension obligations), reduced demand since 9/11, and rising fuel costs. U.S. Airways shifted its pension plan to the PBGC in 2003, as did several failed steel companies. Ultimately, the solvency of the PBGC may come into question and with it the security of pension income for thousands of American workers.

Health Care for the Elderly

In Chapter 6, we examined the basic structure and fiscal pressures affecting the Medicare program. In the following sections we will touch on some specialized issues related to health care for the elderly, including long-term care, rationing health care by age, end-of-life care, and assisted suicide.

Long-Term Care.   As Joshua Weiner notes, "One of the great successes of the twentieth century has been the prevention and treatment of acute illnesses" (1996, p. 51). Unfortunately, this cannot be said of the chronic illnesses that affect millions of elderly Americans. Our health care system has struggled to meet the care needs of those who face lingering illness and disability. Most older adults manage chronic illness by relying on family caregivers, who provide care at considerable personal and financial cost. As we have seen, the Older Americans Act provides some resources to assist in community-based care. In addition, most states use funding available through Medicaid Home and Community-Based Care Waivers to offer limited coverage for in-home services and alternatives to nursing homes, such as assisted living facilities that provide care for elders who need some assistance to live independently (National Association of State Units on Aging, 2005). In part as a result of these initiatives, the number of older adults living in nursing homes for 90 days or longer declined from 1.21 million in 1999 to 1.06 million in 2004 (Kasper & O'Malley, 2007).

But for those who require it, nursing home care is expensive. Private rooms averaged $77,745 per year in 2007 (MetLife, 2007). While a few can pay for nursing homes on their own, either with personal resources or by using long-term care insurance, most nursing home care is paid for by Medicaid.[8] The

---

8. Most states require Medicaid applicants who apply for nursing home admission to be screened to ensure that the placement is appropriate. Individuals who request placement for primarily social reasons (such as the lack of a committed caregiver) or mental health reasons (such as depression) are denied admission.

Kaiser Commission reported that 68 percent of 2004 nursing home costs were paid by Medicaid. Of course, Medicaid has income and asset limits, so patients who need coverage must "spend down." In other words, they must deplete their assets and income until they meet Medicaid's eligibility limits.

Prior to passage of the Medicare Catastrophic Coverage Act of 1988 (MCCA), those who needed Medicaid coverage for long-term care faced a risk known as "spousal impoverishment." In the process of spending down to become eligible themselves, they left the community-dwelling spouse in poverty as well. Under the MCCA and other federal statutes, state Medicaid programs are now required to allow spouses to retain income up to a certain level—usually 150 percent of the federal poverty threshold. The spouse is also permitted to retain some of the couple's assets. Although most MCCA provisions were repealed, these spousal impoverishment measures remain in effect.

Older adults wishing to preserve assets for their heirs sometimes transfer those assets prior to entering a nursing home. As a result, state and federal funds intended to provide medical care of the poor have been spent to cover the care of Americans who are more well-off. State and federal policies discourage this type of transfer, which has become an accepted part of estate planning in legal circles. The MCCA and subsequent federal statutes have stringent provisions governing the transfer of assets. Medicaid eligibility will be delayed if, during the "look-back period" of five years prior to applying for coverage, applicants disposed of assets for less than fair market value. This provision does not ordinarily apply to a house transferred to a spouse or other relatives.[9] Generally, policy in this area is designed to encourage those who can afford it to purchase long-term care insurance rather than relying on Medicaid.

Private insurance companies have offered long-term care policies since 1982. Though long-term care policies are less popular than other forms of health insurance, long-term care coverage is growing both in availability and popularity. Government policy has contributed to that growth as the federal government and several states offer tax and other incentives to encourage the purchase of long-term care coverage.

In the early days of their development, long-term care policies were often problematic. Companies used deceptive sales tactics, and policies had small print that exempted major conditions like Alzheimer's from coverage (National Policy and Resource Center on Women and Aging, 1996). Partly as a result of government intervention and partly due to consumer education, these practices have improved. Still, few older adults have long-term care coverage, and private insurance pays for the care of only a small fraction of long-term nursing home residents—less than 3 percent in 2004 (Kasper & O'Malley, 2007).

---

9. Medicaid eligibility is not affected by the transfer of a house to the following relatives: a spouse, a child under 21 years of age, a disabled or blind adult child, an adult child who lived in the house and cared for the patient for at least two years before the patient was institutionalized, or a sibling who has equity in the house and has lived in it for at least one year before nursing home placement of the homeowner.

BOX 13.3 The Eden Alternative

The Eden Alternative is a new approach to long-term care designed to humanize nursing homes. The movement started in 1991, when Dr. William Thomas founded the first "Edenized" nursing home in New York. Dr. Thomas identifies three "plagues" of old age: loneliness, helplessness, and boredom. Edenized nursing homes are designed to eliminate all three. They look more like homes than medical facilities and include children and pets in their programming. Thomas aggressively promotes his Eden Alternative, which some say is just part of a general trend to humanize care in nursing homes. Although this approach is widely seen as promising, initial research studies provide only limited evidence of improvement on standardized outcome measures (Bergman-Evans, 2004; Coleman et al., 2002). For more information, see Thomas (1996).

Rationing Health Care by Age.   Some people advocate withholding medical care from the elderly on the grounds that their care is expensive and their social contributions are limited. According to this view, the care of the elderly involves lavish expenditures for individuals who have little to contribute to society—a situation that is particularly galling in view of the unmet health needs of infants and children. Former governor Richard Lamm of Colorado and others have suggested that medical treatment be withheld beyond a certain age (see Callahan, 1987, 1990). Through acceptance of a "natural life course," we might allocate scarce resources more effectively (Daniels, 1988). In a less diplomatic statement of the same view, Lamm has been widely quoted as arguing that old people "have a duty to die and get out of the way" (Slater, 1984, p. 1). By doing so, they would presumably free up money for the care of the young.

In opposition to age rationing of health care, Jahnigen and Binstock (1991) have argued that it is wrong to deny lifesaving care to a class of people defined only by their age. According to this view, clinical decisions about care should be based on individual considerations. As C. Everett Koop suggests, "Age is far too loose a criterion. Look at me. One of the main reasons I was rebuffed during my nomination to the office of surgeon general was because I was 'too old.' I was just a youngster of sixty-five. . . . Of course, this did not sit very well with the man who nominated me. President Reagan had just passed his seventieth birthday" (Binstock & Post, 1991, p. ix). Opponents of age-based rationing suggest that denying health care on the basis of age would deny some people life or functioning for significant periods, at a cost not only to the elders themselves but to their family members and friends. They further suggest that the fiscal crisis in health care is caused by systemic factors such as inflation in medical costs and technological developments, as well as the graying of America.

End-of-Life Care.   Although most Americans prefer to die at home, the majority die in hospitals. In 1998 the National Center for Health Statistics reported that 56 percent of deaths occurred in acute care settings (National Center for Health Statistics, 1998b). Although still high, the number of deaths in hospitals has decreased since the 1980s. Public policy decisions were instrumental in this shift, which some attribute to Medicare's prospective payment system and the use of diagnosis-related groups or DRGs (Sager et al., 1989). Under this view, the pressure to discharge patients has moved dying people out of hospitals.

Yet others acknowledge that without community-based supports such as those provided under hospice programs, fewer people would be dying at home (Tolle et al., 1999). Hospice care got a significant boost with the 1982 passage of the Tax Equity and Fiscal Responsibility Act, or TEFRA. This legislation added hospice care to the benefits covered by Medicare, making hospice available to everyone under Medicare Part A who has a life expectancy of six months or less.

Public policy has also established the framework for patients to provide advance directives regarding their end-of-life care. The two approaches most often used are a living will and a durable power of attorney. A living will is designed to outline specific requests about medical procedures that a person may or may not want in the case of incapacity. A durable power of attorney is used to designate a representative for the purpose of directing medical care if a person is unable to express his or her own wishes. Unlike a "simple" power of attorney, the durable power of attorney remains in effect if its executor becomes incompetent or disabled.

All states now recognize the living will as providing legally enforceable instructions regarding medical care. Indeed, the Patient Self-Determination Act of 1990 requires health care institutions participating in Medicare and Medicaid to provide patients with written information regarding living wills. These institutions must ask whether patients have an advance medical directive and document the reply in their medical records.

Assisted Suicide.   Dr. Jack Kevorkian, a retired pathologist in Michigan, probably did more than any individual to bring the topic of assisted suicide to public attention. Dr. Kevorkian has acknowledged assisting in the suicides of at least 92 people since 1990—most of them women, ranging in age from 26 to 89 (ERGO, 1998). In 1999, he was convicted of second-degree homicide for his involvement in the death of 52-year-old Thomas Youk.

Several organizations are working hard to secure legal protection for physicians who help patients commit suicide.[10] These advocates make several arguments in support of their cause. First, they suggest that the suffering associated with some terminal diseases is unbearable and cannot be relieved, stripping such patients of dignity and depriving their life of meaning. Second, advocates argue that physicians (like Dr. Kevorkian) are already helping patients commit suicide and that "decriminalizing" their actions would open them to public scrutiny and ensure that decisions are made in a balanced way that protects the interests of terminally ill patients. Finally, they note that a nation such as the United States,

10. Groups that support assisted suicide include Americans for Death with Dignity;
Choice in Dying; Death with Dignity, National Center; and Euthanasia Research and
Guidance Organization.

which places a high value on individual dignity, should not deprive terminally ill persons of assistance in ending their lives. (See Orentlicher (1996) for a detailed review of legal aspects of these arguments.)

Opponents[11] of assisted suicide offer several arguments. First, they argue that it is the duty of medical practitioners to relieve terminally ill patients of the suffering attendant to their diseases. If physicians have an easy out in the form of assisted suicide, they will not make the heroic efforts necessary to relieve pain. Second, they suggest that assisted suicide is one step down a slippery slope that could lead to euthanasia of undesirable or disabled elders. Finally, they suggest that terminally ill patients who are in unremitting pain are not competent to make an informed decision regarding the value or meaning of their life.

As of this writing, Oregon remains the only state in which physician-assisted suicide is legal. In November 1994, Oregon voters made theirs the first state in the nation to legalize physician-assisted suicide, passing Measure 16 by a slim margin (51 percent in favor and 49 percent opposed). The new law was immediately challenged by a group of patients who declared that it violated their constitutional rights. Federal District Court Judge Hogan ruled in their favor, issuing a permanent injunction against the law. In February 1997, the Federal Ninth Circuit Court reversed Hogan's ruling. The court did not rule on the constitutionality of the statute but decided the patients did not have "standing" to bring the case. In October 1997, the Supreme Court refused to hear the case.

Two cases decided by U.S. courts of appeals offered contradictory opinions. In the first, *Quill v. Vacco,* three New York physicians and their patients challenged the constitutionality of that state's laws prohibiting physicians from providing drugs to hasten death. In April 1996, the U.S. Court of Appeals for the Second Circuit held that "physicians who are willing to do so may prescribe drugs to be self-administered by mentally competent patients who seek to end their lives during the final stages of a terminal illness" (*Quill v. Vacco,* 1995, pp. 2–3). In contrast, the constitutionality of the State of Washington's law against physician-assisted suicide was upheld in a 1995 ruling by the U.S. Court of Appeals for the Ninth Circuit. The opinion states that the court found "no basis for concluding that the statute violates the constitution" (*Compassion in Dying v. State of Washington,* 1995, p. 4).

In 2001, the Bush Administration weighed in when Attorney General John Ashcroft issued a new interpretation of the Controlled Substances Act. Ashcroft held that the act granted him authority to prohibit the prescription of drugs under Oregon's Death with Dignity Act. A lawsuit was filed in Oregon, and a U.S. district court judge ruled against Ashcroft in 2002. The case meandered up to the U.S. Supreme Court, which heard arguments and, on January 17, 2006, affirmed the lower court decision upholding the Death with Dignity Act. (The interested reader will find a summary of laws around the world governing assisted suicide at http://www.assistedsuicide.org/suicide_laws.html.)

---

11. Opponents of assisted suicide include the Roman Catholic Church; Not Dead Yet; the International Anti-Euthanasia Task Force; and Americans Disabled for Attendant Programs Today.

SOCIAL WORK WITH THE ELDERLY

The number of social workers qualified to serve the nation's elderly is insufficient to meet the demand for their services, and the need will become greater in the near future. The Department of Health and Human Services has estimated that between 60,000 and 70,000 professionally trained social workers will he needed to serve older people and their families in the year 2020 (NIA, 1987). Historically the number of social workers providing services to the nation's elderly has been less than half that amount (Greene, 1989; Petersen, 1988). This suggests the need for a significant increase in the supply of social workers trained to work with elderly people.

Few schools of social work offer specialized training in aging, however, and those that do find student interest to be low (Lubben, Damron-Rodriguez, & Beck, 1992; McCaslin, 1987). Unless the production of professional-level social workers prepared to serve the elderly increases, individuals from other fields such as nursing and gerontology will fill roles ordinarily reserved for social workers, such as case manager, counselor, discharge planner, and program administrator. Most social workers in aging find the rewards of working with the nation's elders greater than they anticipated.

SUMMARY: THE OUTLOOK FOR ELDERLY AMERICANS

Public provision for the elderly depends to a great extent on public attitudes. When "compassionate stereotypes" prevail, aging programs tend to expand. In the context of "greedy geezer" rhetoric, they often contract. Apart from attitudes, the material realities of age drive policies and programs.

Twenty-first-century realities for this age group are complex. Foremost is its tremendous growth. The aging of the large baby boom generation will place unprecedented demands on public programs for the elderly. Many in this cohort are economically well-off, enjoying the accumulated benefits of an advantaged life, a phenomenon known as "cumulative advantage" (Crystal and Shea, 1990). These advantages will render suspect the use of age-based eligibility requirements for publicly funded benefits. As a result, programs ranging from Social Security and Medicare to services provided under the OAA are subjected to intense public scrutiny.

At the same time, the cumulative effects of lifelong oppression, termed "cumulative disadvantage" restrict the opportunities and resources available to vulnerable subgroups of the aging population (Crystal & Shea, 1990). Older women of color, like Mrs. Johnson, have extremely high rates of poverty. Age itself brings disadvantages. Even normal physical aging processes can leave a person dependent on health care to limit pain and disability. In the decades to come, a growing proportion of the nation's elderly will be composed of the very old, women, and minorities—the groups most vulnerable to these disadvantages and most likely to depend on public programs and services. It is vitally important that social workers act as advocates for the interests of these disenfranchised and vulnerable elders.

KEYWORDS

Gerontology	Elder abuse	Rural elderly
Meals on Wheels	Elder care	Ageism
America's aging	Mandatory retirement	Think About It

THINK ABOUT IT

1. Consider Mrs. Johnson's experiences with public policies and programs. In what ways do they reflect the themes discussed in the historic sections of this chapter? What modern policies and programs have influenced her? In what ways do gender and race determine the resources available to Mrs. Johnson?

2. Federal, state, and local governments devote considerable resources to measures that assist older people. These range from health services to the popular Meals on Wheels programs. At the same time, many observers feel the nation has neglected the needs of vulnerable children. How would you justify spending public resources on programs for the elderly?

3. A central tension in OAA programs is the need to use scarce funds to serve those in greatest need, while the political viability of these programs stems from their middle-class constituency. If you were the director of a state office on aging, how would you respond to the mandate to serve those in greatest social and economic need?

4. Consider three elderly people, all of whom have incomes below the federal poverty threshold. Helen is a widowed homemaker who raised four children. Her children are all doing well, but her husband's terminal illness in the early 1980s has left her impoverished. Sandra worked all her life in a nonunion factory. She has no pension and now is too disabled to work. Betty is a lifelong alcoholic. Married three times, never for more than three years, she has moved from place to place working at low-paying jobs. She has two children but doesn't know where they are. Describe the public income supports on which these individuals might draw. Now list these three individuals in order of priority—who has the greatest claim on public resources?

5. Medicare currently offers health coverage to elders of all income levels, and this coverage is better than most policies that low- and many middle-income workers could afford to purchase on their own. Yet funding for Medicare comes from a tax on wages. Do you think this is fair? Why or why not? Would you propose to finance health care this way? Or would you recommend a different approach?

WEB-BASED EXERCISE

For a direct link to the site in this exercise, log on to the Student Companion Site for this book at academic.cengage.com/social_work/barusch, and choose Chapter 13.

Go to the Social Security Administration's *Income of the Aged Chartbook: 2004* located at http://www.socialsecurity.gov/policy/docs/chartbooks/income_aged/. Based on the information provided, answer the following questions.

a. In what way do aged households with asset income differ from those without?
b. How do members of various racial and ethnic groups differ in source and amount of retirement income?
c. Does marital status affect retirement income? If so, how?
d. How would you describe the distribution of income in retirement? What are the most common income levels?

SUGGESTED RESOURCES

Achenbaum, W. A. (1986). *Social Security Visions and Revisions*. Cambridge: Cambridge University Press.

Binstock, R. H., & Post, S. G. (Eds.). (1991). *Too Old for Health Care: Controversies in Medicine, Law, Economics and Ethics*. Baltimore: Johns Hopkins University Press.

Hudson, R. B. (Ed.). (1997). *The Future of Age-Based Public Policy*. Baltimore: Johns Hopkins University Press.

Kingson, E. R., & Berkowitz, E. D. (1993). *Social Security and Medicare: A Policy Primer*. Westport, CT: Greenwood Publishing Group.

Richardson, V. E., & Barusch, A. S. (2006). *Gerontological Practice for the Twenty-First Century: A Social Work Perspective*. New York: Columbia University Press.

Schulz, J. H. (1995). *The Economics of Aging* (6th ed.). Westport, CT: Auburn House.

www.aarp.org. The official site of the American Association for Retired Persons, this is a gold mine of information about aging. The AARP's legislative issues link provides up-to-date information about issues that affect the elderly.

www.agingsociety.org. This is the site of the National Academy on Aging, a policy institute operated by the Gerontological Society of America (www.geron.org). The Academy's mission is to promote "education, research, and public understanding" on issues that affect the elderly. Its publications are well balanced and carefully researched.

www.aoa.dhhs.gov. Maintained by the U.S. Administration on Aging, this site is an excellent source of information on programs funded under the Older Americans Act.

14

Working Americans

I can look at history and say that we are evolving into a more
just world. I know that it doesn't look so good today, but over
a hundred years it does change tremendously. But it changes
because millions of people make a decision to make a
difference, to think differently, to demand justice, to demand
justice for other people, to not look the other way, and I just
need to be a part of that.

LAS VEGAS COCKTAIL WAITRESS AND UNION ORGANIZER
(CHANDLER & JONES, 2003)

Most Americans work for a living, bartering time and energy in a market
that favors employers over laborers. It is easy to wax nostalgic about the
"organization man" of the 1950s. Once a figure of disdain, this icon represented
the tight relationship between worker and employer, and the expectation, particularly among white-collar workers, that it would be lifelong. Of course, for
most workers this is not the case, and all too often the interests of employee
and employer are diametrically opposed. Following a discussion of the life experiences of Sam Tobin, this chapter explores historic and contemporary realities
that affect workers in the United States. The chapter closes with a description of
current U.S. labor policies.

LABOR IN AMERICA: A BRIEF HISTORY

The history of labor is the history of our nation, ranging from the forced labor of
slaves to the highly technical work performed by aerospace engineers. In this

A HUMAN PERSPECTIVE Sam Tobin

Sam's hefty frame towers over me as I greet him on the tiny front porch of his new townhouse on the outskirts of Omaha. Dressed casually in an old T-shirt and paint-speckled jeans, he warns that I will need to speak loudly. The rock and roll days of his youth left him with a hearing impairment. Besides that, he has lost all of his hair, so looks a bit older than his 33 years. I increase the volume to compliment him on the little red geraniums planted along the foundation. In a sweet, hopeful gesture, someone—his wife Hannah, as it turns out—has put a lot of effort into those seedlings.

Sam's mother raised him alone, relying mostly on public assistance. His dad worked construction jobs. Sam hated school, finding English and math particularly loathsome. At 14 he started playing drums with a friend after school. His high school music teacher thought he had talent and bought him a set of drums, fueling a dream of rock and roll stardom. After graduation he got a day job as a groundskeeper at a local school, playing drums at night for local bands. Sam earned some good reviews and lots of applause. That's how he met Hannah. She was singing with a band, and they decided to become a team. Attraction flared, and they were married within a month of meeting.

Along with two other music lovers, Sam and Hannah cobbled together a band and set out in a trailer to tour the country. "I was dreaming I was going to be a musician and I left and said, 'I'm never coming back. I'm going on tour. I'm gonna be a rock star. Bye bye!'" Sam recalls. They played at night clubs and colleges and made a demo CD. Sam said it was a fun time, but "it sure didn't pay us much!" In the highly competitive music market they had a hard time getting gigs. Their debts grew and they never did seem to break even, let alone get ahead. "We hardly made $150 a week," Sam explains. "We had a couple of bad tours and realized that music could not fill our stomachs. The band members started getting frustrated and the band disintegrated." He figures, "The system

doesn't support artists. The music industry is not favorable to new artists. It's all about number crunching from foreign companies. That's all they see. So I burned out on music. It was fun as a hobby, but it's another thing when it's your job. It loses its sweetness. I'm not as passionate about it as I used to be. Maybe when I get older. . . ."

Sam and Hannah moved to California and found "real" jobs. She worked in a chocolate factory and he worked in a UPS store. Even without the dream of stardom, life was pleasant and they enjoyed the gentle climate. Then Hannah got pregnant with their daughter, Cecelia. Sam was delighted but soon realized that even on two incomes they could not afford child care. Hannah asked her employer for shift work, but instead she was laid off. Her employer offered no explanation, just "Sorry, we can't do that for you. We're gonna have to let you go." Now there was no way the couple could afford rent and the new baby. Sam had to sell his drum set to pay the rent. So they decided to return to Nebraska where the cost of housing was much lower and Hannah's family could help out in a pinch.

But the return home had its bittersweet moments. The only job Sam could find was his old job—as groundskeeper at the school. So he ate a little crow and is now able to chuckle at the irony. Hannah found a job as a custodian. Sam says, "We did not want to claim bankruptcy, so we planned how much both of us would need to earn to pay off all our debts."

Sam worked for a while without a contract. During this time he broke his ankle at home. He couldn't work, so he had to take leave without pay. He also was hit by the medical bills, since health insurance had not yet been arranged. The family's temporarily reduced income coupled with medical expenses set them back financially. Luckily, they received a good income tax refund that covered their expenses for a while.

section we will briefly focus on key developments in the U.S. labor movement, as well as legislation and court decisions that were pivotal in determining the conditions of American labor. We will then examine in more detail the history of affirmative action, immigration, and policies protecting women and children. This section closes by considering the historic alliance between the social work profession and the labor movement.

"We are not in a position to save any money right now and live from paycheck to paycheck," Sam says, explaining that his job doesn't pay much. But it is full-time and he gets health benefits and has flexible hours. "I get designated breaks and stuff like that. I'm not fired as easily because it's a government job. Not like in a private job, like if a boss doesn't like you he can fire you or lay you off. That happened to me a couple of times. I get all holidays." Sam is determined to keep the job, and hopes that Hannah will be able to go to college and study nursing. Eventually, he would like to go to college too. Sam thinks the American job market favors college-educated people.

School may have to be postponed, since the couple just had another baby, a son named Joshua. Sam plans to tell his son, "Your dad had to cut lawns for ten years because he did not attend school." He says he will caution both children to stay in school and to "create a strong household with a work ethic. Living on minimum wage is not fun. I had no one behind me to support me. There were counselors in school, but they did not give me any direction. Now I will be a counselor for my kids."

Sam is optimistic about the future, saying "I have a lot of faith in my wife, in myself." Still, he acknowledges the growing economic inequality in the United States: "What I see is separation of the classes like back in the old days when there used to be serfs and royalty. It's getting to be more like that, the haves and the have-nots. It's a hard hurdle to get over. Education is the only hope you have. Unless you have a lot of capital or business savvy you're just going to be clawing at the wall. It's all about education."

Sam is glad he did follow his music dream, and hopes to return to it "if I can afford to retire at 50 or 55." His advice for policy makers is, "The main thing is benefits. It's all about benefits. Make sure employees have benefits. . . . America's health system is out of control because of skyrocketing costs of health insurance. . . . Y'know, it costs more, and it's just so easy for the small business owner to lose their money that they just . . . I don't know. . . . It's about insurance. Because like at our work there are 'hourlies' without insurance, like when I was on hourly . . . you've got people working full time with no benefits."

A Social Work Perspective
Sam hit the nail on the head when he said "It's all about benefits." As we will see, union leaders and policy makers agree with him that the rising cost of health care is one of the most important issues affecting working people in America.

Sam is also correct in his assessment that education could make an important difference in the financial security of his family. Of course, in today's labor market professional status does not guarantee financial stability. But in recent decades education has been the one thing standing between workers and income declines. During the 1980s, for example, the only men who saw real wage increases were those with at least six years of college, and women with high school degrees or less experienced wage declines (Bluestone, 1994). The odds may be against Sam, though. In 2003 only 27 percent of the U.S. population over age 25 held college degrees (U.S. Bureau of Census, 2004a). And one study reported that only 6 percent of college students from low-income families complete four-year degrees (Zweig, 2000).

Sam has spent some time in the "secondary labor market," which is characterized by temporary and part-time jobs. This market now accounts for nearly a third of all jobs in the United States (Reisch & Gorin, 2001). Like Sam, most of the people in the secondary labor market do not belong to unions.

The Labor Movement in the United States and Abroad

Many aspects of employment are determined not by laws but by the contracts between employers and employees. Advocates of free enterprise argue that it is inappropriate for the government to intervene in these private contracts. Of course, the power differential between employee and employer is usually so great that the "contract" is less a matter of mutual agreement than of administrative fiat. The traditional role of unions is to shore up the power of employees, bringing greater clout to the bargaining table. Union negotiations have improved conditions for workers in a wide range of industries.

In many ways, the history of the U.S. labor movement is international. As Frank (2004) explains, "[U]nions, the basic institutional unit of 'U.S. labor history,' were transnational from day one" (p. 99). Labor unions crossed borders, in part because of a concern that overseas workers who were not unionized might cross borders and undercut them. Some established international "secretariats" that exchanged information with overseas workers, solicited financial help during strikes, and discouraged foreign workers from becoming scabs. Apart from these practical considerations, some unions shared a vision of working-class solidarity. Recall Karl Marx's famous call, "Proletarians of all countries, unite!" As this quote suggests, in its the early years the U.S. labor movement drew inspiration and direction from communist philosophy and leadership from the socialist movement.

In the 1860s, U.S. unions participated in the International Workingmen's Association (IWA), known as the "First International," sending a delegate from the iron molders' union to the IWA's first congress in Geneva in 1866. Their concerns were both pragmatic and idealistic, combining worries about foreign strikebreakers with a push toward solidarity, but the organizational framework would not survive beyond the 1870s. Still, historians credit the First International with providing an international forum for labor leaders to make contact and develop a common agenda for change. The call for international labor legislation surfaced in the First International and would reappear in subsequent organizations as well (Lorwin, 1929).

The First International was followed by the "Black International," formally known as the International Working People's Association. For a few years in the 1880s, this anarchist group advocated for international worker solidarity. It was followed in 1889 by the "Second International," which began with a congress of socialist labor leaders, primarily from Germany and France. Americans participated in these meetings, but the advent of World War I shattered the organization. As Frank puts it, "Nationalism trumped working-class internationalism abruptly and brutally" (2004, p. 102). Worker organizations that did not support the war effort paid the price in government suppression and public hostility.

Nonetheless, international worker solidarity survived, and a "Third International" was founded in the 1920s to unite socialist and labor leaders. Americans participated in this Soviet-based organization, and during this era many left-thinking intellectuals (like Bertha Reynolds) visited Russia.

Perhaps the most international of U.S. unions was the Industrial Workers of the World, known as IWW or the Wobblies. They organized factory workers, rather than craftsmen, and had locals in South Africa, Australia, Chile, Canada, Mexico, and the United States. Similarly, the Knights of Labor founded several Canadian locals in the 1880s. In contrast, the American Federation of Labor, which has been the dominant union in the United States since the early twentieth century, is primarily a national enterprise.

The years during and immediately following the Great Depression have been described as a "working-class interlude in American labor history" (Greenstone, 1969, p. 71). The 1935 Wagner Act—described by some as the most important labor law in American history—established workers' right to organize unions and negotiate with management (Farhang & Katznelson, 2005). Also known as the National Labor Relations Act (NLRA), this law acknowledged workers' right to organize and join labor unions, to collectively bargain, and to strike. It set up the National Labor Relations Board, an independent federal agency, to administer the act and to certify unions. The act forbade employers from interfering with employees exercising their right to organize and engage in collective bargaining, from attempting to dominate a labor union, from refusing to bargain "in good faith," and from discriminating against union members in hiring. In 1937, the Supreme Court upheld the NLRA (*NLRB v. Jones & Laughlin Steel Corp.*), setting the stage for a period of growth in union membership.

Critics argued that the NLRA did not restrict union tactics, particularly the use of "sit-down strikes," in which workers occupy factories and halt production. The effectiveness of this approach is self-evident, but it was declared unconstitutional by the Supreme Court in 1939 (*NLRB v. Fansteel Metallurgical Corporation*). In the elections of 1946 the Republican Party won majorities in both houses of Congress. Traditionally pro-business, the Republicans set out to dismantle NLRA protections through the Taft-Hartley Act, also known as the Labor-Management Relations Act of 1947.

Taft-Hartley allowed the president to seek a court injunction to block or prevent strikes that he felt would endanger national health or safety.[1] It also created an 80-day "cooling-off" period during which strikes that constituted a "national emergency" could be prohibited. The act prohibited secondary boycotts, sympathy strikes or boycotts, and "closed shops" (which hired only union members). The law permitted "union shops," in which employees are required to join a union, as long as they were not prohibited under state law. This clause set the stage for passage of "right-to-work" laws at the state level that prohibited union shops. Reflecting the times, Taft-Hartley also required that union officers take an oath that they were not communists.

The Cold War

In 1946, more than a third (35 percent) of non-farmworkers in the United States belonged to unions (Cherny, Issel, & Taylor, 2004). By 2006, that figure would drop to 12 percent of wage and salaried workers (Bureau of Labor Statistics, 2007c). While Taft-Hartley contributed to the decline of unions in the United

---

1. Presidents have invoked Taft-Hartley in attempts to stop strikes 35 times, and they were successful on all but two of these occasions. Most recently, President Bush invoked Taft-Hartley when negotiations between port operators and the International Longshore and Warehouse Union broke down (Wagner, 2002).

States, beliefs and attitudes with roots in the Cold War period played a role as well.

The term "McCarthyism" has been used to refer to the anticommunist crusade that held Americans in its thrall during the late 1940s and 1950s. Communists, particularly those with ties to the Soviet Union, were viewed as the enemy, and public furor reached fever pitch in 1956, when Nikita Khrushchev addressed Western ambassadors at a Moscow reception with his famous phrase, "We will bury you." McCarthy himself was a senator from Wisconsin who spearheaded the anticommunist witch hunts that targeted unions which actually were affiliated with the Communist Party. But McCarthy was not alone. The "war on communism" had several fronts, marshalling the efforts of churches, right-wing journalists, employers, and federal officials (Schrecker, 2004). Thousands of workers lost their jobs, and some were blacklisted and unable to find any work in their chosen fields.

McCarthyism was effective. It deprived labor of some of its most talented leaders; and, perhaps more damaging, the pervasive anticommunist rhetoric pulled the ideological rug out from under the movement. Those seeking broad social reform could no longer rally around the banner of worker solidarity. Of course, other issues and other banners would come to fill the void.

The Civil Rights Movement

Two broad social and economic changes set the stage for the civil rights movement of the 1960s: the migration of Southern agricultural workers to Northern cities, and the organizing experiences of African American union members and leaders. Cotton prices dropped sharply during the first half of the twentieth century, and methods for harvesting and processing the fiber were mechanized. As a result, hundreds of thousands of agricultural workers, many of them African Americans, left the rural areas of the South and moved to urban areas in the North. They sought employment in industrial settings, often in union jobs.

This movement to urban settings provided opportunities for socialization and organization. Workers were no longer dependent on planters for employment and goods. It also brought a mandate to many of the nation's unions to support interracial solidarity.

The role of unions in the struggle for racial equality has been debated. Citing examples of racially exclusive unions such as the American Federation of Labor (AFL) and the railroad unions, some argue that the racism of white members made unions hostile to African American workers. Others suggest that racially exclusive unions were the result of pressure from local communities and factory owners. Community hostility to racial integration took the form of anti-union violence. Several leaders of integrated unions, both African American and white, were murdered or lynched with the cooperation of local law enforcement officials. Racism in unions was fostered when factory owners brought in African American workers as strikebreakers.

The history of the union movement also provides examples of strong solidarity between white and African American union members. The United Mine

Diane Perry, front left, and Juan Pena, center, both of the steelworkers union, join hands with Ron Tilman, right, and other members of the United Postal Workers Union at an AFL-CIO solidarity rally in Chicago in 2005.

Workers of America (UMW) enrolled white and African American members who worked side by side in the coal mines of Appalachia. As Foner (1981) notes, African Americans served in leadership roles at both local and national levels of the UMW. The Noble Knights of Labor, a federation of unions, was also deeply committed to racial solidarity, as was the Industrial Workers of the World (IWW). These unions held integrated meetings, even in the South where local statutes prohibited such activities.

Thus, while some leaders and participants in the civil rights movement came from churches and schools, others came from unions. They brought with them the methods and strategies of union organizing as well as considerable financial support. The United Auto Workers, for example, contributed about $160,000 to the Southern Christian Leadership Conference to assist with bail expenses from the Birmingham demonstrations of 1963 (Wilson, 1996).

The civil rights movement effectively brought the federal government into the realm of race relations. Much civil rights legislation had the effect of negating state laws that supported racial oppression. The power of the federal government became a resource in the struggle for racial equality, frequently in conflict with state and local governments.

The era saw the passage of vitally important legislation:

- The Civil Rights Act of 1960 challenged voting discrimination.
- The Civil Rights Act of 1964 prohibited discrimination in public accommodations, employment, and programs receiving federal funds.

B O X   14.1   Title VII of the Civil Rights Act of 1964

"It shall be an unlawful employment practice for an employer . . . to fail or refuse to discharge any individual or otherwise to discriminate against any individual with respect to his compensation, terms, conditions, or privileges of employment, because of such individual's race, color, religion, sex, or national origin; or . . . to limit, segregate, or classify his employees or applicants for employment in any way which would deprive or tend to deprive any individual employee of employment opportunities or otherwise adversely affect his status as an employee, because of such individual's race, color, religion, sex, or national origin."

- The Voting Rights Act of 1965 prohibited discrimination in voting.
- The Fair Housing Act of 1968 prohibited discrimination in housing.

With the passage of the Civil Rights Act of 1964, the federal government assumed a new position with respect to employment. Far from legislating discrimination as was true in an earlier era, the act prohibits it. Its implementation is largely dependent on the political views of the executive branch, with the Reagan and both Bush administrations effectively curtailing activities in this area. Still, the act itself represented substantial legislative progress toward a less segregated labor market.

Affirmative Action

Cedric Herring (1997) offers a succinct definition of "affirmative action": "Affirmative Action consists of activities specifically to identify, recruit, promote and/or retain qualified women and members of disadvantaged minority groups in order to overcome the results of past discrimination and to deter employers from engaging in discriminatory practices" (p. 6). This broad definition was made more specific by two major policy initiatives. The first consisted of executive orders issued under the Kennedy, Johnson, and Nixon administrations requiring that firms doing business with the federal government engage in affirmative action. The second was Title VII of the 1964 Civil Rights Act, which prohibited discrimination by private employers and unions (Pedriana, 1999).

President Kennedy's Executive Order 10925 prohibited government contractors from practicing racial discrimination and required that they take "affirmative action" to ensure that there was no discrimination. The order established the President's Committee on Equal Employment Opportunity (PCEEO) to enforce the law. Although other presidents had issued non-discrimination orders in the past, none had included the clause requiring affirmative action. While establishing an obligation for employers to take action, the order did not specify what this might entail. In essence, it required that federal contractors "do something" without specifying exactly what "something" was. Only one specific action was required: employers had to maintain records of the racial composition of their workforce.

Lockheed was the subject of the first complaint filed under Order 10925. The NAACP complained that the company practiced blatant and pervasive racial discrimination. In response, the firm developed an aggressive "Plan for Progress" that included recruiting and training for people of color, reviewing promotion procedures, and establishing vocational programs in local schools.

Plans for Progress became a watchword for the PCEEO, and companies that voluntarily prepared these plans were guaranteed that they would not be subject to investigation. Many companies did so, but the results were consistently disappointing. An evaluation of the plans' impact, conducted by the Southern Regional Council, concluded that the plans were ineffective. Indeed, there was some evidence that firms completing the plans had worse records on equal employment than those that did not (Pedriana, 1999). Ultimately, the most influential feature of Order 10925 was its record-keeping requirement, which resulted in a "unique national profile of the employment distribution of race" (Graham, 1990, p. 60).

With support from the Kennedy administration, Congress passed Title VII of the Civil Rights Act of 1964. Enforcement of Title VII would move affirmative action out of the realm of vague, voluntary planning into an aggressive approach to equal opportunity that would become characteristic of the Johnson administration.

Title VII prohibited employment discrimination on the basis of gender or race and established the Equal Employment Opportunity Commission (EEOC) to enforce the law. The phrase "affirmative action" was called for in cases of intentional violation. As Pedriana (1999) notes, Title VII included the following language:

> If the court finds that the respondent has intentionally engaged in or is intentionally engaging in an unlawful employment practice . . . the court may enjoin the respondent from engaging in such unlawful employment practice, and order such affirmative action as may be appropriate. (p. 11)

Even this language was fairly broad, and it was left to the courts and the EEOC to interpret and implement the title. Central to their interpretations was defining "discrimination." The law prohibited, but did not define, the practice. Initial interpretations focused on discriminatory intent. Firms that intentionally and obviously discriminated on the basis of race were concentrated in the South, where separate locker, cafeteria, and washroom facilities were the norm, and where African Americans were concentrated in low-paid employment. The approach based on intent was effective at eliminating these more obvious instances of discrimination.

Over time, a focus on institutional discrimination led to redefinition of the term to focus less on intent and more on the consequences of discrimination. Attention shifted to broader employment practices, such as seniority systems and employment testing, that led to racial inequality in the workplace. Indeed, under this view, employment discrimination was part of a broader pattern of oppression that included inferior educational opportunities, exclusion from informal job networks, and limited access to apprenticeship and mentoring opportunities.

Two federal court rulings supported a focus on consequences rather than intent. In *Quarles v. Philip Morris,* the district court ruled against the company's argument that "the present consequences of past discrimination" were not covered by the Civil Rights Act, saying, "Congress did not intend to freeze an entire generation of Negro employees into discriminatory patterns that existed before the act" (Pedriana, 1999, p. 16).

Then, in *Griggs v. Duke Power Company,* the Supreme Court unanimously ruled against the company's promotion requirement of a high school diploma and its use of employment testing. Establishing what is now known as "the Doctrine of Disparate Impact," the Court ruled that

> [t]he objective of Title VII is plain from the language of the statute. It was to achieve equality of employment opportunities and remove barriers that have operated in the past to favor an identifiable group of White employees over other employees. Under the act, practices, procedures or tests neutral on their face and even neutral in terms of intent cannot be maintained if they operate to "freeze" the status quo of prior discriminatory employment practices. . . . Congress directed the thrust of the Act to the consequences of employment practices, not simply the motivation. (Pedriana, 1999, p. 17)

Under the Doctrine of Disparate Impact, businesses that had racial and gender disparities in the workplace could be subject to costly and time-consuming litigation. To avoid litigation, many firms followed the EEOC's guidelines and developed voluntary affirmative action plans. These plans frequently included race-based hiring and promotion goals, now known as "quotas." Few firms were subject to court-ordered affirmative action, and those that were the subject of court mandates had fairly egregious discriminatory practices (Pedriana, 1999).

The use of quotas was much more common in enforcing presidential orders regarding government contractors. In 1965, President Johnson issued Executive Order 11246 to replace Kennedy's Order 10925. This order created the Office of Federal Contract Compliance (OFCC) to enforce nondiscrimination in government contracting. Under the order, firms were frequently required to set and meet hiring quotas. These requirements were especially controversial for construction firms, which traditionally segregated their trades along racial lines. These firms were required to set hiring goals in each of the trades, with the result being the much maligned practice of "hiring by the numbers."

President Nixon's contributions to affirmative action were substantial. Indeed, as Troy Duster (1996) points out,

> Nixon did more than any other president to promote and institutionalize affirmative action. While John Kennedy issued the initially limited

executive orders in 1963, and while Lyndon Johnson had maneuvered through Congress the 1964 civil rights legislation that mandated selected forms in the workplace, it was Nixon who demanded and required that corporate America institute programs of affirmative action. (p. 41)

Insiders' accounts of the Nixon administration have argued that the president's motive was to drive a wedge in the traditional Democratic alliance of labor and blacks (see Ehrlichman, 1982; Haldeman, 1994).

In sum, both Title VII and the presidential orders governing federal contracting increased employment opportunities for people of color. Probably the greatest impact of Title VII came with the courts' establishment of the Doctrine of Disparate Impact. Under this doctrine, even race-neutral practices that resulted in racial disparities were potential subjects of litigation. This led many firms to voluntarily adopt and implement affirmative action plans. The use of hiring quotas was most commonly a response to federal contracting requirements established under presidential orders.

The expansion of affirmative action occurred in an economic climate of expanded opportunity, and, as Duster (1996) and others (Ezorsky, 1991; Northrup, 1970; Quadagno, 1994) have argued, it worked. Affirmative action expanded minorities' access to employment, particularly in public-sector jobs and the building trades. Indeed, as Duster (1996) argues, "It is empirically demonstrable that affirmative action provided a way out of poverty for hundreds of thousands, even millions, of poor blacks" (p. 56).

But by the late 1970s, unemployment rates had risen, real wages were declining, and the time was ripe for a backlash against affirmative action. This backlash was spearheaded by leaders in California (Nixon's home state), who argued that affirmative action was unfair to individuals. Other arguments have been devised against affirmative action:

- It stigmatizes women and minorities whose colleagues perceive them as having been hired not for their qualifications but to satisfy affirmative action quotas.

- It is no longer necessary, as discrimination in employment no longer exists.

- It results in "reverse discrimination" against men and whites.

- It does not help the "truly disadvantaged."

- It is ineffective.

At a time when jobs were disappearing and admission to California's public universities was increasingly competitive, these arguments were persuasive. Affirmative action received a serious challenge in the 1978 case of *Regents of the University of California v. Bakke*. In this case, a 37-year-old white engineer (Allan Bakke) had been twice denied admission to the university's medical school. The school reserved 16 of its 100 entering positions for minorities, and some of the 16 admitted when Bakke was denied had lower admissions scores than he had. The case was decided by the U.S. Supreme Court in a split decision that represented a carefully crafted compromise.[2] The justices held that the California admissions policy was unconstitutional because it used a quota system based on race. The Court left open the question of whether a race-sensitive admissions policy could be crafted that would not be held unconstitutional (Ball, 2000).

In June 2003, the Supreme Court upheld the constitutionality of affirmative action in university admissions by a one-vote margin in the case of *Grutter v. Bollinger.* Arguing that "[u]niversities occupy a special niche," the Court opinion provided strong endorsement of racial diversity on campuses and found there was a compelling state interest in maintaining that diversity: "In order to cultivate a set of leaders with legitimacy in the eyes of the citizenry, it is necessary that the path to leadership be visibly open to talented and qualified individuals of every race and ethnicity." At the same time, in the 2003 case of *Gratz v. Bollinger,* the Court, by a three-vote margin, rejected the use of a point system based on race, finding it was too close to a quota system. The difference between these cases lay in the implementation of affirmative action. In the first case the University of Michigan law school treated race as a factor in an individualized, holistic review of each file. In the second, the University of Michigan undergraduate admissions offices automatically assigned points to applications from people of color.

Other attacks on affirmative action involved the political process. In 1995, the regents of the University of California, under the leadership of Republican governor Pete Wilson, voted to abolish affirmative action in college admissions. A year later, voters in California passed Proposition 209 by a narrow margin. This measure outlawed the use of race, sex, ethnicity, or national origin as a reason for discriminating against or granting preferential treatment to any person or group. Later, similar initiatives passed in Washington State (Initiative 200) and Florida (the One Florida Initiative).

Today there is widespread consensus against the use of racial quotas in hiring, and the phrase itself has taken on negative undertones. As Reverend Davis explained, in our current political environment it will take a creative soul to devise a new approach to equal opportunity in employment that is both effective and politically feasible.

Immigration and Labor

Prior to 1882, the United States had an open immigration policy. Anyone could relocate to this developing nation. But citizenship and voting rights were restricted. Under the Naturalization Acts of the late 1700s only free whites could be citizens, and only free white males could vote (Davis & Cloud-Two Dogs, 2004). Major milestones in U.S. immigration policy are summarized in Table 14.1. For just over a century, the nation has refined its immigration policy in pursuit of three stated goals: exclusion (excluding groups considered undesirable by the majority); economic advancement (promoting domestic economic interests);

---

2. The Supreme Court refused to order the university to admit Bakke, but he did obtain such an order through a California court. Bakke was admitted to the U.C. Davis Medical School and graduated in 1992.

T A B L E 14.1   Legislative Milestones in U.S. Immigration Policy

Naturalization Acts of 1790, 1795, and 1798

- Restricted citizenship to free whites
- Restricted voting to free white males

Chinese Exclusion Act (1882)

- Suspended immigration of Chinese
- Barred Chinese naturalization
- Provided for deportation of Chinese who immigrated illegally into the United States

Immigration Act of 1891

- Provided for national control of immigration
- Established Bureau of Immigration under the Treasury Department
- Provided for deportation of undocumented aliens

Immigration and Naturalization Act of 1924

- Imposed permanent numeric limit on immigration
- Established national origins quota system (favoring northern and western Europeans)

Displaced Persons Act of 1948

- Allowed immigration of WWII victims

Immigration and Naturalization Act of 1952

- Continued national origins quotas
- Established quota for workers with needed skills

Immigration and Naturalization Act Amendments of 1965

- Repealed national origins quotas
- Established seven-category preference system based on family unification and skills
- Set annual limit of 20,000 per country and 170,000 overall on immigrants from Eastern Hemisphere
- Imposed ceiling on immigration from Western Hemisphere (for the first time)

Immigration and Naturalization Act Amendments of 1976

- Extended 20,000 per country limit to Western Hemisphere

Refugee Act of 1980

- Established permanent procedure for admitting refugees
- Removed refugees as a category from preference system
- Defined "refugee" according to international standards
- Established process of domestic resettlement
- Codified asylum status

TABLE 14.1   *Continued*

Immigration Reform and Control Act of 1986

- Instituted employer sanctions for knowingly hiring undocumented workers
- Tripled employment-based immigration
- Created diversity admissions category
- Established temporary protected status

1996 Immigration Acts

- Increased border patrols and barriers
- Denied Supplemental Security Income and food stamps to legal immigrants
- Denied most public services to undocumented immigrants

2001 USA Patriot Act

- Enabled authorities to detain and deport suspected terrorists and those who support them
- Provided humanitarian immigration procedures for foreign victims of the attacks on September 11

Enhanced Border Security and Visa Entry Reform Act of 2001

- Increased background checks required for visas

SOURCE: Fox & Passel (1994); Close Up Foundation (1998); Congressional Research Service (2002).

and humanitarian (providing a haven for the oppressed and permitting families to be together).

Each of these stated goals has implications for workers. As we saw in Chapter 9, exclusion was used in response to economic competition from Chinese laborers. The experiences of Mexican immigrants illustrate the use of immigration to meet U.S. demands for labor. Finally, a worker's ability to bring in family members is conditioned by the nation's humanitarian goals. At the same time, immigration policy reflects American prejudices and bigotry.

Exclusion.   Early immigration restrictions such as the Chinese Exclusion Act of 1882 and the Immigration and Naturalization Act of 1924 were designed to exclude groups considered undesirable by the majority. Recall that the Chinese Exclusion Act suspended immigration from that nation when Chinese laborers were perceived as a threat to American workers.[3] Later, the Naturalization Act established a quota that favored immigrants from western and northern European nations. Based on the argument that immigrants from these nations were more readily assimilated, this act responded to objections raised to immigration from southern and eastern Europe.

---

3. The Chinese Exclusion Act was renewed in 1892 and extended indefinitely in 1902. Its effect ended with the passage of the Immigration and Naturalization Act of 1924.

Ideology and sexual orientation have also been grounds for prohibiting immigration. Fear of communism led to the 1952 passage of the McCarran-Walter Act, which prohibited immigration by people who subscribed to this ideology. This act was overturned in 1990. Until 1990, U.S. immigration policy also allowed for the exclusion of homosexuals.

In the wake of the September 11 attacks, exclusion of suspected terrorists has come to the forefront of U.S. immigration policy. The attacks were perpetrated by non-U.S. citizens, most of whom came from Saudi Arabia. The legislative and executive response has been extensive. Under the 2001 Border Security Act, funding for patrols on the Canadian and Mexican borders increased dramatically. The act also called for fingerprinting foreign visitors from many nations. The Immigration and Naturalization Service (INS) was moved out of the Department of Justice and into the Department of Homeland Security. In 2002, the Enhanced Border Security and Visa Entry Reform Act subjected foreign citizens entering the United States to background checks and made visas more difficult to obtain. Foreign students were required to register with the Department of Homeland Security on a regular basis. Passed in October 2001, the USA Patriot Act gave the attorney general unprecedented powers to detain and deport suspected terrorists.

Economic Advancement. Immigration policies explicitly designed to promote domestic economic goals surfaced in the Immigration and Naturalization Act of 1952, which established quotas for workers with needed skills. This practice is now a well-established part of U.S. immigration policy. Indeed, Microsoft's Bill Gates has argued against further restrictions on immigration, suggesting they would "prevent companies like ours from doing business in the United States" (Close Up Foundation, 1998).

A brief look at the history of U.S. policy responses to Mexican immigrants illustrates how racial prejudice and economic goals interact in U.S. immigration policy. As early as the nineteenth century, Mexican laborers began to organize unions and declare strikes to improve working conditions. The strikes were supported by "*mutualistas,*" which helped members pay for hospitalization and funeral expenses, provided low-interest loans, and offered support in times of need. For example, when 3,500 miners (most of them Mexican) went on strike against the Clifton-Morneci mines, mutualistas gave food, clothing, and other supports to strikers. In this case, despite the use of the National Guard to break the strike, workers were successful at extracting a wage increase.

During the early twentieth century, while laborers in the United States were struggling for wage parity Mexico itself was wracked by civil war. The Diaz government was overthrown in 1911 by Madeira, who was soon overthrown by General Victoriano Huerta. Huerta was forced into exile as two other generals battled revolutionaries Pancho Villa and Emiliano Zapata. The war was especially hard on civilians, and thousands fled north to avoid starvation, torture, or murder.

The migration northward from Mexico continued. Mexican laborers were well received, particularly in southern California and Texas, where they soon

---

B O X 14.2   Cesar Chavez (1927–1993)

Cesar Chavez organized the United Farm Workers (UFW) to advocate on behalf of migrant workers. The UFW has been responsible for improved living condi-tions and benefits for migrant workers throughout the country.

---

made up most of the construction and agricultural labor force. Differential pay scales persisted, and Anglo workers were typically paid more for the same work than Mexican immigrants, referred to as "Chicanos." Chicanos were also restricted to the most unskilled jobs and found it virtually impossible to move into managerial positions.

The Depression ended U.S. demands for Mexican labor, and a policy of "repatriation" was established. Chicanos who applied for welfare were given aid only upon agreeing to return to Mexico. Buses and boxcars were used to transport entire families—including children born in the United States—to Mexico. An estimated 400,000 Chicanos were "repatriated" during the Depression (Moquin, 1972).

World War II brought exploding demand for labor, and in 1942 the "Bracero Program" was introduced to encourage Mexican men to come north and work as contract agricultural laborers. Under an executive agreement between the United States and Mexico, approximately 350,000 men entered the United States to do agricultural work (Chavez, 1991). The program ended in 1960.

Since then national debate about undocumented Mexican immigration has ebbed and flowed, with some observing the huge economic contribution of undocumented workers and others seeking to exclude them as lawbreakers. One recent twist is the move to target employers. The 1986 Immigration Control and Reform Act (IRCA) established sanctions for the "knowing" hiring of undocumented immigrants (see http://migrationpolicy.org/pubs/PolicyBrief_No3_Aug05.pdf for more information on the IRCA).

Low-wage workers tend to rely more extensively on public services. Concern over the cost of services provided to immigrants, particularly undocumented immigrants, has led to policy restrictions on eligibility. Early policy on this topic came from the 1982 U.S. Supreme Court decision in the case of *Plyler v. Doe*. The Court invalidated a Texas law that allowed school districts to charge tuition to undocumented immigrants whose children attended public schools. In its ruling (drafted by Thurgood Marshall) the Court held that depriving these children of education would ultimately prove costly to the government, as uneducated children would be likely to rely on welfare in adulthood.

Political pressure to restrict public services to immigrants culminated in 1996 welfare reform legislation that would have denied Supplemental Security Income (SSI) and food stamps to legal immigrants and excluded undocumented immigrants from most public services. Amid the ensuing uproar, some of the law's more draconian measures were repealed. The Balanced Budget Act of 1997 restored SSI eligibility to most legal immigrants who had lost it under the 1996 law. In 1998, PL 105-185 restored food stamp eligibility to some legal immigrants.[4] Nonetheless, the rights of immigrants, both documented and undocumented, to receive public services that citizens take for granted are now open to dispute.

Humanitarian Goals.   As the inscription on the Statue of Liberty proclaims, the nation was founded in part on the humanitarian principle of serving as a haven for the world's oppressed. Humanitarian goals were explicitly promoted in immigration policy after World War II, when Congress passed the Displaced Persons Act of 1948 to allow some of the war's victims to come to the United States. Later, the Refugee Act of 1980 established a procedure for admitting refugees, legally defining them as people who flee their home nations because of persecution "on account of race, religion, nationality, membership in a particular social group, or political opinion."

U.S. immigration policy is a fascinating example of the nation's response to the demand for labor. It has frequently manifested the prejudices and superstitions of the political majority. At the same time, it is through immigration that the nation has attained, and continues to expand, its diverse cultural heritage.

Protecting Women and Children

A central focus of public debate and public policy during the late nineteenth and early twentieth centuries was the protection of women and children in paid employment.[5] Women have always worked, but under what historians term the "Doctrine of Separate Spheres," middle-class women and girls of the nineteenth century were largely restricted to domestic activities (Lasch, 1979). Children of tender years were kept home, but economic necessity forced some young boys to enter the workforce. In this section we will consider the history of policies that developed in the United States to protect women and children in the workforce.

Women in the U.S. Labor Force.   In the labor market a recurring challenge to public policies supportive of women has been Americans' belief (or hope) that if the free market is left unburdened by government regulation, it will ultimately provide fair conditions for all participants, be they male or female. In the workplace, American public policy has evolved from restricting women's job activities through "protective legislation" to prohibiting discrimination on the basis of gender.

---

4. The Balanced Budget Act was mentioned in Chapter 5.

5. A detailed history of women in the U.S. labor force is beyond the scope of this chapter. The interested reader will find material in Wandersee (1981), Weiner (1985), Kessler-Harris (1990), and Ware (1981). All of these sources were consulted extensively during the preparation of this section.

When women began entering the paid workforce, they were routinely paid less than men who held the same jobs. For example, when the federal government bought its first typewriters in 1867, it established a classification for clerk typists. Within this classification, women received $600 per year and men $1,200 per year (Simpson, 1985).

Working women of this era were excluded from most trade unions, so they established their own organizations. Unions in traditionally female occupations (laundresses, cap makers, and shoe workers) multiplied, and during the early 1900s the Women's Trade Union League was established to promote the formation of women's unions. Women also formed "protective leagues" to enhance working conditions and "abolish the sweatshop." Their successes prompted the development of protective legislation.

Protective Legislation for "Working Girls."   The turn of the century has been characterized as the era of the "working girl." In 1890, roughly one in five women, most of them young and single, were employed outside the home, usually in domestic service. Critics of female employment argued that women were rendering themselves either unfit or unable (if not unwilling) to assume their natural roles as wives and mothers (Weiner, 1985). In 1910 the U.S. Senate's study of employed women and children asked, "Is the trend of modern industry dangerous to the character of women?" (Kessler-Harris, 1990).

Protective labor laws were passed in the United States, Europe, and Australia during the post–World War I era amid rising concern that women were displacing men in manufacturing jobs and popular arguments that work diminished women's reproductive capacity. These laws restricted the number of hours women could work and regulated their wages. Though widely seen as an advance for working women, they had a paternalistic feel, implying that women might be safer if they remained outside the workforce (see Wikander, Kessler-Harris, & Lewis, 1995).

The impact of the laws was debated. Some argued that wage requirements kept women out of middle- and upper-level positions. There were reports of women being fired as soon as they completed apprenticeships and became eligible for higher wages. Women complained that restrictions in the hours they could work limited their ability to compete effectively for jobs (Weiner, 1985).

Ultimately, the wage restrictions established by protective legislation in the United States were overturned by court rulings. In 1923 the Supreme Court overturned the wage regulations in the District of Columbia, invoking the freedom-of-contract argument (*Adkins v. Children's Hospital;* Weiner, 1985). Consequently, protective laws gradually were either overturned or disregarded.

Working Mothers and the New Deal.   The widespread movement of married women into the labor force emerged as a significant trend in the United States during the 1920s. Prior to this period, even in families with very low incomes, less than one in four married women worked outside the home. African American women were the conspicuous exception to this rule. At all economic levels, a much higher proportion of African American wives and mothers worked. Wandersee (1981) argues that the increased employment of married women can be traced to an emerging ethic of consumption. With the emergence of mass marketing, the concept of an "American standard of living" became, as Wandersee puts it, "[something] all could aspire to, many would attain, and some would never know" (p. 21). The changing character of home life also contributed. As the home was transformed from a unit of production to a unit of consumption, women who needed productive roles sought them outside the home.

During the Great Depression, the federal government restricted employment of married women in the civil service through Section 213 of the Federal Economy Act. In the interest of "spreading the wealth," this legislation prohibited more than one member of the same family from working in the civil service. Within a year, more than 1,600 workers lost their government jobs. Although the act did not explicitly target women, three-fourths of those who lost their jobs were women. Nearly every state introduced bills to prevent employment of married women. Most Americans agreed with these practices, according to a 1936 Gallup poll (Abramowitz, 1996).

Despite their presence in the labor force, women were excluded from most New Deal legislation that was enacted on behalf of workers. For example, the Fair Labor Standards Act (FLSA), which regulated working hours, set a minimum wage, and prohibited child labor, specifically exempted domestic service from its provisions. The National Industrial Recovery Act (IRA), designed to "get industrial production moving again," covered only about half of employed women. Indeed, Wandersee notes that women who were most in need of protection—domestic laborers, laundresses not employed in laundries, and dressmakers not employed in factories—were among those explicitly excluded from the IRA's labor protections. Later, the Social Security Act of 1935 excluded domestic workers, thereby precluding coverage for approximately 30 percent of working women, many of them women of color (1981).

Failure of the New Deal legislation to address women's needs reflected strong disapproval of employment among women, particularly those who were married. This attitude was articulated by leaders of unions that supported the Roosevelt administration. Central to their arguments were two concerns: (1) that working women would displace working men, and (2) that, by working, women jeopardized the natural order of civilization.

Samuel Gompers, head of the American Federation of Labor during this era, focused on the first concern when he said, "In industries where the wives and children toil, the man is often idle because he has been supplanted" (Kessler-Harris, 1990, p. 19). The second concern was expressed by a contributor to a labor journal called the *American Federationist*: "Woman's greatest security is to be found in the home, and where rests the security of women rests the security of life, the security of civilization" (Wandersee, 1981, pp. 69–70). Another labor paper argued that "sisters and daughters" should not leave home, even for congenial workshops and factories, and vowed to check this "most unnatural invasion of our firesides" (Abramowitz, 1996, p. 189).

Both concerns were expressed in a 1937 petition by the legislature of North Dakota. In it, legislators asked that the Department of Labor study the growing problem of "home-keeping" women entering paid employment.

Whereas the employment of women in paid work outside the home has increased materially in recent years; and

Whereas the home-keeping women going into commercial and industrial work was mentioned by the report of the Biggers Committee on National Unemployment as one of the causes of the unemployment problem; and . . .

Whereas we all recognize the services rendered by the women of our homes in the building of character: Therefore be it Resolved, that the House of Representatives of the State of North Dakota, the Senate Concurring, hereby petition the . . . Department of Labor . . . to use its influence toward the securing of data on women employed outside the home . . . and thereupon to make a survey and a study of the problems of the home-keeping women, to find the reason for the tendency to leave home for commercial and industrial work and to make recom-

WWII women at work poster. Alfred Palmer, photographer (1943).

mendations to reduce and, so far as possible, eliminate this tendency in modern living. (*Congressional Record,* Vol. 84, p. 1271)

Of course, policies and attitudes toward working women shifted when World War II brought exploding demands for labor. Rosie the Riveter was emblematic of a broad-based campaign to encourage women to abandon their much-vaunted domesticity and contribute to the war effort. Millions responded. About 6 million women entered the workforce for the first time. Women's presence changed U.S. workplaces. For the first time, makers of steel-toed shoes had to produce them in women's sizes. And the women themselves were changed as well. In oral histories from the period many reported that they discovered new capabilities and overcame fears as the result of work experiences (Harvey, n.d.). Though many left the workplace when the war ended, public attitudes toward working women would never be the same (see the Regional Oral History Office of Bancroft Library for oral histories of women of this era at http://bancroft .berkeley.edu/ROHO/projects/rosie/).

Working Women and the Great Society.   Decades later, public policy reflected the shift in attitudes and beliefs about working women during World War II. In 1964, President Johnson signed the first piece of congressional legislation that acknowledged gender discrimination as a significant social problem: Title VII of the Civil Rights Act. Popular myth holds that Title VII was introduced by an opponent of civil rights as a joke, or with the intention of scuttling the act completely. Indeed, the "sex amendment" (as it was known) was introduced by a southern Democrat, Representative Howard W. Smith of Virginia. While the Civil Rights Act was being debated on the House floor, Representative Smith rose and offered a one-word amendment to Title VII, which prohibited discrimination in employment. The word was "sex," and it added women to the categories of individuals protected under the act. Evidently the amendment triggered several hours of "humorous debate," which Jo Freeman (1991) reports was later described as "Ladies' Day in the House." The amendment passed by a vote of 168 to 133.

Freeman and other historians agree that Smith's motivation in introducing the amendment was not humor. Instead, she argues, he was responding to tenacious lobbying by the National Women's Party (NWP). Composed of an elite group of highly educated and well-off women, the NWP was a consistent presence in the Capitol halls. They argued that sex discrimination was pervasive in the U.S. labor market, and if they did not succeed in persuading legislators to adopt their views, they undoubtedly persuaded Congress that the NWP would not go away empty-handed. Thus, when Representative Smith introduced the sex amendment, he was bowing to pressure. As we saw in Chapter 12, the NWP also lobbied for passage of the Equal Rights Amendment (ERA).

As soon as the sex amendment passed the House, women's organizations throughout the nation organized to support it. Unlike the ERA, this provision received the endorsement of the Women's Bureau and the League of Women Voters. It passed the Senate and was signed into law, to the utter indifference of the Equal Employment Opportunity Commission (EEOC). The EEOC considered the inclusion of sex "a fluke" that was "conceived out of wedlock." As Freeman notes, EEOC staff "tried to ignore its existence" despite the fact that one-third of the employment complaints filed during the commission's first year of existence (1965) charged discrimination on the basis of sex (1991, p. 164).

EEOC indifference set the stage for the founding of the National Organization for Women (NOW). As Rhode (1989) tells it, NOW was founded during the 1966 Conference of Commissions on the Status of Women. Frustrated by the EEOC's tolerance of help-wanted advertisements that discriminated on the basis of sex, "twenty-eight disaffected conference participants each paid five dollars to join a group that Betty Friedan spontaneously christened NOW. Its purpose, as recorded on the most accessible napkin, was 'to bring women into full participation in the mainstream of American society now'" (1989, p. 58). NOW's first target was sex-classified help-wanted advertisements. Bowing to NOW's efforts, the EEOC eventually declared that the practice violated Title VII, a view that was upheld by the Supreme Court in 1973.

It is an understatement to say that public attitudes and policies toward working women have changed. Despite these changes, as we will see in later sections of this chapter, working women in the United States have not achieved wage parity with men nor proportionate representation across occupations. Before we explore this topic more thoroughly, let us briefly consider the development of child labor policies in the United States.

Child Labor: A Target of Reform

During the late nineteenth and early twentieth centuries, reformers began to focus on child labor. Their concern reflected changes both in social expectations of childhood and in the conditions under which children were laboring.

The 1900 census revealed about 2 million children working in factories, mines, and other settings in the United States (U.S. National Archives & Records Administration, 2007). This finding triggered a national movement to end child labor. The National Child Labor Committee was founded in 1904 to prevent exploitation of children in the labor market. Their efforts were pivotal in focusing public attention on the issue. Ultimately, labor unions, the Consumer's Union, and eventually even industrial management went on record opposing the practice. Some laws were passed by the states, but there was growing demand for federal legislation.

In 1872, the Prohibition Party included a plank in its platform opposing child labor. Later, Republicans, Democrats, and Progressives all went on record calling for a federal law against the employment of children. Child labor was an early focus of the Children's Bureau, which documented conditions in factories where children worked. In 1906, Senator Beveridge, a Republican from Indiana, proposed to use the federal government's authority to regulate interstate commerce to ban the interstate sale of products made with child labor. The nation's first child labor bill, known as the Keating-Owen Child Labor Act of 1916, was based on this proposal.

BOX 14.3   Child Labor Continues in the United States

After the 1930s, child labor was eliminated from U.S. factories. But millions of children have continued to work illegally (Levine, 2003), and Human Rights Watch (2000) reports that hundreds of thousands of children currently are legally employed as agricultural workers.

The minimum age for a child to work on a farm is 12 years, although younger children can work with parental consent. Agricultural work is the nation's second most hazardous occupation (after mining, from which children are prohibited).

The bill was approved by Congress and signed by President Woodrow Wilson. But it proved controversial and was subjected to a Supreme Court challenge in the case of *Hammer v. Dagenhart*. The same Supreme Court justices who established the principle of "separate but equal" in *Plessy v. Ferguson* declared Keating–Owen unconstitutional. They also invalidated the second child labor law passed as part of the Revenue Act of 1919, which attempted to use the taxing authority of Congress to regulate child labor.

These Supreme Court rulings derailed federal attempts to reform child labor practices for nearly two decades. An attempt to ratify a Child Labor Amendment to the constitution was stalled in the 1920s, and the federal effort to restrict the use of child labor was not resuscitated until the 1938 passage of the Fair Labor Standards Act. This act, too, was the subject of a Supreme Court challenge, and in 1941 the Court upheld the law, reversing its earlier position (see *U.S. v. Darby*). As we will see near the end of this chapter, child labor today is regulated by policies at both the federal and the state levels.

Social Work and the Labor Movement

Social work has a long history of concern for labor issues. As part of the Progressive movement, social work leaders such as Florence Kelley, Lillian Wald, Mary van Kleeck, and Helen Hall supported the cause of workers through their writings and advocacy, and social workers were active in movements to

---

BOX 14.4   Mary van Kleeck

Considered a "communist sympathizer," Mary van Kleeck was pivotal in the left-wing "rank-and-file" movement in social work during the 1930s, arguing that the New Deal reforms did not go far enough in empowering and protecting workers. She resigned shortly after her appointment to the Advisory Council for Roosevelt's National Recovery Administration (NRA) to protest the president's decision to eliminate a clause in the legislation that protected labor's right to strike

in industries covered by NRA codes (Selmi & Hunter, 2001). Many of her insights have relevance today. For instance, in her well-known 1934 paper, *Our Illusions Regarding Government,* van Kleeck held that in a capitalist system "government is essentially dominated by the strongest economic power and becomes the instrument to serve the purposes of the groups possessing that power."

B O X 14.5   **Organizing Guinea Pigs**

In 2006, the largest drug testing site in North America was shut down by fire and health authorities in Florida. Evidently a company known as SFBC International was using the former Holiday Inn to house undocumented immigrants who were paid to participate in drug trials. This was not the first time treatment of "volunteers" in drug trials had come to the attention of authorities. In 1996, the *Wall Street Journal* reported that the Eli Lilly Company was hiring people from a local homeless shelter to test experimental drugs. With growing pressure to bring drugs to market quickly, drug trials are increasingly being carried out by private companies under contract to pharmaceutical companies. These testing firms hire vulnerable workers willing to submit to a range of tests as part of human trials for new drugs. Known as "guinea-pigging," the work is hazardous and largely unregulated. Since 2002, Bob Helms has been involved in "guinea pig activism." A former union organizer, Helms has established a jobzine that provides information and support to these workers. It offers interesting reading at www.guineapigzero.com (Elliott, 2008).

---

support labor (Karger, 1988). Jane Addams insured that the work of Hull House took into account the needs and problems faced by working Americans. As we saw in Chapter 4, Frances Perkins's role in the Roosevelt administration was pivotal, insuring that New Deal programs responded to the needs of workers. This tradition of knowledge and understanding of work's impact on individuals and communities helps distinguish social work from other mental health professions (Reisch, 1987).

It is probably fair to say that since World War II the labor movement has not been a central focus of social work practice and advocacy. The profession's attention to workplace issues has tended to involve employee assistance programs (EAPs), where social workers primarily serve the interests of management. In EAPs, the focus is on personal difficulties, such as substance abuse, that interfere with job performance; rather than with workplace problems such as low wages or discrimination (Chandler & Jones, 2003).

Recent decades have seen a decline in the power of unions throughout the country. As many as 22 states are "right to work" states (sometimes called "right to fire" states), which means that employees may not be required to join a union. Even if a majority votes in favor of union representation, individual employees may elect not to join. This limits the resources available to unions, which are nonetheless required to represent all employees in contract negotiations. Further, most states are "employment at will" states, in which employers can hire and fire at will and are not required to provide justification. Nonetheless, the right to organize and to bargain collectively is still a well-established doctrine in U.S. labor policy.

Of course, many employees are not represented by unions; many are not fluent in English; and many do not understand their rights. These workers are the natural focus of proactive social work intervention. By providing worker education, we can empower these workers and their families and reduce the dissolution, violence, and suffering that result from job stress and disruption. Through partnerships with unions we can help organize for better working conditions and enable workers to secure the rights to which they are entitled. Through our advocacy efforts we can expand (or at least preserve) legal protections for people who work for a living. There is much rewarding work to be done in this field, with great potential for advancing the cause of social justice.

Since the recession of the 1970s, a growing number of social work practitioners and scholars have turned their attention to the labor movement, recognizing that social work and organized labor share common goals and methods (Molloy & Burmeister, 1990; Selmi & Hunter, 2001). The 1996 welfare reform legislation offered further impetus to the alliance between social work and labor by thrusting clients of social workers into paid employment (Chandler & Jones, 2003).

At times it has been unclear what professional roles might be available for social workers in the labor movement. It is all very well to engage in advocacy, but without paid roles for practitioners it is unlikely that labor will become a professional priority (Selmi & Hunter, 2001). Unions have typically not delivered social services and thus have not been in a position to employ social workers.

There are a few examples of successful alliances between social work professionals and organized unions. During World War II, Bertha Reynolds organized a service program for the National Maritime Union that employed social workers on its staff (Reynolds, 1975). In the early 1990s, the Hunter College School of Social Work initiated an action research project in collaboration with Local 1199 of the Hospital and Health Care Employment Union. Researchers documented the needs of home care workers, and results were used in collective bargaining to secure much-needed benefits. The union then funded a service program to meet ongoing needs of its members (Donovan, Kurzman, & Rotman, 1993). After 9/11, Americans cut down on travel and Las Vegas was hit hard. Fifteen thousand members of the Culinary Union were laid off. The union responded by setting up a "Helping Hand Center" housed in a huge tent in their parking lot. Unemployment services set up an office there, as did the power company and United Way. In this way, union members who had been laid off could have a variety of needs met in one site (Chandler & Jones, 2003).

From a broad perspective, social work is part of the social protection afforded to Americans, mitigating the effects of the labor market on workers and their families. Our profession has a strong history of alliances with the labor movement. Given the growing vulnerability of workers in today's economy, it is vitally important that these efforts continue.

CONTEMPORARY REALITIES

Having completed our brief survey of the history of U.S. labor, we now turn to some contemporary realities that affect workers. First, we consider factors of general relevance, including the role of work in preventing poverty; inequality and U.S. workers; unemployment trends; the implications of rising productivity; and the rising cost of employee benefits. Then we will turn focus on conditions specifically affecting women and people of color in the workforce.

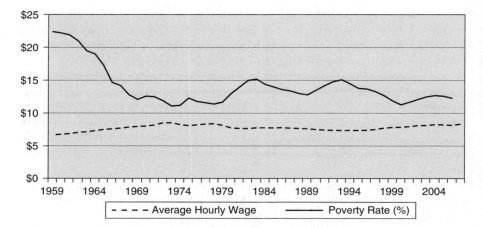

FIGURE 14.1 Wages and poverty in the United States: 1959–2007.

SOURCE: Wages: U.S. Department of Labor, Bureau of Labor Statistics Data. Employment, Hours, and Earnings from Current Employment Statistics Survey, Series ID: eeu0005000049. http://data.bls.gov (accessed February 21, 2008). Poverty figures: http://www.census.gov/hhes/www/poverty/histpov/hstpov2.html (accessed February 8, 2008).

Work as an Antipoverty Strategy

The status of American workers is inextricably linked to the fate of the nation's poor. The close association between poverty and wages is illustrated in Figure 14.1, which presents the percent of the population with incomes below the poverty threshold, as well as the average hourly wage. When hourly wages are high, the number of people living in poverty tends to decline. The converse is also true. (For those inclined toward research, the Pearson correlation between average hourly wages and the number living in poverty from 1959 to 2007 was -0.86, $p < .001$.)

The earnings numbers in Figure 14.1 have been adjusted for inflation and represent constant 1982 dollars. As you can see, hourly wages in the United States rose steadily during the 1960s, reaching a peak of $8.53 in 1973. These gains have not been duplicated. From 1973 wages steadily declined to reach to a historic low of $7.39 in 1995, just before the passage of PRWORA. They have risen slightly since, to $8.36 per hour.

For millions of Americans, work does not provide an exit from poverty. Roughly one in four full-time workers do not earn enough to raise a family of four above the poverty threshold (Mishel, Bernstein, & Boushey, 2004); and at least one person works in the majority of households with incomes below the poverty threshold (U.S. Bureau of the Census, 2003a). Of course, women and people of color are more likely to earn poverty-level wages than men and white Americans.

Inequality and U.S. Workers

Inequality among nations and individual Americans increased during the twentieth century. Further, inequality in the United States was greater at the beginning of the twenty-first century than it had been since the government began monitoring the income gap in 1947 (Blumberg, 1980). This trend had accelerated through the 1980s and persisted (but slowed) during the economic growth of the 1990s. The net effect of the past two decades on family income was to slightly decrease the income of the poor, leave middle-income families with minimal income growth, and tremendously increase the incomes of the most affluent. As the Center on Budget and Policy Priorities (CBPP) reported, "Nationwide, from the late 1970s to the late 1990s, the average income of the lowest-income families fell by over six percent after adjustment for inflation, and the average real income of the middle fifth of families grew by about five percent. By contrast, the average real income of the highest-income fifth of families increased by over 30 percent" (Bernstein et al., 2000, p. vii).

The causes of increased inequality in the United States are complex, involving the transition to a postindustrial economy as well as policy decisions that disadvantage low-income Americans. Researchers have documented stagnation in the lower and middle levels of the wage scale, accompanied by tremendous growth in the wages of highly paid employees such as CEOs (Bernstein et al., 2000; Burtless, 1999). Similarly, economic booms that increase investment income tend to benefit the affluent. Public policy also contributes to inequality. When policy makers unravel the safety net, fail to raise the minimum wage, or diminish labor protections, they further disadvantage low-income Americans. Regressive tax structures at the local, state, and federal levels can accelerate the trend toward greater inequality.

As a result of this economic trend, the United States today is a nation of extremes. In 2005, some 304,000 Americans enjoyed annual incomes in excess of $1 million, and 14,000 reported incomes higher than $100 million. At the other end of the spectrum, over 48 million reported having incomes of $20,000 or less (Internal Revenue Service, 2007). As Mantsios (2001) observes, "It would take the average American, earning $34,000 per year, more than 65 lifetimes to earn $100 million" (p. 170).

According to a recent study by the CBPP, "In the United States as a whole, the poorest 20 percent of families had an average income of $12,990 in the late 1990s, while the average income of families in the top 20 percent of the income distribution was $137,490, or more than 10 times as large" (Bernstein et al., 2000, p. ix). By contrast, the comparable ratio in Japan and Germany was 4 to 1 (World Bank, 2000).

The consequences of inequality, as distinguished from the effects of poverty, are difficult to tease out. There is some evidence that inequality has an independent effect on public health. One study reported that mortality and illness rates are higher in nations with above-average inequality than in those with comparable poverty rates but lower inequality (Burtless, 1999). Growing inequality can also result in greater geographic separation of rich from poor, a factor that contributes to inequalities in housing, public services, and schools (Bernstein et al., 2000). More difficult to measure are the effects of inequality on the cohesiveness of American society, as the wealthy become unable to fathom the plight of low-

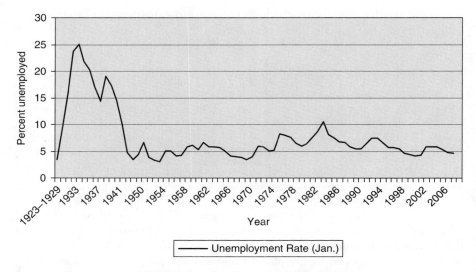

FIGURE 14.2 Unemployment trends in the United States: 1923–2007.

SOURCE: Data from 1923 to 1942: Bureau of Labor Statistics (2003). Compensation from before WWI through the Great Depression. http://www.bls.gov/opub/cwc/cm20030124ar03p1.htm (accessed January 21, 2008). Data from 1948 to the present: Bureau of Labor Statistics. http://www.bls.gov/webapps/legacy/cpsatab7.htm (accessed January 20, 2008).

wage workers and the poor become less able to believe in the American dream that hard work will pay off.

Unemployment in the United States

In 1932, during the height of the Great Depression, one in four U.S. workers was unemployed. Next to that figure, today's rate of 5 percent appears small. In fact, from an international perspective, unemployment is quite low in the United States. Among OECD nations, only Japan has a slightly lower rate (OECD, 2007).[6] Trends in U.S. unemployment rates are illustrated in Figure 14.2.

Unemployment figures are based on a very specific definition and do not include workers who are underemployed, unemployed people who are no longer seeking work ("discouraged" workers). U.S. unemployment figures are based on a monthly survey known as the Current Population Survey, in which a representative sample of about 60,000 U.S. households is interviewed. A person is considered unemployed if he or she is "jobless, looking for jobs, *and* available for work." Actively looking for work is carefully defined to include activities in the previous four weeks such as contacting an employer about an interview, sending out résumés, and answering advertisements. Workers who are temporarily laid off are counted as unemployed (Bureau of Labor Statistics, 2001).

---

6. The European Union uses a similar definition of unemployment (Eurostat, 2007); and when Japan's definition is adjusted to conform to the U.S. concept, Japan still has a lower rate of unemployment (Elder & Sorrentino, 1993).

BOX 14.6   Take Back Your Time Day

In 1926, Henry Ford revolutionized labor practices by introducing the five-day workweek. Ford argued that workers needed leisure time if they were to consume the goods his factories produced. Today America is no longer a leader in reducing the workweek. The average worker in this country puts in about nine weeks more on the job annually than European workers. To protest this reality, several organizations urge Americans to take the day off around October 24, nine weeks prior to the end of the year. The results, they argue, would be more jobs, along with environmental gains that would come from lower consumption. For more information on the movement to reduce the American workweek, visit www.shorterworkweek.com or the Shorter Work Time Action Page (www.swr.org).

The Implications of Rising Productivity

Rising productivity is a long-term trend in the United States. From an economic perspective, productivity can be measured as output per hour worked or output per worker. The U.S. economy has become more productive on both measures. More efficient or "lean" production and technological developments have made it possible to produce both goods and services with less human labor (Head, 1996).

The implications of rising productivity for workers are mixed. One might expect to see wages rise when an hour of work results in greater output. As we have seen, this has not been the case in the United States. One might also expect unemployment to increase as workers are displaced by outsourcing and replaced by technology. But, as we have seen, unemployment does not appear to be on the rise.

Over the centuries, technological advances have led to shorter workweeks. The hours worked each week dropped from 80 to 60 during the nineteenth century and from 60 to 40 during the twentieth century. Faced with rising unemployment, the Commission of the European Union favors shortening the workweek (Commission of the European Communities, 1982). The idea is catching hold in France and other nations, where a four-day workweek has been proposed.

Proposals for a shorter workweek have not been well received in the United States, however, and Americans with full-time jobs are working longer hours than they did in the 1920s (McGaughey, 2007). It is less expensive, even with overtime, to have one worker put in extra hours than to hire an additional worker. Originally designed to allow for rare extensions of the workweek in cases of emergency, overtime is now used to expand the ordinary workweek. This practice reflects the high cost of employee benefits.

"It's All About Benefits."   A recent article distributed by the Heritage Foundation proclaims that "compensation is keeping pace with rising productivity" (Sherk, 2007). How can this be true, given the stagnation in wages? The key term here is "compensation." Although wages have not increased to reflect rising productivity, benefits have risen. The rising cost of employee benefits is absorbing the gains we reap from rising productivity. As Sam said, "It's all about benefits."

Mostly, it's about health care. About half of the U.S. labor force has employer-sponsored health insurance (Bureau of Labor Statistics, 2005). Health premiums are one of the fastest-growing costs faced by U.S. companies. In 2006 alone, employer health insurance premiums rose by 7.7 percent, twice the rate of inflation. Small firms have been especially hard hit, with an increase of 10.5 percent in premiums for 2006. That year, the average premium paid for a family of four was $11,500. And employers are passing these costs on to employees, asking workers to either forgo raises or to pay higher proportions of their premiums. Indeed, the Kaiser Family Foundation reported that premiums for employer-sponsored health insurance have been increasing four times faster, on average, than worker earnings since 2000 (Kaiser Family Foundation, 2006).

Health insurance premiums are frequently on the agenda when union officials sit down with management in collective bargaining situations. Arguing that they are not in the health insurance business, employers ask workers to pay an ever-increasing share of ever-increasing premiums. Unions explore the possibility of providing health insurance themselves. Managers bemoan the rising cost of health care. Some contracts include clauses that release companies from responsibility for health insurance premiums in the event that government-sponsored care becomes available. As a negotiator for the steelworkers explained, "It's all about benefits" (Holland, 2007).

VULNERABLE GROUPS IN THE WORKFORCE

We have explored conditions that affect all workers: the failure of wage-based employment to insulate workers from poverty, rising inequality, pressure for high productivity, and the escalating costs of employee benefits. Now we will consider contemporary realities that particularly affect women and people of color.

Women as Workers in Today's Workforce

The massive involvement of women in the U.S. labor market dates to the latter part of the twentieth century. Prior to World War II, only 28 percent of adult women were in the labor force. By 2007, that figure had increased to 61 percent (Bureau of Labor Statistics, 2007a). Many of these women were mothers. By 1992, most mothers of children under 18 (67.2 percent) were in paid employment (Women's Bureau, U.S. Department of Labor, 1996); and by 2005 the employment rate of married mothers with school-aged children was 75 percent (Cohany & Sok, 2007). Even mothers of very young children are in the labor force. As of 1998, more than half (59 percent) of mothers of children one year old or younger were either working or looking for work (U.S. Bureau of the Census, 2000b).

In this section we will examine issues that have emerged with the growth in women's employment: gender differentials in earnings, child care, and women's pension needs.

Gender Differentials in Earnings.   Women earn less than men. In 2004, the Census Bureau reported the "female-to-male" earnings ratio stood at .77. This means that women who worked full-time earned 77 percent of what men working full-time brought home. To some extent, this reflects occupational segregation by gender.

Table 14.2 presents the distribution of American workers across major occupational groups. While women have made inroads into traditionally male occupations such as law and medicine, most remain in sales and service jobs. There are also important occupational differences between white women and women of color. White and Asian women have greater access to managerial and professional occupations than do African American and Hispanic women.

But even within occupational groupings, women consistently earn less than men. Table 14.3 presents median earnings of men and women within the major occupational groupings. Indeed, when the Census Bureau did a detailed look at earnings within occupations they found only five in which women's earnings nearly equaled those of men: highway maintenance workers, dieticians and nutritionists, engineering managers, other transportation workers, electronic home entertainment equipment installers and repairers, and tire builders (U.S. Bureau of the Census, 2004b).

Proponents of human capital theory (discussed in Chapter 5) would argue that this difference, known as a "wage gap," occurs because women are less

TABLE 14.2   **Occupational Distribution of American Workers: 2006**

Occupation	Percent of African American Men–Women	Percent of Hispanic American Men–Women	Percent of Asian American Men–Women	Percent of White/ Non-Hispanic Men–Women	Total Men–Women
Management and professional	22–31	14–22	49–46	33–39	32–38
Service occupations	20–27	19–31	13–19	12–19	13–20
Sales and office occupations	18–32	14–33	18–27	17–35	17–34
Natural resources, construction, and maintenance (farming)	14–1	31–2	8–1	21–1	20–1
Production and transportation	26–8	22–12	12–8	18–6	18–6

SOURCE: Bureau of Labor Statistics, Household Data, Annual Averages, Employed persons by occupation, race, Hispanic or Latino ethnicity, and sex. http://www.bls.gov/cps/cpsaat10.pdf (accessed February 8, 2008).

TABLE 14.3   Median Earnings of Men and Women in Major Occupational Groups

Occupational	Median Earnings, Men	Median Earnings, Women	Women's Earnings as Group, Percent of Men's
Management, professional, and related	$50,034	$35,654	71.3
Service	$26,000	$17,805	68.5
Sales and office	$35,079	$24,497	69.8
Farming, fishing, and forestry	$20,000	$15,996	80.0
Construction, extraction, and maintenance	$32,000	$29,000	90.6
Production, transportation, and material moving	$30,992	$20,850	67.3

SOURCE: U.S. Bureau of the Census (2003b). *Occupations: 2000*, Census 2000 Brief. http://www.census.gov/prod/2003pubs/c2kbr-25.pdf (accessed February 8, 2008).

committed to their work, receive less education, have interrupted work histories, and fail to build up seniority on the job.

Most studies of the topic, however, have found that these human capital factors do not fully account for the gender difference in wages (Bergmann, 1971; Caputo, 1998; Malkiel & Malkiel, 1973; Mitchell, Levine, & Phillips, 1999; Oaxaca, 1975). As Senator Cranston noted,

> Variables such as attachment to the workforce, level of experience, education, job commitment, and similar factors have been examined in various studies. These studies have attempted to explain the difference in earnings between male and female workers, but they have generally been able to account for less than one-fourth and never more than one-half of the earnings differentials on the basis of different labor force participation patterns of male and female workers. Virtually every research study has concluded that there remains a large gap which can be explained only by the existence of discriminatory employment practices. (*Congressional Record,* July 25, 1984, S9114)

Studies supporting Senator Cranston's views include those by Oaxaca (1975), Malkiel and Malkiel (1973), and Bergmann (1971).

The Equal Pay Act of 1963 required an employer to pay employees holding the same job the same wage. Title VII of the Civil Rights Act of 1964 went one step further, prohibiting wage discrimination on the basis of race, sex, religion, or national origin. A 1981 Supreme Court decision on pay scales for female prison guards in Oregon held that Title VII prohibits wage discrimination even when the jobs are not identical (*Gunther v. County of Washington*).

During the early 1980s, events in the state of Washington brought the high cost of gender discrimination to the fore. In December 1983, U.S. District Court Judge Jack Tanner ordered the state of Washington to raise salaries for workers in fields dominated by women in an effort to correct "pervasive" discrimination among state employees. The state was further ordered to pay back wages to women dating to the time the discrimination was identified. The decision was appealed, and the case was settled out of court.

This case became a catalyst for action at the state level, and other states have since adopted "comparable worth" plans or conducted comparable worth studies. In these studies, jobs are evaluated on the basis of four categories: knowledge and skills, mental demands, accountability, and working conditions. Ratings are assigned within each category and a final score computed for each job. When wages in jobs with equal scores show consistent disparity, advocates argue that gender discrimination is the primary explanation. Rather than lowering the salaries of highly paid employees, remedies consist of increases to underpaid employees each year until their salaries approach parity.

Progress toward comparable worth reflects the longstanding American tradition of using public policy to remedy failures of the free market. The history of attempts to legislate comparable worth reveals profound resistance. At the heart of most objections is a belief that the free market, left unchecked, will eventually provide economic justice. As a result, federal legislation on comparable worth has been introduced, but to date nothing has passed. (For more information on comparable worth, contact the National Committee on Pay Equity listed in the Suggested Resources section at the end of this chapter.) Most progress toward pay equity has been made in the public sector, with cities such as Colorado Springs, Los Angeles, and San Jose and states such as Minnesota and Washington implementing corrected pay scales for public employees.

Child Care.   At the beginning of the twenty-first century, the vast majority of mothers in the United States with children under 13 are employed. Their child care arrangements are, by and large, informal. As Hayes, Palmer, and Zaslow note, "The predominant form of non-parental care for all children 12 years old and under remains relatives" (1990, p. 229). The next most common form of child care is "family day care," in which a woman (usually a neighbor) looks after children in her own home. "Most family day care homes appear to operate in an underground market in which prices are relatively low" (p. 230), and an estimated 10 to 30 percent of these homes are licensed (Hayes et al., 1990). The widespread use of relatives and family day care in 1990 continues today (Kilburn & Hao, 1996; Morrissey & Banghart, 2007).

Federal initiatives in support of child care can take two forms: subsidies that compensate parents for child care expenses and direct payment for care. In recent decades, tax subsidies have represented a growing proportion of federal child care expenditures. In 1972, 80 percent of federal child care dollars were targeted to low-income families through provider subsidies such as Head Start and the Social Services Block Grant (SSBG) programs. By 1995, these combined programs accounted for about 69 percent of the total, while the child and dependent care tax credit alone accounted for 25 percent of federal expenditures in this area. This tax credit represents the single largest federal expenditure for child care (Kilburn & Hao, 1996). Like any tax deduction, child care tax credits now offered by the federal government as well as many states have greatest value to those with the highest federal tax obligation—those who owe the most income tax.

Another innovation, established as part of the Economic Recovery Act of 1981, permits employers to establish "flexible spending accounts" (FSAs) that allow employees to pay for their child care with "pretax dollars." Under these plans (regulated under Section 129 of the IRS code), employees specify their anticipated child care expenses up to $5,000 per year. The specified amount is withheld from gross salary on a regular basis and refunded upon presentation of receipts for child care expenses. Employers save Social Security and unemployment taxes on the portion of the salary allocated for child care, and employees are spared income and payroll taxes. Like the child care tax credit, this benefit is of greatest value to middle- and upper-income workers.

Federal interventions to expand child care availability to low-income women have applied direct expenditures to pay for care. Funding mechanisms have included Temporary Assistance for Needy Families (TANF), Head Start, the SSBG, and other preschool programs (Hayes, Palmer, & Zaslow, 1990; Kilburn & Hao, 1996). Federal programs also provide limited funding for infrastructure subsidies that enhance the supply and quality of available child care by financing increased training and wages for caregivers, improved standards and regulations, and extended resource and referral services.

Women and Pensions.   The disadvantages women experience in the wage market pale in comparison with their lack of employer-provided benefits. As Crystal and Shea (1990) point out, "A 'good' job may be distinguished from less 'good' jobs more sharply by its benefits, such as pension entitlement, than by its salary. The holder of such a 'good' job is more likely to be well-educated, to have a long-term attachment to the job and employer, to be male and to be white" (p. 438). As we will see in the following paragraphs, women are treated differently by private pensions.

Women are less likely to be covered by a pension during their working years, and as a result, less likely to have their retirement income supplemented by pension benefits. This gender difference may be a key factor behind the greater incidence of poverty among elderly women (see Chapter 13). The post–World War II growth in private pensions led to higher retirement incomes for men who retired during the 1980s. As Radner (1991) notes, "Pension income was the only income type that was a substantial positive factor in the growth in mean total income of the aged" (from 1979 to 1989) (p. 11).

A gender gap in pension income persists, however. In today's elderly cohort, men are still more likely than women to receive private pension income and women who do have pensions receive less income. In 2000, median pension income for women 65 and over was roughly half that of older men with pension income (Social Security Administration, 2000).

Some observers explain this gender gap by noting that the industries most likely to employ women (retail trade and nonprofessional services) are among those least likely to offer pension coverage. However, Korczyk (1993) argues that "[b]ased on all characteristics other than earnings, women are still less likely to be covered by pensions than similarly situated men" (p. 28). In her analysis, the gender gap persists among men and women who are similarly situated with respect to job tenure, industry, union membership, age, occupation, and firm size. She suggests that "[w]omen's pension coverage lags behind that of men largely because the labor market treats women differently from men" (p. 32).

The gender gap in pension income should diminish for future cohorts of women. Korczyk (1993) reports that the gender gap tends to be less pronounced among younger workers. Most studies of trends in pensions note that growing numbers of women workers have coverage (Evan & Macpherson, 1994; Wiatrowski, 1993). Of course, the extent to which increased coverage translates into higher retirement income remains to be seen.

In what might now be considered a historical quirk, both contributions and benefits under a private pension plan were once computed based on gender, with women required to contribute more and/or to receive lower monthly benefits. As Gohmann and McClure (1987) note, the practice "seems economically logical," given women's greater life expectancy. Nevertheless, it is now illegal.

In 1978, the Supreme Court used Title VII of the Civil Rights Act of 1964 to conclude that employers could not require women to make larger contributions to a pension plan in order to receive the same benefits a man in their situation would receive (*City of Los Angeles Department of Water and Power v. Marie Manhart*). A 1983 decision extended this ruling to preclude offering lower monthly benefits to women employees (*Arizona Governing Committee for Tax Deferred Annuity and Deferred Compensation Plans v. Nathalie Norris*).

Access to survivors benefits is another significant pension issue for women. Prior to 1974, about one in five covered workers were in plans with no provision for survivors. For wives of workers, the death of a spouse therefore meant complete loss of pension income, as well as a one-third reduction in Social Security benefits. Further, wives of workers whose plans did offer survivors benefits could be divested of those benefits without their knowledge or consent.

With the 1974 passage the Employee Retirement Income Security Act (ERISA), Congress accomplished the nation's first comprehensive pension reform legislation. Three subsequent laws have expanded ERISA protections: the Tax Equity and Fiscal Responsibility Act of 1982 (TEFRA), the Retirement Equity Act of 1984 (REA), and the Tax Reform Act of 1986. (These policies were also discussed in Chapter 13.)

Defined benefit plans must offer employees the opportunity to elect a "joint and survivor option" in which payments are made to survivors following the death of the worker. This option must be provided at the time of retirement. Workers who select it opt for lower retirement income in exchange for coverage that extends for the lifespan of their survivors. ERISA requires that a spouse give "knowing consent" when the worker elects to forgo the survivor annuity. The joint and survivor option is of limited value to low-wage workers who cannot afford to live on a reduced pension. The General Accounting Office reported that in 1989, only 45 percent of those with the lowest pension income elected survivor coverage (U.S. General Accounting Office, 1992). Of course, the growing number of workers who do not have a defined benefit plan do not have the option of electing joint and survivor coverage.

People of Color

In Chapter 9 we considered the role of discrimination and oppression in limiting the resources and opportunities available to people of color in the United States. These twin forces operate in the labor market as well. In particular, African American and Hispanic workers are subject to occupational segregation and elevated risk of unemployment.

African Americans. In Chapter 9 we saw that African Americans have lower household incomes than white Americans. Human capital explanations cannot fully account for this differential. For instance, at comparable levels of education, African Americans receive lower incomes than white Americans. In 2005, the median earnings of a non–Hispanic white American worker with a high school diploma or GED were 19 percent higher than those of an African American worker with similar preparation (U.S. Bureau of the Census, 2006b). The same year, the median income for white workers with a bachelor's degree or more was 12 percent higher than the median income for African American workers with similar preparation (U.S. Bureau of the Census, 2006b).

Some of the difference is clearly associated with occupational segregation. Although recent decades have seen significant gains in the occupational attainment of African Americans, they continue to be overrepresented in service occupations and production and transportation fields. This difference is illustrated in Table 14.2.

Unemployment rates provide another indication of labor force experiences. In 2006, the unemployment rate for African American men was 9.5 percent; more than double the rate for white men, which was 4.0 percent; similarly, African American women had an unemployment rate of 8.4 percent, compared to 4.0 percent for white women (U.S. Bureau of Labor Statistics, 2007b).

Hispanic Americans. Similar trends influence the earnings of Hispanic workers in the United States. Like African American workers, Latinos are overrepresented in the lower-paying service occupations and in production and transportation fields. They are also the group most likely to be employed in natural resources, construction, and maintenance occupations.

Unemployment among Hispanic Americans in 2006 was higher than among whites. The rate for Hispanic American men was 4.8 percent, while the rate for white men was 4.0 percent; for Hispanic women, unemployment was 5.9 percent, compared to 4.0 for white women (Bureau of Labor Statistics, 2007b).

As we have seen, in the United States hard work does not guarantee economic security, and for many it does not ensure a comfortable quality of life. Throughout this volume we have identified some of the factors contributing to this insecurity: limited growth in the average hourly wage, rising numbers of uninsured, and increasing pension insecurity. As we will see in the next section, U.S. labor policy offers limited protections to workers.

CURRENT U.S. LABOR POLICIES

Like most U.S. social policies, labor policy involves the interaction of federal and state laws that have accumulated over decades. They reflect the thinking, not of a single mind, but of hundreds or even thousands of competing perspectives. The result is at times inconsistent, even irrational. A detailed consideration of labor law is clearly beyond the scope of this section, which will focus on policies that commonly apply once a person has been hired. These fit roughly into four categories: laws that govern wages and benefits, protective and antidiscrimination measures, health and safety policies, and laws that govern employee discharges. Finally, the Earned Income Tax Credit stands alone, illustrating an effective use of tax policy to enhance the well-being of low-income workers.

Wages and Benefits

The Minimum Wage.   The minimum wage was established in 1938 through the Fair Labor Standards Act. According to a Department of Labor historian, "When he felt the time was ripe, President Roosevelt asked Secretary of Labor Perkins, 'What happened to that nice unconstitutional bill you had tucked away?'" (Grossman, 1978). Evidently, Perkins's willingness to become secretary of labor was at least partly conditional on Roosevelt's agreement to promote a law that would "put a floor under wages." So, in 1938, despite outraged industrial opposition, the minimum wage was set at 25 cents per hour.

The law is enforced by the Wage and Hour Division of the Department of Labor. The minimum wage is not indexed to inflation, so any increase requires congressional and presidential approval. Since its passage, the minimum wage has been raised 17 times, most recently (at the time of this writing) in July 1997, when it rose to $5.85 per hour.

An estimated 12.5 million workers are affected by the minimum wage (U.S. House of Representatives, 1999). There are a number of exemptions. For example, youth (who are under 20 years of age) are subject to a subminimum wage during their first three months of employment.

Objections to increasing the minimum wage typically come from business representatives and conservative Republicans, who argue that thousands of low-wage workers will lose their jobs. As one advocate argued on the Internet, "Studies suggest that for every 10 percent increase in the minimum wage, a minimum of 100,000 jobs are lost" (Cox, 1997). There is no evidence to support this claim.

Benefits.   Federal law distinguishes between two types of employee benefits: pension benefits and welfare benefits. Pension plans that qualify for favorable tax treatment are subject to "nondiscrimination" rules. This means that an employer cannot arbitrarily provide pension coverage to a few favorite employees while neglecting the rest. Under the Employee Retirement Income Security Act (ERISA) of 1974, as amended, pension plans are also subject to "vesting" requirements. After these requirements have been met, workers have the legal right to receive a pension, even if they leave the job.

Welfare benefits, such as health insurance, life insurance, and disability coverage, are subject to fewer restrictions. Like pension plans, these benefits are also given favorable tax treatment. (They are deductible as a business expense.) But employers enjoy wide discretion in determining how, when, and to whom they will be offered.

Leave is also considered an employee benefit. Some countries stipulate the amount of leave employers must provide. In New Zealand, for example, workers are legally entitled to three weeks of paid leave and 11 paid public holidays each year. Apart from provisions governing family and medical leave, the United States does not enforce policies regarding employee leaves.

Family and Medical Leave.   More than 80 percent of working women are in their prime childbearing years (between the ages of 18 and 44). Further, in 2003, 25.6 percent of all families with children were headed by a single woman, roughly double the 1970 proportion of 13 percent (Mulroy, 1995; U.S. Bureau of the Census, 2004b). Small wonder that in the 1999 Report on the American Workforce, the U.S. secretary of labor declared, "Since 80 percent of families now depend partly or fully on the paychecks of mothers . . . helping families deal with the competing needs of the home and the workplace must also be among our highest priorities" (Herman, 1999).

In 1985 the first family and medical leave bill was introduced during the 99th Congress. Congress adjourned without voting on the bill. During the 100th Congress the bill was reintroduced and amended several times. During the 101st Congress, the bill was amended and passed both the House and the Senate. It was vetoed by President George H. W. Bush on June 29, 1990. A House vote failed to override the veto. During the 102nd Congress, the bill was reintroduced and, after some amendment, passed both the House and the Senate. President Bush again vetoed the bill on September 22, 1992. The Senate voted to override the veto, but the House did not. The Family and Medical Leave Act was introduced on January 21, 1993, passed both houses, and was signed into law by President Clinton on February 5, 1993 (PL 103-3). Thus, debate about family and medical leave continued through eight years and two presidential vetoes before passage of the act in 1993.

Under its current provisions, the Family and Medical Leave Act provides for up to 12 weeks of unpaid, job-protected leave per year—with uninterrupted health insurance coverage—for the birth or adoption of a child or the serious illness of the employee or an immediate family member. Businesses with fewer than 50 employees (a classification that includes most employers) are exempt. Employee eligibility is restricted to those who have worked 1,250 hours (25 hours per week) over the previous 12 months and who have worked at least 12 months. Employers may exempt key employees from coverage. Employees are required to provide 30 days' notice for foreseeable leaves and make a reasonable effort to schedule medical treatments to avoid unduly disrupting employers' operations. Employees must also provide medical certification justifying the need for the leave in the case of illness. Enforcement provisions parallel those of the Fair Labor Standards Act, with damages limited to double actual losses and a "good faith" exception granted to employers with reasonable grounds for believing they have not violated the act.

PROTECTIVE AND ANTIDISCRIMINATION STATUTES

In this section we will briefly review policies that have been developed to protect children in the workplace, as well as antidiscrimination statutes that target women, people with disabilities, and older workers.

Child Labor Laws

Federal laws restrict the hours and types of jobs that children may work. Some states have additional, stricter provisions. Under federal law, restricted hours apply only to children aged 14 and 15. They may work from 7 A.M. to 7 P.M., except when school is in session. During the summer they may work until 9 P.M. They may work no more than 3 hours on a school day, 18 hours in a school week, 8 hours on a nonschool day, and 40 hours in a nonschool week. Children 16 or older are not subject to restrictions in working hours, and these restrictions do not apply to farm labor.

In the United States, children under 13 may work in several positions. They may deliver newspapers, babysit, work as an actor or performer, work in a business solely owned or operated by their parents, and work on a farm owned or operated by their parents. Parents may not employ their children in manufacturing, mining, or any occupation declared hazardous by the secretary of labor. When they turn 14, children may work in offices, grocery stores, retail stores, restaurants, movie theaters, baseball parks, amusement parks, and gas stations. They may not work in several occupations, including construction, driving, manufacturing, and any occupation declared hazardous. When they turn 16, they may work in any occupation not declared hazardous. At 18 years of age, child labor laws no longer apply.

The Pregnancy Discrimination Act

Until 1993, American women had only limited job protection when they became pregnant. What protection they did have dated to the Pregnancy Discrimination Act of 1978, which amended Title VII of the Civil Rights Act of 1964 to ensure that pregnant women would be treated the same as other employees. Essentially, the act required that states and employers extend temporary disability insurance policies to cover pregnant women. The Pregnancy Discrimination Act passed after heated debate, with opponents claiming it would

---

B O X 14.7   The Aging Workforce

The American workforce is aging. In part, this change reflects the reversal of a male trend toward early retirement. Women, on the other hand, have shown a steady increase in late-life employment over the decades. As if anticipating this trend, 80 percent of baby boomers report that they expect to work during their retirement years. Yet many workers—some say as many as one in three—must leave the workforce involuntarily due to ill health, a layoff, or a family problem (Munnell, 2006).

---

substantially increase costs to business, create unfair economic burdens, and even lead to increased discrimination against women of childbearing age.

Accommodation

As we have seen, the Americans with Disabilities Act (ADA) was enacted in 1990 to prohibit discrimination against people with disabilities. Public and private organizations are required to make "reasonable accommodation" to enable people with disabilities to perform job requirements, use transportation services, and access public venues. Accommodation might include changes in existing facilities, restructuring jobs or modifying work schedules, acquiring devices or equipment, or providing readers or interpreters. Companies and organizations may forgo making accommodation if doing so would present them with "undue hardship," a term that is redefined based on the company's size, budget, and operations.

Determining what constitutes a disability is not solely a technical consideration. Politics and philosophy come to bear as well. Today, individuals who are disabled by virtue of addiction to alcohol or drugs are not protected under the ADA, but those who suffer from psychiatric diagnoses are covered. Individuals with contagious diseases such as HIV/AIDS and tuberculosis are covered by the ADA. People whose skills are limited by a learning disability are covered, while those who lack access to learning opportunities are not. Those experiencing stressful lives are not covered by the ADA, but those with a stress disorder that has been diagnosed by a psychiatrist are covered. Since 1994, the ADA has applied to employers with 12 or more employees. Its provisions are enforced by the Department of Justice.

Age Discrimination in Employment

Prior to passage of the Age Discrimination in Employment Act (ADEA) in 1967, help-wanted advertisements could, and did, list age as a basis for hiring. The notion that "older workers need not apply" was widespread and, as Schulz (1995) argues, may have been the cause of longer periods of unemployment experienced by older men. The 1964 Civil Rights Act did not prohibit discrimination on the basis of age. But Congress did direct the Department of Labor to conduct a study of age discrimination. The following year, a report submitted to Congress revealed "a persistent and widespread use of age limits in hiring that in a great many cases can be attributed to arbitrary discrimination against older workers on the basis of age and regardless of ability" (Rich & Baum, 1984, p. 179).

The ADEA prohibits discrimination on the basis of age in hiring, discharge, compensation, benefits, and other terms of employment. Its stated purpose is to "promote employment of older persons based on their ability rather than age; to prohibit arbitrary age discrimination in employment; to help employers and workers find ways of meeting problems arising from the impact of age on employment" (U.S. Labor Code, Title 29, Chapter 14, Section 621, Congressional Statement of Findings and Purpose, http://www.law.cornell.edu/uscode/29/621.html).

ADEA protections originally extended only to workers between the ages of 40 and 65, but the act was amended in 1978 to cover workers up to age 69 and in 1986 to extend to workers of any age. The act applies only to employers with 20 or more employees and allows for discrimination when age is a "bona fide occupational requirement"—that is, when the employer can demonstrate a rational basis for the use of age-based decision making. Typically such requirements have been applied to airplane pilots and air traffic controllers.

As Schulz (1995) notes, "It is difficult to determine the extent to which actual discrimination has in fact lessened" (p. 73). Between 1991 and 1995, an average of 17,000 complaints of age discrimination were filed each year with the Equal Employment Opportunity Commission (EEOC) (Administration on Aging, 1997). These complaints probably represent the tip of the iceberg, and it is fair to say that age-based discrimination remains an elusive social problem. Perhaps the ADEA's greatest impact is symbolic. The simple fact that age discrimination in employment is against the law of the land is, in itself, a statement of American values and expectations regarding the elderly.

Health and Safety Policies

OSHA.   In 1970, Congress passed the Occupational Safety and Health Act to reduce workplace exposure to identified hazards, such as toxic chemicals, excessive noise, mechanical dangers, stressful heat and cold, and unsanitary conditions. The act establishes a "general duty" for employers to eliminate recognized hazards from the workplace. It also requires employers to comply with standards and guidelines issued by the U.S. Occupational Safety and Health Administration (OSHA).

Housed in the Department of Labor, the OSHA oversees enforcement in the 50 states. The OSHA issues detailed standards, such as "safety and health regulations for longshoring," as well as more general guidelines, such as the recent "ergonomic guidelines for the poultry processing industry." Federal and state OSHA officials conduct thousands of workplace inspections each year. These may be triggered by employee complaints, reports from other agencies, or accident reports. All employers are required to display an OSHA poster that informs employees of their safety and health rights. These posters are available in English and Spanish. Employers are encouraged to establish cooperative relationships with the OSHA by seeking consultation about safety issues and accident prevention.

Sexual Harassment. In 1991 many Americans were glued to their televisions, watching Anita Hill, a young law professor, testify that she had experienced sexual harassment at the hands of President Reagan's nominee to the Supreme Court. The experience contributed to a growing awareness of the issue of sexual harassment in the workplace. Since then, thousands of women and some men have filed lawsuits claiming they were sexually harassed. The result has been a potpourri of (sometimes contradictory) judgments and a growing number of "backlash" lawsuits by alleged perpetrators against companies from which they were dismissed.

What is sexual harassment? Current law recognizes two forms of sexual harassment. In "quid pro quo harassment," sexual favors are demanded in exchange for favorable treatment, or rebuffing sexual advances involves the risk of reprisal. Another form of harassment, recognized since a 1986 ruling by the Supreme Court (*Mentor Savings Bank v. Vinson*) involves the creation of an "intimidating, hostile, or offensive" work environment. Both of these types of harassment are recognized by the EEOC as forms of sex-based discrimination. (See EEOC, "Guidelines on Discrimination Because of Sex," Title VII, Section 703, *Federal Register,* 45, April 11, 1980.)

Both forms of sexual harassment are prohibited by Title VII of the Equal Rights Act (Maypole & Skaine, 1983). Title IX of the Higher Educational Amendments of 1972 prohibits sexual harassment on college and university campuses. State laws governing assault and battery or infliction of emotional distress have been applied to cases involving hostile work environments (Thomas, 1991). Finally, most large employers and public agencies have established policies that prohibit sexual harassment and establish procedures for victims to pursue. Often these are "zero tolerance" policies, specifying that the slightest hint of sexual harassment will bring about disciplinary action.

In some cases, men who have been charged with sexual harassment have won large settlements against their former employers. Often these "backlash" cases charge that a man's First Amendment right to freedom of speech has been violated. In one 1993 case (*Silva v. University of New Hampshire*), a court reinstated a professor who had been suspended for using sexual metaphors in his technical writing class. Other backlash cases have resulted in large settlements being awarded to men who were discharged on the basis of allegations of sexual harassment (e.g., *Mackenzie v. Miller Brewing Co.*).

Despite the array of policies and procedures designed to prevent and remedy sexual harassment, judicial practices and employment realities often prevent women from reporting incidents and pursuing legal remedies. In *Mentor Savings Bank v. Vinson,* the Supreme Court ruled that a victim's "sexually provocative" speech or dress was relevant to whether the conduct was offensive. This ruling opened the door to defenses that put women on trial for their relationships, behavior, and attire. Further, some courts have required that women demonstrate they resisted or complained about unwanted sexual demands. Thus women who

were in no position to refuse or complain may be denied access to legal remedies. In 1994, President Clinton signed the Violence Against Women Act, which
restricts the extent to which a plaintiff's personal history can be brought in to
defend against allegations of sexual harassment.

The EEOC and the courts have seen growing numbers of sexual harassment
complaints. Between 1991 and 1998, the number of claims filed with the EEOC
increased from 7,000 to 16,000 (Henetz, 1998).[7] Resolving these cases often
proves difficult, the body of case law regarding sexual harassment is contradictory, cases can degenerate into "he said/she said" allegations that are difficult to
sort out, and there continues to be confusion regarding the distinction between
harassment and discrimination.

As Yale University law professor Vicki Schultz has noted, it is important to
keep in mind that prohibition of sexual harassment does not prohibit sexuality per
se, but gender discrimination. The goal of this policy is to achieve equality in the
workplace, not to prosecute people who tell off-color jokes (Schultz, 1998).

Discharge Policies

Several policies are relevant when a worker leaves a job. These include notice
requirements and measures governing health insurance.

Notice. Under the Worker Adjustment and Retraining Notification of 1988
(WARN), employers of more than 100 workers must provide at least 60 days'
notice of plant closings and mass layoffs. Both terms are defined by the
Department of Labor (see http://www.doleta.gov/programs/factsht/warn.htm).
WARN provisions can also apply to the sale of a business. In addition to these
federal provisions, state laws bear on the nature of notice required when an
employee is laid off. Federal law does not require that employees be given advance notice of individual discharge decisions.

Health Coverage. When employees receive group health coverage, the employer is required to give them notice of their rights under the Consolidated
Omnibus Budget Reconciliation Act (COBRA), passed in 1986. COBRA requires that "qualified beneficiaries" (employees with health coverage) be provided the opportunity to purchase membership in the group health plan when
they lose group coverage due to loss of employment, retirement, divorce, death,
or employer bankruptcy. Keep in mind that bankruptcy does not necessarily
mean a company will go out of business. As we have seen with Kmart and other

---

7. Men, too, have been subjected to sexual harassment. In fact, a 1998 Supreme Court
ruling (*Oncale v. Sundowner Offshore Services*) held that "[t]he prohibition of sexual harassment does not necessarily speak to an individual's gender, but forbids behavior so objectively offensive as to alter the conditions of the victim's employment." In this ruling the
Court focused on the severity and persistence of the harassment. Roughly 12 percent of
sexual harassment claims filed in 1997 involved male victims.

firms, a company can use bankruptcy protection to reorganize its debt and then continue to do business. COBRA applies to voluntary and involuntary departures but not to individuals who are fired for gross misconduct. COBRA restricts the cost of coverage to 102 percent of the actual cost to the employer for people who are similarly situated; and the coverage must be identical to that provided before the "qualifying event." Employees have up to 60 days to decide whether or not to "elect" coverage, and the first premium is due within 45 days of the election. The usual duration of coverage is 18 months, but this can be extended in a range of circumstances. (In cases of divorce or legal separation, COBRA coverage may be required for as many as 36 months.) Coverage may be terminated if an employer terminates all of its group health coverage. The federal COBRA law does not apply to health plans that cover fewer than 20 employees, although some states extend the law to smaller businesses.

Whereas COBRA is designed to help workers maintain their health coverage upon the loss of a job, the Health Insurance Portability and Accountability Act of 1996 (HIPAA) was designed to maintain coverage while employees move to different jobs. HIPAA does this by restricting the extent to which insurers can exclude "preexisting conditions" from coverage. Under HIPAA, no insurer can deny coverage for preexisting conditions for more than 12 months, or 18 months in some cases. Further, the insurer is required to provide "credit" for continuous health coverage prior to enrollment. So a person who is continuously covered by group health insurance in one job should not be subject to exclusion for preexisting conditions when enrolling for coverage with a second employer. HIPAA does not specify the nature or cost of the coverage that is offered. It simply protects the employee from multiple periods without coverage for ongoing conditions. Other HIPAA provisions relate to the privacy of health records.

HIPAA applies to virtually all employers with at least two employees. It prohibits insurers from denying coverage to a group based on the health status of an individual in this group. This was seen as a way to help small companies maintain group health coverage in the event an employee or employee's dependent developed a catastrophic health problem.

Earned Income Tax Credit

Established in 1974, the EITC has become one of the nation's most effective and popular antipoverty initiatives. The EITC is also relatively unknown, to the extent that it could be considered a "hidden entitlement." Some view it as a way to offset the regressive effects of the payroll tax on low-income workers (see Chapter 4 for a discussion of the payroll tax). It also rewards work and supplements the earnings of low-income families with children (Hoffman & Seidman, 1990; Phillips, 2001).

The EITC, which is administered by the Internal Revenue Service (IRS), provides a refundable tax credit to eligible taxpayers. For low-income families, the EITC consistently exceeds their federal income tax obligation. In such cases, the IRS would first apply the credit to any taxes owed and then send the remaining amount directly to the family. In fiscal year 2000, the program distributed approximately $30.4 billion, an amount that exceeded federal expenditures on TANF and roughly equaled the combined federal expenditures for food stamps and SSI. In some states (18, as of this writing), federal EITC benefits are supplemented by state-earned income credits (http://www.cbpp.org/eic2007/EIC_Facts_Text.pdf, accessed February 8, 2008).

The EITC offers substantial gains to low- to moderate-income working families, with the greatest benefits going to families with children. In 2006, a qualifying family with one child could receive a credit worth as much as $2,747 (http://www.irs.gov/individuals/article/0,,id=150513,00.html, accessed February 8, 2008). This amount would have phased out completely when their annual income reached $34,001. Workers without children could have received up to $412 in 2006, with the credit phasing out at an income level of $14,120 (http://www.irs.gov/individuals/article/0,,id=164506,00.html, accessed February 8, 2008).

The EITC is a powerful antidote to poverty. In 2005, more than 22 million taxpayers received $41.4 billion dollars in EITCs, and the credit lifted millions of families out of poverty. Porter and colleagues (1998) report that the EITC has lifted more children out of poverty than all federal assistance programs combined.[8]

Despite its advantages, the EITC has encountered criticism. First, the IRS has reported a 21-percent error rate in EITC payments, which has detractors to claim that it is simply another opportunity for poor people to "work the system." Second, because moderate-income workers experience a high rate of tax on earnings while the EITC is being phased out, opponents of the credit argue that the higher rates represent a disincentive to work; however, there is no evidence to support this view (Hoffman & Seidman, 1990).

SUMMARY: FUTURE PROSPECTS

In *The End of Work,* Jeremy Rifkin argues that "the commodity value of human labor is becoming increasingly tangential and irrelevant." As technology advances and the world's productive processes are restructured, the overall demand for workers may diminish. Some highly skilled and trained workers may be unaffected. But others, particularly those who have earned their living with physical or unskilled labor, are increasingly vulnerable. Clearly social workers must be at the forefront of efforts to sustain these workers and their families.

Over the long term employment trends could force us to rethink the way we value human beings. For centuries the dominant measure of a person's worth has been the market value of his, or more recently, her labor. Given our

---

8. In 2000, nearly four times as many individuals received the EITC as participated in the TANF program. Approximately 5.7 million individuals received TANF in July 2000 (http://ferret.bls.census.gov/macro/032003/pov/new29_100_01.htm).

appreciation of the complex nature of individuals and communities, social workers are especially well positioned to encourage a cultural shift to a new perspective that values human beings as ends in themselves, rather than as means to an economic goal.

KEYWORDS

Employment

Gender equity

Gender gap

Labor Movement

Sexual harrassment and laws

Sexual harrassment and regulations

Unions

THINK ABOUT IT

1. As professionals, social workers are expected to place client needs above self-interest. Yet, as workers, we may need to resort to strikes to improve both working conditions and the quality of the services we provide. Under what circumstances would you be willing to go on strike? Would you ever cross a picket line to deliver services?

2. What changes do you think are needed to reduce the illegal employment of children in the United States?

3. The movement of undocumented workers across the Mexican border has become a hot topic in recent years. How would you explain the current focus on this topic? Is it due to economic changes? To 9/11? To something else?

4. Apply the five-question social justice framework presented in Part I to a proposal to increase the minimum wage. Once you have finished with Question 5, add a sixth question: "Why do I believe this is/is not fair?" Consider how your personal philosophy and experiences have influenced your answer to Question 5.

5. Compare the antipoverty impact of the EITC with that of TANF. Which program more effectively moves families out of poverty? How would you explain this difference? Does your state provide an Earned Income Tax Credit for low-income workers? If not, is this an agenda item for local poverty advocates? Why or why not?

WEB-BASED EXERCISES

For direct links to all the sites in these exercises, log on to the Student Companion Site for this book at academic.cengage.com/social_work/barusch, and choose Chapter 14.

1. Go to http://www.bls.gov/cps/#empstat. Scroll down to the section labeled "Characteristics of the Unemployed." Now answer the following questions using the data provided:
    a. What racial or ethnic group has the highest rate of unemployment?
    b. Does unemployment vary by marital status?
    c. What age group has the longest median duration of unemployment? Why do you think this is so?

2. Go to the website for the U.S. Equal Employment Opportunity Commission (www. EEOC.gov). Click on race under "Discrimination by Type: Facts and Guidance," and review the material under "Race/Color Discrimination" on that page. Now click on "Charge Statistics: Race Discrimination" at the bottom of the page to examine trend data from 1994 to 2004 regarding charges of discrimination (labeled "receipts") as well as the outcome of the case. (These statistics are also available in a more general table at http://www.eeoc.gov/stats/charges.html.) Look at the track record of the Bush administration in this area (years 2001–2004) and answer the following questions:
    a. Did the number of complaints change during this period? ("receipts")
    b. What proportion of complaints resulted in a finding of "no reasonable cause"?
    c. What proportion resulted in a finding of "reasonable cause"?
    d. How did the monetary benefits secured by the EEOC change during this period?
    e. What conclusions can you draw from these figures about the role of the executive branch in implementing antidiscrimination policies?

SUGGESTED RESOURCES

Akabas, S. H., & Kurzman, P. A. (2005). *Work and the Workplace: Innovative Policy and Practice*. New York: Columbia University Press.

Economic Policy Institute. (2007). *The State of Working America, 2006/2007*. Available at http://www.stateofworkingamerica.org/intro_main.html.

Ehrenreich, B. (2001). *Nickel and Dimed: On (Not) Getting by in America*. New York: Metropolitan Books.

Rifkin, J. (1995). *The End of Work: The Decline of the Global Labor Force and the Dawn of the Post-Market Era*. New York: G. P. Putnam's Sons.

Zweig, M. (2000). *The Working Class Majority: America's Best Kept Secret*. Ithaca, NY: Cornell University Press.

www.bls.gov. On this site the U.S. Bureau of Labor Statistics provides a gold mine of information, both current and historic, about labor in the United States.

www.eeoc.gov. This is the official site of the Equal Employment Opportunity Commission. It offers information on federal laws, background on the EEOC, instructions for filing a complaint, and news releases.

www.ufw.org. The United Farm Workers (UFW), now part of the AFL-CIO, continue their advocacy on behalf of migrant workers. At their site you will find action items, news releases, and inspiring quotes from UFW leaders.

Conclusion

Cycles of Liberation

If you have come to help me you are wasting your time. But if
you have come because your liberation is bound up with mine,
then let us work together.
ABORIGINAL WOMAN
FAITHFUL FOOLS STREET MINISTRY

In the conclusion to this text, we will explore possibilities, both frightening
and exhilarating, that lie ahead in social policy and the practice of social
work. We will begin with a brief glance at the concept of liberation.

Liberation is integral to the pursuit of social justice and the practice of social
work. But the advance toward liberation is neither tidy nor linear; instead, it
cycles back and forth between progress and backlash. Progress encompasses personal empowerment, community building, and cultural transformation—social
development in what social workers might call "micro," "meso," and "macro"
systems. Of course, liberation need not necessarily proceed from micro to macro.
Broad social movements contribute to personal empowerment even as personal
change can strengthen communities.

Liberation flourishes on solidarity and love. While noting pervasive domination based on sex, race, and class, bell hooks (2001) describes a process of liberation
based on a loving solidarity across sex, race, and class boundaries. She suggests, "As
we work to be loving, to create a culture that celebrates life, that makes love possible, we move against dehumanization, against domination" (p. 608).

As agents of change, social workers tap into cycles of liberation at various
levels. We work at the interface of individual and community, applying empowerment strategies to transform lives and build communities. We seek to make

policies more responsive to the people they affect, and battle against a tendency to use the force of government to oppress out-groups. In transformative micro practice we help build personal strengths so clients can understand and solve their problems in a broader context. Andrea Ayvazian (2001) describes the transformative potential of our profession well when she notes, "What does seem to create real and lasting change is highly-motivated individuals—usually only a handful at first—who are so clear and consistent on an issue that they serve as a heartbeat in a community, steadily sending out waves that touch and change those in their paths" (p. 609). I hope this book will help prepare you to serve as the heartbeat of liberation.

A GLANCE TOWARD THE FUTURE

As our understanding of the physical and social environment becomes more sophisticated, the connections among people emerge in sharper relief. My liberation is inevitably bound up with yours, and with that of everyone who shares this planet. But this reality is not immediately apparent, and some continue to ignore it.

If you are now entering the social work profession, you can expect to practice well into the twenty-first century. Your work will be influenced by themes that extend deep into the history of the United States, many of which have been described in this book. As we turn to the future, our focus is necessarily speculative, taking into account emerging trends, ideas, and politics likely to shape social welfare and social work practice in coming decades.

GLOBALIZATION AND GLOBAL GOVERNANCE

The term "globalization" refers to the flow of capital, labor, technology, and information across national borders. Taken to its theoretical extreme, the process could make movement across national boundaries as easy as movement within a country. Eventually, nation-states themselves may become irrelevant. Clearly this point has not yet been reached; nonetheless, advanced communication and transportation technologies have enhanced the flow of information and goods between countries, a process that challenges the sovereignty and authority of national governments. It is difficult for a nation to enforce environmental and labor laws within its borders when major corporations can evade these laws by relocating to another country.

This trend toward globalization parallels a trend we considered in Chapter 2. In the United States we see corporations holding local governments hostage—threatening to relocate unless they are granted special tax breaks or exemption from zoning ordinances. In a global context, these domestic issues assume new depth and complexity.

In Chapter 6 we explored the role of global governance in the management of worldwide epidemics. Here we will expand on that discussion, considering the role that international agencies play in global governance. We will focus on three organizations: the United Nations, the International Monetary Fund/World Bank, and the World Trade Organization.

The United Nations

The most widely known of the major international organizations, the United Nations (UN), was founded during the aftermath of World War II, on October 24, 1945. Its original membership included 51 countries, and its stated purpose was "preserving peace through international cooperation and collective security" (see http://www.un.org/aboutun/index.html). With 189 member nations today, the UN includes nearly every country in the world.

The UN is made up of six main entities. Five are located at UN headquarters in New York. They include the General Assembly, the Security Council, the Economic and Social Council, the Trusteeship Council, and the Secretariat. The sixth, the International Court of Justice, is located at The Hague, Netherlands.

The General Assembly serves as a kind of parliament to the UN, with representatives from all member nations. Each nation has one vote, and decisions are made through either simple or two-thirds majority votes. During the Assembly's 2000–2001 session, its representatives considered a wide range of topics, including globalization, nuclear disarmament, social and economic development, protection of the environment, and consolidation of new democracies. Assembly decisions are not binding but do carry the moral authority of the UN.

The Security Council is primarily responsible for maintaining peace and security. It includes 15 members: 5 permanent members (France, China, the Russian Federation, the United Kingdom, and the United States) and 10 elected by the General Assembly for two-year terms. Decisions by the Security Council require nine affirmative votes, and a decision may be vetoed by any one of the five permanent members.

The Economic and Social Council is a natural home for future social work practitioners. The Council addresses issues such as social development, the status of women, crime prevention, drug trafficking, and environmental protection. Its activities are primarily cooperative enterprises with nongovernmental organizations (NGOs). This council has 54 members who are elected from the General Assembly for three-year terms. It holds a major conference in July of each year.

The Trusteeship Council meets rarely, as its work is mostly complete. It was established to provide international supervision to 11 trust territories administered by seven member states. By 1994, all the trust territories had become independent or self-governing. The last one to achieve independence was the trust territory of the Pacific Islands, administered by the United States.

The Secretariat conducts the work of the United Nations. With a staff of approximately 8,900, the Secretariat has its major office in New York, with other locations in Geneva, Vienna, and Nairobi.

The International Court of Justice, also known as the World Court, arbitrates disputes between UN member nations. Nations are not obligated to participate in World Court proceedings, but those who do participate are obligated to comply with the Court's rulings.

One way the UN promotes social justice is by encouraging political independence of areas formerly under colonial rule. Through its Declaration on the Granting of Independence to Colonial Countries and Peoples, the UN has focused world opinion and attention on the status of former colonies. Since the UN was founded in 1945, hundreds of millions of people have moved toward independence. In 1945, 750 million people lived in non–self-governing territories. Today, that number is approximately 1.3 million. The UN also led a 30-year campaign to end apartheid in South Africa and held a World Conference Against Racism, Racial Discrimination, Xenophobia, and Related Intolerance in South Africa in September 2001. The United States did not participate in conference deliberations, objecting to the inclusion of the Israeli–Palestinian conflict and reparations for the trans-Atlantic slave trade as agenda items.

To relieve suffering, the UN provides emergency assistance in the wake of natural disasters and environmental emergencies. Humanitarian aid is also provided through UN refugee programs and food assistance.

The United States plays a pivotal role in the activities of the UN, as a permanent member of the Security Council, the home country of most UN offices, and an important source of financial support. Some Americans distrust the UN, and congressional ambivalence has sometimes resulted in postponed payment of U.S. dues.

The 9/11 attacks and subsequent invasion of Iraq raised Americans' awareness of the UN's role. Many watched on February 5, 2003, as then–secretary of state, Colin Powell, presented the case for invasion before the General Assembly in an attempt to secure international support and avoid condemnation by the UN. Some resented the necessity of this presentation, feeling that the United States should not allow the UN to exert control over its military interventions. In March 2003, the United States, Spain, and the United Kingdom introduced a Security Council resolution authorizing the use of force to secure Iraqi compliance with prior resolutions concerning dismantling weapons programs. Faced with opposition from Germany, France, and Russia, the resolution was subsequently withdrawn. The United States invaded Iraq on March 19, 2003. In May 2003 the Security Council approved Resolution 1483, which had been submitted by the United States and the United Kingdom. This resolution recognized the United States and Great Britain as occupying powers, and called on them to improve security and stability in the country and to provide opportunities for Iraqis to determine their political future. It created the position of UN special representative to Iraq and called for the establishment of a development fund for Iraq.

The 2004 presidential debates saw both candidates agreeing that the United States did not need UN authorization to undertake military campaigns. At the same time, there was general agreement on the need for international cooperation in rebuilding Iraq. Resolution 1483 set the stage for this cooperation. This outcome illustrates the UN's primary source of legitimacy and power. Without a standing military force, the UN cannot demand compliance with international law. Instead, it serves as a forum for dialogue, agreement, and international collaboration.

UN sanctions are a powerful tool for maintaining the peace. Under the charter, the Security Council can call upon member nations to apply measures that do not involve armed force in order to maintain or restore international peace and security. UN sanctions have been applied in 14 cases, involving Afghanistan, Angola, Ethiopia and Eritrea, Haiti, Iraq, Liberia, Libya, Rwanda, Sierra Leone, Somalia, South Africa, Southern Rhodesia, Sudan, and the former Yugoslavia. In most of these cases, sanctions have been fully lifted.

International Financial Organizations

Like the UN, the International Monetary Fund (IMF) was established in the wake of World War II, in 1946. The IMF's purpose is "to promote international monetary cooperation, exchange stability, and orderly exchange arrangements; to foster economic growth and high levels of employment; and to provide temporary financial assistance to countries to help ease the balance of payments adjustment" (see http://www.imf.org/external/about.htm). Most of the nations in the world (a total of 183) belong to the IMF, which provides loans through the World Bank.

The World Bank is a source of development loans to Third World nations. These loans total approximately $16 billion each year, and current loans involve over 100 nations. World Bank loans are controversial because they usually provide financing for major projects such as dams, roads, and power plants. Critics argue that these development loans enrich the elite while providing only social dislocation to the vulnerable.

Also controversial are the structural adjustment programs (SAPs) imposed as conditions for receiving loans. Critics argue that these conditions, which are designed to strengthen free markets in developing nations, actually decrease public investment in social services, education, and health care. SAPs might call, for example, for a nation to reduce its taxes on imported goods and increase interest rates. By opening local markets to imports, such tax reductions disadvantage local producers. Similarly, while higher interest rates combat inflation, they make it difficult for small borrowers to secure needed capital.

Although the IMF and the World Bank have poverty reduction as a stated goal, both organizations have acknowledged that greater inequality has accompanied economic globalization. Critics such as Global Exchange argue that these international financial organizations contribute to inequality by undermining public investment and increasing the wealth of global elites.

The World Trade Organization

Most Americans became aware of the World Trade Organization (WTO) in December 1999 when violence rocked the streets of Seattle. The violence of the Seattle demonstrations may have distracted observers from their fundamental message, which was a critique of the WTO.

The WTO was established in 1994 as a result of negotiations held in Uruguay under the General Agreement on Tariffs and Trade (GATT) as "the only international organization dealing with the global rules of trade between nations. Its main function is to ensure that trade flows as smoothly, predictably, and freely as possible." Representatives of member nations participate in trade negotiations under the auspices of the WTO, which are then submitted to domestic legislative processes for ratification. (For additional information, see www.wto.org.)

In the United States, critics of trade agreements argue that ratification should require the two-thirds vote required to ratify international treaties. Instead, the U.S. Congress typically ratifies these agreements by a simple majority vote.

The WTO argues that it strengthens the international economy and breaks down barriers among people by facilitating trade. The WTO has been a fierce international advocate for the free market. Critics argue that the WTO is the agent of international corporations and that it undermines democratic processes. They suggest that the WTO promotes a "race to the bottom" in labor and environmental protections (see www.globalexchange.org).

The United States ran afoul of the WTO in March 2002 when President George W. Bush imposed tariffs on foreign steel. Designed to shore up the failing domestic steel industry, the measure drew the ire of the WTO, which ruled in November 2003 that the tariffs violated international trade rules. This decision gave other countries the right to impose retaliatory tariffs on U.S. exports, and the European Union (EU) announced that it would apply duties to American motorcycles, citrus fruit, farm equipment, and other goods. This response left Bush an unpleasant choice. If he rolled back the steel tariffs, he would anger voters in key steel states like Pennsylvania and West Virginia. If he maintained the tariffs, he risked jeopardizing other industries. In December 2003, the Bush administration lifted the tariffs, and the EU immediately withdrew its threat of retaliatory tariffs. Relieved observers reported that a "trade war" had been averted.

Globalization has eased the flow of capital and information—but not labor—across national borders. The elites of some nations have managed to take advantage of this trend, consolidating their wealth and power at unprecedented levels. The resulting inequality may simply be an innocuous by-product of this consolidation. But it may destabilize societies, creating a large underclass of disempowered workers and a tiny ruling class that has no interest in their well-being. Multinational corporations may become more powerful than nation-states. Is this an inevitable consequence of the dominance of capitalist philosophy? In the following section we will consider the contrast between capitalist and socialist visions of social welfare.

CONTRASTING VISIONS OF SOCIAL WELFARE

The social welfare system steps in when private markets fail to meet individual needs. In Western industrialized nations, two dominant economic philosophies offer contrasting interpretations of the social welfare state and contrasting approaches to inequality. The first, "welfare capitalism," takes a capitalist economy as given and emphasizes the role of social welfare in support of that economy. The role of social policy in this view is to function as "the enabling state," facilitating individual contributions to economic productivity. The second view, "postindustrial socialism," deemphasizes the role of the market in human life, viewing the social sphere as more important. Under this view the role of social policy is to facilitate the expansion of the social sphere, liberating workers from economic pressures and demands.

The Enabling State

In their classic work *The Enabling State,* Gilbert and Gilbert (1989) offer one of the most coherent visions of welfare capitalism. Observing that public welfare expenditures leveled off in the 1970s and noting the growing use of government lending and tax deductions to accomplish the goals of social policy, these authors argue that the welfare state "has been transformed into the enabling state." They suggest that in the enabling state, "social welfare transfers are interlaced throughout the fabric of modern capitalist society" (p. xii). According to this view, public resources should encourage and support private responsibility. In a distinctively American approach, the enabling state would optimize the efficiencies and vitality of the private market while encouraging individual decisions in support of social policy goals.

The risk, of course, is that the most vulnerable Americans will be left behind. Noting that "there is a tendency for this movement to dilute protection and aid for the weakest, most disadvantaged members of the community," the Gilberts argue that public policy must "temper the increasing concern for private responsibility with greater tolerance for public purpose" (pp. 185–186).

The enabling state is a fundamentally capitalist view of the role and objectives of government. Government serves the purposes of the market, and a primary purpose of social policy is to support personal responsibility. A sharply contrasting view is offered by postindustrial socialists.

The Basic Income

Baker (1987) offers a socialist critique of the welfare state and suggests that "the present welfare state is a compromise which serves many interests. It helps people in need, but it also helps to keep them in their place. It is a system of support but also of control" (p. 10). Thus the modern welfare state is seen as an agent of inequality and a device for sustaining an exploitative economic system. Socialist critiques extend to the free market, noting that it exploits workers and destroys the environment and the social cohesion of a nation. The task of socialism, then, is to free the laborer from the market.

Postindustrial socialists advocate expansion of the social sphere of life. As Gorz (1994) explains, "The societal objective of productivity gains must be to bring about a contraction of the sphere governed by economic calculation and an expansion of the self-determined, self-organized spheres of activity in which human facilities can develop freely" (p. 20). According to this view, the technological developments of the twenty-first century could bring about "the end of work-based society" (Little, 1998, p. 19). Indeed, as a central tenet, postindustrial socialism rejects the strong link between work and survival.

A parallel argument about the impact of the market on the social life of Americans comes in Robert Putnam's book *Bowling Alone* (2000). In an exhaustive analysis, Putnam argues that recent decades have seen a decline in "civic engagement and social capital." This observation is based on declines in Americans' participation in a wide range of activities, including political, volunteer, religious, civic, and informal social events. Putnam traces these changes to the dominance of the economic market and "materialism." He goes further, suggesting that these forces destroy neighborhoods and families, leaving children in jeopardy. Putnam draws an analogy to the end of the nineteenth century, when the "Gilded Age" was marked by dramatic economic growth and threats to social ties. Calling for a return to "social capitalism," Putnam suggests that modern reformers draw inspiration from the early-twentieth-century Progressives, who restored to the nation a measure of social commitment. His incremental approach falls short of the more far-reaching proposals of postindustrial socialists to establish a "basic income."

The notion of a "basic income," advanced by neo-Marxists, was actually introduced by Thomas Paine in his 1795 work, *Agrarian Justice*. The basic (or citizen's) income is a universal, unconditional benefit provided to all members of a society regardless of their work or household status. Supporters argue that the basic income would enhance productivity, in part by eliminating poverty and its attendant social and physical costs, but also by ensuring that those who choose to work (not to avoid poverty, but to increase their affluence and contribute to society) would be better qualified and more motivated. For example, Offe, Muckenberger, and Ostner (1996) argue that

> [i]t does not seem too far-fetched to assume that in wealthy industrial
> societies, citizens might be accorded the right to withdraw from paid
> work without penalty and at only the loss of income (but not poverty!)
> will as a result be better motivated, better qualified, and in a better
> physical and psychic condition to engage in it (for then they would be
> choosing it 'voluntarily') than those from whom this choice is withheld,
> and who must consequently work knowing that non-engagement in
> paid work (or the failure of an attempted engagement in it) carries the
> threat of material need and social stigma. (p. 219)

Some, like Gorz (1985) and Atkinson (1996), have argued that a basic income is not sufficient to restore equity and community to postindustrial societies.

Gorz suggests that, in addition to a more equitable distribution of income, society should provide an equitable distribution of the opportunity to contribute through work. In Gorz's view, an overall reduction in the number of hours worked should accompany the basic income to ensure that no one who is willing to work lacks the opportunity. In another variation on the basic income proposal, Atkinson (1996) suggests that some kind of "social contribution" be the condition for receiving the benefit. This contribution might entail being a good parent, a skilled artist, or an educated voter. Thus, rather than a "basic" income, the social welfare system would provide a "participation benefit."

Welfare capitalism and postindustrial socialism offer sharply contrasting visions. Certainly the enabling state is most compatible with the realities of twentieth-century America. But the new century offers new opportunities, even as it demands new visions. Social workers may apply the notion of a basic income in their efforts to advance the cause of social justice. Of course, the practicality of any social welfare proposals will be largely determined by political realities.

CHANGING POLITICS

The end of the twentieth century rekindled American enthusiasm for capitalism. The dissolution of the Soviet Union, the opening of Chinese markets, and the longest peacetime economic expansion in U.S. history all seemed to signal a victory for the nation's dominant economic philosophy. This victory may have quieted the American Left, and it certainly gave impetus to what some consider the "third wave" of American conservatism. With the 1994 election of a Republican majority in the House of Representatives, the nation seemed poised for a return to the laissez-faire politics of the nineteenth century. The Republican revolution was short-lived, however, and the "compassionate conservatism" of the George W. Bush administration came to sound remarkably like early-twentieth-century Progressivism. George W. Bush's 2001 inaugural address is illustrative:

> While many of our citizens prosper, others doubt the promise—even the justice—of our own country. The ambitions of some Americans are limited by failing schools and hidden prejudice, and the circumstances of their birth. And sometimes our differences run so deep, it seems we share a continent, but not a country.
>
> We do not accept this and will not allow it. Our unity, our union, is the serious work of leaders and citizens in every generation. And this is my solemn pledge: I will work to build a single nation of justice and opportunity. . . .
>
> In the quiet of American conscience, we know that deep, persistent poverty is unworthy of our nation's promise. And whatever our views of its cause, we can agree that children at risk are not at fault. Abandonment and abuse are not acts of God, they are failures of love. . . .

> Where there is suffering, there is duty. Americans in need are not
> strangers, they are citizens; not problems, but priorities; and all of us are
> diminished when any are hopeless.

The president's rhetoric seemed to recognize the problems of the disadvantaged and to promise steps to advance social justice. Although this rhetoric clearly did not predict his future decisions, it did suggest that Bush recognized the power and attraction these ideas hold for the American electorate. Indeed, it may indicate, as E. J. Dionne (1996) argues, that American Progressives "only look dead."

Dionne, like Putnam, draws analogies between this turn of the century and the last. He suggests that during the economic transformation of the early twenty-first century Americans will look to a new Progressivism to restore a balance between the economic and the social spheres of life. Dionne articulated a clear agenda for the New Progressives:

> [T]o succeed, a New Progressivism must be genuinely and not simply
> rhetorically new. Its task is to restore the legitimacy of public life by
> renewing the effectiveness of government and reforming the workings
> of politics. . . . The New Progressives are those who accept the need to
> make another large economic transition, but know that the transition
> will be successful only if government acts creatively, and with a strong
> concern for social justice. (pp. 16, 277)

Dionne's charge to Progressives is equally relevant to social work professionals.

A CLOSING NOTE

In coming years, both policy practice and direct practice of social work will be transformed by global and national trends. Each trend clearly demands advocacy on behalf of vulnerable populations. And each illustrates an essential premise of chaos theory known as the "butterfly effect." Presented by Lorenz in 1972, this premise holds that the flap of a butterfly's wings in Brazil could set off a tornado in Texas. Complex systems can be affected in unpredictable ways by apparently small events. In the post–9/11 world we are forced to see our social environment as a single complex system and to recognize that simple acts of kindness or hatred can have widespread consequences.

On September 11, 2001, American awareness of global issues was transformed by the murder of thousands of civilians. Terrorists attacked the citadels of U.S. economic and military power in a gesture of hatred unlike any this country had ever witnessed. Our nation's struggle to understand and respond to these attacks highlights many of the issues we have explored in this book. Some attributed the violence to the "evil" tenets of Islamic fundamentalism. They labeled Muslims and Arabs "other" and used this as an excuse to persecute and harass them. But those who look beyond simple explanations found themselves reflecting on what social justice means in a global context, asking whether rich nations

—out of "enlightened self-interest," if nothing else—have an obligation to meet the basic needs of the world's disadvantaged. They asked whether the United States could responsibly withdraw from any international dialogue on oppression or social justice.

The terrorist attacks jarred us out of our complacency, awakening Americans to long-standing conditions in the Middle East. Isolated injustices such as the massive accumulation of wealth by elites in oil-rich nations became cause for international concern. Violence in Palestine assumed new relevance, as did the global threat posed by fundamentalist leaders.

Speaking to the realities of this century will require social workers to become conversant not only with the traditional programs and policies of social welfare but also with domestic tax, labor, and financial policies and with global debates about independence and accommodation. We must look beyond labels and rhetoric to offer a vision of social welfare that is compatible with economic and political conditions even as it advances the cause of social justice. As Reisch and Gorin point out, "Social workers need to articulate an alternative vision for our society" (p. 16). We can draw inspiration from the Progressives of the past but must forge our own path, which will require unprecedented ingenuity. Our success will be measured on individual and global scales as we strive to eliminate the causes of hatred and build a world that offers "liberty and justice for all."

KEYWORDS

Social inequality	Employee benefits	World community
Criminal law	Global economy	World poverty
	Global governance	

THINK ABOUT IT

1. Noting that most of the poor in the United States have living space much larger than that of the average Japanese family, some would argue that America's poor are not disadvantaged. Do you agree or disagree with this statement? Why?

2. The twentieth century was marked by rising inequality, both globally and within the United States. Yet life expectancies and, some would argue, the quality of life of the disadvantaged increased during this period. Does this improvement support the notion that inequality is the necessary price for expanding the economic pie? What are the implications of this observation for economic policies aimed at redistributing the nation's wealth?

3. Do you think the term "enabling state" accurately describes the role of the U.S. government in social welfare? Why or why not?

4. Dionne (1996) suggested that it is important for the New Progressives to "embrace the dual concepts of freedom and community." What does this statement mean? Are freedom and community compatible? Does community membership entail responsibilities and roles that limit individual freedom?

5. Do you think the WTO is more powerful than the UN? Consider the case of U.S. steel tariffs. Has the UN ever imposed sanctions on the United States? Has it ever declared a U.S. action in violation of international law?

WEB-BASED EXERCISES

For direct links to all the sites in these exercises, log on to the Student Companion Site for this book at academic.cengage.com/social_work/barusch, and choose Conclusion.

1. What's happening at the UN? Go to http://www.un.org/News/, and read the headlines from the UN News Centre. Select one of the stories to pursue in depth. What social justice implications do you see here? Anything of relevance to social workers and their clients?

2. What policy concerns are important to American manufacturers? Go to http://www.nam.org, the website of the National Association of Manufacturers (NAM). Under Policy Issue Information (and possibly in other locations as well), you will find material that gives a sense of the organization's priorities. How does the NAM feel about government regulations that protect worker safety? Environmental regulations? How about employee benefits? What do you see as the strengths and weaknesses of this organization's positions?

3. Visit www.ifsw.org, and search the site for the definition of social work provided there by the International Federation of Social Workers. Is it congruent with your sense of the profession? Would you revise it in any way?

SUGGESTED RESOURCES

Dominelli, L. (Ed.). (2007). *Revitalising Communities in a Globalising World.* Hampshire, England: Ashgate.

Friere, P. (1973). *Pedagogy of the Oppressed.* New York: Herder & Herder.

Koenig, M., & de Guchteneire, P. (Eds.). (2007). *Democracy and Human Rights in Multicultural Societies.* Hampshire, England: Ashgate.

Loeb, P. R. (1999). *Soul of a Citizen: Living with Conviction in a Cynical Time.* New York: St. Martin's Griffin.

Mapp, S. C. (2008). *Human Rights and Social Justice in a Global Perspective: An Introduction to International Social Work*. New York: Oxford University Press.

Rothenberg, P. S. (2001). *Race, Class, and Gender in the United States: An Integrated Study*. New York: Worth Publishers.

International Social Work, the journal of three international social work organizations: the International Association of Schools of Social Work (IASSW), the International Council on Social Welfare (ICSW), and the International Federation of Social Workers (IFSW).

www.globalexchange.org. For a critical look at the activities of the IMF and the World Bank, visit this site, which is maintained by a human rights organization called Global Exchange. Founded in 1988 in San Francisco, Global Exchange is designed to increase global awareness in the United States.

www.imf.org. This site is maintained by the International Monetary Fund. In addition to a description of IMF activities, it provides research and statistics about economic issues and a link to the World Bank's site (www.worldbank.org).

www.un.org. The website of the United Nations offers a wealth of information about international issues as well as links to other international organizations.

www.wto.org. This site provides a fairly one-sided look at the mission and activities of the World Trade Organization.

References

Abramowitz, M. (1996). *Regulating the Lives of Women: Social Welfare Policy from Colonial Times to the Present.* Boston: South End Press.

Achenbaum, W. A. (1978). *Old Age in the New Land: The American Experience Since 1790.* Baltimore: Johns Hopkins University Press.

Achenbaum, W. A. (1986). *Social Security: Visions and Revisions.* Cambridge: Cambridge University Press.

Adams, M., Bell, L. A., & Griffin, P. (1997). *Teaching for Diversity and Social Justice: A Sourcebook.* New York: Routledge.

Administration for Children and Families. (2005). *Head Start Impact Study: First-Year Findings.* http://www.acf.hhs.gov/programs/opre/hs/impact_study/reports/first_yr_finds/firstyr_finds_title.html (accessed December 30, 2007).

Administration for Children and Youth. (2006). *AFCARS Report #12: Final Estimates for FY1998 through FY2002.* http://www.acf.hhs.gov/programs/cb/stats_research/afcars/tar/report12.htm (accessed December 30, 2007).

Administration for Children and Youth. (2007). *Trends in Foster Care and Adoption. AFCARS Report #13: Preliminary Estimates for 2005.* http://www.acf.hhs.gov/programs/cb/stats_research/afcars/trends.htm (accessed December 30, 2007).

Administration on Aging. (1997). *Age Discrimination: A Pervasive and Damaging Influence.* http://www.aoa.gov/factsheets/ageism.html.

Administration on Aging. (2001). *Older Americans Act Appropriation Information.* http://www.aoa.gov/oaa/oaaapp.html.

Administration on Aging. (2008). *Legislation and Budget.* http://www.aoa.gov/about/legbudg/current_budg/legbudg_current_budg.asp (accessed January 9, 2007).

Alecxih, L., & Kennell, D. (1994). *The Economic Impact of Long-Term Care on Individuals.* Washington, DC: HHS. http://aspe.dhhs.gov/daltcp/reports/ecoimpes.htm.

Alexander, J. C., Eyerman, R., Giesen, B., Smelser, N. J., & Piotr, S. (2004). *Cultural Trauma and Collective Identity.* Berkeley: University of California Press.

Alinsky, S. (1972). *Rules for Radicals: A Pragmatic Primer for Realistic Radicals.* New York: Random House.

Allard, M. A., Albelda, R., Colten, M. E., & Cosenza, C. (1997). *In Harm's Way? Domestic Violence, AFDC Receipt, and Welfare Reform in Massachusetts.* A Report from the University of Massachusetts, Boston.

Altman, D. (1999). Globalization, political economy, and HIV/AIDS. *Theory and Society, 28,* 559–584.

Addresses of websites mentioned in this text may have changed since the manuscript was written. If the specific address doesn't work for you, try using the main address, www.xxx.xxx, and searching for the document by title.

Altmeyer, A. J. (1963). The Development and Status of Social Security in America. In G. G. Somers (Ed.), *Labor, Management and Social Policy: Essays in the John R. Commons Tradition*. University of Wisconsin Press. http://www.ssa.gov/history/aja1963.html.

Amato, P. R., & Zuo, J. (1992). Rural poverty, urban poverty and psychological well-being. *Sociological Quarterly, 33*(2), 229–240.

American Academy of Actuaries. (2007). *Issue Brief: Women and Social Security*. http://www.actuary.org (accessed October 18, 2007).

American Civil Liberties Union (ACLU). (1996). *English Only: ACLU Briefing Paper*. http://www.aclu.org/library/pbp6.html.

American Psychiatric Association. (1990). *Psychiatry and Homeless Mentally Ill Persons: Report of the Task Force on the Homeless Mentally Ill*. Washington, DC: American Psychiatric Association.

Appelbaum, N., Macpherson, A. S., & Rosemblatt, K. A. (Eds.). (2003). *Race and Nation in Modern Latin America*. Chapel Hill, NC: University of North Carolina Press.

Appelbaum, P. S. (1994). *Almost a Revolution: Mental Health Law and the Limits of Change*. New York: Oxford University Press.

Aries, P. (1962). *Centuries of Childhood: A Social History of Family Life*. (Robert Baldick, Trans.). New York: Vintage Books.

Atkinson, A. (1996, January–March). The case for a participation income. *Political Quarterly, 67*, 1.

Avalos, M., Affigne, A. D., & Travis, T. (1997, August). *Race, Land, Money and Power: The Persistence of Racial Stratification in Brazil and the U.S.* Paper presented at the Annual Meeting of the American Political Science Association, Washington, DC. http://www.providence.edu/polisci/affigne/pdf/brasil_u.s.pdf (accessed December 11, 2007).

AVERT. (2005). United States HIV & AIDS Statistics Summary. http://www.avert.org/statsum.htm.

Ayvazian, A. S. (2001). Interrupting the cycle of oppression: The role of allies as agents of change. In P. S. Rothenberg (Ed.), *Race, Class, and Gender in the United States: An Integrated Study* (pp. 609–615). New York: Worth Publishers.

Badgett, L., Donnelly, C., & Kibbe, J. (1992). *Pervasive Patterns of Discrimination Against Lesbians and Gay Men: Evidence from Surveys Across the United States*. New York: National Gay and Lesbian Task Force.

Baker, J. (1987). *Arguing for Equality*. London & New York: Verso.

Ball, H. (2000). *The Bakke Case: Race, Education and Affirmative Action*. Topeka: University Press of Kansas.

Ball, R. M. (1996). Medicare's roots: What Medicare's architects had in mind. *Generations, 20*(2), 13–18.

Bane, S. D. (1991, Fall/Winter). Rural minority populations. *Generations*, 63–65.

Banfield, E. C. (1968). *The Unheavenly City*. Boston: Little, Brown.

Barker, E. (Ed.). (1962). *The Politics of Aristotle*. Cambridge, MA: Oxford University Press.

Barnett, W. (1973). *Sexual Freedom and the Constitution*. Albuquerque: University of New Mexico Press.

Baronov, D. (2003). Colonial rule, AIDS, and social control in Puerto Rico. *Socialism and Democracy, 17*(34, No. 2), 171–189.

Barusch, A. S. (1995). Programming for family care: Mandates, incentives and rationing. *Social Work, 40*(3), 315–322.

Bass, S. A., Caro, F. G., & Chen, Y. (Eds.). (1993). *Achieving a Productive Aging Society*. Westport, CT: Greenwood.

Bean, F., & Tienda, M. (1987). *The Hispanic Population of the United States*. New York: Russell Sage.

Beard, J. H., Propst, R. N., & Malamud, T. J. (1982). The Fountain House model of psychiatric rehabilitation. *Psychosocial Rehabilitation Journal, 5*, 47–53.

Beck, D. L. (2004, January/February). Health, Wealth and the Chinese Oedipus. *Society*, 64–67.

Beers, C. W. (1908). *A Mind That Found Itself: An Autobiography*. Garden City, NJ: Doubleday, Doran, & Co.

Bell, L. A. (1997). Theoretical foundations for social justice education. In M. Adams, L. A. Bell, & P. Griffin (Eds.), *Teaching for Diversity and Social Justice: A Sourcebook* (pp. 3–15). New York: Routledge.

Belle, D. (1984). Inequality and mental health: Low-income and minority women. In L. E. Walker (Ed.), *Women and Mental Health Policy* (pp. 135–150). Beverly Hills: Sage.

Bergman-Evans, B. (2004). Beyond the basics: Effects of the Eden Alternative model on quality of life issues. *Journal of Gerontological Nursing, 30*(6), 27–34.

Bergmann, B. R. (1971). The effect on white incomes of discrimination in employment. *Journal of Political Economy, 79,* 294–313.

Berkowitz, E. D. (1987). *Disabled Policy: America's Programs for the Handicapped.* Cambridge: Cambridge University Press.

Berkowitz, E. D. (2000, July 13). *Disability Policy and History: Statement before the Subcommittee on Social Security of the Committee on Ways and Means.* http://www.ssa.gov/history/edberkdib.html.

Bernstein, J., McNichol, E., Mishel, L., & Zahradnik, R. (2000). *Pulling Apart: A State-by-State Analysis of Income Trends.* Washington, DC: Center on Budget and Policy Priorities. Economic Policy Institute. http://www.cbpp.org/1-18-00sfp-partl.pdf.

Binstock, R. H. (1983). The aged as scapegoat. *Gerontologist, 23,* 136–143.

Binstock, R. H. (1985). Perspectives on measuring hardship: Concepts, dimensions, and implications. *Gerontologist, 26,* 60–62.

Binstock, R. H., & Post, S. G. (Eds.). (1991). *Too Old for Health Care? Controversies in Medicine, Law, and Ethics.* Baltimore: Johns Hopkins University Press.

Blau, J. R., & Blau, P. M. (1982). The cost of inequality: Metropolitan structure and violent crime. *American Sociological Review, 47,* 114–129.

Bluestone, B. (1994). The inequality express. *American Prospect, 20,* 81–93.

Blumberg, P. (1980). *Inequality in an Age of Decline.* New York: Oxford University Press.

Blumenthal, S., & Knupter, D. J. (1988). Overview of early detection and treatment strategies for suicidal behavior in young people. *Journal of Youth and Adolescence, 17*(1), 1–23.

Bostock, D. (2000). *Aristotle's Ethics.* New York: Oxford University Press.

Bouma, D. H., & Hoffman, J. (1968). *The Dynamics of School Integration: Problems and Approaches in a Northern City.* Grand Rapids, MI: Eardmans.

Brace, C. L. (1872). *The Dangerous Classes of New York and Twenty Years' Work Among Them.* New York: Wynkoop & Hallenbeck. (Reprinted in 1973 by NASW Press.)

Bremner, R. H. (Ed.). (1970). *Children and Youth in America: A Documentary History, 1600–1865* (Vol. 1). Cambridge, MA: Harvard University Press.

BBC. (2005). Stars pack Elton "wedding" party. http://news.bbc.co.uk/1/hi/entertainment/4546670.stm (accessed December 27, 2007).

Brody, E. M. (1971). Aging. In *The Encyclopedia of Social Work* (pp. 55–77). New York: National Association of Social Workers Press.

Brown, R. S., Clement, D. G., Hill, J. W., Retchin, S. M., & Bergeron, J. W. (1993). Do health maintenance organizations work for Medicare? *Health Care Financing Review, 15*(1), 7–23.

Brown, T. J. (1998). *Dorothea Dix: New England Reformer.* Cambridge, MA: Harvard University Press.

Bureau of Justice Statistics. (2006). *Prisoners in 2005.* http://www.ojp.usdoj.gov/bjs/abstract/p05.htm (accessed January 10, 2008).

Bureau of Labor Statistics. (2001). *How the Government Measures Unemployment.* http://www.bls.gov/cps/cps_htgm.htm (accessed January 21, 2008).

Bureau of Labor Statistics. (2005). *National Compensation Survey: Employee Benefits in Private Industry in the United States, March 2005.* http://www.bls.gov/ncs/ (accessed January 20, 2008).

Bureau of Labor Statistics. (2007a). *Employment Status of the Civilian Population by Sex and Age,* Table A-1. http://www.bls.gov/news.release/empsit.t01.htm (accessed January 2, 2007).

Bureau of Labor Statistics. (2007b). *Unemployed Persons by Marital Status, Race, Hispanic or Latino Ethnicity, Age and Sex.* http://www.bls.gov/cps/cpsaat24.pdf (accessed December 13, 2007).

Bureau of Labor Statistics. (2007c). *Union Members Summary.* http://www.bls.gov/news.release/union2.nr0.htm (accessed January 20, 2008).

Burt, M. (1992). *Over the Edge: The Growth of Homelessness in the 1980s.* New York: Russell Sage.

Burtless, G. (1999). Growing income inequality: Sources and remedies. In H. J. Aaron & R. D. Reischauer (Eds.), *Setting National Priorities: The 2000 Election and Beyond.* Washington, DC: Brookings Institution Press.

Burtless, G., & Saks, D. (1984, March). *The Decline in Insured Unemployment During the 1980s.* Unpublished Brookings Institution Report to the Department of Labor.

Burton, R. (1621). *Anatomy of Melancholy, What It Is: With All the Symptomes, Prognostickes and Several Cures of It.* Publisher Unknown. Several copies in public domain, available online through Project Gutenberg.

Burton, C. E. (1992). *The Poverty Debate: Politics and the Poor in America*. Westport, CT: Greenwood Press.

Butler, R. N., Oberlink, M. R., & Schechter, M. (Eds.). (1990). *Promise of Productive Aging: From Biology to Social Policy*. New York: Springer.

Butler, S., Lave, J., & Reuschauer, R. D. (1998). *Medicare: Preparing for the Challenges of the 21st Century*. Washington, DC: National Academy of Social Insurance (distributed by Brookings Institution Press).

Byrom, B. (2001). A pupil and a patient: Hospital-schools in progressive America. In P. K. Longmore & L. Umansky (Eds.), *The New Disability History: American Perspectives* (pp. 133–156). New York: New York University Press.

CNN. (2007, December 13). President Bush vetoes child health bill again. http://www.cnn.com/2007/POLITICS/12/12/bush.schip/?iref=mpstoryview (accessed February 5, 2008).

Caffey, J. (1946). Multiple fractures in the long bones of infants suffering from chronic subdural hematoma. *American Journal of Roentgenology, 56*, 163–173.

Callahan, D. (1987). *Setting Limits: Medical Goals in an Aging Society*. New York: Simon & Schuster.

Callahan, D. (1990). *What Kind of Life: The Limits of Medical Progress*. New York: Simon & Schuster.

Camejo, P. (1976). *Racism, Revolution, Reaction, 1861–1877: The Rise and Fall of Radical Reconstruction*. New York: Monad.

Caputo, R. K. (1998). Discrimination and pension income among aging women. *Journal of Aging and Social Policy, 10*(2), 67–83.

Castner, L., & Cody, S. (1999). *Trends in FSP Participation Rates: Focus on September 1999*. http://www.fns.usda.gov/oane/MENU/published/FSP/FILES/trends97.pdf.

Center for Education Reform. (1999). *Just the FAQs—School Choice*. http://www.edreform.com/faq/faqsc.htm.

Center on Juvenile and Criminal Justice. (2007). Race and Juvenile Justice System. http://www.cjcj.org/jjic/race_jj.php (accessed December 31, 2007).

Centers for Disease Control and Prevention (CDC). (1999, August 27). Progress towards the elimination of tuberculosis, United States, 1999. *MMWR,* 48(33), 732–736. http://www.cdc.gov/epo/mmwr/preview/mmwrhtmUmm4833a2.htm.

Centers for Disease Control and Prevention (CDC). (2004). *CDC HIV/AIDS Surveillance Report: HIV Infection and Aids in the United States, 2003*. http://www.cdc.gov/hiv/stats.htm#cumaids.

Centers for Disease Control and Prevention (CDC). (2007a). *American Indian and Alaska Native Populations*. http://www.cdc.gov/omhd/Populations/AIAN/AIAN.htm (accessed December 13, 2007).

Centers for Disease Control and Prevention (CDC). (2007b). *Suicide Trends Among Youths and Young Adults Aged 10-24 Years: United States, 1990–2004*. http://www.cdc.gov/mmwr/preview/mmwrhtml/mm5635a2.htm (accessed December 31, 2007).

Cerne, F. (1995, March 20). Streetwise. *Hospitals and Health Networks, 38*–46.

Chalfant, H. P. (1985). *Sociology of Poverty in the United States: An Annotated Bibliography*. Westport, CT: Greenwood.

Chamberlain, E. (1994, November/December). Blues for single-payer. *Humanist, 54*(6), 3–7.

Chambers, D. (2000). *Social Policy and Social Programs: A Method for the Practical Public Policy Analyst* (3rd ed.). New York: Macmillan.

Chambers, D. E. (1982). The U.S. poverty line: A time for change. *Social Work, 27*(4), 354–358.

Chandler, S., & Jones, J. (2003). Because a better world is possible: Women casino workers, union activism and the creation of a just workplace. *Journal of Sociology and Social Welfare, 30*(4), 57–78.

Chavez, L. (1991). *Out of the Barrio: Toward a New Politics of Hispanic Assimilation*. New York: Basic Books.

Cherny, R. W., Issel, W., & Taylor, K. W. (2004). Introduction. In R. W. Cherny, W. Issel, & K. W. Taylor (Eds.), *American Labor and the Cold War: Grassroots Politics and Postwar Political Culture* (pp. 1–7). Piscataway, NJ: Rutgers University Press.

Child Welfare League of America. (1997). *Breaking the Link Between Child Maltreatment and Juvenile Delinquency*. Washington, DC: CWLA.

Chinn, T., Lai, H. J., & Choy, P. (1969). *A History of the Chinese in California*. San Francisco: Chinese Historical Society of America.

Chipungu, S. S., & Bent-Goodley, T. B. (2004). Meeting the challenges of contemporary foster care.

Future of Children, 14(1), 75–93. http://www.future ofchildren.org.

Church, P., & Minter, S. (2000). *Transgender Equality: A Handbook for Activists and Policymakers.* Washington, DC: National Gay and Lesbian Task Force. http://www.thetaskforce.org.

Churchill, W. (1998). *A Little Matter of Genocide: Holocaust and Denial in the Americas, 1492 to the Present.* San Francisco: City Lights Books.

Citrin, J., Reingold, B., Walters, E., & Green, D. P. (1990). The Official English Movement and the symbolic politics of language in the United States. *Western Political Quarterly, 43*(3), 553–560.

Clement, M. (1997). *The Juvenile Justice System: Law and Process.* Boston, MA: Butterworth Heinemann.

Close Up Foundation. (1998). *U.S. Immigration Policy.* http://www.closeup.org/immigrat.htm.

Cohany, S. R., & Sok, E. (2007). Trends in labor force participation of married mothers of infants. *Monthly Labor Review.* http://www.bls.gov/opub/mlr/2007/02/art2full.pdf (accessed January 2, 2007).

Cohen, W. S. (1994). *Tax Dollars Aiding and Abetting Addiction: Social Security Disability and SSI Cash Benefits to Drug Addicts and Alcoholics.* Investigative Staff Report of the Minority Staff of the Senate Special Committee on Aging.

Coleman, M. T., Looney, S., O'Brien, J., Ziegler, C., Pastorino, C. A., & Turner, C. (2002). The Eden Alternative: Findings after one year of implementation. *Journal of Gerontology: Series A, Biological and Medical Sciences, 57*(7), M422–M427.

Commission of the European Communities. (1982). *Memorandum on the Reduction and Reorganization of Working Time.* Brussels: Author.

Comstock, D. (1991). *Violence against Lesbians and Gay Men.* New York: Columbia University Press.

Conger, R., Elder, G. H., Lorenz, F. O., Simons, R. L., & Whitbeck, L. B. (1994). *Families in Troubled Times: Adapting to Change in Rural America.* New York: Aldine De Gruyter.

Congressional Budget Office (CBO). (1990). *Sources of Support for Adolescent Mothers.* Washington, DC: CBO.

Congressional Budget Office (CBO). (2001). *An Analysis of the President's Budgetary Proposals for FY 2001.* http://www.cbo.gov/showdoc.cfm?index1908 &sequence3&from5.

Congressional Budget Office (CBO). (2004). *Administrative Costs of Private Accounts in Social Security.* http://www.cbo.gov/showdoc.cfm?index5277 &sequence0.

Congressional Budget Office (CBO). (2007, May). *The State Children's Health Insurance Program.* http://www.cbo.gov/publications/collections/collections .cfm?collect=11 (accessed February 5, 2008).

Congressional Research Service. (2002, April 18). *The USA PATRIOT Act: A Sketch.* Order code RS21203. http://www.fas.org/irp/crs/RS21203 .pdf.

Conrad, P. (1986, Summer). The social meaning of AIDS. *Social Policy, 17*(1), 51–56.

Cook, D. (1989). *Rich Law, Poor Law.* Philadelphia, PA: Open University Press.

Cook, F. L. (1996). *Can Public Support for Programs for Older Americans Survive?* http://www.northwestern .edu/IPR/publications/nupr/nuprv0lnl/cook.html.

Coplin, W. D., & O'Leary, M. K. (1998). *Public Policy Skills* (3rd ed.). Croton-on-Hudson, NY: Policy Studies Associates.

Corbett, E. P. J. (1965). *Classical Rhetoric for the Modern Student.* New York: Oxford University Press.

Corson, W., & Nicholson, W. (1988). *An Examination of Declining UI Claims during the 1980s.* Unemployment Insurance Occasional Paper 88-3. Washington, DC: U.S. Department of Labor.

Costin, L. B. (1992). Cruelty to children: A dormant issue and its rediscovery, 1920–1960. *Social Service Review, 66,* 177–198.

Cotchett, J. W. (2004, July 11). Water wars: California's liquid gold shouldn't be entrusted to private conglomerates. *San Francisco Chronicle,* p. E1.

Council on American–Islamic Relations. (2004). *Unpatriotic Acts: The Status of Muslim Civil Rights in the United States.* Washington, DC: CAIR. http://www.cair-net.org.

Cowell, A. J., Broner, N., & Dupont, R. (2004). The cost-effectiveness of criminal justice diversion programs for people with serious mental illness co-occurring with substance abuse: Four case studies. *Journal of Contemporary Criminal Justice, 20*(3), 292–314.

Cox, J. (1997). *The Ugly Truth About the Minimum Wage.* http://www.self-gov.org/cox02.html.

Cox, M. W. (1994). *Make Adoption Policies Colorblind.* http://majorcox.com/columns/adoption.htm.

Cox, O. (1970). *Caste, Class, and Race: A Study in Social Dynamics.* New York: Monthly Review Press.

Crain, R. L. (1968). *The Politics of Desegregation: Comparative Case Studies of Community Structure and Policy-Making.* Chicago: Aldine.

Crawford, J. (1992). *Language Loyalties: A Sourcebook on the Official English Controversy.* Chicago: University of Chicago Press.

Crawford, J. (1996). *Anatomy of the English-only Movement: Social and Ideological Sources of Language Restrictionism in the United States.* Conference on Language Legislation and Linguistic Rights. University of Illinois at Urbana-Champaign. http://ourworld .compuserve.com/homepages/JWCRAWFORD/ anatomy.htm.

Crumbley, J. (1999). *Transracial Adoption and Foster Care: Practice Issues for Professionals.* Washington, DC: Child Welfare League of America.

Crystal, S., & Shea, D. (1990). Cumulative advantage, cumulative disadvantage, and inequality among elderly people. *Gerontologist, 30,* 437–443.

Cuffel, B. J., Bloom, J. R., Wallace, N., Hausman, J. W., & Hu, T. (2002). Two-year outcomes of fee-for-service and capitated Medicaid programs for people with severe mental illness. *Health Services Research, 37*(2), 341–359.

Curcio, W. (1996). *The Passaic County Study of AFDC Recipients in a Welfare to Work Program: A Preliminary Analysis.* Passaic County, NJ: Passaic County Board of Social Services.

Dalaker, J., & Naifeh, M. (1997). *Poverty in the United States: 1997.* U.S. Bureau of the Census, Current Population Reports, Series P60–201. Washington, DC: U.S. Government Printing Office.

Dalton, H. (1925). *Some Aspects of Inequality of Incomes in Modern Communities.* London: Routledge.

Damerell, R. G. (1968). *Triumph in a White Suburb: The Dramatic Story of Teaneck, NJ, the First Town in the Nation to Vote for Integrated Schools.* New York: Morrow.

Daniel, P. (1972). *The Shadow of Slavery: Peonage in the South, 1901–1969.* Chicago: University of Illinois Press.

Daniels, H. (1988). *Am I My Parents' Keeper? An Essay on Justice Between the Young and the Old.* New York: Oxford University Press.

Daniels, R., & Kitano, H. H. L. (1970). *American Racism: Exploration of the Nature of Prejudice.* Englewood Cliffs, NJ: Prentice Hall.

Davidson, L., & Linnoila, M. (1992). Risk factors for youth suicide. *International Social Work, 35*(1), 91–93.

Davies, P. S., Huynh, M., Newcomb, C., O'Leary, P., Rupp, K., & Sears, J. (2002, Summer). Modeling SSI financial eligibility and simulating the effect of policy options—Supplemental Security Income. *Social Security Bulletin.*

Davis, K., & Moore, W. E. (1967). Some principles of stratification. In R. Bendix & S. M. Lipset (Eds.), *Class, Status and Power: Social Stratification in Comparative Perspective* (2nd ed.). London: Routledge.

Davis, K. E., & Cloud-Two Dog, E. I. (2004). Oppression of indigenous tribal populations and Africans in America. In K. E. Davis & T. B. Bent-Goodley (Eds.), *The Color of Social Policy* (pp. 3–20). Alexandria, VA: Council on Social Work Education.

Day, D. (1979). *The Adoption of Black Children: Counteracting Institutional Discrimination.* Lexington: Lexington Books.

Death Penalty Information Center. (2004). *Juvenile Offenders Who Were on Death Row.* http://www .deathpenaltyinfo.org/article.php?did=204&scid=27 (accessed January 1, 2008).

DeCoster, V. A. (2001). Challenges of type 2 diabetes and role of health care social work: A neglected area of practice. *Health and Social Work, 26*(1), 26–36.

Deloria, V., & Lytle, C. M. (1983). *American Indians, American Justice.* Austin, TX: University of Texas Press.

Department of Veterans Affairs. (2004). *Facts about the Department of Veterans Affairs.* http://www1.va.gov/ opa/fact/vafacts.html.

Derlet, R. W., & Kinser, D. (1994, September 29). Access of Medicaid recipients to outpatient care. *New England Journal of Medicine, 331*(13), 877–878.

De Swaan, A. (1988). *In Care of the State: Health Care, Education, and Welfare in Europe and the U.S.A. in the Modern Era.* New York: Oxford University Press.

de Tocqueville, A. (1835). *Democracy in America* (Vols. 1–2). New York: Harper & Row. (Reprinted in 1996).

Diaz, E. (1991, December/January). Public policy, women, and HIV disease. *SIECUS Report,* 4–5.

DiFonzo, J. H. (1997). *Beneath the Fault Line: The Popular and Legal Culture of Divorce in Twentieth-Century America.* Charlottesville, VA: University Press of Virginia.

DiNitto, D. M. (1995). *Social Welfare: Politics and Public Policy* (4th ed.). Needham Heights, MA: Allyn & Bacon.

Dionne, E. J. (1996). *They Only Look Dead: Why Progressives Will Dominate the Next Political Era.* New York: Simon & Schuster.

Dobash, R. E., & Dobash, R. P. (1992). *Women, Violence and Social Change.* London & New York: Routledge.

Dohrenwend, B. P. (1990). Socioeconomic status (SES) and psychiatric disorders: Are the issues still compelling? *Social Psychiatry and Psychiatric Epidemiology, 25,* 4–47.

Dolger, H., & Seeman, B. (1985). *How to Live with Diabetes* (5th ed.). New York: Norton.

Donovan, R., Kurzman, P. A., & Rotman, C. (1993). Improving the lives of home care workers: A partnership of social work and labor. *Social Work, 38*(5), 579–585.

Douglass, D. (1997). Taking the initiative: Anti-homosexual propaganda of the Oregon Citizens' Alliance. In S. L. Witt & S. McCorkle (Eds.), *Anti-Gay Rights: Assessing Voter Initiatives* (pp. 3–32). Westport, CT: Praeger.

Dreyfuss, R. (1996, May–June). The biggest deal: Lobbying to take Social Security private. *American Prospect, 26,* 72–75.

Duster, T. (1996). Individual fairness, group preferences, and the California strategy. *Representations, 55,* 41–58.

Dworak, R. J. (1980). *Taxpayers, Taxes, and Government Spending: Perspectives on the Taxpayer Revolt.* New York: Praeger.

Dye, T. R., & Ziegler, L. H. (1996). *The Irony of Democracy: An Uncommon Introduction to American Politics.* Belmont, CA: Wadsworth.

Eaton, W. W. (1985). *Epidemiologic Field Methods in Psychiatry: The NIMH Epidemiological Catchment Area Program.* Orlando, FL: Academic Press.

Edman, Irwin (Ed). (1956). *The Works of Plato.* New York: Modern Library.

Education Data Partnership. (2007). *The Basics of California's School Finance System.* http://www.edsource.org/pdf/QA_financefinal.pdf (accessed December 30, 2007).

Egan, T. (2004, October 20). Towns hand out tax breaks, then cry foul as jobs leave. *Herald Tribune.* http://www.heraldtribune.com/apps/pbcs.dll/article?AID=/20041020/ZNYT02/410200700; http://www.ed-data.kl2.ca.us/Finance/SFPrime2.asp.

Ehrlichman, J. D. (1982). *Witness to Power: The Nixon Years.* New York: Simon & Schuster.

Eisenberg, J. (1995). Economics. *Journal of the American Medical Association, 273*(21), 1670–1671.

Elder, S., & Sorrentino, C. (1993, October). Japan's low unemployment: A BLS update and revision. United States Bureau of Labor Statistics. *Monthly Labor Review.* http://findarticles.com/p/articles/mi_m1153/is_n10_v116/ai_14668379/pg_1 (accessed January 21, 2008).

Elliott, C. (2008, January 7). Department of Medical Ethics: Guinea-pigging. *The New Yorker,* 36–41.

Engels, F. (1972). *The Origin of the Family, Private Property, and the State.* New York: Pathfinder.

Erickson, S. K., Campbell, A., & Lamberti, J. S. (2006). Variations in mental health courts: Challenges, opportunities, and a call for caution. *Community Mental Health Journal, 42*(4), 335–344.

Erikson, K. (1976). *Everything in Its Path.* New York: Simon & Schuster.

Eskridge, W. N. (1999). *Gaylaw: Challenging the Apartheid of the Closet.* Cambridge, MA: Harvard University Press.

Estes, C. L., Swan, J. H., & Associates. (1993). *The Long-Term Care Crisis: Elders Trapped in the No Care Zone.* Newbury Park, CA: Sage.

Eurostat. (2007). *Harmonized Unemployment.* http://europa.eu.int/estatref/info/sdds/en/une/une_sm.htm#concepts (accessed January 21, 2008).

Euthanasia Research and Guidance Organization (ERGO). (1998). *Dr. Jack Kevorkian.* http://www.efn.org/~ergo/dr.k.html.

Evan, W. E., & Macpherson, D. (1994). *Trends in Individual and Household Pension Coverage. Final Report Submitted to Department of Labor.* Contract No.

41USC252C3. http://www.sba.muohio.edu/evenwe/res%20papers/trends%20in%20ind%20and%20hh.pdf.

Eysenck, H. J. (1973). *The Inequality of Man.* London: Temple Smith.

Ezell, M. (2001). *Advocacy in the Human Services.* Belmont, CA: Brooks/Cole.

Ezorsky, G. (1991). *Racism and Justice: The Case for Affirmative Action.* Ithaca, NY: Cornell University Press.

Faillace, M. (2004). *Disability Law Deskbook: The Americans with Disabilities Act in the Workplace.* New York: Practising Law Institute.

Fanshel, D., & Shinn, E. B. (1978). *Children in Foster Care: A Longitudinal Investigation.* New York: Columbia University Press.

Farhang, S. & Katznelson, I. (2005). The Southern Imposition: Congress and labor in the New Deal and Fair Deal. *Studies in American Political Development, 19,* 1–30.

Farmer, P. (1996). Social inequalities and emerging infectious diseases. *Emerging Infectious Diseases, 2*(4), 259–271.

Federal Bureau of Investigation (FBI). (2004). *Hate Crime Statistics, 2003.* Washington, DC: FBI, U.S. Department of Justice. http://www.fbi.gov/ucr/03hc .pdf (accessed March 14, 2008).

Fee, E., & Porter, D. (1991). Public health, preventive medicine, and professionalization: Britain and the United States in the nineteenth century. In E. B. Fee & R. M. Acheson (Eds.), *A History of Education in Public Health: Health That Mocks the Doctors' Rules* (pp. 15–43). Oxford: Oxford University Press.

Feinson, M. C. (1991). Reexamining some common beliefs about mental health and aging. In B. B. Hess & E. W. Markson (Eds.), *Growing Old in America* (4th ed., pp. 125–136). New Brunswick, NJ: Transaction.

Feld, B. C. (1999). *Bad Kids: Race and the Transformation of the Juvenile Court.* New York: Oxford University Press.

Fernandes, D. C. (2004). Race, socioeconomic development and the educational stratification process in Brazil. *Research in Social Stratification and Mobility, 22,* 365–422.

Fields, B. (1982). Ideology and race in American history. In J. M. Kousser & J. M. McPherson (Eds.), *Region, Race, and Reconstruction: Essays in Honor of C. Vann Woodward* (pp. 143–177). New York: Oxford University Press.

Fischer, D. H. (1977). *Growing Old in America.* New York: Oxford University Press.

Fischer, L. R., & Eustis, N. N. (1989). Quicker and sicker: How changes in Medicare affect the elderly and their families. *Journal of Geriatric Psychiatry, 22*(2), 163–191.

Fisher, G. M. (1997, Spring). Setting American standards of poverty: A look back. *Focus, 19*(2), 47–52. http://www.ssc.wisc.edu/irp/pubs/focl92.pdf.

Fisher, W. F. (1987). *Human Communication as Narration: Toward a Philosophy of Reason, Value, and Action.* Columbia, SC: University of South Carolina Press.

Fisher, W. H., & Drake, R. E. (2007). Forensic mental illness and other policy misadventures. Commentary on "Extending assertive community treatment to criminal justice settings: Origins, current evidence and future directions." *Community Mental Health Journal, 43*(5), 545–548.

Fix, M. E., & Passel, J. S. (2002). *The Scope and Impact of Welfare Reform's Immigrant Provisions.* Urban Institute. New Federalism Discussion Paper No. 02-03. http://www.urban.org/publications/410412.html (accessed February 5, 2008).

Flaks, D. K., Ficher, I., Masterpasqua, F., & Joseph, G. (1995). Lesbians choosing motherhood: A comparative study of lesbian and heterosexual parents and their children. *Developmental Psychology, 31,* 105–114.

Fleischer, D. Z., & Zames, F. (2001). *The Disability Rights Movement: From Charity to Confrontation.* Philadelphia: Temple University Press.

Fleury, R. E., Sullivan, C. M., Bybee, D. I., & Davidson, W. S. (1998). "Why don't they just call the cops?" Reasons for differential police contact among women with abusive partners. *Violence and Victims, 13*(4), 333–346.

Flora, P. (Ed.). (1983). *State, Economy, and Society in Western Europe, 1815–1975: A Data Handbook. Vol. 1, The Growth of Mass Democracies and Welfare States.* Frankfurt: Campus Verlag.

Flora, P., & Heidenheimer, A. J. (Eds.). (1981). *The Development of Welfare States in Europe and America.* New Brunswick and London: Transaction.

Foner, P. S. (1981). *Organized Labor and the Black Worker, 1619–1981.* New York: International Publishers.

Fordyce, E. J. (1996, April–June). Urban mortality: Race or place? *Statistical Bulletin, 77*(2), 2–10.

Fox, M., & Passel, J. S. (1994). *Immigration and Immigrants: Setting the Records Straight.* Washington, DC: Urban Institute. http://www.urban.org.

Fraikor, A. L. (1973). *An Anthropological Analysis of Tay-Sachs Disease: Genetic Drift among the Ashkenazim Jews.* Boulder, CO: University of Colorado Press.

Frank, D. (2004). Where is the history of U.S. labor and international solidarity: Part I: A moveable feast. *Labor: Studies in Working Class History of the Americas, 1*(1), 95–119.

Frank, M. (2007). The evolution of male-male sexual behavior in humans: The Alliance Theory. *Journal of Psychology and Human Sexuality, 18*(4), 275–311.

Freeman, J. (1991). How "sex" got into Title VII: Persistent opportunism as a maker of public policy. *Law and Inequality: A Journal of Theory and Practice, 9*(2), 163–184.

Friedman, M. (1955). The role of government in education. In Robert A. Solo (Ed.), *Economics and the Public Interest.* Princeton, NJ: Trustees of Rutgers College.

Friedman, M. (1962). Excerpt from *Capitalism and Freedom.* Reprinted with permission in Sterba, 1980.

Friedman, M., & Friedman, R. (1979). *Free to Choose.* New York: Harcourt Brace Jovanovich.

Friedman, M. S. (1960). *Martin Buber: The Life of Dialogue.* New York: Harper Torchbook.

Friedman, R. C., & Downey, J. I. (2002). *Sexual Orientation and Psychoanalysis.* New York: Columbia University Press.

Friends Committee on National Legislation. (1987, August/September). With all due respect to the "founding fathers": Indian contributions to the U.S. Constitution. *Indian Report.* http://www.fcnl.org.

Frumkin, P., & Andre-Clark, A. (1999). The rise of the corporate social worker. *Society, 36*(6), 46–52.

Funiciello, T. (1993). *Tyranny of Kindness: Dismantling the Welfare System to End Poverty in America.* New York: Atlantic Monthly Press.

Galas, J. (1996). *Gay Rights.* San Diego, CA: Lucent Books.

Gans, H. (1971, July/August). The uses of poverty: The poor pay all. *Social Policy, 2*(2), 20–24.

Garfinkel, I. (1992a). *Assuring Child Support: An Extension of Social Security.* New York: Russell Sage Foundation.

Garfinkel, I. (1992b). Child-support trends in the U.S. In L. J. Weitzman & M. MacLean (Eds.), *Economic Consequences of Divorce: The International Perspective* (pp. 205–218). New York: Oxford University Press.

Gayle, H. (2000, September). An overview of the global HIV/AIDS epidemic, with a focus on the United States. *AIDS, 14*(suppl. 2), s8–s17.

Gelfand, D. E. (1988). *The Aging Network: Programs and Services.* New York: Springer.

George, C. (2000). *Life Under the Jim Crow Laws.* San Diego, CA: Lucent Books.

George, R. M., & Lee, B. J. (1997). Abuse and neglect of children. In R. A. Maynard (Ed.), *Kids Having Kids: Economic Costs and Social Consequences of Teen Pregnancy* (pp. 181–203). Washington, DC: Urban Institute Press.

Gibelman, M., & Schervish, P. H. (1995). Pay equity in social work: Not! *Social Work, 40*(5), 622–629.

Gibelman, M., & Schervish, P. H. (1997). *Who We Are: A Second Look.* Washington, DC: NASW Press.

Gil, D. G. (1992). *Unravelling Social Policy: Theory, Analysis, and Political Action Towards Social Equality* (5th ed.). Rochester, VT: Schenkman Books.

Gil, D. G. (1998). *Confronting Injustice and Oppression: Concepts and Strategies for Social Workers.* New York: Columbia University Press.

Gilbert, N., & Gilbert, B. (1989). *The Enabling State: Modern Welfare Capitalism in America.* New York: Oxford University Press.

Gilbert, N., & Terrell, P. (2002). *Dimensions of Social Welfare Policy.* Boston: Allyn & Bacon.

Gilder, G. (1981). *Wealth and Poverty.* New York: Basic Books.

Gilovich, T. (1991). *How We Know What Isn't So: The Fallibility of Human Reason in Everyday Life.* New York: Free Press.

Gohmann, S. F., & McClure, J. E. (1987). Supreme Court rulings on pension plans: The effect on retirement age and wealth of single people. *Gerontologist, 27,* 471–477.

Goldberg, D. T. (1993). *Racist Culture: Philosophy and the Politics of Meaning.* Cambridge, MA: Blackwell.

Good, H. G. (1962). *A History of American Education* (2nd ed.). New York: Macmillan.

Gordon, M. (1964). *Assimilation in American Life: The Role of Race, Religion, and National Origins*. New York: Oxford University Press.

Gorz, A. (1985). *Paths to Paradise: On the Liberation from Work*. London: Pluto Press.

Gorz, A. (1994). *Capitalism, Socialism, Ecology*. London: Verso.

Gossett, T. (1965). *Race: The History of an Idea in America*. New York: Oxford University Press.

Gottfried, A. E., & Gottfried, A. W. (Eds.). (1994). *Redefining Families: Implications for Children's Development*. New York: Plenum Press.

Graetz, M. J., & Schenk, D. H. (1995). *Federal Income Taxation: Principles and Policies*. Westbury, NY: Foundation Press.

Graham, H. D. (1990). *The Civil Rights Era: Origins and Development of National Policy, 1960–1972*. New York: Oxford University Press.

Grambs, J. D. (1989). *Women Over Forty: Visions and Realities*. Springer: New York.

Graves, E. J. (1995). 1993 Summary: National Hospital Discharge Survey. *Advance Data from Vital and Health Statistics*, No. 264. Hyattsville, MD: National Center for Health Statistics.

Gray, G. (1985). *National Commission on Unemployment and Mental Health. Resource Papers to the Report of the National Mental Health Association Commission on the Prevention of Mental Emotional Disabilities*. Alexandria, VA: National Mental Health Association.

Greenberg, D. F. (1988). *The Construction of Homosexuality*. Chicago: University of Chicago Press.

Greene, R. (1989). The growing need for social work services for the aged in 2020. In B. S. Vourlekis & C. G. Leukefeld (Eds.), *Making Our Case: A Resource Book of Selected Materials for Social Workers in Health Care* (pp. 11–17). Silver Spring, MD: National Association of Social Workers.

Greenhouse, L. (2005, March 2). Supreme Court, 5–4, forbids execution in juvenile crime. *New York Times*, p. A1.

Greenstone, J. D. (1969). *Labor in American Politics*. New York: Knopf.

Gresenz, C. R., Watkins, K., & Podus, D. (1998). Supplemental Security Income (SSI), Disability Insurance (DI), and substance abusers. *Community Mental Health Journal, 34*(4), 337–350.

Grob, G. N. (1994). *The Mad Among Us: A History of the Care of America's Mentally Ill*. New York: The Free Press.

Grossman, J. (1978, June). Fair Labor Standards Act of 1938: Maximum struggle for a minimum wage. *Monthly Labor Review*, 22–30.

Gurr, T. R. (1989). The history of violent crime in America: An overview. In T. R. Gurr (Ed.), *Violence in America: The History of Crime*. Newbury Park, CA: Sage.

Gutman, H. (1976). *The Black Family in Slavery and Freedom, 1750–1925*. New York: Pantheon Books.

Guttmacher Institute. (2002). *Teen Pregnancy: Trends and Lessons Learned*. http://www.guttmacher.org/pubs/tgr/05/1/gr050107.html (accessed December 31, 2007).

Guttmacher Institute. (2006). *U.S. Teenage Pregnancy Statistics: National and State Trends and Trends by Race and Ethnicity*. http://www.guttmacher.org/pubs/2006/09/12/USTPstats.pdf (accessed December 31, 2007).

Haber, C. (1983). *Beyond Sixty-Five: The Dilemma of Old Age in America's Past*. Cambridge: Cambridge University Press.

Haber, C., & Gratton, B. (1994). *Old Age and the Search for Security: An American Social History*. Bloomington: Indiana University Press.

Haldeman, H. R. (1994). *The Haldeman Diaries: Inside the Nixon White House*. New York: G.P. Putnam's Sons.

Hanlon, J. J., & Pickett, G. E. (1979). *Public Health Administration and Practice*. St. Louis: Mosby.

Hardcastle, D. A., Wenocur, S., & Powers, P. R. (1996). *Community Practice: Theories and Skills for Social Workers*. New York: Oxford University Press.

Harrington, M. (1984). *The New American Poverty*. New York: Holt, Rinehart & Winston.

Hartwell, S. (2003). Short-term outcomes for offenders with mental illness released from incarceration. *International Journal of Offender Therapy and Comparative Criminology, 47*(2), 145–158.

Harvard Law Review Editors. (1990). *Sexual Orientation and the Law*. Cambridge, MA: Harvard University Press.

Harvey, S. (n.d). *Rosie the Riveter: Real Women Workers in World War II.* http://www.loc.gov/rr/program/journey/rosie-transcript.html (accessed January 18, 2007).

Hattersley, J., Hosking, G. P., Morrow, D., & Myers, M. (1987). *People with Mental Handicap: Perspectives on Intellectual Disability.* London: Faber & Faber.

Hayashi, R. (2004). The environment of disability today. In G. May & M. Raske (Eds.), *Ending Disability Discrimination: Strategies for Social Workers* (pp. 45–70). Boston: Allyn & Bacon.

Hayashi, R. (2007). MiCASSA—My Home. *Journal of Social Work in Disability and Rehabilitation. 6*(1–2), 35–52.

Hayek, F. A. (1960). Excerpt from *The Constitution of Liberty.* Reprinted with permission in Sterba, 1980.

Hayes, C. D., Palmer, J. L., & Zaslow, M. J. (1990). *Who Cares for America's Children? Child Care Policy for the 1990s.* Washington, DC: National Academy Press.

Head, S. (1996, February 29). The new ruthless economy. *New York Review of Books,* 47–52.

Hefetz, A., & Warner, M. (2004). Privatization and its reverse: Explaining the dynamics of the government contracting process. *Journal of Public Administration Research and Theory, 14*(2), 171–190.

Heffler, S., Smith, S., Keehan, S., Borger, C., Clemens, M. K., & Truffer, C. (2005). Trends: U.S. Health Spending Projections for 2004–2014. *Health Affairs.* http://content.healthaffairs.org/cgi/reprint/hlthaff.w5.74v1.

Henetz, P. (1998, March 15). Getting to the roots of gender discrimination. *Salt Lake Tribune,* p. A1.

Hening, W. W. (Ed.). (1809–1823). *The Statutes at Large: Being a Collection of All the Laws of Virginia from the First Session of the Legislature in the Year 1619* (Vols. 1–13). Richmond, VA: Samuel Pleasants. Cited by Grob, 1994.

Henry J. Kaiser Foundation. (2006). *Race, Ethnicity and Health Care Fact Sheet: Young African American Men in the United States.* www.kff.org/minorityhealth/upload/7541.pdf (accessed October 27, 2007).

Henry J. Kaiser Family Foundation. (2007). *HIV/AIDS Policy Fact Sheet.* http://www.kff.org/hivaids/upload/3029-071.pdf (accessed November 3, 2007).

Herman, A. (1999). *Report on the American Workforce.* Secretary of Labor. http://stats.bls.gov/opub/rtaw/message.htm.

Herring, C. (Ed.). (1997). *African Americans and the Public Agenda: The Paradoxes of Public Policy.* Thousand Oaks, CA: Sage.

Herrnstein, R., & Murray, C. (1994). *The Bell Curve: Intelligence and Class Structure in American Life.* New York: Free Press.

Herzog, A. R. (1989). Physical and mental health in older women: Selected research issues and data sources. In J. A. Hendricks (Ed.), *Health and Economic Status of Older Women* (pp. 35–91). New York: Baywood.

Himmelstein, D., & Woolhandler, S. (1995). Care denied: US residents who are unable to obtain needed medical services. *American Journal of Public Health, 85*(3), 341–344.

Hodgins, S. (1992). Mental disorder, intellectual deficiency, and crime. *Archives of General Psychiatry, 49,* 476–483.

Hoff, R. (1988). *I Can See You Naked: A Fearless Guide to Making Great Presentations.* Kansas City: Andrews & McMeel.

Hoffman, S. D., & Seidman, L. S. (1990). *The Earned Income Tax Credit: Antipoverty Effectiveness and Labor Market Effects.* Kalamazoo, MI: W.E. Upjohn Institute for Employment Research.

Hoffman, W. (2000). The trouble with Medicare HMOs: Health plans say money is the key but critics see other problems. *ACP-ASIM Observer.* http://www.acponline.org/journals/news/dec00/medicarehmos.htm.

Holden, K., & Smeeding, T. (1990). The poor, the rich, and the insecure elderly caught in between. *Milbank Quarterly, 16,* 227–239.

Holinger, P. C., Offer, D., Barter, J. T., & Bell, C. C. (1994). *Suicide and Homicide Among Adolescents.* New York: Guilford Press.

Holland, W. (2007). Negotiator for Steelworkers Union; Executive Director, Utah Democratic Party. Personal communication.

Holzer, C., Shea, B., Swanson, J., Leaf, P., Myers, J., George, L., Weissman, M., & Bednarski, P. (1986). The increased risk for specific psychiatric disorders among persons of low socioeconomic status. *American Journal of Social Psychiatry, 6,* 259–271.

Holzer, C. E., Leaf, P. J., & Weissman, M. M. (1985). Living with depression. In M. R. Haug, A. B. Ford, & M. Sheafor (Eds.), *The Physical and Mental Health of Aged Women* (pp. 101–116). New York: Springer.

hooks, b. (2001). Feminism: A transformational politic. In P. S. Rothenberg (Ed.), *Race, Class, and Gender in the United States: An Integrated Study* (pp. 601–608). New York: Worth Publishers.

Horney, J., & Spohn, C. (1991). Rape law reform and instrumental change in six urban jurisdictions. *Law and Society Review, 25*(1), 117–153.

Human Rights Campaign. (2000). *State of the Workplace for Lesbian, Gay, Bisexual, and Transgendered Americans: 2000.* http://www.hrc.org/worknet/publications/stateworkplace/2000/sow2000.pdf.

Human Rights Campaign. (2001). Hewlett-Packard, General Mills, and others back federal employment non-discrimination bill. http://www.hrc.org/worknet/workalert/2001/0408/article01.asp.

Human Rights Watch. (2000). *Fingers to the Bone: United States Failure to Protect Child Farmworkers.* http://www.hrw.org/reports/2000/frmwrkr/ (accessed January 21, 2008).

Humphreys, K., & Rosenheck, R. (1995). Sequential validation of cluster analytic subtypes of homeless veterans. *American Journal of Community Psychology, 23*(1), 75–98.

Hunter, N., & Rubenstein, W. (1992). AIDS and civil rights: The new agenda. *AIDS and Public Policy Journals, 7*(4), 204–208.

Internal Revenue Service. (2007, Fall). Individual Income Tax Returns, Figure F, *Statistics of Income Bulletin.* http://taxprof.typepad.com/taxprof_blog/2007/12/irs-releases-fa.html (accessed January 18, 2008).

Jacobson, P. H. (1959). *American Marriage and Divorce.* New York: Rinehart & Company.

Jacoby, R. (1975). *Social Amnesia: A Critique of Conformist Psychology from Adler to Laing.* Boston: Beach Press.

Jahnigen, D., & Binstock, R. H. (1991). Economic and clinical realities: Health care for older people. In R. H. Binstock & S. G. Post (Eds.), *Too Old for Health Care: Controversies in Medicine, Law, Economics and Ethics.* Baltimore: Johns Hopkins University Press.

Jamison, K. R. (1993). *Touched With Fire: Manic-Depressive Illness and the Artistic Temperament.* New York: Macmillan.

Jansson, B. (1999). *Becoming an Effective Policy Advocate: From Policy Practice to Social Justice* (3rd ed.). Pacific Grove: Brooks/Cole.

Jansson, B. (2002) *Becoming an Effective Policy Advocate: From Policy Practice to Social Justice* (4th ed.). Belmont, CA: Wadsworth.

Jefferson, T. (1854). Letter from Thomas Jefferson to Mr. Correa, Nov. 25, 1817. In H. A. Washington (Ed.), *The Writings of Thomas Jefferson.* New York: Riker, Thorne & Co. Cited by U.S. Commission on Civil Rights, 1967.

Jensen, A. R. (1973). *Educability and Group Differences.* London: Methuen.

Johansen, B. (2002). Native Americans in the 2000 census: Far from the "vanishing race." *Native Americas, 19*(1/2), 42–45.

Johnson, J. C., & Smith, N. H. (2002, Fall). Health and social issues associated with racial, ethnic, and cultural disparities. *Generations,* 25–32.

Johnston, D. D. (1994). *The Art and Science of Persuasion.* Boston: McGraw-Hill.

Jonas, S., & Kovner, A. (2002). *Health Care Delivery in the United States* (7th ed.). New York: Springer Publishing Company.

Jones, G. W. (Ed.). (1972). *Cotton Mather, The Angel of Bethesda.* Bane, MA: American Antiquarian Society and Bane Publishers. Cited by Grob, 1994.

Jurik, N. J. (2004). Imagining justice: Challenging the privatization of public life. *Social Problems, 51*(1), 1–15.

Kadushin, A. (1974). *Child Welfare Services* (2nd ed.). New York: Macmillan.

Kaiser Commission on the Future of Medicaid. (1993). *The Medicaid Cost Explosion: Causes and Consequences.* Baltimore: Kaiser Family Foundation.

Kaiser Family Foundation. (n.d.). *Total Medicaid Spending, FY 2006.* http://www.statehealthfacts.org/comparetable.jsp?ind=177&cat=4 (accessed February 12, 2008).

Kaiser Family Foundation. (2006). *Employee Health Benefits: 2006 Annual Survey.* http://www.kff.org/insurance/7315.cfm (accessed January 21, 2008).

Kaiser Family Foundation (2007). *The HIV/AIDS Epidemic in the United States.* http://www.kff.org/hivaids/upload/3029-071.pdf (accessed December 27, 2007).

Kaplan, M., & Krell-Long, L. (1993). AIDS, health policy, and ethics. *Affilia, 8*(2), 157–170.

Karabanow, J. (2004). *Being Young and Homeless: Understanding How You Enter and Exit Street Life*. New York: Peter Lang.

Karger, H. (1988). *Social Workers and Labor Unions*. New York: Greenwood Press.

Karger, H. J., & Stoesz, D. (2002). *American Social Welfare Policy: A Pluralist Approach*. Boston: Allyn & Bacon.

Kasper, J., & O'Malley, M. (2007). *Changes in Characteristics, Needs, and Payment for Care of Elderly Nursing Home Residents: 1999 to 2004*. Kaiser Commission on Medicaid and the Uninsured. http://www.kff .org/medicaid/7663.cfm (accessed January 10, 2008).

Kates, B. (1985). *The Murder of a Shopping Bag Lady*. New York: Harcourt Brace Jovanovich.

Katz, H. J. (1994, February 19). *Statement Before the Subcommittees on Social Security and Human Resources of the House Committee on Ways and Means. Hearing on Exploring Means of Achieving Higher Rates of Treatment and Rehabilitation Among Alcoholics and Drug Addicts Receiving Federal Disability Benefits*. 103rd Congress, 2nd Session. Cited by Gresenz, Watkins, & Podus, 1998.

Kaye, H. S. (Ed.). (2000). *Disability Watch: The Status of People with Disabilities in the United States*. http:// www.dralegal.org/publications/dw/.

Kaye, H. S., Kang, T., & LaPlante, M. P. (2002, May). Wheelchair use in the United States. *Disability Statistics Abstract, 23*. http://dsc.ucsf.edu/pub_listing .php?pub_typeabstract.

Kaye, H. S., LaPlante, M. P., Carlson, D., & Wenger, B. L. (1996). Trends in disability rates in the United States, 1970–1994. *Disability Statistics Abstract, 17*. http://dsc.ucsf.edu/pub_listing.php?pub_ typeabstract.

Kelley, M. (1999, April 28). American Indian boarding schools: "That hurt never goes away." CNEWS-Canada's Internet Network. http://www.canoe.ca/ CNEWSFeatures9904/28_indians.html.

Kelly, M. A., Perloff, J. D., Morris, N. M., & Liu, W. (1993). Access to primary care among young African-American children in Chicago. *Journal of Health and Social Policy, 5*(2), 35–48.

Kempe, C. H., Silverman, F., Steel, B., Droegemueller, W., & Silver, (1962). The battered child syndrome. *Journal of the American Medical Association, 181*, 17–24.

Kessler, R. C., McGonagle, K. A., Zhao, S., Nelson, C. B., Hughes, M., Eshleman, S., Wittchen, H. U., & Kendler, K. S. (1994). Lifetime and 12-month prevalence of DSM-III-R psychiatric disorders in the United States: Results from the National Comorbidity Survey. *Archives of General Psychiatry, 51*, 8–19.

Kessler-Harris, A. (1990). *A Woman's Wage: Historical Meanings and Social Consequences*. Lexington: University of Kentucky Press.

Kilburn, M. R., & Hao, L. (1996). *The Impact of Federal and State Policy Changes on Child Care in California*. Rand Corporation Report. http://www.rand.org/ publications/CF/CFI23/kilburn/.

Kingson, E. R., & Berkowitz, E. D. (1993). *Social Security and Medicare: A Policy Primer*. Westport, CT: Auburn House.

Kingson, E., & Quadagno, J. (1997). Social Security: Marketing radical reform. In R. B. Hudson (Ed.), *The Future of Age-Based Public Policy* (pp. 117–133). Baltimore: The Johns Hopkins University Press.

Kinsey, A. C., Pomeroy, W. B., & Martin, C. E. (1948). *Sexual Behavior in the Human Male*. Philadelphia: W. B. Saunders.

Kinsey, A. C., Pomeroy, W. B., Martin, C. E., & Gebhard, P. H. (1953). *Sexual Behavior in the Human Female*. Philadelphia: W. B. Saunders.

Klein, J. D., Woods, A. H., Wilson, K. M., Prospero, M., Greene, J., & Ringwalt, C. (2000). Homeless and runaway youths' access to health care. *Journal of Adolescent Health, 27*, 331–339.

Klerman, G. L. (1987). Clinical epidemiology of suicide. *Journal of Clinical Psychiatry, 48*(suppl.), 33–38.

Kloss, H. (1998). *The American Bilingual Tradition* (2nd ed.). Washington, DC: ERIC, Clearinghouse on Language and Linguistics.

Koebel, C. T. (1998). Nonprofit housing: Theory, research, and policy. In C. T. Koebel (Ed.), *Shelter and Society: Theory, Research and Policy for Nonprofit Housing* (pp. 3–20). New York: State University of New York Press.

Koegel, P., Burnham, M. A., & Baumohl, J. (1996). The causes of homelessness. In J. Baumohl (Ed.), *Homelessness in America*. Phoenix: Oryx Press.

Korczyk, S. M. (1993). *Why Has Women's Pension Coverage Improved?* Paper presented at the 1993 meeting of the Eastern Economic Association.

Kozol, J. (1991). *Savage Inequalities: Children in America's Schools*. New York: Crown Publishers.

Krause, N. (1986). Stress and sex differences in depressive symptoms among older adults. *Journal of Gerontology, 41,* 727–731.

Ku, L., & Broaddus, M. (2003). *Why Are States' Medicaid Expenditures Rising?* Center on Budget and Policy Priorities. http://www.cbpp.org/1-13-03health .htm (accessed February 12, 2008).

Ku, L., & Garrett, B. (2000). *How Welfare Reform and Economic Factors Affected Medicaid Participation*. Washington, DC: Urban Institute. http://www.urban.org/ Template.cfm?NavMenuID24&template/Tagged Content/ViewPublication.cfm&PublicationID7369.

Kupers, T. (1999). *Prison Madness*. San Francisco: Jossey-Bass.

LaBruzza, A. L., with Mendez-Villarrubia, J. M. (1994). *Using DSM-IV: A Clinician's Guide to Psychiatric Diagnosis*. Northvale, NJ: Jason Aronson.

Lamb, R. H., Weinberger, L. E., & Reston-Parham, C. (1996). Court intervention to address the mental health needs of mentally ill offenders. *Psychiatric Services, 47,* 275–281.

LaRue, A., Dessonville, C., & Jarvik, L. F. (1985). Aging and mental disorders. In J. E. Birren & K. W. Shaie (Eds.), *Handbook of the Psychology of Aging* (pp. 664–702). New York: Van Nostrand Reinhold.

Lasch, C. (1979). *Haven in a Heartless World: The Family Besieged*. New York: Basic Books.

Lee, K., & Dodgson, R. (2000). Globalization and cholera: Implications for global governance. *Global Governance, 6*(2), 213–236.

Leibowitz, A. H. (1969). English literacy: Legal sanction for discrimination. *Notre Dame Lawyer, 45*(7), 7–76.

Leiby, J. (1978). *A History of Social Welfare and Social Work in the United States*. New York: Columbia University Press.

Leighninger, L. (1990). Professionalism in British and American social work. *Current Research on Occupations and Professions, 5,* 29–42.

Lemann, N. (1986). The origins of the underclass. *Atlantic Monthly* (June), 31–55; (July), 54–68.

Leonard, K. K., Pope, C. E., & Feyerherm, W. H. (Eds.). (1995). *Minorities in the Juvenile Justice System*. Thousand Oaks, CA: Sage.

Levine, D. (1997). The Constitution as rhetorical symbol in Western anti-gay-rights initiatives: The case of

Idaho. In S. L. Witt & S. McCorkle (Eds.), *Anti-Gay Rights: Assessing Voter Initiatives* (pp. 33–50). Westport, CT: Praeger.

Levine, M. J. (2003). *Children for Hire: The Perils of Child Labor in the United States*. Westwood, CT: Praeger Publishers.

Lewin Group. (1998). *Policy Evaluation of the Effect of Legislation Prohibiting the Payment of Disability Benefits to Individuals Whose Disability Is Based on Drug Addiction and Alcoholism: Interim Report, April 28, 1998*. Washington, DC: Social Security Administration.

Lewis, M. A., & Widerquist, K. (2002). *Economics for Social Workers: The Application of Economic Theory to Social Policy and the Human Services*. New York: Columbia University Press.

Lewis, O. (1965). *La Vida*. New York: Harper & Row.

Lichtenberg, F. S., & Sun, S. X. (2007, November/December). The impact of Medicare Part D on prescription drug use by the elderly. *Health Affairs,* 1735–1744.

Lichtenstein, A. (1996). *Twice the Work of Free Labor: The Political Economy of Convict Labor in the New South*. New York: Verso.

Limerick, P. N. (1987). *The Legacy of Conquest: The Unbroken Past of the American West*. New York: Norton.

Link, B., Phelan, J., Bresnahan, M., Stueve, A., Moore, R., & Susser, E. (1995, July). Lifetime and five-year prevalence of homelessness in the United States: New evidence on an old debate. *American Journal of Orthopsychiatry, 65*(3), 347–354.

Link, B. G., Andrews, H., & Cullen, F. T. (1992). The violent and illegal behavior of mental patients reconsidered. *American Sociological Review, 57,* 275–292.

Liptak, A. (2004, November 12). Caution in the court for gay rights groups: Fearing backlash, legal challenges will focus on civil unions. *New York Times,* p. A16.

Littell, J. (1995). Debates with authors: Evidence or assertions? The outcomes of family preservation services. *Social Service Review, 69,* 344–351.

Little, A. (1998). *Post-Industrial Socialism: Towards a New Politics of Welfare*. London: Routledge.

Loewen, J. (1995). *Lies My Teacher Told Me*. New York: Simon & Schuster.

Longman, P. (1987). *Born to Pay: The New Politics of Aging in America*. Boston: Houghton Mifflin.

Longmore, P. K. (2000). Introduction. In H. S. Kaye (Ed.), *Disability Watch: The Status of People with Disabilities in the United States*. http://www.dralegal.org/publications/dw/.

Longmore, P. K., & Umansky, L. (2001). Disability history: From the margins to the mainstream. In P. K. Longmore & L. Umansky (Eds.), *The New Disability History: American Perspectives* (pp. 1–33). New York: New York University Press.

Lorwin, L. (1929). *Labor and Internationalism*. New York: Macmillan.

Lubben, J. E., Damron-Rodriguez, J. A., & Beck, J. C. (1992). A national survey of aging curriculum in schools of social work. *Geriatric Social Work Education, 18,* 157–171.

Lubbers, J. S. (1998). *A Guide to Federal Rulemaking*. Washington, DC: Government and Public Sector Lawyers Division of the American Bar Association.

Maas, H. S., & Engler, R. E. (1959). *Children in Need of Parents*. New York: Columbia University Press.

MacAskill, E. (2007, August 13). U.S. tumbles down the world ratings list for life expectancy. *The Guardian*. http://www.guardian.co.uk/world/2007/aug/13/usa.ewenmacaskill (accessed February 20, 2008).

Malkiel, B. G., & Malkiel, J. A. (1973). Male–female pay differentials in professional employment. *American Economic Review, 63,* 693–705.

Mandel, J. (1992). *Not Slave, Not Free: The African American Economic Experience*. Durham, NC: Duke University Press.

Mantsios, G. (2001). Class in America: Myths and realities. In P. S. Rothenberg (Ed.), *Race, Class, and Gender in the United States: An Integrated Study* (5th ed., pp. 168–182). New York: Worth.

Mark, T. L., Levit, K. R., Coffey, R. M., McKusick, D. R., Harwood, H. J., King, E. C., Bouhery, E., Genuardi, J. S., Vandivort-Warren, R., Buck, J. A., & Ryan, K. (2007). *National Expenditures for Mental Health Services and Substance Abuse Treatment, 1993–2003*. SAMHSA Publication No. SMA 07-4227. Rockville, MD: Substance Abuse and Mental Health Services Administration. http://www.samhsa.gov.

Marx, K. (1888). *The Communist Manifesto* (Friedrich Engels, Trans.). Reprinted with permission in Sterba, 1980.

Marzuk, P. M. (1996). Violence, crime, and mental illness: How strong a link? *Archives of General Psychiatry, 53,* 481–486.

Mason, M. (1994). *From Father's Property to Children's Rights*. New York: Cambridge University Press.

Mathematica. (2000). *Reaching Those in Need: Food Stamp Participation Rates in the States*. http://www.mathematics-mpr.com/3rdLevel/fins2ndbrochurehot.htm.

Mayfield, C. (Ed.). (1981). *Growing Up Southern: Southern Exposure Looks at Childhood, Then and Now*. New York: Pantheon Books.

Maynard, R. A. (Ed.). (1996). *Kids Having Kids: A Robin Hood Foundation Special Report on the Costs of Adolescent Childbearing*. New York: Robin Hood Foundation.

Maypole, D. E., & Skaine, R. (1983, September/October). Sexual harassment in the workplace. *Social Work, 28*(5), 385–390.

McCallum, D. M., & Bolland, J. M. (2001). Homelessness. In D. L. Peck & N. A. Dolch (Eds.), *Extraordinary Behavior: A Case Study Approach to Understanding Social Problems* (pp. 156–176). Westport, CT: Praeger.

McCaslin, R. (1987). Substantive specialization in masters level social work curricula. *Journal of Social Work Education, 23*(2), 8–18.

McGaughey, W. (2007). *Reviving an Economic Argument in the 21st Century: Information and Writings Which Favor Government Action to Reduce Work Time*. http://www.shorterworkweek.com/ (accessed January 20, 2008).

McLeod, H. R. (1995, Spring). The sale of a generation. American Prospect. http://www.prospect.org/web/page.ww?sectionroot&nameViewPrint&articleId5024.

McMurrer, D. P., & Chasanov, A. B. (1995, September). Trends in unemployment insurance benefits. *Monthly Labor Review,* 30–39.

Mechanic, D. (1962). Some factors in identifying and defining mental illness. *Mental Hygiene, 46,* 66–74.

Mechanic, D. (1999). *Mental Health and Social Policy: The Emergence of Managed Care*. Needham Heights, MA: Allyn & Bacon.

Melich, T. (1998). *The Republican War against Women*. New York: Bantam Books.

Merck Manual of Diagnosis and Therapy (16th ed.). (1992). Rahway, NJ: Merck.

MetLife. (2007). *Private and Semi-Private Room Nursing Home Rates Increase 3% in 2007*. http://www.metlife.com/Applications/Corporate/WPS/CDA/

PageGenerator/0,4773,P250%5ES1010,00.html? FILTERNAME=@URL\&FILTERVALUE=/ WPS/\&IMAGE2.X=0\&IMAGE2.Y=0 (accessed January 9, 2008).

Michael, R. T., Gagnon, J. H., Laumann, E. O., and Kolata, G. (1994). *Sex in America: A Definitive Survey.* Boston: Little, Brown.

Michlethwait, J., & Wooldridge, A. (2004). *The Right Nation: Conservative Power in America.* New York: Penguin Press.

Migration Policy Institute. (2005). *Lessons from the Immigration Reform and Control Act of 1986.* http:// migrationpolicy.org/pubs/PolicyBrief_No3_Aug05 .pdf (accessed January 20, 2008).

Mill, J. S. (1863). *Utilitarianism.* Reprinted in Sterba, 1980.

Miller, D. (1976). *Social Justice.* Oxford: Clarendon Press.

Miller, D. (1999). *Principles of Social Justice.* Cambridge: Oxford University Press.

Miller, R., & Luft, H. (1994). Managed care plan performance since 1980: A literature analysis. *Journal of the American Medical Association, 271*(19), 1512–1516.

Mintz, S., & Kellogg, S. (1988). *Domestic Revolutions: A Social History of American Family Life.* New York: Free Press.

Mishel, L., Bernstein, J., & Boushey, H. (2004). *The State of Working America: 2002/2003.* Washington, DC: Economic Policy Institute.

Mitchell, O. S., Levine, P. B., & Phillips, J. W. (1999). *The Impact of Pay Inequality, Occupational Segregation, and Lifetime Work Experience on the Retirement Income of Women and Minorities.* Washington, DC: AARP. http://research.aarp.org/econ/9910_women_l.html.

Mitteness, L. S. (1987). The treatment of urinary incontinence by community living elderly. *Gerontologist, 27,* 185–193.

Molloy, D., & Burmeister, L. (1990). Social workers in union-based programs. In Straussner, S. L. A. (Ed.), *Occupational Social Work Today* (pp. 37–51). Binghamton, NY: Haworth Press.

Monahan, J. (1992). Mental disorder and violent behavior. *American Psychologist, 47,* 511–521.

Monti, D. J. (1994). *Wannabe: Gangs in Suburbs and Schools.* Cambridge: Blackwell Publishers.

Moon, M. (1990, Summer). Public policies: Are they gender neutral? *Generations,* 59–63.

Moore, J. P. (1995). *Highlights of the 1995 Youth Gang Survey.* Office of Juvenile Justice and Delinquency Prevention (OJJDP). http://www.ncjrs.org/.

Moquin, W. (Ed.). (1972). *A Documentary History of Mexican Americans.* New York: Bantam Books.

Morgan, E. (1975). *American Slavery, American Freedom: The Ordeal of Colonial Virginia.* New York: Norton.

Morrissey, J. P., & Goldman, H. H. (1986). Care and treatment of the mentally ill in the United States: Historical developments and reforms. *Annals of the American Academy of Political and Social Science, 484,* 12–27.

Morrissey, T. W., & Banghart, P. (2007). *Family Child Care in the United States.* Child Care Bureau, U.S. Dept. of Health and Human Services. http://www .childcareresearch.org/SendPdf?resourceId=12036 (accessed February 27, 2008).

Morrow-Howell, N., Hinterlong, J., & Sherraden, M. (Eds.). (2001). *Productive Aging: Concepts and Challenges.* Baltimore: Johns Hopkins University Press.

Mulroy, E. (1990). Single-parent families and the housing crisis. *Social Work, 35,* 542–546.

Mulroy, E. A. (1995). *The New Uprooted: Single Mothers in Urban Life.* Westport, CT: Auburn House.

Munnell, A. H. (2006). *Policies to Promote Labor Force Participation of Older People.* Chestnut Hill, MA: Center for Retirement Research at Boston College. http://crr.bc.edu/working_papers/policies_to_ promote_labor_force_participation_of_older_ people.html (accessed January 21, 2008).

Muntaner, C., Eaton, W. W., Diala, C., Kessler, R. C., & Sorlie, P. D. (1998). Social class, assets, organizational control, and the prevalence of common groups of psychiatric disorders. *Social Science and Medicine, 47*(12), 2043–2053.

Murphy, J. M., Olivier, D. C., Monson, R. R., Sobol, A. M., Federman, E. B., & Leighton, A. H. (1991). Depression and anxiety in relation to social status: A prospective epidemiologic study. *Archives of General Psychiatry, 48*(3), 223–229.

Murphy, T. F. (2005). The search for the gay gene. *British Medical Journal: International Edition, 330*(7498), 1033.

Murray, C. (1994). *Losing Ground: American Social Policy, 1950–1980.* New York: Basic Books.

Mustard, D. B. (2001). Racial, ethnic, and gender disparities in sentencing: Evidence from the U.S.

federal courts. *The Journal of Law and Economics, 44*(1), 285–314.

National Advisory Mental Health Council. (1991). *Building Social Work Knowledge for Effective Services and Policies: A Plan for Research Development.* Washington, DC: NIMH. Available from IASWR, 750 First Street, NE, Suite 700, Washington, DC 20002–4241.

National Association for the Advancement of Colored People (NAACP). (1969). *Thirty Years of Lynching in the United States, 1889–1918.* New York: Arno Press.

National Association of Black Social Workers (NABSW). (1994). *Position Statement: Preserving African American Families.* Detroit: Author.

National Association of Social Workers (NASW). (1999). *Code of Ethics of the National Association of Social Workers.* Washington, DC: NASW.

National Association of State Units on Aging. (2005). *Quality in Medicaid Waiver Assisted Living: The Ombudsman Program's Role and Perspective.* http://www.nasua.org/Medicaid_Assisted_Living_Waiver.pdf (accessed January 9, 2007).

National Center for Education Statistics (NCES). (2004). *Digest of Education Statistics, 2003.* http://nces.ed.gov//programs/digest/d03/.

National Center for Education Statistics (NCES). (2007). *Digest of Education Statistics, 2005.* http://nces.ed.gov/programs/digest/d05/ (accessed August 29, 2007).

National Center for Health Statistics. (1998a). Births, Marriages, Divorces, and Deaths for August 1998. *National Vital Statistics Report, 47*(14). Hyattsville, MD: Author.

National Center for Health Statistics. (1998b). *National Mortality Followback Survey.* http://www.cdc.gov/nchs/about/major/nmfs/nmfs.htm (accessed January 15, 2003).

National Center for Health Statistics. (1998c). *Teen Birth Rates Down in All States: New Government Report on Teenage Birth Rates Includes State Rates by Race and Ethnicity.* http://www.cdc.gov/nchs/releases/98news/98news/teenrel.htm.

National Center for Health Statistics. (2004). *Fast Facts A-Z.* http://www.cdc.gov/nchs/fastats/teenbrth.htm (accessed August 29, 2007).

National Center for Health Statistics. (2007). *Overall Infant Mortality Rate in U.S. Largely Unchanged.* http://www.cdc.gov/nchs/pressroom/07newsreleases/infantmortality.htm (accessed January 13, 2007).

National Coalition for the Homeless. (1999). *The McKinney Act.* Fact sheet #19. http://www.nationalhomeless.org/mckinneyfacts.html.

National Conference of State Legislatures. (2007). *Managed Behavioral Health Care Carve-outs.* Health Chairs Project. http://www.ncsl.org/programs/health/forum/chairs/carveout.htm (accessed December 3, 2007).

National Education Association. (n.d.). *NEA Offers Plan to Improve NCLB.* http://www.nea.org/esea/index.html (accessed December 30, 2007).

National Indian Health Board. (2004). *Fiscal Year 2005 AI/AN National Budget Perspective.* www.nihb.org.

National Institute of Mental Health (NIMH). (1992, May 8). Social Work Research and Development Centers: Program Announcement. *NIH Guide, 21*(17). http://www.nimh.gov/grants/research/920078.cfm.

National Institute of Mental Health (NIMH). (2000). *Insurance Parity for Mental Health: Cost, Access, and Quality. Final Report to Congress by the National Advisory Mental Health Council.* NIH Publication No: 00-4787. http://nimh.nih.gov/publicat/nimhparity.pdf.

National Institute on Aging (NIA), National Institutes of Health. (1987). *Personnel for Health Needs of the Elderly Through the Year 2020.* DHHS-NIAH Pub. No. 87-2950. Washington, DC: U.S. Department of Health and Human Services.

National Policy and Resource Center on Women and Aging. (1996). "A big decision for women: Should I buy long-term care insurance?" *Women & Aging Letter, 1*(6). http://www.heller.brandeis.edu/national/ind.html.

Navarro, V. (1991, September). Class and race: Life and death situations. *Monthly Review, 43*(4), 1–13.

Nelson, F. H., Rosenberg, B., & Van Meter, N. (2004). *Charter School Achievement on the 2003 National Assessment of Educational Progress.* http://www.aft.org/pubs-reports/downloads/teachers/NAEPCharterSchoolReport.pdf.

Nicholson-Crotty, S. (2004). The politics and administration of privatization: contracting out for corrections management in the United States. *Policy Studies Journal, 32*(1), 41–57.

Noji, E. K. (2001). The global resurgence of infectious diseases. *Journal of Contingencies and Case Management, 9*(4), 223–232.

North American Association of State and Provincial Lotteries (NASPL). (1999). *Lottery History*. http://www.naspl.org/history.html.

Northrup, H. R. (1970). *Negro Employment in Southern Industry: A Study of Racial Policies in Five Industries*. Philadelphia: Industrial Research Unit, Wharton School of Finance and Commerce, University of Pennsylvania.

Nozick, R. (1974). *Anarchy, State, and Utopia*. New York: Basic Books.

North American Association of State and Provincial Lotteries (NASPL). (1999). *Lottery History*. http://www.naspl.org/history.html.

Nuschler, D. (2002). *Social Security Benefit Enhancements for Women Act of 2002* (HR 4069). Congressional Research Service Report for Congress. Report No: RS21228.

Nussbaum, M. (2001). The costs of tragedy: Some moral limits of cost–benefit analysis. In M. D. Adler & E. A. Posner (Eds.), *Cost–Benefit Analysis: Legal, Economic, and Philosophical Perspectives* (pp. 169–200). Chicago: University of Chicago Press.

Oaxaca, R. (1975). Sex discrimination in wages. In O. Ashenfelter & A. Rees (Eds.), *Discrimination in Labor Markets* (pp. 124–151). Princeton, NJ: Princeton University Press.

Offe, C., Muckenberger, U., & Ostner, I. (1996). A basic income guaranteed by the state: A need of the moment in social policy. In C. Offe (Ed.), *Modernity and the State: East, West*. Cambridge: Polity Press.

Office of Economic Development (OECD). (2007, May). *Main Economic Indicators 2005*. Paris: OECD.

Office of Management and Budget (OMB). (n.d.). *OMB Circular CFDA 17.225 Unemployemnt Insurance (UI) Program*. http://www.whitehouse.gov/omb/circulars/a133_compliance/17225.html (accessed March 14, 2008).

Office of Management and Budget (OMB). (2001a). *A Citizen's Guide to the Federal Budget: Budget of the United States Government, Fiscal Year 2001*. http://w3.access.gpo.gov/usbudget/FY2001/guidetoc.html.

Ogunwole, S. U. (2002). *The American Indian and Alaska Native Population: 2000. Census 2000 Brief*. Washington, DC: U.S. Bureau of the Census. http://www.census.gov/prod/2002pubs/c2kbr01-15.pdf (accessed February 24, 2003).

O'Keefe, B. J., & Shepherd, G. J. (1987). The pursuit of multiple objectives in face-to-face persuasive interactions: Effects of construct differentiation on message organization. *Communication Monographs, 54*, 396–419.

O'Keefe, D. (1992). *Persuasion: Theory and Research*. Newbury Park, CA: Sage.

Okin, S. (1989). *Justice, Gender and the Family*. Reprinted with permission in Sterba, 1980.

Oliver, M. L., & Shapiro, T. (1990). Wealth of a nation: A reassessment of asset inequality in America shows at least one third of households are asset poor. *American Journal of Economics and Sociology, 49*(2), 129–152.

Olshansky, S. J., Passaro, D. J., Hershow, R. C., Layden, J., Carnes, B. A., Brody, J., Hayflick, L., Butler, R. N., Allison, D. B., & Ludwig, D. S. (2005). A potential decline in life expectancy in the United States in the 21st century. *New England Journal of Medicine, 352*(11), 1138–1145.

Omi, M., & Winaut, H. (1994). *Racial Formation in the United States: From the 1960s to the 1990s* (2nd ed.). New York: Routledge.

Orentlicher, D. (1996, August 29). The legalization of physician-assisted suicide. *New England Journal of Medicine, 335*(9), 663–667.

Organization for Economic Cooperation and Development (OECD). (2007). *OECD Health Data 2007*. http://www.oecd.org/document/30/0,3343,en_2649_37407_12968734_1_1_1_37407,00.html (accessed March 14, 2008).

O'Rourke, S. P., & Dellinger, L. K. L. (1997). Romer v. Evans: The centerpiece of the American gay rights debate. In S. L. Witt & S. McCorkle (Eds.), *Anti-Gay Rights: Assessing Voter Initiatives* (pp. 133–140). Westport, CT: Praeger.

Orshansky, M. (1965). Counting the poor: Another look at the poverty profile. *Social Security Bulletin, 28*(1), 3–29.

Osborne, R. (1993). *Freud for Beginners*. New York: Writer's and Reader's Publishing.

Osipow, S. H., & Fitzgerald, L. F. (1993). Unemployment and mental health: A neglected relationship. *Applied and Preventive Psychology, 2*, 59–63.

Osumi, M. D. (1982). Asians and California's Anti-Miscegenation Laws. In N. Tsuchida (Ed.), *Asian and Pacific American Experiences: Women's Perspectives*. Minneapolis: Asian/Pacific American Learning

Resource Center and General College, University of Minnesota.

Overfield, T. (1995). *Biologic Variation in Health and Illness: Race, Age, and Sex Differences*. New York: CRC Press.

Owens, L. H. (1976). *This Species of Property: Slave Life and Culture in the Old South*. New York: Oxford University Press.

Owens, M. J. (1999). Battered women and their children: A public policy response. *AFFILLA: Journal of Women and Social Work, 14*(4), 439–459.

Paine, T. (1795). *Agrarian Justice*. http://www.ssa.gov/history/paine4.html.

Park, R. (1974). *The Collected Papers of Robert Ezra Park*. New York: Arno.

Parker, A. C. (1916). *The Constitution of the Five Nations, or the Iroquois Book of the Great Law*. Albany, NY: A.C. Irocrafts, reprinted by Iroquois Reprints.

Patterson, C. J. (1995). Lesbian mothers, gay fathers, and their children. In A. R. D'Augelli & C. J. York (Eds.), *Lesbian, Gay, and Bisexual Identities Across the Lifespan* (pp. 262–290). New York: Oxford University Press.

Patterson, C. J., & Redding, R. E. (1996). Lesbian and gay families with children: Implications of social science research for policy. *Journal of Social Issues, 52*(3), 29–50.

Pearson, J., & Griswold, E. A. (1997). Child support policies and domestic violence. *Public Welfare, 55*(1), 26–32.

Pearson, S. D., Sabin, J. E., & Emanuel, E. J. (1998). Ethical guidelines for physician compensation based on capitation. *New England Journal of Medicine: Sounding Board, 339,* 689–693.

Pecora, P., Fraser, M., Nelson, K., McCroskey, J., & Meezan, W. (Eds.). (1995). *Evaluating Family Based Services*. Hawthorne, NY: Aldine de Gruyter.

Pecora, P., Whittaker, J. K., Maluccio, A. N., & Barth, R. P. (2000). *The Child Welfare Challenge: Policy, Practice and Research*. New York: Aldine de Gruyter.

Pedriana, N. (1999). The historical foundations of affirmative action, 1961–1971. *Research in Social Stratification and Mobility, 17,* 3–32.

Pension Benefit Guarantee Corporation (PBGC). (1998). *Pension Insurance Data Book, 1998*. www.pbgc.gov/publications/databook/databk98.pdf (accessed January 6, 2005).

Pension Benefit Guarantee Corporation (PBGC). (2001). *Pension Benefit Guarantee Corporation: History*. http://www.pbgc.gov/about_pbgc/history/hptext.htm.

Perkins, J., Olson, K., & Rivera, L. (1996). *Making the Consumers' Voice Heard in Medicaid Managed Care: Increasing Participation, Protection and Satisfaction*. National Health Law Program. http://www.healthlaw.org/pubs/19970128consumersvoice.html.

Perlmutter, M. (Ed.). (1990). *Late Life Potential*. Washington, DC: Gerontological Society of America.

Perloff, J. D. (1996). Medicaid managed care and urban poor people: Implications for social work. *Health and Social Work, 21*(3), 189–195.

Perry, M. J. (1996). The relationship between social class and mental disorder. *Journal of Primary Prevention, 17*(1), 17–30.

Petchey, R. (1987). Health maintenance organizations: Just what the doctor ordered? *Journal of Social Policy, 16*(4), 489–507.

Petersen, D. A. (1988). *Personnel to Serve the Aging in the Field of Social Work*. A report prepared by the Andrus Gerontology Center, University of Southern California, Los Angeles, CA, and the Association for Gerontology in Higher Education, Washington, DC.

Petr, C. G., & Johnson, I. C. (1999). Privatization of foster care in Kansas: A cautionary tale. *Social Work, 44*(3), 262–267.

Philips, F. (2007, June 14). Legislators vote to defeat same-sex marriage ban. *Boston Globe*. http://www.boston.com/news/globe/city_region/breaking_news/2007/06/legislators_vot_1.html (accessed December 27, 2007).

Phillips, K. R. (2001). *Who Knows About the Earned Income Tax Credit?* Washington, DC: Urban Institute. http://newfederalism.urban.org/html/series_b/b27/b27.html.

Phillips, W. D., & Phillips, C. R. (1992). *The Worlds of Christopher Columbus*. Cambridge: Cambridge University Press.

Physician Payment Review Commission. (1991, April). *Annual Report to Congress: 1991*. Washington, DC: Author.

Piketty, T., & Saez, E. (2003). Income inequality in the United States, 1913–1998. *Quarterly Journal of Economics, 118*(1), 1–39.

Piven, F. F., & Cloward, R. A. (1971). *Regulating the Poor: The Functions of Public Welfare*. New York: Pantheon Books.

Piven, F. F., & Cloward, R. A. (1997). *The Breaking of the American Social Compact.* New York: New Press.

Ploughman, P. (1995/1996). Public policy versus private rights: The medical, social, ethical, and legal implications of the testing of newborns for HIV. *AIDS & Public Social Policy Journal, 10*(4), 182–204.

Pollard, L. J. (1980, September). Black beneficial societies and the Home for Aged and Infirm Colored Persons: A research note. *Phylon, 41*(3), 230–234.

Porter, K. H., Latin, K., & Primus, W. (1999). *Social Security and Poverty Among the Elderly: A National and State Perspective.* Washington, DC: Center on Budget and Policy Priorities. http://www.cbpp.org/4-8-99socsec.htm.

Princeton Survey Research Associates. (1997). *National Omnibus Survey Questions About Teen Pregnancy, for the Association of Reproductive Health Professionals and the National Campaign to Prevent Teen Pregnancy.* Washington, DC: Author.

Prospective Payment Assessment Commission. (1995). *PPRC Annual Report to Congress, 1995.* Washington, DC: U.S. Government Printing Office.

Public Citizen. (2003). *The Other Drug War 2003: Drug Companies Deploy an Army of 675 Lobbyists to Protect Profits.* http://www.citizen.org/_Drug_War2003.pdf.

Putnam, R. D. (2000). *Bowling Alone: The Collapse and Revival of American Community.* New York: Simon & Schuster.

Qazy, R. (2006). Biobehavioral science research on human sexual orientation. In D. Yip, *Psychology of Gender Identity: An International Perspective* (pp. 1–34). Hauppauge, NY: NOVA Science Publishers.

Quadagno, J. (1989). Generational equity and the politics of the welfare state. *Politics and Society, 17,* 360–376.

Quadagno, J. (1994). *The Color of Welfare: How Racism Undermined the War on Poverty.* New York: Oxford University Press.

Quadagno, J., & Meyer, M. H. (1990, Summer). Gender and public policy. *Generations,* 64–66.

Quinn, J. F., & Mitchell, O. S. (1996, May–June). Social security on the table. *American Prospect, 26,* 76–81.

Radner, D. B. (1991). Changes in the incomes of age groups, 1984–89. *Social Security Bulletin, 54,* 2–18.

Ramirez, J. D., Yuen, S. D., & Ramey, D. R. (1991). *Final Report: Longitudinal Study of Structured English Immersion Strategy, Early-Exit, and Late-Exit Transitional Bilingual Education Programs for Language-Minority Children.* San Mateo, CA: Aguirre International.

Raphael, J. (1996). *Prisoners of Abuse: Domestic Violence and Welfare Receipt.* A second report of the Women, Welfare and Abuse Project. Chicago: Taylor Institute.

Rasell, E., & Weller, C. E. (2001). *Trust Funds' Rainy Day Postponed, Again: Trustees' Reports Provide No Justification for Radical Changes in Social Security and Medicare.* Washington, DC: Economic Policy Institute. http://www.epinet.org.

Rawls, J. (1971). *A Theory of Justice.* Cambridge, MA: Harvard University Press.

Reegan, L. J. (1997). *When Abortion Was a Crime: Women, Medicine and Law in the United States, 1867–1973.* Berkeley: University of California Press.

Regier, D. A., Narrow, W., Rae, D., Manderscheid, R., Locke, B., & Goodwin, F. (1993). The de facto U.S. mental and addictive disorders service system: Epidemiological Catchment Area prospective one-year prevalence rates of disorders and services. *Archives of General Psychiatry, 50,* 85–94.

Reichmann, R. (1999). *Race in Contemporary Brazil: From Indifference to Inequality.* University Park, PA: Pennsylvania State University Press.

Reisch, M. (1987). *The Unique Contribution of Social Work to the Mental Health Professions.* Paper presented at the regional meeting of the California Council on Psychiatry, Social Work, and Nursing. San Francisco. Cited in Reisch & Gorin, 2001.

Reisch, M., & Gorin, S. H. (2001). Nature of work and future of the social work profession. *Social Work, 46*(1), 9–19.

Reynolds, B. C. (1963). *An Uncharted Journey: Fifty Years of Growth in Social Work.* New York: Citadel Press.

Reynolds, B. C. (1975). *Social Work and Social Living.* Washington, DC: National Association of Social Workers. (Original work published 1951).

Rhode, D. (1989). *Justice and Gender Sex Discrimination and the Law.* Cambridge, MA: Harvard University Press.

Rice, D. P. (1991). Ethics and equity in U.S. health care: The data. *International Journal of Health Services, 21*(4), 637–651.

Rich, B. M., & Baum, M. (1984). *The Aging: A Guide to Public Policy.* Pittsburgh: University of Pittsburgh Press.

Richards, D. A. J. (1999). *Identity and the Case for Gay Rights: Race, Gender, and Religion as Analogies.* Chicago: University of Chicago Press.

Richardson, T. R. (1989). *The Century of the Child: The Mental Hygiene Movement and Social Policy in the United States and Canada.* Albany: State University of New York Press.

Richmond, M. (1917). *Social Diagnosis.* New York: Russell Sage Foundation.

Rimlinger, G. V. (1971). *Welfare Policy and Industrialization in Europe, America, and Russia.* New York: Wiley.

Rimmerman, C. A. (2000). A "friend" in the White House? Reflections on the Clinton presidency. In J. D'Emilio, W. B. Turner, & U. Vaid (Eds.), *Creating Change: Sexuality Public Policy, and Civil Rights* (pp. 43–56). New York: St. Martin's Press.

Roberts, A. R., & Kurtz, L. F. (1987). Historical perspectives on the care and treatment of the men tally ill. *Journal of Sociology and Social Welfare, 14*(4), 75–94.

Robertson, A. H., & Merrills, J. G. (1996). *Human Rights in the World: An Introduction to the Study of the International Protection of Human Rights.* Manchester, UK: Manchester University Press.

Robins, L. N., Helzer, J. E., Weissman, M. M., Orvaschel, H., Gruenberg, E., Burke, J. D., Jr., & Regier, D. A. (1984). Lifetime prevalence of specific psychiatric disorders in three sites. *Archives of General Psychiatry, 41,* 949–956.

Robins, L. N., & Regier, D. A. (Eds.). (1991). *Psychiatric Disorders in America: The Epidemiological Catchment Area Study.* New York: Free Press.

Robinson, G. (1999). *Parental Consent/Notification for Teen Abortions.* http://www.religioustolerance.org/abo_pare.htm.

Roemer, M. I. (1993). *National Health Systems of the World, Volume II: The Issues.* New York: Oxford University Press.

Roscoe, M., & Morton, R. (1994). *Disproportionate Minority Confinement.* Office of Juvenile Justice and Delinquency Prevention (OJJDP). http://www.ncjrs.org/txtfiles/fe-9411.txt.

Rose, N. (1996). Psychiatry as a political science: Advanced liberalism and the administration of risk. *History of the Human Sciences, 9*(2), 1–23.

Rosen, G. (1993). *A History of Public Health* (Expanded ed.). Baltimore: Johns Hopkins University Press.

Rosenbaum, D. (2000). *Improving Access to Food Stamps: New Reporting Options Can Reduce Administrative Burdens and Error Rates.* Washington, DC: Center on Budget and Policy Priorities. http://www.cbpp.org/9-1-00fs.htm.

Rosenbaum, S., Hughes, D., Butler, E., & Howard, D. (1988). Incantations in the dark: Medicaid, managed care and maternity care. *Milbank Quarterly, 66*(4), 661–693.

Rosenthal, M. G. (2000). Public or private children's services? Privatization in retrospect. *Social Service Review, 74*(2), 281–305.

Roubideaux, Y. (2002). Perspectives on American Indian health. *American Journal of Public Health, 92*(9), 1401–1403.

Rowe, J. W., & Kahn, R. L. (1998). *Successful Aging.* New York: Pantheon Books.

Rowland, D., & Hanson, K. (1996). Medicaid: Moving to managed care. *Health Affairs, 15*(3), 150–152.

Rowland, D., & Salganicoff, A. (1994). Commentary: Lessons from Medicaid: Improving access to office-based physician care for the low-income population. *American Journal of Public Health, 84*(4), 550–552.

Rubin, A., & Babbie, E. (2001). *Research Methods for Social Work* (4th ed.). Belmont, CA: Wadsworth.

Rubin, I. S. (1998). *Class, Tax, and Power: Municipal Budgeting in the United States.* Chatham, NJ: Chatham House Publishers.

Rubin, L. B. (1972). *Busing and Backlash: White Against White in a California School District.* Berkeley: University of California Press.

Ruggles, P. (1990). *Drawing the Line: Alternative Poverty Measures and Their Implications for Public Policy.* Washington, DC: Urban Institute Press.

Russell, L. A. (1998). *Child Maltreatment and Psychological Distress Among Urban Homeless Youth.* New York: Garland.

Russell, P. (1996). *The Gay 100: A Ranking of the Most Influential Gay Men and Lesbians, Past and Present.* Secaucus, NJ: Citadel Press.

Sager, M. A., Easterline, D. V., Kindig, D. A., & Anderson, O. W. (1989). Changes in the location of death after passage of Medicare's prospective payment system: A national study. *New England Journal of Medicine, 320,* 433–439.

Saleebey, D. (1990). Philosophical disputes in social work: Social justice denied. *Journal of Sociology and Social Work, 17*(2), 29–40.

Salmon, J. (1995). A perspective on the corporate transformation of health care. *International Journal of Health Services, 25*(1), 11–42.

Schaaf, G. (1990). *Wampum Belts and Peace Trees: George Morgan, Native Americans and Revolutionary Diplomacy.* Golden, CO: Fulcrum.

Schmid, C. (1992). The English-only movement: Social bases of support and opposition among Anglos and Latinos. In J. Crawford (Ed.), *Language Loyalties: A Sourcebook on the Official English Controversy* (pp. 202–209). Chicago: University of Chicago Press.

Schneider, C. (1991). Discretion, rules, and law: Child custody and the UMDA's best-interest standard. *Michigan Law Review, 89,* 2215–2298.

Schrecker, E. (Ed.). (2004). *Cold War Triumphalism: Exposing the Misuse of History After the Fall of Communism.* New York: New Press.

Schultz, V. (1998). Reconceptualizing sexual harassment. *Yale Law Review, 107,* 1683–1806.

Schulz, J. H. (1995). *The Economics of Aging* (6th ed.). Westport, CT: Auburn House.

Scotch, R. K. (2001). American disability policy in the twentieth century. In P. K. Longmore & L. Umansky (Eds.), *The New Disability History: American Perspectives* (pp. 375–397). New York: New York University Press.

Scott, R. (2003). Five decades of federal initiatives concerning school desegregatory effects: What have we learned? *Journal of Social, Political, and Economic Studies, 28*(2), 177–215.

Segalman, R., & Basu, A. (1981). *Poverty in America: The Welfare Dilemma.* Westport, CT: Greenwood Press.

Selmi, P., & Hunter, R. (2001). Beyond the rank and file movement: Mary van Kleeck and social work radicalism in the Great Depression, 1931–1942. *Journal of Sociology and Social Welfare, 28*(2), 75–100.

Senate Finance Committee. (1995, March 27). Hearing on SSI program.

The Sentencing Project (2002). *Mentally Ill Offenders in the Criminal Justice System: An Analysis and Prescription.* Washington, DC: The Sentencing Project.

Shanas, E. (1968). *Old People in Three Industrial Societies.* New York: Atherton Press.

Shanas, E. (1980). Older people and their families: The new pioneers. *Journal of Marriage and the Family, 42*(1), 9–15.

Sherk, J. (2007). *Analyzing Economic Mobility: Compensation Is Keeping Pace with Rising Productivity.* http:// www.heritage.org/Research/Labor/bg2040.cfm (accessed January 20, 2008).

Shilts, R. (1993). *Conduct Unbecoming: Gays and Lesbians in the U.S. Military.* New York: St. Martin's Press.

Shinn, M. (1997). Family homelessness: State or Trait? *American Journal of Community Psychology, 25*(6), 755–769.

Short, J. F. (1997). *Poverty, Ethnicity, and Violent Crime.* Boulder, CO: Westview Press.

Sierminska, E., Brandolini, A., & Smeeding, T. (2007). *Cross-National Comparison of Income and Wealth Status in Retirement: First Results from the Luxembourg Wealth Study (LWS) Center for Retirement Research at Boston College.* http://ideas.repec.org/p/crr/crrwps/wp2007-03.html (accessed January 8, 2007).

Siminoff, I. (1986). Competition and primary care in the US: Separating fact from fantasy. *International Journal of Health Studies, 16*(1), 57–69.

Simmons, L. W. (1945). *The Role of the Aged in Primitive Societies.* New Haven, CT: Yale University Press.

Simon, R. J. (1994). Transracial adoption: The American experience. In I. Gabor & A. J. Long (Eds.), *In the Best Interests of the Child: Culture, Identity and Transracial Adoption* (pp. 135–150). London: Free Association Books.

Simpson, P. (1985, October). If the wage system doesn't work, fix it. *Working Woman,* 118–159.

Sisk, J. E., Gorman, S. A., Reisinger, A. L., Glied, S. A., DuMouchel, W. H., & Hynes, M. M. (1996, July 3). Evaluation of Medicaid managed care: Satisfaction, access, and use. *Journal of the American Medical Association, 276*(1), 50–55.

Skocpol, J. (1995). *Social Policy in the United States: Future Possibilities in Historical Perspective.* Princeton, NJ: Princeton University Press.

Slater, W. (1984, March 29). Latest Lamm remark angers the elderly. *Arizona Daily Star,* p. 1.

Slesnick, N. (2004). *Our Runaway and Homeless Youth: A Guide to Understanding.* Westport CT: Praeger.

Social Security Administration. (n.d.). *A Quarter-Century of Service to Children: Katharine F. Lenroot.* http:// www.socialsecurity.gov/history/kl25.html (accessed March 14, 2008).

Social Security Administration. (2000). *Income of the Population 55 or Older, 2000.* Table 5.C2. http:// www.ssa.gov/policy/docs/statcomps/income_ pop55/2000/sect5c.html.

Social Security Administration. (2004). *Substantial Gainful Activity*. http://www.ssa.gov/OACT/COLA/SGA .html.

Social Security Administration. (2006). *Income of the Aged Chartbook, 2004*. http://www.socialsecurity.gov/ policy/docs/chartbooks/income_aged/#toc (accessed January 8, 2007).

Southern Poverty Law Center (SPLC). (1999, Spring). *Intelligence Report. Hate Crimes: Serious Violence Against Gays Said to Rise*. http://www.splcenter .org/intelligenceproject/ip-4j10.html.

Sowell, T. (1981). *Markets and Minorities*. New York: Basic Books.

Sowers, W. E. (1998). Parallel process: Moral failure, addiction, and society. *Community Mental Health Journal, 34*(4), 331–336.

Sowers-Hoag, K. M., & Harrison, D. F. (1991). Women in social work education: Progress or promise? *Journal of Social Work Education, 27*, 320–328.

Specht, H., & Courtney, M. (1994). *Unfaithful Angels: How Social Work Has Abandoned Its Mission*. New York: Free Press.

Stampp, K. M. (1956). *The Peculiar Institution: Slavery in the Ante-Bellum South*. New York: Vintage.

Stavis, P. F. (1995, July 21). *Civil Commitment: Past, Present, and Future*. An address by Paul F. Stavis at the National Conference of the National Alliance for the Mentally Ill, Washington, DC. http://www .cqc.state.ny.us/cc64.htm.

Steadman, H. J., Barbera, S., & Dennis, D. (1994). A national survey of jail diversion programs for mentally ill detainees. *Hospital and Community Psychiatry, 45*, 1109–1113.

Steele, E., & Redding, W. C. (1962). The American value system. *Western Speech, 26*, 83–91.

Stein, T. (1995). Disability-based employment discrimination against individuals perceived to have AIDS and individuals infected with HIV or diagnosed with AIDS: Federal and New York statutes and case law. *AIDS & Public Policy Journal, 10*(3), 123–139.

Stein, T. J. (1996). Child custody and visitation: The rights of lesbian and gay parents. *Social Service Review, 70*, 435–450.

Steinwachs, D. M., Kasper, J. D., & Skinner, E. A. (1992). *Family Perspectives on Meeting the Needs for Care of Severely Mentally Ill Relatives: A National Survey*. Arlington, VA: National Alliance for the Mentally Ill.

Sterba, J. (1980). *Justice: Alternative Political Perspectives*. Belmont, CA: Wadsworth.

Sterba, J. P. (1998). *Justice for Here and Now*. New York: Cambridge University Press.

Sternleib, G., & Hughes, J. (1981). *The Future of Rental Housing*. New Brunswick, NJ: Center for Urban Policy Research, Rutgers.

Stillwagon, E. (2000). HIV transmission in Latin America: Comparison with Africa and policy implications. *South African Journal of Economics, 68*(5), 985–1011.

Stone, C., Greenstein, R., & Coven, M. (2007). *Addressing Longstanding Gaps in Unemployment Insurance Coverage*. Center on Budget and Policy Priorities. http://www.cbpp.org/7-20-07ui.htm (accessed February 21, 2008).

Stoner, M. (1995). Intervention and policies to serve homeless people infected by HIV and AIDS. *Journal of Health and Social Policy, 7*(1), 53–68.

Straznickas, K. A., McNeil, D., & Binder, R. L. (1993). Violence toward family caregivers by mentally ill relatives. *Hospital and Community Psychiatry, 44*, 385–387.

Strouse, J. (1998, November 23). The brilliant bailout. *The New Yorker*, 62–77.

Stuart, P. (1997). Community care and the origins of psychiatric social work. *Social Work in Health Care, 25*(3), 25–36.

Sullivan, A. (1995). Policy issues. In *Issues in Gay and Lesbian Adoption: Proceedings of the Fourth Annual Peirce-Warwick Adoption Symposium*. Washington, DC: Child Welfare League of America.

Supreme Court of the United States. (1937). Opinion in *Helvering et al. v. Davis*. http://www.ssa.gov/ history/supremel html.

Surgeon General. (1999). *Mental Health: A Report of the Surgeon General*. http://www.surgeongeneral.gov/ library/mentalhealth.

Swanson, J. W., Holzer, C. E., Ganju, V. K., & Jono, R. T. (1990). Violence and psychiatric disorder in the community: Evidence from the Epidemiologic Catchment Area surveys. *Hospital and Community Psychiatry, 41*, 761–770.

Swartz, M. S., & Swanson, J. W. (2004, September). Involuntary outpatient commitment, community treatment orders, and assisted outpatient treatment: What's in the data? *The Canadian Journal of Psychiatry.* http://www.cpa-apc.org/Publications/Archives/CJP/2004/september/swartz.asp.

Sweeney, J. (1999, June 24). Statement by AFL-CIO President John Sweeney on the Employment Non-Discrimination Act. http://igc.org/prideatwork/enda.html#2.

Szasz, T. (1960). The myth of mental illness. *American Psychologist, 15,* 113–118.

Takaki, R. (1993). *A Different Mirror: A History of Multicultural America.* New York: Little, Brown.

Task Force on Social Work Research. (1991). *Building Social Work Knowledge for Effective Services and Policies.* Washington, DC: NASW.

Tasker, F., & Golumbok, S. (1997). *Growing Up in a Lesbian Family: Effects on Child Development.* New York: Guilford Press.

Taylor, M. J., & Barusch, A. S. (2004). Personal, family and multiple barriers of long-term welfare recipients. *Social Work, 49*(2), 175–183.

Tedeschi, J. T., & Rosenfeld, P. (1980). Communication in bargaining and negotiation. In M. E. Roloff & G. E. Miller (Eds.), *Persuasion: New Directions in Theory and Research.* Beverly Hills: Sage.

Temkin-Greener, H., & Winchell, M. (1991). Medicaid beneficiaries under managed care: Provider choice and satisfaction. *Health Services Research, 26*(4), 509–529.

Thomas, C. S. (1991). *Sex Discrimination in a Nutshell* (2nd ed.). St. Paul: West.

Thomas, M. P. (1972). Child abuse and neglect: Part 1. Historical overview, legal matrix, and social perspectives. *North Carolina Law Review, 50,* 293–349. Cited by Watkins, 1990.

Thomas, W. H. (1996). *Life Worth Living: How Someone You Love Can Still Enjoy Life in a Nursing Home: The Eden Alternative in Action.* Acton, MA: VanderWyk & Burnham.

Thornberry, T., & Burch, J. H., II. (1997). *Gang Members and Delinquent Behavior.* Office of Juvenile Justice and Delinquency Prevention (OJJDP). http://www.ncirs.org/txtfiles/165154.txt.

Thornton, R. (1987). *American Indian Holocaust and Survival: A Population History Since 1492.* Norman, OK: University of Oklahoma Press.

Thornton, R. (1996). Tribal membership requirements and the demography of "old" and "new" Native Americans. In G. D. Sandefur, R. R. Rindfuss, & B. Cohen (Eds.), *Changing Numbers, Changing Needs: American Indian Demography and Public Health* (pp. 103–112). Washington, DC: National Academy Press.

Titmuss, R. (1971). *The Gift Relationship.* New York: Pantheon Books.

Tolle, S. W., Rosenfeld, A. G., Tilden, V. P., & Park, Y. (1999). Oregon's low in hospital death rates: What determines where people die and satisfaction with decisions on place of death? *Annals of Internal Medicine, 130,* 681–685.

Torrey, E. F. (1997). *Out of the Shadows: Confronting America's Mental Illness Crisis.* New York: John Wiley & Sons.

Torrey, E. F., & Kaplan, R. J. (1995). A National Survey of the Use of Outpatient Commitment. *Psychiatric Services, 46,* 778–784.

Transgender Law and Policy Institute. (2005). *Nondiscrimination Laws That Include Gender Identity and Expression and Hate Crime Laws.* www.transgenderlaw.org.

Trattner, W. I. (1989). *From Poor Law to Welfare State: A History of Social Welfare in America.* New York: Free Press.

Troy, D. E. (1998, October 19). Rule of law: Hate crime laws make some more equal than others. *Wall Street Journal.* http://www.aei.org/ra/ratroy3.htm.

Trupin, L., Sebesta, D. S., & Yelin, E. (2000). *Transitions in Employment and Disability Among People Ages 51 to 61.* University of San Francisco, Disability Statistics Center. http://dsc.ucsf.edu/publication.php?pub_id=3 (accessed December 6, 2007).

Trupin, L. & Yelin, E. (2005). *Multiple Jeopardies in the California Labor Market: The Conjoint Role of Disability, Race, Gender, and Age.* Final Report to the Disability Research Institute, University of Illinois at Urbana-Champaign. http://www.dri.uiuc.edu/research/p05-08c/Yelin_Trupin_Final_Report.doc (accessed December 6, 2007).

Urban Dynamics. (1999). *Gangs 101.* http://www.lincolnnet.net/users/lrttrapp/block/gang101.htm.

U.S. Bureau of the Census. (2000a). Disability Status 2000: Census 2000 Brief. http://www.census.gov/hhes/www/disability/disabstat2k.html.

U.S. Bureau of the Census. (2000b). *Methodology and Assumptions for the Population Projections of the United States: 1999–2100.* http://www.census.gov/population/www/documentation/twps0038.pdf.

U.S. Bureau of the Census. (2001). *Overview of Race and Hispanic Origin 2000. Census 2000 Brief.* http://www.census.gov/prod/2001pubs/c2kbr01-1.pdf.

U.S. Bureau of the Census. (2002). *Statistical Abstract of the United States* (1116th ed.). www.census.gov/population/www/socdemo/race/indian.html (accessed February 24, 2003).

U.S. Bureau of the Census. (2003a). *Current Population Survey, 2003 Annual Social and Economic Supplement.* http://ferret.bls.census.gov/macro/032003/pov/new06_100_01.htm.

U.S. Bureau of the Census. (2003b). *Occupations: 2000, Census 2000 Brief.* http://www.census.gov/prod/2003pubs/c2kbr-25.pdf (accessed February 8, 2008).

U.S. Bureau of the Census. (2003c). *Poverty Tables.* http://ferret.bls.census.gov/macro/032003/pov/toc.htm.

U.S. Bureau of the Census. (2003d). Poverty Tables Based on Current Population Surveys. http://www.census.gov/hhes/poverty/poverty02/pov2_and_3-yr_avgs.html.

U.S. Bureau of the Census. (2004a). *Educational Attainment in the United States: Current Population Reports.* www.census.gov/prod/2004pubs/p20-550.pdf (accessed January 15, 2008).

U.S. Bureau of the Census. (2004b). *Evidence from Census 2000 About Earnings by Detailed Occupation for Men and Women.* Census 2000 Special Reports. www.census.gov (accessed January 21, 2008).

U.S. Bureau of the Census. (2005a). *Factfinder: Disability Linked to Poverty.* http://factfinder.census.gov/jsp/saff/SAFFInfo.jsp?_pageId=tp4_disability (accessed February 13, 2008).

U.S. Bureau of the Census. (2005b). *General Demographic Characteristics: 2005.* http://factfinder.census.gov/servlet/ADPTable?_bm=y&-geo_id=01000US&-ds_name=ACS_2005_EST_G00_&-_lang=en&-_caller=geoselect&-format= (accessed December 11, 2007).

U.S. Bureau of the Census. (2005c). *65+ in the United States: 2005.* http://www.census.gov/prod/2006pubs/p23-209.pdf (accessed March 14, 2008).

U.S. Bureau of the Census. (2006a). *Current Population Survey, 2006 Annual Social and Economic Supplement,* Table HINC-05. http://pubdb3.census.gov/macro/032006/hhinc/new05_000.htm (accessed December 13, 2007).

U.S. Bureau of the Census. (2006b). *Educational Attainment in the United States: 2006.* Table 9. http://www.census.gov/population/www/socdemo/education/cps2006.html (accessed December 11, 2007).

U.S. Bureau of the Census. (2007a). *American Community Survey.* http://factfinder.census.gov/servlet/DTSubjectShowTablesServlet?_ts=207669128216 (accessed August 31, 2007).

U.S. Bureau of the Census. (2007b). *Current Population Survey, Annual Social and Economic (ASEC) Supplement,* Tables POV01 and Pov02. http://pubdb3.census.gov/macro/032007/pov/toc.htm (accessed February 5, 2008).

U.S. Bureau of the Census. (2007c). *Household Income Rises, Poverty Rate Declines, Number of Uninsured Up.* http://www.census.gov/Press-Release/www/releases/archives/income_wealth/010583.html (accessed January 8, 2007); http://www.census.gov/prod/2006pubs/p23-209.pdf (accessed January 8, 2008).

U.S. Commission on Civil Rights. (1967). *Racial Isolation in the Public Schools.* Washington, DC: U.S. Government Printing Office.

U.S. Congress, Office of Technology Assessment. (1994, September). *International Comparisons of Administrative Costs in Health Care* (BP-H-135). Washington, DC: U.S. Government Printing Office. http://www.ota.nap.edu/pdf/data/1994/9417.pdf.

U.S. Department of Agriculture. (n.d.). Food Stamp Program FAQs. http://www.fns.usda.gov/fsp/faqs.htm (accessed February 5, 2008).

U.S. Department of Agriculture. (2000a). *Food Stamps: Income Chart.* http://www.fns.usda.gov/fsp/MENU/APPS/ELIGIBILITY/income/INCOMECHART.HTM.

U.S. Department of Agriculture. (2000b). *Food Stamps: Allotment Chart.* http://www.fns.usda.gov/fsp/CHARTS/ALLOTMENTCHART.HTM.

U.S. Department of Commerce, Economics and Statistics Administration, Bureau of the Census. (1992).

Statistical Abstract of the United States, 1993 (112th ed.). Washington, DC: U.S. Government Printing Office.

U.S. Department of Health and Human Services, Social Security Administration. (1992, September 4). *Supplemental Security Income Modernization Project: Final Report; Notice* (Federal Register). Washington, DC: U.S. Government Printing Office.

U.S. Department of Health and Human Services. (1994). Office of the Inspector General. *Requirements for Drug Addicts and Alcoholics on SSI,* OEI-01-94-001 10.

U.S. Department of Health and Human Services. (2000, June 5). *HHS Fact Sheet: Clinton Administration Record on HIV/AIDS.* http://www.thebody.com/hhs/clinton.html.

U.S. Department of Health and Human Services. (2006). *Medicare Fact Sheet: Medicare Premiums and Deductibles for 2007.* www.hcca-info.org.

U.S. Department of Housing and Urban Development. (1993, October). *Creating Communities of Opportunity: Priorities of U.S. Department of Housing and Urban Development: Executive Summary.* Washington, DC: HUD.

U.S. Department of Housing and Urban Development. (1999). *The Widening Gap: New Findings on Housing Affordability in America.* http://www.hud.gov/library/bookshelf18/pressrel/afford/afford.html.

U.S. Department of Justice, Bureau of Justice Statistics. (1994, February). *Race of Prisoners Admitted to State and Federal Prisons, 1926–1986.* Table 7. http://www.ncjrs.gov/pdffiles1/nij/125618.pdf.

U.S. Department of Justice, Bureau of Justice Statistics. (2005). *Homicide Trends in the U.S.: Age, Gender and Race Trends.* http://www.ojp.usdoj.gov/bjs/homicide/tables/varstab.htm (accessed December 31, 2007).

U.S. Department of Justice. (2006a). *Crime in the United States: 2004.* http://www.fbi.gov/ucr/cius_04/offenses_reported/violent_crime/index.html (accessed October 27, 2007).

U.S. Department of Justice. (2006b). *Mental Health Problems of Prison and Jail Inmates.* http://www.ojp.usdoj.gov/bjs/pub/pdf/mhppji.pdf (accessed February 12, 2008).

U.S. Department of Justice. (2007a). *Crime in the United States: 2006.* http://www.fbi.gov/ucr/cius2006/offenses/violent_crime/index.html (accessed February 5, 2008).

U.S. Department of Justice, Bureau of Justice Statistics. (2007b). *Prisoners in 2006.* http://www.ojp.usdoj.gov/bjs/pub/pdf/p06.pdf (accessed December 13, 2007).

U.S. Department of Justice. (2007c). *Juvenile Offenders and Victims: 2006 National Report.* Office of Juvenile Justice and Delinquency Prevention. http://ojjdp.ncjrs.org/ojstatbb/nr2006/index.html (accessed December 31, 2007).

U.S. Department of Veterans Affairs. (n.d.). *A Brief History of the V.A.* http://www.va.gov/facmgt/historic/Brief_VA_History.asp (accessed February 12, 2008).

U.S. General Accounting Office (GAO). (1980). *Section 8 Subsidized Housing: Some Observations on Its High Rents, Costs and Inequities.* Report to Congress by the Comptroller General of the United States, CED-80-59. Washington, DC: U.S. Government Printing Office.

U.S. General Accounting Office (GAO). (1992, February). *Pension Plans: Survivor Benefit Coverage for Wives Increased After 1984 Pension Law.* Report to the Chairman, Subcommittee on Retirement Income and Employment, Select Committee on Aging, House of Representatives, GAO/HRD-92-49. Washington, DC: U.S. Government Printing Office.

U.S. General Accounting Office (GAO). (1994a). *Social Security: Major Changes Needed for Disability Benefits for Addicts.* GAO/HEHS-94-128. Washington, DC: U.S. Government Printing Office.

U.S. General Accounting Office (GAO). (1994b). *Tax Gap: Many Actions Taken but a Cohesive Compliance Strategy Needed.* GGD 94-123. http://www.unclefed.com/GAOReports/gao94-123sum.html.

U.S. General Accounting Office (GAO). (1995). *Supplemental Security Income: Recent Growth in Rolls Raises Fundamental Program Concerns.* GAO/T-HEHS-95-67. Washington, DC: U.S. Government Printing Office.

U.S. General Accounting Office (GAO). (2000). *Mental Health: Community-Based Care Increases for People with Serious Mental Illness.* Report to the Committee on Finance, U.S. Senate. GAO 01-224. http://www.gao.gov/new.items/d01224.pdf.

U.S. General Accounting Office (GAO). (2004). *No Child Left Behind Act: Education Needs to Provide Additional Technical Assistance and Conduct Implementation Studies for School Choice Provision.* Report to the Secretary of Education. http://www.gao.gov/new.items/d057.pdf (accessed December 30, 2007).

U.S. House of Representatives. (1999). *Hot Topic: Minimum Wage. A Report from the Democratic Leadership.* www.house.gov/democrats/ht_min_wage.html.

U.S. House of Representatives, Select Committee on Aging. (1990). *Medicare and Medicaid's 25th Anniversary: Much Promised, Accomplished, and Left Unfinished.* Committee Publication No. 101-762. Washington, DC: U.S. Government Printing Office.

U.S. House of Representatives, Select Committee on Aging, Subcommittee on Human Services. (1988). *Older Americans Act: A Staff Summary.* Committee Publication No 100-683. Washington, DC: U.S. Government Printing Office.

U.S. National Archives and Records Administration. (2007). *Keating-Owen Child Labor Act of 1916.* http://www.ourdocuments.gov/doc.php?doc=59 (accessed December 30, 2007).

U.S. Senate, Special Committee on Aging. (1988, February 26). *Developments in Aging* (Vol. 1). Washington, DC: U.S. Government Printing Office.

U.S. Sentencing Commission. (2007). *Special Report to Congress: Cocaine and Federal Sentencing Policy.* Washington, DC: U.S. Sentencing Commission.

Van Soest, D., & Garcia, B. (2003). *Diversity Education for Social Justice: Mastering Teaching Skills.* Alexandria, VA: Council on Social Work Education.

Van Tassel, E. F., Wirtz, B. H., and Wonders, P. (1993). *Why Judges Resign: Influences on Federal Judicial Service, 1789 to 1992.* Federal Judicial History Office.

Van Wormer, K. (2004). *Confronting Oppression, Restoring Justice: From Policy Analysis to Social Action.* Alexandria, VA: Council on Social Work Education.

Vasak, K., & Alston, P. (Eds.). (1982). *The International Dimensions of Human Rights.* Westport, CT: Greenwood Press.

Verbugge, L. M. (1985). An epidemiological profile of older women. In M. R. Haug, A. B. Ford, & M. Sheafor (Eds.), *The Physical and Mental Health of Aged Women* (pp. 41–64). New York: Springer.

Vernon, R., & Lynch, D. (2000). *Social Work and the Web.* Belmont, CA: Wadsworth.

Vonk, E. (2001). Cultural competence for transracial adoptive parents. *Social Work, 46,* 246–255.

Wade, P. (1997). *Race and Ethnicity in Latin America.* London: Pluto Press.

Wagner, S. (2002). *How Did the Taft-Hartley Act Come About?* http://hnn.us/articles/1036.html (accessed November 8, 2007).

Wakefield, J. (1988, June). Psychotherapy, distributive justice, and social work. Part 1: Distributive justice as a conceptual framework for social work. *Social Service Review,* 187–210.

Walker, F. A. (1874). *The Indian Question.* Boston: J. R. Osgood.

Walters, K. L. (1999). Urban American Indian identity attitudes and acculturation styles. *Journal of Human Behavior and the Social Environment, 2*(1/2), 163–178.

Wandersee, W. D. (1981). *Women's Work and Family Values: 1920–1940.* Cambridge, MA: Harvard University Press.

Ward, M. J. (1946). *The Snake Pit.* New York: Random House.

Ware, S. (1981). *Beyond Suffrage: Women in the New Deal.* Cambridge, MA: Harvard University Press.

Watkins, S. (1990). The Mary Ellen Myth: Correcting child welfare history. *Social Work, 35*(6), 500–503.

Waxman, L., & Trupin, R. (1997). *A Status Report on Hunger and Homelessness in America's Cities: 1997.* Washington, DC: U.S. Conference of Mayors.

Wayne, L., & Petersen, M. (2001). A muscular lobby rolls up its sleeves. *New York Times.* http://query.nytimes.com/gst/fullpage.html?res=9E02E5DF1639F937A35752C1A9679C8B63 (accessed February 12, 2008).

Weatherford, J. (1988). *Indian Givers: How the Indians of the Americas Transformed the World.* New York: Crown Publishers.

Weaver, H., & Brave Heart, M. Y. (1999). Examining two facets of American Indian identity: Exposure to other cultures and the influence of historical trauma. *Journal of Human Behavior and the Social Environment, 1*(1/2), 19–33.

Weil, A. (1997). *The New Children's Health Insurance Program: Should States Expand Medicaid?* New Federalism Series, Paper A-13. Washington, DC: Urban Institute. http://newfederalism.urban.org/html/anfa113.htm.

Weiner, J. M. (1996). Managed care and long-term care: The integration of financing and services. *Generations, 20*(2), 47–52.

Weiner, L. Y. (1985). *From Working Girl to Working Mother: The Female Labor Force in the United States, 1820–1980.* Chapel Hill: University of North Carolina Press.

Weitzman, L. J., & Maclean, M. (1992). *Economic Consequences of Divorce: The International Perspective.* Oxford, England: Clarendon Press.

Welfare Policy Organization. (1997). *Comparison of Prior Law and the PRWORA Statute.* http://www.welfare-policy.org/aspesum.htm.

Wells, K. (1995, September). Proceedings of the NIMH Conference on Service Research in Washington, DC.

Wexler, D. E., & Winnick, B. J. (1996). *Law in a Therapeutic Key: Developments in Therapeutic Jurisprudence.* Durham, NC: Carolina Academic Press.

Whiteside, A. (2002). Poverty and HIV/ AIDS in Africa. *Third World Quarterly, 23*(2), 313–332.

Wiatrowski, W. J. (1993). Factors affecting retirement income. *Monthly Labor Review, 116*(3). http://stats.bls.gov/opub/mlr/1993/03/art2abs.htm.

Wiehe, V. R., & Richards, A. L. (1995). *Intimate Betrayal: Understanding and Responding to the Trauma of Acquaintance Rape.* Thousand Oaks, CA: Sage.

Wikander, U., Kessler-Harris, A., & Lewis, J. (1995). *Protecting Women: Labor Legislation in Europe, the United States, and Australia, 1880–1920.* Urbana: University of Illinois Press.

Willhelm, S. (1970). *Who Needs the Negro.* Cambridge, MA: Schenkman.

Williams, D. D. (1993). Barriers to achieving health. *Child and Adolescent Social Work Journal, 10*(5), 355–363.

Wilson, C. A. (1996). *Racism: From Slavery to Advanced Capitalism.* Thousand Oaks, CA: Sage.

Wilson, W. J. (1987). *The Truly Disadvantaged.* Chicago: University of Chicago Press.

Wiener, J. M., Freiman, M. P., & Brown, D. (2007). *Nursing Home Care Quality: Twenty Years After the Omnibus Budget Reconciliation Act of 1987.* Kaiser Family Foundation. http://www.kff.org/medicare/7717.cfm (accessed February 4, 2008).

Wingfield, K., Petit, M., & Klempner, T. (1999). *Mortality Trends Among U.S. Children and Youth: An Issue Brief.* Washington, DC: Child Welfare League of America.

Winicki, J. (2003). Children in homes below poverty: Changes in program participation since welfare reform. *Children and Youth Services Review, 25*(8), 651–668.

Wolfe, B., & Perozek, M. (1997). Teen children's health and health care use. In R. A. Maynard (Ed.), *Kids Having Kids: Economic Costs and Social Consequences of Teen Pregnancy* (pp. 181–203). Washington, DC: Urban Institute Press.

Women's Bureau, U.S. Department of Labor. (1996, September). *Facts on Working Women.* No. 96-2.

Wood, J. C., & Woods, R. N. (1990). *Milton Friedman: Critical Assessments.* London: Routledge.

World Bank. (1994). *World Development Report.* New York: Oxford University Press.

World Bank. (2000). *World Development Report, 1999/2000: Entering the 21st Century.* Herndon, VA: World Bank Publications.

World Health Organization. (2002). *World Report on Violence and Health.* http://www.who.int/violence_injury_prevention/en/ (accessed December 31, 2007).

World Health Organization. (2005). *3 by 5 June 2005 Report.* http://www.who.int/3by5/progressreport June2005/en/ (accessed February 12, 2008).

Wright, M. H. (1928). The removal of the Choctaws to the Indian Territory: 1830–1833. *Chronicles of Oklahoma, 6*(2), 103–128.

Yell, M. L., Rogers, D., & Lodge Rodgers, E. (1998). The legal history of special education. *Remedial and Special Education, 19*(4), 219–228.

Yellow Bird, M. J. (1999). Indian, American Indian, and Native Americans: Counterfeit identities. *Winds of Change: A Magazine for American Indian Education and Opportunity, 14*(1), 86.

Yellow Bird, M. J. (2001). Critical values and First Nations Peoples. In R. Fong & S. Furuto (Eds.), *Culturally Competent Social Work Practice: Practice Skills, Interventions, and Evaluation* (pp. 61–74). Boston: Allyn & Bacon.

Zedlewski, S. R., & Meyer, J. A. (1987). *Toward Ending Poverty Among the Elderly and Disabled: Policy and Financing Options*. Washington, DC: Urban Institute.

Zhang, A. Y., & Snowden, L. (1999). Ethnic characteristics of mental disorders in five U.S. communities. *Cultural Diversity and Ethnic Minority Psychology, 5*(2), 134–146.

Zorza, J. (1991). Woman battering: A major cause of homelessness. *Clearinghouse Review, 25*(4), 421.

Zuckerman, S., Evans, A., & Holahan, J. (1997). *Questions for States as They Turn to Medicaid Managed Care* (Series A, No. A-11). Washington, DC: Urban Institute.

Zweig, M. (2000). *The Working Class Majority: America's Best Kept Secret*. Ithaca, NY: Cornell University Press.

Name Index

Subject Index